ENTERTAINING RACE

ALSO BY MICHAEL ERIC DYSON

Long Time Coming (2020)

JAY-Z (2019)

What Truth Sounds Like (2018)

Tears We Cannot Stop (2017)

The Black Presidency:
Barack Obama and the Politics of Race in America (2016)

Born to Use Mics:
Reading Nas's Illmatic, *edited with Sohail Daulatzai* (2010)

Can You Hear Me Now?
The Inspiration, Wisdom, and Insight of Michael Eric Dyson (2009)

April 4, 1968:
Martin Luther King, Jr.'s Death and How It Changed America (2008)

Know What I Mean? Reflections on Hip Hop (2007)

Debating Race with Michael Eric Dyson (2007)

Pride: The Seven Deadly Sins (2006)

Come Hell or High Water:
Hurricane Katrina and the Color of Disaster (2006)

Is Bill Cosby Right? Or Has the Black Middle Class Lost Its Mind? (2005)

Mercy, Mercy Me:
The Art, Loves, and Demons of Marvin Gaye (2004)

The Michael Eric Dyson Reader (2004)

Open Mike:
Reflections on Philosophy, Race, Sex, Culture, and Religion (2003)

Why I Love Black Women (2003)

Holler If You Hear Me: Searching for Tupac Shakur (2001)

I May Not Get There with You: The True Martin Luther King, Jr. (2000)

Race Rules: Navigating the Color Line (1996)

Between God and Gangsta Rap: Bearing Witness to Black Culture (1996)

Making Malcolm: The Myth and Meaning of Malcolm X (1995)

Reflecting Black: African-American Cultural Criticism (1993)

ENTERTAINING RACE

Performing Blackness in America

Michael Eric Dyson

St. Martin's Press ⚏ New York

First published in the United States by St. Martin's Press, an imprint of
St. Martin's Publishing Group

www.stmartins.com

Design by Meryl Sussman Levavi

Library of Congress Cataloging-in-Publication Data is available from the Library
of Congress.

ISBN 978-1-250-13597-1 (hardcover)
ISBN 978-1-250-13598-8 (ebook)

Our books may be purchased in bulk for promotional, educational, or business
use. Please contact your local bookseller or the Macmillan Corporate and
Premium Sales Department at 1-800-221-7945, extension 5442, or by email at
MacmillanSpecialMarkets@macmillan.com.

First Edition: 2021

1   3   5   7   9   10   8   6   4   2

To
Bobby Joe Leonard
Faithful cousin, more like a brother, who taught me the
game of manhood on the basketball courts of Detroit
And
David N. Redman
Whose profound support as a graduate school dean at
Princeton got me in and saw me through

Contents

RELIGION

BODIES IN MOTION

PUBLICS

ENTERTAINING RACE

Introduction

Command Performance

An illustration captures a fate that is at once jarring and sadly familiar. A white man with an official title commits a wicked act that leads to the death of a fifteen-year-old Black girl. The image might have easily accompanied a recent newspaper story about a cop assaulting a Black teenager. Instead, the colored print by Scottish caricaturist Isaac Cruikshank was engraved in 1792. The drawing was originally captioned, "The Abolition of the Slave Trade Or the inhumanity of dealers in human flesh exemplified in Captn. Kimber's treatment of a young Negro girl of 15 for her virjen [sic] modesty."

In 1791, John Kimber, the captain of the slave ship Recovery, departed New Calabar, known today as Nigeria, headed for Grenada, West Indies. After weeks of torturing a young captive girl, Kimber used a whip to mercilessly flog the nearly naked teen as she was suspended in midair by a single ankle; she died shortly thereafter. British abolitionist William Wilberforce gave a speech in the House of Commons in 1792 condemning Kimber for the killing. Wilberforce's oration led to Cruikshank's illustration and Kimber's arrest and trial for the girl's death, and that of a second girl, before the High Court of Admiralty in June 1792.

The true reason for the captain's cruelty, outlined by Wilberforce in his speech, came to light at trial in the testimony of surgeon Thomas Dowling and shipmate Stephen Devereux, the only witnesses: "The girl would not get up to dance with the other girls and women." It was common to "dance the captives" aboard a slave vessel to keep them in shape, to provoke sexual excitement in the crew, and to offer mostly white men entertainment on the long journey to the Americas.

The demand for Black entertainment by white folk continued in the New World.

Dowling testified that the girl came aboard "in a diseased state" with a "very severe" case of gonorrhea that led to "a lethargy or drowsy complaint."

According to other shipmates, Dowling had raped and infected the girl before leaving the Calabar region. Her illness left her weary and unwilling, perhaps unable, to perform.

It should come as no surprise that Kimber was quickly acquitted of murder. The jury concluded that it was disease and not mistreatment that led to the young girl's death. The ugly truth is as simple as it is tragic: The Black girl was sentenced to death for refusing to entertain a white audience. It was hardly the first, and surely not the last, time that Black folk had to perform because their lives depended on it.

Even before the Atlantic slave trade began, Europeans traveling through Africa were introduced to Black performance. They viewed the folklore and rituals that inspired African song and dance through a distorted lens, seeing African art as inferior and its creators as deviant. Yet, Africans were often envied for the very reasons they were despised: their freedom of movement, their sensual confidence, their enthusiastic exploration of identity, their fearless performance.

Despite their alleged superiority, Europeans and Americans neither fully understood nor completely controlled Black culture. These same whites, as stewards of Western civilization, might at times acknowledge a Black upper hand, as long as that hand could be kept from strangling white throats or stifling white identity. Blacks were deemed bad at science and society, a lot better at song and dance, though of a crude, uncivilized character, and better still at sports and sex because these demanded little motive beyond the exercise of muscles and passion.

Such thinking willfully ignored the extraordinary craft, complexity, and care that marked Black performance in different regions of Africa. And most whites were not curious about how, for example, West African dance and song evoked one's profession, spirituality, the history of a populace, and the area's natural resources, as well as its customs, habits, traits, dispositions, myths, legends, and wisdom.

All cultures sing about their companionship with or alienation from the universe. All peoples dance their wonder or worry about the worlds that shape us or that we create. The stereotype that Blacks in particular are born to sing and dance denies our creative intelligence and fuels the myth that Blacks and whites are inherently different. Such views make it easier to dismiss the seriousness of Black art and reduce Black folk to amusement for white eyes and ears. Black folk became an entertaining race—on slave ships, on plantations where masters competed for the most gifted performers, and, later, in freedom, when Black entertainment offered Black artists a measure of independence and financial reward as their performances were coveted and exploited by the white world.

The terms of Black performance trace back to that fateful ship and carry on in the name of that anonymous Black girl who was murdered for refusing to dance for people who viewed her movement in vulgar terms. Black performance since then has sought to heal the traumatic rift between the quality and source of African art and the violent coercion to entertain myopic white folk in the New World. Black performers forged a complex racial identity and preserved ties to a cultural heritage under relentless fire. White folk used Black art to construct stereotypes of docile Sambos, happy Negroes, witless buffoons, and classless coons, character types that populated the minstrel shows that first darkened the culture in the 1830s.

Racial paradox flooded, and united, the slave ship, the plantation, and the minstrel stage: white people yearned to be near a Blackness they mocked, that made them feel superior. White folk insisted that Blackness be staged when and how they saw best and performed in a manner that brought them the greatest pleasure. Black folk performed a sly and signifying style of Blackness that seemed to say "yes" to stereotypes even as they secretly said "no" in their hearts. Black people often rolled their eyes to parody the white belief that they were clowns or fools. Blacks who performed found the means to entertain "massa" while helping to emancipate the masses. This is most clearly heard when the enslaved sang spirituals about a heavenly destination with veiled information about escape to earthly freedom. Harriet Tubman used spirituals to signal hiding places, danger zones, and safe escape. To be sure, the genuinely gifted Black performer always stood out. But the myth of the innately talented Black person persuaded white folk to command and choreograph performance from the masses of Blacks. In an inspired example of the Kantian concept of making a virtue of necessity, the enslaved got great at the performance that was demanded of them. They routinely turned the misfortunes of color into a stronger and richer Black identity.

Contemporary Black performance carries the weight of this history, the imprint of these struggles and tensions, in both exceptional and everyday expressions. Black performance is singing or dancing on Broadway or at the local talent show, making music for the Philharmonic or the nursing home, preaching at Washington National Cathedral or taking a dry run in a homiletics class, lecturing at a prestigious university or speaking to a sorority gathering at a junior college, launching a three-pointer in the NBA Finals or shooting hoops at the neighborhood YMCA, and presiding over the wedding of Harry and Meghan at Windsor Castle or blessing the nuptials of Hakim and Monifa at a modest Baptist church.

Black performance is how Black folk greet each other, go to work, sell lemonade, bird-watch, barbecue in the park, style our hair, direct the church choir, sling slang, write with a certain flourish, stand on the porch, drive, get arrested, or even die at the hands of cops. Black folk read or ad lib from a racial script centuries in the making. Black performance is both formal and informal, standard and vernacular, professional and amateur, planned and spontaneous. It is driven by Black love, joy, pleasure, pain, purpose, grief, freedom, justice, democratic hunger, moral necessity, and electrifying experimentation. It is shaped by white terror, delight, demand, appropriation, curiosity, anger, appreciation, greed, voyeurism, dominance, hatred, control, and insecurity.

Black performance is a paradox, wrapped in a conundrum, inside a contradiction; surely there must be a key. Black folk are forced to entertain race, engage the idea of it, its social expressions and its personal consequences. But as a people forced to be an entertaining race, we are, by definition, not just performers but a performance of many sorts, of fictions and fantasies, of design and chaos, of ideals and moral sentiments, of possibility and romance and dead ends and dashed hopes and snuffed ambitions. Black performance embodies the ceaseless churn of life pitched against its lethal limits.

On the surface, the very idea of performance seems to lose its distinction and merit when tied to Black life. If every act is a performance, and every word vibrates in performance, and if every life is bathed in performance, then the word ceases to separate spheres of activity and instead is a synonym for Black breath and being. In such a view, the term "performance" might reasonably be omitted without losing the meaning of Blackness.

That may all make sense when looking from the outside into Black culture. Black life takes shape in a white world where stereotypes empty Blackness of all meaning except what benefits the broader world. That means that Black folk only exist when they are forced to adopt a narrow philosophy of life that is part Descartes, part Nas: *Ut praestare, ergo sum*, I perform, therefore I am.

If we go back to the ship *Recovery*, to the plantation, to the sharecropping field, to the southern backroad, or come forward to Central Park or Starbucks, or the urban street corner commanded by cops, it is clear that Black life is tolerated only if Black folk submit to the white will at all times.

It is the white world's demand to bow to racial hierarchy that grinds every Black limb, every Black thought, every Black word to performance inside the white world.

But Black folk found escape and solace in their own culture. Black performance fed on the inspiration that flowed in the bosom of Africa. As each generation got further away from the motherland, performance became an even greater source of identity, strength, value, and survival. This is why many Black folk who headed north in dramatic numbers in the first half of the twentieth century clung more tenaciously to communal and culinary habits than some of their southern kin. Nothing feeds the hunger for home like nostalgia and alienation. And, in a way, Black performance that was further in land and clock from its African origins became an alluring tertium quid. This is in sharp contrast to W. E. B. Du Bois's opposition to the racist belief that "between men and cattle, God created a tertium quid, and called it a Negro."

The Black performance I have in mind is a vibrant third thing sandwiched between its edifying African character and its greatly undervalued expression in the white world. The purpose of Black performance in the New World is to restore a Black universe and to reestablish Black humanity. The yearning for positivity is nearly absent at Black America's African roots. Before the Scramble for Africa starting in the nineteenth century, Africans possessed the freedom to explore the good, the bad, and the ugly of Black identity. They felt no need to justify or explain their existence beyond acknowledging the ethics or deities that governed their society.

When the white world kidnapped African bodies to the Americas, elements of Black performance both traveled along and were cast overboard; Africans both adjusted and resisted. Black performers felt the need to fend off the white gaze and to re-create a sense of home while forging new expressions in the belly of a racist beast. We became preoccupied with positive representations of Black culture in a way we had not been before. We policed our own culture for fugitive expressions of Blackness that jeopardized our perception in the world. We reserved the greatest disdain for disloyal enslaved figures who dropped dime on our plans for escape or revolution.

Black folk became obsessed with the quality and character of Black American performance. They worried whether a given person was a coon or Tom whose performances were mindless updates of blackface minstrelsy or sellout behavior, on the plantation or at the political podium. This held true whether figures were fictional, like Samuel L. Jackson's character

Stephen, who was an eager traitor in Quentin Tarantino's slavery revenge fantasy *Django Unchained*, or true life, like Supreme Court Justice Clarence Thomas, who practices chronic betrayal from the bench.

The quest for restoration has tightened the seams in the narrowing quilt of acceptable Black performance. It was tragic that white folk sought to impose their restrictive views of race on Black culture; it was just as tragic for Black folk to promote suffocating racial visions of their own.

Thus, every Black performance carries far more weight than it should. Every film, every album, every play, every speech, every political decision, every book, every essay, every song, every tweet, every word we utter, every notion we entertain, means more than it ought to mean on the surface. This is in sharp contrast to the broader culture. There is the white given, which is the cultural starting point of knowledge. This perspective boasts an *a priori* manner of evaluating white ideas and actions. Whiteness is seen as inherently valid. Reason itself is a servant of the white world and endorses white experience. And then there is the Black given, in which knowledge of Black ways of being and thinking follows an *a posteriori* path and cannot be taken for granted. Black people must produce in each generation fresh evidence of our intelligence and humanity.

Black performance in the New World has attempted to bridge the chasm between Africa and America, between a Blackness presumed and a Blackness pressured. It has been charged with these imperatives: to recover Africa, which is to say, to reestablish the humanity and intelligence of Black folk and a Black universe as norm; to entertain the world, including white folk, while liberating Black folk; and to generate a political vocabulary specific to the circumstances of our existence in America.

Those imperatives weave through four vital dimensions of contemporary Black performance: echo, shadow, spark, and register. In each case, there is what is given to the white world—what is performed as shield, face, and deflection—and there is what is given to, and taken from, Black culture, as the exploration and emancipation of Black life.

ECHO

Echo is the sound that Black folk make as we perform our humanity by talking, singing or making music, across many centuries, cultures, and countries. Black music is the sound of Black people embracing a heritage from which we could never be completely separated. The drum is the percussive seed planted in African earth and sprouting in Black American soil. But the drum didn't belong to Africa alone. It was used by white slavers in

European colonies and the West Indies to announce the beginning of an auction "scramble," in which buyers scurried frantically to pick and choose among newly arrived Africans in the pen where they were herded. The drum also signaled throughout the Middle Passage the enforced performance of the Black enslaved.

But Africans snatched the drumbeats to communicate. The drum blended their tongues into a percussive language that vibrated truths that transcended tribes. The drum amplified a lingua franca of rebellion and escape. That is why the drum was outlawed throughout the New World. Beyond its emancipatory effects, the drum gained a great hearing in Black America. More recently, the drum has echoed in the frenetic rhythms of James Brown and in the fierce backbeats of hip hop.

Two centuries ago, Thomas Jefferson contended that Blacks are more gifted than whites with "accurate ears for tune and time," though he said it remained to be seen whether they could compose extensive melodies and complicated harmonies. Jefferson also contended that misery produced moving poetry, and while he acknowledged that Black folk suffered great misery, he maintained that we lacked poetry. Jefferson wasn't alone: long before Monticello's venerable polymath weighed in, and for quite some time afterward, our music has been used to prove Black inferiority, despite the resonant echo of our musical mastery. His prejudice aside, Jefferson was at least open to the possibility that Black folk might achieve even a little of the refined sentiment and highbrow tastes of Europeans.

Black music is more than electrifying rhythms and entrancing beats, more than lyrical invention lifted by vivid imagination. Black music is even more than the glorious harmonies of the R&B girl group The Sweet Inspirations or the majestic melodies of Earth, Wind and Fire, proving Jefferson's worries about Black melody and harmony quaint. Black music is also the sound of Black folk battling beliefs about Black savagery. It is also the aching rhythms and yearning beats that measure the passion and hunger for human affirmation.

Black music is the faithful score to a culture composed of soothing social melodies or bruising racial discord. The music of the late John Coltrane is a resonant example. Coltrane mastered, then abandoned, the mellow modulations and cool chords of modal jazz and the staccato rhythms of bebop and hard bop. He later experimented with what critic Ira Gitler termed "sheets of sound" as notes cascaded down jagged time signatures into shrieking sonic vortexes. Coltrane opted for the mood disorders evoked by violent variations of sound, shifts in timbre, and wind shears of acoustic energy that rip through self-contained notes and themes. Coltrane was playing toward a sort of unified field theory of Black sound that constructed dense improvisation from the sensual thump of random melody and brooding dissonance.

Black music in this vein might be heard as the effort to tame racial chaos by modifying sound. Coltrane's avant-garde riffs were the perfect contrast to the melancholy of sorrow songs and the worry of the blues. If Coltrane's musical menu satisfied a different sonic taste than the offerings of spirituals and the blues, all these sounds fed a larger appetite for the poetry of Black self-expression. Coltrane's poetry found voice as he blew through cacophony in the quest for musical beauty that echoed the struggle to hear the sweet strains of social justice in racial disharmony. The poetry of spirituals and the blues speaks more directly in the lyrics on which their musical fates rest. Indeed, the poetry that Jefferson said Black folk lacked speaks in the hidden messages of spirituals. That poetry also echoes in the ironic and comic tones of the blues. The blues pokes fun at imperfection and invites heartbreak to dance with joy, representing the noisy diversity of Black humanity. The poetry of Blackness resonates as well in the verse and literary devices of hip hop. Rap music reflects how Black culture demands that song supply not only artistic but political satisfaction as well.

The political urge of Black music cannot compensate for our lack of power: we cannot control the white man, so we arguably fill the air with our resentful sounds. But Black music nurtures our humanity and supports our engagement with society. I learned this up close in the sixties and seventies in Detroit, the city of my birth.

When the Motown Record Corporation rolled out of the Detroit factory of Berry Gordy's imagination in 1960, it was fueled by the goal of all great Black art: to thrill the senses and light the mind in one blessed gesture. Motown engineered its unique model of musical genius to navigate the twists of a tortured racial history and the turns of a Black culture at once accommodating, resisting, and redefining American identity. It was no small feat for an upstart Black record label to so quickly live up to its courageous and, at the time, brazen slogan: The Sound of Young America. Gordy dared the nation to deny the Motor City tunes floating from their car radios—a sound that Motown's engineers perfected by building in the studio a small tinny-sounding radio to mimic what came tumbling from automobile speakers and pocket-size transistor radios. Gordy's gospel of racial harmony was brilliantly exhorted by solo evangelists like Smokey

Robinson, Mary Wells, and Stevie Wonder and supported by angelic choirs like the Temptations, the Supremes, and the Four Tops.

Hungry to spread its message around the globe, Motown hit the road in the sixties for a series of concerts that featured its leading stars in the Motortown Revue. More than once during that decade of seismic social change, the Motortown Revue alighted on Harlem's legendary Apollo Theater. The storied community that hosted a Black literary renaissance in the twenties and thirties seemed the perfect witness to the flowering of its musical equivalent thirty years later. The first of four albums issued by Motown that featured live recordings of the Motortown Revue was recorded at the Apollo during a weeklong stint in 1962 and released in 1963. This deepened the symbolic ties of Detroit and Harlem, two great Black meccas. It also underscored how crucial Motown was in reshaping the image of Black folk to the world. The stereotype of the uncouth darky gave way to the glamor and glory of men and women singing of Black love and social change. Motown's artists were imbued with the panache of Marvin Gaye and the elegance of Diana Ross, both of whom exemplified exquisite Black style and performed their songs to make a better world.

Black sound, the performance of Blackness in sound, is, thus, the echo of the Black Atlantic in modern American culture. The music thrives on a Blackness that feels no need to prove that we are whole or appropriate. Irreverence is born when Black folk are free to be themselves. The unapologetic irreverence of Black music drives its vibrant sexuality and erotic intensity. Black sound rebukes white claims of Black pathology by making a virtue of the things that whites find offensive. The performance of Black irreverence filters brilliantly through the blues, hip hop, and moments of R&B in between. It roars in Millie Jackson's raw explicitness, and it purrs in Grace Jones's sometimes humorous probing beneath the sexual surface.

The irreverence of Black sound is also heard in "mumble rap," the hip hop style du jour. Classic hip hop is proud of its clever wordplay and lyrical creativity. Mumble rap turns its back on clarity and artfully muddies sound and obscures literary meaning in its postmodern Black urban communication. For James Brown, the sonic godfather of hip hop, the percussive was a powerful instrument of expression. In mumble rap, its artists favor the sonic over the rational and prize melody above poetry as a language of performance. It is all part of the sound of the Black Atlantic.

The Black Atlantic sound resonates across the cultures of Blackness and affirms our common humanity while respecting our differences. As much as there is a dialogue between, say, Lagos, Nigeria, and Augusta, Georgia, between Fela Kuti and James Brown, there is something distinct in the American scene that does not merely capture Africa but transforms it. Pockets of the Black Atlantic hear the irreverent as crucial to our complicated identities.

Jazz, for instance, was born in irreverence, expressing the unrespectable thoughts, outlaw perspectives, and outside-the-box beliefs of Black life. It eventually came to represent Black genius and humanity in the battle over the cultural status of Black art. It is now widely viewed as the quintessential American art form to which other Black art is compared and often found wanting. Hip hop has been blasted out of sound systems and by critics who hear it amplifying the worst features of American life. Legendary jazz artist Wynton Marsalis famously assailed the culture on aesthetic grounds: sounding like a latter-day Thomas Jefferson, he contended that the best songwriting blends harmony, melody, and rhythm, disqualifying rap because it is rooted in an artless repetition of beat that signals a lack of musical invention and imagination. The gifted late jazz critic Stanley Crouch called rappers "thugs" and compared the art form to the infamous racist 1915 D. W. Griffith film when he lambasted hip hop as "*Birth of a Nation* with a backbeat." Such a view ignores the origins of jazz partly in the brothels of New Orleans and in the same economic squalor that birthed hip hop. The sonic warfare inside Black culture, and the one between Black culture and the white world, echoes the tensions of earlier generations over art that is a redemptive representation of Black humanity. The tension has never ended.

SHADOW

Black performance, too, is about what is seen, but resides in the shadow cast by race. The shadow is symbolic of Black skin. It is also shorthand for how the optics of Blackness color the sights and sites of culture and society. For example, the performance of Blackness in film and television has both reinforced and interrupted racial stereotypes.

Racial demands shadow the Black visual arts with pressure to address conflicting desires. On the one hand, there is the desire for Black art to be positive, redemptive, reverent, and inspirational. On the other hand, Black art is urged to challenge convention and to freely explore complicated Black experience and complex Black identities. Black folk have heated debates about Black film and television because those images circulate widely and influence white eyes. The effort to perform in a way that rings true to Black culture while ringing the white cash register is in perennial tension.

At times, the way Black performance is staged, and seen, magnifies its impact. Politically incorrect Black voices are perhaps better appreciated when they resound from the stage rather than from the pulpit or the political podium. This message came home to me when Barack Obama and his then pastor Jeremiah Wright faced off over the meaning of racism during Obama's first run for president. Snippets of Wright's prophetic sermons had surfaced, especially his profane attack on the hypocrisy of American politics. The airing of Wright's sermons threatened Obama's political fate while also calling his patriotism into question. In a single weekend during the controversy, while in New York sampling the tangy postmodern Blackness of the Broadway play *Passing Strange*, I also caught rapper JAY-Z and comedian Chris Rock in concerts as each reflected on presidential politics.

Rock brilliantly launched into the political controversies that engulfed Obama and Wright, calling the beleaguered former pastor a seventy-five-year-old Black man who didn't like whites (he was actually sixty-six at the time). "Is there any other kind of seventy-five-year-old Black man?" Rock slyly asked, alluding to his well-known earlier bit that said that elderly Black men are the biggest racists in the nation because of lingering bitterness toward racist whites. But Rock made it clear that he shared some of Wright's skepticism about the Bush administration's political exploitation of terror when he questioned the very existence of Osama bin Laden—"a seven-foot-tall Muslim who gets electricity in a cave." In comedy, conspiracy theory is baptized in wit and reborn as common sense.

But Rock took aim at Black folk, too, wryly noting hoopla over the NAACP's symbolic burial of the "N" word. "Well, tonight, I'm its resurrection," Rock claimed to echoing howls. And he chided Blacks who failed to support Obama. "Only we would do that," Rock lamented. He vigorously argued that the likelihood of another credible Black candidate was so far off that it made no sense for Black folk to pass on the chance to vote one of their own into the presidency.

JAY-Z weighed in on Bush and Obama, too. With a huge portrait of President Bush projected on the screen behind him, the sophisticated griot stopped the music so that his words would sink in as deep as the waters that soaked the Gulf Coast during Katrina, the subject of his riveting song "Minority Report." After declaring in compelling cadence that his people "were poor before the hurricane came," the rapper defended those survivors who were demonized by asking in a powerful couplet: "Wouldn't you loot, if you didn't have the loot?/ Baby needed food and you stuck on the roof." JAY-Z noted the bitter irony of how a helicopter "swooped down just to get a scoop/ Through his telescopic lens but he didn't scoop you."

But the rapper reserved his greatest criticism for an indifferent "commander-in-chief [who] just flew by" and refused to share even the space in his plane with the suffering survivors. JAY-Z imagined what might have happened "if he ran out of jet fuel and just dropped, Huh, that woulda been something to watch/ Helicopters doing fly-bys to take a couple of shots, Couple of portraits then ignored 'em, He'd be just another bush surrounded by a couple orchids/ Poor kids just 'cause they were poor kids, Left 'em on they porches same old story in New Orleans." After asking his throng of revelers if they were ready for change, JAY-Z flashed a picture of Obama on-screen as his audience roared its approval.

The politics of race devoured the terrain laid out in rock maverick Stew's introspective musical *Passing Strange*. The conceit of the play, its troubling trope, is the pursuit of The Black Real, or how Black folk define what's racially and culturally authentic. In Stew's hands, it's at the heart of the various explorations and transgressions of Blackness as a young rock musician traipses from his native haunt of '70s Los Angeles, stoked by fervent Black religious ideas of purity and danger, to Amsterdam's insistent free love and on to '80s Berlin agitprop. The play marries high cultural jargon and pop cultural signifying to probe the meanings of authentic Blackness and who can be said to own them. As the narrator says, he is concerned with the "reinvention, transformation and the limits of Blackness." Or as one song's chorus contends, "I let my pain f*** my joy and I call the bastard art." Portraying a Black rock musician as the arbiter of authentic Blackness is to embrace a complex and irreverent Black identity. That variety of Blackness is as challenging to those inside the boundaries of Black culture as it is for those on the outside.

I glimpsed another dimension of the shadow of Blackness on Broadway in 2004. I sat in the Royale Theatre and witnessed a remarkable ensemble cast bring fresh urgency to the sublime poetry of Lorraine Hansberry's *A Raisin in the Sun*. Sean "P. Diddy" Combs, playing Walter Lee Younger, lent his heavyweight hip hop status to bring younger and Blacker faces to the Great White Way. Audra McDonald let loose with a stirring performance as Ruth Younger that garnered her a Tony for best featured actress in a play. Sanaa Lathan brought her sultry charm and thespian grit to bear on her Broadway debut, snagging a Tony nomination and a Theater World Award for her role as Beneatha Younger. And the regal Phylicia Rashad, recently named dean of the newly christened Chadwick A. Boseman College of Fine Arts at her alma mater, Howard University, plied her majestic talents as matriarch Lena Younger to win the first Tony Award for best actress in a play given to a Black woman. Rashad also made her Los Angeles directorial debut in 2011, adding considerable heft to the Ebony Repertory Theatre's timely production of *Raisin*.

The 2004 Broadway revival of Hansberry's classic portrayal of Black family life took place as President George W. Bush's compassionate conservatism left many Black families unprotected, the renewed attack on poor Black families was about to get heated up, and the mortgage crisis that would bleed off more Black wealth than any other event in history was about to descend on vulnerable Black households. In 2011, in the Age of Obama, *Raisin*'s relevance remained strong. The Black family was still buffeted by brutal economic forces, from the fallout over the subprime mortgage scandal to the overincarceration of Black males.

In a supposedly post-racial era—a term Obama deemed wrongheaded—the remnants of racial inequality littered the political landscape: Blacks lagged behind in education and employment but led the pack in poor health and mortality. And the gritty battles between Walter Lee and his mama were just as poignant as when Hansberry first sketched them in 1959. Walter Lee was throttled by hip ambition and instant gratification. Mama remained a dignified advocate of cautious tradition and heroic history. The performance of Blackness was undiminished in the years between the debut of Hansberry's work and contemporary Black life. The shadow of Black performance casts light, paradoxically, on both our representative and our unorthodox cultural expressions.

SPARK

In Black life, spark names the way Black performers blend head and heart to explore Black identity. Spark inspires Black performers to test the full range of thought and feeling in their craft, even if they sometimes rub against the grain. It also encourages ordinary Black folk to grapple with their emotions, especially trauma, as they master the psychology of race.

The late Chadwick Boseman addressed pressing issues in Black art and life. Boseman insisted that artists don't need permission to perform beyond the audience their talent brings them. "It only takes me and an audience," Boseman told me. "[If] we're talking about Greek theater, even, or some ritual theater, you only need one person, and the person you're talking to, in that exchange. If we have two people, it's even greater. If you have a chorus, it's even greater. But you only need [yourself] in order to [practice your craft]."

Boseman also disputed the common misperception, even among many Black folk, that there is a surplus of films that address slavery. "I hear people saying they're tired of movies about us being enslaved. But when you really think about it, there haven't been that many of them. If you compared it with the number of movies about white men who have affected history, there's no end to them commemorating those people and those ideas." Boseman found it "weird" in light of the celebration of white achievement that the artistic recognition of Black struggles was frowned on, expressing disappointment in those "who don't want to see us advance to another step in American society."

Boseman also decried an artistic landscape that often limits Black performers to the issue of race. "Very often, when you get a journalist, they're still trying to frame it as if this [film] is about race. This is about your oppression. No, this is just about our lives." Boseman pushed back on the notion that Black existence is lived primarily in reaction to the white world. "I'm not, every minute of my existence, thinking about myself in the context of you. I would be enslaved if [that were true]." Boseman called on eminent scholars to support his point. "It's essentially the double consciousness that was talked about by W. E. B. Du Bois, and that Frantz Fanon expounded upon. I think that's why you hear actors very often saying, 'I want to play a role that doesn't have to be Black.' That's part of what they're saying."

Boseman embraced the idea that Black artists should explore their interests beyond race. "Even though I've played characters that are the first black person to do [something historic], or James Brown, who creates music styles, I still feel the same way as other actors about that. Maybe I just want to do a horror film, because I'm free enough to do that too. Maybe I want to do a comedy. I'm free enough to do that as well." For Boseman, such freedom did not negate his Blackness. "All of those things somehow are part of what it means to be an African American artist, or an African artist, and fully express yourself."

At times the limitations on Black performance are imposed from within the culture. When JAY-Z decided to work with the NFL to boost their quality of pregame and halftime musical performers and social justice agendas, many matched him against Colin Kaepernick, the blackballed NFL quarterback who grated on white team owners' nerves because of his courageous stand against racial oppression. But the same double consciousness that Boseman cited came into play in the unyielding opposition between the two figures. The scenario pitted a great Black performer in one realm against a noted Black performer in another arena. But both of them are in search of the most effective ideas in support of Black identity and social justice. It posed the question: Can someone come inside and work for the change he demanded on the outside?

"I think there is an important role for being on the outside and agitating and holding people's feet to the fire, and making it clear that we all have to do better," says Hillary Clinton, whose 2016 presidential campaign JAY-Z and his wife endorsed and supported with a concert. "But I also think there's an important role for being on the inside. Because once you agitate and once you make the point that you expect changes, somebody's gotta be there to keep the pressure on and actually do the negotiations to reach their changes. And what's so remarkable about JAY-Z is [that] he's played both. He's been the outside voice and he's been the inside negotiator."

There is little tolerance for strategy and nuance in an era that lusts for immediate ideological gratification or political moralizing. The emcee Rapsody, who released a critically acclaimed album, *Eve*, in 2019, argues that "there's more than one way to do things. In the same way we had a Martin Luther King, and a Malcolm X is the same way we need a JAY-Z and Colin Kaepernick. We have to be patient in allowing people to show us [who they are] through their actions, and not necessarily following the herd of people that go off quickly in emotions."

Not that emotions are useless. Neither are they limited to the disarray suggested by the phrase, now popular in Black circles, that a given person is lost "in their feelings." Emotion is the flip side of enlightenment on the coin of spark. Feeling and thought are wed in a psychology of race that permits us to peer into the Black psyche and to probe mass white psychology.

Trauma, more than any emotion, links Black Americans to Black folk from the continent. Trauma contains the oceans of agony in which enslaved Black bodies suffered or drowned. The act of being seized from their motherland or being ripped with white hands from their mother's wombs devastated generations of Black folk. The traumas were cascading: the trauma of being alienated at birth and later separated from one's family, the trauma of being forced into lifelong labor without compensation, the trauma of being denied to flourish as an agent of one's own destiny, and the trauma of being repeatedly punished, and often killed, at the hands of white folk. Black performance was marked by trauma in the sorrow songs "Nobody Knows the Trouble I've Seen," "Sometimes I Feel Like a Motherless Child," and the post–Civil War spiritual "Oh Freedom!," where the protagonist testifies, "And before I'd be a slave/I'd be buried in my grave/And go home to my Lord and be free."

The emotional odyssey of surviving trauma persisted long after slavery. But Black folk didn't just express the pain and suffering of Blackness; they also gave voice to inexplicable joy and defiant hope. The blues squeezed comedy from tragedy with witty self-deprecation. Jazz, meanwhile, denied sorrow emotional sovereignty over Black life by channeling delight through the vocal cords of Billie Holiday and Sarah Vaughan and trumpeting the defeat of anguish through the horns of Louis Armstrong and Miles Davis.

The gridiron and the court have been sacred ground for the performance of Black emotion. Football players trample on ancient agonies and blocked feelings through end zone dances. Basketball players tap the suppressed zeal of captive souls in a fit of chest thumping after scoring a three-pointer.

When Serena Williams famously did the Crip Walk dance to celebrate her sixth Wimbledon victory, she indulged a triple irreverence: a Black woman appropriating a Black male celebration; a searing twist of a gang ritual into a cultural performance of Black genius and bliss; and the projection of supreme body control into a rigorous choreography of Black female swag.

Emotional Black performance frees Black folk from a culture that harshly judges Black feeling and perception. The tropes of the Angry Black Woman and the Volatile Black Male chastise Black folk for the same emotions that flow freely in the white world. Or Black folk are disdained for supposedly favoring the heart over the head when our emotions emerge. For instance, Google honored the abolitionist and writer Ignatius Sancho with a Doodle in 2020 to commemorate British Black History Month, whom Thomas Jefferson had damned with faint praise by noting that his writings "do more honour to the heart than the head," that his "imagination is wild and extravagant, escapes incessantly from every restraint of reason and taste," and that he is found "always substituting sentiment for demonstration." Perhaps Jefferson couldn't stomach the gall of a Black writer casting a critical eye on the untoward passions and violent emotions of white life, as Sancho wrote of the Gordon Riots of June 1780 (not unlike the insurrectionary riot of January 6, 2021, in Washington, D.C.) where Protestants angry at the parliamentary extension of Roman Catholic enfranchisement morphed into a mob that looted and burned parts of London: "There is at this present moment at least a hundred thousand poor, miserable, ragged rabble, from 12 to 60 years of age, with blue cockades in their hats—besides half as many women and children, all parading the streets, the bridge, the park, ready for any and every mischief."

The Black emotional landscape is glutted with grief and knotted with injury. Trauma dominates our Age of Black Siege. We are forced to see Black death recycled in videos of Black fatalities on the streets, a spectacle that retraumatizes Black folk with each viewing. Some of us shield ourselves from repeated exposure to trauma while others refuse to watch the first time. This is part of the psychology of self-defense in an era of self-care.

One of the most compelling dimensions of spark is the psychology of Black performance, where Black folk must be strategic, and therefore measured, in order to beat white folk at their own game. There is a relentless masking of Black effort: Black folk deliberately disguise their intentions and misrepresent their motives to psych out their counterparts in the mainstream. The Black enslaved constantly played their supposedly smarter masters for fools when they feigned ignorance or illness to get the upper hand in a game of psychological warfare. When Black folk signify, they are performing not simply a grammatical ruse, but a psychological strategy, too, a place where Chomsky mingles with Freud.

The psychology of self-care grows from the performance of Black self-regard, a timely lesson passed on by the Black Lives Matter movement. The withdrawal of tennis champ Naomi Osaka from the 2021 French Open over concern for her mental health is one of the most dramatic performances of the psychology of Black self-care. The criticism she got was muted by a surprising show of solidarity and sympathy for the Black star. Osaka prized self-regard over athletic performance. Her dilemma recalled the bitter conflict between Black self-preservation and performance for the white world at great peril to oneself. If the enslaved girl's refusal to dance led to her death, then Osaka's withdrawal, which may be her greatest performance yet, vindicated the enslaved girl's choice. While both of them exercised self-care in refusing to perform, one died for her choice so that the other one could live with her decision.

Of course, that same Black Lives Matter movement has criticized the performative, where one offers an emotionally charged or politically correct performance of social awareness while not following through with a commitment to true justice. The performative must be viewed in bigger and more positive terms than the negative meaning it has gained.

The performative in Black life has social value and political merit. For instance, the performative is handy in the use of mass psychology to pressure whites to justly transform the culture. The performative might involve, for example, a Black artist like Amanda Seales making an Instagram post of herself on a trampoline, suggesting that she is taking a necessary mental health break and isn't available to answer the questions of white folk about how to address social injustice, questions they should research for themselves. Such a performance may have forced some white allies to admit the debilitating psychic toll of placing that burden on Black folk.

It might also offer the occasion to probe the white psyche: how does one explain white dependence on the very people who have endured great harm? The appeal to psychological strategies of social resistance are important sparks of Black performance. This kind of Black performance surely doesn't undo the European denigration of Black life and art. But it does present the opportunity to reverse the white gaze and ask pointed questions about the psychology of whiteness, an effort that draws on the intellectual heft, emotional energy, and psychological insight of Black culture.

REGISTER

Register is the constantly evolving manner in which cultural meanings of Blackness flow through gestures of style and spirit. Style recycles the spirit of Black freedom and restores the dignity of Black humanity. Style flows especially strong in dancing. Dance encompasses both formal and vernacular performance in the theater, on stage, whether jazz or ballet, and in street dance like twerking, a sensually charged dance performed in a low squatting stance that grew out of the hip hop bounce music scene in New Orleans in the late 1980s. Twerking connects Black female movement and sexuality to a long history of cultural expression that has often been condemned as licentious.

Other gestures of Black style have also been deplored: the Black male rhythmic walk and sensuous gait, which conjures the fear of sexual prowess, and the exuberant and colorful way Black bodies occupy all sorts of public spaces. In the performance of Black existence, the moderation, adjustment, and restriction of gestures of Black style are crucial to Black self-preservation.

The register of Black performance is about more than personal survival. Styles of political movement also signify the Black performance of justice and democracy. Black bodies marching in the streets brought color and style to the performance of Black resistance—from escape from slavery to armed rebellion against enslavement, to principled protest in public rallies against Jim Crow and southern apartheid to dramatic civil disobedience against racial terror. Ella Baker, John Lewis, Fannie Lou Hamer, Diane Nash, Jim Lawson, Rosa Parks, Martin Luther King, Jr., and countless anonymous souls performed all kinds of Black resistance: Black bodies marching across bridges, sitting-in at lunch counters, confronting snarling police dogs, being washed against buildings with fire hoses, being beaten on court steps, singing in jails, and speaking at movement podiums.

Styles of Black protest filter through art forms as well. As original *Hamilton* cast member Renée Elise Goldsberry told me, Black artists invent and then abandon art forms because they no longer embody Black resistance. "[Black art is] no longer valid protest [when] the establishment has fallen in love with the brilliance of the form, and so they take it over," Goldsberry says. "The blues section, and the gospel section, when you used to go to the record store, were now [filled with] all these white artists. So, we keep abandoning [these art forms] because there's no protest in that, and we have to keep finding a new art form, a new genre of music to speak our truth." Goldsberry says that hip hop has managed to avoid being discarded: "What I find really amazing is that this form of music continues to work. It continues to satisfy. It continues to offend. We haven't needed to [abandon it] because it's something that continues to evolve. That's why it's so needed in this America."

The grammar of Black style encourages the ongoing exploration of a rich range of ideas, identities, and performances. Styles of Black passing— whether on the basketball court, where a Black player throws the ball without looking, part of a ritualized expression of Black cool; in perilous racial situations where Blackness is, paradoxically enough, erased, so that a Black body that passes for white won't suffer the same fate of erasure; or when a Black body dies and passes from one world to the next—archive performances of both Black survival and death.

Styles of Black performance transform Black genius into political capital. As actor Daveed Diggs told me: "[Black art] has opened a lot of eyes to [the fact] that there is genius in places where maybe classically it wasn't thought that there was. It's happened before. The Harlem Renaissance, and the Jazz Era. It happens again and again that the popular art of the time is where black folks are allowed to be brilliant first. And then it seems like that can open doors to getting a seat at the table." As if on cue, in 2016 noted singer-songwriter Solange Knowles released *A Seat at the Table*, an album that grappled with these ideas.

Black performance opens us as well to spirit. Performance can make us sensitive to the register of Black religious ecstasy, effort, and effect. Spirituality can redeem Black performance. Register emphasizes the public performance of Black spirituality, from singing in choirs, to praying, to preaching. The performance of sacred music in church nurtures Black liturgy, ritual, and ceremony. But Black spirituality registers far beyond the sanctuary when Black religious music is performed in secular spaces. Recordings of Black choirs spread the religious message of Black salvation and redemption. But you don't have to be a church member to appreciate Kirk Franklin's mesmerizing melodies and hypnotic harmonies.

Neither do you have to subscribe to the Holy Trinity for your spirit to register the riveting rhetoric of Gardner Taylor, T. D. Jakes, Gina Stewart, Emilie M. Townes, Frederick Douglass Haynes III, Lance Watson, and thousands of other Black preachers. Black preaching is the public performance of sacred speech that offers both spiritual nurture and social support. When Black believers face illness, unemployment, or family crises, the preacher's words become God's Word and create an expectation of "blessing," which might translate as psychological relief and moral solidarity.

The prophetic performance of ministers like Martin Luther King, Jr., Jesse Jackson, Al Sharpton, Prathia Hall, and Vashti McKenzie carries the moral energy of Black sacred speech into secular arenas in the demand for freedom and equality. Their contributions fundamentally reshape national destiny. America could never mean what it does today without Martin Luther King's stirring performance of civic virtue and radical democracy.

"I think that my first obligation is to keep the King tradition of social justice that I learned under Reverend Jackson and Reverend [William August] Jones alive," Al Sharpton tells me. "So, I'm looking at the landscape of the challenges of my time. Continued criminal justice [transformation] from Trayvon Martin to Stop and Frisk in New York to Stand Your Ground to George Floyd and beyond. I look at all of that and I say, 'Now how do we deal with it?' You have to dramatize it. Our whole thing was demonstration, then legislation, then reconciliation. That was how we were trained . . . right out of the [Martin Luther King–led] SCLC [Southern Christian Leadership Conference] manual."

King's "I Have a Dream" speech at the 1963 March on Washington and Jesse Jackson's "Our Time Has Come" speech before the 1984 Democratic National Convention are remarkable performances of Black religious belief. Their Black sacred rhetoric amplified the spiritual aspirations and moral imagination of Black America. Black preaching registers a complex world of style and spirit that represents Black performance at its best.

* * *

Black performance shapes America to this day. In fact, the current performance of Blackness links us to the nation's origins and affirms Black life.

The jury in the 1792 trial of Captain Kimber quickly absolved him of legal responsibility for the death of the anonymous enslaved girl. Two hundred and thirty years later, in 2021, another jury weighed the death of a Black man caused by the actions of a white man with an official title. This time the jury didn't fall for the prior illness ruse and convicted Derek Chauvin for the murder of George Floyd.

Floyd's last performance—sadly, it was a performance of death—embodied all the elements that make Black performance resonate. Floyd's voice echoed around the world as he repeatedly declared, "I can't breathe." The shadow of his dark skin captured on a cellphone video lit up the globe and made the world see the injustice it hadn't seen before. His death sparked millions of commentaries, reflections, meditations, and think pieces about the nature of systemic racism and how we must change our culture to embrace genuine democracy. The trauma of Floyd's death, and the death of so many others, continues to haunt the country. Floyd's public murder unleashed seismic gestures across the globe. His gentle spirit registered on our collective consciousness and inspired us to achieve a moral maturity we have too long refused.

Black performance has in many ways been the measure of the American soul. What we have said, sung, seen, written, rapped, filmed, recorded, danced, preached, run, dribbled, painted, marched, and so much more has made the nation incalculably richer, deeper, and better. We have entertained the country with our gifts and used those gifts to entertain the idea of race, indeed, the idea of America, with a redemptive love that is both unquenchable and nearly incomprehensible. No matter what goes down, our loyalty to America only grows stronger as we shape the nation with our blood and brains, our limbs and lives.

This book collects some of my efforts to both embody and interpret Black performance and to test the limits of the American imagination against Black life and culture. I have performed my Blackness and American identity in a number of roles: preacher, writer, pastor, university professor, public intellectual, lecturer, cultural critic, author, social activist, newspaper columnist, radio talk show host, political analyst, and media commentator. I have tried to live up to the high ideals and noble aspirations of the figures who have blazed the path for me. I have tried to keep faith with the traditions and examples that have given me and millions more inspiration to keep performing. Without Black performance, on every level, on every field, in every endeavor, at every period of history, America will not achieve its truest and best identity or begin to reach the most just meaning of its monumental experiment in democracy.

NOTA BENE

With rare exception, and unless otherwise noted, the sermons, lectures, speeches, interviews, and addresses published here were delivered extemporaneously and then transcribed. I have grown up in a Black rhetorical environment of call-and-response, where the moment of delivery—of a sermon, a lecture, a speech, a rally oration, an interview, and the like—is met, accented by, and responded to with often hearty reaction from the audience, punctuating the speech act with all sorts of passionate affirmation, delightful interruptions, and other excited verbal cues. Often, I, or many other (Black) figures, thrive on the electric interaction between audience and speaker, and sometimes the folk listening end up shaping in part the message they receive. In this collection, I have noted the verbal responses and other reactions from the audience in parentheses to give as great a sense as I can of what it was like to experience the live rhetorical moment. (Of course, Black folk often talk back to actors on stage in live performance, or even voice their thoughts about the action on-screen as they take in a film and verbally react to what they see or feel.) Some of the chapters herein have been edited for length and/or focus; these elisions are indicated by a bracketed ellipsis [. . .]. From piece to piece, the reader may note some stylistic variations; these variations have been retained to be truthful to time and place. The grammar, including the colorful vernacular expressions and the sublimely curious tenses of African American Vernacular English (AAVE), has remained to give the fullest meaning possible of what it was like to hear the words as they were delivered. In a sense this hints at the rhetorical democracy that prevails in live moments of Black performance where the audience literally has its say. I felt this was the best way to communicate the dynamic character and the dramatic twists and turns of thought and expression that typify one man's engagement with, and embodiment of, the improvised and back-and-forth nature of Black performance.

THE ARTS

Exposing film is a delicate process—artful, scientific, and entangled in forms of social and political vulnerability and risk. Who is seen and under what terms holds a mirror onto more far-reaching forms of power and inequality. Far from being neutral or simply aesthetic, images have been one of the primary weapons in reinforcing and opposing social oppression. From the development of photography in the Victorian era to the image-filtering techniques in social media apps today, visual technologies and racial taxonomies fashion each other.

—Ruha Benjamin, *Race After Technology*

Right now I'm just aware that my job is to speak the truth of my experience and my corner of the world. I can't be afraid of that truth or mute it in any way, even as it becomes confronting for others or exposing of myself. The only way to remind us of our collective humanity is to keep pushing for more stories from the disenfranchised to have equal voice and support socially as those in positions of privilege. Balance of storytelling is all of our responsibility because we all ultimately benefit from it.

—Dominique Morisseau

In March 1987, when I was a second-year graduate student at Princeton University, I published, on my mother's fiftieth birthday, my first professional piece of writing, "Rap, Race, and Reality," for *Christianity & Crisis*, founded in 1941 by immortal theologian Reinhold Niebuhr.

As a budding scholar of modest means, I tried my best to fund my voracious habit of collecting music in the relatively new form of compact discs. While I appreciated my precious, if fading, vinyl, and my stash of cassette tapes, I was too poor to afford a generous stack of CDs on my graduate school stipend and first jobs out of graduate school. While I didn't collect my doctorate until 1993, I left Princeton in 1988 to take a job running an anti-poverty project, and teaching a few classes, at Hartford Seminary.

I also began writing an occasional music column in the free weekly newspaper *The Hartford Advocate*, for which I got no money but, to me, something equally important: free review copies of compact discs. And every now and then I'd write about figures like the late, legendary Luther Vandross and the great Anita Baker appearing locally in concert. By hook or crook, I was determined to replenish my music catalogue in the transition from albums and cassette tapes to the shiny new and wondrous form that slid smoothly into a large stereo or clicked snugly into a portable CD player. Later I also wrote occasional pieces for the *Hartford Courant* newspaper, catching Freddie Jackson or Karyn White in concert and writing about their electrifying performances.

Ever since the late 1980s I have avidly sampled broad varieties of music and consumed all manner of concerts, and, as a few more coins jangled in my pocket, I gained access to the marvels of Broadway, witnessing Denzel Washington's Great White Way debut as Sylvester Williams in 1988's Broadway premiere of *Checkmates*. I didn't know as I sat there enthralled by Denzel's performance, and those of the great Paul Winfield and the all-time-great Ruby Dee, that I'd be invited in coming years to lead several "talkbacks" for various Broadway plays and that I'd meet Dee and Denzel and call them friends. Denzel is one of the greatest actors of all time; from Spike Lee's incandescent biopic *Malcolm X* to Antoine Fuqua's splendidly bad-tempered *Training Day*, he shines no matter where he appears.

I extended my active patronage of the arts by taking in galleries and witnessing the wonders of drawings, paintings, and photography, whether at Harlem's Studio Museum or the Guggenheim on Manhattan's Upper East Side. When I moved to Chicago in the late 1980s, I enlivened my interest in architecture, too, and imbibed the incredible diversity of the city's built environment and cast eager eyes on its remarkably varied and intricate edifices.

And always, since the time I was a twelve-year-old kid and our neighbor Vivian volunteered in 1971 to take a few of us to the theater to see the film *Willard*—"get your grits together," she playfully admonished us in collecting the necessary funds to attend—I have been a film nut. In fact, the next year, I saw, in the backseat of our family car at the drive-in theater, the greatest film ever made, the epic touchstone for my quip, "everything you need to know in life can be gleaned from the Bible and *The Godfather*." I catch this Francis Ford Coppola masterpiece when I can in revival film houses that feature it in its outsize glory on the big screen. I watch *The Godfather: Part II* nearly as frequently, and like it nearly as much, although younger generations favor Al Pacino's portrayal of Michael Corleone's ruthless reign as the crucial predecessor to Brian De Palma's brilliantly bloody 1983 gangster film classic, *Scarface*, which also starred Pacino. But the young folk have it wrong: Marlon Brando's turn as Don Vito Corleone, despite his relatively brief appearance on screen, is so dominant a performance that it echoes across movie vistas to this day. Brando is the reason I watch *The Godfather* several times a year: to remind me of great art, to remind us all of the outsider's role in making America—the opening line, after all, from an immigrant, is "I believe in America"—and to remember the importance of honor, respect, and family. Salut!

I Love Music

On the Concert Stage

1

The King of Pop and the Queen of Everything

This piece appeared in Queen Bey, *an essay collection edited by my dear friend Veronica Chambers. It incorporates a briefer essay I penned as the foreword for Beyoncé's 2017 coffee table book,* How to Make Lemonade. *I saw Michael Jackson perform in person: he was legendary—his body lithe, his limbs rubbery, his dancing epic, his singing powerful. But Beyoncé, whom I have seen in concert many, many times, is all of that and more! As a musical artist, Michael's body of work is unexcelled. But as a performer, onstage, Beyoncé is the King!*

Beyoncé symbolically snatched from Michael Jackson the crown of best entertainer on the globe, ever, when, ironically enough, the curls atop her glorious crown got snatched into the blades of an electric fan. While that event had hardly anything to do with her ascent, it certainly had a lot to do with the performance of a Black and female identity that could meet any challenge on any stage at any time as she maintained her dignity and cool.

Sure, a fateful elevator would descend in her future, in which she proved the same point, but that was a different stage with very different stakes. And yes, she had stumbled and fallen down a set of stairs six years before her hair got entangled in the fan, but that was long before she became a global icon who would revolutionize the music industry with the release of two monumental visual albums, *Beyoncé* and *Lemonade*, without so much as a peep that they were on the way.

There, in Montreal, Canada, on July 22, 2013, at the Bell Centre, on the North American leg of her Mrs. Carter world tour, in the same year she released *Beyoncé*, Beyoncé's golden locks got caught in a circular high-powered fan as she descended stairs during an encore performance to get closer to her adoring audience. As she continued belting the tune "Halo," Beyoncé's bodyguard, Julius de Boer, tugged at the tufts of hair lodged in the screen of the fan, attempting to dislodge his most famous client's tresses at the very moment she mouthed the lyrics that gravity "can't forget / To pull me back to the ground again." De Boer was joined by a man and a woman from a security detail; the man handed de Boer a sharp implement and he was able, finally, to free Beyoncé from the fan's remorseless suction. Beyoncé didn't miss a note and kept singing throughout, and once free, received a hearty applause from her fans. She even parodied her predicament when she posted on her Instagram account rewritten lyrics to the song, changing them from "It's like I've been awakened / Every rule I've had you breakin'" to "I felt my hair was yankin' / From the fan that's always hatin.'"

In case it's not clear, my saying that she got caught in a fan while show-ing love for the fans who adore her is not simply a clever literary homage to homonyms and puns. And it's more than the truism that her hair symbol-izes her crown; it's that her mane is a metaphor, maybe even a metonym, for how often women, doing encores, which means working overtime, are sliced by patriarchy and sexism as they do twice the work of men and get only half the credit. It's not even that Beyoncé and Michael Jackson are an update of the gender inequality spotlighted in a 1982 *Frank and Ernest* cartoon, which was memorably paraphrased by the late maverick treasurer, and then governor, of Texas, Ann Richards, when she said to the 1988 Democratic National Convention, "Ginger Rogers did everything that Fred Astaire did. She just did it backwards and in high heels." Beyoncé is not simply doing at a higher level what Michael Jackson so brilliantly did. She's doing what no one before her has done. She is a cunning master who leaves others in her trail, whether she is singing, dancing, or perform-ing. Michael's musical body of work is unrivaled, but Beyoncé's work of her musical body on stage and in videos as a singer-dancer-performer is unsurpassed.

Beyoncé and Michael seemed to share a kinetic performance gene passed on to them by brilliant Black bodies in motion, from Bill "Bojan-gles" Robinson to Josephine Baker, from Sammy Davis, Jr., to Katherine Dunham. Beyoncé saw her first concert in April 1988 at the age of six when she witnessed Michael Jackson perform at the Summit in Houston, Texas. As a budding artist, Beyoncé spent countless hours absorbing Michael Jackson videos, gleaning dance moves and ideas and a grammar of elastic and electrifying entertainment. Michael Jackson's magnetic performances featured a lean frame that articulated a fluid esthetic of clean lines and mathematically precise gestures that Beyoncé embraced in her own rep-ertoire. But she upped the ante. As she matured, Beyoncé expanded the vocabulary of motion with a voluptuous frame that accentuates a combustible physical expressiveness and a more intense poetry of flexibility.

Michael brilliantly integrated street dance into his performance, most famously in his epic moonwalk, which bent time and collapsed space in a spasm of optical illusion that seemed to reverse motion and defy gravity. He was Einstein in a fedora. Beyoncé feminizes the geometry of flow in her surreally pliable limbs. She brings sweet antagonism to her dance discipline in a regimen of fiercely maintained and beautifully unresolved terpsichorean tensions: between formal and vernacular dance styles, between ballet and hip hop, jazz and krumping as she pivots between bust thrusts, overhead fist pumps, graceful chair choreography, head tosses, braid whips, shoulder shaking, frenetic breakdowns, tiptoe gestures, booty bumping, body rolls, hip grinding, sinuous floor crawls, double sidesteps, power stomping, spread eagles, lascivious tongue licks, runway prances, double hair flips, deep groove gyrations, arm extended airplane simulations, finger twirls and wrist twists, belly dance stomach manipulations, rubbery backbends, shimmying, air kicks, sensual undulations, twerking and booty popping, sashays and so much more. She is Euclid in an asymmetrical leotard.

Michael's signature moonwalk dance move may have anticipated dramatic attempts later in life to reverse the inevitable march of his aging, and perhaps, vicariously, in our celebration of him, our own, in clinging desperately to the childhood that both molded and maimed him. By the time Michael gave up the ghost at 50 years old on Thursday, June 25, 2009, the same day another pop cultural icon, Farrah Fawcett, lost her battle with cancer, we may have witnessed an eerie embodiment of *The Curious Case of Benjamin Button*. In both F. Scott Fitzgerald's novel and the Oscar-nominated film version starring Brad Pitt, Benjamin Button ages in reverse: born a shriveled old man, he dies a newborn baby. As an 11-year-old prodigy, Jackson burst into the public as a miniature adult seemingly immune to small talk and child's play. His singing erupted in a volcano of sound that buried his youth beneath an implausible, irresistible sophistication. If he knew too much for his age, he may have also known too much for his own good. Jackson's art opened a window onto emotions he couldn't possibly have understood. As he got older, he repented of his precociousness and took refuge in a childlike persona that at first amused and then provoked pity and horror. He eventually flaunted a penchant for sharing his bed with children, leading to accusations of molestation. Although he was acquitted of the charges, Jackson failed to persuade skeptics in the court of public opinion. By the time he died, Michael was both loved and loathed by millions because he refused in some ways to grow up. To twist Fitzgerald's words, Jackson proved that there are no second childhoods in America.

The truth may be that both of Jackson's childhoods were imagined: the first childhood snuffed by the inspiring and imperious demands of his father, Joseph; the second childhood carved from an occasionally dangerous nostalgia for the youth he largely missed. Beyoncé had an equally energetic and engaged childhood in Houston, though in a far more stable setting than that of the working-class Jackson clan in Gary, Indiana. Beyoncé is the daughter of former sales representative Mathew and former cosmetologist Tina, Black middle-class professionals who reared Beyoncé and her younger sister, Solange, in relative comfort. Beyoncé was quite shy and had few friends, prompting her parents to sign her up for a dance class when she was seven years old. Mathew and Tina were caught by great surprise a short while later at a community show when they first witnessed Beyoncé sing and dance with a self-confidence and vibrancy they had never seen in her.

It is true that at six years old she had come home bursting with enthusiasm for the new song her first-grade teacher had taught her, unabashedly performing it for Tina while looking her squarely in the eye and brimming with vocal authority. But the kitchen was one thing, the public platform a different animal. Like Michael, Beyoncé was most alive on stage, and like him, she found her esteem and métier in performance, in the public exhibition of privately held joys through song and dance. Beyoncé entered and won many talent show contests and beauty pageants. When she was nine, she won membership in the singing group Girls Tyme, performing with them at local competitions and national showcases, displaying her precocious talent and her prodigious work ethic while learning to compartmentalize the personal and professional, a trait that famously survived her teenaged years as a star in the phenomenal girl group Destiny's Child, the successor to Girls Tyme, and into adulthood with her legendary solo career.

What Michael and Beyoncé did with their voices was noteworthy too. As a youth, Michael displayed a precocious desire to plumb the depths of his voice that harkened back to Mozart's early genius. His soaring, soulful arpeggios as he ran up and down scales like a music track star; his poignant moaning and cooing and humming that formed a golden tunnel of sound in which his notes found blissful escape; and his naked wailing and fearless vulnerability all marked his vocal magic. As Michael grew older, his voice dramatically changed; his tone radically shifted. He no longer belted out R&B tunes in a blues-drenched melisma. Instead, Jackson as a solo artist spiced his undulating tenor with sonic hiccups, parenthetical yelps, falsetto sighs, and melodic grunts, all akin to musical Tourette's. Jackson created a set of pop songs that transformed American music and evaded the racial pigeonhole. Embellishing disco, fomenting funk, and dabbling in light rock on his superb 1979 album *Off the Wall*, Jackson reached his commercial peak with 1982's *Thriller*, the bestselling album in the world of all time.

As incredible a singer as Michael was—Jackson, for instance, stylistically echoed James Brown and Jackie Wilson, and yes, Otis Redding and William Hart—Beyoncé has rivalled him with her ecstatic experimentalism that has sparked her stylistic evolution of off-kilter syncopations, rhizomes of jutting rhythms layered atop one another, and the fertile fusion of talk-rap-singing. Beyoncé can arguably be said to be the matriarch and precursor to the mumble rap style, if not its content or themes, then its slinky, esoteric phrasing and its obscuring panache that revels in elided syllables; blurred, then fused, consonants; and conjoined, or contrapuntal, ellipses. It produces a sound where meaning is destroyed and re-created, where sense is intuited, inferred, implied, and percussively insinuated rather than explicitly, or clearly, drummed into our hearing. Beyoncé's vocal prowess, now, as a mature songstress—and in her case it must be said that she *stresses* song, pressing and shaping it in the magic of her sonic embrace—matches Michael's artistic heights.

Michael's most dynamic, explosive vocal performances, on record and on stage, occurred between the ages of 8 and 21, before the prodigious weight of his transcendent singing gifts gave way to an airier sonic shimmer that he ingeniously achieved in a softer and higher register of notes. When Michael came into full possession of his musical genius as auteur, he no longer possessed the range and resonance of his more brutally soulful and bluesy sound. Beyoncé, however, has grown from vocal grace to vocal grace in a steady procession from prodigy to master, mining a volatile sonic terrain that has only increased its range, depth, and power. Beyoncé's voice unleashes a cascade of notes down mountains of styles, some craggy with delightfully hostile hip hop beats that disrespect linear rhythms, others smoothed in R&B melodies and harmonies that form an archipelago of gospel grooves in her acoustic topography. Michael on stage, singing, after he reached his global fame, is no match for Beyoncé, on stage, singing, after she attained international recognition. The sheer quality of sound emanating from her durable instrument well into her thirties puts Beyoncé in a vocal stratosphere beyond Michael and her contemporaries. And when the dazzling range of her song meets the furious freedom of her body on stage, Beyoncé is in a league all her own.

But there is more to her craft than its sonic surface: Beyoncé renders pop songs as tone poems, transforming her art through stories of female aspiration, feminist resistance, and racial pride. Both Michael, starting as a child, and Beyoncé, largely as an adult, helped in their own ways to challenge and change racial and gender perceptions in America. The Jackson 5 singing group Michael formed with four of his brothers was signed to Motown Records in 1968, the year Martin Luther King, Jr., was murdered. Their string of hits starting in 1969 helped to usher in a post–civil rights version of Blackness that exploded on record with their electrifying sound and on stage with their fashionable expression of race pride. The Jackson 5 didn't have to give speeches or attend rallies to certify their authentic Blackness; the way they grew their hair and moved their bodies spelled love of their people in bold letters. Michael was a chocolate, cherubic-faced genius with an Afro halo. He and his brothers offered an image of Black masculinity that had all the style of the Black Panthers, and the broad appeal of Tony the Tiger, which is why their own cartoon series— their animated artistry—helped to integrate Saturday morning television in the early '70s. To be sure it was bubblegum, but their Blow Pops were spiked: coming only a few years after the Moynihan Report famously concluded in 1965 that the Black family was in shambles, the Jackson 5 presented an intact unit whose image of togetherness was as revolutionary in its own way as what was happening in the courts and streets. Blacks and whites rode Michael Jackson's vocal cords into musical ecstasy and absorbed the soft racial catechism of Motown universalism without protest or resistance.

Beyoncé's Blackness has been, from the start, complicated and contested, from her time as a little girl at school when she was targeted for her light skin and hair, to her time as an adult when her racial identity and gender politics have been relentlessly questioned, both within Black life and feminist circles and far beyond. Beyoncé's Blackness has been both subliminal and subversive, both implicit and explicit, both central and incidental, nearly accidental, both taken for granted and rendered invisible, or, at the very least, innocuous. Her pop aesthetic in the white world has been read, or been interpreted, as non-Black, or nonracial, universal, transcendent. She's not a color, not a race, not a genre, not a style, not a moment in the culture's self-reckoning; she's Beyoncé, a language, a medium, an identity, a category of existence and consciousness all her own.

But her Black acts have occasionally shattered the compact of racelessness for a Black artist in America, namely, that they swear off any hint of

Blackness and instead view Blackness as instrumental, that is, as critical in realizing the means to an artistic end, rather than substantive, that is, as grounding both one's approach and music—and one's themes, ideas, and identity, one's politics even—in that Blackness. Beyoncé's Black roots, her unapologetic embrace of her heritage and social protest, were displayed clearly in the video for her song "Formation." This led the legendary ensemble comedy television show *Saturday Night Live* to poke fun at the white panic the video inspired, with racial obliviousness referenced in the title of the segment: "The Day Beyoncé Turned Black."

Of course, white folk weren't the only ones worrying about Beyoncé's Blackness. Her mother, Tina Knowles-Lawson, feared that the predominantly white audience at the music festival Coachella wouldn't understand all the Black cultural references, especially those associated with Black college life, that Beyoncé brilliantly explored in her Coachella sets on successive weekends in the spring of 2018. But, according to her mother, Beyoncé rebuffed her: "I have worked very hard to get to the point where I have a true voice, and at this point in my life and career, I have a responsibility to do what's best for the world and not what is most popular." This squares with Beyoncé's response to those who accused her of anti-cop sentiment during her February 2016 Super Bowl halftime performance of "Formation"—a song where she embraced Black Lives Matter and criticized police misconduct. She later insisted she admired police but drew a distinction between good and bad cops: "But let's be clear: I am against police brutality and injustice. Those are two separate things. If celebrating my roots and culture during Black History Month made anyone uncomfortable, those feelings were there long before a video and long before me. I'm proud of what we created and I'm proud to be part of a conversation that is pushing things forward in a positive way." Later, Beyoncé offered an astute diagnosis of the tragic conflation of whiteness and national identity: "It's been said that racism is so American that when we protest racism, some assume we're protesting America."

All of this concern about Beyoncé came about after she skyrocketed to fame. The more popular she became, the more she dominated global media, and art, and culture, the less Black she became in the eyes of whites here and around the world. Beyoncé overcame one of the biggest barriers of Blackness: a whiteness that fantasizes that its racial identity is neutral and that its values are universal. In such a world, even the Black object of white fantasy is transmuted into a lifestyle, a goal, an aspiration, and, finally, an icon of perfection untainted by any particular identity. Such an illusory vision can only be challenged when one is willing to contest the terms of elevation and reject the projection onto one's flesh of the apolitical ideals such a status bestows. One must be eager to embrace an identity that is seen as ineligible for cultural deification: a dirty, dark, polluted Blackness that literally rises from the dust of Western civilization to reshape the institutions of society and culture.

To paraphrase the Bible, the rejected stone of Blackness has become the cornerstone of a civilization that was suspicious of its worth and merit. Beyoncé's body is a busy intersection where dangerous collisions occur between the cranky particularity of a Blackness rooted in the skin and skill of everyday Black folk and, from another direction, a colonized and curtailed Blackness, a fetishized and toothless Blackness, a subservient and symbolic Blackness. Hers is the irreverent and irresistible Blackness of artists who come bearing the gifts of their civilizations and tribes and are willing to remake the institutions they confront through the lens of the Blackness they convey. That is how the hallowed Super Bowl stage Beyoncé commanded became an opportunity to stage an insurrectionary Blackness that jettisoned dominant meanings and substituted resistive ones. That is how Coachella went overnight from being one of the whitest showcases for artistic expression to a prominent platform for unhinged, uncontained Blackness, for metastatic Blackness, for a Blackness rooted in Black cultural styles and norms, in Black intellectual ferment, in Black college mores and folkways, and in the process got memorably rebranded as "Beychella."

Indeed, in the midst of one of the most turbulent periods in American history, where a reckless, soon to be twice-impeached president teetered on the brink of self-destruction, and a nation was thrust into racial cataclysm by the alarming resurgence of white supremacy, a shining artistic beacon called *Homecoming* arrived. The concert, and then its filmed record, diverted our eyes and ears to the sounds of Black genius and the hopeful specter of racial healing. Beyoncé, the most celebrated entertainer on the globe, planted herself deeply and unapologetically in the rich soil of her culture. She offered the world a glimpse of the magnificent flowering of talent that grows from the roots of the nation's historically Black colleges and universities.

Homecoming highlights the serpentine rhythms, staccato cadences, dramatic percussions and soulful voices that are beautifully amplified in the blaring horns of marching bands on Black college campuses. *Homecoming* captures the frenetic expressions and willful creativity of Black America at its best. We see it in Beyoncé's colorful array of costumes, and those of her female colleagues. And we see it in the spot-on replica of the gear donned by pledges vying to gain acceptance to a number of Black Greek fraternities and sororities. And we see it in the forbiddingly complex routines many of these students hone on pliable limbs that jut and strut at freakish abandon.

Homecoming is a spectacular concert film. But it is also a rousing behind-the-scenes recording of what it takes to pull off such a remarkable display of Black girl magic and Black boy joy. We learn of Beyoncé's valiant fight against gravity and carbs in her singular determination to rescue her body from the rigors of childbirth. And we see the perils of giving birth too, as Beyonce describes the toxemia, preeclampsia and high blood pressure that plagued her journey to delivering twins. She spices her epic performances with the wise words of literary saints like Maya Angelou and Toni Morrison. These figures remind us that Black women may have different roles, but they share a virtuosity that is often ignored by the larger world. *Homecoming* captures the trials and tribulations of the world's greatest performer and serves as a feminist inspiration for ordinary women.

Still, it is as a work of artistic imagination and stunning aesthetic vision that *Homecoming* bowls us over. Yes, it is an ethnography of female labor. Yes, it documents the bountiful artistic blessings of a still underappreciated Black world. Yes, it is a spiritual rejection of the racism that thumps its chest on social media and the bigotry that screams from the nation's bully pulpit. Yes, it revels in the moral beauty of a people whose only wish has been to live free of hate and violence. Yes, it delights in channeling resistance through rhythm and celebrates a culture that sometimes makes beats out of cultural beat downs. But the most remarkable feature of *Homecoming* is how it showcases Beyoncé reimagining her entire oeuvre through the horns, head nods, harmonies, heritage, humor, and hustle of HBCU culture—from the electrifying vamp of her first big solo hit "Crazy in Love," which is deliberately slowed to emphasize the kinetic trumpets that ride the song's cantankerous rhythms, to the precise martial phrasing that highlights the orchestrated combustion of "Formation," one of her most recent hits.

Homecoming effortlessly evokes the courage and discipline it takes for a singular artist to command the attention of her peers. The film records Beyoncé directing her formidable chorus of musical and acrobatic compatriots to make an incredible piece of art that pays homage to the culture that they share. It is a culture that has nurtured the liberating desires and emancipating ideas of a people once locked in chains, but who now stand tall to celebrate the ancestors who produced and inspired them.

Every sound we hear, every sight we view, in this majestic slice of Blackness, and indeed, Americana, resonates, because *Homecoming* brings us back home to our roots as a race, as a culture, as a people, and, finally, as a country. Beyoncé in this film is the president of a nation of hope that spans the geography of imagination and includes anyone willing to listen and learn.

If Beyoncé's image was enlarged with *Lemonade* and *Homecoming*, Michael's image also underwent rapid transformation as he matured: his Afro got relaxed and curled, then straightened; his nose got smaller and sharper; and his skin got lighter and whiter. None of that spared Jackson racial travail. In 1980, after a *Rolling Stone* magazine publicist declined Jackson's request for a cover story, he fumed, "I've been told over and over that Black people on the cover of magazines doesn't sell copies . . . Just wait. Someday those magazines are going to be *begging* me for an interview. Maybe I'll give them one. And maybe I won't." In 1983, Jackson and his music label had to put the screws to MTV to air the video for his landmark single "Billie Jean," which opened the door for other Black artists and gave the fledgling music channel cultural cachet. Jackson essentially had to beg MTV for the opportunity to help make it rich and successful.

While Beyoncé has been widely recognized as the globe's greatest star, she has faced her own version of artistic apartheid. Although she has garnered a gang of Grammys, she has been denied the most prestigious of those awards, including those for Record and Album of the Year. After the release of her pathbreaking album *Lemonade*—a dizzying amalgam of musical genres, Black cultural allusions and references, Black iconography, carnal and spiritual desires, African female deities, serpentine phrases, trap beats, staccato cadences, and existential and institutional marital angst, all in the service of channeling rage at social inequities, especially the machinery of toxic masculinities and traitorous patriarchies in defense of vulnerable-turned-vengeful feminisms that settle scores by naming injustices without ever having to name the men who perpetuate them, thus making it the greatest diss album of all time because in naming no guilty man it essentially names all guilty men—Beyoncé was nominated for nine Grammy awards, including in the Album, Record, and Song of the Year categories.

To get a sense of just how epic Beyoncé's sixth studio album is, Google the word "lemonade." What pops up first, and second, and third, and fourth and fifth, and on and on, is not a drink that traces back to AD 1000 Egypt. Instead, there is reference after reference to what isn't so much a compact disc as it is an explosion of Black sight and sound. "Lemonade" is a revolutionary rush of experiences that are at once eye-catching and ear pleasing. *Lemonade* redefined what recording artists are capable of achieving when they dream as widely as the bold world they imagine.

Lemonade leapt right to the forefront of great concept albums. Think Sinatra's *In the Wee Small Hours*, which bathes in the bluesy introspection and sad loneliness that hug the midnight hour. Think Marvin Gaye's *What's Going On*, a haunting, jazzy probe of war, environmental distress, drug abuse and social injustice. *Lemonade* doubled down on the technical inventiveness of those classics. Sinatra's disc was one of the first pop albums to be issued as a single 12-inch record LP. Gaye layered his vocals in one of the first instances of an artist multi-tracking his own voice. Beyoncé's second visual album stormed the horizon of what could possibly be seen and heard and married them in seamless combination.

Lemonade also gave us the zesty maturity of one of history's greatest auteurs. Beyoncé waged war against demons and forces that might have laid waste to a lesser woman, that might have stifled a less gifted artist, that might have crushed her younger self. But *Lemonade* served notice that Beyoncé was more than a survivor. To paraphrase Faulkner's immortal words, *Lemonade* proved that she had not only endured, but that she had prevailed. She had evolved from a child of destiny to become its ferocious and protective mother. She mercifully brought us along for the ride and it changed us too. After Beyoncé served the world *Lemonade*, nothing again tasted the same. We couldn't be satisfied gulping the pop confections of cookie-cutter ingénues. Not after Beyoncé's righteous anger at oppression quenched our thirst. A slug of Beyoncé's tart vengeance washed away the bitter infidelities of a straying mate. And a swig of Beyoncé's healing elixir tasted like justice after an officer's gun had swallowed our loved one.

It's the colorful and unique way that *Lemonade* blended so many pungent musical flavors and disparate styles that made it such a creative monster. It's fashionable these days to talk of "intersectionality." That means that you can't explain your existence as a woman or a person of color by citing a single force, a single urge, a single slice of disadvantage or mistreatment. It's also trendy to speak of how great thinkers swerve between genres. Yet another impulse in Black intellectual circles is to embrace the Diaspora beyond one's own homeland. *Lemonade* manages, brilliantly, with orchestrated effortlessness, to synthesize all three. It is intersectional because it revels without hesitation in a feminist worldview. It unapologetically embraces a Blackness that scorns racist tyranny. And it delights, in memorable words spoken by Queen of Bounce Big Freedia on "Formation," in the visceral pleasures of queer identity.

Lemonade heartily, perhaps defiantly, swerves between genres. It is at once a pure pop amalgam of competing melodies and dense harmonies, as "Pray You Catch Me" and "Daddy Lessons" amply show. Yet it never sheds its undeniably Black voice. It trades in slinky, serpentine, and slippery phrases, like those on "6 Inch," and at times, brusque and staccato cadences, as on "Sorry," as Beyoncé restlessly mines Black sound and Black life. She also cites, samples, experiments with, and absorbs blues, rock, funk, soul, pop, country, gospel and electronic. She falls with great purpose into trap music too. Beyoncé is hardly ever given credit for how she slips in nearly imperceptible fashion, in unremarked utility, from singing to speaking—that is, if the speech is hip hop, as the flourish and bravura she generates on "Hold Up" proves. She at once spits and spirits us along, rap-singing her way to insights she delivers with as much mirth and gravity as the best emcees.

Beyoncé's Blackness has never been in question. Still, with *Lemonade*, she expanded and grew it, sparking off a Blackness that is bigger than her immediate roots. On *Beyoncé* she amplified the words of Nigerian novelist and feminist Chimamanda Ngozi Adichie. On *Lemonade* Beyoncé features Warsan Shire, a Kenyan born, London raised poet with Somali parents. If all the Blacks have been men, all the women white, and all the citizens American, Beyoncé on *Lemonade* shifted the vehicle of difference into reverse and put Black ladies on top of feminism, race and nation, flaunting a feminized globalism. We have had to remind the nation that Black lives matter because it has too often forgot. But we have forgotten even more how little Black women and girls have mattered. One of *Lemonade*'s greatest gifts is to redeem the moral worth of Black women and restore their recognition as the fertile womb of creative genius.

It may be the "at-onceness" of *Lemonade* that most leaves our mouths agape, our spirits agog, our minds blown. Yes, it is at once a sonic masterpiece and an astonishing visual feast. It is at once sacred and profane. It is a paean to the edifying art that spiritual sight gives rise to. It also thrives on the beautifully profane insistence on flinging obscenities to combat the vulgarities of modern existence. If, in the eclectic Knowlesian grammar, Diva is another word for hustler, then pop star is another word for prophet. As Jeremiah Wright proved, sometimes a prophet has got to say goddamn—and make no mistake, Beyoncé carries the prophetic mantle with goo gobs of swag. And even within the spiritual realm there is a sublime at-onceness too. Beyoncé's Christian roots always nourish rather than strangle. They are less about proselytizing folk to her cause than performing the love that grips her heart. But that doesn't mean she can't bow to

African deities and goddesses, whether the sexual, fertility and dance deity Oshun, on "Don't Hurt Yourself" (enthusiastically endorsed by rocker Jack White in his plea to "Love God Herself"), or Yemoja, the water deity that births humanity, glimpsed in the electrifying Black anthem "Freedom."

Lemonade is at once personal and political. It is at once a searing meditation on marital betrayal while also probing the boundaries and burdens of a nation's unfaithfulness to some of its most loyal citizens. It is at once a tell-all exposé of the moral turmoil of a woman working out her soul's salvation in public, in concert, and in conflict, with another human being, a phantom partner, a mystery mate who could be any—and indeed every—one. Hence its universal appeal, despite being seemingly rooted in a particular story. But it is also a tight-lipped romp through existential suffering and emotional trauma without revealing a single source. It is at once a wink and a nod, a shout and a shush, an "ah hah" and a "shhh," a public declaration of bristling angst and torturous skepticism, and a tender embrace of relentless, unexpected hope.

If *Lemonade* sizzled on the screen, and popped in our ears, it unleashed a riot of spectacle on stage. In city after city, *Lemonade* reminded us that it wasn't just a visual album. It was, too, a movement of women sweeping themselves into the tour Formation, armed, while in formation, with information Beyoncé prolifically and generously and robustly and without apology shared with them. Like any great work of art—remember *The Godfather* gave us memorable clichés like "I'm gonna make him an offer he can't refuse"—*Lemonade* condenses its logic of insurrection into pithy and memorable phrases: "Boy Bye" or "What's worse, looking jealous or crazy?" or "Becky with the good hair," or "I slay." Or the ruthlessly apt summary of retribution capitalism: "Always stay gracious, best revenge is your paper."

What was most profoundly on display, just as it was in her world-changing, life-altering performance at Super Bowl 50—where she and a gorgeous gaggle of women clad in Black paid homage to the Black Panthers and the fight against unjust Black death at the hands of the boys in blue—was Beyoncé's body of work. And, quite simply, and spectacularly, the work of her body. The forever in motion body. The disciplined and impossibly pliable body. The sacrificing, and performing, body. Beyoncé pushed herself harder, and with greater velocity, and more force, under incalculable pressure, and with greater skill, arguably, than anyone ever. Including Michael Jackson at his height, whom I witnessed, in person, on stage. As great as he was, he could not conjure the splendid vexation and bewildering frenzy of rubbery body parts brought to market with the inexhaustible energy and transcendent terpsichorean trance evoked by Beyoncé Knowles Carter. She is without question the greatest entertainer this globe has seen. She is a world apart from everyone else, existing in her own Beyonciverse. It is our blessing that, as she has snared us in her incomprehensible omnicompetence—where denied awards become the occasion of even more celebration of her astonishing genius, where elevators grow wings and scurry her to even greater heights of success—she has shared with us some sweet, sassy, tangy, satisfying *Lemonade*.

Despite that, the Recording Academy didn't drink the *Lemonade*; the masterly album was tartly shut out of the big awards, winning only a Best Music Video Grammy and one for Best Urban Contemporary Album. In a year in which her artistic genius soared, shattered conceptual barriers, and transgressed social boundaries, Beyoncé was ghettoized and given an award to match the official musical culture's estimation of her value, as if to remind her of the narrow definitions of Blackness in which she should remain cocooned. (It was this failed recognition by the music establishment that led Kanye West to infamously protest Beyoncé's snubbing at the 2009 Video Music Awards when Taylor Swift's "You Belong With Me" was awarded the iconic Moonman statue for Best Female Video over Beyoncé's "Single Ladies [Put a Ring on It]." West leapt on stage as Swift made her acceptance speech and broke in, saying, "Yo Taylor, I'm really happy for you. I'm a let you finish, but Beyoncé has one of the best videos of all time. One of the best videos of all time!" It was a startling gesture that occasioned great criticism of West, but it shone a harsh light on the unjust denial of recognition to Black artists.)

It is insufficient to recognize the value of Blackness in the art one consumes if you fail to recognize the value of Black art to the American enterprise. Giving Beyoncé a Grammy for Best Urban Contemporary while denying her the recognition for her American genius with the specific Grammy awards that transcend genre is to slight her Blackness and ignore her Americanness. Thus Adele, the British singer who won Album of the Year for her rousing *25*, asked, incredulously, backstage at the awards in a post-victory interview: "What the fuck does [Beyoncé] have to do to win album of the year?" Obviously be white and European.

Perhaps that fundamental recognition drove to a great degree Michael Jackson's experiments in radical self-reimagining. Michael reshaped his face in his own image, that is, the one planted in his mind by a father who teased him as a child that he was ugly. Jackson grew to believe that he was too dark and that his nose was too broad. His relentless self-mutilation through reconstructive surgery was in part a bitter projection of the self-hatred that slices the Black psyche. Although Jackson claimed to suffer from vitiligo, the disease that causes one's skin to lose pigment, he may have sought to bleach his skin to rid his face of its offending Blackness. Jackson's deconstructed face became a geography of distorted, possible faces, a fleshly region of racial ideals invaded by spooky European traits that rendered him ethnically opaque.

Beyoncé's light skin has, too, played a role in her life, in her public perception, in the politics of colorism that track her. "Sometimes in the Black community, it's the lighter girls who are picked on," said Beyoncé's mother, Tina Knowles-Lawson. "Of course, the opposite is often true as well, sadly—the darker girls are also picked on. It's a shame, but it's a fact of life. Beyoncé would often come home crying that the other girls were making fun of her. 'I wish I was darker,' she would say. I wanted her to embrace who she was. 'Don't wish to be anything other than what you are,' I would tell her. I know it's easy for adults to say such things, but harder for little girls to understand." Beyoncé's ethnic and racial identity has been a source of fascination on Google over the years: the search engine receives more than two thousand inquiries per month wondering "Is Beyoncé Black?" while two hundred more queries ask, "Is Beyoncé full Black?" and the same number pose the question "Is Beyoncé white?" One of Beyoncé's biographers even refers to her as of mixed descent because her father is Black and her mother is "of French Creole ancestry," an observation that would render millions of Black folks of mixed descent. Beyoncé has been accused of lightening her skin. But the charge says less about Beyoncé and more about the deeply entrenched politics of colorism that dog Black culture: how lighter-skinned Black folk have enjoyed more cultural advantages than darker-skinned Blacks because of the presumption of higher intelligence, more sophisticated culture, and greater moral standing.

Despite Michael's perilous skin politics, it wasn't difficult to see the Blackness and greatness of the music he made and the broad humanity of the globally popular brand of entertainment he championed. Michael Jackson didn't get from his father the nurture, love, and unconditional affirmation he wanted in his first childhood. At times he recklessly pursued them in his failed second childhood. Still, he offered the world a glimpse of an extremely disciplined genius who was willing to share his gifts so that he could give to millions of others what he couldn't enjoy himself. That may not qualify him for martyrdom, but it does make him a remarkable, if tortured, soul who transformed his suffering into transcendent song and dance.

When Michael Jackson perished at age 50, our greatest consolation at the time was that Prince, the other Black musical genius born in the Midwest the same year as Jackson, still strode the earth in fashionable platforms. His Royal Badness's death on April 21, 2016, just as Beyoncé on April 23, 2016, poured her latest musical elixir on the world, lacked, perhaps, the synchrony of astrology and region that shaped his gentle rivalry with the King of Pop. Yet, in retrospect, we can take solace in another royal succession: as we drank the bitter dregs of a Prince leaving the scene too early, a Queen emerged in her fullest complexity yet to serve us *Lemonade* and further claim her throne as the globe's greatest entertainer. Despite their instructive differences, Prince and Beyoncé, and Michael too, remind us that the pieties of faith enflame, and heal, the flesh, that musical boundaries, and those between the political and personal, can be brilliantly transgressed, and that the extravagant performances of race and gender, and sexual identity as well, often threaten the vain sovereignty of power and monoculture. Beyoncé now reigns supreme, alone, atop a kingdom of performance that she inherited from a Prince and a King but which she has made even greater.

Beyoncé's extraordinary career reflects the convergence of furious racial and gender forces as she reigns as the planet's most magnificent performer. Beyoncé has managed to command the artistic respect of her peers and the adoration of millions of fans the world over while expressing her distinct brand of feminism: the insistence that women's lives count, that their issues matter, that they be treated with respect, and that women achieve social and economic equality. Beyoncé's formidable politics of fusion—of musical styles and rhythms, of Black female deities and cultural icons, of material aspirations and spiritual desires—has reinforced her expansion of Black artistic identity by embracing queer sensibilities, amplifying progressive racial interpretations of Black suffering, and centering existence in a Black female worldview. Beyoncé is the greatest performer ever because she has absorbed and extended the best traits and wisest lessons of Michael Jackson in her ever-evolving, tirelessly shapeshifting hunger for excellence. Whether singing, dancing, rapping, making videos or documentaries, or using her art to protest, rally, signify, edify, and, above all, to entertain, Beyoncé is an outsize genius whose quest for greatness has blazed a path that no one before her has traveled and, undoubtedly, few, if any, after her can successfully pursue.

CHAPTER

2

"One Love," Two Brothers, Three Verses

This essay is from Born to Use Mics, *a book I co-edited with Sohail Daulatzai, dedicated to interpreting each song on Nas's debut,* Illmatic, *one of the greatest hip hop albums ever. It is even more meaningful to me because the song I explore is about letters from, and to, prisoners, and at the time, my brother Everett Dyson-Bey, prisoner #212687, was serving life in prison for a murder my family is convinced he didn't commit. He died at fifty-six years old in prison in 2019, after spending the last thirty years of his life incarcerated. It hurts to this day. It stings even more because the church in which he was reared denied us the right to hold his funeral there because he had become a member of the Moorish Science Temple of America. This is one reason why I insist that my real religion is love—even beyond the confines of the church and faith I hold dear. Love you, Everett. Rest in Peace.*

[One Love] just came from life, it's a song about letters to prison inmates, friends of mine, shout-outs to childhood friends and their uncles and people who were like family to me. I was, again, too young to be going through all of that. That's what I think about when I hear that album. I was too young to be going through all of that.

Nas, *Rolling Stone*, 2007

When I first heard Nas's "One Love," cast in the form of letters to friends locked in prison, I thought immediately of my brother Everett, who is serving a life sentence for a murder I believe he didn't commit. Sure, he sold drugs on the tough Detroit streets on which we both hustled and matured. But that doesn't justify his incarceration for a crime he's innocent of, even as he takes responsibility for his errors and manages to find the good in his bad circumstance. "I've not always made the best of choices," Everett says, "and therefore I must suffer the results thereof. I've learned that. However, I've come to learn also that going through this does not negate the fact that I can become what I choose to become." By the time Nas's song appeared in 1994, Everett had already been in the "stone hotel" for five years. Now he's been locked down for twenty years, his plight captured in a nationally televised 2008 CNN special on Black men hosted by Soledad O'Brien that ended by focusing on me and Everett.

Whenever the segment on me and Everett aired in a screening across the country, I invariably received an email, call or comment from another Black person, telling me that *our* story is *their* story. Not necessarily our particular truth—one brother an author and professor, the other a prisoner incarcerated with a life sentence. But so many Black families are plagued by a similar mathematics of misery: prospering members are divided from loved ones behind steel bars, multiplying the cruel twists of fate. One may teach, as I did for years, at Penn. The other is locked away in the pen.

The temptation is to believe that the individual choice Everett spoke of accounts for such differences in destiny. Successful Black family members did their work and played by the rules; suffering family members ran afoul of the law and were justly locked away, as they are in "One Love." Of course, that is true in many cases, but in far too many cases, that's not the entire truth. There is a vicious prison system that hungers for young Black and brown bodies. In America, the more young Black and brown folk are thrown in jail, the more cells are built, and the more money is made. It has been well documented that we spend far more money on penitentiaries than university education for poor Black and brown males. During the 1980s and 1990s, state spending for corrections grew at six times the rate of state spending on higher education.[1]

Even as two million Americans occupy prisons and jails, prison and jail have come to occupy the American imagination in everything from sobering foundation reports to fiery rap lyrics. According to a 2008 Pew Center report, there are 1,596,127 adults stowed in state or federal prisons, and another 723,131 locked in local jails. The total of 2,319,258 sums up an astonishing statistic: more than 1 in every 100 Americans is incarcerated in America. Predictably, the news is even worse for Blacks and Latinos. For white men over 18, 1 in 106 are behind bars. For Latino men, the number is 1 in 36, and for Black men, it's 1 in 15 locked up. Sadder still, for Black men between the ages of 20 and 34, the number is a startling 1 in 9 behind bars. In light of these depressing numbers, it is no mystery why incarcerated young Black males occupy so much space in hip hop's lyrical universe.[2]

Nas's sonic epistle "One Love" trades on conventions established in hip hop—remembering one's "homies" locked away, speaking about the harsh circumstances of their incarceration, decrying the social forces that left them little choice but to pursue an illegal path that ended in prison. But it also occupies territory staked out by the Apostle Paul and Martin Luther King, Jr.—and by figures as diverse as Mahatma Gandhi, Malcolm X, Dietrich Bonhoeffer, George Jackson, the Marquis de Sade, Mumia Abu-Jamal, Fidel Castro, Wei Jingsheng, Imam Jamil Al-Amin, Thomas More, Jean Genet, Birtukan Midekssa and Antonio Gramsci. Their letters and other writings from prison offer wisdom, express political dissent, explore the criminal mind and lifestyle, proclaim their innocence, analyze social ills, trumpet religious conversion, tout spiritual awakening, uplift fellow believers, or spark civil disobedience and social protest.

Nas also reverses the trend: instead of writing, better yet, speaking the letters as an inmate, he writes to imprisoned comrades, offering them if not quite a way out, at least a view outside the prison walls that confine them. If prison means the restriction of sight and sound from the world beyond bars, and limited information about its happenings too, Nas's narration casts a sharp eye and literate tongue on the streets from which his mates have been temporarily banned. "One Love" teems with gritty details of unfaithful lovers, menacing rivals, criminal apprentices, unseen offspring, mourning mothers, troubled siblings—and a neighborhood fraught with murder and other moral mayhem. It probes what Sohail Daulatzai terms "the carceral imagination" with lyrical elegance.[3]

"One Love" is both reportage and pep talk, a morality tale of lost innocence and lost life in degrees and proportions, a missive that smoothly melds empathy and caution. "One Love" captures poignant moments of Black male intimacy and vulnerability forged in the crucible of urban desperation and poverty. In telling his friends stories, Nas manages to tell his friends' stories. "One Love" reflects on lives carved from suffering and struggle, interpreting their experience in a tale that marries vernacular and formal poetic devices. Nas's plea not only moves me intellectually and artistically, but touches close to home as I struggle with my brother serving an unjust life sentence for murder.

"One Love" takes root, from its opening sounds, in classic Black literary and musical territory. The voices of several Black inmates can be heard in a prison yard during recreational activities as one prisoner excitedly speaks of "a letter I got from my man Nas." His boast not only establishes the song's epistolary conceit, linking its sonic fictional ambitions to works like Alice Walker's *The Color Purple*, but "One Love" harkens back to another

Black music classic: Marvin Gaye's "What's Going On." Gaye's 1970 song begins with the party banter of his friends Mel Farr and Lem Barney, who were then football stars for the Detroit Lions. In sweetly dramatic contrast to his pals' playful mood, Gaye denounces war and generational strife, and pleads for love in a heavenly tenor that weaves inside the jovial atmosphere.

Nas, however, amplifies the tone and theme of his intimates' yard exchange to comment on their plight and that of hundreds of thousands more Black males. While Gaye laments the age bias of elders who distort youth culture through a moralistic lens—"who are they to judge us/simply 'cause our hair is long?" the crooner asked—Nas jumps back a generation to ride the beats of a soul jazz classic by the Heath Brothers, "Smilin' Billy Suite, Part II." Rapper Q-Tip, who produced "One Love," cleverly selected a sample of the Heath Brothers track that underscores the dulcet tones of Stanley Cowell's Mbira thumb piano and a nimble Percy Heath double bassline that metastasizes across the melody. Q-Tip spices the sonic stew with a deftly disguised drum track borrowed from Parliament's "Come In Out of the Rain."

Nas's letter opens a window to the world his friends left behind, keeping them abreast of changes that directly bear on their personal lives and their former street hustling. In both instances, Nas's lyrics resonate with his hearers because they tap existential and epistemic roots: his knowledge of the world they inhabited is joined to his knowledge of the people and events that matter to them, making Nas a rhetorical hinge on which their insight and information swings. As their eyes and ears, Nas spins poetry on the pavement of their existence, drawn from the textures of their stories and the threads of their ambitions and aspirations, which archives and distributes happenings in the hood and home.

The point of framing "One Love" as a letter is to root his reflections on prison in existential soil by accounting for the shifting allegiances, shattered affections, and the sustaining alliances too, which sprout in the aftermath of incarceration. The point of telling us about "Jerome's niece," and "Little Rob," and "Born's" brother is to convey the menace that dogs the lives of even the youngest ghetto resident. The point of telling us about an unfaithful girlfriend and disappearing friends is to portray how hood relationships crumble under the pressures of survival and cutthroat competition. And the point of making things so personal is to make them universal; beyond the chaos of urban violence and poverty, Nas expresses care for vulnerable children, hurting parents, wayward youth, and suffering friends, just as members of the broader society do. This may be the "other" America, but in the grammar of human aspiration and social desire, the noun is just as important as the adjective.

It makes demographic sense for rappers to seriously grapple with prison and jail, especially since hip hop culture is largely created by the young males who are most vulnerable to incarceration. Just as they grapple with the plagues of poverty and police brutality, hip hop artists contend with the prison bars that seal the fate of many of their peers, and in some visible cases, that of rappers too. Hip hop's roots in working class and poor Black communities make its artists attuned to the hard-scrabble conditions that either become fodder for rap careers or an expressway to incarceration. The lyrics of rap artists are flooded by references to prison, making up an informal incarceration canon, including songs as varied as Ice-T's "The Tower," Public Enemy's "Black Steel in the Hour of Chaos," Akon and Styles P's "Locked Up," AZ's "Fan Mail" and JAY-Z's "Do U Wanna Ride."

In 1995, a distinct shift occurred: no longer rapping *about* prison, hip hop's artists were themselves increasingly rapping *from* prison, or at least releasing records while they were accumulating prison records. That year Tupac Shakur stalled in a prison cell on a sexual abuse conviction as his CD *Me Against the World* rocketed in its first week of release to the top of the pop charts. Nearly a decade later, rapper Shyne was in prison on a first-degree assault and reckless endangerment conviction as his CD *Godfather Buried Alive* debuted at No. 3 on Billboard's album charts. He even recorded a remix of a single from his CD in his jail cell. In 2005 rapper Cassidy, incarcerated and facing first-degree murder charges (he was later cleared), released his CD *I'm a Hustla,* which debuted at No. 5 on Billboard's album charts. Rapper Beanie Siegel's *The B. Coming* CD debuted at No. 3 on the music charts in 2005 while he was incarcerated on a federal weapons charge. And Lil' Kim released her CD *The Naked Truth*, which debuted at No. 6 on the Billboard 200 charts, while she was imprisoned on a perjury conviction.[4]

The list of other rappers who have served time doesn't just include superstars like T.I., who went to jail on a weapons conviction at the height of his career, and men like John Forté, DMX, DJ Quik and Prodigy. The roll call also includes female rappers like Foxy Brown, Da Brat and Remy Ma. Beyond the realm of rap, doing time has become a tragic rite of passage for too many young Black males, often harming their chances for sound employment and stable family life after getting snagged inside the machinery of the prison-industrial complex. Thus, prison supplies a metaphorical and literal destination for Black males who, partially in self-defense, drape poetry around their imprisoned limbs, or those of their jailed loved ones, and offer a sometimes negative glory to the prison cell as an unavoidable stop on their journey to manhood.

In "One Love's" opening verse, Nas regrets that his unnamed letter recipient hadn't come to his house to escape the cops in his scrape with the law, but says that there's "no time for looking back it's done." Since prisoners are often poorly served by an obsession with how things might have turned out differently, Nas smartly chases away such thoughts with a focus on the present. Nas quickly communicates, or confirms, a number of facts to his friend: the birth of his son, the disdain his son's mother feels toward him since his imprisonment, the existence of a group of males who are his friend's bitter rivals, and the disloyalty of his son's mother who fails to write him yet manages to fraternize with his enemies.

Nas's knowledge of his confined comrade is similarly confined to particular quarters of his life—he hasn't yet seen his friend's son, though he knows of his existence. Nas's knowledge is instead targeted and functional, serving ethical priorities generated in an urban male culture where loyalty and bloodline are a big deal. Nas need not have seen his friend's newborn son to acknowledge his importance in a masculine stronghold where Black males endure social suffering but nevertheless claim patriarchal privilege within their own clans and circles. To be a Black male means to be a king and a pariah all at once. When Nas congratulates his friend for having a son, he acknowledges the pride a Black male often takes in having a seed to carry his life further.

The miracle of birth for any child is heightened when Black male infants announce their existence in a cry that reverberates in moans and shrieks later in life. It is the wonder and brokenness of Black male life in the ghetto that Nas implicitly grasps and shares as an unspoken bond with his jailed compatriot. Still, Nas's failure to see the son is an unavoidable metaphor for how many Black males fail to witness the growth and maturity of their own sons and daughters, whether they are locked in jail or imprisoned in narrow visions of family and manhood. Having *a* son is sometimes more important than *my* son.

"One Love" configures, and then complicates, the poor relations between young Black men and women, relations which are often already pressured by poverty before they are further strained by an extended stay in prison. Harsh judgments of women are standard in hip hop, making it difficult to separate the wheat of natural gender conflict from the chaff of misogyny.

Nas avoids the sexist trap by framing his friend's loss of his lady with the facts of male prison life: lovers and wives often lose momentum or fall away under the unforgiving silences and distances incarceration brings. As his friend's rhetorical double and symbolic substitute, Nas speaks to, and for, his isolated brother in arms, scorning his woman's traitorous behavior while relieving him of the burden to say it himself.

Nas speaks for his friend's lady too as she indicts her lover for his rough behavior and his failure to heed her advice—a point that is given graphic illustration in the video for "One Love" where a female character mouths Nas's words as he spits them. In other cases, such an act might appear little more than patriarchal ventriloquism—a woman's mouth is moving but a man's views are spoken. But Nas ties her complaint about her lover's hard-headedness into a nasty trick of subversion: the apparent concern for her man expressed in her diatribe is but a deceitful prelude to stabbing him in the back by taking to his rivals' side. The less his friend has to reckon with his lover joining forces with his enemies, the more time he has to adjust to a life of curbed desires and severe restrictions. His friend can claim vicarious victory, without breaking a sweat or busting a gut, because Nas defeats her treachery by calling her out and naming her fatal flaw.

Nas extends his charge of betrayal beyond the female realm in the second verse of "One Love," addressed to his homeboy Born, as he highlights another example of a friend joining a foe, in this case, a former associate of Born's who gives Born's Glock to a man he shot a year earlier. Instead of a baby in common, these men shared a "block" on which they hustled and committed crime as a crew. Nas satisfies Born's unspoken wish for justice, and relieves his imprisoned friend's burdened heart, by emphasizing the responsibility that comes with his liberty, pledging to Born that he would handle things for his imprisoned friend.

In this verse, and throughout the song, especially as he shouts out other friends locked away from society, Nas signifies on a lively and expansive conception of brotherhood: his "brothers" in prison; the brotherhood of males who struggle to escape the desperate circumstances of the projects; and the brotherhood of mankind implied in his complex vision of a just community that flows throughout his CD. By conceiving of his neighborhood as a brotherhood, Nas contests a strand of social criticism—one that, ironically, could be supported by his lyrics that cite the lethal competition that undermines community—that views the 'hood as a zone of unrelieved terror. By acting as his brothers' keeper, their eyes and ears, their scribe and conscience, Nas generates a holistic vision of Black brotherhood that reflects the goodness and potential of one man reflected in the eyes of the other, despite the prevalence of negative circumstances.

I hear Nas's understanding of brotherhood reflected in my own brother's words. "Whenever I see Michael," Everett says, "it becomes testament to the fact that I could have done this, that or the other. It becomes a testament to the fact that I can *still* do this, that or the other."[5] Everett also argues that despite the trauma of prison, it was perhaps the path he had to take to become his best self, just as my own path permitted my talents to shine.

> I've come to see that each man must work out his own path of life. The experiences that Michael has had, that have taken him to where he is right now, is a great and beautiful thing. Michael couldn't have been in the streets doing what I was doing, and become who he is. That's not the experiences he needed to unfold, spiritually, mentally, socially, physically. However, I couldn't have gone to Princeton, taught at Chicago Theological Seminary. I couldn't have been a critically acclaimed author and learnt the lessons that I needed to learn.

Beyond our own bond, Everett reflected on the forces that erode Black brotherhood, acknowledging how his drug dealing was a blight to the community.

> The law states, under the Fourteenth amendment, that [Blacks] aren't official persons. So when we go to our neighborhoods and we see death, destruction, when we see crime at a rampant pace, more so than elsewhere, when we see the mortality rate of our babies, higher than some third world nations, then you ask the question, "Why?" And it boils down to this, simply: if we knew who we are, and had something to look to greater than the South for pride, then we would understand that we're the builders of civilizations . . . Now isn't that sad, that I had to come to prison to learn this? Why couldn't I have been taught this in the streets? Why wasn't I taught this in our school system?

Just as Everett "had to [go] to prison" to learn his lessons, "One Love" implies that Born's prison predicament leaves him open to Nas's wisdom and the virtues of self-examination.

Nas's pledge to Born, and his earlier defense of his unnamed chum, is an example of lateral love, where hustling together in a crew creates bonds of masculine intimacy and loyalty. As omniscient street narrator, Nas is deliberately ambiguous about his role in the hustling he observes, though his knowledge of the details of their lives—his friend fleeing the cops, which in the video for "One Love" Nas views from his apartment window, and Born having shot a rival—suggests Nas's deep connection to his underground peers. Nas's understanding of what his imprisoned peers should know is one of the few acceptable displays of love and intimacy that even hardened men might show each other in the face of vulnerability.

In this guise, gestures of intimacy, and an ethic of care for the lives of Nas's beloved "boys," bathe the lyrics of "One Love." Nas asks his unnamed pal about mutual friends and sends his greetings to others. Nas reminds his friend of the practical function of their intimate bond—that men who forged connections on the street can sustain each other and try to make prison a scene of extended intimacy and care. In case there's any doubt about how Nas feels about his jailed partner, he proves that money—literal capital—can be made into the symbolic capital of emotional and spiritual intimacy when it is offered in fraternity and gratitude. "I left a half a hundred in your commissary/You was my nigga when push came to shove/ One what? One love." Short of having their sentences reversed, there is nothing prisoners need more than cash and visits. Nas offers the former to his unnamed friend, and the latter to Born.

The bond between Nas and Born, like all such courted and constructed intimacies, has collateral advantage, and links Nas to Born's mother. Offering only half a bar's progress report on Born's troubled sibling, Nas pivots from the cool grief of meditations on lost innocence, and the loss of innocent life, wounded aspirations, arrested developments and imprisoned hope, to the hot grief evoked by a mourning mother. "I hate it when your moms cries/It kinda makes me wanna murder, for real-a/I even got a mask and gloves to bust slugs/But one love." The tears of Born's mother unleash in Nas a murderous empathy. Ironically, that leads him to the brink of an emotional identification with her that is so strong that it threatens to overwhelm a reasoned refrain, both musically and morally, from the same crime that Born may have attempted. Nas escapes such a fate, at least lyrically, through a crucial conjunction—"But one love." Even in the projects, love is a superior force that, more often than it is credited, brings order and encourages strategic restraint.

Nas's care shows up too in the events he chooses to report on, especially the urban catastrophe that plagues young victims. "But yo, guess who got shot in the dome-piece?/Jerome's niece, on her way home from Jones

Beach—it's bugged." The tragedy of the young lady getting shot in the head is compounded because she isn't involved in the criminal activity that gets Nas's friends sent up the river. Nas adds dramatic urgency to his reporting by naming the geographies that are the site of terror, which is all the more devastating because the locales are familiar to New York natives. It's local knowledge and inside code for the cognoscenti.

Nas extends the reach of his inside signifying, and reinforces the repetitive trauma to young lives of the events he describes, with internal rhyming—where rhymes impatiently repeat near the beginning and middle of sentences, and then at the end, as in "piece . . . niece . . . Beach," or in the line to Born that issues an abbreviated State of New York for the urban poor in the not-quite post-crack mid-90s: "The crack-heads stalking, loud-mouths is talking." Nas reports, too, on another young victim who got sucked into the drug game already crowded by adolescent peers: "Plus little Rob is selling drugs on the dime/Hangin' out with young thugs that all carry 9s." At the heart of Nas's description is a veiled lament of the illicit lifestyle that snares young lives, and not a boast of the drug seller's gain or glory.

Hip hop's artists have often defended themselves against the charge of adding glory to carnage by insisting that they are not making the news but reporting it. Of course, every act of reportage is also an act of interpretation, of selecting what events merit coverage and how to state what happened and why, a valuable recognition for reporters as well as rappers. Nas's reportage, even at the tender age of 19, is long since done with the objectivity and neutrality that are ostensibly among the reporter's greatest goals. Nas is aware that he is not merely transmitting, but transforming, knowledge. He is both reporting and editorializing; he spits facts and provides frameworks to interpret the facts he chooses to share.

Nas's version of interested reporting—of reporting invested in the values, priorities, biases and interests of the community from which he speaks—and his adoption of the epistolary form, gives him intellectual space to breathe in rhymes that "drop science" and share wisdom. In his sonic missive, Nas wars against religious and educational authority in a brilliantly condensed and breathtakingly acute four bars: "Sometimes I sit back with a Buddha sack/Mind's in another world thinking about how we can exist through the facts/Written in school text books, bibles, et cetera/ Fuck a school lecture, the lies get me vexed-er."

Nas's wordplay is masterly and unmistakable: the Buddha sack he references—that takes him to another world, another frame of mind, an alternate intellectual vision, a competing conceptual order, a rival paradigm of experience—is a variety of weed. He's mellow and his higher reasoning is freed from the constraints of conventional wisdom. But Buddhism, too, takes us to another religious world outside of the hegemony of Western versions of Christianity. That tack is important, not simply because it references the Five Percenter theology Nas dabbles in, but it also gives him the intellectual courage to link, then challenge, canonical religious and educational texts. The separation of church and state might be a constitutional promise, but Nas understands the collusion between schoolrooms and church sanctuaries in extolling narrow versions of shared truths, especially about the poor Black communities Nas represents.

Nas's poetically ambiguous phrasing underscores the breadth of his dispute: when he starts "thinking how we can exist through the facts/Written in school textbooks, bibles, et cetera," it is both a cosmological and sociological query. Nas is questioning the religious creation narratives that specify the origins of human existence. He is also interrogating the validity of school history textbooks that underplay, isolate, or leave aside altogether the existence of Black culture and the "Afrocentric Asian" as Nas refers to Black folk on his track "It Ain't Hard to Tell." Local knowledge trumps traditional knowledge; the knowledge of the streets, the commonsense of communities whose character shines in wise sayings, sound moral habits and skeptical inquiry is to be trusted more than institutional knowledge that denies the humanity of Black folk.

Everett appealed to the local racial and theological knowledge of the minority religious group to which he belongs, the Moorish Temple, to make this same point.

> We're classed as undesirables. We not second class citizens. This is the law; this is not me talking. If you're calling yourself Black, it's no different than calling yourself a Negro or a colored man or an Ethiopian. These are slave names. And if so, then you're classed as an undesirable [and you will get] all the mistreatment and the inferiority that the citizens care to bestow upon you. This is why this system is as full as it is . . . Look it up lawfully. See how serious it is to proclaim your nationality, to proclaim your free national name, in this nation. If you were to ask, "What is your free national name?" the majority of us, as a people, would say "Blacks." Where is Blackland? What is the flag that represents Black? There is none. We don't exist, in truth, except as a fiction in law. But you see, a fiction in law gets you put in a place like this right there, with no evidence, trumped up, and here you sit for as long as they choose to keep you here.

Nas bravely enters the fray and draws an important distinction between schooling and education: "Fuck a school lecture, the lies get me vexed-er." The fact of Nas's inquiry, the existence of his intellectual curiosity, shows he's interested in learning and knowledge. His problem, like that of many Black youth, is with the schools in which the transmission of knowledge is institutionally embedded, and too often, in which cultural distortions and racial myths take on the force of fact.

> First month of ninth grade, that was my last month. School ain't shit, the teachers is full of shit, the whole system is bullshit, to me. I'm there riffin' with the teachers, dissin' the teachers. I mean, I wanted to finish school, I didn't want to drop out of school, I wanted to finish school and do something. I was drawin' and shit, I wanted to do that, or write a movie, some ill shit. I used to write all type of shit when I was young, I thought I was blessed. But they crushed that type of shit, they crushed that in my head. I dropped out of school, start to smoke weed, that's what that was all about.[6]

The lies vexed Nas so much that he dropped out of school but added a suffix to the end of the adjective, "vexed-er" in his vernacular rendering, to underscore his agitated state. Too often schools that train poor young Blacks are sites of shortsightedness, or outright sightlessness, about the aims and ambitions of young learners. It is small wonder that Nas and millions more reach for the Buddha sack to weed out the lies, myths and distortions that riddle their existence.

Nas's wisdom sings most memorably when he offers advice to Born, and to a young thug to save him from his errant ways. Nas cautioned his friend Born to "chill" after he'd used an "ox"—a blade or razor—to assault a fellow prisoner. Nas pleads with Born to "stay civilized, time flies/Though incarcerated your mind dies." Nas realizes the cruel psychic and mental effects of prison, that incarceration often doesn't just bind the body but kills the mind and deadens intellectual energy. (2Pac said as much when he revealed that, contrary to popular belief, he found little creative inspiration in prison.)

Nas still says that Born's prison sentence might pass more quickly were he to "stay civilized," arguably in the eyes of the prison authorities and in the interior space of his personal identity. Prison often fails to offer true penitence to prisoners, much less a civilizing or rehabilitative influence. Often those who are deemed savage and beyond correction before they get locked down find an internal moral compass to navigate through the perils of prison. That may be one meaning of the civilizing impulse Nas seeks to strengthen in his friend. It is just as likely that Nas is alluding to the Five Percenter view that imprisonment, as a tool of white supremacy, can make a "civilized" god "savage" again.

When Nas turns his attention to his young charge on the street corner, his verbal mastery roars. Grabbing his weed and getting "ghost" for a couple of days respite from the projects, Nas leaves his phone and gun behind to recharge his batteries. The stress of the streets, he says, can lead to a choice between prison, and the emergency or psych wards, and can "have a nigga up in Bellevue/Or HDM, hit with numbers from 8 to 10/A future in a maximum state pen is grim," he says in a dazzling display of synecdoche and metonymy. Upon his return, Nas is greeted by a youngster rolling blunts and wearing a bulletproof vest and sporting a .32 caliber pistol for protection as he slings crack. Nas's description is novelistic, even cinematic; indeed, this verse inspired a scene in the Hype Williams–directed Black crime film *Belly*, in which Nas starred with fellow rapper DMX.

The video clip for "One Love" is equally dramatic. Directed by legendary graffiti artist and hip hop aficionado Fab Five Freddy, "One Love" brings to life Nas's lyrics with a skillful use of flashback scenes, and interwoven visual threads of parallel events in prison and the free world. "One Love" also intercuts various shots of Nas in full color with drained black-and-white landscapes, largely in prison and in the hood, signifying the lifelessness that threatens to stifle the incarcerated and those stuck in the ghetto alike. "One Love's" video also portrays the precocious youngster whose illicit actions are rendered more ironic and painful by his baby-faced adolescence. As Nas's words race to catch up to the images of his young apprentice's destructive behavior, the scenes quickly shift from black-and-white to color to paint the conflicting, and often confused, moral energy that fuels criminal activity in the hood.

In the song "One Love," Nas's internal rhymes unfold furiously as he vividly portrays the life of the criminal prodigy whose ambitious corner agenda prods Nas to offer him brotherly advice from a mature hustler.

I had to school him, told him don't let niggaz fool him
Cause when the pistol blows the ones that's murdered be the cool one
Tough luck when niggaz is struck, families fucked up
Coulda caught
your man, but didn't look when you bucked up
Mistakes happen, so take heed never bust up
At the crowd catch him solo, make the right man bleed

In a gesture of ethical triage, Nas starts with the given, that the young man, whom he calls "Shorty," is committed to a life of crime which will have negative effects on his community. In offering his advice, based on his experience in the streets, Nas seeks to influence his young peer's thinking and minimize the devastation of his drug dealing. Nas's narrative poignantly captures the moral complications of the hustling lifestyle: it is at once an erosion of the bonds of community, even as it sometimes seeks to answer the social and racial inequalities that make hustling necessary and useful to so many poor men of color. The tender age of Nas's hardened student hustler is a crime in itself. It is an offense that Nas brilliantly underscores as he wrestles with the question of whether he was schooling the youngster, or if he was schooling Nas. The elder is taken by the young man's surprisingly confident reaction to his advice.

Nas poetically acknowledges the jarring contrast between "Shorty's" youth and his exuberant worldliness, compelling Nas to conclude his impromptu lesson and his weed smoking. Nas understands, like St. Paul understood, that he planted the seeds, another man watered them, but only God, or destiny, or fate, could make them grow. Having done his part, Nas rises to depart, but not before releasing the inhaled smoke of a final hit of blunt, and not before acknowledging, in a beautiful metaphor, that he left "some jewels in the skull that he could sell if he chose," highlighting Nas's urban altruism. Shorty was free to treasure the precious knowledge Nas had deposited in his brain, or, like the crack he pumped, he could trade it later for cash or influence or power.

But it is not until Nas announces his final words of wisdom that it becomes clear that he is attempting to keep Shorty out of prison. As he cautions Shorty to watch out for Jake, slang for police, Nas brings "One Love" full circle and ends where he began: he couldn't prevent his unnamed friend from being caught by cops and sent to jail, but he could try to keep another youngster free of their grasp and that of the pen. Proving useful as a secular benediction after the fact of incarceration, "one love" also becomes a gesture of preventive maintenance, a cry of survival uttered from a loving friend or brother.

It is the same phrase I often share with Everett before we hang up from a collect phone call or a prison visit. It pains me deeply—often, by myself, to tears—to see him suffering so long for a crime that he didn't commit. I feel the hot grief that Nas felt when he confronted the tears of Born's mother. It hurts as well to know that prisons are being built to fit the failures and struggles of other young Black and brown men just like him. Like Nas in

"One Love," I feel an obligation to raise my voice in defense of millions of young Black and brown men and women who may one day follow his path. I want to warn them away from the destructive personal habits that make them vulnerable to prison, much as Nas warned Shorty. But I must also cry out against a society that would punish them in such unforgiving fashion while extending mercy to millions more who aren't poor or Black. In my mind, that inequality and racial injustice are the real crimes.

Besides hearing from my brother, I get a lot of mail from many other prisoners. Recently one wrote me: "I have followed you for years. I actually grew interested in who you were when I heard a song by this rapper named Nas and he mentioned your name." I suppose I feel tied to Nas because of my brother Everett, and that other prisoners may feel a tie to me because of Nas, and because of Everett. The three of us enjoy a brotherhood formed by our common experience of prison, either being incarcerated or loving those behind bars. And because our stories have reached millions more—Nas through "One Love," me and Everett because of our segment on CNN, and my open letter to him published in 1996—we have formed a brotherhood, and a sisterhood of sorts, with thousands of other prisoners, and those who support them as they endure their plight. That feeling of intimacy and hurt, of love and grief, is what makes "One Love"—like the Bob Marley song whose title it borrows—a rhetorical tour de force and a poetic blast of sonic consolation.

3

Mission Accomplished

In 1996, I drew from Danyel Smith, the music editor of Vibe *magazine (and, later, the magazine's first Black and first female editor-in-chief), a plum assignment to cover the career revival of the Isley Brothers, a group that then had its first hit record since 1983's* Between the Sheets. *I caught up with them at a '70s soul night at the Hampton Jazz Festival, which also featured soul music saints Isaac Hayes, Millie Jackson, and Harold Melvin and the Blue Notes. When the Isley Brothers and Earth, Wind and Fire participated in a 2021 Verzuz—the unique musical product of the global pandemic where two legendary acts amiably and digitally square off with each other—I was reminded of their staying power. Given that millions of (female) fans swooned over the 79-year-old Ron Isley's performance during Verzuz, but especially cited his newly grown and gorgeous gray beard, it's only right to quote the Notorious B.I.G.—who sampled "Between the Sheets" on his 1994 song "Big Poppa"—when he bragged on the remix to "One More Chance" something about himself that is equally true of Isley: "True playa for real."*

"Ooh, that's Mr. Biggs," the young Black housekeeper coos as she and her coworker spot Ronald Isley approaching an elevator in a Hampton, Virginia, hotel.

"No, it ain't, girl," the coworker whispers, half disbelieving, half hoping it might be true. After all, how likely is it that they'd see an R&B legend—who, after nearly 40 years in the business, is perhaps best known these days for his role as crime kingpin Mr. Biggs in R. Kelly's "Down Low (Nobody Has to Know)" video—traipsing through their terrain?

All the while, Isley, 55, glides through the hotel hallway as smoothly as one of his sensuous ballads. His white jogging suit sets off his glowing chocolate face and immaculately preened jet-black locks. A scaled-down version of his crew is in tow—his wife, sultry songstress Angela Winbush;

their assistant; guitar-legend brother Ernie, 44, with his daughter, Alexandra; and a record label executive. (Brother Marvin, 43, the Isleys' bassist and percussionist, is home sick.)

But faster than you can say "Fight the Power"—nah, not Public Enemy's summer of '89 anthem, but the Isley Brothers' 1975 smash—Isley gives away his secret with an impish, hammy come-on.

"Yeah, I'm Mr. Biggs," he purrs in mock hipness as he steps into the elevator.

As the doors close, Isley flicks on his dark shades and flashes a mega-kilowatt smile. The elevator may be going down, but the Isley Brothers' fortunes—thanks in part to Mr. Biggs—are going nowhere but up.

Some soul masters from the old school might resent the minor musical roads they have to travel to regain popularity: having a snatch of your voice or a lick of your guitar sampled on a hip hop joint; adding vocal flourishes to a new star's hit single; or making a for-old-time's-sake cameo appearance in a video. But the Isleys aren't your typical legends. They're not content to sit on their assets, heads swollen from decades of praise. The group is still hungry.

They may have sailed into the Rock and Roll Hall of Fame alongside former band member Jimi Hendrix, but the Isley Brothers are still hustling to win new fans with their magical blend of sex and soul. And they've still got the touch: This year's already gold *Mission to Please* (their first studio album in four years) is the group's first bona fide hit since 1983's *Between the Sheets*.

"[The durability of our music] is really a gift from the Lord," Ron says as he kicks back on the sofa in his luxury hotel suite. "And the competitiveness from wanting to be first. I don't know what we would do if we couldn't do music."

The hunger has brought the Isleys South to headline a '70s soul night at the Hampton Jazz Festival, on a bill that includes Isaac Hayes, Millie Jackson, and Harold Melvin and the Blue Notes. And the love has kept them going for nearly four decades, stretching from 1959's *Shout*, the archetypal rhythm and blues record, to this year's "Let's Lay Together," a lovely '90s update of the Isleys' signature sound: Ron's haunting falsetto arching over a sweet melody surrounded by velvet, undulating grooves.

That Isley sound, enhanced by Ernie's wicked wah-wahs and stinging, soaring guitar riffs, has provided the rhythmic bottom for countless hip hop tracks—from A Tribe Called Quest's "Bonita Applebum" and the Notorious B.I.G.'s "Big Poppa" to Bone Thugs-N-Harmony's "Tha Crossroads."

And as an R&B band—a self-contained musical force that has shown that rock, soul, funk, and gospel go together as naturally as the blindness and bigotry that prevent such a recognition—the Isleys are also the musical foreparents of D'Angelo and Dionne Farris, of Prince and Maxwell.

But if the Isley sound is sprinkled over the fragmented sonic landscape of urban music—"Between the Sheets" is perhaps the most sampled song in contemporary rap—their influence washes most thoroughly over records by Jodeci, Keith Sweat, and especially R. Kelly's tightly wound grooves, his yearning, pleading vocals, and his obsession with making the flesh obey the spirit.

But Kelly hasn't just hit the Isleys up for ideas. He made the next step, one that is as often overlooked as the artists who inspire young Turks: He went back to the source to see what they have to say now.

"Kelly had taken off on some of our stuff with the album *12 Play*," Ron explains. (In fact, Kelly's remix of "Bump n' Grind" contains a dead-on reprise of the lilting melody from the Isleys' "Make Me Say It Again Girl.") After bringing in Ron to harmonize on "Down Low," Kelly was really inspired.

"He said, 'I wanna be involved in y'all's next album,'" Ron says. "I said, 'Cool, man. Let's write some songs and get in the studio and throw down.'" They did just that, resulting in three numbers on *Mission to Please*. "When I started singing, R. Kelly fell all out on the floor, saying, 'I can't believe this. It's really him,'" Ron says, his eyes dancing with obvious pride. "He paid me my props and all that. I just love that out of young people."

If respect is based on talent and tenacity, then the Isleys deserve mad props indeed. They're true soul survivors who've weathered their share of personal and professional heartaches on the way to becoming pop icons. Reared in Cincinnati, the Isley boys—six in all—were almost literally born in rhythm. Their father was a former vaudevillian; their mother, a church choir director and music teacher.

"When I was two years old, my mother and father wanted a quartet," Ron recalls. The oldest brothers—Rudolph, Ronald, O'Kelly, and Vernon— sang gospel music in local churches in the early '50s, but after Vernon was killed in a bicycle accident in 1955, the foursome broke up.

A year later, Ronald, O'Kelly, and Rudolph teamed up again, expanding their repertoire to include everything from Dinah Washington to Frank Sinatra. They won several local talent contests and were encouraged to go to New York by, among others, rhythm and blues legend Clyde McPhatter. The Isleys journeyed to the city in 1957, recording several singles for independent labels that failed to make any noise. In 1959 Howard Bloom of RCA Records caught an Isley performance at the Howard Theater in Washington, D.C., and signed them immediately. Their first record, *Turn Me On*, bombed, despite the work of Sam Cooke's former producers Hugo & Luigi.

The follow-up, though, titled *Shout*, not only sold more than 1 million copies but also helped shape the direction of Black pop music. *Shout* turned loose on the secular world the unfiltered zeal and frenetic passion of Black gospel music. And like Cooke and Ray Charles before them, the Isleys came under attack from the Black religious world.

"A lot of the churches at the time called the radio stations," Ron recalls, "[saying] 'I don't know if it's right for them to be doing that song "Shout." . . . People are shouting on a song that's not a gospel song.'" Of course, "Shout" is now a classic, as is the Isleys' 1962 single "Twist and Shout," which has been covered most prominently by the Beatles (who most pop listeners probably assume wrote the song).

The Isleys followed with a string of lackluster singles for a series of record companies—Atlantic, Wand, and United Artists. After their relationship with United soured, the Isleys (who had since relocated to Teaneck, N.J.) formed their own label, punningly named T-Neck Records, in the early '60s.

The first version of T-Neck spawned a single, 1964's "Testify," which is important only because it's one of the first records on which Jimi Hendrix played. Jimi's influence on Ernie is obvious, but most people don't know how great an opportunity the younger Isley had to peep his idol's fretwork up close.

"He lived at the house," Ernie recalls animatedly, his yellow T-shirt and white jeans hugging his muscular frame as he snaps to attention on the couch in Ron's suite. "He was in the band for four years."

Because he was 10 years younger than Hendrix, Ernie never got the chance to study directly with the guitar wizard, but he soaked up the pyrotechnic vibes Hendrix sent rippling through the homeplace. "Basically, I would be peepin' around the hall while he was playing," Ernie says. "But Marvin was asking him everything he could think of," he adds with a grin. Still, the shadow of Hendrix's Stratocaster falls mightily on Ernie's majestic craft: the psychedelic, bluesy intensity of Ernie's long, lacerating licks on Isley ballads like 1973's "Summer Breeze"; his atmospheric, weeping phrases that jut just above the melody of mid-tempo grooves; and the dropkick-to-the-chest ferocity of his staccato picks on such up-tempo Isley jams as 1973's "That Lady."

It wasn't until 1969—after the Isleys had come and gone from Motown, where they enjoyed moderate success, and then revamped the T-Neck label and released the Grammy-winning "It's Your Thing"—that the addition of Ernie, Marvin, Isley brother-in-law/keyboardist Chris Jasper, and drummer Everett Collins made the group a soul septet, or, more to the point, a funk band. Although Ernie calls "It's Your Thing" the group's foundation, it didn't have enough kick to give them a distinct, recognizable sound.

Still, "It's Your Thing" was an important musical nod to the group's eventual direction. In the early '70s the Isley Brothers began to contribute their considerable skills to the Funk Revolution—joining General James Brown and Field Marshall Sly Stone and the genre's best weapon of attack, George Clinton's P-Funk Mothership. What the Isleys had in common with these and other funk groups is crucial, something often lost on today's heads: They weren't just a singing group, they were a band. And like all great funk bands, they wrote, produced, arranged, played, and sang their own material.

It was in 1973 that the Isley Brothers found their musical identity, their *sound*—and extraordinary commercial success to boot—with the release of *3+3*, the first of 10 gold or platinum albums the band would release over the next decade. They damn near reinvented the soul ballad—taking apart its prepackaged sentimentality, rebuilding it from the ground up, and handing it back to us full of honest, edifying emotion in songs like "For the Love of You."

But their success couldn't stem the tide of trouble that eventually floods all groups blessed—and burdened—by longevity. When I ask Ron about the group's split in 1984—when Chris, Ernie, and Marvin formed their own band, Isley, Jasper, Isley—he's forthright about his and his older brothers' roles in the breakup.

"The older brothers [O'Kelly, Rudolph, and Ron], being like fathers to the younger brothers, didn't give them the attention we should have," Ron confesses. From Ernie's point of view, it all boiled down to "a lot of miscommunication and noncommunication" between the younger and older brothers. Whatever happened, it led to a bitter breakup that lasted nearly six years. (Marvin and Ernie returned to the fold in 1990.) Isley, Jasper, Isley had two huge hits—"Caravan of Love" and "Insatiable Woman"—while the Isley Brothers wouldn't score again until "Smooth Sailin' Tonight" in 1987. In the meantime, the unexpected death of Kelly (who had dropped the "O'" from his name) in 1986 from a heart attack, at the age of 48, had a profound impact on the brothers.

"[When he passed] it was like somebody had reached inside me and pulled my living guts out," Ernie painfully remembers, gesturing with hands more familiar with stroking a guitar than pantomiming grief. "He was the center of the wheel, and after that the spokes started flying everywhere."

Rudolph decided to study for the ministry with his wife. He virtually gave up secular recording. Kelly's death hit Ron even harder. With Ernie, Chris, and Marvin in their own group, Ron was left all alone. Shortly afterward, he sought out Angela Winbush, then part of the R&B duo René and Angela (who were in the process of splitting), to produce tracks for the *Smooth Sailin'* album. Impressed by Winbush's vocal gifts, but especially by her songwriting and production skills, Isley discovered in her not only an enthusiastic fan but also a comforting shoulder and sympathetic ear.

"We started straightening each other's problems out," Ron says, as Winbush, seated next to him in a limo headed to one more in an endless series of radio interviews, blushes. Married three years ago, after a seven-year courtship, Isley and Winbush (who is about 20 years younger than her husband) are a deeply spiritual couple. After Kelly's death, Ron reclaimed his religious roots, returned to church, and now sprinkles his conversation with frequent references to "the Lord." But in hanging with Isley and Winbush, you don't get the sense—at least I didn't, and as a Baptist preacher my antennae are finely tuned—that when they're coming your way, as one wag put it, you're tempted to give three cheers for sin.

Ron claims not to feel any tension between his religious beliefs and his secular, sensual singing. "None whatsoever," he emphatically declares. "Because I always let the Lord know how appreciative I am for Him letting me do certain things. I want to use this instrument that He's given me to perform."

If that's the case, the Isleys' performance that night—with Angela as one of the backup singers—is not only a family affair, it's a faithful exercise of their gifts as well. It really is, at the risk of sounding corny, a mission to please—with an emphasis on "mission."

When I meet the crew at the Hampton Coliseum, Ron is already dressed to the nines—shrouded in a black suit, black shirt, and black shoes, with his trademark cane in hand. Like a preacher before he delivers the word, he sits, for the most part, silent and alone, soaking up the energy that only his mind and soul can give to him. I go over to make small talk. He cordially obliges, but he's distracted, slightly distant. After all, he's getting ready to perform, and, in his own understanding, to serve. Since I know something about that sort of concentration, I leave him to his thoughts.

Minutes later, the Isleys are unleashing pandemonium on Hampton Coliseum's stage. Kicking off their 45-minute set with "Harvest for the World," they cruise through 10 of their biggest hits and crowd pleasers, including "Between the Sheets," which draws massive screams from the audience, and a jazzed-up version of their remake of the Todd Rundgren song, "Hello It's Me."

But after a grinding rendition of "Twist and Shout," the Isleys tear into "Shout," a surefire climax that winds gradually to the song's sanctified though hardly sanctimonious sentiments, only to uncoil in an orgy of hand clapping and foot stomping. And of course, the enraptured crowd mouths, even mimics, Ron's every vocal twist. And why shouldn't they? After all, this is one of pop music's enduring standards.

"Hey-ey-ey-ey," he calls.

"Hey-ey-ey-ey," the crowd hollers back.

At the peak of the frenzy, as the audience rhythmically assaults the air with their arms and hands, I briefly pause to think about Ron's desire to use his God-given talent to perform. He must be in heaven, I think, as I resume my enthusiastic responses to his gruffly voiced calls. And right about now, so am I.

CHAPTER

4

Hello Like Before

Bill Withers was one of the greatest poets of the twentieth century and surely one of its greatest singers and songwriters. I was incredibly honored to be invited to pen these liner notes to the box set that collected his nine studio albums in 2012. Interviewing him for the liner notes was pure ecstasy; he retained the wit and wisdom that poured through his transcendent lyrics. I established a warm friendship with him that lasted until his death in 2020.

"Let me tell you a story," Bill Withers says, offering a phrase that perfectly encapsulates his storied career as a gifted storyteller and wise philosopher whose lyrical genius ranges over big subjects. Love. Art. Work. Spirituality. The story of language itself.

"Let me tell you a story," he says, the phrase floating like a heavenly harp plucked by his cherished accompanist Dorothy Ashby on a Withers gem like "Stories."

Bill Withers justified his legendary status a long time ago, establishing his artistic pedigree with some of the best poetry set to music in the last half-century. Yet Withers, like fellow poets T. S. Eliot and Rita Dove, is also a first-rate critic of the creative process.

"The ideal role of the artist is that of curator," he says, "but their actual role is narrator. Everybody is narrating from their own personal information. With me, there's a tendency to draw from the upbringing I had back in West Virginia. But by the time I started making music I had been around the world. I had not only been innocent in West Virginia, I had been a drunken sailor in Guam," alluding to his time in the Navy.

Withers sounds like Tennyson—*I am a part of all that I have met*—and sings the poet's insight in his own voice. "The artist is a composite of all the places you've been, everybody that you've met, and everything that affects you."

Referring to his childhood in coal mining camps and the nuggets of self-knowledge he unearthed, he says: "I learned that I had an innate facility for the English language. I learned that I could write things, which is probably what caused me to eventually wander into songwriting. And that was challenging because you didn't have a long time to say things. You had four minutes, max, and whatever you said had to be profound or funny or interesting."

No small task when you consider that Withers's work has effortlessly crossed borders, and as the literary critics say, swerved between genres. Withers brought his rural blue-collar aesthetic, his lunch pail work ethic, and even the sounds of labor, to his singer-songwriter workshop. His boundary-crashing 1971 debut *Just As I Am* is a prime example of the formidable fusion of *folksouljazzfunk* that he mastered and refined in a concentrated decade-and-a-half of kaleidoscopic expression.

"Some of the Black stations would say, 'Ah, this sounds too white,' and the white stations would say, 'We can't play this, it's too Black.'

"All the work that I did had rhythms and sounds. Airplanes make noise. I was an aircraft mechanic for nine years. I remember writing songs like 'Use Me' and 'Grandma's Hands' while working at McDonnell Douglas. I rushed home trying not to forget it before I could get home and write it down. So I never separated work from writing because our interactions with people cause us to write and think things."

Let's not forget that Withers is also the auteur of *+Justments*, an unjustly neglected classic of American pop that ruminates on relationships, passion and narrative as seamlessly as Marvin Gaye meditated on war, love and politics with the masterful *What's Going On*. One need only listen to the onomatopoeia of Withers slinging gravel on "Railroad Man" to literally hear how work and writing mingle in his mouth.

"When you're trying to be successful at songwriting, you have to be clever. It's not always deep thinking. Sometimes you're just trying to rhyme something with something else. You get the thought down, and then you go back and say, 'I've got to make this interesting.' And when you turn a phrase, you go, 'That's it.'

"There's one phrase that I'm most proud of, because I've never heard anybody else use it: 'Hello like before.' In my whole life, I've never heard academics, pimps or cops use that phrase. It's only in that song. But you know what it means."

We got it immediately because it touches on one of Withers's perennial themes and our culture's magnificent obsessions: love. Withers writes with forensic and visceral intensity about love's guises and poses, its frantic fluctuations and its soothing, surprising stability.

He writes about love of one's lover ("Ain't No Sunshine") and love of one's fellow man ("Lean On Me").

About jealous love ("Who Is He? And What Is He To You?") and paradoxical love ("The Same Love That Made Me Laugh").

About cerebral love ("Make Love To Your Mind"), metropolitan love ("City of Angels") and meteorological love ("Lovely Day").

About tender love ("Dedicated To You My Love"). Hopeful love ("We Could Be Sweet Lovers"). Restorative love ("Make A Smile For Me").

He writes about addictive love ("Use Me") and love soiled by self-sabotage ("Better Off Dead").

Even love crushed by snobbery and class grudges ("You").

"In order to speak of love from a complete place," he observes, "I think you have to have needed it, and didn't have it.

"Or, you find yourself in one of those goofy-in-love situations, where you're dumber than a wooden watch but you just think you've found this wonderful thing. And then as you go on, the reality is that you're not going to have tomorrow with this woman you just met. But the world's not going to come to an end, either. It's going to all come down to earth, because there's a reality to it—the actual practice of love, versus people that fall in love with a photo.

"Either way, it's just one episode in your life."

Withers is equally eloquent about another form of love—religion—that is often corrupted and exploited. He prefers intimate spirituality rather than institutional religion; small churches more than big ones; the Pentecostals, whose electric energy uncoils in many of his rhythms, to the Baptists and Methodists. The message of brotherly love found in the Sanctified church also breathes in Withers's lyrics. "Grandma's Hands" surely comes to mind, which in word celebrates his grandmother's tambourine wielding ecstasy though the song's serpentine cadence snakes more heavily into our ears in the opening notes of Blackstreet's "No Diggity" sampled a generation later.

"The pageantry of organized religion confuses me," he says. "If we're talking about worship based on the whole Jesus Christ thing, who was always down there on the ground, how do you translate the worship of such a humble, ultimately sacrificial figure into all that pageantry and wealth?"

Withers sounds like an updated Max Weber when he diagnoses the misuse of charisma in religious circles. "This is show business. You got to have some charisma, whether it's correct, or correctly incorrect, because one of the basic requirements of leading anything is get somebody to follow you. When Jim Jones got all those people to commit suicide, he had his leadership down."

Withers nailed that same correct incorrectness on his maiden recordings. "One of the first songs I wrote was called 'Harlem.' *A crooked delegation wants a donation to send the preacher to the Holy Land/Come on sugar, don't give your money to a lying, cheating man.* How do you sort that out, especially when you get older?" It's a question that resonates for Withers as he creeps closer to the end.

"I'm at the age of mortality and I really want to sort it out. You get old and get aches and pains, and you need somewhere emotionally to go, for solace. I want to go somewhere. I want to be part of it. Because mortality whips a whole 'nother game on you. You want to be alright."

Withers has also been fighting the mortal threat of racism his entire life, a peril so real that it may have cut short his brilliant career.

"The challenge is to survive through the apprehension and try to create a value for yourself. Make sure that it doesn't shut you down and turn you so angry and bitter. Now if I had been able to do that, I probably would've made more music. Because when I went to a larger record company and they had all this Black/white stuff, I just shut down. And that's the best education you can give somebody on race—to make allowances for what somebody else doesn't know, to make allowances for somebody else's ignorance. So whatever you gotta do, persevere and motivate yourself so that it doesn't interrupt you from creating your own value."

The magnitude of Bill Withers's own value can't be denied. His stories have shaped a generation's understanding of itself. His poetry has touched the lives of millions around the globe whose tongues can barely express what their hearts so deeply feel.

5

The Church of Aretha Franklin

For the last fifteen years of her colossal and regal existence, I had the great fortune of knowing, listening to, talking to, and spending time with the one and only Queen of Soul, Aretha Franklin. Her voice, the greatest we have heard, echoes still in the majestic command and sonic explosions that characterized her craft and spill from hi-fis, stereos, CD players, iPods, iPhones, streaming services, and wherever else the human voice can be heard. Her friendship was an oasis of refined elegance mixed with gutbucket humor and a zestful joie de vivre. She loved talking politics, and would text me, sometimes in all caps, or, even more humorously, would send complete messages in the subject lines of emails. Seeing her perform in all sorts of venues, from Virginia's Wolf Trap, to the Essence Festival in New Orleans, or in front of the pope in Philadelphia, was always a thrilling experience. It may be a cliché—I once heard Toni Morrison say that clichés are clichés for a reason, they contain a truth—but she was truly one of a kind. A version of this essay appeared in the op-ed pages of The New York Times *after her death in August 2018.*

In 2015, Aretha Franklin invited me and a few others to join her in Philadelphia as she sang for the Pope. I was certainly thrilled to see the Pontiff up close. But, I must confess, after many years of friendship, I was still more excited to watch the Queen of Soul once again exult in her vocal majesty. Even at 73, Franklin could trap lightning in her mouth at a moment's notice and shout down fire to earth. Her throat was a magical theater where notes undulated to soaring rhythms. Her runs up and down the scale exhausted the horizon of sound until it yielded as her musical footstool. It was Franklin's astonishing virtuosity and unrepeatable voice that left *Rolling Stone* magazine no choice but to crown her the greatest singer ever.

Just the mention of Aretha Franklin's name cast a spell and conjured transcendent sonic fury. She came to it honestly. Her father, the Reverend

C. L. Franklin, was one of the most storied preachers of his day. His rhetorical genius unspooled in a homiletical frenzy that tracked onto more than seventy-six recordings. His sermons on vinyl were treasured as sacred touchstones in Black communities across the nation. Rev. Franklin crossed the country as an electrifying evangelist, gathering a group of friends that read like a who's who of Black America, from singers like Sam Cooke and leaders like Martin Luther King, Jr. Young Aretha absorbed the rich atmosphere of Black excellence decades before the term gained currency. She was nurtured in a womb of Black accomplishment that fed her desire to spread her wings and fly as high as her genius could take her.

I grew up in Detroit, where Rev. Franklin lived, but I first sampled the minister's seductive moan and his wicked hum on my grandfather's Alabama farm. I was barely six years old, and I sat, transfixed, as Franklin's rhetorical charm spilled onto the turntable of the archaic record player that I found stashed near the fireplace in the living room. Franklin was a down home preacher whose homilies showcased his earthy squall that could resolve in dramatic whisper. He was a past master of "whooping," or the chanted sermon, where articulation is artfully coarsened, diction is skillfully striated, and words are put under pressure of music and speech bursts into song. The freakishly precocious Aretha gestated in her father's verbal womb and then came forth full blown as a bronze gospel wunderkind.

If Aretha got her gift from her father, I inherited my love for Aretha from my mother. When she migrated to Detroit from Alabama in the mid-1950s, my mother frequented the New Bethel Baptist church where C. L. Franklin held forth every Sunday. She told me how, after Rev. Franklin mesmerized the congregation with his poetic homilies, his teenaged daughter would rise behind him to ratchet up the spirit to more thrilling heights. Her uncanny aptitude rang in a theological clairvoyance so compelling that the congregation knew that greatness and the Spirit rested in double portion on this fearless young woman. One can hear her gargantuan gift on her first gospel recording at age fourteen, "Never Grow Old." Aretha was light years ahead of Chronos, or time as told by a clock, and had plunged headlong into Kairos, or the fullness of time, a time where fulfillment of destiny seemed clearly at hand.

When it came time for her to switch from sacred to secular, a seismic shift occurred, a great wound was inflicted. When she invested religious fervor in her quest for fulfillment in affairs of the heart, and joy in the senses, a bruising rift opened up between the church and the world. Ray Charles had already tested that gap, and so had Sam Cooke after him. Their departure from the pews eased the path for Aretha. When it came time for her to switch from sacred to secular, to head for the soul music charts after she had brilliantly charted the path of the soul in gospel music, she confronted great gusts of resentment and brutal blowback from Black believers.

They thought that she had betrayed her first love and her true calling. But they were wrong. After experimenting with numerous genres, from blues to jazz, Aretha found a bigger canvas to sketch her artistic vision on that drew both from ancient soul passions and progressive moral possibilities. Thus, she transformed Otis Redding's punchy "Respect" into a transcendent anthem for racial pride and a cry of feminist self-recognition. Her church got larger, her congregation composed of millions of people in search of a soulful vision of spiritual direction beyond choir stands and sanctuary doors.

When she returned to the world of gospel in 1972, and again fifteen years later, her embrace of the phrases and emotion of the sanctuary put at rest those who may have feared that she had somehow lost it, or that God had somehow forsaken her. Her father let the world know, in spirited remarks on her landmark 1972 album, *Amazing Grace*, that his daughter "never really left the church." And clearly it had never left her.

If Aretha blessed Black America as an artist, she blessed Black women even more as a model of thriving in what James Brown famously sang of as a "man's world." He may have been the Godfather of Soul, but Aretha was the Queen of Soul, proving time and again that she could beat the men at their own game. Who can forget the great Otis Redding's reaction to hearing Aretha belt out his memorable tune, "Respect?" Redding was naturally funky, but Aretha brought a feel to the song that was at once earthy and uplifting. If Redding's version was memorable, Aretha's was transcendent.

She sang the song like her life depended on it. And in many ways, it did. She confronted domestic violence in her first marriage early on in her career, and her version of "Respect" can be read as an early declaration of #MeToo—her testimony in song about the need, and in her rendering, the demand, to be heard and respected. She literally spelled it out in a way that Redding hadn't done—in a way he hadn't needed to do. Aretha gave the song a female urgency that neither Redding's throat nor pen could capture. In 1967, when he performed the song at the Monterey Pop Festival, he said, "This next song is a song that a girl took away from me. A good friend of mine, this girl, she just took the song."

But Aretha didn't just take Redding's song; she also seized the power to tell her own story, and thus, inspired generations of women that came behind her to tell their own stories in song too. There would be no Chaka Khan, Whitney Houston, Mariah Carey or Beyoncé without Aretha. As much as her love for her people shines through in all that she did, her love and advocacy for Black women was even more striking, and arguably, more necessary. The way she fashioned her hair in an Afro sparked pride in Black women to embrace a hairstyle that was very much controversial when she first embraced it. Her lavish threads were preceded by the African themed gowns that she adopted, a flourish that helped to inspire the Black embrace of flowing African-centered clothes.

If she inspired Black women in strong self-expression, style and fash-ion, she also displayed extraordinary political courage too. One remarkable flash of Aretha's political bravery was captured in an article in *Jet* magazine, the bible of everyday Black folk in the sixties and seventies. "Aretha Says She'll Go Angela's Bond If Permitted," the title declared. The Angela it ref-erenced is Angela Davis, the jailed social rebel who had made it onto the FBI's 10 most wanted list in 1970. She was charged with murder, kidnap-ping and conspiracy for her role in the escape attempt of political prisoners from a California courtroom. Aretha went against her father's wishes in offering to pay Davis's bond.

"My daddy says I don't know what I'm doing," Franklin said. "Well, I respect him, of course, but I'm going to stick by my beliefs." She didn't call herself a feminist; the term was barely in circulation, yet Aretha was clearly acting as an independent and assertive woman intent on helping another woman, another sister. "Angela Davis must go free . . . I'm going to see her free if there is any justice in our courts . . . because she's a Black woman and she wants freedom for Black people."

Aretha brilliantly linked the freedom and plight of Black women with the freedom and plight of Black America. She also believed that her role as a wealthy celebrity obligated her to help other Black folk, especially Black women. "I have the money; I got it from Black people—they've made me financially able to have it—and I want to use it in ways that will help our people."

Franklin's concern for social justice and redemptive politics also flashed as she performed at civil rights fundraisers for dear family friend Dr. Martin Luther King in the sixties, and to benefit the efforts of her close comrade Reverend Jesse Jackson in the 1970s and beyond. Adorned in a spectacular hat, Franklin famously sang "My Country, 'Tis of Thee" at the first inaugu-ration of Barack Obama in 2009. I was fortunate to know Aretha Franklin personally, and she would often call me to discuss current events. She had a crisp comprehension of the political machinations of our time, and offered considered opinions about one figure or another. She reveled in the prospects of the first Black president, and registered grief at the polarization of his successor.

Her sense of humor was sharp. I cracked up each time she recalled how Dr. King, as a guest in her father's home in the sixties, encountered the family maid one morning who laid out the options for breakfast. (Franklin's mother Barbara separated from the preacher when Aretha was barely six but stayed in contact with her children until she died of a heart attack right before Aretha's tenth birthday in 1952.) "There are scrambled eggs, and grits, and *soychig*," Franklin recalls the maid saying. Having discerned that she was offering her unique pronunciation of sausage, King, without missing a beat, replied that he'd have the eggs and grits, "and some of that *soychig*." We both laughed until tears streamed down our faces. Franklin used the anecdote to cherish the sublime humanity of a great friend, while I absorbed, vicariously, yet another display of an adored leader's profound humility.

From time to time, Franklin would summon me and my wife to celebrate her birthdays in grand style at a hotel ballroom or tony restaurant. We would see Tony Bennett fete her with a personal painting, or the late great Dennis Edwards crooning for her in his unmistakable musical signature, a sweet, roughhewn plaint at the center of his volcanic melismas. Franklin and Edwards, then the lead singer of the Temptations, dated in the early seventies, when Franklin penned the classic "Day Dreaming" with him in mind, praising a lover who is "the kind of guy that you give your everything."

I hungered for personal knowledge of the wellsprings of her father's homiletical artistry. My close study of his craft led Franklin to invite me on stage with her at the Trumpet Awards in Atlanta in 2012 to offer my brief appreciation for his formidable arsenal of oratorical talents and spiritual effects. She took great pride in her father's legendary command of Black sacred speech, and she was especially grateful that a younger generation took note of his epic gifts. As we stood on stage, we both realized, as we remarked later, that we were a long way from Detroit, but we both drew sustenance from its artistic and rhetorical contributions all these years later.

We both fiercely loved Detroit, and Detroit, in turn, was exceedingly proud of her fearless evangelism for a city that was often spurned for its daring embrace of unapologetic Black identity and leadership. The Baptist church that we both sprang from eventually took great delight in her reign as the most dominant force in American music while never forgetting her roots in the energetic spirituality that bathed her style. The preacher in me believed that hers was the best way to tell our story to a world that might never darken our doors but was sorely in need of a dose of the Spirit.

Franklin had a huge intellectual appetite as well. She would often call me after reading an article about politics, or watching a documentary about, say, geological digs that unearthed some Biblical relic, or simply to praise me for my words on television, on page, or in the pulpit. No words can possibly convey the sense of divine affirmation I heard in the words of a woman I had grown up idolizing as making the greatest sound I had heard a human voice sing.

Aretha Franklin had a famous fear of flying. But now, like one of her legendary compositions, she has shattered the ethers and ascended to a heavenly domain in which she passionately believed, and to which her immortal art, both in the church and beyond, always pointed.

Do You See What I See?

In the Photograph

CHAPTER

6

August March

My former student and assistant, and now gifted curator, historian and educator, Paul Farber, invited me to write the lead essay in This Is the Day, *a 2013 book that collected the photography of Leonard Freed from the March on Washington in 1963. Freed's photographs invite us to think deeply and passionately about the philosophical character of the lens and what it does to dark or Black skin—how it features or obscures us, how it radiates power or distributes punishment. Freed's Black ocular focus in particular extended an aesthetics of redemption, and his photographs offered me the opportunity to reflect on Black flesh revealed in its beauty and power, and on Martin Luther King, Jr., the greatest freedom fighter in the nation's history, who appeared in but one Freed photo from the day, and that from a far distance. But there was a lesson even in his distance from King, a lesson that I cite here.*

There have been many marches since, and several before, but no other march to the nation's capital captured our collective imagination like the March on Washington of August 28, 1963. It was undoubtedly one of the greatest gatherings of American citizens since the republic's birth. The March on Washington branded the protest march like Xerox branded copying machines, like Apple branded computers. The circumstances of the march make it remarkable that it came off at all. The march was composed of eclectic groups with varying purposes: the moderate National Urban League, for instance, sought to rescue the Negro from urban peril, while the insurgent Student Nonviolent Coordinating Committee wanted to protect the Negro from white terror. The march also exploited colorful if tenuous alliances between Jews and Blacks, between labor and civil rights groups, and between religious believers and secular activists. The drama that engulfed the planning of the march put soap operas to shame: the leadership class nursed petty jealousies and ugly rivalries while jostling for position before television cameras. The momentous pilgrimage also showcased an inspired pairing: Martin Luther King, Jr., the celebrated leader of Black America who hadn't yet delivered an entire speech that the nation had listened to, and Bayard Rustin, whose organizational genius drew the masses to D.C. despite the open secret of his homosexuality.

The internal problems that plagued the march were mild compared to the intimidation of ordinary Black people. In the Deep South most whites saw joining the NAACP as racial surliness, a defiant and uppity gesture worthy of brisk unemployment and a kick in the pants, or worse yet, a literal shot in the dark. If local organizing provoked white anger, a national protest aimed at winning jobs and freedom for Black folk was utterly infuriating. The routine brutality that stalked Black life also leapt over white borders: many whites were attacked or murdered for their solidarity with Black struggle.

Powerful whites who sympathized with Black life often did so in an abstract fashion. They passed the liberal smell test, but when scratched they often bled in faint spots of moderation. They were typically more spooked by strong Black protest against injustice than by the white violence that caused Blacks to resist. King faced this challenge in 1963 from eight white clergymen who implored him to take the gradual approach to social revolution in Alabama. King's response was his famous "Letter from Birmingham Jail," trumpeting Black folks' "legitimate and unavoidable impatience." The civil rights leader reprinted his searing missive in a book whose title said it all: *Why We Can't Wait.*

King and other leaders also met stiff resistance from President John F. Kennedy, who wasn't nearly as progressive as the figure he played on television. Kennedy lamented in a Presidential meeting three months before the march that "King is so hot these days that it's like Marx coming to the White House." Although King didn't pen it, the title of Nick Bryant's book *The Bystander* neatly summarizes Kennedy's equivocating stance on civil rights. Kennedy didn't hide his opposition to the march from King and his colleagues. "We want success in the Congress, not a big show on the Capitol," Kennedy argued in a meeting with civil rights leaders. It was only after the triumph of the march that the young commander in chief greeted the even younger civil rights hero in the White House on the very afternoon of King's glorious achievement with the magical refrain from his instantly immortal oration: "I have a dream," the president said as he beamed a smile at King.

The march's resounding success made all the paranoia about any possible trouble seem typically overplayed: Washington police and the U.S.

military were poised as if for an insurrection. Such fears have hardly died even in our day. The tragic death in February 2012 of Florida teen Trayvon Martin is sad proof of racism's bitter persistence. Trayvon was a 17-year-old Black youth shot to death by George Zimmerman, a neighborhood watch volunteer who got drunk on the poisonous brew of Black suspicion. Zimmerman killed Trayvon because he looked like he was up to no good as he walked back to the home of his father's fiancée in a gated community, armed only with Skittles and iced tea. Zimmerman claimed self-defense, but Trayvon's only crime seems to be that he was young and Black. Outrage at Trayvon's senseless death sparked protests across the nation.

Trayvon's death echoes the epic loss of another Black teen, Emmett Till, whose 14-year-old body was mutilated, murdered and tossed into Mississippi's Tallahatchie River in 1955 with a 70-pound cotton gin fan tied around his neck, held in place by barbed wire. Till's death unleashed tidal waves of mourning and memory that swept thousands of activists into the titanic struggle for justice. Rustin and his colleague surely weren't oblivious to the poignant symbolism of holding the march on the eighth anniversary of Till's epochal sacrifice.

While Till's premature martyrdom surely haunted the movement, A. Philip Randolph furnished the march's enduring political rationale. Randolph's long and colorful odyssey as a civil rights and labor leader culminated in organizing and heading the Brotherhood of Sleeping Car Porters, the nation's first predominantly Black labor union. Along with Rustin, Randolph organized the March on Washington Movement (MOWM), which lasted from the mid-thirties to the late forties. The purpose of the MOWM was to pressure the government to desegregate the armed forces and to provide fair employment opportunities for Black folk. In 1941 Randolph, Rustin and pacifist A. J. Muste called for a march on Washington to highlight Black grievances and to call for concerted government action. After national organizing efforts led to the prediction that more than one hundred thousand marchers might descend on the nation's capital in protest, President Franklin D. Roosevelt issued Executive Order 8802. Roosevelt's action established the first Fair Employment Practices Committee (FEPC), leading Randolph, Rustin and Muste to call off the march less than a week before it was scheduled to take place, but only after they made sure that government employment for Blacks was also covered in the presidential order. Although the MOWM was founded to call for a march on Washington, it lasted until the late 1940s as a force to urge the federal government into just action on behalf of beleaguered Blacks.

More than twenty years after Randolph's initial organizing for a March on Washington, and in the centennial year of the Emancipation Proclamation, the time seemed right for a renewed effort to dramatize the Negro's demand for jobs and freedom by flocking en masse to the nation's capital. By 1963, Randolph's visionary activism, strategic acumen, organizational talent, stentorian voice, stirring oratory and regal bearing made him, at 74 years of age, the great old man of Black leadership and the titular head of the March on Washington. Rustin was the perfect organizer. He was a distinguished social activist and theoretician of nonviolence who had worked alongside Randolph in many causes. Rustin later served as an adviser to Martin Luther King, Jr., whose potential he spotted early on before heading south to help the young minister understand and implement Gandhian tactics of nonviolence in the 1956 Montgomery Bus Boycott. A year later Rustin helped King to organize the Southern Christian Leadership Conference.

Rustin had the unenviable task of corralling competing forces to make the march a success. The Black male leaders of major civil rights groups formed the march's organizational core. Dubbed "The Big Six," they included Randolph, King, Congress of Racial Equality head James Farmer, SNCC chairman John Lewis, NAACP leader Roy Wilkins, and National Urban League head Whitney Young. These men had at times conflicting ideas about the best route to racial redemption. For instance, the gifted Roy Wilkins favored action in the courts rather than activism in the streets, and had a special distaste for King's style and approach to social justice. Whitney Young was a talented organizer who awakened the group from its social slumber and made it relevant to the Black freedom struggle. He was also chummy with white corporate titans, a close adviser to Kennedy, and later, to Presidents Johnson and Nixon. Young's proximity to the White House was a sore spot later on when King criticized the Vietnam War and Johnson played the two leaders against each other.

There were many hurt egos about who would and would not speak. The leaders omitted noted writer James Baldwin, and Rustin only belatedly invited the Birmingham movement hero Rev. Fred Shuttlesworth to the podium when the other speakers were in tense negotiations over the controversial elements of John Lewis's speech. The absence of women was a glaring omission. The wives of the male leaders weren't allowed to march with their husbands, and no woman spoke during the proceedings except expatriate performer Josephine Baker. Two Black female stars managed to take the stage. Opera great Marian Anderson performed "He's Got the Whole World in His Hands," and gospel legend Mahalia Jackson let loose with "I Been 'Buked and I Been Scorned," an ironic if unintended commentary on the treatment of women as well. A token "Tribute to Women" called on notable women activists to take a bow, including Rosa Parks, Daisy Bates, Diane Nash Bevel and Gloria Richardson. Even the great Dorothy Height, a presidential adviser and head of the National Council of Negro Women, who surely qualified as one of the "big" leaders, wasn't invited to speak. Women were barely seen and largely unheard that day.

The rhetorical and symbolic centerpiece of the march remains Martin Luther King, Jr. His remarkable oration that day still resonates at the heights of American rhetoric, though behind-the-scenes drama surrounded his speech as well. As Black leaders jockeyed to appear early in the program to assure television coverage, and to avoid speaking after King, they had little idea of how quickly the march's magnitude would capture the nation's attention. By the time King stood to deliver his speech, after being memorably introduced by Randolph as the "moral leader of our nation," ABC and NBC joined CBS, the only station scheduled to cover the march. Together they provided full network coverage of an event that grew well beyond its predicted impact on the approximately two hundred and fifty thousand protesters gathered. The march registered around the globe as a seismic shift in the presentation and portrayal of Black intelligence in the service of social justice and the public good.

King started slowly and deliberately, his rich baritone resounding throughout the crowd as he self-consciously linked himself to Lincoln's legacy by alluding to Lincoln's language in the Gettysburg Address, counting years clumped together in arcane bushels of scores. Lincoln began his 1863 oration "Four score and seven years ago," referring to the American Revolution in 1776, while King began his 1963 oration "Five score years ago," referring to Lincoln's signing of the Emancipation Proclamation. King gained immediate purchase on the dynamics of American democracy and the dilemmas of American race in one fell rhetorical swoop.

King steadily built his oration—or in the language of Black preachers he "argued his case"—on a series of metaphors that clarified his moral rendering of history from the angle of democracy's delayed beneficiaries. The nation had bounced a check to Black people that King and his colleagues had come to collect for us all. Millions of Black folk had been unjustly marooned on an island of poverty in the midst of an ocean of prosperity— material prosperity he was careful to say, suggesting that other forms of well-doing were meager consolation at this historical juncture, anticipating President Lyndon B. Johnson's War on Poverty less than a year later.

King's measured cadence and euphonious delivery masked the radical character of his speech. King said that there would be "neither rest nor tranquility in America" until Negroes gained full citizenship, and he spoke of the "whirlwinds of revolt" that would continue to "shake the foundations of our nation" until justice is done. King railed against police brutality, the stunted social mobility of poor Blacks in urban ghettoes, and the chronic assault on Black selfhood and personal dignity.

Women may have been barred from the speaker's stage, but at least one of their voices ranged far beyond where their bodies had been exiled. Mahalia Jackson noted that King's usual rhetorical freedom had been stifled under the weight of history and the demands of a written speech. She evoked a bit of holy boisterousness and encouraged her friend to depart from paper and soar to oratorical heights in the careful improvisation that marks Black speech at its best. "Tell 'em about the dream, Martin," she bellowed from the background, rescuing King and changing history on the strength of a verbal interjection, a sweet call and response not uncommon in the Black church.

And respond to her call King did. Even if his ears didn't hear her, his soul did. King cast aside his prepared speech and offered the world a glimpse of Black rhetorical genius. King conjured bits and pieces of other orations to weave the dream metaphor into the tapestry of the nation's self-image, and in the process, he grafted Black folk to the heart of American democracy. He dreamed about his children being judged on character, not color. He dreamed of the day when the offspring of slaves and the offspring of their former owners might enjoy each other's humanity. He dreamed that Mississippi might be made over in the image of justice and that Alabama might redeem its destiny because its youngest citizens joined hands. He dreamed that true biblical inspiration might spill over into the corridors of hope and faith and baptize the freedom songs of suffering servants. He dreamed that his dream might be recognized as America's dream, and that freedom might ring from the great peaks and resound in the downcast valleys of the American soul. And he dreamed in such a way that the blues and the spirituals were reconciled in an exhilarating moment of moral synergy that mirrored the unity he wished on the American people.

If King's thrilling and masterly oration rose from the belly of Black suffering, bounded over hurdles of national power, and captured American moral aspiration, then the folk gathered on the National Mall put body and face to King's resilient dream. Leonard Freed's moving photography offers still images of an America at once frozen in time and marching restlessly to its multicultural and multiracial future through the lens of a visionary artist. Freed's photographs are more than snapshots; they are portraits of social possibility set against the backdrop of a nation grappling with the exclusionary obsessions of one race, one gender, one sexuality, one age, one religion and one region. Freed's photographs of the day offer instead the expansive possibilities of many races, many genders, many sexualities, many ages, many religions, and many regions gathered on the Mall to call for change.

But he does something more, without either agenda or political motivation, making his visual testimony that much more powerful: He photographs the rainbow of Blackness that floats above prescribed definitions of beauty and intelligence. Dark-skinned Blacks that were usually only photographed in buffoonish extravagance get from Freed a forgiving realism that rescues the Blackest Blacks from the wasteland of stereotype and restores them to majestic ordinariness. They are marching as much for the freedom to breathe the air of their luminous darkness—with their chocolate skin and their neatly cut kinky hair or their freshly pressed coifs—as for the right to live free of the lynch mob or the poll tax.

Freed also captures white faces and bodies as a drop in a Black ocean, not the other way around, reinforcing the fact that the global majority even then were people of color. But the subtle politics of capturing such portraits suggest justice, or the search for it, as the basis for peaceful coexistence. What Freed's photos do, too, is document white investment without the pretense of superiority or the encumbrance of nobility. The aims of King's speech find forceful symmetry in the aim of Freed's camera.

The moral beauty of Freed's photographs bathes the aesthetic that guides his flow of images. The folk here are neat, dignified, well-dressed—in a word, *sharp*, with all the surplus meaning the word summons, since Black dress can never be divorced from political consequence. The Black desire to dress elegantly, or failing that, to dress noticeably, reflecting a sartorial instinct rooted in complicated dimensions of Black life and aspiration, marked our existence then as surely as it does now. Well-dressed Black folk decked-out in their Sunday go-to-church clothes, or their Saturday go-to-party glad rags, often offended whites who resented even a thread of evidence that Black folk were prospering beyond their desert, or beyond comparative white means. Freed captures the simple dignity and the protocols of cool—the ethics of decorum—that characterize large swaths of Black life. And when his camera swings wide to include a vision of America too rarely noticed in the mainstream press at the time, and in some cases even now, he records almost mundanely, and hence, rather heroically, the everydayness of the encounters between white and Black. He allows the images to steep in the crucible of American race. One can almost hear the subliminal suggestion: This is what it should always be like. The photograph of Blacks and whites linking arms in the culminating rendition of "We Shall Overcome" is sweet "I sing" on the cake of unity.

The single Freed photograph from the march that includes King's presence, if not his discernible image, is instructive in its courageous stinginess and in its polar distance from the iconic figure. A year later Freed captured King in one of the most famous shots of the leader as a throng of admirers lay hands on him in a passing motorcade celebrating King's receipt of the Nobel Peace Prize in 1964. But on the day of the march, Freed positions himself far off and below the steps of the Lincoln Memorial as King delivers his speech. Freed thus achieves visually what scholars have labored to do intellectually: to show that no matter how dominant a figure King was, he wasn't the only, and often not even the primary, vehicle for the civil rights movement. Freed's photo also suggests that no matter how much we think we know King, how close we thought we were to him, he was in truth a far more complicated man who struggled with personal demons and unpopular political ideas as he tapped the vein of social revolution.

Like Freed's photographs, the movement didn't stop in 1963 on the National Mall. The civil rights movement's struggles for nonviolent social change continued to unfold in political corridors and popular culture years after its most ballyhooed achievements. The legacy of the March on Washington is still being written, still being contested, still being fought for in the soul of the nation. Conservatives who once ridiculed the movement's goals and gains now sample its rhetoric out of context to perversely oppose the ongoing struggle for justice by contemporary social activists. And folk of every political stripe and ideology who march to Washington, from Minister Louis Farrakhan to conservative media figure Glenn Beck, have to pay homage to the iconic expression of social protest on August 28, 1963. When the National Park Service dedicated an inscription in stone to the spot where King delivered his speech, the march's imprint went from symbolic to literal.

Twenty years after the March on Washington, a commemorative gathering sought to recapture the old spirit of struggle and to infuse renewed energy into a flagging movement that was under assault. Freed's photos of the 1983 march show King looming even larger in death than in life. The pensive pose of Jesse Jackson, King's former aide and his successor as the preeminent leader of Black folk, also contrasts the styles and times of leadership and of movement building: a more casual atmosphere is glimpsed in Jackson's leisure suit and in the dress of the thousands gathered on the Mall. To be sure, there were still well-dressed men and women, in particular, as photographed by Freed, the immaculately attired men of the Fruit of Islam, the security arm of the Nation of Islam. But there were far more T-shirts and blue jeans as well, suggesting the changed trends and styles in American dress. It also hinted at the relaxing of a Black urge to always be properly clothed to avert misfortune—misfortunes that seem to happen more frequently when Black folk are deemed to be under-dressed, or improperly dressed, when police or vigilantes see them as thugs or hoods in fashions that, by the way, pass for casual dress in white America.

Freed's camera captures the signs of the times at the 1983 march: the presence of placards calling for President Reagan to cut the military budget, sweatshirts urging Jackson to run for the presidency, which he would announce almost three months later, and ubiquitous images of King. Most Blacks believed that Ronald Reagan was hostile to Black interests, except when he signed the King Holiday legislation into law in November 1983, although he had earlier revived baseless and hoary rumors of King's Communist dealings. The 1983 March on Washington reminded the nation of King's vital legacy and reinforced Jackson's standing as the most visible Black leader in America. His presidential runs in 1984 and 1988 would shortly establish Jackson's standing as a creative public moralist while transforming American politics and paving the way for Barack Obama to become the nation's first Black president.

King's legacy looms large in Obama's life and shadowed his presidency. In 2010, I interviewed President Obama in the White House. As my interview wrapped with him in the Oval Office, he led me to the bust of Martin Luther King, Jr., by Harlem Renaissance sculptor Charles Alston that he had installed near a bust of Abraham Lincoln. Obama's gaunt visage creased in delight as we gazed in silent awe on the face of a man the two of us baby boomers have acknowledged as a great inspiration. In 2011, Obama participated in a far more public recognition of the martyr's meaning when he spoke at the dedication of the Martin Luther King, Jr., Memorial on the National Mall. King became the first individual African American to occupy the sacred civic space dominated by beloved Presidents like George Washington and Franklin Delano Roosevelt. King's image on the Mall is a sturdy reminder that his story, and the story of the people for whom he died, helped to rescue American democracy and make justice a living creed. King's memorial is even more impressive because his statue rises 30 feet high on a direct line between the likenesses of Jefferson and Lincoln; dwarfing those memorials by 11 feet, it is one of the tallest on the Mall. Even in death, King is still breaking barriers.

It was both fitting and ironic that Obama presided over the cementing of King's status as an icon in the national political memory. Obama's historic presidency is unthinkable without King's assassination and the Black masses' bloodstained resistance to racial terror. Obama embraced King's rhetoric of justice during his presidential campaign while eschewing his role as prophet. Presidents uphold the country; prophets often hold up an unflattering mirror to the nation. King may now be widely regarded as a saint of American equality, but he often had to criticize his nation's politics and social habits to inspire and, at times, to force reform. As its loving but unyielding prophet, he helped to make America better by making it bend to its ideals when it got off course. Had he lived, King certainly would have hailed Obama's historic feat even as he took issue with some of the President's policies toward Black and poor people. It would have been principled criticism rooted in an obsession with improving the lives of the vulnerable.

As King rises on the Mall, and even higher in our national consciousness, he is forever linked to the 1963 March on Washington that made him a household name and a living icon for resistance to racial injustice. King gave his life to transform American society, and, as his martyr's blood sank deep in the soil of national history, new life and political possibilities sprang up from his valiant sacrifice. The 1963 March on Washington offered the nation its first extended hearing of a man whose words would change how we understand race in America. Leonard Freed's images document the poignant impact the march had on those Americans who were fortunate enough to hear the beginning of that change in person.

7

Photobombing Mandela

Meeting Nelson Mandela in 1990 has been one of the great thrills of my life. Even though I had studied his life and thought, nothing I read quite prepared me for the majesty and grandeur of this larger-than-legend figure—since, as Toni Morrison said, no one is larger than life! Seeing him, Winnie Mandela, Oliver Tambo, and Jesse Jackson in one small room seized my imagination and reminded me of what is possible when human beings submit to a higher purpose to change the world. This essay is from the February 2014 special edition of Ebony *dedicated to Mandela's memory.*

Just two months after his release in February 1990 from decades in a South African jail cell, I had an opportunity to meet Mandela, a legendary figure so globally celebrated that only a single name had to be uttered. Chanted is more like it, since there was often a percussive quality to the pronunciation of his last name. I was a thirty-one-year-old seminary professor who tagged along as the not-so-ghost writer of the autobiography of Jesse Jackson, a legend himself. We left Chicago for the United Kingdom, my first trip to Europe, to greet Nelson and Winnie Mandela in the north London home of exiled freedom fighter Oliver Tambo and his wife Adelaide.

I knew I was breathing history as I inhaled the warm greeting between Jesse Jackson and the Mandelas in the Tambos' spacious home. They enjoyed a respectful yet spirited conversation around a table in a room small enough to feel the heat of their intimate interaction. As their two-hour meeting drew to a close, Mandela gracefully lifted his lean septuagenarian frame from his chair as he prepared to leave for his next appointment. I sensed that my chance to capture immortality had arrived as I angled myself between Mandela and Jackson while they shared parting thoughts. I even shook the great man's hand and spoke briefly to him. I prayed the photographer who was snapping away had caught me in his flurry of flashes, but I was disappointed to discover that God had ignored my pleas.

This was long before the smartphone camera turned everybody into an amateur Gordon Parks.

My disappointment didn't last long. Later that day I was again in the presence of the Mandelas at a swank soiree thrown by the media mogul Robert Maxwell, who, as a socialist billionaire, was a sweet slice of political contradiction. I spied the Mandelas across the room in a makeshift receiving line and thought I might finally get proof of having met greatness. This time I wouldn't leave things to fate. I begged the peeved photographer to record my momentary brush with two social giants. I couldn't break the long line because I was there with Jackson and didn't want to embarrass him. Since I was neither dignitary nor waiter, I had no good reason to barge in on the couple to glad-hand them or pass them a drink. The best I could do was to lean back slightly while the Mandelas greeted their well wishers and hope that I didn't come off like a stalker or idiot. Just as I bent backwards, the photographer immortalized my delirious dip. I had just photobombed the Mandelas.

I am not alone. There has been a great deal of intellectual and ideological photobombing of Mandela over the years, and some rhetorical airbrushing as well. His political portrait has been widely distorted and broadly manipulated. Mandela's image has been used as the backdrop of one claim or another in political debate, efforts which will no doubt intensify in death as his legacy and memory are bitterly contested.

From the start of his efforts to defeat injustice, racist forces have manufactured a portrait of Mandela as a figure disloyal to the state and a threat to South African culture and civilization. The South African government was deeply entrenched in apartheid, which in the formerly ruling language of Afrikaans means "the state of being apart." They portrayed Mandela and his fellow Black activists as terrorists for their willingness to violently oppose brutal subjugation.

It must not be forgotten that terror dressed as law is terror no less. Mandela the freedom fighter was committed to the use of violence to combat state terror against defenseless Black folk. He embraced this strategic violence as a necessary tool of struggle, not to grab power, but to force whites to negotiate in good faith, only when it was clear that nothing else would stop the state's brutal assault on Black citizens.

Neither should we forget that many American conservatives helped to portray Mandela as a terrorist and advocated a repulsive policy that lived up to neither of its terms: constructive engagement. Ronald Reagan put

Mandela on the U.S. international terrorist list, a dishonor that wasn't fixed until he was finally removed in 2008. The Reagan administration violated a U.N. arms embargo by inviting senior South African security officials to the United States. They also vetoed a U.N. Security Council resolution that called for economic sanctions on South Africa's capital city of Pretoria.

Constructive engagement rested on the questionable belief that white moderates could reform their racist government from within while making overtures to the ANC. It was little more than a wild-eyed political fantasy that never materialized. Instead, constructive engagement appeased the unjust status quo that doubled its efforts to violently contain the Black masses. President Reagan's policy was neither constructive nor did it engage the poisonous roots of apartheid.

Reagan eventually vetoed legislation aimed at imposing stern sanctions on South Africa and lambasted the effort as "immoral" and "repugnant." But Nobel Peace Prize–winning activist Bishop Desmond Tutu beat him to the rhetorical punch, labeling constructive engagement "an abomination" and lashing out at Reagan's strong support for Pretoria as "immoral, evil and totally un-Christian." Former Vice President Dick Cheney, then a Wyoming congressman, voted in 1986 against a congressional resolution demanding Mandela's release from prison. After Mandela went to his reward, the Ronald Reagan Presidential Foundation and Library said on its website that it was "saddened" by Mandela's death and that Reagan had "called for his release on numerous occasions." Reagan's veto went unmentioned as his library heaped posthumous praise on the fallen South African president. Photobombing for sure.

Of course, the communist canard has been used to distort Mandela's portrait and to manipulate public opinion against him. This strategy was a holdover from the Cold War era when communist support for anti-colonial struggle united citizens across national lines. Mandela's relation to communism was a practical political commitment rather than a strictly ideological affair. It made sense for Mandela and the ANC to embrace those who embraced them, to support those forces that supported them. Reagan, for instance, defended his treacherous alliance with South Africa in 1981 when he asked: "Can we abandon a country that has stood by us in every war we've fought, a country that is strategically essential to the free world?"

The ANC and its military wing, Umkhonto we Sizwe, stood by their communist benefactors because they reaped huge material and political support from their association with the former Soviet Union, Fidel Castro and Cuba, and Libya and Muammar Gaddafi. There's little mystery to why Mandela and his compatriots viewed communism and its stalwarts in a positive light. The burden of proof of humanity rests on the shoulders of self-proclaimed democracies like the United States and South Africa (one shudders to think that the latter is one of only a few countries to ever officially call itself a Christian nation) that failed to protect the Black population. The effort to impose a complex bulwark of political beliefs on Mandela to stain his reputation is an act of ideological photobombing. That's especially true because conservative views of communism are at once self-serving and willfully ahistorical.

The flip side of dishonoring Mandela is the portrayal of him as a toothless tiger with his claws clipped. Mandela's enemies ultimately embraced him to shield themselves from the knowledge that they had treated so noble a human being, and the Black people he loved, with utter barbarity. The reflex of many whites to make Mandela a hero draws in large part from a will to psychological survival by the white minority. They must sanitize him in order to grudgingly admire him. They must turn him into a saintly icon whose future grows more beatific by the moment because the story of their brutal past is diminished with each telling. The memory of the more aggressive Mandela is a danger to a society premised on reconciliation. Such a dangerous memory demands a reckoning that threatens the accord that thrust South Africa into the only future it could have without choking the nation in a frenzy of Black vengeance.

To be sure, Mandela's allies and followers are at fault too. They have altered Mandela's portrait by subtracting unsavory elements and adding new interpretations in the effort to gussy up a picture of the man with softer characterizations and a less controversial background. This puts Mandela's legacy in a bind. On the one hand are enemies who obsessively stress Mandela's advocacy of armed struggle and his strategic embrace of communist allies. On the other hand, allies are tempted to airbrush his complicated thinking and action, and his discomfiting evolution. They dance gingerly around his advocacy as president of neoliberal economic principles pushed by business elites, a practice that didn't sit well with many of his former comrades in the freedom struggle.

The lessons of Mandela's journey are clear: If he could do hard time in little space while chasing freedom and plotting South Africa's destiny, then activists and leaders must take the long view of history and struggle. Mandela's movement from the outside to the inside of the social order also presaged the political arc of our first Black American president.

I was reminded of just how torturous the transfer from resistance to governance can be, and how heavy symbolism weighs in the exercise of power, when I attended the White House screening in November 2013 of the affecting film *Long Walk to Freedom* based on Mandela's autobiography. President Obama introduced the film, acknowledging the presence of star Idris Elba, among others, and averring the deep inspiration of Madiba (which Mandela was endearingly called, after the isiXhosa word for "father") on his own activism and political career.

Without saying so, without even having to try, the parallels between Obama and Mandela fairly screamed, despite the different fingerprints that time and circumstance left on their respective rise to power. Like Mandela, Obama has been the subject of distortions and manipulations, even disfiguring misportrayals, as well as airbrushed efforts from far friendlier quarters. I couldn't help but think of those parallels as the White House photographer buzzed about, capturing Obama, who had stopped to greet me with a brotherly Black man embrace. This time I didn't have to photobomb the man in power, though I spotted several others, smartphones in hand, selfies in the offing, who were champing at the bit.

8

Of Mic and Lens

The sheer volume of hip hop's output since its beginnings more than forty years ago makes it both important and impossible to record its dynamic foundations in a single project, and yet David Scheinbaum's evocative portraiture communicates the will and verve of a transformative genre of artistic expression. It aims at doing for hip hop pioneers what Roy DeCarava did for a generation of jazz greats in his iconic photographic collection, The Sound I Saw. *I was honored to contribute this essay to Scheinbaum's 2013 book,* Hip Hop: Portraits of an Urban Hymn.

Hip hop didn't invent the word, although one of its earliest benedictions radiates literary aspiration: Word. Some linguists argue that language burst on the human scene a hundred thousand years ago through a single chance mutation in one individual that spread like a verbal prairie fire to others in the breeding circle. Other linguists say that language evolved over long stretches of time and circumstance and emerged in *Homo sapiens* less than two hundred thousand years ago. If you believe biblical scribes, The Word stretches all the way back to God and the beginning of time and space and the universe. In the beginning was the word. In religious genealogy, then, grammar begets gravity, so to speak. Literally.

Neither did hip hop invent the beat. If it doesn't quite have the celestial bragging rights of speech, rhythm's origins are hardly less primitive, tucked inside our bodies where our hearts measure our existence one beat at a time. Blending word and beat as part of hip hop's own creation myth means that an art form that dates back just to the seventies connects to the creation myth of the universe itself.

Depending on how you view hip hop culture, such a belief is heady, arrogant, or delusional, or a brazen remix of all three. From the start hip hop has been unwilling to settle for anything less than cosmic significance and global influence, even when it could barely make it from its Bronx bedroom to a train stop in Brooklyn, much less travel from Long Island to London. Hip hop's reach often exceeded its grasp, or else what's a cipher for? All of its bombast and outsize boasts seem to flow in the traffic between hood saviors and their divine inspiration in project flats that doubled as modern birthplaces for artistic gods.

If that comparison seems far too self-important and spiked with hyperbole, then consider this equally ambitious parallel: At least one holy book declares that God got his start on earth as the son of a single mother who got knocked up by someone out of the picture, leaving a brave man to step in and love the mother and raise the boy who would be delivered in harsh circumstances among the poor because the establishment barred them from comfortable birth.

Jesus meet Jay-Hova. Nazareth meet New York. Manger meet Marcy. Mother Mary meet Afeni Shakur. Swaddling cloths meet Underoos. Scripture meet scribbling in note pads. Missing years between adolescence and adulthood learning to bear the weight of the world as the messiah meet missing years between high school and rap career spent pushing weight before saving hip hop. Overturned tables in the temple meet the temple of hip hop and its turntables. Forty days in the wilderness meet no church in the wild. The list of such similarities could literally go on, if not ad infinitum, then at least ad nauseam.

Like sacred texts and the spiritual figures they reveal, the speech, rhythms, and representatives of hip hop battled mighty opposition to forge artistic triumph and commercial dominance. Hip hop has endured significant ridicule because the primary makers of its talk and beats are Black. Black art has been relentlessly mocked as a hodgepodge of inferior form and puerile content. Thomas Jefferson savaged the artistic pedigree of Black music; before him David Hume denied the existence of Black arts at all. Black art was widely viewed as a Black mark on what little humanity and intelligence Black folk were said to possess.

The initial thorns in hip hop's flesh grew from the same bush-league criticism that has always dressed down Black culture while its opposition is dressed up as highfalutin theory or scientific analysis. It is chilling to recall, for instance, that the same society that in the name of science sponsored the Tuskegee experiment and allowed disease to spread in three hundred Black men without treatment is the same society that tried to convince us that Tupac's meditations on Black manhood were morally diseased. The Tuskegee experiment ended in 1972; 'Pac's life began in 1971. There is no relation between the two dates, except the relation forced on random events in history by human beings out to do harm or to relieve suffering through their words and actions. In a world where the Tuskegee experiment could exist to hurt Black men, their sometime noble artistic defender Tupac had to be born.

That may be putting the proverbial sociological cart before the artistic horse. Hip hop has rarely had the freedom to just be, as Common allusively suggests in the title of one of his greatest albums, because it got dragged so quickly into political arguments about its right to exist, and because hip hop is widely viewed as the soundtrack to Black pathology. Perhaps the condition of its emergence had something to do with how the shadow of politics has cloaked the roots and rise of hip hop culture. The messiah in a manger, metaphor aside; hip hop's birth is no less miraculous for taking place in crushing social, political and racial conditions.

Hip hop got its start less than a decade after a defining and cataclysmic event: The death of Martin Luther King, Jr. King's death rocked our culture like few deaths ever have—Lincoln's death shook the nation of course, and so did the death of the Kennedy brothers, but all of them were presidents or politicians who had the blessing of the state and the resources of government at their call. King magnetized the needle of America's moral compass as a private citizen and quite literally as a minister without portfolio. King challenged America's musty racial views through vibrant social struggle, and like the hip hoppers who came after him he moved the crowd through the power of his melodic speech.

King's death cast a pall of deep grief on Black America and led many folk to question whether the nation was willing to genuinely support ideals of fairness and equality that it paid lip service to but steadily undercut. The racial miasma that triggered King's assassination briefly gave way to fleeting Black empathy before hardening into white backlash. As the civil rights movement sputtered, the Black power movement picked up steam to proclaim the beauty of Blackness and the need for more aggressive resistance. On the cultural front the Black Arts Movement (BAM), sparked by the tragic death in 1965 of another seminal Black leader, Malcolm X, had already begun to fight the power of white superiority by painting the canvas of history and aesthetics in bold Black strokes.

By the time BAM reached its end in the mid-seventies, the battle against white resentment and, later, the fight over affirmative action would reenergize the civil rights movement. Together the waning Black power movement and the revived civil rights movement flooded the ballot boxes of northern cities to elect Black mayors in Newark and Detroit in the early seventies after successfully electing mayors in Cleveland and Gary, Indiana, in the year of King's death. The South and West got on board with Black mayors in Atlanta and Los Angeles. At the same time Black folk flexed their electoral muscles at the polls to sweep into office many more Black members of Congress.

If Black folk gained on the political front, they continued to knock down barriers in television, film and radio, and in sports and entertainment as well. Bill Cosby and Diahann Carroll integrated the small screen while Sidney Poitier continued lighting up the big screen. And the original Foxy Brown—Pam Grier—torched the local Cineplex with her erotic charisma before Blaxploitation symbolically burned it down. The expansion of FM in the seventies garnered a bigger audience for Black radio and its corps of spirited DJs. The ranks of major league baseball swelled with Black players less than a quarter century after Jackie Robinson ended apartheid on the diamond. And Black basketball players eclipsed white athletes in the NBA in the mid-seventies, but not before the New York Knickerbockers were derided as the New York "Niggerbockers." The NFL got a lot more color too, paving the way for a league that today is nearly 70 percent Black.

Motown and Philadelphia International Records enlivened the culture as recording beacons, and R&B artists began to break free of commercial ghettos and cultural constraints. Marvin Gaye brought conscience to Black pop with the groundbreaking *What's Going On,* a theme album meditating on war, spirituality, the ecology, God, and the salvation of children. Disco stars Donna Summer and Sylvester gave spirited voice to an art form that unapologetically traded on raucous female energy and gay bravura. Aretha Franklin amplified her sixties cries for respect at home and in society and returned to her spiritual roots with the landmark *Amazing Grace.* Stevie Wonder pled for universal love, cosmic enlightenment, social justice, and Black equality on the monumental *Songs in the Key of Life.* And Michael Jackson released *Off the Wall* in 1979, a sonic harbinger of the eclecticism that made him the dominant musical artist of the 1980s and the greatest entertainer in the world.

In the same year, on September 16, a single dropped that forever changed the musical landscape: The Sugarhill Gang's "Rapper's Delight," the first hip hop recording to popularize an art form that later won international acclaim. In the meantime, "rap"—the talking part of hip hop culture—was largely viewed as a temporary musical trend that would eventually disappear like dolphin earrings and K-Swiss sneakers. But the music and the culture that supported it struck a nerve with youth in New York City and then around the country. For better and worse, males created hip hop and it is still a *testosterocentric* affair often booming with patriarchal ambitions. Hip hop culture can therefore be heard and seen through four metonyms that relate the artist to the accoutrements used to craft his art: Man and mat, man and machine, man and marker, and man and microphone.

Man and mat—referring to the *breakdancer*—conjures the cardboard mats used by breakdancers on the streets to cushion their acrobatic moves as they spin on shoulders or heads in sync with the break beats isolated and looped on sound recordings. Man and machine—referring to the *DJ* and then the *producer*—summons images of the DJ's turntables that were central in the early sound of hip hop and, later, the machines used by hip hop's sonic architects to produce and perfect sound. Among the recent favorites are the Auto-Tune voice processor preferred by T-Pain and Lil Wayne and famously bashed by JAY-Z on "D.O.A. (Death of Auto-Tune)." Of earlier vintage is the Roland TR-808 drum machine which, along with Auto-Tune, is used by Kanye West on his fourth studio album and even cited in the title of that searing reflection on love, loss, and loneliness, *808s & Heartbreak*—a seething musical stew of electronica, synthpop, R&B, electropop, and hip hop. Man and marker—referring to the *graffiti* artist—pictures the magic markers and other utensils employed by graffiti artists to scar the tissue of public space while inscribing their existence. And man and microphone—referring to the *rapper* or *MC*—symbolizes the sole possession necessary to project the voice and amplify the lyrical ambition of the rap artist to the world, as Nas immortally proclaimed in his classic "One Mic."

The MC is the heart of hip hop, the centripetal force that draws the varied elements of the culture to its rhetorical center. The MC's story is hip hop's story, and vice versa, since they came up together in the same hoods and either floundered or prospered under the same racial and economic forces. The MC has carried the symbolic weight of hip hop in his throat from the start as the art form rode the golden throats and silver tongues of its greatest artists all the way to platinum success. That success, however, is not the greatest measure of hip hop's achievement. The honor belongs to the genre's most gifted creators who obsess over the complicated lyrical content and complex rhythmic flows of hip hop at its best.

A few of hip hop's best MCs may sport gold teeth, but the bulk of rap's most talented artists surely weren't born with a silver spoon in their mouths. Their lives often tracked the evolution of the genre itself, which matured in the 1980s as budding MCs faced the cruel consequences of Ronald Reagan's voodoo economics, the alleged benefits of which never trickled down to working and poor people as advertised. Hip hop's original MCs often grappled with the low economic growth of the seventies and a vicious recession in the early eighties, high inflation and interest rates, energy crises, unforgivably high unemployment rates for Black males, and the bottoming out of the manufacturing sector in an economy that brutally transitioned to a service industry where the high end excluded poor and undereducated people of color. The public school system was equally abysmal: Talented Black students were steered toward vocational tracks while their white peers were over prepped for college. To make matters worse, budgets for visual art and musical training were ruthlessly slashed, hampering the musical and artistic prospects of Black and brown youth for generations to come.

It is no small wonder that Black youth experimented with technology and literacy in creating an art form that has reclaimed poetry for common folk and opened the ears of the world to beautifully chaotic meters, spectacular cadences, and snaking rhythms. The argument about whether hip hop was even music raged for a spell, until the spell of hip hop became the rage of the world. The children of white snobs and Black moralizers often made their parents' objections to hip hop obsolete with their discerning consumption and sophisticated analysis of rap music and the culture in which it was spawned.

The MC is the lightning rod and arbiter of hip hop's meaning in a world where lyrics matter so much that their creators are sometimes dragged before congressional committees and made to account for their menace to youth. MCs aren't alone in such ventures. Perhaps there's a fifth element, another metonym, that's gone unrecognized, but which is crucial to hip hop's fortunes: Man and Mac—that is, the journalist, writer, and intellectual who uses his or her computer or notepad to critically engage a seminal art form. (Knowledge already unofficially exists as hip hop's fifth element alongside graffiti, breakdancing, DJing, and rapping, and can easily be absorbed in my proposed fifth metonym.)

My own pilgrimage is an example, though my journey as a critic, scholar, journalist, and writer on hip hop surely isn't unique. My experience as a curious intellectual grappling with rap music is not unlike the struggle of many thinkers to define, defend, and deconstruct an artistic juggernaut that often barrels into the social and political arena. I began writing about rap music as a graduate student at Princeton University in the mid-eighties, publishing articles in magazines and journals that explored the history, politics, ethics, and aesthetics of rap. My first book, published in 1993, included several essays on hip hop culture, and I've returned to the subject in my subsequent work, especially my critical estimation of the life and legacy of Tupac Shakur, my interview reflections on various elements of the culture, and my edited treatment of Nas's classic debut album, *Illmatic*. I've also taught college courses on hip hop culture since the mid-nineties at the University of North Carolina at Chapel Hill, Columbia University, DePaul University, the University of Pennsylvania, and now at Georgetown University, where my course on JAY-Z drew national media interest and ire.

I've written about rap for the *New York Times*, discussed hip hop on countless television shows, including the *MacNeil/Lehrer NewsHour* on PBS and on HBO's *Real Time with Bill Maher*, and talked about rap on nearly every major radio show in the country. I've debated hip hop in lecture halls across America and, indeed, around the globe, most recently in London, where I was the advocate for hip hop in an international debate on the genre's virtues and vices that was broadcast on Google. And I've appeared before Congress on three separate occasions to debate rap: Before the U.S. Senate in 1994 and again in 2000, and before the House of Representatives in 2007.

My Senate testimony and vigorous exchange with Senator John McCain in 2000 was published in my book *Debating Race*. But my unpublished maiden voyage in congressional hearings before the Senate in 1994 at the invitation of Senator Carol Moseley-Braun captures the stormy debate about hip hop at the height of the cultural resistance and political revulsion to rap music. The hearing took place before the Senate Subcommittee on Juvenile Justice, with the purpose, it was stated, of examining "the effects of violent and demeaning imagery in popular music on American youth."

I was called on to offer my analysis of rap music, along with figures like political activist C. Delores Tucker, who would gain her greatest fame for taking on the misogyny and obscenity in rap, and legendary entertainer Dionne Warwick, who, like Tucker, was appalled at the vicious portrayals of women in rap music. While I was respectful of Tucker and Warwick, I attempted to place hip hop culture in its broader historical and political context without dismissing its troubling aspects, especially the gangsta rap of figures like Snoop Dogg, who had in particular sparked the outrage of Tucker and Warwick. I submitted a formal testimony, but my words that day flowed extemporaneously from my heart and head, and I ended by saying:

What we must not forget is that gangsta rappers represent a population that
is among the most politically invisible, politically underrepresented, culturally maligned populations in American culture—young Black males.
How dare we [not] remember that . . . a culture that not a century and
a half ago put Black men on an auction block to sell them by describing
them in the most crass, materialistic, consumerist [fashion] . . . driven by
an American desire to dominate Black men's lives—[is] now hypocritically,
less than a century and a half later . . . decry[ing] them for the very
same . . . beliefs that it held . . . as precious principles of American
culture. How dare we do that? We have to be more sensitive. We have
to . . . [understand] that we cannot simply stigmatize the victims. We
have to speak for them.

I might add, if we really want to get to the source of demonizing Black
women: Young Black men don't have the power. This is why Senator
Moseley-Braun ran for the Senate, because it was a white-dominated
male Senate that had castigated Black women's lives and made sure that
the glass ceiling that was on their lives would turn into cement. This is
the real enemy in American culture. Black bourgeois institutions, white
male culture, and certain forms of gangsta rap all have certain things in
common.

So, as we expand the palette of colors from which we draw to paint upon
the canvas of life the forces that we want to oppose, let us remember that
gangsta rap is not simply an objective revelation or narration of the coming
racial apocalypse. I don't believe in the moral neutrality of gangsta rap,
as I don't believe in the moral neutrality of the Senate, as I don't believe
in the moral neutrality of the recording industry. All of us must be held
responsible for the circulation of vicious, misogynistic, sexist and
homophobic lyrics, ideas and ideologies. . . .

I would not dare come here and defend any attempt to, in any way, desecrate
Black women. But if we are honest about it, Senator Moseley-Braun,
Stokely Carmichael, as part of the movement during the 1960s, said
that the best position for a Black woman [in the movement] was prone.
Civil rights organizations were notoriously sexist. Highly trained Black
women were sent to work in civil rights organizations, and they were
made carriers of coffee and pencil sharpeners. [Women, despite] . . . their
extraordinary talent, were. . . . sexually objectified, and we know across
this culture that women have been treated that way.

So, what I argue . . . is that we must deal with an honest assessment of the

conditions that lead to gangsta [rap]. If we listen to Snoop Doggy Dog
when he says, "Wake up, jumped out my bed/I'm in a two-man cell with
my homie Lil' Half Dead/Murder was the case that they gave me/Dear
God, I wonder can you save me"—what you have in Snoop Doggy Dog is
a [male with a] second-generation Mississippi drawl in the post-industrial
collapse of L.A. trying to come to grips with . . . the transition from a stable
life to one that has been undermined by forces of . . . economic immiseration
and class division. Those are the real culprits here.

Although these words were spoken nearly twenty years ago, they
communicate a raw passion about the defense of vulnerable Black youth
that burns in me to this day. The flaws of hip hop must be acknowledged and opposed; rap music's often-poisonous views of women and
gays must be resisted. Rap music has too often twisted James Brown's
patriarchal cry into a wretched paean to male supremacy and misogyny:
"This is a man's world/But it wouldn't be nothin' if we couldn't diss a
woman or a girl."

But the best of hip hop culture looks beyond bigotry to embrace the
heroic use of words and beats to cast light on the dark places of the Black
experience and the American soul. At their noblest hip hop artists carry
the weight of the Black and poor in their speech and rhythms and exorcise demons as they encounter them in their own minds and in the world
around them. It is in performance that rap's rhetorical royalty often massage the grief and encourage the ecstasy of their audiences and cast word
spells over a transfixed constituency.

This is the world that David Scheinbaum captures with effortless brilliance and transcendent beauty. His images stick in the eye for their lean
and muscular portrayals of bodies in motion, and for their voluptuous
characterizations of mouths in movement. He catches speech the moment
it spills from lips fixed around sentences that rush in staccato fury or fall
back in asymmetrical repose.

Scheinbaum's aesthetic voice and visual language speak through images
that zing, blur, haze, identify, splatter, brush, clarify, and even coagulate
like celluloid blood on fleshly surfaces. If renowned photographer Roy De-
Carava famously shot the sound he saw when Coltrane blew his horn, then
David Scheinbaum shoots the music he tastes when his eyes are hungry for
poetic truth. If hip hop artists are ghetto deities born to fly the artistic coop
and soar to the musical heavens and back, then Scheinbaum is one of their

most faithful chroniclers, recording their ascent and return one gesture, one image, at a time. To paraphrase the holy book: In the beginning was the word, and the word became flesh and spoke among us through pavement prophets. What they said is on record; how they looked when they said what they said is on record, too. Turn these pages and see.

Act Like You Know

In the Theater

9

King at Midnight

I have written two books on Dr. King, and in each, I addressed his perilous journey to manhood and iconic status, and how he spent his relatively short life changing the world while fighting his own demons. In my mind he is the greatest American to ever live—greater than any president, because he transformed America and gained global recognition as a private citizen. His words have changed lives, cultures, and politics, and his example has inspired millions around the world. In my first book on King, I grappled with his plagiarism and his promiscuity in relations outside of his marriage. Some Black critics deemed me a disloyal sellout, but I knew then, as I know now, that the culture's views of Dr. King may well change in dramatic fashion after sealed documents in the FBI's file are released in 2027. We got a taste of that already when King biographer David Garrow detailed in 2019 recently published FBI documents on King that suggest potentially disturbing sexual conduct. I wanted to address what we know of Dr. King now so that such revelations won't be so shocking—and to say that, despite what might be revealed, despite his flaws, faults, foibles, and failures, which he shares with most great figures, he is still the greatest American ever. Katori Hall's remarkably prescient and provocative Broadway play is a fictional portrayal of King's last night on earth, and it wrestles with his deep humanity and his profound vulnerability and undeniable imperfections, and yet it captures his nobility in the face of imminent death. A version of this essay appeared as the foreword to the 2009 published version of her landmark play.

When I went to see Samuel Jackson and Angela Bassett on Broadway in Katori Hall's *The Mountaintop*, it hit me hard: this play is artistic dynamite. It explodes the myths that bury Martin Luther King, Jr.'s humanity and shatters his image as a stoic martyr. *The Mountaintop* invites us to see King as a flesh-and-blood genius with flaws who worked fiendishly to end Black oppression while fighting for liberty and justice for all. The play teems with wisdom about the Black, and therefore, the human condition, but it isn't served up in musty language or reverent grammar. The dialogue pops off the stage in vernacular wit and folk philosophy; its lines are laced with humor, irony, paradox, signifying and magic. It's not the sort of magic that rescues us from the grip of grief; rather it's the kind of magic that conquers tragedy by facing it head on. *The Mountaintop* portrays a man who is much more interesting and useful when his blemishes and virtues are shown together.

One might ask why we would turn to the dramatic arts when the best scholarship on King has already warned against smothering him in fable. Sometimes poetry tells more truth about history than either science or religion. Poetry is Hall's greatest weapon in her loving war against the lazy deification of Martin Luther King, Jr. Her words snap and jolt, and at times, they even pounce in delicious ridicule of the hollow, deadening worship of King, insisting instead that we take him at his word. Not the immortal words he uttered in public that have won the favor of history, but the words we never got to hear him say, the words that fear pried from his lips, or the words that tumbled from a tongue that depression turned into a staircase of spiraling doubt near the end of his life. That's a side of King that only his closest compatriots glimpsed. And most of them only saw snapshots of King's inner turmoil as the movement for justice lurched in seizures of resistance, sputtering and then taking off again as heroic freedom fighters battled evil in some far-flung corner of the Black universe. Memphis in March and April of 1968 was such a moment. King had been summoned for the umpteenth time to channel, or truth be told, to catch on to the resurging spirit of a battered movement.

Hall draws a literary circle around the next-to-last day of King's bitterly shortened life, a life, like the movement he led, riddled by chaos and transition. How could it be otherwise? All roads for the Nobel Prize–winning evangelist of hope led to death. The government harassed King to death. White supremacists hounded him to death. His followers loved him to death. And King worked himself to death. When the coroner opened his body after a bullet felled the 39-year-old prodigy of protest, it was his heart that lodged the greatest resistance: it looked to be that of a 60-year-old man.

This fact makes its way into Hall's drama, as do other telling details which are skillfully woven into the narrative: King's vicious bouts of hiccups, which disappeared when he spoke, and which resumed after his oration was done; King's chain smoking; his artful and relentless bending of the elbow (and my God why not, given what he was up against?); his vanity about being *the* Black leader (we must tell all those who compare Jesse Jackson and Al Sharpton unfavorably to King that, at least on this score, they're dead wrong); King sending his wife artificial flowers only once—a few days before his demise, another sign of premonition blooming in his brain; King's fear of flying, and given how much he flew, a fear that underscored his courage; King's haunting anxiety near the end of his life of being in rooms with windows that might present his potential assassin clear opportunity; and King's brutal battle with depression.

Hall may not be a historian, but her art is eerily accurate. She conjures fictional scenes that nourish us with an understanding that dry facts alone starve us of. Hall's dramatic license also opens the door to hotly contested truths that range far beyond King's life and death: the gender of God; how class colors social relations in Black life; the belief in an afterlife, and the shape it might take; and the inscrutable ways of God, as Hall's theatrical meditations amount to a grassroots theodicy of sorts.

Hall peers brilliantly into the shadows of King's last night on earth and lights briefly on the monumental speech he pulled from the core of his soul. King's words dripped in death, but Hall convinces us that King wasn't simply addressing his immediate circumstances, but speaking to the specter of imminent death that dogged him most of his life. That's entirely plausible since he was being pursued relentlessly by crack pots, and crack shots, across the land. King is seen here begging off the bravery he displayed in his last speech where he declared he wasn't worried about anything or fearing any man. This doesn't make him a hypocrite, but a man struggling with his mortality. Even Jesus begged God to spare him from drinking the bitter cup of his destiny, a destiny he had previously proclaimed with full readiness to die. But when the moment of death looms near, words of certainty crumble beneath the tangible threat of nonbeing.

Still, words uttered in higher, clearer moments provide a touchstone of faith to thwart the doubt that inevitably creeps in when the rubber meets the road, when death swagger gives way to death stagger, at least for a while. Besides, only those who know the transcendent heights to which oratory can take you, not only as a hearer, but as a giver of the word, can possibly understand how one can literally speak oneself into courage and vision that are less apparent in mundane moments. This is not simply a matter of being whipped into frenzy, or driven to flights of fancy, by the power of words. Speech gives individuals and societies a sense of who we are, and what we are capable of; words give life, order existence and clarify destiny. "In the beginning was the Word . . ."

By spotlighting King's last night, Hall illumines our nights too: the time of reckoning, the time of wrestling, like Jacob in the Hebrew Bible, with powerful, wounding forces below, only to discover we were wrestling with a messenger from above. Hall magically sweeps us into King's cramped, pinched, smoky, desolate, and dingy temporary living quarters to show us a picture of a human soul struggling with death—his death, the death of a way of life in the South, the death of personal and vocational hopes and aspirations, and the death of theological certainties and pulpit proclamations. The cussing, smoking and gallows humor are spiritual anesthesia to endure mortal peril—the awareness that one's life is being snuffed out—and from that mixture rises a truth, or perhaps many of them, that costs one's life to learn.

King was profoundly familiar with late night. One of his most famous sermons is "A Knock at Midnight." In it, King says, "You can have some strange experiences at midnight." Hall proves King right and summons a fateful late-night encounter to imagine her way into his heart and mind as he surrenders his life for a greater purpose. It does no disservice to King, and in fact helps the rest of us, that King's human side gets the long view here. Only a King who has faced his own fears, nursed his own psychic wounds, stirred in private remorse at his own sins, and yes, reveled in defiant mischief, can possibly speak to the masses of folk who will never wear the victor's crown nor taste the sweet adoration of millions. Only a King who has descended to the depths of hell and stared at his own mortality can possibly inspire the rest of us to overcome our flaws and failures and rise to our best futures. King had to do that daily, perhaps even before a woman in New York tried to take his life near the beginning of his pilgrimage.

On March 7, 2015, Izola Ware Curry, the mentally ill Black woman who stabbed Martin Luther King, Jr., at a Harlem book signing in 1958, died at ninety-eight in a Jamaica, Queens, nursing home. King forgave the itinerant housekeeper from Georgia—"I . . . know that thoughtful people will do all in their power to see that she gets the help that she apparently needs if she is to become a free and constructive member of society"—and afterward brilliantly transmuted Curry's homicidal urge into a riveting anecdote in a speech delivered in 1968, the night before assassin James Earl Ray blasted him to his heavenly reward. Curry's passing the baton to Ray in the decade-long race to murder King paid bitter and ironic homage to the remorseless efficacy of integration.

That is hardly all that has been made of King's death in the nearly half century since he gave up the ghost on a motel balcony splattered with his martyr's blood. The same society that killed King now seeks to resurrect him in its material and mythological image. Every year during his holiday celebration King's troubling memory is smothered by the deadening imperatives of capital—"Would you like some fries with your burger on your King place mat?"—and the stifling hagiography of his devout worshippers.

King was a magician of words—he made hope appear where there had been none, especially among people grounded by the ruthless sweep of Jim Crow's wicked wings. King's intellectual inheritance offered ordinary Negroes a foretaste of the existential and political riches they could enjoy—first, vicariously through him, and then, because of the work he did, the life he lived, and the way his death opened horizons of even more opportunity than he could provide in his last years on earth. King walked into the teeth of lethal racism while some of his northern Black competitors mocked the nonviolent revolution he led. In the end, he made the world safer and more negotiable for them, too, while proving that southern Black rituals of survival perfectly fit American rhythms of change: a little here, some there—and then, bang, the whole thing gave way to new ways of thinking and living in spaces that not that long ago were haunted by racial tyranny.

Those whites that hated King—some of whom are still alive, and some of whom still despise him—cannot as easily, and certainly not as openly, express their fearsome beliefs nor find solace in the state to make their case and to protect their bigotry. That kind of change emerged from both the will of King—revealed in his last days in all its trenchant moral beauty— and that of the common Black person who fought from the pits of poverty to win noble station for all of their kind, all of the despised "hambones" cluttered in the darkest regions of Memphis and throughout the South.

Alas, as Hall's play makes palpably clear, King must be rescued from his true believers as well, those who mean well but who do harm when they fail to face King's flaws and imperfections. It is easy to understand why Black folk who have had our leaders taken down by the bullet or hounded by unprincipled demonization should fear looking squarely at King's humanity. But there is no other way to keep King from being merchandised for cultural amnesia and marketed for easy political consumption as a docile and toothless spokesman for change unless we dip into the swirling vortex of grief and its glorious transcendence that Hall reveals in her play.

King died in Memphis fighting for the poor. To be sure, the King of the Lincoln Memorial understandably enchants many still, the King whose stirring oratory called the nation to honor its democratic legacy and to renounce its shameful past. But the latter-day King is a figure who, like his Lord, is "a man of sorrows and acquainted with grief." The King who speaks after death is a man whose legacy of struggle can't be exhausted by carefully redacted sentences that are stripped of suffering and disappointment.

The King who got killed wasn't targeted because he promoted a safe and comforting dream of racial transformation. That King, with his limits and warts, was a man obsessed with making the pain of the vulnerable sing; he wanted to shine a light on the ignoble indifference to those who couldn't talk the talk he learned in school. His doctorate, no matter how much it was doctored with, was their passport to respect. King's greatest achievement was never meant to lie between the borders of his own life—but in the legacy of love and transformation he left behind. The restoration of King to his complicated humanity is way too much to ask of even a work as poignant as *The Mountaintop*. But it is a sign of its dramatic genius that, after reading it and witnessing its performance, it makes us believe that the task is necessary, and that this play is as good a place as any to start the journey.

10

The Blues of August Wilson

The pen of August Wilson was a mighty sword of truth—about Black life, but especially about Black male life. I met Wilson once, in 1993, when he was awarded an honorary doctorate, the Doctor of Fine Arts, by Princeton University, the year I earned my doctorate in religion there. He was a man of impressive genius and yet a mild soul who was shy and self-effacing. His work has had an enormous influence in the twentieth and twenty-first centuries, and fueled the Oscar-winning performance of Viola Davis in the 2016 Denzel Washington–directed film adaptation of Fences *and in her ripsnorting turn as the title character in the 2020 film version of* Ma Rainey's Black Bottom, *directed by George C. Wolfe, which also featured the epic swan song of the late Chadwick Boseman. A version of this essay appeared in 2015 in* Humanities, *the magazine for the National Endowment for the Humanities.*

If the blues is the wash of Black suffering hung up to dry in the sun of pitiless self-reflection, then August Wilson was our greatest lyrical washerman. He was also the most gifted blues poet on the American stage. He bathed the soil of bigotry in the rhetoric of Black spirituality. He wrung out American tragedy in the tubs of Black metaphor. Wilson scrubbed racial trauma on the washboard of Black humor. And he made raucous Black vernacular an agitator to stir hope into motion.

"I think the blues is the best literature that we as Blacks have created since we've been here," Wilson said. "And it's a lot of philosophical ideas. I call it our sacred book. So what I've attempted to do is mine that field, to mine those cultural ideas and attitudes and give them to my characters."

To say the blues are literature is more controversial than it sounds. The argument sternly rebukes highbrow guardians of the Western canon. Many literary gatekeepers questioned Black art because they doubted our humanity and intelligence too. These doubts prompted political efforts to contain the unwashed Black masses. Racist perceptions of Black art were decidedly political even as the mainstream often sought to keep art free of polemics. Those perceptions didn't just corrupt the thinking of figures like David Hume and Thomas Jefferson; they flared, too, in Saul Bellow's bitter dispute with multiculturalism, as he doubted that the Zulus had produced a Tolstoy or the Papua New Guineans had come up with a Marcel Proust.

When Wilson says the blues are literature, he is not exaggerating its importance but underscoring the blues' sublime literary qualities. The blues are brief bursts of sonic fiction that vibrate with signifying lyrics, double entendres, and the effortless interplay between personal and social forces. The blues give lyrical shape to the hurts and affections that stymie and transform Black life. The blues tap comedy to temper tragedy—and to tame the absurd. Wilson's characters mouth those truths with moral clarity.

"White folks don't understand the blues," Gertrude "Ma" Rainey, dubbed the "Mother of the Blues," says in *Ma Rainey's Black Bottom* to Levee and her other sidemen during a lull in recording in a white-run studio. "They hear it come out, but they don't know how it got there. They don't understand it's life's way of talkin'. You don't sing to feel better. You sing 'cause that's a way of understanding life. The blues help you get out of bed in the mornin'. You get up knowin' you ain't alone. There's something else in the world. Somethin's been added by that song. This'd be an empty world without the blues. I take that emptiness and I try to fill it up with somethin'."

Not only do the blues sound literary, but, Wilson contends, the blues breathe philosophy too. Some philosophers think that literature, or at least literary theory, does the work that philosophy should do when it gets rid of the idea that there's some deep difference in the kind of knowledge you get from philosophy and the kind you get from literature. "I think critics would do better to realize that philosophy is no more likely to produce 'definitive results' . . . than is literary criticism itself," philosopher Richard Rorty argued. Wilson's philosophical bent is decidedly Rortyian: he refuses to draw distinctions between the kind of wisdom we get by the blues and the kind we get by philosophy. In Wilson's work blues artists are grassroots philosophers. Some of them are gutbucket epistemologists who make and analyze claims of knowledge grounded in Black experience. Others are earthy ethicists who grapple with the evils that mar their lives and those of their loved ones. When the philosophy of knowledge streams through the blues it sounds like the Ma Rainey soliloquy cited above. The problem of evil screams in another bit of dialogue from *Ma Rainey's Black Bottom* that features the character Levee.

Ma Rainey's speech argues two interlocking ideas: that whites lack knowledge of the blues while Black folk know little else. Blacks have the blues because whites have, in large measure, given Blacks the blues while striving to have as little of the blues as possible. It's clear in Ma Rainey's soliloquy that epistemology and anthropology are linked. Rainey asserts the moral priority and social privilege of Black knowledge, that is, what Black folk know is more important than what white folk know; it is important for Black survival, and important, too, for acknowledging white humanity. When whites recognize Black humanity it's to grudgingly concede that Blacks are like them, a recognition that takes Blacks up a notch or two in white books from their unjustly degraded status. When Black folk recognize white humanity it's to recognize that whites are no different than Blacks, which brings them down a notch or two from their unjustly elevated status. In short, when Black folk say that white folk are human it's to say that they're not gods; when white folk say that Black folk are human it's to say they're not animals. For white folk the recognition of Black humanity is a concession; for Black folk the recognition of white humanity is a revelation. The blues bravely sing the knowledge of Black and white humanity.

When Rainey says that white folk don't understand the blues, she's making an argument about how they've managed to escape the knowledge that Black folk can't escape—that the blues is knowledge that Black folk can't help having and that white folk can't possibly possess. To be sure white folk can have their version of the blues, but they don't have the blues the way Black folk have them. The circumstances of Black life compose the blues; the conditions of Black life create its artists; the constraints of Black life shape its forms; and the content of Black life supplies its themes and vision. When Rainey says white folk don't understand the blues, it's another way of saying they don't understand the scope and sweep of Black life; they don't understand its goals and methods, its aspirations and inspirations alike.

Rainey says white folk hear the blues but don't know how they got there, that is, in Black life, in Black lore, in Black legend, and especially in Black throats and Black bodies. Rainey's statement is as much about creativity as it is about procedure—as much about the mystery of beginnings, and origin myths, as about the means of artistic production. Rainey claims that epistemology and cosmology are connected since life itself speaks through the blues. Rainey also claims that whites don't understand that the blues aren't essentially about catharsis or performance, at least not performance on the stage, but rather, the blues involve the performance of knowledge and interpretation, making the blues, in technical terms, a hermeneutical experience. Rainey says the blues give Black folk a reason to keep going, to keep living, and offers them a consoling companion in a lonely universe. The blues artist fills the empty spaces of existence with meaningful music. Wilson's blues poetry has the same effect.

If Wilson grappled with epistemology in *Ma Rainey*, he also confronted theodicy, or the philosophical and theological question of evil, of how one could claim God to be good, or all-powerful, or all-knowing, while Black pain persisted. Wilson's blues captured the harrowing intensity of Black suffering while giving voice to its victims. Like a contemporary book of Job, Wilson's blues permitted sufferers to talk back to God. What the poet W. H. Auden was to the painter Pieter Bruegel's iconic *Landscape with the Fall of Icarus*, Wilson was to the canvas of Black existence: the interpreter of its often unobserved heartbreak, calling attention to Black Icaruses who'd flown too high, or the Black folk who had to ignore them as they went on with their daily work so that they could make it through the night.

"God," the character Levee says in *Ma Rainey's Black Bottom*, waiting a beat after the utterance of the word God, letting "God" hang in the air for a few seconds, realizing, through the mechanics of speech, its timing and rhythms, what James Weldon Johnson in *God's Trombones* meant when he said that God was lonely. Levee then weighs in with counterevidence of God's greatness with beat two in the syncopation of suffering.

"God take a nigga's prayers and throw them in the garbage." And then beat three.

"God don't pay niggas no mind."

Every beat contains a repetition—the mention of God—and an enlarging awareness and argument. First there is the assertion of divinity. Then there is the divine disposal of human pleas for relief and the callous disregard for the Black condition, which rests in part on the solicitation through religion of such pleas in the first place, and the lunacy, the sheer idiocy, of pursuing God down the corridor of time when God disregards your history, treats it like toilet paper to wipe the cosmic behind, and then discards it as waste. And then beat four.

"In fact," he bellows, "God hate niggas."

That's it, that's the suppressed premise of the logic of Black suffering, the truth that Black religious folk dare not speak: that the God you love may hate you. William R. Jones argued—in a book with one of the bravest and most controversial titles a Black intellectual has ever conjured, *Is God a White Racist?*—that one must be willing to consider that God just doesn't love Black folk, a consideration one can entertain only if one is intellectually honest and wants to avoid insanity by squaring the facts to the case at hand. Levee was beyond considering it; he embraced the idea at full rage. And then beat five.

"Hate niggas with all the fury in his," Levee screams, unable to even finish the thought—at least when Charles Dutton played him on stage in 1984—because the thought is so disgusting, and so disgustingly obvious, that its opposite seems unnecessary to state or complete.

"Jesus don't love you nigga," he protests. "Jesus hate your Black ass."

Just in case he failed to get across his message by referring to God, Levee looped in Jesus. That's two of the three figures in the Godhead: The Father and now the son. Only the Holy Ghost was missing, and Levee's vengeful manner seemed to suggest that the only spirit in the room was quite unholy. Given the lively Christocentric lens through which Black Christians view the world, bringing Jesus into the mix makes it a more intimate, and therefore a more troubling, association, a greater insult, a more deadly species of divine rejection.

"Come talkin' that shit to me about burnin' in hell."

That's the second premise: going down to the lake of fire that consumes a soul for its disbelief in God leaves aside a more disturbing query: What about God's disbelief in us? Levee seems to be saying that that's hell enough. And thus the threat of hell is really the threat of *another* hell, because the first one is one that is too dangerous, too dark, for us to consider—that hell is not other people, as Sartre said; hell is the belief that there's a hell other than the one we're in but refuse to see. 2Pac expressed that belief when he rapped: "We probably in Hell already, our dumb asses not knowin'/Everybody kissin' ass to go to heaven ain't goin." 2Pac is also skeptical of religious claims of a hell to come, and the angry religious figures who denounce him for showing their ruse and for proclaiming hell on earth in the form of suffering Black bodies: "The preacher want me buried why? Cause I know he a liar/Have you ever seen a crackhead, that's eternal fire."

"Nigga, God can kiss my ass." Levee prefaces his blasphemous dismissal of God with a vernacular, and for some, a vulgar reference to Black folk that expresses the only redemption in that sentence—a term of racial derision transmuted to a term of endearment. But "Nigga" is also seen by many folk as the opposite of all that religion suggests; thus Levee's statement expresses pervasive secularism and the repudiation of piety that Levee sees as the most effective way to destroy the illusion of religion.

Wilson often filled the lips of his characters with powerful ideas in their vernacular, which didn't simply refer to language, but also embraced their

native haunts where commerce and culture collaborated, and sometimes collided: the jitney station, the barbershop, the backyard, the parlor, the pool
hall, and the diner where Wilson took his notebook as a homespun philosopher and as an eerily accurate ethnographer. Those gathering places—and
the accoutrements and implements we find there, including a fence, or a
piano, each of which is a synecdoche of racial memory and struggle in
Wilson's plays—are sacred spaces where Black life is worked on, worked
out, and worked into fighting shape, or at least good enough shape to face
our problems and to sing the best blues possible.

In *Fences*, for example, star athlete Cory asks his garbage collector father
Troy, an embittered former Negro baseball league player who crushes Cory's
collegiate gridiron dreams, why he never liked him. "Who in the hell ever
said I got to like you?" Troy says that Cory poses a "damn fool ass question,"
assails the logic of such a query, and then asks Cory if he ate every day, had
a roof over his head, and clothes on his back. When he answers yes, Troy
asks his son, "Why you think that is?" "Because you like me," Cory says.
Troy's ire is only slightly tempered. In their tense interaction Wilson stages
a seminal moment where the meaning of the implicit casts its robes on the
floor and gets emotionally naked.

"Like you," Troy says reflectively, slightly mournfully, in gentle anger, "I
go outta here every mornin' and bust my butt, puttin' up with them crackas
all day long. Because I like you," Troy says, repeating Cory's phrase in disbelief. "You is the biggest fool I ever saw." Troy makes explicit what is often
left unsaid between fathers and sons. "It is my job. It is my responsibility.
You understand that? A man got to take care of his family. You live in my
house. You sleep your behind on my bed clothes. You put my food in your
belly, because you are my son, you're my flesh and blood. *Not* because I
like you. It is my duty to take care of you. I owe a responsibility to you."
Troy demands Cory's full attention as he hammers the central point like
he hammers nails in the fence of the play's title. "I ain't got to like you. Mr.
Rand don't give me my money come payday because he like me. He give
it to me because he owe me. Now I done give you everything I had to give
you. I give you your life. Your mama and me worked it out between us. And
likin' your Black ass was not a part of the bargain and don't you *trrryyy* and
go through life worried if somebody like you or not. You best make sure
that they are doin' right by you."

Wilson lays bare the logic of Black devotion to kin and fights the myth
of universal Black male irresponsibility. Troy growls his commitment to
Cory and gives voice to the tension between obligation and affection, and

argues that duty is the highest expression of love, that the bottom line in rearing and loving kids is, indeed, the bottom line: providing shelter as a metaphor for housing the bodies of Black children and protecting them from natural and manmade elements. And teaching them that respect is the coin of the realm in the wider, whiter world.

Wilson's blues were surprisingly feminist, too, and imagined how women chafed under a gender double standard as men failed to understand that women live in the same world of desire as they do, although female desires are often thwarted by their greater sense of responsibility.

"I gave 18 years of my life to stand in the same spot with you," Troy's wife, Rose, says to him. "Don't you think I ever wanted other things? Don't you think I had dreams and hopes? What about my life? What about me? Don't you think it ever crossed my mind to want to know other men? That I wanted to lay up somewhere and forget about my responsibilities? I wanted someone to make me laugh so I could feel good. You're not the only one who's got wants and needs."

Wilson's domestic blues shapes his ability, in *King Hedley II*, to intertwine complicated social issues: the grief of a mother after her son dies at the hands of the police while another woman wrestles with her decision to abort a baby without telling the father. Tonya justifies her decision to abort King's unborn child because Tonya's still growing, hasn't been able to teach the daughter she already has about life, fully, and wants to spend time mothering herself and not raising more children or grandchildren. This is the sort of self-maintenance that men need never justify, nor worry that in embracing it they will appear selfish. Tonya has battled bruising doubt and comes, finally, to her decision to abort with radiant finality, thinking that she might have kept her unborn child from a life of misery or, paradoxically, of dying violently before its time. If some Blacks justify corporal punishment by arguing that they're disciplining Black children so they won't step out of line and lose their lives by arguing with police, then Tonya's logic goes a step further as the ultimate gesture of Black social protection. It's not unlike Black mothers aborting their babies in slavery to keep another soul from toiling in chains in this world.

"I'm through with babies," Tonya says. "I ain't raisin' no more. I ain't raisin' no grandkids. I'm looking out for Tonya. I ain't raising no kid to have somebody shoot 'em. To have his friend shoot 'em. To have the police shoot 'em." In those three staccato phrases Wilson rebuts the alleged indifference of Black folk killing other Black folk. Tonya can't see the difference between death at the hands of the police or from mayhem with "friends" when the result is the same: one's child is dead, or one's child is the killer. "Why you wanna bring another life into this world that don't respect life. I don't wanna raise no more babies when you got to fight to keep them alive. You take little Buddy Row's mother up on Bryn Mawr Road. What she got? Her heartache that don't never go away. She up there now sittin' down in the living room. She got to sit down 'cause she can't stand up. She sitting down tryin' to figure it out. Trying to figure out what happened. One minute her house is full of life. The next minute it's full of death. She was waitin' for him to come home and they bring her a corpse. I ain't goin' through that. I ain't havin' this baby and I ain't got to explain it to nobody."

Wilson's blues not only underscore the right of women to own their bodies, but the pain of seeing the bodies of their babies perish at the hands of friends or foes and not being able to do a thing but cry bitter tears and try to explain the unexplainable. Though written decades before the tragic murders of Trayvon Martin and Michael Brown, Wilson manages to capture the sentiments of their mothers, Sybrina Fulton and Lezley McSpadden, women made famous because their sons didn't come home but perished at the hands of a private citizen and a cop under extremely suspicious, and apparently unjust, circumstances—deaths that helped to spark a movement against Black death at non-Black hands, especially those of the police. Far less famous are those mothers and fathers who bury children taken from them by other Black folk. Both varieties of death visit incalculable hurt on Black communities and bring inconsolable grief to Black mothers.

In light of the shattering pain so many Black mothers have confronted, and still face today, Tonya insisted, on their behalf, too, that she need not explain her decision to abort to anyone but herself. Thus in the most organic, most aesthetically transparent fashion, Wilson showed the feminist credo that the personal is the political, and thus, enlivened the debate about the way art invites us to reflect on how society shapes individual lives. The philosophical blues of August Wilson takes stock of how the social world draws on, and drains, the personal, a dynamic that shapes Black life at every stage of our collective existence. That's why a critic of Wilson's politically charged aesthetic like Robert Brustein fails to grasp the blues sensibilities that color a Black world where art can't avoid politics, because those politics have so profoundly shaped the stuff of life that artists forever tap in their creative process.

August Wilson's grand vision is, arguably, the most sophisticated expression of the Black Arts Movement's hunger to meld politics and art, to marry the pen and the sword, or at least the protest placard. Wilson's work is not the playwright's equivalent of James Baldwin's version of the protest novel that ultimately fails because it denies the complicated humanity of Black folk:

> For Bigger's tragedy is not that he is cold or Black or hungry, not even that he is American, Black; but that he has accepted a theology that denies him life, that he admits the possibility of his being sub-human and feels constrained, therefore, to battle for his humanity according to those brutal criteria bequeathed him at his birth. But our humanity is our burden, our life; we need not battle for it; we need only to do what is infinitely more difficult—that is, accept it. The failure of the protest novel lies in its rejection of life, the human being, the denial of his beauty, dread, power, in its insistence that it is his categorization alone which is real and which cannot be transcended.

By tracing the shape-shifting Black Zeitgeist that lighted on the twentieth century—by discerning, in 10 plays set in each decade, its anatomy, and its logic, rationale, varied artistic and social expressions and its virtues and promises, its joys and hopes, its pains and torments—August Wilson gave us as thrilling, complex, and synoptic a view of Black life as any artist has rendered. By choosing the philosophically and literarily suggestive blues as a medium of expression, or more likely, being claimed, and therefore inspired, by the moral arc of the blues, Wilson grasped the simple yet surpassing humanity of Black life and gathered its component agonies and aspirations in the majestic sweep of his gritty and graceful poetry. As shaman and showman, as poet and playwright, as philosopher, anthropologist and literary craftsman and critic, August Wilson was a twentieth-century giant who not only bestrode the culture like a colossus, but who composed words and characters that made Black folk understand just who we are as our lives played out on stage for the world to see.

Represent

On the Silver Screen

11

Trump L'oeil of Race

This essay addresses American film and race in the Trump era. Ed Norton is not only one of the greatest actors of his generation but also a profound thinker whose craft reflects his intellectual gifts. Motherless Brooklyn *is more than a creative adaptation of Jonathan Lethem's novel, it is also a soulful meditation on politics, place, and the geography of race. The engrossing film* Antebellum *debuted during the resurgence of white nationalism and white supremacy under the Trump presidency. It is an intriguing movie that forces us to see how the history of anti-Blackness relentlessly impinges on American life and society. The* Motherless Brooklyn *portion of this essay appeared in 2019 online for* Esquire *magazine, and the* Antebellum *section appeared in 2020 online on the website* Blavity.

I

When President Trump recently tweeted that the impeachment inquiry he faces is a "lynching," it underscored his cynical manipulation of racial rhetoric for political benefit. It also exposed what a poor medium politics is for many white guys to offer nuanced perspectives on race. Trump's racial politics are morally stingy. His views of life are botched and malevolent. Tragically he is not alone. He is matched in his erosive incompetency by hordes of white male politicos who can't tell the truth about race to save their careers. It's not only that they lack insight. After all, they could get that if they really wanted to. It's that they are unwilling to dispute the rampant mendacity that dresses up as undeniable fact. Politics seems a barren racial landscape for the marriage of imagination and perfect duty for white men. That is a lesson, by the way, that rings true as white men on both sides of the political aisle fumble or stammer their way through race. Art seems to be a better place where white men can entertain complex views of race and Blackness.

Of course, we have to remind ourselves of this truth every so often. We must remember Bob Dylan damning unadorned hatred in his song "The

Death of Emmett Till," cursing lynching in his feral "Black Cross," or de-crying the murder of a Black hotel barmaid by a white socialite in the bit-ing "The Lonesome Death of Hattie Carroll." Filmmaker Norman Jewison grappled with hard boiled Southern bigotry in the riveting crime drama *In the Heat of the Night*.

Now we have the sharp eye and sublime talent of Edward Norton. The actor's actor both stars in and directs the majestic film noir *Motherless Brooklyn*, adapted from the evocative Jonathan Lethem novel of the same name. Lethem lathered his tale of Lionel Essrog (played in the film by Nor-ton), a Tourette's afflicted gumshoe in search of his mentor's murder, with the linguistic jouissance that shapes his compulsively repetitive verbal con-vulsions. Norton brilliantly pairs Lionel's misfit rhetorical riffing with the currents of bebop, with its lightning-quick tempos, chord progressions and key changes, and hard bop, which borrows the feisty tones of R&B, the un-dulating rhythms of gospel, and the sweet hypnotism of the blues to com-plement Lionel's percussive disorder. The jazz-like shape of Norton's story shifts the terrain of experience and amplifies the path of flaw to virtue, or, at least, helps us to hear the melody in our malady.

In Norton's film, we feel and hear race before we wrestle with its sinister implications. We feel it in the piercing tones and hear it in the throbbing beats and swaying rhythms of the film's musical scenes. We absorb it in the contrasting portrayals of communities bounded by race and those at-tempting to impose borders of color. We experience it in the luxurious flow of sensibilities crafted to contain difference, and those forged to overcome it. It rattles in the exchange of glances and utterances across a divide made of Black and white identity. We hear it in the language of characters con-sumed by issues bigger than their bodies and native tongues.

If the film goes straight for the jugular of race, it does so by approach-ing the issue organically, thoughtfully, lovingly, by remembering that the best film aspires to great art and satisfying entertainment, and *then* it can persuade, cajole, inspire. *Motherless Brooklyn* is refreshingly free of cant and dogma; it unfolds without grueling didacticism and finger-wagging wokeness. Because of that, it offers us brilliant and disturbing insight into the machinations of race on the ground, and in buildings erected to scrape the skies of whiteness, even as Black clouds rain down fierce meanings of race that intermittently interrupt the parade of privilege.

Norton traces his noir on a canvas that straddles, aesthetically, the present and the resonant past, bridging into *Chinatown* and *L.A. Confi-dential*, where noir literally meets, in this case, well, noir, or Blackness, and teases out the implications of race in a highly intriguing and entertaining fashion.

"I have always been drawn to the serious and, I think, important intention in noir as a genre to remind us that under the mainstream American narrative, there is a shadow narrative in which things are happening that we should be paying attention to and expose," Norton tells me. "The theme [in the film] that interested me was the danger, and tragedy, in not seeing things, and people, for what they are." This is where race fuses with a vision of the mainstream that has nothing to do with namby-pamby, we-are-the-world multiculturalism, or dreadfully colorless universalism.

Instead, in Norton's view, it is a vigorous nod to the ill effects of an America that discards its darker side. It is a film that measures our failure to see how what happens in the Black world reflects the tensions and possibilities in the white world. The reason Black culture has resonated so powerfully in some white circles is because it forces the nation to confront issues of difference that we'd rather sidestep. It encourages the culture to see parts of itself in our struggles for acceptance, in our efforts to find our footing in the country. There is some give and take, too, and Black folk see the relationship between our struggles and the struggle of white folk to grapple with difference among themselves, whether because of Tourette's or class or geography or region.

The cast of characters in the film sheds considerable light on this point. Lionel is underestimated because he's a "freak show" despite being smart and tough. Laura (Gugu Mbatha-Raw), around whom the ultimate mystery of the film revolves, is marginalized as a Black woman and dismissed as a "secretary" despite being a lawyer and activist. Paul (Willem Dafoe) seems to be a bum and a crank despite being a brilliant engineer and, finally, a moral hero of sorts.

But it works in reverse, too: Paul's brother Moses Randolph (Alec Baldwin) is viewed as a public servant, the Parks Commissioner and a hero of the people, not as the unelected, autocratic power broker and racist bully that he turns out to be. *Motherless Brooklyn* makes clear that great damage is done to people and the communities that nurture or stifle them when we fail to see folk for what they are. The film's title, *Motherless Brooklyn*, fairly screams the absence of love, the absence of public care, the absence of social concern of the often-seedy world it depicts. It is a harsh universe populated by orphaned people and orphaned places.

But films ain't books; cinema isn't scholarship. We must respect the genre of presentation—well, technically, of representation—and pay homage to the artistic conventions that shape the messages auteurs want us to get. Race is an issue that works best when we are not preached to. (I say this as an ordained minister for 40 years who values preaching in its rightful, righteous place.) Instead, we must be engaged and uplifted, inspired to think and reflect.

Motherless Brooklyn does that wonderfully. It's not a polemic. Nor is it a dose of cinematic medicine intended to heal the ills of race and color. It is a rousing piece of entertainment that takes us back in time to take us forward. It is a film whose music, language, style, panache, mystery, and daring transport us to an era in the forties and fifties with impressive scale and fine detail, with colorful and diverse characters that defy stereotype and cliché and keep us guessing to the very end.

It may sound hokey, and hopelessly nostalgic, but this is what the best cinema used to do for us: treat us like grownups and seduce us with its charm and magic. The best of those films hypnotized us. Instead of telling us they showed us. They gripped us with narrative and didn't coerce us with guilt. I'm a professor, too, but this is surely no staid lecture either. Still, the film offers the benefits of deep thinking while wearing its learning lightly. And its punch packs that much more of a wallop.

For instance, the character Moses Randolph sucks up a lot of the film's dramatic oxygen. It's an ingenious move on Norton's part to give Randolph plenty of room to breathe fire into his villainous rampage from the thirties until the sixties through the urban geography of New York. This is Norton's brilliant cinematic gambit: he uses Lethem's novel as the springboard, but he lands in a place that Lethem doesn't conjure in his book, one that introduces Randolph as a foil, and as a thinly disguised version of the "master builder" Robert Moses. You will recall that Robert Moses was the unelected New York Parks Commissioner, among 12 other titles he held. It is in Randolph's character that Norton explores race in a timely and provocative fashion.

There is presently, in the culture, a great deal of discussion about gentrification and urban renewal. In Los Angeles, the slain rapper Nipsey Hussle was trying to prevent the takeover of his inner-city community by strategically investing in neighborhood businesses before he was senselessly gunned down. In Washington, D.C., Howard University was scolded that it should move its address if it was offended by white gentrifiers turning the school's grounds into a dog park.

Motherless Brooklyn tackles urban renewal in one of its most notorious instances in New York City, especially in Brooklyn. What Moses did to

Black folk there is far more brutal than the politer forms of erasure and dis-placement that the term "gentrification" summons. Moses wreaked havoc and wrought wholesale dislocation, a kind of gnarled deconstruction of Black urban space that undercut the beauty of Black intimacy in formerly stable Black communities, and, on their dismantled bones, constructed the worst slums in America, and named them, in a classic clinical euphemism that was far less benign than it sounded: The Projects. (It reminds me of JAY-Z's lyrics: "You know why they call the projects a project/Because it's a project!/An experiment, we're in it, only as objects." As Jay said in his memoir: "Housing projects are a great metaphor for the government's rela-tionship to poor folks: these huge islands built mostly in the middle of no-where, designed to warehouse lives." Those words may literally be applied to Moses, whose willful urban undoing fueled the construction of the Marcy Projects in which JAY-Z came to maturity.)

Norton brilliantly shows how Moses rode the gravy train of federal cap-ital to further consolidate his nondemocratic power and to ghettoize mi-norities. Moses's biographer Robert Caro makes the compelling case of his sturdy racist pedigree (including opposing Black war veterans from mov-ing after World War II into a Manhattan residential development complex designed to house veterans). Norton's film shows it in granular but grip-ping detail. *Motherless Brooklyn* depicts how Moses set bridges too low for buses so that minorities couldn't go to beaches. It gives us a view of the in-tentional dislocation and ghettoization of Black life that surely debunks the argument that our crises flow from the intrinsic complexities of urban life.

"One of the most perverse psychological tactics of racists of all kinds is to use distance from their worst historical atrocities to deny the actual severity of that history and to, appallingly, suggest that anything *that* bad is implausi-ble," Norton tells me. "The Holocaust denier tries to jiujitsu the inconceivable scale of the horror into proof that it's a fabrication. So, too, do the people try-ing to shout down Black Lives Matter, or any other attempt to assert that the dark symbiosis of poverty and discrimination [and] dehumanization [that] flows from the legacy of institutionalized racism are 'conspiracy theories' and rationalizations for character deficiencies in a whole community of people." Norton communicates these blame-the-victim strategies through drama and character development. What otherwise might be a dry dissertation about human motive and the factors that lie behind abhorrent behavior is made far more interesting and salient.

"I think films can approach these themes about who we want to be and what our values are in a way that's very different from academic or journalistic assessment," Norton says. "We can depict the emotional and psychological landscape and connect the audience with their empathy, make them feel the pain of brutality, instigate the anger and disgust that motivates determination to resist. The one thing I didn't want to revert to was the cliché of cynicism in noir. I don't think we can afford it right now. I wanted a noir with an arc toward moral evolution and acceptance of responsibility to act by the gumshoe."

Fortunately, that's exactly what *Motherless Brooklyn* does: it entertains us while inviting us to engage a world of racial hierarchy built on criminal levels of systemic injustice. The film refuses to throw red meat to the merchants of racial cynicism. It doesn't truck in the easy shibboleths of the enlightened. Both options are poor substitutes for dramatic flair and storytelling with a compelling moral arc.

In the Age of Trump, the foolish prevarications of some white men drive what often gets passed off as righteous resistance to political correctness. It is downright inspiring to encounter an artist who embraces old fashioned moviemaking to tell a beautifully complicated story of human striving and moral suffering. Along the way, he never forgets that it's a picture first, and only then, yes, perhaps, especially then, a poignant reflection on our all too human condition.

II

Norton's film ranges back over several decades to grasp hold of our racial chaos and to offer a cinematic genealogy of anti-Blackness that, in form at least, would make both Nietzsche and Foucault proud. The directors of *Antebellum* warp time with Einsteinian elegance as they leap back into the nineteenth century to conjure a racial dystopia that is filled with even greater horror for Black folk because we cannot determine when, or if, it will end. In a world where George Floyd's death has sparked a social movement that addresses the nation's long and brutal racial history, the Lost Cause has gained renewed currency as activists wrestle with statues and flags that testify to the bitter struggle over national identity. The cultural clash over the Confederacy is taking place as we redefine the racial landscape and argue about what makes us uniquely American. Beyond that, the prominence of the *New York Times'* 1619 Project forces us to turn once again to America's original sin.

Slavery still ignites heated debates about how the past affects the present, and how bitter disagreement over enslaved Black people led kinfolk to take up arms against one another on bloody battlefields in the Civil War.

That "Late Unpleasantness," as southern historians took to calling the Civil War, has so deeply stained the American consciousness that thousands of folks each year participate in reenactments of its most notable conflicts. White Southerners who lost the war but won the battle to interpret the war's meaning can't seem to let go of that war, or the Confederacy, or, for that matter, the idea of slavery that backed it all.

But what if they didn't have to surrender slavery? What if they could find a way to get us back to the old days where Black folk were shackled and had to obey the ruthless will of white overseers and owners? That sounds like a horror film, and that's just what *Antebellum* is—a brilliant, disturbing piece of visual magic and historical imagination wrapped inside of a highly charged thriller that keeps us on the edge of our seats precisely because it yanks us from the present and transports us into a dark, foreboding, and hateful racial past. Or does it?

"Look, obviously we don't want to finger wag," says Gerard Bush, who co-wrote and co-directed the film with Christopher Renz. "We want people to go in and get the thrill of the movie. However, we would be gutted as artists if we felt, or if it ended up happening, that that's all people got was the thrill. The point is to [also] give you this medicine."

The medicine hardly tastes bitter and goes down smoothly. That's because the acting is superb, the storyline intensely intriguing, if downright scary, and the conceit of the movie altogether plausible. I won't give it away here, but suffice it to say that it makes sense because white supremacy has reared its ugly head again as we teeter on the edge of social tumult and neo-fascist politics in a racially divided society. Let's just say when certain folk get nostalgic for the past, the virtue of their nostalgia depends on exactly what past they have in mind.

The nation is presently torn between a vision of national thriving that borrows from the demented and twisted mindset encouraged by neo-Nazis and assorted bigots, and one that owes a debt to confronting our worst instincts and communing with the better angels of our nature. *Antebellum* forces us to confront the fact that in the midst of such epic seizures of social discontent, the choice to revert back to a racist past without hopping in a time machine to get there is a truly horrifying thought—and according to this film, a realistic prospect. "We think it's plausible," Bush says. "That's what is most scary about it."

A great deal of thought clearly went into grappling with our present racial malaise, one that exploded on the neck of George Floyd but was centuries in the making. "We're fascinated by the collective psychopathy that is so pernicious and stubborn and durable within civilizations," Bush says. "The Nazis actually got so many of their ideas from coming over to America and seeing what the South was doing in the Jim Crow era."

By drawing the line from Berlin to Birmingham, Bush and Renz insist that the deformities of racism unite a confederation of bigots the world over. Moreover, the fantasy of snatching Black folk from their creature comforts as they enjoy enormous Black progress and fixing them in their natural habitat of total subordination to superior white folk is a fantasy that just won't die. But in order for the fantasy to become real, some Black bodies just well might have to perish. That's a prospect that plays out on the screen as *Antebellum* offers a glimpse of the horrors of slavery in the bodies of some of its memorable male characters like Eli, played by the sublime Tongayi Chirisa.

Bush and Renz aim to take us back in time to move us forward in vision by effecting a shift in perception. "When you're in what you think is the antebellum South, everything looks and feels the way it would have then," Bush says. "It's impossible to take your mind out of that and to imagine that it could for even a second be modern."

But the shift in perception isn't simply about chronology and era; it is also about gender and womanhood. Bush is especially sensitive to the portrayals of Black women in media and film because he watched his grandmother, among other women, embody extraordinary grace and abounding dignity.

"[Her dignity] was impossible to smother and to extinguish," Bush says. "And we hope that within this film our depiction of the Black woman is turned on its ear from what is normally on offer." Of course, the theme of dignity threads through the exquisite performance of Janelle Monáe as the highly successful author Veronica Henley, in the radiant presence of Kiersey Clemons as Julia, and in the grit and determination of Gabourey Sidibe as Dawn.

The way Black women are presented, the way they are seen, is a microcosm of the film's broader project of refiguring how Black bodies intended for the auction block and the sun-drenched plantation are created for more noble purposes than the white supremacist imagination can abide. And yet, the horrors of racism and slavery are most clearly seen when lives otherwise meant for excellence and greatness and freedom are subject to subservience, oppression and humiliation. The white supremacist imagination has featured Black bodies in its fantasies as stuck perpetually in slavery, and if there was any way that such an imagination could have its way, Black folk in 2020 would be somehow transported back in time when the rawhide whip of the malevolent overseer lashed bodies with a message of brutal domination.

It is the yen for such authenticity of representation, for seeing how Black bodies were distorted through the lens of a white worldview, that led Bush and Renz to make a decisive choice. "We actually insisted on shooting the movie with the lenses from *Gone with the Wind*," Bush says. "We wanted to take the same weaponry that was used to shoot propaganda, and to misinform, to correct the record." Even as the great poet and critic Audre Lorde insisted that "the master's tools will never dismantle the master's house," Bush and Renz believe that the master's lens may indeed help correct the master's distortions.

It is crucial to correct such distortions lest our discomfort with the truth lead to a historical void filled by harmful fantasy and lies. "As soon as we don't amplify the stories, that's when the erasure slips in," Bush says. "When suddenly the textbooks in Texas are saying that Africans were servants brought over to cultivate the land when, in fact, that's completely false." Even though Bush never thought he'd do a slave narrative, he was drawn to it precisely because he wanted to turn the usual arc of slavery on its ear and make us listen acutely to different dimensions of being stolen away from our destinies. But if this nifty and riveting horror mystery of a thriller comes off as a nightmare, that's because it began in Bush's dreams.

"I wish that I could take credit for the story and the way that it was laid out," Bush says. "We didn't. My father passed away about a year before we moved to LA. I was really traumatized by that. My brother died shortly thereafter, here in LA. And I had this terrible nightmare, and in that nightmare, I was not the star of my dream, and I'm normally the star of my own dream. It was this woman Veronica. And the dream that happened is essentially what you see in *Antebellum*."

If *Antebellum* is not quite a fever dream, it is a film born of nightmare—in the mind of its creator, and in the national imagination from which we scarcely seem able to awaken. It is to the filmmakers' credit that we feel the trauma and thrill, the horror and catastrophe, of the racial nightmare of slavery. With their provocative films, Norton, and Bush and Renz, have managed to throw fresh light on the ancient malady of race in a way that is both mysterious and as clear as day, both scary and compelling.

12

Bigelow's General Method

Kathryn Bigelow is the first of only two women to win an Oscar for directing, in 2010 for The Hurt Locker. *Bigelow has never shied away from engaging big issues, like war, terror, and violence, and has insisted all along that she be judged on her creative genius and not her gender. In so doing, she has paved the way for female directors including Chloé Zhao, Greta Gerwig, Ava DuVernay, Emerald Fennell, and Regina King. I hung out with Bigelow in Detroit, Los Angeles, and New York for this profile, which appeared in* Elle *magazine in 2017.*

"You think that's him?" the director Kathryn Bigelow furtively whispered to me as yet another aging, crumpled Black man passed us by.

We were in Detroit, standing outside a weathered apartment building near the waterfront. It sat in the shadow of the on-the-comeback downtown, once the fourth-largest city in the country and a teeming hive of entrepreneurial energy fueled by the automobile industry. If the apartment house didn't quite scrape the sky, it at least pointed to the heavens in a glory that seemed to have faded eons ago.

We were looking for a man whose life story would be featured in Bigelow's latest film, about a bloody siege of police terror at a seedy motel during the epic upheaval in Detroit known as the '67 riots. He'd been one of the victims, and Bigelow wanted to talk to him about his memories of that night to better shape his character onscreen. Although he'd spoken to her team during preproduction, he proved to be pretty elusive when it came to actually meeting. So we set out to bag a reluctant star. Call it guerrilla astronomy: Larry Reed. Black male. In his late sixties. Sang second tenor with the soul-music sextet the Dramatics before they made it big. (And to prove how big-hearted I was, I pitched in despite the fact that the eventual lead singer of the group, the great L. J. Reynolds, had tried to holler at my fiancée one night in the late 1970s in a small west side Detroit jazz spot, Watts Club Mozambique.)

Bigelow and I did our best imitations of Columbo, chatting up a few brothers in the effort to find Reed, who wasn't returning calls or answering buzzers. It was hard to make an appointment with a phantom. So we stealthily made our way past security and onto the elevator to the wrong floor, then up a more convenient flight of stairs to the right floor, and left a culinary goody bag at Reed's door when he failed to answer. I was quietly impressed that Bigelow wouldn't just send a hireling to do this kind of grunt work. But I guess you learn to pay attention to the smallest details when you hang around eagle-eye military types like those Bigelow met filming the landmark war flick *The Hurt Locker*, focusing on a bomb-disposal unit in Baghdad—a movie that won her the Academy Award for directing—and the harrowing *Zero Dark Thirty*, about the global hunt for Osama bin Laden.

At Hollywood events, the tall, lanky Bigelow is a model of elegance, with a wholesome beauty that defies the arithmetic of her 65 years. But Detroit ain't Hollywood. That day, when we were looking for Reed, and most other times we met while she was working, she wore gray Nike running shoes; dark blue, cropped skinny jeans; and a lightweight black quilted puffer over a black T-shirt. (The exception was when she dressed up to hear me preach in New York in the spring of 2016; I'd urged her to get a flavor of Black-church criticism of racial terror to prep for her film.) Her face was sometimes partly obscured by gold-rimmed aviators, their dark tint hiding her hazel eyes; her light brunette hair was parted in the middle and lightly tousled, falling just below her shoulders. Whether in Hollywood or the hood, she never looked out of place, especially in Detroit, where her sleek but casual look mingled effortlessly with the working- and lower-middle-class practical wash-and-wear of no-nonsense strivers.

* * *

At one point, I broke away from Bigelow to see if I could ply my homeboy instincts to locate Reed better on my own. That's where I met the truth, disguised in crinkly Black flesh.

"But do the white girl really know what these crackas did to us?" a wizened old man asked me. It was more threat than question. I'd just told him that Bigelow was directing a movie about the Algiers Motel incident, in which racist white cops killed three Black men—Carl Cooper, Aubrey Pollard, and Fred Temple—and viciously beat another eight, as well as two white women.

From the looks of it, the man had seen more than his share of suffering. His radiant, purple-black face was perforated by eerie, glistening sockets of merciless knowingness where eyes should have been. He'd witnessed the halcyon days of dizzy capital taking luxurious rides down tree-lined streets in the latest Cadillac to roll off the assembly line, each year's design more terrific, more decked out than the one before. But he'd also witnessed the vengeance of whites, including newly arrived European immigrants, who clashed with the surging population of Black people continually migrating to Detroit from the South. (My father booked passage to the northern promised land from Georgia in the late '40s; my mother, from Alabama, in the mid-'50s.) As car manufacturers converted to the war effort in the late 1930s, the competition for jobs and housing became increasingly intense, and the race riot of 1943 in Detroit was a foreshadowing of the '67 rebellion. A common denominator linked both antagonisms: a ruthless white police force that waged war against a captive, vulnerable Black community.

All of that seeing and knowing bubbled to the surface in the words that the old man hurled as much as spoke. And then came, slowly, his dagger of a query: "What she know 'bout niggas anyway?"

The man's challenge gnawed at me as I made my way back to Bigelow. (We left without finding Reed, but she managed to connect with him a few weeks later.) I grew up in Detroit, and now I'd come back to help Bigelow find her man, and to scout my beloved birthplace for sites to shoot her film. I'd traveled these streets as a schoolboy, a gang member, an expelled prep-school student, a teen father, a janitor, a crime victim, and, for a brief stint, a factory laborer before I entered the ministry at 21 and headed south to college. I'd walked these streets when Detroit wore the dubious crown of "murder capital of the world." I was born less than three months before Berry Gordy first amplified the aching melodies and sparkling harmonies of Motown, in January 1959.

I vividly remember the wigged-out jubilance after the Tigers captured the 1968 World Series. That victory consoled a city that, a few months earlier, briefly erupted in futile homage to a lonely prophet who was murdered at another desolate motel, this one in Memphis. And the year before that, my eight-year-old eyes watched plumes of smoke billow above a horizon hazed by the flames of Black desperation. And exasperation too. I was frightened; my mother explained that it had all been caused by a police raid of a "blind pig," but my young mind couldn't comprehend what a sightless mammal had to do with the chaos I saw. When adults were forced to come inside earlier than normal, I turned to my tattered gray hardback Merriam-Webster in search of the meaning of "curfew." I saw Black folk scampering down my ghetto street, dollar bills precariously stashed in their blooming Afros, nutritional booty tucked into their pockets, hustling radios and televisions and couches and chairs to homes that hadn't seen newer versions of any of that in a while. There was an eerie mix of glee and grief. Black folk were plain tired of sinking into what John Bunyan had three centuries earlier called the "slough of despond." In the looming postindustrial economy, Black brawn was quickly becoming unnecessary, Black skill devalued, and persistent racism would handcuff new educational and economic opportunities, as police continued to flash their batons and guns with menacing regularity.

All of that hurt and pain is what led to the uprising, the rebellion, the riots, and even earlier, the Civil War. Black folk were tired of being bossed and beaten by the police, of being killed by them. Just like we are today. In that sense, Bigelow's film couldn't be more timely.

"When [screenplay writer, producer, and sometime collaborator] Mark Boal presented the idea of the incident at the Algiers Motel, it was right on the heels, sadly, of the death of Michael Brown," in Ferguson, Missouri, Bigelow tells me on a break from the editing room at Sony Pictures Studios in Culver City. "It crystallized the need to add, from my vantage point, more volume to that conversation. Because it's a conversation that I believe needs to be had."

Indeed it does. Black folk have it every day, all the time, in ways that are probably difficult for many white folk to imagine. That's because if your ass is being kicked, it's in your interest to talk about it, to make as much commotion as possible to get the beaters up off you. One of the most confounding elements of the recent uproar over police brutality is that, despite the smartphone video recordings, cops' hostility toward Blacks seems to refresh itself without abatement, without shame, and with the belief that getting caught on camera bashing or cursing or taking precious Black life will likely cost them nothing more than the inconvenience of being put on paid leave. Or, at worst, getting fired. And, oh so rarely, charged with a crime—say, manslaughter, for which they're often exonerated. Or they'll plead guilty to excessive force, a slap on the wrist that doesn't begin to make up for the poetics of destruction they so callously practice on Black life.

That poetics must be met by higher, deeper art—art lifted by theory from its academic trenches without showing off. In that sense, Bigelow is working similar ground as virtuosos like Kendrick Lamar, whose primal scream of Black humanity against its jaundiced denial on *To Pimp a Butterfly* offered a measure of vicarious release from both police brutality and neighbor-to-neighbor mayhem. And worse, from the soul-gutting experience of playing by the rules, of seeking redress through the courts, only to be met with state-sponsored obfuscation, rationalization, and rebuff. Tragically, our only answer, sometimes our only pipeline to justice—yes, at times, our revenge—is art.

Bigelow doesn't often get credit for just how sophisticated her craft is, how theoretically informed; how alluring the palette of ideas from which she draws. That may have in part to do with the more commercial or, at times, quirky films she directed early on, such as *Point Break* and *Blue Steel*. But the thread that runs through all her work is an attraction to story. "Finding stories that speak to you, and imbuing them with artistic integrity, is a challenge for every filmmaker," Bigelow says. "I look for substantive stories that are informational, set against a canvas that is worth viewing. My choice of projects is primarily instinctive."

The narrative that coalesces around Bigelow hinges on her being a female director, but that doesn't do justice to how adroitly she's traversed the tightrope between art and politics. She began as a painter, studying at the San Francisco Art Institute, and, upon graduating in 1972, decamped for New York City and an independent study program at the Whitney Museum of American Art. She started hanging with highbrow thinkers like conceptual artists Lawrence Weiner and Jeffrey Lew, and the intellectuals who produced the seminal critical theory journal *Semio-text(e)*. Bigelow took up philosophy and film theory at Columbia, where she earned an MFA in 1981. But her desire to probe the interface of art and politics can be traced to her roots in California during a turbulent decade.

"I was in high school in the '60s," Bigelow says. "Obviously, there was a lot going on, especially in the San Francisco area. And then I went to New York to study art. One of my advisers was Susan Sontag. And my work got more and more and more politicized." In the mid-'70s, Bigelow's baptism in aesthetics and postmodern theory instigated a gradual migration from paint to film. At 26, she made a movie called *Psychological Operations in Support of Unconventional Warfare*, which critiqued American counterinsurgency methods and death squads. "When I moved into film," she says, "I never drifted away from that."

For Bigelow, taking on the stories of *The Hurt Locker, Zero Dark Thirty*, and now, *Detroit*, seemed like a natural extension of her interest in the thorny intersections of the aesthetic and the social. Her work with Sontag and other professors inspired her to think about what we see onscreen:

why we like it, feel repulsed by it, or both, and what that conflict says about who we are.

"Sontag had just written *On Photography*, and it was about how you identify not just a photographic image, but an image on film. That informed the longest film I had done thus far, called *Set-Up*." It's her 17-minute thesis film, and it kicks off with two men tussling in a dark alley, though the images are shrewdly sabotaged in a continuous voice-over by two of her Columbia professors, Sylvère Lotringer and Marshall Blonsky. Bigelow instructed her teachers to explain what was simultaneously intriguing and disconcerting about the violence onscreen. "It was an attempt to deconstruct [what Lotringer calls] 'scopophilia,' which is why you are attracted to an image, a character. You're trying to undercut that attraction. That's what *Set-Up* tried to do, in real time." It has certainly set the pattern for her subsequent work.

"What is the tension that's created between the viewer and the screen? What is that 'contract,' as [Jacques] Lacan calls it in the world of deconstruction? So Susan Sontag was a kind of bridge to thinking in more complex and elaborate terms about 'Why do you make art? Why do you write books?' I think we make art, we write books, to further understand why we make art and write books. It's a conversation we have with ourselves."

And it's a conversation Bigelow will now have with the nation. The bigger story—of which the Algiers tragedy was part—was bad enough, and Bigelow shrewdly begins *Detroit* there, tapping into the cumulative anguish that exploded in the city in the wee hours of Sunday, July 23, 1967. The police had assailed an illegal after-hours drinking joint, the "blind pig" my mother told me about, expecting only a small group. To their surprise, more than 80 Black revelers had gathered to celebrate the safe return of two local Vietnam vets. A bullheaded cop decided to arrest the whole lot of them, and as the police awaited vehicles to haul everyone in, a crowd of 200 Black folk amassed, venting their rage at the barbarous treatment they were routinely subjected to. Taunts and jeers led to bottles being tossed, and in quick order, stores being looted and burned. The powder keg of racial oppression, and Black chafing at structural inequality, blew up, the fuse lit by cops who had the temerity to shut down a party for a couple of Black men who'd fought for their country. By the end of the five-day riot, 43 people were dead—25 killed by police—7,231 were arrested, more than 1,000 injured, and about the same number of citizens, mostly Black, were left homeless.

Bigelow plays this opening skillfully, and thunderingly, to viscerally evoke the violence that has seeped into the seams of Black existence. The bodies of Black people are herded and harassed, and the need for the hashtag, the battle cry, the rallying plea, "Black Lives Matter," becomes agonizingly clear. There's a long history here, one that Bigelow memorably communicates through the images of the battering, and the battered, that stalk the screen.

Where Bigelow's rich theoretical background is most palpable—where her understanding of what violence does to us, how it at once makes us cringe and crane our necks, how it reveals our submerged fears and our truest, most confusing, sometimes destructive desires—is in her treatment of the events at the Algiers: home to a dubious though largely innocuous enclave of stragglers, pimps, hustlers, prostitutes, and people on the make and on the run. It was there, at the corner of Virginia Park and Woodward Avenue, about a mile southeast of where the riot had begun, that a report of a sniper led police to raid the motel and perpetrate their murderous assault.

While Bigelow doesn't make the connection explicit in *Detroit*—it is, after all, a period piece—Wayne State University historian Danielle McGuire, the author of a forthcoming book about the Algiers incident called *Murder in the Motor City*, says that what happened at the motel "contextualizes, and echoes, the recent spate of police killings of Black boys and young Black men like Laquan McDonald in Chicago, Tamir Rice in Cleveland, Michael Brown in Ferguson, and Akai Gurley in New York City, to name just a few."

Rutgers University professor Brittney Cooper, author of *Beyond Respectability: The Intellectual Thought of Race Women*, seconds McGuire, noting that the quest for a model of policing that "protects rather than destroys Black lives is a multigenerational struggle." The film goes broader, too, Cooper says, implicitly documenting the historical buildup of forces that still weigh on the city's future: disinvestment, gentrification, and the government's utter abandonment of its citizens in a time of crisis. (A sip of Flint's drinking water, anyone?)

Of course, there were competing explanations for what happened at the Algiers that night. The cops claimed self-defense, although even then that was considered highly suspicious. But if it's hard to prove that a police officer murdered a Black person now, when there's ample video evidence of a kid being shot within two seconds of being approached, of a man's back being filled with lead as he flees, imagine how hard it was to prove police execution of unarmed Blacks at a time when the contentions of white cops were virtually irrefutable? From the evidence that can be pieced together, following the conclusions of Pulitzer Prize–winning author John Hersey, the police giddily engaged in a kind of "death game," toying with Black lives and riddling Black bodies with bullets, like so many bull's-eyes on a target.

Bigelow's peripatetic and, at times, slightly jittery camera puts us right in the middle of this chaotic, chilling encounter, shifting anxiously from the perspectives of the perpetrators to that of the victims. And she vividly captures the psychosexual jealousy that spurred the white cops to perform what was in essence an extended castration for the crime of carousing with white girls.

If Bigelow's photographic lens destabilizes the audience—refusing to let us be lulled into unspoken complicity with the status quo—her impact on the set is the opposite. "She made each and every actor feel not only safe, but empowered," says Jason Mitchell, who plays Carl, one of the young men gunned down inside the motel. "Kathryn creates a world, then just lets you do you. She does the same with her cameramen; things are constantly moving." Before the shoot, Jacob Latimore, who stars as another victim, Fred, says the white and Black actors "all came together and really built a strong brotherhood," a buffer for when things "got physical" and "emotionally exhausting." Bigelow, if anything, encouraged the intensity. "I never read a full script and was unaware of what happens to the other characters, which put us in a very vulnerable place," Latimore says, a strategy that likely contributed to the authentic mystery and urgent drama of the film. "She always kept us in the scene," he adds. "There weren't any distractions."

But there is a distraction the director may not be able to block: Bigelow knows that some people question her ability as a white woman to accurately, justly, and effectively tell this story, just like the old Black man I encountered.

"I'll admit that I'm automatically skeptical when a white woman is tasked with a story that depicts Black life, particularly as it relates to how Black women are portrayed," cultural critic Jamilah Lemieux tells me. While that attitude is often warranted, there are no Black women prominently featured in *Detroit* because none figured into what happened at the Algiers that night.

Lemieux continues: "What might her lens be? Does she have even a limited understanding of the complicated politics of interracial dating from our side? Will she rely on the comfortable tropes so often employed by her male counterparts—hell, by Black men?" Lemieux is no doubt referring to the conventional liberal wisdom that interracial sex is an act of resistance to bigotry. The idea can't help but disturb Black women, who are often thrust into competition with white women—whose beauty and worth are at a cultural premium—for a relatively small pool of "eligible" Black men. To her credit, Bigelow tells the story straightforwardly, just as it happened that night, according to the best accounts. You don't have to invent a Freudian quagmire of sexual resentment of Black men when the facts are this harsh: White cops who, like the rest of society, trafficked in stereotypes of Black sexual prowess couldn't control their rage and attacked the Black males, and slapped around and sexually humiliated the two white women. "Why you gotta fuck them, huh?" one of the officers asked the girls. Later another snarls, "Honestly, it doesn't bother you, the Afro Sheen in the hair?" The truth was more hurtful than any fiction or mythology.

Bigelow doesn't shy away from parsing the meaning of her advantage: "Am I the ideal person to direct this movie? No. Having lived with a certain amount of privilege, how can I truly, truly get into the DNA of somebody who has experienced social injustice?" But she decided to not let the best be the enemy of the good. "Is this a story that needs to be told? Yes. And so I felt like, well, let's just add more noise to the conversation and hopefully there will be many more movies."

And let's be honest: However much her race limits her perspective, Bigelow had the power to get the project green-lighted. Not to mention that her ability to tell vivid, complicated war stories isn't trivial to the project at hand: If *Detroit* is anything, it's a tale of domestic terrorism.

McGuire thinks of the matter this way: "It is important for white people to tackle these stories about white supremacy. After all, it is up to white people to end systemic and institutional racism." Cooper goes so far as to suggest that there might be a benefit, even penance, in "one of the most celebrated female directors in the game" wielding her considerable influence to prod the nation to think seriously about race. "Given the 2016 election in which white women threw their lot in with white supremacy in support of Trump, it matters that a white woman is helping to recover this history," she says. "Hopefully it will lead not to easy calls for reconciliation, but more to an authentic kind of racial reckoning."

As for Bigelow herself, she laments the underrepresentation of people of color, as well as women, in the directorial ranks, but she believes we've got to keep confronting and exploring racial themes . . . by any means necessary, you might say. Her initial impression of the Algiers Motel tragedy was, "That's 50 years ago. Surely something has changed." But she almost immediately recognized she was wrong. "Oh, no, it hasn't [changed]. I feel that from a sociopolitical standpoint, we're just trapped unless there's a political will to change this paradigm of subjugation." She pauses and sits back in her chair. "And I feel pain," she says. And then a sincere confession, as much for herself as for her fellow citizens: "And shame."

Back to the old man and his questions. Is Bigelow going to tell what cynical racists, and systemic racism, did to Black folk? Yes. She probes white paranoia and fear, white privilege and innocence, white hate and resentment, white-on-Black violence, with jarring fidelity to the facts of the case. And what does she know about Black folk? Enough to limn our fragile, beautiful, worthy humanity with a discerning eye, and enough to know that telling the truth about the devastating consequences of structural racism and police brutality is one of the greatest gifts we can be given.

Oh, and the red gators. They make an appearance on Carl Cooper's feet about 40 minutes into the film: round-toed, Merlot-colored, crocodile-skin loafers with matching laces and black soles. Those gators were a wet kiss from Bigelow to Black Detroit, to the men who lost their lives, to the Black men who struggle daily to keep their heads above water, to the Black men who take pride in sporting their finest threads amid estranging and repulsive conditions. Nothing says I know working-class Black Detroit better than a pair of gators. "Pink gators/My Detroit players," The Notorious B.I.G. once rapped. Add Bigelow to the Detroit shout-out hall of fame for that splendid recognition and powerful metaphor. It's as fine a use of her high cultural theory as might be imagined.

RELIGION

Because I sit in the academy, the church, the classroom, and the community, I must explore socioeconomic class and globalization as it moves in and out of Black life with blazing speed—taking the poor *and* the wealthy out of sight . . . I must listen to the different rhythms of Blackness that come from the different geographies that shape people's bodies and health. I am drawn, sometimes with enormous reservation and circumspection, to understand the different ways the religious—beyond my own Christian identity— has shaped me and my communities, and to understand what is at stake when we have lost, forgotten, or been stolen away from the rich medleys of the religious in Black life.

—Emilie M. Townes, *Womanist Ethics and the Cultural Production of Evil*

For those of us who are descendants of enslaved Africans, it was the spoken word that enslaved and liberated us . . . How can we de-center ourselves from our privileged positions of preacherly comfort, while simultaneously placing at the center of our sermons, teachings, thoughts, and actions, the constructive envisioning offered to us by the most marginalized amongst us?

—Stacey Floyd-Thomas, "That We May Dare to Suffer: The Moral Muster and Theological Urgency of Human Flourishing"

I fought my calling to the ministry for years. I would read the Bible and heed its warnings of the dire consequences for shepherds who misled their flocks. I didn't want to be in their number. But the example of my church's pastor, Dr. Frederick G. Sampson, II, proved irresistible. He was a tall, dashing, Romantic figure who preached without a single note before him, a habit I quickly acquired and thought was standard until I saw ministers read their homilies from manuscripts. He quoted from memory long passages of Shakespeare, Bertrand Russell, and W. E. B. Du Bois in the pulpit. He also recited from heart reams of poetry, from Thomas Gray's "Elegy Written in a Country Churchyard" to Langston Hughes's "The Negro Speaks of Rivers," both of which we performed in his study, at church or home, as we traded verses of the masters from memory. Sampson's profound combination of high intelligence and spiritual conviction convinced me that I should follow him into the ministry.

Even though I acknowledged "God's call on my life" at eighteen, it wasn't until just after my twenty-first birthday—after I had already become a teen father and husband, and then got divorced, and worked as an emergency substitute janitor, a clerk in the wood forms shop of an automobile company, a factory laborer, and then got accepted into a historically Black college in Knoxville just before my twenty-first year—that I got licensed to preach. I came home from college during the beginning of my freshman year for Thanksgiving break, in part to see my year-and-a-half-old son, to offer my maiden sermon. I warned my congregation of about 300 about the danger of divorcing technology from morality in the Age of Anxiety:

> Every age has a word that characterizes it, that expresses what Hegel called the Zeitgeist, the spirit of the times. Our age has been characterized by a word that sounds the plumb line of man's contemporary existence: anxiety. And this is not without reason. The twentieth century has been witness to amazing technological and industrial advantages . . .
>
> But we have not trained our moral lives to parallel the leaps and bounds of science into what Dr. Kenneth B. Clark has called a "moral technology." The attitude of many scientists doing the science is that morals are increasingly irrelevant in the pursuit of truth. They feel that morals should decrease as scientific research increases. This critically refutes the existence of the spiritual, and historically this has been dangerous.

I suppose the twenty-one-year-old me presaged my mature belief that knowledge cut off from ethics is potentially disastrous. After my ordination to the ministry, I pastored three churches in Tennessee, the last of which, in the early eighties, booted me when I decided, after teaching and preparing my congregation for a year, to ordain three women as deacons. Deciding against fighting gender oppression, the leadership of the church, egged on by local ministers who thought I was bringing shame to the male-dominated clergy, decided to fight me instead.

I returned to the southern Baptist college to which I had transferred—and from which I had been kicked out for protesting the dearth of Black speakers by skipping mandatory chapels—and graduated with a degree in philosophy. I attended graduate school in religion at Princeton University, and since then, I've taught at a number of schools, in a number of academic departments. At Vanderbilt University I have been reunited with my religious roots in African American Studies and the Divinity School.

No matter what academic department I've been associated with, I've always kept my feet planted in pulpits across the land, preaching the gospel extemporaneously, with rare exceptions, with no notes or manuscript after meditating on a passage of scripture. After all, that was the way Dr. Sampson preached. At times I headed to the pulpit to console mourners. At other times I challenged myself to grow in the same way that I challenged the congregations I'm privileged to address. I've tried in parts of my scholarship, and while donning my public intellectual hat, to wrestle with the philosophical and theological consequences of Christian faith, even as I've tried to subject my beliefs to rigorous self-examination, and even the doubt of non-believers, in the effort to tell as much truth as possible.

Holy Hallways

In Divinity School

13

What's Derrida Got to Do with Jesus?

I remember, as an undergraduate student, mentioning Jacques Derrida, Deconstruction's founder, as I was on the line with Cornel West. In 1983, I had used my last several dollars of quarters to call him at Union Theological Seminary in New York from a pay phone in Tennessee to introduce myself and discuss his first book. To my great surprise, he answered the phone. "I'm beginning to read Jacques Derrida," I said, pronouncing his last name as Duh-Ride-uh. "That's Derrida, Brother," he corrected me, pronouncing it as Dare-ree-dah. Ever since then, besides getting his name right, I've been trying to get his ideas right, too. This essay is from a late-1990s conference on religion at Harvard and is included in One Nation Under God? *co-edited in 1999 by Marjorie Garber, one of the conference's convenors.*

Rhetoric is an indispensable force in shaping narratives of Black cultural identity. Indeed, the narrativity of Black experience—the ways that stories constitute self-understanding and enable self-revelation—is powerfully glimpsed in a variety of rhetorical forms, from autobiographies to sermons, from novels to hip hop culture. These forms embody in complex and conflicting ways the collective racial effort to articulate the goals of survival, resistance, and excellence through the literacy of representative figures.[1] If we acknowledge the unavoidable storyness of human existence, then narrative can be viewed as a dominant shape of Black intelligence; speaking and writing can be viewed as the crucial rhetorical surfaces on which Black identity is inscribed.

This is particularly true with Black religious identities. Among its many functions, religious rhetoric is deployed to reinforce racial aspirations, situate intellectual and cultural expressions, articulate moral expectations and norms, and combat social evils, especially white supremacy. Although religious rhetoric is among the most vital spheres of cultural expression, it is virtually ignored by cultural studies, critical social and race theory, and poststructuralist theory.[2] This essay has a modest ambition: to examine Black sacred rhetoric—its ecclesiastical expression and its public moral function—through the lens of theory. I will begin by briefly addressing the racial and social function of Black rhetoric, especially oral traditions, since they are key to understanding Black sacred rhetoric. I will then discuss the importance of theory for Black discursive practices, particularly religious discourse. I will conclude by briefly reading through the lens of theory the public moral performance of Black sacred rhetoric in the speech of Malcolm X and Martin Luther King, Jr.

I

Oral traditions are a significant aspect of Black rhetoric. They serve a crucial genealogical function: They index how Blacks have passed history, memory, and culture over to contemporaries and down to the next generation. Of course, these processes of oral transmission are not static. People who engage rhetorical forms transform what they inherit. In that sense, these oral traditions exemplify Nietzschean and Foucauldian elements of genealogy as well: They mark how and when ideas, beliefs, values, and practices emerge and flourish.[3]

The genealogical effect of these oral traditions accentuates the essential constructedness of rhetorical practices, since such practices rely to a large degree on invented traditions of racial memory.[4] Such invented traditions suggest that racial memory is shaped by the intellectual parameters, social circumstances, historical limitations, and existential needs of a particular group or society.

Then, too, given the racist cultural context in which Black rhetorical practices have evolved, Black oral traditions have been deployed to mobilize racial agency against the ideology of white supremacy. White supremacy is shorthand for the institutional and cultural practices of white racial dominance that are intellectually justified by its exponents as normal and natural. In such a cultural milieu, Black rhetorical acts are read as unavoidable gestures of political contestation.

The social circumstances in which Black rhetoric has survived have also given Black oral traditions a surplus utility: supplying empirical verification of Black humanity while enabling the struggle for Black identity and liberation. Black rhetoric is thus implicated in bitter cultural debates about the value and status of Black intelligence. In many ways, orality and literacy, in Walter J. Ong's memorable phrase, are flip sides of rhetorical articulation.[5] In the contentious social climate in which Black rhetoric has usually functioned, it is central to claims about Black intelligence as evidenced in Black facility with reading, writing, and speaking.

Very often, however, beliefs about how Black intelligence and identity are marked by literacy and speech are not engaged in an explicit manner that reveals the ideological stakes and political predicates of such beliefs.[6] In this light, it makes sense to think of the paradoxical functions of Black rhetoric in two ways. First, Black rhetoric is used to assault the dominant culture's ideological *inarticulateness*—that is, the suppressed features and unspoken dimensions of its hegemony over Black culture. Second, Black rhetoric is fashioned to resist the *overarticulation* of negative readings and distorted images of Black life in the dominant culture's political economy of representations.[7]

Finally, Black rhetorical practices are shaped in an international and multiethnic context. As cultural theorists have recently argued, Black cultural meanings are generated in the intersection of diasporic cultures in the Black Atlantic—comprised of the United Kingdom, Caribbean, and the United States.[8] Hence, Black rhetorical practices are likewise polyvocal and multiarticulative: They register the accents of a variety of simultaneous, mutually reinforcing cultural voicings in a transnational zone of exchange, appropriation, and emulation. All in all, this emphasizes the radical mobility of Black narratives. The meanings and mediators of Black rhetoric move back and forth along—and certainly across—an ever enlarging circumference of ethnic experience and racial identity.

II

In theorizing the relation of race to rhetoric, intellectuals have largely drawn upon cultural studies, literary criticism, feminist theory, and critical race and social theory.[9] While the contribution of cultural studies scholars, literary critics, and critical race and social theorists to debates about race and language is well established—although not without controversy—it is neither obvious nor acceptable to some Black critics that they should employ European theories in explicating Black culture.[10] I think that French poststructuralist theory, for example, has a great deal to offer critics who interrogate the complex meanings of African American discursive and rhetorical practices.[11]

Of course, those French critics must not be fetishized or given undue deference. Nor should their thought be uncritically adapted to Black life without acknowledging the complicated process by which European theory has historically been deployed to colonize the psychic, intellectual, and ideological spaces of Black culture.[12] Colonization as a corollary to European theoretical transgression against indigenous, native, and subaltern populations—or more precisely, theoretical transgression as an adjunct to European colonial expansion—is reason enough for a healthy skepticism about such matters.[13] Still, the critical appropriation of poststructuralist theory by Black intellectuals can prove beneficial.

For example, parts of Jacques Derrida's theory of deconstruction might help illumine the relation of Black identity to rhetorical expression.[14] Derrida's critique of the conception of speech as expression independent of a transcendental object of inquiry rather than as a mode of articulation constitutive of its object of inquiry might strengthen the liberation of African American critical discourse from the quest for transcendental epistemic security within a framework of universal reason. This is helpful in at least two ways.

First, it relieves the "burden of representation," so that African American criticism is not viewed as the effort to suture the gaping theoretical wound produced by splitting truth from its discursive mode of expression.[15] Representational theories of truth are only relevant when one believes that accurate pictures of the world are possible.[16] Once one dismisses the quest for such a transcendental basis of epistemic authority and representational accuracy, one clears discursive space for a new conception of truth as a function of justifying beliefs by referring to the contingent practices of human reason. Truth cannot be known apart from the linguistic resources and intellectual grounds at our disposal. Hence, Black critics need not fear that by contending that truth is produced and known by fallible human beings that they are fatefully departing from epistemic strategies and philosophical procedures that allow others to know with certainty the objective world. On the view I have discussed, *all* human efforts to discover truth are similarly circumscribed, despite the apparently authoritative character of many epistemological claims.

The second consequence flows from the first: The political fallout of such a theory of truth is that all linguistic assertions, and the grounds of reason and morality that support them, are provisional rhetorical practices subject to revision as the telos of the social order is transformed through conflict and struggle. Thus, differential assertions about race are often predicated on conflicting social or group values within a hierarchy of racial perspectives that reflects a structural validation of certain views as more legitimate, hence more *reasonable*, than others.

This conception of reasonableness is widely viewed as the adjudicative force that resolves disputes, or that restores an illusory balance between rival claims to racial common sense. As a result, a contingent set of racial norms is made to appear natural and universal. In the process, supplying the necessary condition of the relative social and intellectual merits of racial claims is deceptively portrayed as the sufficient condition of such arguments. There is in turn a neat, even elegant, justification of the inherent superiority—i.e., the self-evident and logically irresistible character—of certain racial claims. By highlighting the logical means, rhetorical strategies and political ends that structure hegemonic racial practices—showing how the contingent is rendered permanent—Black critics help demystify the complex procedures by which racial hierarchy is maintained.

Another relevant feature of Derrida's theory of deconstruction is the accent on multiple meanings of sentential rationality and linguistic practice. This means that the horizon of meaning—and here, Gadamer's and Ricoeur's work is of paramount importance as well—is not closed by definitive hermeneutic acts or absolute notations of truth.[17] In determining a text's *meanings*—already that's a polemical plural, suggesting a break of the powerful link between authorial intentionality and textual interpretation, while also suggesting that a text might be a book, a social convention, a rhetorical practice, a film and so on—the emphasis is not on the singular meaning, the decisive reading, or the right interpretation, ideas premised on the belief that it is possible to exhaust the ways one might understand (*verstehen*) a text.[18] Rather, the question one asks of a text is not "What does it mean?" but "How does it signify?"[19] This is linked to Black critical reflections on signifying practices within Black diasporic cultures.[20] The simultaneous convergence of possible meanings underscores the multiple valences a text may generate. These valences index a political economy of expressive culture that produces a thick network of flexible readings which are an exercise in hermeneutical warfare.

Indeed, competing schemas of explaining and knowing the world are implicated in the readings, *re*readings, *mis*readings, and *anti*readings that flow from poststructuralism's jouissance. It might be useful as well to remember Michel Foucault's notion of the "insurrection of subjugated knowledges."[21] Such a notion sheds light on how marginalized discourses, suppressed rhetorics, decentered voicings, and subaltern speech have erupted along a trajectory of political struggles and discursive quests for self-justification, since the search for other-validation is arrested by the recognition that truth is contingent. In short, all quests for truth are interested and biased. The rise of such knowledges—signifying in part what Althusser termed an "epistemic break" with previous epistemological conditions, positions, and authorities—enables the articulative possibilities and rhetorical resources of minority cultures.[22]

But borrowing from my own theological tradition, I think we must baptize European cultural and social theories. It is not that Derrida, Foucault, Guattari, Deleuze, Lyotard, Kristeva, Irigaray, Baudrillard, and Barthes must be subject to a xenophobic rearticulation of American nationalist values. Neither is it the case that we should force them to show, as it were, their theoretical passports in order to traverse the semiotic or ideological borders of (African) American theory. Rather, we should shape poststructuralist theory to the peculiar demands of (African) American intellectual and social life. The translation of poststructuralist theorists with our rhetorical resonances, linguistic tics, and discursive habits challenges national biases and intellectual insularities on all sides of the Atlantic. We must make gritty the smooth surface of poststructuralist theories—which often enjoy untroubled travel to our intellectual shores—with the specificities of our racial and political struggles. This is especially the case as we theorize the links between rhetoric and Black identities.

III

In light of the intellectual richness of contemporary debates about Black rhetoric, and drawing on recent theory, I want to posit four crucial features of Black religious rhetoric: its *ontological mediation*, its *performative epistemology*, its *hermeneutical ubiquity*, and its *dense materiality*.[23] Ontological mediation stresses how Black religious narratives help structure relations between beings: horizontal relations between human beings, and vertical relations between human beings and God. Black religious discourse helps define, and mediate, the moral status of human existence. It also helps clarify the ethical ends human beings should adopt in forming human community, and the moral means they should employ in its defense. Black religious narratives define a relationship of human subordination to divine authority as the linchpin of personal redemption, while asserting moral transformation as the consequence of spiritual rebirth. Black religious narratives support the claim that human emancipation is rooted in observation of, and obedience to, divine imperatives of justice and equality.

The performative epistemology of Black religious narratives underscores the intimate relation between religious knowledge and social practice, and secondarily, the link between belief and behavior. In Black sacred rhetoric, a crucial distinction is made between *knowing about* God and *knowing* God. The former represents a strictly intellectual exercise devoid of fideistic commitments; the latter is rooted in the faithful assertion of a cognitive and personal relationship with the supreme supernatural being. The consequence of such cognition is the *performance of faith*, the *dramatization of devotion*, and the *behaving of belief*. In Black religious discourse, there is little substance or benefit to knowing God without *doing*, or performing, one's knowledge of God.[24]

Moreover, performative epistemology emphasizes that knowledge is not produced by having an accurate account of the relationship between truth and its representation, but by the relation of knowing to a grounding ideal of truth whose justification depends in part upon an appeal to human praxis. Performative epistemology also accents the engaged, humane, and political character of religious curiosity, linking the experience of knowing and loving God to knowing and loving human beings. Black religious discourse suggests that it is difficult, and indeed morally noxious, to know God and not do right in the world.

The hermeneutical ubiquity of Black religious discourse highlights the fecund interpretive properties to be found in all forms of Black sacred rhetoric, from homiletics to Sunday school pedagogy. I mean this in three ways. First, Black sacred rhetoric gives religious believers vast opportunity and great variety in interpreting their religious experience. Black religious narratives secrete interpretation as a function of their justification of a sacred cosmology. Black sacred rhetoric encourages the interpretation of faith in the light of reasoned articulation of the grounds of belief. Second, hermeneutical ubiquity suggests how Black religious narratives shape the interpretive activities of believers in secular intellectual and cultural environments. This encompasses two elements: the religious interpretation of ideas and events, including, for example, abortion, civil rights, the Million Man March, and feminism; and the interpretive strategies that believers adapt in the public square, including, for instance, the translation of religious passion into political language and the voicing of religious dissent to political policies and cultural practices in protest rallies.

Third, hermeneutical ubiquity casts light on how Black religious rhetoric seizes any event, crisis, idea, or movement as grist for its interpretive mill. Black sacred rhetoricians, especially Black preachers, constantly view, and interpret, the world through the prism of moral narratives generated in Black churches. Black religious narratives are relentlessly deployed by

Black sacred rhetoricians to carve an interpretive niche in political behaviors, social movements, cultural organizations, and institutional operations. Black sacred rhetoricians are interpretive cartographers as well: They map prophetic criticism onto social practice with an eye to reconstructing the geography of national identity.

Finally, Black sacred rhetoric, especially Black preaching, exhibits dense materiality, which refers to the rhythms, tones, lyricisms, and textures of Black religious language. Because the narrative generativity, semiotic strategies, and linguistic adaptability of Black religious discourse have influenced Black scholars, preachers, lawyers, doctors, scientists, and entertainers, Black sacred rhetoric should be much more rigorously examined and theorized.[25] Two brief examples, C. L. Franklin and Charles Gilchrist Adams, will illustrate Black sacred rhetoric's dense materiality (and the other features I have described) as it is institutionalized in ecclesiastical functions. Franklin and Adams are towering pulpiteers who, while they possess sharply contrasting styles, are formidable practitioners of Black homiletical art.[26]

Franklin, the late father of soul music idol Aretha Franklin, was a legendary preacher and pastor who was uniquely gifted in the style of Black preaching known technically as the "chanted sermon," and more colloquially as "whooping."[27] As a species of Black sacred rhetoric, whooping is characterized by the repetition of rhythmic patterns of speech whose effect is achieved by variation of pitch, speed, and rhythm. The "whooped" sermon climaxes in an artful enjambment or artificial elongation of syllables, a dramatic shift in meter and often a coarsening of timbre, producing tuneful speech. In the sacred spaces of Black worship, the performative dimension of Black rhetoric is acutely accented in whooping.

Moreover, the antiphonal character of Black ecclesiastical settings means that congregational participation is ritually sanctioned in the call-and-response between preacher and pew-dweller. The interactive character of Black worship exerts a profound rhetorical and material pressure on the preacher to integrate into her sermon hermeneutical gestures, semantic cues, and linguistic opportunities that evoke verbal response and vocal validation from the congregation. Franklin was a past master at deploying his vast rhetorical skills to orchestrate the religious rites and ecclesiastical practices of Black Christendom with flair and drama.

Charles Adams, who pastors a landmark Detroit religious institution, Hartford Avenue Memorial Baptist Church, is equally gifted. Adams was dubbed "The Harvard Whooper" because of his uncanny fusion of an intellectual acuity honed as a student at the Harvard Divinity School and a charismatic quality of folk preaching gleaned from his immersion as a youth in the colorful cadences of Black religious rhetoric. Adams's riveting sermonic style is characterized by a rapid-fire delivery; keen exegetical analyses of Biblical texts; the merger of spiritual and political themes; a far-ranging exploration of the varied sources of African American identity; and a rhythmic, melodic tone that, at its height, is a piercing rhetorical ensemble composed of deliberately striated diction, staccato sentences, stressed syllabic construction, alliterative cultural allusion, and percussive phrasing.

Further, Adams sacralizes the inherent drama of Black religious rhetoric by embodying its edifying theatrical dimensions. As preacher, he is both *shaman* and *showman*. In his brilliant pulpit oratory, Adams nurtures the sacrament of performance: the ritualized reinvestment of ordinary time and event with the theological utility of spectacle. Adams, for instance, has not only preached the Biblical story of a woman searching for a lost coin; he took a broom into the pulpit and dramatized the search for lost meaning in life and the need to reorder existential priorities.

Franklin and Adams provide a brilliant peek into Black preaching's dense materiality (and of its ontological mediation, its performative epistemology, and its hermeneutical ubiquity). Their art illumines as well Black sacred rhetoric's polysemous power, and the sanctification of language and imagination for salvific ends. They embody the ecclesiastical functions of eloquence, and the racial utility of religious articulation. They also show how Black sacred rhetoric's dense materiality does not negate its other linguistic features. For instance, these figures' rhetorical practices underscore the phenomenological merit of linguisticality—that sacred rhetoric possesses a self-reflexive quality that allows its users to reflect on and refine its constitutive elements. Such figures also highlight how words can lend ontological credence to racial identity, and how religious language can house an existential weight, a self-regenerating energy, that can be levied against the denials of Black being expressed in racist sentiment and practice. If Franklin and Adams embody the multiple utilities of Black sacred rhetoric in an ecclesiastical context, two other figures, Malcolm X and Martin Luther King, Jr., articulate its public moral posture. Both Malcolm and King sought to shape public moral discourse with the rhetorical resources of their respective religious traditions. After a brief discussion of theories of the public sphere and discourse, I will examine the public uses of Malcolm's and King's sacred rhetoric and moral discourse.

IV

Theories of the public sphere have received a great deal of attention in a variety of disciplines, primarily because of the influential work of Jürgen Habermas.[28] On the one hand, the public sphere has been conceptualized as a crucial component in explications of democratic theory. On the other hand, the exclusions of the bodies of women and (other) Blacks, for instance, from the theoretical articulations of the constitutive elements of the *res publica* (the common good), highlights the unjust, antidemocratic dimensions of conceptions of the public sphere.[29] Theorists like Nancy Fraser and Craig Calhoun have imaginatively extended and criticized Habermas's concept of the public sphere.

Fraser explores the philosophical and social consequences of Habermas's conception of the public sphere as a space where discourse constitutes public opinion; where issues of common concern are debated by members of the public as they deploy reason-giving as a means of rational persuasion; and where political decision making is energized by public opinions.[30] Fraser also presses Habermas as to how critical theory functions to enlighten or reinforce gender hierarchy in modern societies; how it either resists or replicates the ideological justification and rationalization for such hierarchy; and how it can clarify or muddy the terrain of struggle for contemporary women's movements.[31] A similar project—one that theorizes the multiple locations and uses of the public sphere—has been taken up with regard to the Black diaspora.[32]

Calhoun engages Habermas's notion of the public sphere by exploring how the public good is distinguished from private interest; by noting the institutions and means by which people are permitted to participate in the public sphere independent of patronage or political power; and by accentuating the conditions and forms of private existence that make it possible for individuals to act autonomously as critical agents in the public sphere.[33] Calhoun argues convincingly, and against Habermas, that there is not a single, authoritative public sphere, but a "sphere of publics"—matched by Fraser's conception of subaltern counter-publics, and "multiple publics" (including "strong" and weak" publics), distinguished by ideology, gender, class, profession, central mobilizing issue, and relative power.[34] They both argue that the multiple lines of interaction between publics must be tracked.

Fraser and Calhoun both criticize Habermas for his failure to acknowledge alternate publics and alternate routes of public life (such as were constructed by various groups of women in the nineteenth century).[35] And both Calhoun and Fraser recognize that the question of "identity-formation," or the "politics of recognition," must be viewed as a public, not a private, matter, and that they must be theorized within the public spheres in which they are constructed and reproduced.[36]

Discourse is also a crucial concept in social and cultural theory. Poststructuralist thought, especially the work of Foucault, has generated tremendous interest in the conceptual and social functions of discourse. Despite the influence of structuralism on his early work, Foucault's conception of discourse marked a break with the marginalization in structuralism of acute analysis of social phenomena and thick historical detail. Instead, structuralists highlighted governing laws, forms, and structures. Foucault attempted to transcend—or better yet, discard—binaristic thinking, taking a leap of discursive imagination beyond a Kierkegaardian either/or, accentuating instead the variable, subjective character of linguistic and social phenomena.[37] Foucault eventually embraced a genealogical project—derived in name and nature from Nietzsche—an intellectual enterprise that discarded metaphysics, grand theories, foundational myths, timeless epistemic warrants, teleological philosophies, deep structures, unyielding essences, unifying centers of reason, and *Heilsgeschichte* (sacred history).[38]

Counterposed to Enlightenment reason's obsession with uncovering the basis of unmediated truth—a project undermined by Derrida's deconstruction of metaphysical dualism, rationalist epistemology, and hierarchical ontology in his attack on logocentrism—Foucault's genealogical project attempts to bring to light how dominant discourses render certain ideas normative, certain practices natural, certain interests invisible, and certain powers discrete. Discourse underscores the construction of meanings that shape and organize both individual and social actions and self-conceptions.[39] Discourse aids us in comprehending how what is thought and spoken is situated within a matrix with its own particular history and its peculiar grounds and conditions of existence.[40]

Foucault viewed discourse as a successor concept to Marx's concept of ideology.[41] Foucault claimed that ideology was a problematic concept because it presupposes the existence of truth in opposition to the untruth, or lies, that the concept of ideology is used to uncover;[42] that the concept refers to the subject (whose intellectual death Foucault's work proclaimed); and finally, that ideology is a secondary effect of a primary, determinative economic and material infrastructure.[43] Instead, for Foucault, normalization, regulation, and surveillance are the conceptual hat-trick that registers how power is dispersed over a field of discursive practices. The institutionalization of rival discursive regimes of truth produces effects of domination marked in power operations that fix normative gazes (a historicization of Sartrean ontology, especially "le regard"); regulate the dispersal of knowledges (a pluralization and politicization of Cartesian epistemology); and that rationalize surveillance as an ineluctable and necessary condition of social reality (a technologization of Benthamite penology). But as Stuart Hall points out, Foucauldian genealogy, with discourse at its analytical heart, is not significantly different from notions of domination that can be explored through the concept of ideology.[44]

Theories of the public, and of discourse—and other postcolonial, political and critical social and race theories—should be kept in mind as we explore the public functions of the religious rhetoric of Malcolm X and Martin Luther King, Jr.[45] Malcolm X was supremely skilled in several aspects of Black oral artistry. Indeed, his "broad familiarity with the devices of African-American oral culture—the saucy put-down, the feigned agreement turned to oppositional advantage, the hyperbolic expression generously employed to make a point, the fetish for powerful metaphor—marks his public rhetoric."[46] Furthermore, Malcolm articulated a powerful "Black public theodicy" that was "rooted in a theological vision that lent religious significance to the unequal relationship between whites and Blacks," and that rejected the belief that "Black people should redeem white people through bloodshed, sacrifice and suffering."[47] Malcolm's Black public theodicy led him to the conclusion that "white violence must be met with intelligent opposition and committed resistance, even if potentially violent means must be adopted in self-defense against white racism."[48]

Central to Malcolm's religious beliefs was a vehement verbal assault on white supremacy. Through his rhetoric of opposition, Malcolm helped constitute and articulate a Black counter-public that revealed itself through the discursive practices of an alternative Black religious *Weltanschauung*.[49] For Malcolm—and for the Nation of Islam to which he belonged—the Black public sphere was not only obsessed with resisting white attacks on Black being, but with bitterly opposing the discourse of Black Christian piety, and its public counterpart, civil rights ideology. By emphasizing the "tricknology" and the brainwashing of Black people, achieved by the discursive deceit and rhetorical duplicity of white society, Malcolm meant to underscore the destructive consequences of Blacks adopting white religious rhetoric and belief.

Malcolm also wanted to ridicule the discourse of Black bourgeois public morality, which he thought was predicated on Black capitulation to white intellectual hegemony. Further, the rhetoric of civil rights implied an accommodationist posture to the very political structures that had made Blacks "victims of democracy." In that specific sense, Malcolm's public rhetoric of opposition to the ideological articulation of white supremacy—and his rhetorical resistance to Black moral surrender to cultural hegemony—evinced an appreciation for what some orthodox Marxists would term "false consciousness."[50] Malcolm's Black counter-public—constituted by Black Islamic religious belief, racial rhetoric, and the discursive practices of Black nationalism—was not only articulated against the discursive practices of white romantic nationalism (the uncritical celebration of all things deemed purely American); but it also countered Black Christian practices articulated in public as the ethical expression of religious narratives of charity and redemptive suffering.

Within the discursive practices and narrative strategies that comprised the Black Islamic counter-public, Malcolm X articulated three rhetorics: the rhetoric of reinventions, the rhetoric of rage, and the rhetoric of violence. For Malcolm, the rhetoric of reinvention had to do with the discursive distance between white religious rhetoric and moral indoctrination, and the racial reconstruction, religious rebirth, and moral transformation forged in the crucible of Islam. The rhetoric of reinvention had to do with conversion, the remaking of the ego, and the ideal spiritual self in light of the religious narratives that are crucial to sustaining Black dignity, identity, and survival. For Malcolm, this meant a direct repudiation of the ideological distortions, rhetorical fallacies, and racial corruptions associated with white Christianity.

For Malcolm, the rhetoric of rage was enabled by the rhetoric of reinvention: It was not until Malcolm was able to secede from the discursive union of false consciousness and distorted self-identity that he could embrace the righteous anger that is the consequence of Black spiritual rebirth.[51] Prior to being reborn within the womb of Black Islamic belief, Malcolm lacked the rhetorical resources and intellectual discipline to surgically analyze the discursive operations of white domination and to pinpoint the massive public articulation of the discourse of white superiority. His rhetoric of rage against the machinery of white distortions and dogmatisms was matched by his relentless verbal denunciations of Black apathy and racial surrender. In one sense, Malcolm's anger at white foes and Black folks was made possible because he shed the secular seductions attached to the hustling life he previously prized and clung to the moral puritanism of the Nation of Islam. The cultic dimensions of the religious group generated for him a discursive framework, rhetorical weaponry, and an existential raison d'être that countered the erosion of Black self-confidence, and the promotion of Black self-loathing, in the religious cul-de-sacs of the white public sphere.

Finally, Malcolm's use of the rhetoric of violence has been much maligned and misunderstood. Malcolm's fundamental point was that Black people should be prepared to defend themselves in the face of white hostility. In Malcolm's view, America was created because a group of citizens refused any longer to be oppressed and exploited, and violently defended their self-interests, and their burgeoning collective national awareness, in war. In short, violence was a profoundly American tradition. It was a central force in national self-definition and social practice. Malcolm insisted that the same logic of social practice, group identification, and ideological consolidation be applied to the Black liberation struggle.

In this light, Malcolm held that the white demand for Blacks to forgo their birthright as American citizens to violently defend their interests in the face of unprincipled, systematic attack was logically flawed and morally indefensible. The rhetoric of violence became a way for Malcolm to use American self-definition and identity as tropes. He posited his reading of American history as the intellectual corrective to the distorting pedagogy of oppression being perpetuated in the white public sphere. For Malcolm, Black violence was a morally justifiable reaction to an already existing condition of spiritual and physical violence that threatened the self-hood and, literally, the safety of Black people.

In sharp contrast, King's rhetorical opposition to the discursive and material provinces of violent white public spheres—with their discourses of moral purity, intellectual superiority, and racial supremacy—was predicated on the effort to fuse Black public spheres with the morally enlightened white public.[52] King sought to transform the white American public sphere by appealing to a broadly shared set of beliefs that held national citizenship and identity together.[53]

King's public moral discourse was inherited from a Black discursive and rhetorical tradition in which religious narratives of unearned suffering, patient protest, and political accommodation were juxtaposed to narratives of radical social resistance, violent self-defense, and justifiable subversion of the civil order. In so doing, King deployed a number of rhetorical strategies gleaned from his Black Baptist heritage.

First, a crucial rhetorical strategy that King adapted involved the ingenious public performance of the intradiscursive character of Black Christian religious discourse: that human speech can lead to more speech, or different speech, that can help alter human behavior. The gist of this strategy is to convince the participants and opponents of a moral crusade—*through rhetoric*—that spiritual and moral rhetoric has the capacity to catalyze human action toward the transformation of the public sphere.[54] Rhetoric can be used to morally energize participants to revive their flagging efforts; and it can be employed to motivate opponents to change their hateful, destructive behavior, and to alter customs, habits, and traditions that prevent Black liberation.

The belief in rhetoric's power to transform human behavior and social relations was linked to religious narratives that advocated transformation through moral trial, reinvention through self-examination, conversion through confrontation with the ultimate good, and redemption through suffering. For King and other Black religious figures, their rhetoric rang with moral authority because its ethical claims and public performances were inspired by imminent contact with a transcendent God. King often spoke of civil rights devotees enjoying "cosmic companionship." Thus, their rhetoric and social practices were motivated by belief in a God who gave believers the power to speak and act in ways that transform personal sentiments, group thinking, and social structures. Religious rhetoric—and its translations in civil society and its articulations in other public spheres— was an important vehicle for such transformation.

This latter feature highlights another rhetorical strategy employed by King: He fused the language, rhythms, and modes of Black sacred rhetoric with civic rhetoric and civil religious symbols in American society. In short, King bombarded the white public sphere with discursive remnants from hegemonic civil culture to argue for the inclusion of Black counterpublics, suppressed rhetorics, and subjugated knowledges. His ingenuity consisted in arguing that such publics, knowledges, and rhetorics were not only crucial resources to sustain and refashion American democracy; but that they were indeed a more faithful, authentic articulation of the original meanings and high moral intent of the American republic. When King appealed to the Declaration of Independence and the Constitution, he did so with an eye to making religiously inspired uses of the secular documents that undergird civil society and that codify its basic beliefs about the character of American citizenship. He deployed those documents—along with the beliefs about democracy they encouraged and the rhetoric of equality they mobilized—as a rhetorical vehicle to express his religious interpretations of justice, freedom, and equality. King's religious beliefs were the impetus for his rhetorical efforts to translate an ethic of *love as justice* in public discourse and practice. King linked his understanding of social transformation to the quest for the public good through the language of civic virtue and civil rights.

The public moral discourse deployed by Malcolm and King reveals the multiple utilities of Black religious rhetoric. By viewing their speech—and the rhetoric of Black religion in general—through the prism of theory, several aims can be achieved. First, we can further locate and illumine how their rhetoric functions within Black discursive practices. Second, we can isolate examples of their ideological abridgments of Black sacred rhetoric in the translation from ecclesiastical to public contexts. Third, we can examine the aesthetic and stylistic repertoire of religious figures who make imaginative use of Black sacred rhetoric. Fourth, we can cast a brighter intellectual light on the complex forms of intertextuality, intradiscursivity, and intersubjectivity constituted through Black religious narratives.

And finally, we can better grasp the ritualized mediation of polyvalent racial significations through Black religious practices, such as heteroglossia or "speaking in diverse tongues." In fact, heteroglossia can serve as a metaphor for the psychic, social, and discursive distance between competing vocabularies of rationality within American, indeed, Western, culture.[55] But perhaps most important, theory will be baptized in the fires of Black culture, transformed by the lived, material force of Black religious practices.

14

The Prophetic Passions of a Black Radical Evangelical

I first met William August Jones—twice named one of Ebony *maga- zine's fifteen greatest Black preachers—in 1980, when he preached at the Knoxville, Tennessee, church where I served as a pulpit assistant and eventually minister of visitation. It was my job to pick him up from his hotel, and I was excited to meet this linguistic wizard and transcendent wordsmith. As he packed his suitcase, he shared with me wise words. "Young man, it is easier as a young preacher to damn people to the heap pile of fallen humanity than it is to get in there and help them out. The older I get, the more I preach about grace. I sup- pose it's because I need more of it." His brilliant theological manifesto,* God in the Ghetto, *was re-released in 2021, and I had the privilege to write this foreword.*

I

His room-rattling voice is what first impressed you about William August Jones, Jr. It was a rich, rumbling, basso profondo that resonated in sanc- tuaries and auditoriums across the world. His dulcet tone recalled a story about Southern Baptist preacher Carlyle Marney that was true of Jones too: he had a voice like God's, only deeper. Sure, he was tall and beige and handsome with a regal bearing. Yes, he was sublimely self-confident in a way that only Black men can be when their gifts demand a stature that the white world worked hard to deny. But his vocal register suggested that his voice was a divine instrument to make people listen.

His rhetorical gifts would have tickled Kenneth Burke and made Aristo- tle proud. His vocabulary was spiced with "ineluctable," "lustrous," "bi- furcated," "vitiate," and "truncated," words that might have easily turned up on an SAT exam. But in his golden throat those words sounded strangely familiar. His alluring alliteration delighted his eager listeners.

As a Brooklyn divine, Jones shared the spotlight with Gardner Taylor, another legendary pulpiteer. Taylor's art was expansive, his craft encyclopedic, his method expository. He carved conceptual pathways through a dense forest of lively language. His sermons made masterful use of pregnant pauses and strategic silence. What was heard wasn't always what was said, but rather, what was implied in his dramatically shifting cadences. Jones's masterly artistry rested on a relentless will to knowledge. He effortlessly translated theology and social theory into accessible rhetoric. He brilliantly blended ancient Black wisdom and rigorous philosophical reflection in his melodic verbal quilt. His craft borrowed from the blues in turning melancholy to hope and by comically bending tragedy to the shape of irony. Jones's blues epistemology flashed in shifting paces and modulated tempos as he offered lyrical ripostes to Black suffering and racial injustice. His speech and passion could rise or fall in a flutter of phrases that unspooled in staccato fury. Or his insight could flow in a flurry of words that glided along his poetic trajectory. Taylor's sweeping verbal compositions nimbly arranged a Duke Ellington–like symphony of words. Jones's laconic bursts of witty scatting and the intermezzo flights of formal fancy were all Louis Armstrong.

Jones's deeply imaginative sermon "The Low Way Up," for instance, glitters in interpretive magic and rhetorical invention. Jones poignantly paints the occasion as the Lord's circle of intimates heatedly debated their place in holy history. The disciples, Jones says, "sit after sundown at supper, wondering who's going to be the bigshot in the Kingdom of God." Jones's lively alliteration proves to be the literary appetizer. His poetic license thrusts him into the fray between divine destiny and human desire. Jones dramatically sets the scene in "the sweeping slopes of Hermon," as "the Master prayed" that the ominous cup of death might pass him. Jones captures the fateful tension between disciple and master as Peter rejects Jesus's prophecy of his own imminent demise by saying, according to Jones, "Lord, this can't happen to you," which draws a stern rebuke from the Messiah.

Jones rachets up the rhetorical fury even more as he portrays the epic theological battle between human circumstance and divine will. "And then, with the crisis swelling to bewildering proportion," Jones says, his voice climbing precipitously to a thundering crescendo. "With the shepherd about to be slain, and the sheep about to be scattered!" Finally, the pressure relents, Jones's voice gently recedes, and Jesus's fate resolves as he embraces the destiny he was sent to earth to fulfill. This epochal upheaval and cosmic reversal are brilliantly telegraphed in Jones's dramatic declaration of "Gethsemane beckoning and Calvary calling."

"The Low Way Up" doesn't just address the churning urgency of an earthly aspiration toward heavenly reward. It also knowingly glosses the perilous pilgrimage of Peter, and by extension, all of us, toward spiritual maturity. Jones's reading out loud the passage that grounds his sermon is a lesson in the ethics of the public rendering of Holy Writ. It is as an exercise in Black signifying where recitation, through manipulation of tone and pace, is at once exposition and homiletical deconstruction. Jones reverse engineers the King James Version and reconstructs it in the crucible of Black voice, Black vision, Black virtue. "And the Lord said, Simon, Simon, behold, Satan hath desired to have you, that he may sift you as wheat: But I have prayed for *thee*"—Jones's Kentucky brogue resounds in quaint emphasis on that archaic one-syllable replacement for "you"—"that thy faith fail not: and when thou art converted, strengthen thy brethren."

Jones interprets the passage to eloquently chastise the self-righteous. "When you get up there real close to God, where you can smell the sweet incense burning on the heavenly altar—watch out!" Jones fairly threatens. And he alerts the pious about the hazards awaiting them as they scale the mountain of faith. "While you're climbing, watch your footing, for even the heights of spirituality are slick and slippery." Jones offers commonsense wisdom gleaned from the ethical imperatives of ordinary Black folk. "Every day, as you make your way, build up some credits that God can't take away: Treat people right. Love everybody. Speak no evil."

Jones was justly hailed for his rhetorical genius and linguistic mastery, but his prophetic passions were equally impressive. Jones believed that human affairs must be shaped by the ethical demands of the Gospel. He agreed with his colleague and former Riverside Church pastor, Ernest T. Campbell, that Christians shouldn't "retreat into the womb of an ahistorical piety." His Black radical evangelical faith encouraged him, as theologian Karl Barth counseled, to head to the pulpit with a Bible in one hand and the newspaper in the other. The part of the Barth quote usually not cited is that one must read the newspaper in light of the Bible, and that Jones routinely did.

He read what human beings did in court, or in the concrete jungles of the nation, or in cathedrals and sanctuaries—all of which was reported in the papers—through the moral lens of the Gospel. Jones insisted that the radical demands of justice be met by political figures and unjust administrations or regimes. As he argued in his sermon "On Prophets and Potentates," the "Christian's first loyalty ought always to be to God and not to government." Jones also praised the prophet Jeremiah for confronting "evil men and sinful structures in the name of the Lord." Jones preached that Jeremiah was "God's prophet, and without trembling he preached to potentates," and "remained faithful to the prophetic function." The same can be said of Jones himself.

II

And yet, as much as Jones's prophecy held sway in the pulpit, it can be argued that we were not quite prepared for the rigorous and exacting sociological analysis, ethical reflection, and theological meditation Jones offers in his scholarly 1979 book, *God in the Ghetto*. The sheer audacity to send that seminal work into the world without a subtitle is noteworthy. There were no theoretical justifications offered to qualify his assertion about the divine presence in the ghetto. There was no query as to the efficacy of the proposition that God might be found in such scandalous surroundings.

The theological scandal of particularity is one thing, that is, that God decided to take up residence in human history in one human being by putting on the flesh of Jesus. But the suggestion that God might be housed in the trauma and brutality of the ghetto is unthinkable to many. Neither was Jones using the term ironically, or sarcastically, or with paternalistic condescension. He insisted that Jesus's birth in Bethlehem was eerily similar to what we call a ghetto: a zone of habitation shaped by racial injustice and deliberately depleted of social resource and subject to stigma and exposed to cruel systemic inequality.

By the time he published his book, there had been many sociological classics on the ghetto. There was Elliot Liebow's pioneering ethnography *Tally's Corner: A Study of Negro Streetcorner Men*, penned more than a decade before Jones's book in 1967, and two years before that, in 1965, Kenneth Clark's searing *Dark Ghetto: Dilemmas of Social Power*. Jones's book arrived almost a decade before William Julius Wilson's magisterial 1987 study *The Truly Disadvantaged: The Inner City, the Underclass, and Public Policy*. Their revealing subtitles emphasize even more the heuristic courage of Jones leaving his title naked and untethered before the world. Jones's colorful and prophetic social ethical analysis of the ghetto was a genuinely insightful addition to the literature.

Jones's book was published in the last year of a heady decade of political progress after the bruising sixties when the Kennedy brothers succumbed to assassins' bullets and Martin Luther King, Jr., was cut down on a desolate balcony in Memphis in 1968. By 1970, Kenneth Gibson was elected as the first Black mayor of a major Northeastern city when he took the helm of Newark, New Jersey. In 1971, the Congressional Black Caucus was formed with 13 founding members, including Shirley Chisholm, John Conyers, and Ron Dellums. Later that year Jesse Jackson, King's most formidable mentee, founded Operation PUSH. In 1972, Chisholm became the first Black person to run for the Democratic presidential nomination. That year the first National Black Political Convention convened in Gary, Indiana. Amiri Baraka was a driving force and Jesse Jackson famously asked, and answered, what many there repeated: "What time is it? Nation time."

In 1973, Maynard Jackson became the first Black mayor of Atlanta. A few months earlier, Tom Bradley became the first Black mayor of Los Angeles. He was re-elected four times, but he was defeated in his run for governor in '82 (and '86) despite being ahead in the polls. This resulted in "the Bradley effect," where white voters pledge support of a Black candidate for fear of being thought of as racist but fail to back them in the voting booth. In 1974, Coleman Young became the first Black mayor of Detroit. In 1976, Barbara Jordan was the first Black woman to offer a keynote address at the Democratic National Convention, and the next year, Patricia Roberts Harris became the first Black woman to hold a cabinet position as Secretary of Housing and Urban Development. Harris was confirmed shortly before the miniseries *Roots* aired on national television and broke ratings records as it schooled the nation about slavery. In 1979, the year Jones published his book, mainstream hip hop enjoyed its first blush of popularity with the release of the Sugarhill Gang's "Rapper's Delight."

The social and political gains of upwardly mobile and high-achieving Black Americans were aided by affirmative action policies. But the economic outlook for the most vulnerable remained dismal. Inflation and a downturn in the economy because of a recession drove unemployment dramatically higher, pushed real income down, and exacerbated the poverty rates for those at the bottom. Deindustrialization, the precipitous shift from manufacturing to service industries, the grip of the steel collar with automated technology that hemorrhaged resources and shed jobs—all of this happened while white racial resentment intensified. The seventies were greeted by Nixon's southern strategy, and his racially pernicious war on drugs, at the decade's start, while Ronald Reagan's brutal continuation of that war, and his callous war against the poor and the masses of Black folk, loomed large at its end. Jones's *God in the Ghetto* provided a theological lifeline for Black pastors who sought to link ministry with prophetic thought and social activism.

Jones brought his homiletical skills to bear on his thesis—both his premise that a prophetic religion must combat social injustice in the ghetto, and on this book, the revised dissertation he submitted in 1975 to complete his Doctor of Ministry degree at Colgate Rochester Divinity School under the leadership of legendary scholar Henry H. Mitchell. But Jones also flexed his considerable scholarly muscles. There are many remarkably gifted preachers who hone their rhetorical gifts and harness their oratorical abilities in the discipline of delivering sermons. There are many extremely talented scholars who reflect brilliantly on the social and moral forces that beleaguer Black life, including our religious institutions. And there are many superb writers who command nouns and verbs and other parts of speech to tell as much Black truth as possible. It is rare enough that any given figure can do one of these well. It is rarer still that a figure can do two of these well. It is inarguably most rare that a figure can do all three, or, in the vernacular, that they can say it, think it and write it. Jones was a past master of Black sacred speech, a talented scholar of social ethics, and a fluid writer of the Black experience.

Jones brings together his considerable gifts in *God in the Ghetto*. It is remarkable how Jones uncannily anticipates subsequent scholarly trends. He is a harbinger for the discourse of Ibram X. Kendi in 2019, as Jones summarizes a strain of racism that perversely sees its vision as truly American: "To be antiracist is to be anti-American." He anticipates Andrew Hacker's 1992 *Two Nations* book that was inspired by the Kerner Commission when Jones writes that the "two Americas of which the Kerner Commission speaks are in fact already existing." He anticipates Eric Holder's controversial argument in 2009 that we are "a nation of cowards" because "outside the workplace . . . there is almost no significant interaction between us." Jones writes that "the basic institutions of American society remain sharply segregated. Blacks and whites do not work or play on a peer basis." And before Isabel Wilkerson's 2010 *Warmth of Other Suns*, her epic narrative about the migrations of Black folk from the South, Jones wrote that these "erratic wanderings typified the deep thirst and the insatiable appetite for full freedom impossible to realize in the cruel and callous South." But there is much more.

In seven vigorously argued chapters, Jones addresses forces that sap the economic vitality and social viability from Black life. Jones builds his case carefully, logically and systematically. He posits an ideological superstructure—"The System"—that regulates the flow of capital to the wealthy, destabilizes the economic situation of the poor, deprives the Black masses of social legitimacy, and overdetermines the racial prospects of striving African Americans.

In "The Ghetto: Symbol of the System," Jones specifies how the ghetto is the system writ small, or better yet, the system as an ideological minstrel rendered in political blackface. Jones looks at the plantation while keeping an eye on economic circumstances that harm the life chances of the Black poor. In doing so, Jones traces a genealogy of the ghetto that is both Nietzschean, linking the morality of its constitutive elements to the very power to create it, and Foucauldian, offering a counter-history of the ghetto that sketches the idea's development through subversive history.

In "The Larger Ghetto," Jones tracks the global reach of imperialism as so-called third-world nations and peoples of color contend with what Colin Morris calls the "unyoung, uncolored and unpoor." In "Social Aberrations in Ghetto Life," Jones walks a fine line between what Daniel Patrick Moynihan termed the "tangle of pathology" that ensnared poor Black families, and a vigorous unmasking of the structural forces that plague the Black ghetto.

In "The Involvement of Racistic Religion," Jones's Black radical evangelicalism rings out as he hammers white evangelicals for justifying and reinforcing white supremacy. Jones says bluntly that the "ghetto is a creation of white America with its racist religion." In "God and the Ghetto," Jones's prophetic vision gathers near-apocalyptic intensity as he unleashes holy venom on those who deny democracy and justice to God's darker devotees. Jones envisions the poor enjoying favored nation status with God and not citizens of imperial powers. The ghetto becomes a metaphor for all of those locked out of society's economic and moral resources. God is familiar with the ghetto. "He grew up in a ghetto," Jones writes of Jesus. "He sat and supped with sinners. He and his men went without wallets and lived mainly on handouts. In a real sense, they were on the Galilee welfare rolls."

"Confronting the System" is Jones's most in-depth analysis of the American empire. It is his most sophisticated demystification of American exceptionalism. And it is a searing demythologization of manifest destiny. Jones offers a trenchant indictment of a religion that is, if not the opiate of the masses, at least their intoxicating elixir. Jones provides a political demonology that charts the vices of both white and Black religious practice. The downfall of white evangelical belief is the arrogance of whiteness and the erasure of any difference between the status quo and the Kingdom of God. But Jones also accuses many Black preachers of being "a hindrance to the advancement of the Black cause." He says they are "inactive in the struggle because of their failure to see the social implications of the Gospel," concluding that they "are unconscious allies of racistic religion." Jones writes that to "awaken many Black preachers to the prophetic task is an awesome but necessary responsibility." His book remains a stirring call to such a task.

William August Jones, Jr., inspired thousands of ministers with his prophetic ministry. Two supremely gifted men in particular, mentored by Jones, carry his majestic vision and prophetic vocation into civil rights and the pastoral pulpit. Al Sharpton's brilliant political oratory owes a debt to Jones, who baptized him into the Baptist tribe and offered him an edifying model of public ministry. Sharpton's genius resides in his ability to wring deep wisdom from both the vernacular formulations of Black folk culture and the high-minded principles of the Black elite.

Sharpton's social activism is a bridge between prophetic demands of the Gospel and charismatic forms of Black Protestant worship. Sharpton was a rhetorical prodigy, a boy preacher and homiletic wunderkind who began to speak the Word at four years of age. His Pentecostal pedigree intersected vividly with his Baptist prophetism to yield an intriguing mixture of mournful lamentations and incisive jeremiads. While many have heard Sharpton's canny and daring exegeses of civil rights traumas visited upon the souls of Black folk, fewer in the mainstream know the Sharpton who can "tune," "whoop," or preach the "chanted sermon": a practice where spoken words are melded in magical melodies that rip from the preacher's mouth in pleasing rhythms and charming cadence.

Beyond his sweet speech, Sharpton has used his itinerant pulpit to call a nation to repentance for its racial sins as the foremost Black leader of this age. The mark of William August Jones, Jr., is imprinted in his rhetoric, his responsible civil disobedience and his relentless advocacy for the vulnerable.

Like his nineteenth-century namesake, Frederick Douglass Haynes, III, a Jones acolyte, is an orator of surpassing gifts who commands the stage with prophetic panache. His rhetorical genius is evident to all who hear him. His superior grasp of the English language is abundantly clear. He weaves in and out of sermons in sentences loaded with verbs that carry the interpretive work and adjectives that modify the actions he encourages us to undertake. His use of metaphor and alliteration lulls us to "peep"—the insights that brim in each line of oratory he shares; the profound analysis he offers in either brief verbal scope or extended linguistic trajectory; and the consummate control of story to illustrate the mysteries of faith.

Haynes flows in the holy bombast of relentless religious rhetoric geared toward rapid-fire delivery. He effortlessly switches to staccato bursts of electrifying cadence that conduct the train of truth on the rails of reasoned speech. Haynes's rhetoric is a seamless fusion of jazz-like riffs and hip hop bars. His verbal debts range from Harlem Renaissance New Negro creations to postmodern Black vernacular. He can warm himself in old-school Black homiletical fires. Or he can bring new-school flavor in sermons that declare war on pedantry and obfuscation. And his poetic meter spills forth in sonic eloquence as he measures out the feet of hip hop verse while he traverses the scriptural terrain with the beautiful feet of the prophet.

Haynes's prophetic imagination forms a pregnant cloud above the literary landscape. He routinely rains down the righteous fury of God on the systemic sin and structural inequality that strain mercy and stain grace. Some white evangelicals attempt to kidnap God. Others attempt a theological heist of the Kingdom's hermeneutical riches. Haynes carpet bombs their liturgical strongholds and ritual outposts through kerygmatic guerrilla combat to liberate our conception of the Almighty. He takes no prisoners in holy warfare against the distortions and misinterpretations of the Word that suggest that God is on the side of the oppressor.

Both Sharpton and Haynes, and many, many more, owe huge gratitude to the formidable ministry of one of our greatest preachers and thinkers ever. Jones was an incomparable wordsmith, and, like his words about Jesus, a "prophet without peer [and] priest without equal." We have a great deal to thank him for. His rhetorical prowess. His majestic homilies. His haunting eloquence. His inspiring advocacy for the weak and lonely, the neglected and abused. And, especially at this moment, a powerful book that unequivocally states and convincingly argues that God is, indeed, in, and for, the ghetto. All of this makes William Augustus Jones, Jr., one of the foremost advocates of Black radical evangelical belief in our nation's history. And like those other highly touted rhetoricians from Brooklyn, Christopher Wallace and Shawn Corey Carter, he ranks among the greatest poets and prophets to ever call the Brook their home.

Do You Hear What I Hear?

God in the Public Square

15

Abraham, Isaac, and Us

(and Hagar and Ishmael and Trayvon and Michael Brown, Too)

The biblical story of Abraham and Isaac is often cited to suggest that God always has a ram in the bush, a last-minute substitute for us as we are spared a cruel fate. And yet, far too often, especially for Black and other children of color in our society, there is no sparing them a tragic fate. This essay appeared in 2015 in The Good Book: Writers Reflect on Favorite Bible Passages, *edited by Andrew Blauner.*

The story of Abraham being commanded by God to surrender his son as a burnt offering as proof of his love for the Almighty has always bothered me. It's not that I think that God doesn't have the right to put those of us who believe in God to the test. After all, I'm a university professor who tests his students all the time, even if the stakes aren't nearly as high. One might think by the horrified reaction of some of them that I was asking them to sacrifice their firstborn. That's a curious sight to see since most of them aren't yet parents.

To be fair, many of my students have been victims of a culture of high stakes testing in our public schools that has got way out of hand. The debate about what we take to be standard, and about the standards we observe in the pursuit of solid education, is plagued by racial injuries and cultural scars that have never fully healed. In many schools across the nation, the stakes are too high when standardized tests are used to determine promotion to the next grade, or what courses one might take, or what curriculum might be followed, or even if one graduates from school. I spent many days in Florida with activists arguing that the Florida Comprehensive Assessment Test (FCAT) was unjustly used to block the high school graduation of Black and Latino students who failed the test but successfully completed their course work. Testing is never devoid of social forces and political choices that test our commitment to equality and justice for all children.

God's tests are steeped in politics, too, and a fair bit of philosophy and theology as well. That's especially true in the case of Abraham, who believes he heard the voice of God tell him to sacrifice his only son. How does Abraham, or any of us, ever really know that we've heard God's voice and not our own desires or fears, our own hatreds and suspicions, or our own intuitions and dreams dressed up as divine will? How do we know we're not merely sanctifying our social norms or deifying our political instincts when we say that God is telling us to believe or behave a certain way?

Take, for instance, trying to decide between moving to Michigan and moving to Minnesota for work. What roles do my racial identity and political ideology play in how I discern God's will? Does God work within my biases to protect me from exposure to ideas that I find harmful or distasteful, while upholding my preferences and validating my experiences? Is that why few Black pastors feel called to white churches in Maine, or why few white churches in New Hampshire extend a call to Black pastors, despite Martin Luther King, Jr., immortalizing their "prodigious hilltops" in his famous "I Have a Dream" speech? Does the divine will merely track human intention, and how do we know the difference between the two?

One answer to this question subscribes to the notion that there is a transcendent truth that eclipses the limits of our human understanding. Many believers seek to avoid the quicksand of subjective ideas of truth and goodness by endorsing an objective point of reference to ground their moral beliefs and ethical practices. These believers get nervous when they think that what they say or do lacks the seal of divine approval or the signature of godly intention. Oddly enough, many believers think that the Bible offers them unqualified access to transcendent truth. I say oddly because if there's any book that's proved to be the product of its time and place in history, it's the Bible. The scriptures capture ancient folk fighting for meaning in a world that either oppressed or inspired them, or sometimes both; we see glimpses of the humble trading places with the exalted and stories that show how power can be both redeeming and corrupting.

David, for instance, rises from shepherd to king by slaying a menacing giant, only to arrange the murder of a loyal soldier and steal his wife while leaving his kingdom in shambles. The Bible scolds injustice in the mouths of the prophets, yet amplifies it in the throat of Paul, whose *Haustafeln* (household codes) reinforce the social inequality of women as a way to reassure the Roman Empire that Christianity wouldn't undermine the social order. The Bible is in heated conversation with the culture that shaped it, at times as a faithful mirror of its virtues and biases, and at other times as a window onto a liberating social landscape.

The Bible's complicated cultural status makes it impossible to conclude that the scriptures offer an ironclad version of transcendence that resolves clashing views of truth. The Bible is intimately bound to those clashes; its words are used to support one truth claim or another in vastly different communities with greatly opposed theological, moral, and political agendas. Even if the transcendence police break down the front door of faith and arrest theological interlopers, enough dissenters will escape out the back door to challenge the Bible's link to truth.

The only meaningful interpretation of transcendence we might propose is to strip the term of its philosophical and theological orthodoxy and offer instead a more forceful definition. Truth can be described as transcendent if it illumines the time and place of its emergence as well as other places and periods. Truth's transcendence is not pegged to its authoritative reflection of an unchanging reality that everyone would agree on if they had access to it. Truth happens when we recognize the expression of a compelling and irrefutable description of reality. Truth is not irrefutable because it appeals to ideals that escape the fingerprints of time and reason. Truth is irrefutable because it is morally coherent and socially irresistible.

That's why Martin Luther King, Jr., and his comrades could challenge the transcendent truths of white supremacy and Black inferiority, truths seen by their advocates as true for all times and places, and truths that were rooted in religion and reason. But King and company offered a more compelling version of truth that ultimately proved to be more reasonable, more morally coherent, and more socially irresistible than the tribal truths it sought to displace. They didn't prove their vision of truth was superior by appealing to a transcendent truth that rang through the universe as self-evident, even though King spoke of Black folk enjoying "cosmic companionship" in our struggle for equality and justice.

Rather, King and his companions worked to show that they had a more edifying grasp of truth—that their moral vision was clearer, their ethical energy more uplifting, their description of democracy more meaningful, and their alliance with other truth tellers more cogent than those who bonded around the moral and legal justification of oppression. Thus, irrefutability is provisional, and may change with the appearance of other compelling views of truth that are rooted in reason and affirmed by morality. Such is the case, for instance, with gay marriage: traditional views of marriage that rest on religious and social orthodoxy are slowly giving way to superior versions of the truth that support gay and lesbian domestic intimacy and family values.

Closely yoked to the idea of a transcendent truth, of course, is biblical literalism, a plague that has often robbed Christianity of its liberating power and inspirational appeal. Believers who turn to the Bible for a transcription of God's thoughts, word for word, have arguably done more to harm the reputation of the Good Book than a million heretics.

I suppose the fear that some misguided soul would hear God telling him to sacrifice his children is a major reason I've worried about the meaning and interpretation of Abraham and Isaac's story over the years. Scores upon scores of mentally ill folk have done just that, telling us that God instructed them to drown, stab, shoot, or otherwise murder their offspring. Instead of reading this story metaphorically, as one that asks human beings to clarify the priority that God holds in our lives, too many folk afflicted with demons seek to purge their spirits by spilling the blood of innocent children. The tragedy is that literalism fails us when we need it most, when even naysayers to the doctrine wouldn't mind being wrong for once. Alas, no angel descends to keep many fathers from slaughtering their children in the name of God; no lamb is caught in the bush to exchange for the sacrifice of a child.

The story makes it clear that Isaac was an unwitting victim of religious sacrifice. He trusted his father to protect him, like millions of children around the globe expect their fathers to do. Isaac had no idea that the man who had crept into his centennial before fathering the only son he had with his wife, Sarah, would be the one who thought he must kill the future he had helped to make possible. The tragedy was doubled because Abraham had already lost one son, Ishmael, the child he fathered with his slave Hagar, whom Sarah had forced Abraham to cast out with his mother in a fit of pique, making certain that Isaac was his father's sole heir. (One can't help but note that too many children of the oppressed, who are the legitimate heirs of American freedoms for which Black folk bled and died, are treated as outcasts, their rightful share of equality divided among members of the majority culture, who are viewed, with all the protections it brings, as the sole heirs of our national bounty.) Now all of Abraham's plans would go up in smoke on an altar whose components Abraham compelled Isaac to tote on his back, making his son the vehicle for his own destruction.

In retrospect, I'm sure that as I got older I read this story through my own pain and suffering. My father believed, like many other Black fathers do, that God dictated not the sacrifice but surely the punishment of his children. Brutal measures of corporal punishment feel like symbolic sacrifices of one's children, a snuffing out of their self-esteem, a mortal unbodying of their fragile, vulnerable flesh.

The indictment of famed football player Adrian Peterson by a Texas grand jury for reckless or negligent injury to a child—he subsequently pleaded no contest to a misdemeanor charge of reckless assault—set into relief the harmful disciplinary practices of some Black families. Peterson used a "switch," a slim, leafless tree branch, to beat his four-year-old son, raising welts on the youngster's legs, buttocks, and scrotum. This is child abuse dressed up as acceptable punishment.

While 70 percent of Americans approve of corporal punishment, Black Americans have a distinct history with the subject. Beating children has been a depressingly familiar habit in Black families since our arrival in the New World. As the Black psychiatrists William H. Grier and Price M. Cobbs wrote in *Black Rage*, their 1968 examination of psychological Black life:

> Beating in child-rearing actually has its psychological roots in slavery and even yet Black parents will feel that, just as they have suffered beatings as children, so it is right that their children be so treated.

The lash of the plantation overseer fell heavily on children to whip them into fear of white authority. Terror in the field often gave way to parents beating Black children in the shack, or at times in the presence of the slave owner in forced cooperation to break a rebellious child's spirit. Black parents beat their children to keep them from misbehaving in the eyes of whites who had the power to send Black youth to their deaths for the slightest offense. Today, many Black parents fear that a loose tongue or flash of temper could get their child killed by a trigger-happy cop. They would rather beat their offspring than bury them.

If beating children began, paradoxically, as a violent preventive of even greater violence, it was enthusiastically embraced in Black culture, especially when God was recruited. As an ordained Baptist minister with a doctorate in religion, I have heard all sorts of religious excuses for whippings.

And I have borne the physical and psychic scars of beatings myself. I can't forget the feeling, as a 16-year-old, of my body being lifted from the floor in my father's muscular grip as he cocked back his fist to hammer me until my mother's cry called him off. I loved my father, but his aggressive brand of reproof left in me a trail of uncried tears.

Like many biblical literalists, lots of Black believers are fond of quoting scriptures to justify corporal punishment. Many Christians often cite what they think is a verse of scripture that supports beating their children,

"Spare the rod and spoil the child." But that is a line from *Hudibras*, a mock epic poem penned in 1664 by English poet and satirist Samuel Butler to ridicule the Puritans. To be sure, there are plenty of scriptures that bolster corporal punishment, particularly the verse in Proverbs 13:24 that says, *"He who spares the rod hates his son, but he who loves him is careful to discipline him."* And Proverbs 23:13–14 says, *"Withhold not correction from the child: for if thou beatest him with the rod, he shall not die. Thou shalt beat him with the rod, and shalt deliver his soul from hell."*

But in Hebrew, the word translated as "rod" is the same word used in Psalms 23:4, *"thy rod and thy staff, they comfort me."* The shepherd's rod was used to guide the sheep, not to beat them. Of course, the Bible, in Exodus 21:20–21, accepts slavery, in part by referring to the death of slaves by the same rod used to beat children. *"Anyone who beats their male or female slave with a rod must be punished if the slave dies as a direct result, but they are not to be punished if the slave recovers after a day or two, since the slave is their property."*

The passive acceptance of slavery and the ringing endorsement of child beatings are flip sides of the same biblical coin; the same literal interpretation of the Bible that justifies beating a child justifies enslaving her as well. In the end the believer is faced with a choice to worship either the Bible or the God who inspired it. Arguing for biblical literalism in the case of punishment—although certainly not in the case of slavery, as one is often forced by biblical literalism to pick and choose which verses really do apply—casts the Black Christian in an uncomfortable role of supporting his own oppression.

Many believers—including Peterson, a vocal Christian—have confused the correction of children's behavior with corporal punishment. The word "discipline" comes from the Latin *discipulus*, which means "student" or "disciple," suggesting a teacher-pupil relationship. Punishment comes from the Greek word *poine* and its Latin derivative *poena*, which mean "revenge," and form the root words of "pain," "penalty," and "penitentiary." The point of discipline is to transmit values to children. The purpose of punishment is to coerce compliance and secure control, and, failing that, to inflict pain as a form of revenge, a realm the Bible says belongs to God alone.

Yet secular Black culture thrives on colorful stories of punishment that are passed along as myths of ancient wisdom—a type of moral glue that holds together varying communities in Black life across time and circumstance. Black comedians cut their teeth on dramatically recalling "whoopings" with belts, switches, extension cords, hairbrushes, or whatever implement was at hand. Even as genial a comic as Bill Cosby offered a riff in his legendary 1983 routine that left no doubt about the deadly threat of Black punishment. "My father established our relationship when I was seven years old," Cosby joked. "He looked at me and says, 'You know, I brought you in this world, I'll take you out. And it don't make no difference to me, cause I'll make another one look just like you.'"

The humor is blunted when we recall that Marvin Gaye's life ended violently in 1984 at the hands of his father, a minister who brutalized him mercilessly as a child before shooting him to death in a chilling echo of Cosby's words. Perhaps comedians make us laugh to keep us from crying, but no humor can mask the suffering that studies say our children endure when they are beaten: feelings of sadness and worthlessness, difficulties sleeping, suicidal thoughts, bouts of anxiety, outbursts of aggression, diminished concentration, intense dislike of authority, frayed relations with peers, and negative high-risk behavior.

Equally tragic is that those who are beaten become beaters, too. And many Black folks are reluctant to seek therapy for their troubles because they may be seen as spiritually or mentally weak. The pathology of beatings festers in the psychic wounds of Black people that often go untreated in silence.

Adrian Peterson's brutal behavior toward his four-year-old son is, in truth, the violent amplification of the belief of many Blacks that beatings made them better people, a sad and bleak justification for the continuation of the practice in younger generations. After Peterson's indictment, the comedian D. L. Hughley tweeted: "A father's belt hurts a lot less then a cop's bullet!" He is right, of course, but only in a forensic, not a moral or psychological sense. What hurts far less than either is the loving correction of our children's misbehavior, so they become healthy adults who speak against violence wherever they find it—in the barrel of a policeman's gun, the fist of a lover, or the switch of a misguided parent. Far too often a literal interpretation of the Bible has tragically reinforced violence against loved ones and prevented Christians from embracing the emancipating elements of the stories we read.

Ironically, the siege of biblical literalism keeps us from identifying with the son of Abraham who, like many Black children, is referred to, though not by name, and certainly not heard from. Hagar was the slave mistress of Abraham, just as Sally Hemings was the slave mistress to Thomas Jefferson. Hagar's son, Ishmael, was prophesied by an angel to become *a wild donkey of a man; his hand will be against everyone and everyone's hand against him, and he will live in hostility toward all his brothers.*" That angel's message delivered Isaac but damned Ishmael. That reality rings true today.

There are still few angels to deliver the children of the socially disposable and despised. Isaac is kept from death by divine intervention; Ishmael is condemned to bitter circumstances with no relief in sight. There are far too many Hagars in our time who are social outcasts: single Black mothers who bear the stigma of shame and disrespect, who scrap for every single resource they can muster to provide for children who are marked for tough and brutal lives. Our present-day Ishmaels are prophesied, or stereotyped, as failures, when in truth they enjoy few of the privileges of the Isaacs in our culture. The same drug use by contemporary Isaacs that leads them to be lightly admonished about their bad behavior leads our Ishmaels to be harshly reprimanded and sent to prison. The same adolescent pranks in school that land the Isaacs of our time in the principal's office land our Ishmaels in detention or lead to outright expulsion. And far too frequently the Isaacs of our age are free to grow into fruitful adulthood while our Ishmaels are harassed and policed to death.

Our present-day Ishmaels, and our young Hagars, too, suffer the wounds of persistent and subtle racial injustice. The nation's foster care system, like most other institutions in America, reflects the racial dynamics that plague our society. Although Black children are only 15 percent of the U.S. population, they make up 24 percent of the children in foster care. Not only are Black children more likely to be reported, investigated, and relegated to foster care, but once they are there, they face prohibitive barriers: Black children are far more likely to endure longer placements in out-of-home care, are on the short end of comprehensive services, and reunify with their families far less than white children. In Los Angeles County, for example, eight out of every 100 children are Black, but 29 out of every 100 children are in foster care. When Black children in Los Angeles County are placed in foster care, they are trapped there 50 percent longer than children of other races. More troubling is the fact that Black children are mistreated by family members and die at a higher rate than children of other races.

Young Hagars are also targeted by the epidemic of sexual abuse in our communities: 60 percent of Black girls are sexually abused before they turn eighteen, while 40 percent of Black women suffer sexual assault in their lifetimes. Their suffering is compounded by the virtual silence that clouds the issue and the reluctance of Black female victims to seek counseling. Black women are raped at a higher rate than white women yet are less likely to report it. Then, too, the myth that they are "fast girls" has made Black girls who are victims of sexual exploitation wary of coming forward. As long as the culture at large, and Black culture in particular, perpetuates stereotypes of inappropriate Black female sexual desire, Black girls and women will endure their sexual suffering in silence.

Although "hashtag activism" has been widely assailed as a virtual substitute for substantive social action on the ground, it can have helpful, even therapeutic, results. Such was the case with #fasttailedgirls, the idea of *Hood Feminism* author and cofounder Mikki Kendall, a topic that trended nationally on Twitter as survivors of sexual abuse detailed their hesitation to speak up for fear they would be labeled "fast-tailed girls." From the pulpit to the playground, we must educate our communities and fight vicious stereotypes of Black women as Jezebels and loose women who bring harm to boys and men.

But the battles over our children don't end there. Sixty years after the Supreme Court ruled in the *Brown* decision that Blacks should receive the same education as whites, educational disparities between the Isaacs and the Ishmaels of our nation loom larger than ever. Black and brown students are less likely to gain access to advanced math and science courses and experienced instructors. Black students, even preschoolers, are more likely to be suspended than other students. That's not the entire story of educational inequities: 25 percent of high schools containing the greatest percentage of Black and brown students don't offer Algebra 2, while a third of such schools don't offer chemistry. As our civil rights groups and other bands of activists advocate for broader social justice, and the fuller participation of Black folk in our society, these educational disparities must be targeted to ensure that the next generation of Isaacs thrive.

Even more proof of the failure of biblical literalism can be seen in how elements of Isaac's and Ishmael's stories are conflated in narratives about the social suffering of Black youth. Our Ishmaels, like the biblical Isaac, are also victims of misguided theology. Our nation's political fathers have left our Black youth vulnerable, convinced, like Abraham, that they are listening to the voice of God when leading our youth to their downfall, saddling them with vicious beliefs about their own lack of worth in a culture that doesn't prize or respect them.

Trayvon Martin and Michael Brown are but the most recent examples of our national failure of will to protect our Isaacs from sacrifice. Trayvon deserved the dignity of normalcy. He deserved the protection that comes with the presumption that one is a regular kid, a child with no malicious intent, one who will experiment his way to adulthood by making the same immature choices many children make when they pose as rebels on social media or smoke some weed. And, like any red-blooded youth, Trayvon deserved the right to defend himself when recklessly pursued, and then shot to death, by a cowardly bully masquerading as a community savior named George Zimmerman.

Michael Brown was an unarmed Black youth who, like many Isaacs, like any youth, really, made mistakes, none of which he should have perished for. Brown was gunned down in the street by a relentless, and apparently remorseless, policeman named Darren Wilson. The officer fired several shots into Brown's body, including one into his head, as he was positioned beneath Wilson. A friend of Brown's who witnessed the killing said his friend pleaded with Wilson, "I don't have a gun, stop shooting," to no avail. After Zimmerman shot Trayvon, his killer claims that Trayvon's final words were "Okay, you got it." If true, what could Trayvon have meant by "it"? That Zimmerman had the presumption of innocence on his side despite being out of order in pursuing Trayvon? That Zimmerman had the right to kill any Black youth he wanted because their negative images flooded the culture? That Zimmerman had the advantage because he brought a gun to a fistfight that he provoked?

Trayvon Martin and Michael Brown both perished on the altar of an American history that has exploited and expelled Black youth from school—and from existence. Uncaring political fathers have repeatedly compelled Black youth to carry the instruments of their own demise, such as unjustified reputations for wrongdoing, on their backs. Or, in turn, they see, like so much of society sees, what is on their backs, and their faces, and their bodies—their Black skin—as cause for suspicion and death. (How, indeed, can we distinguish God's will from cultural suspicions and racial intuitions? The question has far greater existential weight when asked in relationship to Black bodies that have been deemed threatening and perishable in our culture.)

The Black *New York Times* writer John Eligon summed up the harmful view of Black youth in a sentence that was published the morning of Michael Brown's funeral: "Michael Brown . . . was no angel." In sharp contrast, the *Times* ran a concurrent story that praised Brown's killer, Darren Wilson, as a "well-mannered, relatively soft-spoken, even bland person." It may as well have called him an angel.

There is another sense, however, in which Eligon's phrase is quite fitting: "no angel" showed up to save Brown, or Trayvon, or thousands of other Black youth. Even though it had been drilled into the collective unconscious of Black American youth that no ram would be waiting for them in the bush, that no angel would deliver them, Michael Brown's and Trayvon Martin's last words were, tragically and paradoxically, a stubborn belief that the lamb might come, that it should, somehow, be in place, or that their last-breath attempt to snatch hold of its wings might make the angel descend to their aid. Their final words were gasps of protest at the horrifying and unjust absence of help, and also the undying affirmation of a crude optimism, equally unjustified, that they shouldn't perish this way; that, by surrendering to their victimizers, they'd done what was necessary to live past the rage of an armed assailant who sought to impose his one-man judgment—his steely, bullet-riddled narrative—on their lives and bring the story of their youthful existence to a violent end in the barrel of a gun.

As a sign of how even bad stories feature glimmers of hope, Eligon also offers us, in the same piece that disparaged the youth, a heartening glimpse of Michael Brown's theology of divine intervention:

It was 1:00 A.M. and Michael Brown, Jr., called his father, his voice trembling. He had seen something overpowering. In the thick gray clouds that lingered from a passing storm this past June, he made out an angel. And he saw Satan chasing the angel and the angel running into the face of God. Mr. Brown was a prankster, so his father and stepmother chuckled at first. "No, no, Dad! No!" the elder Mr. Brown remembered his son protesting. "I'm serious." And the Black teenager from this suburb of St. Louis, who had just graduated from high school, sent his father and stepmother a picture of the sky from his cell phone. "Now I believe," he told them.

Sadly, Brown's budding belief was killed and left to fester in the same body that lay prostrate on the street for *four hours* after his death. If Michael Brown is Isaac, and his father, Michael Brown, Sr., is Abraham, imagine the suffering the father endures as he realizes he was unable to keep his son from being sacrificed, that no angel spoke to rescue his son from peril, that no lamb was exchanged as his son was sent to his bloody demise.

The story of Abraham and Isaac offers us a powerful lesson about the tests of God, and what we do with them, and our own tests, and how we sometimes abuse them. The story opens the possibilities of a broader view of truth, and the contrasting perils of biblical literalism. It highlights the virtue of rescuing narratives from the grasp of the powerful and the parochial as we read them to rescue in ourselves the excitement and vigor of fresh interpretation—and an uplifting, if sobering, application of the Word to our words, and to the worlds we make of them.

Above all, Abraham and Isaac, and Hagar and Ishmael, too, remind us that Trayvon Martin and Michael Brown, and countless other Black youth besides, are daily sacrificed on the altar of unmerited suspicion and fear of Black identity, pushing them into early graves. We must be the angels our children seek. We must keep them from destructive discipline at our own hands. And we must shield our children from death at the hands of those who think, bizarrely, often in veiled manner, though sometimes in fatally explicit terms, that they are doing God's will to kill them.

CHAPTER

16

George Floyd and the Politics
of Black Automortology

When working on my second book on Dr. King, addressing his death and its impact on American society, I came up with the term "automortology" to describe the forecasting and foretelling of one's death. One of the most haunting features of Floyd's murder by former officer Derek Chauvin is the way it elicits from Floyd a narration of his own demise, so that automortology becomes Black obituary on the make. A version of this essay appeared in 2021 online in The New Yorker.

George Floyd's death may be the most consequential police killing to have occurred since smartphones gave us the ability to document the realities of police violence. The details, captured on recordings by several passersby, are by now familiar. On March 25, 2020, Floyd, a forty-six-year-old bouncer forced out of work by the pandemic, was accused of passing off a fake twenty-dollar bill at a convenience store in Minneapolis, Minnesota. When the police officers Thomas Lane and J. Alexander Kueng arrived at the scene, employees of the store pointed them to Floyd's car across the street, where he was waiting. Lane quickly drew his weapon and dragged Floyd from the vehicle. Floyd was a large man at six feet six inches and two hundred and twenty-three pounds. He quickly told the cops that he had been shot before, and asked them not to shoot him this time, perhaps hoping to make himself seem less threatening, more vulnerable. The officers soon cuffed him and tried to put him in their cruiser. He told them that he was claustrophobic and resisted. To restrain him, the cops held him to the ground. Kueng rested his knees on Floyd's torso, and Lane placed his knees on Floyd's legs. Derek Chauvin, another officer who had arrived on the scene, dug his knee into Floyd's neck.

At this point, Floyd began foretelling his own death. "Y'all, I'm going to die in here," he said. "I'm going to die, man." He cried out that he couldn't breathe. "Please, the knee in my neck . . . I'll probably die this way." As

Floyd continued to plead for his life, Chauvin announced that he was under arrest. "All right, all right. Oh my God," Floyd acknowledged in utter exasperation. But he also eerily prophesied his fate in a post-mortem declaration as if the deed of death was already done. "Tell my kids I love them. I'm dead." He soon fell unconscious and was hustled into an ambulance and sent to the hospital. He died of cardiac arrest an hour later.

In 2008, while working on a book about Martin Luther King, I was struck by what I came to call King's "automortology"—the manner in which he seemed to forecast his own death, at times even narrating it as if it had already happened. This rhetorical form dates back at least to the life of Jesus, the founder of the religion King and Floyd followed. Jesus resisted Roman oppression of the Jews; as Biblical scholar Obery Hendricks notes in his book *The Politics of Jesus*, "Jesus was put to death by the Roman state for advocating—if not actually waging—social disruption and political revolution." Jesus knew that the state was mustering its forces against him. In Mark, the earliest Gospel, he begins predicting that his death is imminent, telling his followers that he will be "killed and after three days rise again." He narrates the particulars of his death, saying that he will be "mocked and flogged and crucified." He describes all of this as if it were in the past, speaking the not-yet as the already-was, and giving him rhetorical leverage to shape how his death, and therefore his life, would be understood in the future. He makes clear that his crucifixion will not be a victory for the Romans and the end of his movement, as they seem to think. Instead, it will form part of God's larger plan, leading to the salvation of humankind and the spread of Christianity around the world.

Like Jesus, King did his own work under the specter of violence. Several of his colleagues were murdered for their agitation on behalf of civil rights and Black emancipation: Medgar Evers was assassinated in 1963, and Malcolm X in 1965. King faced direct threats to his own life. When he was in his mid-twenties, his home in Montgomery, Alabama, was bombed by a white supremacist. In 1958, at a book signing in Harlem, a woman stabbed him with a letter opener. In 1965, as he attempted to register at a formerly all-white hotel in Selma, Alabama, King was punched several times by a white anti-integration advocate. When he led a demonstration for fair housing in Chicago, he had a knife thrown at him and was knocked to the ground by a brick. Hardly a day passed when he didn't receive death threats. He soon began to speak as if his death were inevitable. In 1965, on a brief trek to the gravesite of martyred church deacon Jimmie Lee Jackson, with Joseph Lowery, a board member of the Southern Christian Leadership

Conference, King said, "This may be my last walk." When John F. Kennedy was assassinated in Dallas, Texas, King insisted to his wife, Coretta, "This is what is going to happen to me also." Coretta later said, "I had no word to comfort my husband. I could not say, 'It won't happen to you.' I felt he was right." When a plane that King was on was targeted with a bomb threat, in 1964, he said to Coretta and his aide Dorothy Cotton, "I've told you all that I don't expect to survive this revolution."

Early on, he made clear that his death would not be a defeat for the project of integration. "If I am stopped, our work will not stop," King said in Montgomery, in 1956, at the height of the bus boycott. "For what we are doing is right." He even predicted that his martyrdom might propel the movement, as he told interviewer Alex Haley in *Playboy* in January 1965 that his cause was so moral "that if I should lose my life, in some way it would aid the cause." In 1968, he travelled to Memphis to march and speak on behalf of striking sanitation workers. "Like anybody, I'd like to live a long life," he said. "But I'm not concerned about that now." He instead trumpeted his divine priority. "I just want to do God's will. And He's allowed me to go up to the mountain. And I've looked over. And I've seen the Promised Land. I may not get there with you. But I want you to know tonight that we as a people will *get* to the Promised Land."

The next evening, an assassin's bullet cut him down on his balcony at the Lorraine Motel. By the time he perished, he had become a pariah within the country's political landscape. He was unpopular with white moderates because he criticized America's role in the Vietnam War, and he had been largely upstaged within Black activist circles by younger Black Power advocates. But in death, he became a martyr, and what Hegel called a "world historical individual": the primary symbol of the fight for racial justice in America. As Jon Meacham and Vern E. Smith contend, in *Newsweek*, while King "lay dying, the popular beatification was already underway."

In hip hop's golden era, the rapper 2Pac, né Tupac Shakur, became similarly obsessed with his own death. 2Pac carved out a career that was an intriguing amalgam of Black edification and thuggish bravado—he was as likely to encourage young girls to keep their heads up as he was to boast of blasting rivals with weapons. Tupac was born in 1971 in New York as a child of Black Panthers, reared partly in Baltimore, and transplanted to the Bay Area by the time he was 17. 2Pac was an iconic figure in West Coast hip hop who moved to Los Angeles in 1993 and forged an epic career before he was killed in Vegas during a still-unsolved drive-by shooting.

Violence tracked Shakur as well. In 1991, two Oakland policemen bloodied and bruised the young rapper and slammed him to the ground in a chokehold and arrested him for jaywalking. He later sued the Oakland Police Department and won a $42,000 settlement. In 1993, 2Pac was charged with two counts of aggravated assault when he shot two off-duty police officers who had menaced people in an incident involving two cars in Atlanta. The charges were later dropped when witnesses confirmed that the cops had been the initial aggressors. That same year the temperamental 2Pac got into a fistfight with director Allen Hughes, who charged the rapper with assault, landing him in jail in 1994 for 15 days. That same year, 2Pac was shot five times during a robbery at Manhattan's Quad Studios, sparking a feud between Shakur and rapper the Notorious B.I.G. That fatal disagreement shadowed the two iconic figures before they were both gunned down, 2Pac in 1996 and the Notorious B.I.G. the following year in a still-unsolved drive-by shooting in Los Angeles.

In whatever form it came, Shakur seemed to believe that he wouldn't be around long. At times he welcomed death's deliverance from the hell of earth. "My only fear of death is reincarnation," 2Pac says on "Reincarnation." In his song "Unconditional Love," 2Pac baldly asked, "Mama why I got this urge to die." Shakur also stated that "I either will be in jail or dead or be so fucking stressed out from not going to jail or dying or on crack that I'd just pop a vessel. I'll just die from a heart attack. All the deaths are not going to be from the police killing you." In his song, "Only God Can Judge Me," Tupac describes an attempt on his life, and confesses to regretting that it doesn't succeed, saying, "I wish they didn't miss." The director Vondie Curtis Hall, who directed Tupac in the film *Gridlock'd*, said that the rapper and actor "knew he was never going to hit thirty," and that such a belief "allows you to live with a certain level of abandonment" and to "accept destiny without fear." Maxine Waters, a Democratic Congresswoman from Los Angeles who knew Tupac the few years he lived in her city, told me that Tupac was "wild and unpredictable, and even troubled," but that he "stared danger in the eye and didn't flinch one bit."

If King channeled the moral energy of Black resistance in the argot of the Black bourgeois, Tupac spoke for the masses of Black folk hustling in the underground economy and contending with everyday realities of police violence. In "Point the Finga," Tupac describes himself getting lynched by cops, who then face no consequences and stay on the state's payroll. When people got their paychecks, he says, the government was "taking tax out / So, we payin' for these [cops] to knock the Blacks out." On "Hellrazor," Tupac speaks of police officers who seek him for investigation, because, he says, "I'm marked for death," but "I'm a spark 'til I lose my breath." On "Only Fear of Death," Tupac confesses that "I see visions of me dead." On "How Long Will They Mourn Me?" he says that "I know soon one day I'll be in the dirt," and that all his people will "be mournin'."

Some critics may disparage rappers who see their urban plight as part of "the struggle." Still, a case can be made that the struggle for visibility and legitimacy by young Black folk in the streets is every bit as compelling as their forebears' fights for civil rights and Black freedom. Thus, the martyrs of the movement of the sixties aren't in that sense entirely divorced from those figures in the inner city who perish in a society that sees them as disposable. Tupac viewed his potential martyrdom as more important than surrendering his life on foreign soil for a nation that cared little for poor Black folk. "It would be an honor to die in the 'hood," Tupac told writer Veronica Chambers. "Don't let me die in Saudi Arabia . . . I'd rather die in the 'hood, where I get my love. I'm not saying I want to die, but if I got to die, let me die in the line of duty; the duty of the 'hood."

Tupac functioned as a hip hop Jeremiah, an urban prophet who spoke up in defense of the vulnerable at-risk souls who congregated around him and formed a sonic discipleship. He heard their pain and amplified it; he heard their cries for relief and echoed them. On his song "Black Jesus," Tupac proclaimed that, "In times of war we need somebody raw, rally the troops like a Saint that we can trust." At the end of the song, one of Tupac's comrades prays for a Black Jesus who is "like a Saint that we pray to in the ghetto." In many ways, Tupac became a ghetto saint. As soon as his bullet-ridden body was cremated rumors began to circulate that Tupac had faked his death, that he was still alive, retreating into anonymity to escape the encumbrances of his fraught existence.

Perhaps one of the points of the rumor that Tupac staged his death is to deny the power of death by denying it had occurred at all. Is it all that different than the followers of a Jewish messiah denying that he truly died, that he shed his death clothes and was resurrected to save the world? Tupac's followers developed urban legends of his posthumous persona as a way to combat the crushing inevitability that pointed to their deaths—from guns, from gangs, from the government's police. If Tupac could escape, so could they. If Tupac wasn't really dead, maybe they wouldn't have to die so early either. Maybe they wouldn't have to plan their funerals at 18 and be surprised they lived to be 25. Even now Tupac remains a resonant cultural presence: murals—in Miami, Florida, and Brixton, London, all over California from Melrose and Fresno to San Francisco and Los Angeles, to Melbourne and Sydney, Australia, to Madrid and Sevilla, Spain, to Cape Town, South Africa, to Korea—testify to his artistic and cultural immortality.

"He was a martyr before it even happened," Robin Kelley, a historian at UCLA, told me. "So much of his music was about the inevitability of his demise, and at the same time he also had this almost Jesus-like voice, where he would preach and, in his own body and experience, would articulate all this pain and hope."

Unlike King or Shakur, most Black folks are neither Nobel laureates nor internationally acclaimed hip hop artists. But all live under the threat of violence. Black people, on average, live 4 fewer years than white people—although in some areas, like Baltimore, there is a 20-year gap in life expectancy between mostly poor Black communities where folk die on average at 67 and tonier white areas where they live on average to be 87. The reason is simple: systemic racism, which affects the economic circumstances, medical and behavioral forces and geographic and environmental conditions that affect health and determine life expectancy. If you're too poor to routinely see a physician; if the ghetto grocer stocks high-sugar cereals and unhealthier cuts of meats; if you can't afford to develop an exercise routine because of multiple jobs or lack of financial support for gym membership, then you're likely to be Black and unhealthy and die earlier. Add to that the chronic stresses of racial oppression—from the microaggressions of sundry "Karens" calling the cops on us to police killings of Black people—and the sources of the disparity in racial life expectancy become unavoidably clear.

This disparity has been laid bare during the pandemic: Black people in America are 37 percent more likely to die from COVID-19 than white people. Black Americans are 6 times more likely to be murdered than white Americans. And they are anywhere from 3 to 6 times more likely than whites to be killed during a police encounter. In a further injustice, when Black people are killed by the police, they are often posthumously smeared in an attempt to justify the killing. After Mike Brown was killed by a cop on the streets of Ferguson, Missouri, a security video was released that appeared to show Brown stealing cigarillos from a convenience store moments before he was killed; a subsequent video of an earlier encounter suggests that, in fact, he may instead have been giving a small bag of marijuana to store employees and receiving the cigarillos in return. After Breonna Taylor was killed by police officers in Louisville, Kentucky, she was falsely rumored to have been living with a drug dealer. Automortology offers the chance that a fallen figure will have, if not the last word, then at least a lasting one.

Automortology is in some cases more muted than explicit, more subtle than transparent, and can be a vehicle to not only mourn individual loss but also to anticipate collective freedom. King foretold his own death but also pointed to the emancipation of Black folk. Although he did so in a dramatically different register, with a different set of skills, the legendary singer Sam Cooke may have achieved the same end. Cooke was shot to death on December 11, 1964, at age 33 by a motel manager. She claimed it was in self-defense as Cooke tussled with her after he had angrily forced his way into her office in search of a female companion. A month after his death, arguably Cooke's most famous song was released, "A Change Is Gonna Come." The song's lyrics steep in premonition and yearn for Black liberation. Like King, Cooke casts his reflections in personal terms. "It's been too hard living/But I'm afraid to die," Cooke poignantly confesses. Later he admits that "there been times that I thought I couldn't last for long."

Although he might not last, the movement, it seems, would carry on and the hoped-for deliverance would finally arrive. "It's been a long/A long time coming/But I know a change gon' come." When Cooke played the song for his wife, Barbara, and friend, singer Bobby Womack, they, in the words of Womack, told him it "feels like death," it feels like "something terrible's gonna happen." The cultural studies scholar Dhanveer Singh Brar says that for Womack and Barbara Cooke, the song's "eeriness was both the sound of futurity and the sound of death," allowing them "to posthumously reinvent it as a premonition of death" because the song "sounded like freedom but it also sounded like death." Brar argues that King's "Mountaintop" speech and Cooke's song "have become evidence of their quasi-mystical powers" because they "were able to experience a time of Black freedom, as well as their own demises."

But more than eerie premonition is at stake. Automortology is Black obituary on the sly. It allows a person, living under a threat of violence, to acknowledge this sense of impending doom, and to feel that she is exerting some agency over it. And it allows the person, who has little control over the circumstances of the death, to at least exercise some control over the narrative that will attend the death. Floyd was an imposing Black man with a history of arrests for drug use, and his death might ordinarily have been cast as the necessary killing of a threatening suspect. His killers might have been taken as heroes. But, because there was video footage of Floyd being docile and solicitous, asking the officers not to kill him, and repeatedly saying "I can't breathe," it became clear that he was being victimized.

And the fact that he could tell that his death was coming early on in the encounter and repeatedly predicted it seemed to underscore the inevitability of violence in encounters between police officers and Black suspects. It preemptively framed Floyd's death as a police killing of an innocent Black man, and one in a sordid series.

Floyd became a global icon for social justice, and a spur to wrestle with systemic racism. There have been protest marches all over the world in the wake of Floyd's death—from Sydney to Beirut, from Istanbul to London, and Berlin to Brazil. There are murals of Floyd's strong African features plastered on walls across the globe, and countless quilts bear his striking image—while the skin of many bodies bears the tattoo "I Can't Breathe." And since Floyd was killed, nearly 60 Confederate symbols have been removed. Floyd's death also sparked the largest protests for racial justice in the history of this nation. The same nation that failed him and couldn't keep him breathing to enjoy his life, and yet, paradoxically enough, his death has given this nation new life—a renewed desire to exorcise our racial demons, a fresh will to rid our land of systemic racism. Only if we keep their memories alive will King's and Floyd's prophecies of Black mortality set us free and help wash their blood from our hands.

17

Black Love in a Time of Coronavirus

The global pandemic swept upon us with devastating suddenness. This essay offered me the opportunity to reflect philosophically on the intertwined pandemics, the syndemic, that we Black folk, and other people of color, confront: one a vicious virus that attacks our bodies and the other a virulent strain of anti-Blackness that smothers the body politic and American society. It appears as the foreword to the book Religion, Race, and COVID-19, *edited by religious ethicist Stacey Floyd-Thomas.*

Technically, I suppose, every living being dies when we cannot breathe. Our heart stops pumping, our brain's light disappears, our breath, perhaps the most fragile means to sustain our bodies, our very existence, leaves our lungs for the last time. The disappearance of breath marks the end of life in the same way that the presence of breath signals its beginning. James Weldon Johnson, at the end of his immortal poem "The Creation," says that God shaped a lump of clay into the divine image to create human life.

> *Then into it he blew the breath of life,*
> *And man became a living soul.*

Most human beings want to keep breathing. Some, in cases of extreme or extended emergency, or in cursed spells of self-destruction, conclude that breathing is no longer worth the effort to keep alive the myth of happiness, or the elusive song of delight that long ago escaped their lips to find no fruitful return in joy or satisfaction. Entire societies fight furiously, even ruthlessly, to get better ways of breathing. They establish political orders to get the better-off people in cleaner and healthier environments. They secure social and economic protections where they and their kind can literally, and figuratively, breathe easier. But such breathing often comes at the expense of the poor and destitute. The achingly vulnerable can't breathe easy at any time as they are pushed further into precarity, and further away from the safety and stability that the well-off enjoy. For Black folk, breathing has always been biological and metaphoric, both literal and symbolic.

From the start of our forced intimacy with North America, Black folk have been trying to breathe air that is free of the pollution of captivity, of coerced transport, of enslavement, of white supremacy, of social inequality and perennial second-class citizenship. When our captors crashed the shores of Africa to ensnare us, we ceased enjoying the air of freedom. While it is true that our breath had been snatched with bouts of unfreedom in tribal disputes and local seizures, those crucial losses approached nothing like the wholesale rejection of our liberty in chattel slavery. When we were kidnapped from our native haunts, we were denied more than the African air we breathed. We were also deprived of the oxygen of opportunities to deepen our ties to our cruelly estranged motherland. And we had withheld from us the nitrogen of nourishment from the land and limbs of our kin and loved ones.

When we were packed into seafaring vessels of mobile terror for passage to the New World, the air we breathed was polluted by the feces and urine of our fellow captives. We imbibed the stench of vomit from souls who couldn't stomach the sadistic and cruel treatment. We could barely breathe, and many of us gave up the ghost on the perilous journey as we succumbed to sickness and suffering. Some of us had our breath snatched from us at the end of a blunt instrument or in the barrel of a weapon. Some of us stopped breathing as we jumped, or were pushed, overboard. When we arrived at our various ports of call, we were deposited into zones of suffering and grounds of grief to provide relief for the white masses. We could barely breathe free air for centuries afterward. Even when we were finally granted the opportunity to inhale freedom, the relentless spray of contaminants polluted the emancipated air around us.

This backdrop helps to explain a popular saying in Black circles that when America has a cold, Black America has pneumonia. It is no accident that the analogy that best captures the suffering of Black folk in comparison to the ills of white folk has to do in large measure with labored breathing. (Even the runner-up analogy shares the same trait. True, it reverses the order of racial citation by arguing that Black folk are the proverbial canary in the coal mine. In short, it suggests that what happens to us first will happen eventually to white folk and the rest of the nation. And that homespun maxim, too, rests on the deadly effect of Black lungs analogously ingesting toxins from the atmosphere.) And neither was it a surprise that those same Black lungs were more likely to quit when hit by the spread of a lethal virus.

The disappearance of Black breath ties together the global outbreak of coronavirus and the ongoing plague of Black oppression into a syndemic, or the convergence of dual pandemics. The fatalities that result from this syndemic are expressed in a common cry: I can't breathe, whether from lungs turned to sponge because of the disease's virulent spread, or, for instance, Black bodies suffocated in the merciless embrace of conscienceless cops. The syndemic reminds us that we must be vigilant in underscoring the poor health care systems that render Black and Brown bodies more vulnerable to dying from COVID-19, all because poor and working people often lack health care insurance that provides them the opportunity to prevent the spread of disease or to reduce its lethal effects. And the plague of racism certainly isn't quarantined to cops: the 45th president of the United States used his bully pulpit to perpetuate legacies of white supremacy, ideas of white nationalism, and practices of xenophobia that aimed contempt at immigrants from Africa, Asia and South and Central America.

The global pandemic has dramatically shifted the way the nation and the world do business. Until mid-2021, we could not go out to eat in packed restaurants, watch in person live sporting events with thousands of others, take in a movie at the local cineplex, or applaud our favorite artists on the concert stage. The separation anxiety engendered by our forced apartness has driven us to rely even more heavily on our technology. Whether connected to a smartphone, computer, iPad, or other tablets and devices, screens have brought us into unexpected and counterintuitive communion. After all, hadn't we for years been warned of the seductions of gadgets and the distraction of contraptions that rob us of face-to-face experiences? We have been thrust into electronic encounters that not a month before we could have never imagined cherishing as much as we do now. Our screens are also salvation and healing when they bring us preachers or physicians or therapists with reassuring words from above or within. Sadly, as the pandemic has separated families more dramatically than any force since the Civil War, the afflicted turn to digital surfaces that are the only medium to bring their loved ones within sight for their final goodbyes.

At the same time, the pandemic offers us irresistible metaphors for a particular form of Black oppression, the plague of terrorizing policing that not even COVID-19 could eclipse. No masks could hide the fear and hate of Blackness nor stop the spread of viral anti-Blackness. No volume of hand sanitizer could cleanse the grime of diseased Blackness from the hands or knees of loathsome cops. No study of viral ontology could relieve the ontological spite that many cops feel for Black being. No determination to flee the clutches of angry cops could escape the contact trace of bigoted policing. No amount of social distancing, a racially colored idea that sought, more than a century ago, to measure the amount of space that white folk would maintain from Black people in their everyday existence, could keep cops from brutalizing and killing the bodies of Blacks.

All of this came to a fateful head in the killing of George Floyd on May 25, 2020. To witness his killing captured on a mobile phone video was to watch Black breath disappear into the racist ether. It was to watch the plague of poisonous policing play out before our very eyes in the shape of a cop who gave America's racist history a glaring face. Yes, it was the specter of a grown Black man begging for his mother that broke the hearts of millions of people the world over. The sounds he made ripped the psychic gestalt of a white society deceitfully premised on the unimpeachable gulf between white supremacy and ordinary whiteness. Floyd's unconscionable death suggested that it was all of a piece. The primal form of violence of kneeling on a man's neck to kill him was so precise and cruelly efficient and tragically ordinary that it revealed the shameless rot at the core of a system that has never valued or loved Black bodies beyond sheer exploitation. Black breath could be squeezed out of Black lungs at will with as little care for Black well-being or worry of moral or legal consequence as Chauvin expressed that fateful day.

Floyd's loss of breath, loss of body, loss of life, fueled social rebellion and historic forms of social protest. The crisis of color forced the nation to reckon with the unaddressed and unrelieved suffering this nation has endured ever since it decided to kidnap African citizens from their homes and enslave them in the New World. Ever since 1619, the emblematic year the savage theft of Black bodies became visible, to this day, when systemic racism is deeply entrenched in every nook and cranny of the culture, our original sin has continued to lash the national soul. The peril and terror unleashed by the election in 2016 of a president who embraced the spirit and impulse of white nationalists, and white supremacy, shocks and sickens even those who predicted the tragedy of his ascent to power.

Floyd's death happened in the same period as crowds of mostly white folk stormed state capitols with their weapons flashing to protest governors shutting down their states because of the virus. Once it became clear to them that the disproportionate impact of COVID-19 on Black lungs made it a "Black disease," all bets, and masks, and in some cases, sheets were off.

Once the preexisting health problems that Black and Brown folk share, from heart disease to diabetes and asthma, came into focus, white rage was sparked. Once it became apparent that Black breath was even more at risk, and that the pandemic endangered Black folk who worked on front lines, prepared food, and delivered health care, the tolerance for restrictions on mobility collapsed. Once it was clear that their chronic lack of access to health care, and the crushing economic and social barriers they confront, made the steady evaporation of Black breath a national concern, the performance of white ressentiment was in full gear. All of this was exacerbated by a president who stoked the flames of racism, racial intolerance, and racial bigotry, and who advocated for nationalism and affirmed the virtue of "white power."

Now is the time to rediscover Black love in a time of coronavirus. Now is the time for the nation to take a hard look at its racist practices, beliefs, ideals, goals and aspirations. Now is the time to examine its folkways and mores, and its norms and social and political habits, too, that have for too long been overlooked, ignored or denied, or, worse yet, accepted as the necessary status quo. The time for racial reckoning is upon us, and we have an incredible opportunity to grapple with our nation's shameful and tragic racial history in meaningful and enlightening ways. It is true that we must move beyond symbolic gestures of racial comity to substantive discussions of genuine equity. We must dig deep and uproot the causes of systemic racism and inequality. And we must recognize the progress betokened in removing statues of Confederate figures and racist political icons that dot our physical and psychological landscapes.

But we must move from statues to statutes, from culture to law. This will ensure that we address draconian measures like stand your ground laws that put Black and Brown lives at risk. We must also unravel the troubling legal webs that bind local prosecutors and district attorneys to the very law enforcement upon whom they depend to solve cases. These same cops often mistreat, harm and unjustly kill Black and Brown citizens. The likelihood of those cops being held to account by the same prosecutors and district attorneys is almost nonexistent.

But we must resist racial temptations from within the stream of Black breath too. This is not the time to witch hunt our way across the racial landscape to provide "gotcha" moments of past racial embarrassment for white "offenders." This is not the time to obsess over their mistakes in racial protocol, or to trigger outrage by focusing exclusively or primarily on what can be heard and read as racially improper. We have bigger fish to fry. The very foundation of deeply entrenched racist practice and behavior, and of profoundly disturbing racist thought and reflection, is finally under pressure. We must keep the pressure up and go after the real culprits of racist culture: the institutional, systemic and structural dynamics that preserve white racial hierarchy and that maintain white racial privilege. These are the forces that routinely and with criminal skillfulness take away Black breath.

A bigger fish we must fry is to have a genuine racial reckoning amidst a rash of unjust cop killings of Black folk. The rash has continued, becoming a rush of foul racist behavior and fatal police action that has resulted in a crisis that we can no longer ignore. The cop crisis in America is driven in large measure by racial animus, conscious or not, and sustained by other deeply rooted and glaring racial inequalities in our society. We will experience no genuine relief from these plagues until we confront them. If we have not come full circle, we have at least been shown the interrelated character of the crises we confront in our present syndemic: COVID-19 has ravaged the bodies of Black and Brown people, but it has also spread in the broader population in devastating fashion. The racial pandemic began with the enslavement of Black folk, but it soon sank the entire society with an undertow of racist brutality from which we have yet to escape. While the election of Trump seemed at first only to insult the Brown, Black, immigrant, Muslim and LGBTQIA communities, the plague of the Trumpian doctrine—which, no matter where it flares, has two basic components of mendacity and mediocrity—swept the entire nation into its traumatizing arc.

Religion, Race and COVID-19 is a book, really a manual, that helps us to brilliantly negotiate the nefarious forces that intersect on Black, Brown and Indigenous bodies, and that threaten to weaponize a viral pandemic into a willfully racist one. By flushing from our collective system of thought and governance the spiritual, moral and political detritus of toxic Americanity, it offers an ennobling and redeeming call to conscience in the age of coronavirus. The book strikes a Whitmanesque note by singing the Body Infected, in all its coarse and vulnerable parts, not to celebrate it, but to properly diagnose it in order to bring it to fuller health and better breathing. The lungs of American democracy are turned to mush by systemic racism and social inequity. They must be Blacksinated from the further spread of the virus of anti-Blackness. This book is a huge dose of moral medicine for the maladies of our nation.

If the perils of Black breathing show us anything, it is that what happens first to Black folk will eventually happen to the rest of the nation. Yes, we are the canaries in the coal mine of American social and political life. But the good news is that if we solve the persistent problems of Black breath, of Black breathing, of the loss of Black breath, we will, like James Weldon Johnson suggested, breathe new meaning into the lungs of American democracy. If we can turn to Black entertainers and athletes to artistically enliven our national spirit—and often to deepen our collective conscience—we can turn to Black Lives Matter and Stacey Abrams and Stacey Floyd-Thomas and others to strengthen our national will and our democratic practice. Blackness has often saved this nation, and if we engage it in our day and time, it may well do it again when we need it most. And then, at long last, we may all be able to breathe a sigh of collective relief.

I Love to Tell the Story

In the Pulpit

18

What Have I Left?

I preached this sermon the Sunday after the terrorist attacks of 9/11. Sitting in the front row was my dear friend Congresswoman Barbara Lee, the only member of Congress to vote "No" on the Authorization for Use of Military Force Against Terrorists (AUMF). With striking prescience, Lee warned her fellow members of Congress to be "careful not to embark on an open-ended war with neither an exit strategy nor a focused target." She argued that such authorization was "a blank check to the president to attack anyone involved in the September 11 events—anywhere, in any country, without regard to our nation's long-term foreign policy, economic and national security interests, and without time limit." President Biden seems now to agree with what Lee argued twenty years ago: "We cannot continue the cycle of extending or expanding our military presence in Afghanistan, hoping to create ideal conditions for the withdrawal, and expecting a different outcome . . . I will not pass this responsibility to a fifth [president] . . . I have concluded that it's time for American troops to come home." This sermon appeared in 9.11.01: African American Leaders Respond to an American Tragedy, *edited in 2001 by homiletics teachers Martha Simmons and Frank A. Thomas.*

I want to say [thank you] to Congresswoman Barbara Lee. [When I heard about the vote,] I leaned over to Dr. Wilson and I said, "Is she really *the* only person in the United States Congress to stand up against the machinery of war and vote 'No'?" And at a time, be reminded, when our sentiments and passions have been shaped by the media to make us believe that the only alternative is to stick that colossal military foot on the necks of people throughout the world without trying to negotiate—which is the reason why we left Durban [South Africa], and couldn't even talk at the table at the World Conference on Racism. This is the same government that refuses to acknowledge your pain and the domestic terrorism that we confront on a daily basis in Watts, Oakland, Harlem and Detroit. The same government that refuses to stop racial profiling and police brutality—that's terrorism, too. And now we, as a people of color, are being seduced into believing that the only alternative is to do to them what has been done to us, to bomb them as they have bombed us.

So, I want to thank Congresswoman Barbara Lee for her bravery and for her courage. God bless you. Because we ain't trying to act like bin Laden is our buddy. He started off in Africa. We ain't stupid. But we're caught in the midst of this. American imperialism and colonialism are an old tradition. In fact, America trained bin Laden as part of the Afghanistan movement against the Soviet Union. The CIA, the Central Intelligence Agency of America, trained him to do battle. Now he turns that weaponry on America. Don't hate the player, hate the game.

Oh, America's got a short memory. Not to suggest we don't have to have a strategic response to terrorism throughout the world. Of course we do. But the question is how will we hold ourselves accountable for creating the conditions where folks are clapping when they hear about America [being attacked]? Don't get it twisted, see, because Negroes were clapping when O.J. got off. White America thought we had lost our minds. We ain't thought O.J. was innocent; we just didn't believe he was guilty. Because we have been trying to tell America for years: you can't mistreat people in an unjust system and expect us to celebrate the way in which you've hurt us. So, when O.J. came along, we knew he was perfect for white America. O.J. was a substitute white man in American society. There wasn't nothing Black on him but the bottom of his shoes. But since they loved him, that was our time to say, "Yeah, this is wrong and we're glad the brother got off because you didn't prove your case." Let's talk about balanced reporting and the need to give history and perspective to all of the warfare going on in the Middle East. They are our brothers and sisters as well.

And so, yes, we need to respond to terrorism, but we have to be responsible for the way in which we are a part of a nation that has hurt other people in the name of democracy. And we know we've been mad at America, too. And still be mad. Right? Because as soon as all of the unity fades away in the face of the love, affirmative action still ain't getting passed. Reparations, according to Condoleezza Rice, *your* representative of national security in the Bush administration, will still be put down.

So my point is, yes, we are American, but we've been telling America we've been American from the beginning. And if you're really American, you ought to tell the truth about America. Loving America doesn't mean uncritically celebrating everything she does. If Martin Luther King, Jr., said, "I love America enough to tell her the truth," and the truth is we've been wrong, then we've got to deal with that as well. It ain't just bin Laden; it's the "been lying" we've been doing and now we've got to straighten that up, too.

And, see, this book I just wrote on Tupac [Shakur], that's another young brother who was subjected to the American media trying to dis him. But Tupac dropped science. Long before racial profiling became an issue, he was talking about that, talking about police officers getting paid to beat up on Blacks, talking about his taxes going toward paying those same cops. And he didn't say "nigger." He said, "Nigga." N-i-g-g-a—Never Ignorant Getting Goals Accomplished. Don't get it twisted.

So, one of the things Black youth culture helps to remind us is the degree to which America will descend to try to denigrate our integrity. Tupac was telling the truth about that. Yeah, he might have been cussing, but that ain't the first cuss word you've heard. And what's more profane and vulgar, saying "m—f—" or treating somebody like one? So, you've got hip hoppers with their jeans slung way down low to their behind who are talking about stuff, but really acting like love because they're selling wolf tickets. Or, you have an American government with suit and tie that will blow to smithereens its enemies without compunction and refuse to acknowledge its own perpetration of global domination and of white supremacy. That's the reality we must always confront. Thank God for the hip hoppers who tell the truth about that.

Let's look now at our text from Judges 18:24, from the Revised Standard Version: "And he said, 'You take my gods which I made, and the priest, and go away, and what have I left? How then do you ask me, 'What ails you?'" I just want to preach a bit about, "What have I left?"

In Ephraim's hill country, the central highland of Palestine, the site of so much controversy and confusion today, a woman had saved eleven hundred shekels or pieces of silver that amounted really to her life's savings. That was a whole lot of cheddar for those times. And she saved it up and accumulated it over years of hard work and extracting her savings and the dowry she might have inherited to create her little personal fortune. And one day somebody stole that personal fortune. All of the accumulated wealth that she had managed to sock aside was now depleted by a barbaric act of thievery. And so—like many of us whose wealth is depleted by a singular act of extraordinary degradation and depravity—she cursed (with a holy curse, we're told) the folk who stole her money. She said, "Curses be upon those who have taken my money."

Money is always more than money. Currency is a symbol of an accumulated wealth that will never altogether be exhausted by the currency that symbolizes it. That's why they're always making arguments about do we have gold in Fort Knox to back up the money we've got circulating. Because the currency you hold is no better than the accumulated wealth that it symbolizes. You can have a whole lot of checks, but if you ain't got no money in the bank, the checks ain't really worth nothing. Now that don't stop some of us from still using them, but that's another sermon! Money is really always altogether more than money. It symbolizes how we relate to one another. It is a token of how we create relationships with one another. At the root of so much of the fratricide and the genocide in our world is the question of the use or abuse of money and wealth.

That's why when we talk about prosperity, it should always be within the context of God's plan. God is not interested in the unfettered, uncritical accumulation of wealth for self-aggrandizing purposes, for self-absorbed, narcissistic me-ism. It's about helping Black folk. It's about helping this nation. It's about helping Africa. It's about helping our people.

And so she cursed those people who had stolen her money. Her son, Micah—which means "he who is like God"—turned out to be the person most shaken by her curse. Micah, whom she had reared with intense attention to nurturing in him the spirit of truth and of godliness, was shaken by that curse. Micah was convicted by her curse. He was convicted because he had stolen his mama's money.

How our children sometimes disappoint us. Of course, she probably would have said, "You didn't have to steal it. You could've asked me for it and I'd've gave it to you." I know that's bad grammar but that's some serious theology. "I'd have given it to you. You didn't have to pilfer it. You didn't have to steal it. You didn't have to, in the cover of night, sneak into my tent and remove my accumulated wealth—the wealth that had we used wisely would not only have helped me, but you. But in deference to immediate gratification, you ripped off not only my money, but also your future." We do that 'cause we're shortsighted. But see, sometimes that shortsightedness is a real road to some revelation that we have to confront.

So Micah ripped off his mama, stole her purse, and then when she uttered that curse, something deep in him was convicted. (Thank God for training and rearing your kids in the way they ought to go, for planting something in them. It might not come out when you think it ought to, but sometimes the Word of God that you give to them will resound in them, maybe not now but later.) And so, Micah goes to his mama and he says, "Mama, I am the one that stole that money." And his mama is so overwhelmed that he's told the truth that together they decide what to do. So they invest about two hundred shekels of that money and take it to a silversmith to melt it down into a molten and graven image.

Now, the tricky part here is that the money that was stolen is now replaced and restored, and now it is melted down into an idol to worship God. They're on touchy ground there because idol worship in that ancient world is already a source of enormous strain and consternation with the real God. So idol worship was already on the wrong footing, and in acknowledgment of the blessing of God, they do something to contradict the spirit of God, who gave them the blessing to begin with—because that's how messy human relationships are.

So in light of that, they melt down the gold into a god, into a molten image, and Micah even hires his son. He sets up his son as the priest of the temple he establishes in his home, a shrine to God. But then, another priest comes along—an educated Levite priest. The Levite priest had some serious learning and so Micah says to him, "I want you to be my priest. I'll give you ten pieces of silver a year." That was some serious money back then. "I'll give you a place to stay and some food to eat and some nice clothes if you will be *my* priest." Not God's priest, not God's prophet, not God's servant, but *my* priest. And so, the Levite signs on and he begins to become the priest of Micah in their homemade shrine in their tent.

A few months later along comes the traveling, roaming Danite tribe. The tribe of Danite, who is homeless. Ain't got no home, looking for a home, looking for the Promised Land. And part of what was going on in the Middle East then is what's going on now, people arguing over geography as destiny, as Ralph Waldo Emerson put it. Trying to argue about whose land belongs to who. And when you're already in a land and people claim it to be their Promised Land, that's a problem with you because you've already got the land. And God ain't told you about the deed God might have given to them. But in the name of God, they claim to own your land.

And so the Danites see the beautiful shrine in the house of Micah. And they see that silver god shining there and they see the priest and they want both of them. And so they steal the shrine of god. At first the priest puts up a battle, but then they say, "What do you want? Do you want to be pastor of a church with one person, with four people, or do you want six hundred members in your congregation? Plus, we're going to pay you more and give you a better retirement package." He said, "See you, Micah. Got to get with the Danites."

And so the priest went with them. And you know Micah was deeply upset and he said, "Oh my God, what have they done?" So, he got some of his villagers and took some knives and some sickles. You know they didn't have that much armament back then because they were victims of their enemies. And one of the tragedies of minority people in a majority situation is that they've got to borrow the very armament they use from their enemies. And so they took up arms and they went out against these six hundred Danites, and they said, "Give us our stuff back." And [the Danites] laughed at them. "What are you doing? Don't play with us. There are six hundred people out here and you've got about, what, twenty-five people?" And Micah said, "You have taken my gods; you have taken the priest who is my personal priest and you have taken them. What have I left? And that's the reason I'm asking you to give them back. Why then do you ask me what ails me? That's what ails me."

That question that Micah asks is really a question that all of us have to come to. In the middle of devastation, what have I left? But if you examine it, it was an opportune time for them to really dig deep into the spiritual resources that God had given to them. Because, after all, if God is going to be God, you've got to get rid of your other gods. And sometimes God does a jack move on your gods, just rips them off; just used your enemies to take them away from you. I know we don't like that, but you know what Paul Sherer said? "Real worship is bringing gods we've made to bow down to the God who made us." Oh, but what do we do? We attempt to make God bow down before our gods. Oh, we know how we create our own gods—our gods of materialism. We know some of us are worshipping bling bling. Some of us are worshipping platinum. Some of us are worshipping Lexus and Rolls-Royce. Some of us are worshipping materialism.

Now we know we live in a world where we need to have some accumulated wealth. I ain't stupid. Right? And the problem with so many Black people is that we ain't got wealth. We've got a whole lot of income, but no wealth. Right? See, if you've got some serious wealth, you ain't got to have much of an income 'cause your wealth is going to make money. Your money is going to make wealth. Your wealth is going to create wealth. If you don't go to work today, you don't miss nothing. But most of us miss work, miss money, miss meal. Right? "Oh yeah, I'm making $500,000 but ain't got no wealth created." And so Black communities have been wealth poor. And because we've been wealth poor, the infrastructure of the ghetto economy means we have to engage in underground economies: illicit materials, thieving, thugging, and other activities as opposed to creating entrepreneurial expertise to perpetuate wealth to pass on to our children and to our grandchildren.

Now you might not like it, but some of the best examples of wealth creation in the Black community come out of the hip hop community. I ain't just talking about P. Diddy. He says, "I ain't got to write rhymes, I write checks." But I'm talking about Master P down in New Orleans. This man has created extraordinary opportunities for the poor people in his community. And now *Forbes* magazine has to acknowledge his entrepreneurial genius. Maybe he should be teaching over here at the Wharton School or over here at Georgetown University. So, I'm not against that. But what I am against is this kind of uncritical celebration of the goods and services and materials of life as if they are themselves the sign of God's blessing to you.

See, the problem with that is that, when you ain't got no goods, are you not blessed by God? When you ain't living like Big Willie, does that mean God has not blessed you? We have to be very careful about talking about how God blesses us—even in our theology when it says "I was spared." I was supposed to be at the World Trade Center doing a book signing the day it went down. And then, I was in Boston Monday night, could've been on that plane Tuesday morning. Some of my friends and family said, "God blessed you." And I said, "Yeah, hold on, I am blessed by God, but not because I was spared." What kind of theology is that? So the people who went down to their deaths were not blessed? Blessing is not determined by possession of material wealth or even by your life. Blessing is determined by your relationship with God. Blessing is determined by your consciousness to know you need God. Blessing is determined by your intimate contact with the Almighty. Whether you are dead or alive, you are blessed, if you have that.

We have all these theologies that just sanctify materialism. We're mad at JAY-Z for talking about all this stuff and we say that's problematic. But JAY-Z ain't never claimed to be no prophet nor no preacher nor no teacher from God. But we've got people in the pulpit across America and the globe saying that, if God has blessed you, you ought to have a certain amount of money in the bank automatically—and if you don't, you're not blessed by God. Yes, we need the accumulation of wealth. Yes, we need to leverage our authority so that we can get out of poverty. Ain't nobody sanctifying this poverty except a capitalistic system that wants to keep us poor. But don't get it twisted. Don't identify God with the things you possess. God is not your car, not your house, not your clothes, not your capital, not your jewelry, not your ice, not your platinum, not your record deal, not your book deal, not your title. God is God by God's self.

So, sometimes God has to send the Danites to rip off your gods. And maybe God is telling America that you've been worshipping your power too long. You've been worshipping your nuclear capability too long. What is a nuclear bomb going to do to somebody who doesn't care whether he lives or dies? Which is why I study some of these kids in the ghetto, because some of them are like that, too. Ain't got nothing to lose. Don't care about you or themselves. That's why they're in love with death. So much of their music talks about death. You know, like they're addicted to death. They *are* addicted to death because they live in a death-dealing culture that sees them as nothing but thugs and throwaways, so they begin to wear proudly the labels they are given. "You call me a thug? Darn right I'm going to be a thug." So we live in a culture that refuses to acknowledge their legitimacy or their centrality as human beings.

And then it's not just the white supremacists and mainstream culture that do it. Black people do it, too, to our own kids because they *is* your kids. Yeah, you may be afraid of them and yeah, some of them are misled and misdirected and got devil all up in it. Ain't no doubt about that. But these are your children. And if you are only concerned about the accumulation of your wealth, wanting your priest, wanting your preacher and not God's priest and God's preacher, you'll have ministers preaching a gospel that will reproduce your wealth while the masses of Black people are going down the drain, to hell in a hand basket.

And those young people begin to spring up like Tupac, like Biggie, like Nas, and they begin to tell. They begin to use words because all they have is words. They have no wealth. They have no accumulated capital. They're living in an enclave of civic horror called the ghetto and the slum, and Black people who are wanting to distance themselves from them because they're the wrong kind of niggas. They ain't our kind of niggas. They're project niggas. And I'll tell you why so many Black folk are upset with the rap music: the wrong niggas have got the microphone. Them ain't the folks we want to speak for us: Snoop Dog, Lil' Kim, Foxy Brown. I understand ya, I feel ya. But here's the point, when they were anonymous, nobody knew their names. Many of us were not concerned about their plight, predicament, and culture. So as a result of that, they feel no moral responsibility to accede to our moral wishes now that they're on their own, away from our help; they've managed to rise up. So now you want them to be responsible when you weren't responsible for helping them from the beginning. They feel that. Don't always just give scholarships to the A students. Be worried about the C and D students, too.

I ain't justifying sexism and patriarchy [and] homophobia. I am not justifying beating up on women, calling them nasty names, 'cause that stuff is evil and problematic and wrong. But it didn't just begin with hip hop culture. In most Baptist churches this morning, you can't find a female sitting up on the pulpit. Right? Because we are practicing patriarchy. Ain't nobody calling you no bitch but they're treating you like one if they don't let you into the place of power. You mean to tell me that the Black church, which is 75 to 80 percent female, can't be run by a female? God ain't blessed her? God said, "If you don't cry out, the rocks will cry out." You mean God can call a rock "Reverend" but not a woman? What kind of theology is that? God comes in whatever form God chooses to.

And so, Micah said, "You've taken away my gods and you've taken away my priest. I done had my private Reverend, Mr., Dr., Professor, and now you done taken him. And, not only did you take my god, you took my priest that helped me with my god, which may be a good thing." Because, if you are a priest on somebody's payroll, you've got to say what they want you to say. You've got to do what they want you to do. And the problem with too many of us is that we've got too many priests and prophets on the payroll. Can't speak truth to power.

Don't get me wrong. It's hard to speak truth to power because you know you like going to the White House. I've been there and done that. You like being in the halls of power. They may not call you because you're a little bit too uppity, a little bit too Afrocentric, a little bit too Black for them, a little bit too discourteous in the face of romantic idealization of power. And he's our friend. He is our friend, so you end up saying everything like he's said it. Because you can't be a priest or a prophet on payroll. And if you are a priest on payroll, you've got to go to the National Cathedral and say it's all right to simply drop a bomb and commit war as opposed to saying, "Slow down. There ain't but one God. We understand domestic policy. We understand the political machinations of governmental authorities who are appointed to represent the people. But that notwithstanding, there's somebody else's voice that's got to be up in the mix." That maybe we ought to slow down and do as Psalm 46 says: "Be still and know that *I* am God." And maybe the problem is God is whipping us by saying "you have been worshipping at the altar of your supremacy, your superiority, your power, your terrorism throughout the world. Stop!"

But if you are a preacher on the payroll, you can't say that. If you want to be on C-SPAN next week, you can't say that; want to be on CNN, can't say that; want to be on *Nightline*, can't say that; want to write another book, can't say that; want to still make money on the lecture circuit, can't say that; want to deliver some more preachers, can't say that; can't go to the revival next week if the other preacher doesn't believe in that stuff. You can't say that, but you've got to say that 'cause the only payroll you should be worrying about is the payroll of God, the economy of the kingdom. That's why when you listen to most of these preachers, if you wake up and turn on the TV, Martin Luther King couldn't get up in their church. Right? Martin Luther King with his prophetic gospel saying "what thus sayeth the Lord." The average church that's preaching this kind of gospel, he can't get up in there. Now, King wasn't perfect, but King was powerful and prophetic and told the truth and bore witness to the truth of God. And he said it in season and out of season. He said it when white folk wanted to hear it; he said it when they didn't want to hear it. He said it when Negroes wanted to hear it; he said it when Negroes didn't want to hear it.

Your job as a preacher, as a priest, as a prophet is to deepen people's consciousness of God. It's to nurture their spiritual awareness. It's to lead them to be self-critical and to preach justice. That ain't easy—especially when you are pastoring Black folks. You've got to love Black folk enough not to be scared of them. Because Black folk don't appreciate nobody scared of them. Right? But if you'd stand up and tell the truth about what you think, even if they don't agree with you, they're going to appreciate the fact that you're telling the truth.

And so that kind of gospel means we challenge our own xenophobia, our own homophobia, our own viciousness towards women. You've got to be unafraid of Black people enough, and love them enough, to tell them the truth. And, yes, maybe we are doing something in our inner-city communities that needs to be reconstructed because we are killing each other. We've got to tell the truth about that. But we don't cave in to white supremacy that tries to make us pawns to beat up other Negroes. A real prophet uses his or her education in defense of the best interest of the people by preaching prophetically to them.

You cannot afford to be on the payroll of anybody but God. And the reason is not because we're perfect, not because we have a direct pipeline to God, but because we are under judgment ourselves, if we do not preach the gospel. If we are not being responsible for what God has given to us, we are sinning ourselves. And that means we have to oppose the wisdom of the world. Sometimes, like Representative Lee, you've got to stand up by yourself. It looks like nobody else is going to help you; nobody else is with you. Even your former allies think you're crazy for what you're doing. If God has told you to do it, you've got to stand up to it.

And then when Micah asked that question, "What have I left?"—Oh, that's a good time. When your gods are destroyed and your priests have gone, who are on your private payroll, that's a good time to hear God. What you got left? Just you and God. But that's all right. Ain't no harm in that. See you done got rid of the unnecessary. You done got rid of the contention. You done got rid of the non-vital. You know what's left? Just you and your God. And when that's left, you've got everything left.

What have I left when my gods are gone? What have I left when my preacher is gone? Me and my Savior. Just a walk in the garden. I talk with him and I walk with him and he tells me I am his own. And the joy I share, my God, and the peace I know. I'll tell you what you've got left. You've become a prisoner of the permanent. And when you become a prisoner of the permanent, that's God in you. No matter what buildings crumble, no matter what lies are told, no matter what opposes you, God is in you. That's what we have left: A love for our Lord, a love for our God, our Priest, and our Christ. Peace.

19

Hard Out Here for a P.I.M.P.

I preached this sermon as part of an appearance at a conference, "Nurturing the Prophetic Imagination," at Point Loma Nazarene University. At the time, the song "Hard Out Here for a Pimp," recorded four years earlier by the Memphis rap group Three 6 Mafia and made famous when it was performed by stars Terrence Howard and Taraji P. Henson as their characters DJay and Shug in the film Hustle & Flow *(and which snagged the Memphis crew an Oscar in 2006 for best original song), was still resonant enough to make an impression with my audience. The subtitle of my sermon, turned into an acronym, quickly made plain my intent with P.I.M.P.: (a Prophet who Imagines Moral Possibilities). The sermon appears in* Nurturing the Prophetic Imagination, *edited in 2012 by Jamie Gates and Mark H. Mann.*

Thank you so kindly, Vice President Carr, for that gracious introduction. It is an honor to be here today at Point Loma to have this opportunity to chat with you a bit about some important things, and, as I'm wont to say in my tradition, what the Lord has laid on my heart. I want to thank Drs. Nelson and Mann for their gracious hospitality and for their brilliant leadership here at this institution and of course over this conference.

Now I ain't got but thirty minutes. I am a Baptist preacher. Usually, I introduce myself in thirty minutes, then start preaching. But Bart Ehrman, who has gained quite a bit of notice lately as a biblical scholar, and who has deconstructed some of the beliefs about scriptures, argues that we can't assume that people have a certain level of biblical literacy anymore, because we're living in a different era. He didn't say we're living in a postmodern era where we have really challenged the stability of certain understandings of the Word. So, with that in mind, I want to take a bit of time to read from the nineteenth chapter of Kings, in the Hebrew Bible, what we call the Old Testament:

[1] Now Ahab told Jezebel everything Elijah had done and how he had killed all the prophets with the sword. [2] So Jezebel sent a messenger to Elijah to

say, "May the gods deal with me, be it ever so severely, if by this time to-morrow I do not make your life like that of one of them."

³ Elijah was afraid and ran for his life. When he came to Beersheba in Judah, he left his servant there, ⁴ while he himself went a day's journey into the desert. He came to a broom tree, sat down under it and prayed that he might die. "I have had enough, LORD," he said. "Take my life; I am no better than my ancestors." ⁵ Then he lay down under the tree and fell asleep.

All at once an angel touched him and said, "Get up and eat." ⁶ He looked around, and there by his head was a cake of bread baked over hot coals, and a jar of water. He ate and drank and then lay down again.

⁷ The angel of the LORD came back a second time and touched him and said, "Get up and eat, for the journey is too much for you." ⁸ So he got up and ate and drank. Strengthened by that food, he traveled forty days and forty nights until he reached Horeb, the mountain of God. ⁹ There he went into a cave and spent the night.

And the word of the LORD came to him: "What are you doing here, Elijah?"

¹⁰ He replied, "I have been very zealous for the LORD God Almighty. The Israelites have rejected your covenant, broken down your altars, and put your prophets to death with the sword. I am the only one left, and now they are trying to kill me too."

¹¹ The LORD said, "Go out and stand on the mountain in the presence of the LORD, for the LORD is about to pass by."

Then a great and powerful wind tore the mountains apart and shattered the rocks before the LORD, but the LORD was not in the wind. After the wind there was an earthquake, but the LORD was not in the earthquake. ¹² After the earthquake came a fire, but the LORD was not in the fire. And after the fire came a gentle whisper. ¹³ When Elijah heard it, he pulled his cloak over his face and went out and stood at the mouth of the cave.

Then a voice said to him, "What are you doing here, Elijah?"

¹⁴ He replied, "I have been very zealous for the LORD God Almighty. The Israelites have rejected your covenant, broken down your altars, and put your prophets to death with the sword. I am the only one left, and now they are trying to kill me too."

¹⁵ The LORD said to him, "Go back the way you came, and go to the Desert of Damascus. When you get there, anoint Hazael king over Aram. ¹⁶ Also, anoint Jehu son of Nimshi king over Israel, and anoint Elisha son of Shaphat from Abel Meholah to succeed you as prophet. ¹⁷ Jehu will put to death any who escape the sword of Hazael, and Elisha will put to death any

who escape the sword of Jehu. [18] Yet I reserve seven thousand in Israel—all whose knees have not bowed down to Baal and all whose mouths have not kissed him."

Excuse me for that rather lengthy reading of the Scripture. The great southern historian C. Vann Woodward says a title is a contract between an author or a speaker and his or her audience. So, I want to reflect on "It's Hard Out Here for a P.I.M.P." Now in my mind, P.I.M.P. is not pimp. It's an acronym. P.I.M.P.—A Prophet who Imagines Moral Possibilities. Elijah has been doing battle with the forces, as he sees them, of evil. The people of Israel have been seduced by a god who has not made them but is purely of their making, a god foreign to their tradition, bowing their knees down to Baal. And it has been horrible for those who are the faithful, because they have been slaughtered. And Elijah has been sent a death threat by Jezebel, who says, "I'm making it my intention and my greatest duty to make sure that by this time tomorrow, you are dead. And like those other prophets, you too will die." And Elijah is afraid for his life. People think that prophets are built of steel, that they have bulletproof hearts.

To engage in an act of prophecy is not simply trying to predict the future—that's not even what biblical prophecy ultimately is about. If you try to have a one-to-one correlation between what some prophet said and what God subsequently did, you'd be hard-pressed to see the level of fulfillment really be extraordinary. But what is more important about prophecy is to get deep into the mind and imagination of God—to have the audacity to risk the belief that God somehow communicates to human beings and that you can tap into the imagination of God or you can be overrun by the imagination of God. You can be hit like a Mack truck by God's will, by God's desire, by the energy and imagination of God's mind. That's a rather, if you will, not humble, not characteristically gentle, but that's a rather—some would argue—arrogant way to assume that one can exist in life. That you can actually know the mind of God. That you can feel the pulse of God. That you can be driven by God. After all, in the name of that vision, many people have done evil and desperate things; many people thinking they have served God have murdered and created mayhem. And so Elijah, feeling that he is in the grip of God's imagination, knowing that he has been pushed forward by what he feels God wants him to do, runs for his life, because now he's been threatened.

Prophets are often a threat to the social and civil order. Prophets are not simply there to make people feel good. Prophets often don't make kings feel very good. In fact, prophets are the ones saying, you know, "You da man." But "you da man" like you're the man who's messing up. You're the man who's engaged in all kinds of nefarious activities. You are the man who's contradicting your very principles. Remember Nathan going to King David, saying that very thing. Once you were the apple of God's eye and you were riding high, and now because of your own particular lust and the consumption of desires that have not been disciplined, you are messing up big time and contradicting your very principles. And so, you da man all right, but not "You da man." No, no, no—you da man. No, no, no—you're the man. Not that kind of celebratory back-slapping celebration, but it is a challenge to those who are in power, if we are really prophetic, if we really have the imagination of God at stake.

God often opposes those who are in power, and, ironically enough, the biblical record tells us time and time again that God is responsible for getting people in power, but people who are in power tend to forget what they are in power for. Folk get elected, selected, and then they tend to forget what they were there for—what they were sent for—because the voices around them begin to squeeze out that divine anointment and possibility. A host of people who are advisors begin to crowd out the ability of this particular prophet or this anointed leader to hear the voice of God. And it's difficult, and none of us need be arrogant about it, because all of us are tempted by the traps of life. All of us are seduced by power. All of us are seduced by influence. You don't know until your name is up in lights. You don't know until people bow down in your presence. You don't know until they acclaim you as a great singer or great entertainer or great thinker. You don't know that temptation until then.

And so here it is that Elijah is running for his life, because the prophetic imagination often runs counter to what the world of power wants. And as a result, there's a conflict, and the person who pays the price is often the prophet. And so now Elijah is running for his life, and he comes to the mouth of a cave and the angel speaks to him, asking, "What are you doing here?" He says, "Look, it is enough oh Lord, now take away my life." I've read to you from the New International Version, but the King James Version says, "It is enough oh Lord, now take away my life for I am not better than my fathers." He said, they've beat up on the prophets, they've murdered them, they've thrown down your altars, they bow their knees to a foreign god; they are no longer listening to the prophetic narrative that I have enunciated. Just take my life; it's over. It's a wrap. It's done. I don't want to live anymore.

It's hard out here for a prophet who imagines moral possibilities because you're often thinking, dadgum, I'm just trying to do the right thing. How come folk can't hear me? How come they just can't do what I tell them to do because God has inspired me to say what I'm saying? Because perhaps one of the reasons people can't hear a prophet is because they don't want to hear the truth about their circumstances or situations. And so, it is difficult for us to hear, so sometimes we turn to entertainers or we turn to artists, we turn to visual artists and artists of the word. Because we can't sometimes take the truth from prophets who stand to proclaim the Word. Now sometimes a prophet is a bit arrogant or self-important, confident beyond any measure of reasonable expectation. You know, when you got the Word of God, you figure that you're the dude, you're the one who's walking around, you're the woman. Look, I got the Word of the Lord, step off. You know I'm that person.

And yet what Elijah discovers is that it's hard out here for a prophet, because prophets are often alienated from the structures of society that would give them commendation. Society doesn't celebrate what they do; they don't get the national awards to celebrate their prophetic integrity or imagination. They are often running counter to the prevailing logic of the times, or what Eric Hoffer used to call the temper of the times. And so now it is not a comfortable position, and it ain't well paid. Ain't a long line of people signing up to be no prophet. The job description is awful tough. You don't have much money, not much social acclaim; you may die in the process. I think I am going to be a nurse practitioner, thank you very much. And so, the long line of prophets diminishes or is diminished, is eroded, is lessened, because the demands are so high. And those who are called to such a duty often find themselves in direct contradiction to the society around them, and that leads to depression and grief.

Martin Luther King, Jr., was a deeply depressed human being. Why? Because he was called by God to speak a word of prophecy to an era that didn't want to hear it. Now that we celebrate Martin Luther King, Jr.'s birthday as a national holiday, it is hard for you to imagine that it was hard for Martin Luther King, Jr. But here was a man who for the last three years of his life was persona non grata. He could hardly get a speaking engagement at universities. No American publisher wanted to publish his book. His own staff spoke out against him or disagreed with him. His own organization initially said, when he spoke out against the war in Vietnam, "That represents Dr. King; that doesn't represent the board of the SCLC" (Southern Christian Leadership Conference). And then when he spoke out against the war in Vietnam a year or two later, Whitney Young, who was then the head of the National Urban League, and Roy Wilkins, who was head of the National Association for the Advancement of Colored People, said, "You're wrong, you're problematic, to break precedent. The man in power, Lyndon Baines Johnson, has done more to help Black people than any recent president, and here you are speaking out against him, here you are taking a stand against him. It will lead to grief!"

It leads to depression. King was deeply depressed, not because he wasn't sure of his vocation, though he tried to figure it out. He said, "Maybe I need to go back to teaching. Maybe I need to retire and give up this prophetic vocation. Maybe I need to stop staying on the road 360-some-odd days a year. Giving something like 380 speeches a year. Never at home, the children don't even know me; my wife is a stranger to me. My home will not even receive me gladly." You can romanticize what it means to be a prophet, but to pay the price for that prophecy is another thing, and often the price of prophecy is grief and suffering and depression. And so Elijah is there like Martin Luther King, Jr., was there, Martin Luther King, Jr., wondering what would be his end. It got so tough at the end that he could never stand to be in a room that had windows. Because he was wondering, "Is it going to be now that I will be murdered? Some bullet will come crashing through the window?" He was very uncomfortable. This man was not even forty years old. When they did an autopsy on his body, they said he had a heart of a sixty-year-old man. Distress was too deep; the pain was too penetrating and poignant. The depression was so profound.

It's hard out here for a prophet who imagines moral possibilities that are against the era in which we live and against the logic of those who are in power. Prophets would rather be on the payroll, paid, supplemented, stipends, foundation grants. Prophets would rather live in nice homes and drive nice cars, this prosperity gospel that has choked Christian belief in the last fifteen to twenty years. But it's just a recycling of what happened. Even the great Harry Emerson Fosdick was victim to some of this stuff back in the '30s. You think about the fact of this—the more things change, the more they stay the same. People think that God is about cosigning your home, God is about getting a better car, driving a nice car. I'm not mad about driving no nice car. I'm trying to get one, too. Trying to live in a nice crib. Ain't nobody mad about that. But the point is, don't worship at the altar of materialism, because it blocks prophetic enunciation. They make you more comfortable in the world in which you're trying to deliver judgment and have analysis, and you become compromised with the trinkets of power, with the seductions of access, with the powerful poignancy of influence. Name in lights, on books, on marquees and you become quiet, compromise what you want to say.

And so Dr. King was depressed because he was in the land of grief, because he was grieving and lamenting the steep decline of the American moral imagination and that America was in the grip of a notion called white supremacy. That some people believe that just because they were of one race, they were better than others. That they were superior, that they were more intelligent and more likely to be the recipient of God's favor. He said, I don't even know that god. The God I worship is a God of love that believes in justice, and justice is what we do when we think about love. As I've often tried to say, "Justice is what love sounds like when it speaks in public." And so, we've got to figure out a way to love people in public spaces that allows justice to roll down like waters and righteousness like a mighty stream, King said, and for that, the head of the FBI—or at least his second in command—said that King was the most dangerous leader in America. For that, for the desire to not have one person drink at a white water fountain and another person drink at a Black water fountain, he was considered to be a threat to American society. Because he wanted white children and Black children to go to the same school, he was seen as a threat to America.

And so he was deeply and profoundly grieving and depressed; the mortality descended upon him with rushing fervor. And like Elijah, he withdrew as well, as Elijah withdraws and says, "Lord it's enough to take away my life; they've killed your prophets, torn down your altars, they've bowed at another god." And God led Elijah to get something to eat. Because you've got to feed the prophetic imagination, but you've got to feed the prophetic body as well. That means sometimes there's a relationship between your nervous system and folk who get on your nerves. If you're not healthy, if you're not in your right mind, you're not in the mind to hear the word of God or even to put on the mind of God, the imagination of God. There is a strict relationship between physical resource and physical stability, and material resource and hearing the godly imagination. That's why some people who are subject to poverty, that's why some people who are viciously relegated to the periphery of American society, that's why some people who go to schools where they don't have any resources, books that are second- and third-hand, pages ripped out, their bathrooms don't even work, their toilets are in disrepair, their teachers are working in overcrowded rooms—and those kids are acting up because they didn't even eat breakfast that morning. Lead paint and asbestos is their common companion. And then we wonder why those children have attention deficit disorders. We wonder why they can't pay attention in significant fashion. Their stomachs are grumbling. They are physically malnourished; they can't even hear or consume the mental nourishment because they have been psychologically depleted and physically assaulted.

God says to Elijah, "You can't even understand what a prophetic poignancy you possess. You can't even understand your great imagination because you are tired, worn out, worn down." And so even though he is grieved and depressed, God wants to speak to him. God wants to lift him up. But God can only do that by feeding the prophetic imagination, by feeding the prophetic body. That's why some people who try to get into this abstract spirituality that enunciates and articulates this vast notion of God being some spiritual being and we are all floating on high are not relevant. If your God ain't got nothin' to do with the redistribution of wealth and trying to get people paid right and at a decent wage, if your God ain't got nothin' to do with folk having their bellies filled because they are hungry, if your God ain't got nothin' to do with trying to help folk out of the misery they're in—then that God is not relevant. Then that God is not of much use to those of us who are struggling down here on the ground.

Gottfried Wilhelm Leibniz, the great philosopher, said that some try to see God *sub specie aeternitatis*, that we see God from above and the eternal perspective. But I'm with the Wes Montgomery crowd. That's a jazz musician. Down here on the ground. You all don't know nothin' about that. You're all into JAY-Z and Britney Spears. I ain't mad at none of them. Taylor Swift. Or Kanye. Now this ain't got nothin' to do with my sermon this morning, but I got to defend Kanye just a little bit up in here today. I'm talking about prophets and how tough it is. It's hard to be a prophet. I ain't saying Kanye was no prophet. He didn't intend nothing edifying. But he was mad at the fact, because he had this stupid notion that people who got awards should actually deserve them. We ain't sayin' Taylor Swift ain't cool. We ain't saying that Taylor Swift ain't got no skills. But Taylor Swift on video of the year, up against oh-oh, oh-oh, come on.

> All my single ladies, All my single ladies,
> All my single ladies, All my single ladies,
> Oh, oh, oh, oh, oh, oh, oh
> Come on, come on.

So Kanye seizes the microphone. It was rude, it was ridiculous, like prophets often are. You don't want to live next door to no prophet—they're ridiculous people. They don't brush their teeth, they don't shave, they don't sometimes put on their proper adornment. But boy, when that word comes out of them, it's ridiculous and cantankerous. And so, Kanye seizes the microphone, and he starts to speak, and people are pissed. How dare he? How many young Black and Latino and First Nation people are Taylor Swifted every day? Except they don't even get a chance to get the microphone to speak back. And, guess what, I bet you Chuck Berry was watching, saying, "Do it!" Chuck Berry was going, "Where were you when Elvis was getting my awards?" Huh? I bet you Little Richard was saying, "Do that! Shut up, give me my Grammy. Whhhooo!" 'Cause Little Richard said, "Pat Boone got my award!"

So, Kanye wasn't intentionally engaging in a prophetic act. But the consequences were prophetic because what it did was try to compensate for the denial of legitimate and authentic recognition of Black artistry in the world, where their superior achievements were not recognized. Now, that don't mean then that Taylor Swift ain't got no skills. What it means is that sometimes we are not sensitive to other children who have been Taylor Swifted. Those who are denied opportunity, but don't have amplification from the same tribe that dissed them. Beyoncé gave her the microphone later. But many people of the same tribe who have dissed the others have not allowed them to amplify their pain and misery.

And so if I were to link that back into this—rather suspiciously—Elijah is out there saying it's enough, cancel tomorrow, it's done, it's a wrap. We try to pass over the mournful passages of our souls, the dark night of the soul. Because when you are a prophet, sometimes that darkness must be calculated as the price to be paid in order for the advance to go forth, and sometimes to your own detriment you are a vehicle for a transcendent blessing. But the problem is that you just don't want to get trapped there. Sometimes cynicism is the luxury of those who have the time to think and calculate, but those whose backs are against the wall got to stand up.

And so, God says to Elijah, "What are you doing here?" Elijah says, "Look, I'm representing you. I know you know. Don't tell me you too? I'm here because they've messed up." God says, "Get something to eat. You're tired, you're weary, your nervous system is painfully overwrought." Howard Thurman, the great prophet, said, "We must yield the nerve center of our consent to God." That means at the center of your soul, like Dag Hammarskjöld, the great U.N. secretary, said: "There must be a yes, even in the midst of no." Even in the midst of denial, even in the midst of lapsed opportunity, even when you think everybody else is gone and you the only one left.

And he says to God, "I'm the only one left." Be careful when you telling God that you the only one, 'cause God be making more that look just like you. Right? Remember that Bill Cosby used to have that thing with the children—"I'll get rid of you and make another one that looks just like you." Oh, parents are terrorists, aren't we? You're telling God you the only one left—slow down. Is God still God? Part of the prophetic imagination is to imagine that you got a successor and some company. And so sometimes the temptation is to believe that we're the only one. I'm the only Michael Eric Dyson. Well hope I am, but I ain't the only one God sent. I'm the only Desmond Tutu, I am the only Martin Luther King, Jr., I'm the only Prathia Hall Wynn, and I'm the only Stanley Hauerwas. You are, but you ain't the only one that God sent. You're not the only one with the Word. God said, "There are 7,000 others who have not bowed their knees to Baal. They have not been seduced. You just don't know them."

And so, what you have to do is not to imagine you the only one left, because when you think that you the only one, you start making mistakes. You are on the court and think that you are the only one that can shoot, and you are trying to toss up threes, and here is a dude under that basket who can dunk it if you just pass him the ball. Man. And so you're not the only one. There's a team, but sometimes that team is invisible. So, you have to use your prophetic imagination to organize a colloquium, a congregation of fellow sufferers and servants who are here to do God's work, and never have the audacious assumption in the negative sense to assume that you are the only one. God says to him, "You're tired, and because you're tired and your nervous system is overwrought, you don't understand that there are others out here who are working in different venues." Remember Jesus later said, "I got sheep you know not of." There are other folk working out here. You think that your church is the only one, your denomination's the only one, you think your religion is the only one. You think your way of knowing God is the only way. You ain't the only one. You're not the only person, you're not the only people, and Elijah was especially distraught because he says, I thought I was better than those white supremacists who trained me. Thought I was better than those crackers and rednecks that I left behind. Those were the real racists. But I am pure. I am part of the Why? Generation. I listen to JAY-Z. I listen to Snoop Dogg.

> Follow me, follow me, follow me, follow me, but don't lose your grip
> Nine-trizzay's the yizzear to f*** up s***
> So I ain't holdin' nuthin' back

And motherf***** I got five on the twenty sack
I said a Rat-tat-tat-tat
Right . . .
Falling back on that . . .
With a heck-a-fied gangsta lean
Gettin' funky-on-the mic like an old batch o' collard greens
It's the capital S, oh yes, I'm fresh N double O P
D O double G Y D O double G ya' see
Showin' much flex when it's time to wreck a mic'
Pimpin' what and clockin' a grip like my name is Dolomite.
Yeah.

Well. I got Black friends. I know a couple of Negroes, some Native Americans, and some Asian brothers and sisters. I'm down. I'm cool. I eat at Mexican restaurants. I go to concerts that feature diversity. I am cool. I am not like my ancestors. Then you discover that I'm no better than them. Why? Because some of them did the best they knew how, their moral intestines gutted by blinding bigotry. And we think we're better, and yet here we are living in a so-called post-racial era. And we still live in abject poverty and misery. And if you push even enlightened young white brothers and sisters hard enough, how much are we willing to admit that our privilege rests upon the denial of opportunity for so many others?

I am not better than my fathers. That recognition will make it difficult for you to even deliver your prophecy, because if I am no better, then I might as well end it. No. 'Cause ain't nobody perfect, and ain't nobody got the ultimate truth, but you are humble enough to admit that just like your mothers and fathers you have your impediments and obstacles, then that opens a pathway for divine revelation. And so God says to Elijah, He says, "Check out the seven other thousand who ain't bent their knees to Baal. Go anoint another king to take over them that's messing up, then anoint your successor, who is going to be the prophet after you. 'Cause you ain't the only one."

It's hard out here for a prophet if you think that you the only one. This is a long-distance race. You got to pass the baton on. You think Jordan is great, but then comes Kobe Bryant. Okay, LeBron James too. You think you're FloJo, and then comes somebody else—started to say Marion Jones, but that would be difficult right now. Wilma Rudolph before them all. You think that you're the only one, that you're the zenith, you're the high point, you're the apotheosis? You are the prophetic imagination, you are the cat's pajamas from God? You are not the only one, and it's hard sometimes, and we get stuck in grief. And we must go through grief; you cannot avoid it. But what ultimately saves you, even in the midst of your grief, is to recognize that you have a community of co-aspirants who desire the same thing you do, but you must imagine their existence in order for your own to be made more worthy. And for you to become an ultimate instrument of God, you must imagine that there are others who possess an equal measure of God's grace.

And as I end, that's why it's so important even as a prophet not to assume that your way is the only way. Howard Thurman said, "You can go to the Atlantic Ocean, you can dip your glass in the Atlantic Ocean. It may be full of the Atlantic Ocean, but it ain't all the Atlantic Ocean." Sometimes we're depressed and grieved because we're trying to do it all by ourselves, thinking our way is the only way. I deal with my conservative brothers and sisters all the time and they are so sometimes mind-numbingly self-righteous and self-assured and confident that they have God's word, and they know what the deal is, and they're against abortion—they are pro-life, but they ain't pro-livin'. I ain't mad. Choose your moral position; I respect you; but don't assume you got the only way. Don't assume you the only one. Why do you assume that because you live in Montana, or Idaho, you got God's number on speed dial? And you assume that those poor Black and brown and red and yellow people who are beyond the pale—literally—of your imagination are somehow not as blessed by God. You must realize you are not the only one.

And so, it's hard out here for a prophet who fails to recognize you are in a great community with a great cloud of witnesses. And as I end then, you must recognize, no matter where you are, no matter what generation you're in, no matter what kind of music moves you, no matter what kind of spirituality that you have, it's not the only one. It's not the only way. It's not the only path. And the God we worship is bigger and more powerful and calls us to a prophetic vocation and to imagine others who are there with us, who can check us, who can challenge us, and who may ultimately change us. God bless you.

Eulogizing Ancestors

In the Grieving Sanctuary

CHAPTER

20

A Key, a Song, a Bridge

Amiri Baraka and I enjoyed what can only be termed a cantankerous relationship. I greatly admired his literary genius and his political courage, even if I didn't always agree with him. In fact, we had a televised debate—about Manning Marable's posthumously published biography of Malcolm X—that was full of verbal fireworks and rhetorical pugilism, mostly as he assailed Manning and opposed me. Baraka and I—and Dr. Betty Shabazz, Malcolm's widow—had appeared together to speak at New York's Abyssinian Baptist Church in celebration of Malcolm's mighty memory. I was honored to deliver this eulogy in 2014 at Baraka's spirited and inspiring funeral at Newark Symphony Hall.

I will not be long. I'm honored to be here today. You ever had a telephone conversation with somebody, and you thought they hung up? And you said what you really believed? That was Amiri Baraka all day long. He said what he meant the first time around. He had no excuse for the articulation and expression of profound truth.

He was three things at least to me. First of all, he was a key. He was a key to the revolutionary transformation of Black and American consciousness in the time in which he lived. He was a man who was self-critical, like the best of Martin and Malcolm. He moved from Afro-bohemian embrace of a Beat poetry movement onto a cultural nationalism, onto a revolutionary nationalism, onto a revolutionary political practice—a Communist and Marxist practice. The man was constantly evolving because he was self-critical. Too many of us fail to look into the mirror to see the flaws we point out in somebody else. But Amiri Baraka was the key to that revolutionary transformation, and it was relentless interrogation of his practice in light of the best ideals that he nurtured in the bosom of Black resistance to white supremacy, social injustice and economic inequality.

But not only that, he wasn't just a key, he was a song. How do you divorce and divide the poetic meters, iambic pentameters, the avant-garde, the free verse, the beauty of his language from the music you heard [at his funeral] here today? You don't. His very language was music. His very poetry was intense. His very investment in the belief that Black people meant something was a gift to those who felt that they were nothing in a universe that did not respect them. And so, his language was powerful. The way he used commas and ampersands, the way he used vernacular traditions, that was a beautiful gift to suggest that Black people would not be dehumanized by an uncritical comparison to an American standard that [devalued] us to begin with and that should never be elevated. That's why his language was beautiful—because it was rooted in our vernacular tradition. The ugly, nasty, indignant realities that we confronted.

And then, finally, he was a bridge. He was a bridge between those in the streets and those in the academy. Now, a whole lot of people like to be anti-intellectual and say, "You ain't got to have no Ph.D." That's true. 'Cause you got to have something deeper than that. But don't sleep on the Ph.D. [Applause] Don't sleep on the schooling. You can be edified and intelligent, and you can be debased and ignorant. Choose what you will do. He understood the beauty and the intelligence of making scholarly inquiry in conjunction with revolutionary transformation. Before there were Black public intellectuals, Amiri Baraka was a Black public intellectual telling the truth and speaking back to the ignominious defeat of Black survival in a post-racial culture. It ain't post-racial. We still racist in American society. [Applause]

We still in love with pigment and pedigree. He was a bridge—as I take my seat—between slam poetry, so to speak, and hip hop and so-called old school. I'll tell you what: I see the beauty of Amiri Baraka in these young people we saw [perform here] today. But also, out there in the streets. And in Tupac. In a Nas. And in a JAY-Z. They could not do what they do without Amiri Baraka doing what he did. Because sometimes you can't just call upon your intellectual credibility to articulate your resistance to the world in which you live. Sometimes only a curse word will do. Sometimes only a sacred profanity will be able to articulate what we believe. As I take my seat, I believe in Amiri Baraka's spirit because he believed in us. We love him. We embrace him. And sometimes all you can say is, "nigga," or "motherfucker," because that's the ultimate reality we confront.

Peace! [Applause]

21

Long Live the Queen

Aretha Franklin was one of my dearest friends. No matter how many times she told me to call her "Aretha," I always called her "Miss Franklin." She and I shared a great appreciation for the variety and genius of Black preachers: I introduced her to the thrilling homiletical artist Freddy Haynes, whom she greeted with joy in a personal meeting in Baltimore, and I told her about the majestic old-school artistry of the late, great preacher Caesar Arthur Walter Clark. We took great delight in listening live to legendary preachers like Donald Parsons in Chicago. We also partied, and hung out, too, all while she fought pancreatic cancer with sublime grace and serene determination to keep going. I miss her every day, but I am consoled by listening to her voice, that voice, the voice, of a people, of a generation, of an age, of all time. I spoke these words at her epic, nearly nine-hour 2018 funeral at Detroit's Greater Grace Temple. I know she would have got a kick out of this tidbit tweeted by Merriam-Webster Dictionary about my eulogy for her: "Searches for 'lugubrious' jumped 3200% during Michael Eric Dyson's speech at #ArethaHomegoing."

To Bishop Ellis and Reverend Smith, to President Clinton and her husband, Bill [laughter and applause], to Attorney General soon-to-be-president Holder, and to Reverend Jackson. [Applause]

If some cosmic ethnographer were to drop down here and do a biopsy, an extract of living tissue, of Black genius, here today would be the veritable cornucopia of its radical expression. [Applause] We done had all kind of "*sanging*" up in here, from high European-derived classical composition to the gutbucket gospel [and] grueling reality of our blues and soul traditions. We have heard singers hit high notes and pan the depths of the diapason scale of American music. But we are here for one voice, one reason, one woman, who was a freakishly precocious woman. A bronze wunderkind of the gospel. Born in the legendary rhetorical womb she gestated in—of her father, Clarence LaVaughn Franklin.

She took me one day to the Trumpet Awards [in Atlanta] and there she had me attempt to explain his genius. C. L. Franklin practiced the species of Black sacred speech called whooping. How does one explain whooping? The coarsened articulation. The striated diction. The elastic grammar. Speech pressured by music that turns into song. You will quickly see one of the greatest exemplars of that rhetorical form in the presence of the Reverend Dr. Jasper Williams.

But it was in that womb that she was born, and [from] that Mississippi mud arrived Detroit deity. Aretha Franklin, at 14, sang "Never Grow Old." And in singing it, you could feel the theological prescience and the clairvoyance that God gave to her. She became a vehicle of the on high purpose that was radiated in that beautiful brown body. When Aretha sang at 14, she convinced people that, indeed, she would never grow old.

But then, she recorded the song again, when she was 30 years old. And in recording that song on her epic [gospel album] *Amazing Grace*, she gave us a vision of a return to the gospel world that her father claimed she had never left anyhow. And then, when she sang that song, about five minutes and twenty-one seconds in, on a nine minute and fifty-seven second song, you felt the volcanic eruption, the *glissando*, the *melisma*, stretching a single note across several syllables so that she can articulate the deep and profound realities that only song could capture. Aretha sang that song at 30 in a different way than she sang it at 14. Why is that? Between 14 and 30 there was a whole bunch of living. She never loved a man the way she loved that man. She said, if you gon' be a man demanding a do right woman, you better be a do right man. [Applause]

Now we know the great scholar Farah Jasmine Griffin speaks about [her] inchoate feminist perspective, never calling her a feminist, because Aretha Franklin never called herself a feminist. But she had feminist sensibilities; the independent autonomous reach of Black female identity was regnant in her rhetoric. She was Black girl magic before there was Black girl magic. [Applause]

And so, between 14 and 30 there was a lot of living. There was a chain of fools that she was conscribed into. There was the reality of the hurt and pain, the ardor, the ecstasy, the suffering and the reality that we have to confront as a Black people.

And don't get it twisted: she was Black without apology or excuse. And she was American without argument or exception. She was Black 'cause she was from the Blackest city in the world, Detroit. I know y'all jealous. You from Chicago, Philadelphia, Pittsburgh. You good, but you ain't got the D. [Laughter and applause]

Dot & Etta's Shrimp Hut.

Faygo Red Pop.

Vernors Ginger Ale.

Coney Island hot dog. [Applause]

The future hitched a ride in a Cadillac and found its destiny in a Ford. We had Motown music. I know everybody else had music, but y'all ain't had it like Detroit had it. [Applause] The greatest artist ever produced, Mr. Stevie Wonder. [Applause] The greatest songwriter ever, Smokey Robinson. [Applause] And for a long while, the greatest entertainer, Mr. Michael Jackson. [Applause] And the greatest singer in the world, Aretha Franklin. [Applause]

She was an edifying thief. She took other people's songs and made 'em her own. When Otis Redding heard her sing he said, she done took my song. Oh yes, she did, and he was glad she took it. Because she spelled out in a way he never spelled out Respect. She had to articulate it and enunciate it so folk could understand what she was talking about. Then in that belly of Blackness in Detroit, without apology or excuse, that embrace of her Blackness led her to be political. We got all kind of music now that ain't got nothin' to do with nothin' except cars and money and glory. [Applause] I ain't mad at that, but she was about getting Angela Davis out of jail. She was about working with Martin Luther King, Jr., and Jesse Jackson and Al Sharpton. She was about transforming the existence of Black America.

Now Negroes scared to say they Black. Scared to show up at a too-Black place. That's why some Black folk ain't here today. They sendin' letters. They don't want to get up in this Blackness. They don't want to feel the nasty power of this Blackness. We are Black in Detroit. We don't care. Take your shoes off. Dip it in the water. Get baptized. [Applause]

And then, this orange apparition had the nerve to say she worked for him.

You lugubrious leech. [Applause]

You dopey doppelganger of deceit and deviance.

You lethal liar.

You dimwitted dictator.

You foolish fascist. [Applause]

She ain't worked *for* you. She worked *above* you. She worked *beyond* you. Get your preposition right. [Applause]

Then, he got the nerve to say he gone grab it. That ain't what Aretha Franklin said. I'm-a *give* you something you can feel. [Applause] Like the brothers in the street say, tap lightly, like a woodpecker with a headache. [Applause]

So, don't you sully the memory of our great queen. Aretha Franklin was an original. Never one like her before, never another like her afterward. She was bold and brilliant and courageous and beautiful and indebted to the traditions that spark our renewal. She refused to sell out. She remained herself all along in her life.

And so, as I take my seat, you got to remember Aretha Franklin gave us something deep and powerful. When [Aretha] made her transition, Farah Jasmine Griffin, the professor at Columbia, said she was doing work even after she died. When she made her transition, convictions came down. Immunity pleas were made. Folk got sent to jail. Even as an ancestor she doin' work. She moved from being the Queen of Soul to the Queen of Souls. She is indeed looking over us as our ancestor, never forgetting that she will walk with us.

I had to go the other day from South Bend, Indiana, into Chicago. Leaving Notre Dame going to Chicago to speak. My ticket said the plane left at 4:33. But it arrived at 4:20. I had landed before I took off. [Applause] If you ain't already at where you goin', you ain't gonna be there when you arrive. You got to already know where you heading. Aretha Franklin ain't just made no transition, she been building up her housing equity in another place, with a God who loved her so. She was already there. She said a prayer for us. She loved us. And now she is the Queen of Our Souls.

Long live the Queen. Long live the Queen.

22

When She

Jessye Norman possessed a regal bearing and a magnificent voice, and she was every bit the diva that one might imagine any globally recognized opera star would be. But she was also a warm, down-to-earth woman who sought to use her considerable platform to advance knowledge of Black people and culture and an appreciation of our history and struggles in America. She curated a remarkable event at Carnegie Hall: Honor! A Celebration of the African American Cultural Legacy, *which she invited me to participate in as a speaker. I joked with her that I knew I'd play Carnegie Hall one day and that she made my dream come true. I wasn't the only one: she fulfilled the dreams of millions of folks who longed to see a Black woman of noble stature perform with confidence and verve on the world stage while never forgetting her roots. This eulogy was delivered at her funeral in October 2019 at the William B. Bell Auditorium in Augusta, Georgia.*

To the Norman and Sturkey family. To Dr. Hill. To Elder Sturkey. To Rev. Jesse Jackson, Dr. James Forbes. And to Vernon Jordan and all of the incredible brothers and sisters gathered here today. Especially Bishop Williams. Now, for those who are unfamiliar with the act and gesture of Black sacred rhetoric, that was an act of feminist resistance to patriarchal exclusion. [Laughter] The suppressed female voice not well represented in the formal edifice of Black rhetoric seized its central space, and ended everything before it began. [Applause]

If I were to give a title to my few minutes of reflection upon my dear friend and great colleague Jessye Norman, it would be, "When She."

When she entered, it was a great occasion. Six-feet-one-inch of pure Black woman. [Applause] All majesty and grace. Her limbs, symphonic extensions of a divine music to which she kept incredible time. Her beautiful face, her chocolate charm, her radiant smile, her active and curious eyes. She was Black girl magic before the term ever existed. Before there was Oprah and before there was Beyoncé and before there was Michelle Obama, there was Jessye Norman. [Applause]

When she swept in, the epic tides of grief in the ocean of haunting pain that Black people felt, resolved in her beautiful, symphonic, orchestral operatic expression. She transmuted the hurt and sorrow of Black people that she learned in part from a racist society here in Augusta, Georgia, where James Brown also emerged from the soil, and Mr. [Laurence] Fishburne. 1945 when she came. Bob Marley and Rod Stewart in the same year. When she arrived, when she made an entrance, we knew that God had blessed us with a majestic diva. And she was a diva. One of her fellow opera stars said that she insisted once that, as she was walking, the air ahead of her be spritzed with water to keep down the dust. [Laughter] When she entered, the race entered with her. Her people entered with her. When she entered, what entered was the architecture of God's divine imagination, blessing us with such power and beauty.

And when she spoke it was tremendous. She spoke unafraid and unapologetic about being Black in America. Yes, she attained the summit and the heights of ecstatic proclamation as one of the world's greatest singers. And yet she never forgot where she came from. [Applause] She never forgot this Southern terrain of terror, where white supremacy repudiated the very fundamental premise of Black humanity—she stood as eloquent declamation against that nonsense. And she held on long enough to see this era of insouciant, insipid ignorance and lethal unintelligence and unenlightenment that has grasped the nation in Washington, D.C. Her very speech is a rejection of that nonsense. [Applause]

When she spoke, [as she wrote] in her eloquent memoirs, *Stand Up Straight and Sing!*, as her mother often told her, she wrote with the pen of an eloquent author because it had been dipped into the existential experience of her people. And so, when she spoke, we felt the amplification of our deepest desires and our most cherished and intimate feelings as Black people, the transaction between us and God manifest in the beauty of her language.

And finally, when she sang. My God, when she sang, a volcano of sound erupted. Clouds of possibility poured down on us. That voice, that soprano voice, between a high, arching soprano, and the mezzo soprano that she occupied, that rare intermediate space. Because she was used to negotiating as an intermediary between competing and rival communities. She sang European music: Schubert, Gustav Mahler. She listened to Donizetti's opera *Lucia di Lammermoor* performed by the great Joan Sutherland on her radio in her bedroom when she was ten years old. She dipped herself into German and French and Italian, but she was straight up and unapologetically rooted in the very Black base that gave her voice, that gave her significance, that gave her style, that gave her panache and that gave her the spirit to overcome.

When she sang, she reinterpreted words that had been written by others, music that had been articulated from a foreign soil, and she baptized it in the beautiful womb of Black existence, and out of her poured the power, the beauty, the intelligence and the wise persistence of what it meant to be Black.

We celebrate you, Jessye Norman, a citizen of the world. A Black woman without apology, and a citizen of this city without excuse. [Applause]

BODIES IN MOTION

Black people's humanity is a profoundly insistent expression discernible throughout the cartographies of the new world, which took shape as stomped earth through dance as well as melodies of resistant song. Yet there . . . [is] no clear division between play and work. One of the most spectacular and prized performances of this combination is in sports. This is contest play, which includes organized and pickup sports, physical skill, and the chance and strategy that often separate good athletes from great ones . . . Societal concerns and orders are played out on the field and court as well as the street and workplace, making for a continuation of the hierarchies that organize all sociopolitical spaces.

—Shana Redmond, *Everything Man:*
The Form and Function of Paul Robeson

American democracy's promise is a means of narrating, and at times normalizing, the routinized practices of violence that have been essential to the operation of commerce, industry, and capital in the United States. In this respect, the Black political leader as a racial icon mirrors the tensions and contradictions between the rhetoric of democracy's promise and the violence of our racial state.

—Nicole Fleetwood, *On Racial Icons:*
Blackness and the Public Imagination

When I was a ten-year-old boy in Detroit, my cousin Bobby Joe Leonard, five years my senior, would collect me from my house, a couple of blocks from his own, and we would make the half-mile trek to the outdoor hoops at the junior high school that I later attended. At fifteen, Bobby was already a playground legend. On any given summer day, he would let loose with a sweet jump shot that arched near the heavens as it found its target in a hoop from what would now count as the three-point line. Bobby schooled me in the mechanics of movement on the court, learning to juke here, jab step there, and fake out my opponents with a spin move that found me leveraging my undersize body to great advantage as I slithered through more muscular and older frames to swish the ball in the nets.

Of course, more than basketball was happening on that ghetto court, and thousands more like it around the country. We were hoping, yearning, pleading, to make a safe transition from boys to men, to become like the figures we admired, those we looked up to for examples of mature manhood, the men we saw working in factories, laboring in fields, preaching in pulpits, digging ditches, washing cars, raking leaves, painting houses, shoveling snow, measuring walls, making blueprints, engineering buildings, cleaning floors, balancing wheel brakes, and hundreds more jobs to support their families. Bobby Joe was giving me more than the gift of game, or rather, the game he was teaching me was bigger than basketball. Indeed, it was the game of life, and here I mean game in the way Wittgenstein meant it when describing a language-game, so that you don't understand the meaning of a word or sentence until you grasp the rules of the game being played.

Bobby didn't just get me ready for bigger boys on the court, but he got me ready for games that are played in political and social circles. He taught me to discern an opposing player's intentions, the way they gave clues about their moves with their eyes or their bodily gestures. He also taught me how I might use a feint—imply a move with a head fake and then head in the opposite direction. His wisdom migrated to other arenas of engagement and served me well as I interpreted the moves, gestures, and implications that flourished in legislative and political bodies, and in other spheres of society where power and influence are at stake. And just as I grew to appreciate the placement and movement of bodies on the court, I grew to respect how men, and women, situate themselves to uplift our people and amplify our need for representation. And, especially, for justice and freedom.

I often reflect on the crucial lessons I gleaned from Bobby Joe, particularly as I sit in a floor seat to watch some of the most gifted athletes in the world do things with their bodies that most of us can only conjure in our fiercest fantasies. While the relentless assault on Black life, in many instances on Black male life, has left some believing that we are pariahs and misfits, my cousin Bobby planted in me the confidence to deploy Black male cunning and shrewdness to slice through defenses put up by fearful and ignorant opponents, thwarting their strategies to contain and, too often, to destroy Black life. I have managed to engage and advise presidents, players, politicians, and prominent leaders, but what I learned from my cousin Bobby Joe Leonard was the best possible preparation to walk the halls of power and play with a swag that can never be completely explained or permanently contained.

Balling Out

In the Arena

23

Pound for Pound

Although I had been an avid basketball fan since my youth, one player finally drove me to get season tickets to watch his on-court wizardry: Allen Iverson. By the time I arrived in Philadelphia to teach at Penn in 2002, Iverson, also known as "The Answer," and by his initials, AI, had just won the regular season and All-Star game MVPs in his fifth year as a member of the Philadelphia 76ers. For three years, I saw him soar, weave, and get knocked down only to bounce back up and make his way to the basket again, all while performing his version of a move he didn't invent but that he perfected: the crossover, which involves artfully, and in Iverson's case with a mesmerizing feint, rapidly switching the ball from one hand to the other while simultaneously changing direction of travel and speed of motion. It was indeed a metaphor for how he had switched directions in life and faked out would-be opponents to his thriving while putting a storied franchise on his back. I got to know the man behind the legend a bit, including when we served Thanksgiving dinner to the vulnerable in Philadelphia. He remains one of the most beloved professional athletes of all time. He was only six feet tall. Kobe Bryant, who admitted that Iverson's exceptional play drove him to higher heights, said, "We all should be fortunate that Allen Iverson wasn't 6'5." A version of this essay appeared in September 2016 as one of two collectible cover stories for Slam *magazine's 200th issue. The other cover featured Michael Jordan.*

It was one of the most iconic plays in NBA history, although it only lasted a few seconds. Michael Jordan, the greatest basketball player in the world, many say of all time, applied his suffocating defensive skills to Allen Iverson, a truculent prodigy whose approach to the game couldn't have been more different. That night Iverson came off a screen with the ball at the top of the key as Jordan guarded his man. Bulls Coach Phil Jackson hollered "Michael, Michael," signaling for his superstar guard to switch off of his man onto Iverson. AI spied Michael through his peripheral vision as he came near, and everyone in the crowd stood up in eager anticipation of Jordan clamping down on Iverson with his swarming defense. It was a moment thick with drama and dripping with excitement. Iverson hit Jordan with a little feint of a crossover first just to set him up. He didn't intend to rehearse his move in front of MJ. He simply didn't get it right. Despite his initial failure, Jordan bit the bait and fell for Iverson's faux crossover. Iverson said to himself, "Oh shit, I didn't even do it for real, and he went for it." That boosted his confidence and fueled his drive to topple the master with his signature move. So Iverson cocked it back and hit him with it. Boom! It was lightning quick and left Jordan's legs twisted as he thought Iverson was heading one way, but he actually went in the opposite direction toward the basket and made his mid-range jump shot. The crowd erupted in applause.

That Iverson bested Jordan and "broke his ankles" underscores an athletic truism: basketball is a game where youngsters grow up to battle their heroes. "I remember the first time I played against him—he didn't even look human," Iverson tells me. "He looked to me on that court the same way he looked when I was a ten-year-old kid looking at him on television. This is the man I wanted to be like." Almost fifteen years later, the move inspired hip hop superstar Drake to drop a couplet that summarized the ruthless manner in which the transition between styles and generations is often made: "And that's around the time that your idols become your rivals / you make friends with Mike but gotta AI him for your survival."

On that night, Iverson lived up to his nickname "The Answer" as he solved the riddle of Jordan's hardwood omniscience, at least for a play, badgering the basketball deity with a devilish move that left him flummoxed in his sneakers. Iverson had practiced the move at Georgetown as a collegiate star before refining it in the league. But at this game, the Chosen One, and through the miracle of the media, the nation at large, too, got a taste of Iverson's wicked crossover—a term that conjures Iverson's complicated, even tortured, odyssey to mainstream success as he held fast to the tenets of his hardscrabble youth. The crossover, a move that Iverson didn't patent but brilliantly reinvented, is far more difficult than it looks. One must master the physics of momentum, the calculus of velocity, the geometry of space and the esthetics of illusion. The crossover is equal parts magic and science.

"That was the first time that people saw [Jordan] vulnerable," Iverson tells me of the huge reaction it garnered in the press and among basketball cognoscenti and casual fans alike. "That was the first time people saw something that they never thought they would see. I always compare it to the night Mike Tyson got knocked out. Everybody was in shock. Nobody could believe it. Everybody knew that it was a possibility that it could happen. Everybody knew that with a right punch any boxer can get knocked out. But you never expected Mike Tyson to ever get knocked out."

Iverson didn't initially think much of the play—the crowd always went crazy whenever he crossed over any player—until he got home and flicked on the tube to discover it was all over the local news and on frantic repeat on national sports television. That's when it hit him that this was something truly special. In the 24-hour sports media machine, events that happen locally take on national significance when they're isolated and examined and endlessly looped so that their meaning is either exaggerated or rescued from potential erasure. ESPN's *SportsCenter* is a major outlet for such events; they're the unofficial curators of outsize sports moments. Their iconic segment "Top 10 Plays" catalogues great sports achievements across the athletic spectrum. *SportsCenter* seized on Iverson's crossover move on Michael Jordan and looped it with archival intensity. *SportsCenter*'s coverage gave the move gravitas and made it a legendary gesture because it happened against the game's greatest player.

But if the information-starved, details-hungry 24-hour sports news cycle benefited Iverson, it also turned on him too. He was everything Jordan wasn't—and everything the NBA was ill prepared to handle. Jordan and Iverson hailed from two different galaxies. Jordan was a clean-shaven, suit-and-tie wearing, All-American face of the league—if not the logo, as some believe he should have been, Jordan was at least the game's gold standard. Iverson, on the other hand, was a tattoo-bearing, cornrow-sporting, starter-gear wearing wunderkind who shook the nervous guardians of the league's image. Jordan's courtly elegance reflected eighties quiet storm rhythm and blues and smooth jazz. Iverson was unvarnished nineties hip hop, and his rat-a-tat pace and staccato rhythm of play mimicked the music, and urban culture, from which they both sprang. Jordan was Kenny G; Iverson was Notorious B.I.G. Iverson may have never won any titles, but he championed street style and hood smarts while forging a durable link with millions who vicariously lived through him and proclaimed him a ghetto god. Their showdown was epic, not because Jordan and Iverson met in a game where a new victor would be crowned, but because two competing universes of Black identity came crashing down on an insignificant encounter and lent it transcendent meaning.

To be sure, Iverson is remembered for his dazzling acrobatics performed in dingy gyms and cavernous arenas across America, and for his fearless drives to the basket on domineering forces in the paint like Shaq. His fans nostalgically replay his legendary shootouts with fellow All-Stars Ray Allen and Vince Carter. They fondly remember his relentless flurry of short-and-long jump shots that arched over the outstretched arms of taller defenders. But those aren't the only images that remain. Burnt into the nation's memory of Iverson are the braids, the body-ink, the baggy hip hop fashion, the flashy jewelry, and the bad boy reputation, one that started with a high-school brawl in a bowling alley that unjustly landed him behind bars and almost ended his storied career before it got started. The man who gave Iverson a second chance played a huge role in his life and career and proved the virtue of Black belief in redemption.

But a lot of what we think we know about Iverson simply isn't true, is easily misunderstood, or is sometimes deliberately misinterpreted, either because the media was lazy, or he was occasionally his own worst enemy. More often than not, Iverson was viewed through the distorted lens of a culture that had little tolerance for young Black men who bolted suddenly from abject poverty to astonishing wealth and fame.

Iverson admits that the fast come-up that he experienced, that so many other ballers and rappers experienced before and after him, often leads to a head rush that is at once intoxicating and disorienting. "Just being young, twenty-one, twenty-two years old, never having nothing, then all of a sudden you've got millions of dollars, you're going to do what you want to do," he ruefully remembers. "You're going to make mistakes, you're going to walk around like your shit don't stink when everybody in the world know it do. You never went to class for that." Iverson admits that get-and-spend was the watchword for his ilk; living in poverty can often, without discipline and training, lead to satisfying the thirst for acquisition and material rewards—from a life of want to a life of everything I want. "That's the first thing you think about: getting everything that you always wanted, all the things that you dreamed that you were going to have in your life. And I was no different from anybody else. And then they started destroying me over it."

"They" also destroyed Iverson for hanging with his boys from the hood, which to him was just reward for loyal friends who stuck by his side when he was poor and anonymous. Now that he was rich and famous it would be heartless and cold to abandon them and deny his friends the payoff for their faith in him. "You see me with five or six guys from my neighborhood?

That's what you're supposed to do when you make it. The guys you grew up with, and that you've been friends with and been with every day. Why can't they come up to Philly and come to games with me and hang out? It was something that they had never seen before. And it wasn't malicious. I thought I was doing what I was supposed to be doing. It didn't sit well with people, and they started killing me over it. But that's what made me feel so good about seeing LeBron and these different guys [bring their guys with them from the hood]."

Iverson became the poster boy for all that was wrong in the NBA, when in truth he reflected his generation and their way of negotiating the world. He was by no means perfect, but, to paraphrase Grace Jones, he was perfect for the times in which he became a troubled star as the NBA underwent a profound transformation and hip hop style surged to its center. Two years after Iverson joined the NBA, *Sports Illustrated* ran a cover story on him under the heading "Allen Iverson: Not as Bad as You Think." If that was true then, it's perhaps even truer now, as Iverson continues to combat public perceptions of him rooted in ignorance and distortion.

Iverson's attire, for instance, wasn't meant to flash a brazen indifference to the respectability politics of the NBA—though it certainly did—as much as embrace without apology or self-consciousness the style of dress of his age and his neighborhood cohort. He may have loved the way Earvin Johnson threaded the needle with a pass, but he passed on his idols' needles and threads. "As much as I wanted to be like Michael Jordan, that wasn't how I dressed," Iverson tells me. "I wanted to shoot like Bird. I wanted to pass like Magic. I wanted to be fast like Isaiah. I wanted to jump like Mike, rebound like Rodman. I tried to add all of that edge to my game. But who I am as a person, and my overall style, and the way I dress, and the people that I hang around, it's nothing like that. That was a part of their life that I didn't want to emulate. Because I was satisfied with my own."

Iverson's self-satisfaction got under the skin of some of his elders and the NBA office, but spilled rapidly onto his own flesh with purposeful expression. (Most people don't know that when AI entered the NBA, he only had one tattoo: a bulldog, a nod to the mascot of his college team, the Georgetown Hoyas, with his nickname "The Answer" written above it.) "And then I got a tattoo . . . and then I got addicted to them. I got another one. Then I got another one." Iverson was especially upset when *Hoop* magazine, an official NBA publication, decided to airbrush his jewelry and tattoos from its January 2000 cover photo of the Philadelphia 76ers superstar. Those tattoos had been inked into his body with the design and desire to honor his loved ones. "That was a big thing with me when they airbrushed my tattoos on the cover of that magazine," Iverson says. "That's what hurt me the most. I don't just have tattoos like a rainbow on my body, [or] designs . . . [but I have] my mother, my grandmother, my kids, my wife. Those [tattoos] mean something to me."

Ironically, Iverson's body was the gateway—more precisely the sacrifice—for the acceptance of tattoos on ball players' bodies; it is rare today to see basketball players without an inked message on their skin. They have Allen Iverson to thank for that. "LeBron [is] considered the greatest player on planet earth, but he's flooded with tattoos," Iverson points out in satisfying confirmation of his influence. "And it's [seen as] no big deal. I had to take the ass whipping for them guys to be able to be themselves, for them to be able to look like they want and be accepted." Just think, despite the NBA imposing a dress code, in no small part due to Iverson's dress habits, there'd be no Dwyane Wade or Russell Westbrook style flourishes without the precedent-setting sartorial insurrection of Iverson.

Iverson's hairstyle, too, meant something, even if he kept his locks plaited for far more practical reasons—not because he was a hooligan. "I didn't get cornrows because of no thug shit," Iverson protests to me. "My whole thing with the cornrows was just—I would go on the road, and barbers in different cities would mess my hair up. So I figured, shit, if I get my hair cornrowed, I wouldn't have to worry about that. It's a long season. Then that turned out to be some thug thing." But Iverson saw how quickly the so-called thug look caught on and even spread among the general population. "I had cornrows and [then] everybody had cornrows, and [we] started seeing guys in different sports wearing cornrows. You never seen no boxer or football players wearing cornrows. And then everybody had them, and eventually you're seeing teachers with cornrows, you're seeing police officers with cornrows. I'm like, 'Damn, I thought that was supposed to be the look of the suspect.'" Iverson has a clinical approach to what was once a huge sore spot. "If you [saw] a guy with a suit on walking side by side with a guy with the cornrows and the baggy pants on, and the sneakers and pants hanging off his ass, first thing you're going to think is, 'Snatch up him.' But it made me feel so good that I could see a damn police officer with cornrows, or a teacher. I look at it like I changed that [from an] epidemic."

What he couldn't so easily change, perhaps to this day, is the perception that he hated practice—an impression left by the same media that had lifted him to glory because of his crossover on Jordan. Iverson's ballyhooed "practice" incident got heavy rotation on *SportsCenter*. The endless looping of his words surely marked them down in the annals of sports as one of the most infamous athletic quotes of all time. Most people don't know the story behind the "practice" riff that gives it a far more sensible context, even if it is still admittedly funny after all these years.

Iverson's comments came after a 2002 campaign where he had to contend with the constant drumbeat of trade rumors. The noise was at first irritating, but the sheer volume of speculation left him bewildered and frustrated. The most public round of speculation had been set off with the incendiary words of his head coach, Larry Brown. Iverson adored Larry Brown as a man and admired him as a coach, but he felt that Brown made some ill-advised comments about not being able to coach Allen and about Iverson missing a single practice. That single miss somehow got translated into Iverson ditching practice and dodging his responsibilities as a team leader. Iverson believed that Brown's comments should have been made to him in private so that they wouldn't compromise the chemistry they had built as a team.

Iverson was a young player when trade rumors flared. Had he been more mature, he might have handled the situation with greater wisdom. At the time he was all of twenty-six years old and the relentless speculation got inside his head. His best friend had just been killed and Iverson and the 76ers got booted out of the playoffs, which made matters even worse. The Sixers brass finally sat down with Iverson and assured him that he'd remain with the team for the foreseeable future. Iverson felt that he had dodged a bullet and was determined to justify the front office's faith in him. He knew he hadn't been perfect and wanted to right the ship and calm the tumultuous waters by setting a good example for his teammates. The news that he would stay was a great relief for Iverson and he wanted to share it with his family and fans. Iverson and the Sixers called a press conference to give the world the scoop. But things quickly went south and took a turn for the worse. The media was obsessed with all the rumors that led to the speculation that he'd be traded and not the news that he wouldn't get shipped to another team. Those circumstances made this perhaps the most infamous NBA press conference ever.

Sixers PR rep Karen Frascona tried to shut down the press conference when she saw that the media was determined to focus on anything and everything except the fact that Iverson would be returning to the team. Iverson, however, insisted that they field as many questions as possible to quiet the rumble of rumor that had shaken the team's locker room. That's where the trouble began. It appeared the media were asking the same ques-

tion, and it all had to do with the misperception that Allen wasn't interested in discipline and practice. It finally got to him. He lost it.

"Could you be clear about your practicing habits since we can't see you
practice?" a reporter quizzed him.

"If Coach tells you that I missed practice, then that's that," Iverson
stated as matter-of-factly as he could. "I may have missed one practice this
year. But if somebody says he missed one practice of all the practices this
year, then that's enough to get a whole lot started. I told Coach Brown that
you don't have to give the people of Philadelphia a reason to think about
trading me or anything like that. If you trade somebody, you trade them to
make the team better. Simple as that."

"So you and Coach Brown got caught up on Saturday about practice?"
yet another follow-up question rang out.

And thus Iverson's rant on practice began. The sheer repetition of the
word itself took on a mantra-like quality. It did appear for a moment that
Allen was caught in a trance where he exploited every nuance of the word's
meaning by inflecting his voice and stressing different pronunciations as
much for poetic meter as for rhetorical emphasis.

"If I can't *practice*, I can't *practice*," he insisted. "It is as simple as that. It
ain't about that at all. It's easy to sum it up if you're just talking about *practice*. We're sitting here, and I'm supposed to be the franchise player, and
we're talking about *practice*."

Iverson felt the surge of repetition coming on and there was nothing
he could do about it. He was swept into a stream of consciousness and his
mouth was the voice of his bruised soul.

"I mean listen, we're sitting here talking about *practice*. Not a game. Not
a game. Not a game. But we're talking about *practice*. Not the game that I go
out there and die for and play every game like it's my last. But we're talking
about *practice* man. How silly is that?"

It's obvious that "game" was a runner-up to practice in Iverson's grammar of agitation. Had it not been for the media pressing him on practice,
"game" might have been a decent contender for parody as well. But the
deluge of "practices" simply couldn't be avoided. Iverson was clearly exas-
perated, and once it got started, he seemed incapable of quenching the rush
of words that centered on the word the media kept tossing at him.

"Now I know that I'm supposed to lead by example . . . I know it's important, I honestly do. But we're talking about *practice*. We're talking about
practice man."

The room bust out in laughter as Iverson repeatedly rolled "practice" from his tongue with an impish grin on his face, taking refuge in humor to combat the absurdity of the situation.

"We're talking about *practice*. We're talking about *practice*. We're not talking about the game. We're talking about *practice*. When you come to the arena, and you see me play . . . You've seen me play right? You've seen me give everything I've got, but we're talking about *practice* right now."

The media laughed again. They got Allen's point. Even though the press conference lasted for several more minutes after that outburst, and Iverson addressed the issue yet again, the backdrop for his mini-tirade was lost in the performance art of his protest. He didn't realize at the time that his infamous words would take on epic meaning in the media machinery that replayed his words outside of their clarifying context and made it look as if he were protesting the very work ethic that got him to the top of his profession as the reigning MVP. The clip of him talking about practice soon went viral, a casualty of the culture's athletic obsession that had helped to launch his reputation when he had his encounter with Jordan a few years earlier.

Iverson eventually learned to laugh at his words, words that seem to have taken their place, alongside NFL football coach Jim Moran's "playoffs" rant, as perhaps the two most easily laughable and spontaneous combustions of speech in the history of professional athletics. When Iverson got home the night of the press conference, he watched himself on *SportsCenter*, and even his wife got on his case!

"Why the hell did you keep saying practice?" she asked him.

Iverson explained to her what had gone on behind the scenes, and let her in on his rationale for repetition. But that didn't stop them from cracking up at his performance. Iverson regrets the rant because it gave the wrong impression of his work ethic and underplayed his efforts to get better every day.

"If I could take it back, I would, a thousand times, but I can't," Iverson tells me. "The whole thing . . . made it out that I didn't like practice. And my whole thing was, how in the hell do you become an MVP and a multi-year All-Star player and accomplish all the things that I've accomplished in basketball if I didn't practice?"

Iverson's record of achievement, and the hard work on which it rested, speaks for itself: NBA Rookie of the Year. NBA All-Rookie first team. Three-time All-NBA first team. Three-time All-NBA second team. One-time All-NBA third team. Three-time NBA steals leader. Eleven-times NBA All-Star. Two-time NBA All-Star Game MVP. Four-time NBA scoring champion. And NBA Most Valuable Player.

The practice incident is really a metaphor for how Iverson was beset by problems of distorted perception, and those of his own making, although, on balance, as King Lear declared, he is more sinned against than sinning.

One of the most egregious sins against him happened on February 14, 1993, when Iverson and several of his teammates were in a bowling alley blowing off steam and having fun like any red-blooded American youth. Not only was it Valentine's Day, a time to celebrate love, but it was also abolitionist Frederick Douglass's birthday, a day of history. As things turned out, it would be a day of history for Iverson, and a bad one at that, but love was nowhere in the mix.

The lanes were across the street from the projects and most of the crowd that night was Black. There were also several white folk between twenty-five and thirty years old tossing back a few brews. The white folk were from a part of town where Blacks knew they wouldn't be welcome. That night a couple of Black guys got into an argument with a couple of white guys, and before you know it, things got ugly as racial slurs and punches got thrown in rapid succession.

The brawl escalated when chairs were hurled, but by then, Iverson had long since left the building for fear that he'd get caught up in trouble that might taint his future. It wasn't a big surprise that none of the white people were locked up for the clash, but it was bitterly disappointing that Iverson and three Black friends were eventually arrested. Iverson was accused of hitting a white woman in the head with a chair. Fortunately someone had videotaped the incident, clearly showing he wasn't involved in the mayhem. But it wouldn't do him much good because the powers that be didn't allow the tape in court to prove his innocence.

It's clear that Iverson's success as an All-State football and basketball player and state champion bred envy and resentment in some whites. Not necessarily the ordinary whites, but those with power and something to prove to powerless Blacks about their lowly station in life. The prosecutors were so determined to nab Iverson that they waited more than six months to try him as an adult, even though the brawl took place when he was a minor. The usual course of action would have been to slap Iverson on his wrist since this was his first skirmish with the law. But that wasn't to be. Iverson was later convicted of the felony charge of "maiming by mob," a rarely used Virginia statute to combat lynching after the Civil War that was resurrected just for him.

One can't but think of the irony that a law designed to aid Black folk wasn't used much to help us when we needed it most. Now the law was being dragged from the musty depths of the Jim Crow era to target a youth whose biggest crime seemed to be that he was Black and on his way somewhere out of the hole that most local folk couldn't escape. They threw the book at Iverson and gave him 15 years in prison, with 10 years suspended, to make sure that he wouldn't escape either. Iverson defiantly held his head up high when he got shipped off to the Newport News City Farm correctional facility. He didn't want his fellow inmates to sense any fear or weakness in him that they could exploit while he was imprisoned. Four months into his sentence, Virginia's first Black governor, L. Douglas Wilder, granted him clemency. As a condition of his release Iverson couldn't play any sports and had to enroll in an alternative high school. That was a bitter pill to swallow, but it beat languishing in his cell by a long shot. It wasn't long before Iverson met a man who would change the course of his life—a giant of a man who had a heart as big as Mother Teresa's and a mouth as colorful as Richard Pryor's.

Iverson's mother, Ann, managed a sit-down with legendary Georgetown University coach John Thompson when it was rumored that Allen might receive early release from prison. Allen and Ann and their circle of advisors knew that he'd need a strong-minded coach, somebody who would protect him from all of the harsh scrutiny he'd certainly face when he got to school. Coach Thompson's reputation as a tough but fair coach, as a man who watched over his players like a mother hen shielding her young ones from marauding foxes even as she kept her brood in line, appealed to Ann Iverson. She knew Allen needed tough love and a person who wouldn't be afraid to get in his face but who always had his back.

It also appealed to Ann and Allen that in the eighties the Georgetown Hoyas became Black America's team in the same way that the Dallas Cowboys became America's team in the seventies. Coach Thompson instilled pride in a Black style of play that rattled the cages of college basketball and brought to prominence the skills of Black boys who might otherwise go unnoticed. Georgetown seemed like a good fit with Iverson's style of play and his demeanor, especially since he'd borne the stigma of Blackness with his arrest. It made sense that America's Blackest coach, and one of the nation's Blackest players, were destined to work together. Ann went to Coach Thompson and pled for Allen's life. She persuaded him to give Iverson a spot on his roster once he was free and finished with his high school requirements.

At Georgetown Iverson knew it was going to be serious business. He caught sight of Coach Thompson from afar as he walked into the gym while he was speaking to Alonzo Mourning, the former Georgetown center who had been selected second in the NBA draft behind Shaquille O'Neal two years earlier. Mourning's success, and that of Dikembe Mutombo alongside him, and of Patrick Ewing before them, confirmed Coach Thompson's reputation as a big man's friend. That made Iverson more than a little skittish about joining a program where guards didn't seem to matter as much as the man in the middle. A lot of people Allen consulted told him not to go to Georgetown for fear that he'd get lost in Coach Thompson's focus on exotic skyscrapers while neglecting dynamic but smaller buildings.

When Iverson got to school, Coach Thompson proved he was supremely adaptable to the talent on hand. He changed his approach, at least during Iverson's tenure. Before Allen arrived, the direction of play had always been inside out from the center to the perimeter players: The ball would always go inside first, to Patrick, to Alonzo and to Dikembe, and then, if they had limited options, back outside to forwards and guards. When Iverson arrived it was quite literally a changing of the guard. Coach Thompson valiantly put Allen in a position to succeed. He sought to exploit his strengths to the team's advantage by building the squad's flow around Iverson's creative playmaking, crafty ball handling and explosive scoring.

All of this came after Iverson established himself at Georgetown as a force to be reckoned with on the hardwood. The day he arrived in the nation's capital and met Coach Thompson for the first time, Thompson let him know who was in control and gave him a hint of the discipline and respect that were crucial for his success. Iverson approached Coach Thompson as he was sitting on a training table. He had his hat on, and he didn't yet know that you didn't wear your hat in the gym. Alonzo grabbed his hat and unceremoniously ripped it off his head without explanation. Iverson snatched his hat back and cocked it back on his head. And then he heard his first words from Coach Thompson.

"Boy, if you don't take that got damned hat off your head," he barked, with no need to finish his statement. Iverson quickly removed his lid before he could say more. Then a wide smile creased the face of this stern six-foot-ten Black man who had played a couple of years as Bill Russell's backup center for the Celtics before later becoming an iconic fixture on collegiate sidelines.

"How you doing? You alright?" he quizzed Iverson, making sure he'd get settled in without a hitch. They had a pleasant but brief conversation. Iverson had class the next morning and he sent Allen up the hill to his dorm room so that he'd be wide-awake and prepared to hit the books.

Later that evening, Iverson was in the apartment of one of his teammates' friends, playing cards and drinking with the fellas. Suddenly there was loud banging at the door.

"Allen, Allen, Coach Thompson is looking for you," somebody shouted out to Iverson. Iverson froze. He was scared as hell. He thought to himself, "Damn, I just got out of jail, and as soon as I get here, I'm about to get in trouble on my first day in school!"

Iverson headed outside where Coach Thompson was sitting in the car with assistant coach Craig Esherick.

"You alright boy?" Coach Thompson asked him. "You cool?"

"Yeah!" Iverson replied.

"How you feel? Everybody treating you right?"

"Yeah."

"Alright. I just came up here to check on you."

As quickly and unexpectedly as he had come, he was gone. Iverson's Georgetown era began in a way that symbolized his time at the school under Coach Thompson: ready discipline, the demand for respect, the expectation of greatness and preparation, and the offer of concern and support. He immediately felt at home. Thompson was a big-time father figure who was very protective of Iverson. He spotted a lot of mess coming Allen's way, but he was determined to never let it get to Iverson. In a sense they reversed roles: Iverson was the center of his attention and Thompson guarded Allen from harm.

That was no small feat, especially since he'd just spent four months of his life in prison with the threat of losing his career in sports forever. When Iverson was in prison, he received a ton of death threats each day. Once a scarecrow with his jersey was hung on a tree outside the prison with the strong suggestion of lynching. It was a rude awakening for Allen to go from hundreds of recruiting letters to hundreds of daily death threats.

The death threats and hostility continued at Georgetown. Coach Thompson kept most of that stuff away from Iverson. When reporters sidled up to him to ask about his time in prison, and not his performance on court, Coach Thompson shut them down.

When the Hoyas played Villanova Iverson's freshman year, they were greeted by four guys in the stands festooned in orange jumpsuits, shackles and chains, holding up signs that said "Allen Iverson, the Next MJ," but the MJ had a line struck through it, and written under it were the initials "OJ," referring to the former football star and broadcast personality turned accused murderer. Coach Thompson corralled the entire team and whisked them off the court while getting in the referees' faces and heatedly insisting that they weren't going to play the game if those guys weren't kicked out of the arena. Coach Thompson went nuts and then apologized to Iverson for the incident.

Coach Thompson's willingness to battle for Allen made him even more determined to do battle for him and the team. Iverson was already a very tough competitor, and the hostility he faced made him even tougher. He would be on the free throw line playing a team, and the chants would begin, "jail bird, jail bird." But he'd block it out and attempt to reward their jeering with the sweet swish of the net. "The basketball court is for me a dance floor, and when I'm out there, the cheers and boos all sound the same. I get adrenaline either way. I honestly can't figure out if I like it better playing away or at home. With the away crowd, I want to send them home upset, and with the home crowd, I want to send them away happy."

It's hard to overestimate Coach Thompson's impact on Iverson's career. He provided perhaps the greatest moment in Iverson's life as a basketball player. It was an incident that shaped his self-confidence in a profound manner. It was like a scene from a Hollywood movie. In his second and final year in the program, the Hoyas were on the road in the middle of a grueling effort to make it back to the top of the Big East. The coaches had informally assembled in the bathroom, thinking that they were the only ones present. What they didn't know was that Jerry Nichols, one of Iverson's teammates, was posted on the toilet in a stall. As soon as the coaches disbanded, Nichols rushed to tell Allen of the conversation the coaches had in their makeshift training room.

"Man, I was in the bathroom and you wouldn't believe what happened," Nichols breathlessly blurted out to Iverson.

"What man?" he impatiently implored.

"The coaches were in there talking about you."

Iverson thought that it was surely negative. He steeled himself for the criticism, making up his mind to improve his play based on the insight his eavesdropping could offer. But his preemptive worry proved unnecessary.

"Coach Thompson said, 'That little motherfucker is a *baaad* motherfucker.'"

There have been undoubtedly more eloquent words written about Iverson's play, his impact on the game, his remarkable skills, and his killer instinct. But in the end, Thompson's words are as fitting a summary of Iverson's basketball career as might be penned.

24

He the Best

Admittedly, one of the reasons I loved Kobe Bryant so much had nothing to do with his otherworldly basketball skill but with the fact that he reminded me of my youngest son, Michael. Both were born in 1978, my son almost exactly three months earlier; both of them became very handsome young men; and both were blessed from birth with a sharp intelligence. When Kobe came into the league, in the same 1996 draft that brought us number-one pick Allen Iverson, and other greats like Ray Allen and Steve Nash, he was selected number thirteen overall, having leapt straight from high school to the pros when such a thing was still possible. He played all twenty years of his professional career for the Los Angeles Lakers, a team I'd grown to love as a boy, mostly listening to their games on radio and catching them on television when I could, enjoying Jerry West, Gail Goodrich, Elgin Baylor, Happy Hairston, and, especially, the Big Dipper himself, Wilt Chamberlain. Later, when my fellow Michigander Earvin "Magic" Johnson joined the team, alongside the inimitable Kareem Abdul-Jabbar, James Worthy, and Norm Nixon, it only cemented my love. Still, I always had love for my local Detroit Pistons, particularly when Dave Bing came out of the backcourt to pop his patented pretty jumper as the radio announcer stretched his last name in thrilling melisma: "Dave Biiiiiiiiiiiing!" While many folks say that Kobe was a brilliant knockoff of Michael Jordan, the game's widely acknowledged GOAT—Greatest of All Time—such a knock ignores how Jordan "stole" from Connie Hawkins, Julius "Dr. J" Erving, and particularly David "Skywalker" Thompson, about whom Jordan said, "The whole meaning of vertical leap began with David Thompson." Kobe was an athletic wonder and a basketball savant, and his genius poured into an obsessive focus on honing his skills. I have said that Jordan was the greatest force the game has seen, Kobe the greatest player—ball on floor, footwork, shots—and LeBron the

*greatest athlete to ever play the game. (Of course, if we throw in off-
court conscience and using one's platform for social justice advocacy,
LeBron is in a class by himself.) When I wrote this piece, Kobe was,
to my mind, the best in the way I've specified here. Jordan occupies a
unique spot because when he came along he gave the game a global
push, athletically and commercially. I adore Kobe still for the way
he parlayed his incredible drive to succeed into hoops immortality.
It may be that LeBron eclipses them both. (Several years ago, at the
beginning of LBJ's career, when I was arguing about GOATs at dinner
with a few people, including the late and great Flip Saunders, Washington Wizards coach at the time, Saunders said, "There's a guy in Cleveland who might make the conversation moot.") I loved Kobe greatly,
and his untimely death in January 2020 hurts me, and millions more,
to this day. This essay appeared as the cover story in April 2016 for*
Slam *magazine upon Kobe's retirement.*

When I was a 24-year-old pastor, I was booted from leading an East
Tennessee congregation in 1983 because I committed an act of blasphemy: I sought to ordain three women as deacons in a male-dominated
Baptist church. More than 30 years later, I can't seem to shake the charge
of blasphemy as I defy the roundball gods and their mortal mouthpieces
and argue that Kobe Bean Bryant is the greatest basketball player this globe
has seen. For many hardcourt acolytes, such a declaration surely calls for
me to repent of my sin and get baptized in the River Jordan. Even Larry
"The Hick from French Lick" Bird, after his Celtics barely weathered the
relentless downpour of 63 points by His Airness in a 1986 double-overtime
playoff game, declared that, "It's just God disguised as Michael Jordan."
Jerry West's silhouette may form the NBA's official logo, but Jordan's body
of work is where many believe that hoops greatness paused most memorably to lace up its sneakers.

It's impossible, and unnecessary, to deny Jordan's God-like status.
Jordan has no peer as the greatest commercial and cultural force the game
has seen. But saying that Jordan is the greatest basketball player ever—
ball dribbled on floor, ball in hoop, footwork, shot selection, discipline,
work ethic and the like—well, that's a different argument altogether. Despite
the golden consensus that hugs Jordan's head like a halo, the insistence
that he's the GOAT has always been an article of faith, an exercise in

groupthink, grading on a curve, or an act of rebellious deconstruction in shaping the facts to fit one's interpretation. Think about it: Bill Russell damn near doubled Jordan's ring count, and Kareem Abdul-Jabbar scored the most points ever, won more regular season MVPs and collected just as many titles. Why aren't they universally proclaimed the greatest? The stubborn orthodoxy of Jordan's singular greatness appears ripe for a paradigm shift. As the idea's originator, Thomas Kuhn, argued, a paradigm is a theory about how the world operates, and when disconfirming evidence steals our confidence in that theory, we've got a crisis on our hands, which leads us, if we're open and honest, to shift paradigms and adopt a more compelling explanation about what's true. Here's the truth: In most of the categories that matter, Kobe is equally as good as Jordan, and in some cases, even better.

"You've never seen anyone with the footwork [Kobe] has, the athleticism, the shooting ability," Kevin Durant tells me. "Being able to shoot the three off the dribble, off the catch and shoot, off the post. You've never seen that many skills in one person, outside of Michael Jordan. Of course, he doesn't have six Finals MVPs, or six titles, but skill for skill he's unmatched."

It's that six-six-six spell of perfection that bedevils those who would dispute Jordan's supremacy: six trips to the Finals, six rings, six Finals MVPs, a lyrical and morally neat rounding out of the terms of unrivaled greatness. But what seems at the time as a necessary proclamation of superiority may later be exposed as arbitrary, or at the very least, an assertion colored by preferences that are neither logical nor objective. There is, for instance, Russell's ethical arc of 11 Championships when he was a controversial center of attention—an outspoken Black man leading one of the whitest teams in all of sport to the throne of grace by first forcing it to hear the groans of race. Russell's Celtics more than doubled Jordan's three-peat by winning eight straight Championship trophies and 11 chips in 13 years. Russell also equaled Jordan's five regular season MVPs. From the beginning there's been a nod to a mystical, je ne sais quoi quality when asserting Jordan's unchallengeable greatness; there is the appeal to something intangible, something that transcends statistics. Let's call it analytics in service of a broader, more satisfying sense of athletic completeness, an omni-competence that reflects a level of mastery that is not only physical but spiritual and emotional as well. Beyond shooting percentages, Championship hardware and MVPs there is basketball intelligence, killer instinct, Herculean work ethic, a nimble intuitiveness about the game's improvised elegance, all of which Jordan had, and Kobe, too, though, arguably, in greater abundance.

Of course, we must battle the hackneyed notion that Kobe could never be as great as Jordan because Mike first embodied the kind of greatness they together share, and therefore, Kobe was a carbon copy of the original. Depends on what you mean by original: Jordan was a chip off of some blocks that came before him.

"I never held true to that argument," says former All-Star, Warriors coach and current ESPN on ABC analyst Mark Jackson. "And the fact of the matter is that there was Dr. J before Jordan. Jordan will tell you that. We don't say there was no way Jordan could be better than Dr. J. because he emulated him. It makes no sense. At the end of the day, Kobe has put himself in the discussion because of his greatness, how hard he's worked. You have to be that good. Larry Holmes isn't Ali, not because he didn't work his tail off. He's just not Ali because he wasn't as great as him. Let's give Kobe his credit."

Lakers fan and rapper/actor/director Ice Cube does just that. "Dr. J got something to say about Jordan's game, too—Elgin Baylor, and the Ice Man [George Gervin] and all those great dudes who showed style, grace and creativity on the court. And power and strength."

While it may be a tribute to Jordan's sheer genius and originality that he eclipses those who came before him, we may cut a better and simpler explanation with Occam's razor: just as John F. Kennedy maximized his advantages over Richard Nixon on television in their pioneering debates—the medium was relatively new and Kennedy's telegenic appeal made him seem a more natural fit with the American public than the twitchy, self-conscious Nixon—so Jordan made the most of a birth order he couldn't bribe, but which he could certainly exploit: the players most like him in the past largely peaked before the NBA became a powerhouse league full of stars with household names. The NBA was then plagued by low ratings, tape delays for Championship games and a turbulent transition of the Association from a white man's fantasy league to a Black man's dreamscape. All of these factors—plus the fact that the players Jordan cribbed from were past their primes when they got some shine on TV—conspired against Jordan's predecessors and thrust him into the spotlight while obscuring just how much of his game was borrowed from the greats who came before him. Kobe cribbed from Jordan the way Jordan cribbed from Dr. J and David Thompson. It takes nothing away from Bryant that his work resembles the master who came before him.

Jordan, for his part, nods to Kobe's brilliance, and by strong inference his own, when he says he could beat everyone in today's game in one-on-one matchups except Kobe, "because he steals all my moves."

"I agree with him," Kobe tells me with a laugh. "I'm a big historian, and I understand a lot of Michael's game is built off of how Jerry West played: pull-up shots, the stop-and-gos and things of that sort. So it's interesting—if you follow the lineage of players it's easy to see who they watched and who they learned from. Because those games are really the same, tactically. The only thing that changes is the person that's executing them."

Brian Shaw, who first faced Kobe on a court in Italy when Bryant was a preteen, and who later played with, and then helped to coach, Kobe, argues that Kobe and Jordan are nearly dead even and that MJ gets the slightest of nods for what is essentially a forensic matter: Jordan has six rings, Kobe five. Still, interestingly, complicatedly, almost contradictorily, he argues that because Kobe benefited from seeing Jordan play, he may actually be a better player. "I think that Kobe may have exceeded Michael in terms of just development of overall game," Shaw says. That's getting closer to my argument: Kobe's level of skill is simply unmatched in the history of the game, even by Jordan. Kobe took even more time than Jordan to develop his game; he was monastic and monomaniacal about mastering the game.

"Jordan was obsessed, but Jordan did other things," Jackson says. "Jordan played golf. Jordan played cards. Jordan went out. He played baseball. With Kobe Bryant, it's been strictly basketball 24/7. His crazed work ethic is historic. We've seen nothing like it: how hard he's worked and how he has chased perfection throughout his life."

Kobe's former Lakers teammate and now Hall of Famer Shaquille O'Neal can attest to that. "He has a tremendous willpower and tremendous focus," O'Neal tells me. "Much more than I ever did. Put it this way: I probably had 30 parties a year. Kobe never went to any of them. He's like, 'Naw, man, I'm cool.' We come back at 2, 3 [a.m.], we see Kobe and his trainer coming up, and we say, 'Damn. This dude working out at 3 in the morning?' So he had a crazy, crazy, crazy work ethic."

When I ask Kobe about his magnificent obsession, he's downright abstract and cerebral. "I think it's a constant curiosity," he says. "It's constantly trying to figure out why things happen, why things work. Having the strength to honestly assess things and honestly assess yourself, see what you did wrong and what you could do better. And what you did great. And just being really honest with yourself. And then from that point you can then move forward to try to be better."

Jordan has been rightly given credit for getting better year after year and working on his game, adding weapons to his arsenal, including a killer fade-away jumper that he could shoot over taller defenders. Kobe did the same thing. At the dawn of his career, Jordan was a determined yet relatively limited scorer, relying heavily on his dunk, a solid low-post game and a reasonable mid-range game, but he didn't have much of a three-point game. Kobe's arsenal from the start was far more complete and well rounded. Shaw argues that Bryant really had no weakness. Shaw played against Jordan but says he never saw anyone have the ability to quickly absorb new information and alter his game to compensate for even a perceived deficiency like Kobe had. Shaw recalls Kobe being told by a reporter from Seattle that his daughter thought Bryant was the game's greatest player, but that he didn't have a three-point game. She thought that was his only weakness. Shaw remembers the day clearly. "And he said to the reporter: 'Oh, is that right?' So after the reporters left he stayed in the gym and he just shot three after three after three after three. And the next night when we played the SuperSonics, he set the three-point record. He hit 12 threes."

As good as Jordan's footwork was, Kobe's is even better, the product of a boyhood spent in Italy where soccer was dominant and where Kobe honed his skills. His yen for perfection started early. Listen: "Once I started playing soccer, I watched it every day. I watched basketball, too. Then I started making the connection between the two of them. So certain things that I may see [Diego] Maradona do, I'd come out on the court and try to do a basketball version of it. So it was conscious on my part, trying to migrate [one sport to the other], to bring together both of those disciplines."

Like Jordan, Kobe's incredible discipline and work ethic led him to practice like he played. For Kobe, practice was the game; he was shooting an endless string of jumpers long before anyone deigned to come to the gym to work on their craft. Kobe always came earlier and stayed later than anyone else, busying himself in honing his skills. He not only tried everything he tried in a game in practice first, but he tried it at the actual speed of the game.

"As a coach you try to teach young players, and even your kids when they play, that it doesn't do you any good to practice something at a lesser speed than what you're going to be faced with doing it in a game," Shaw says. "And, over and over again, not only with the ball but, more importantly, without a ball, Kobe would practice his footwork and practice his moves at game speed."

If Kobe had an even greater desire than Jordan to master the game in itself, some have argued that the game Kobe mastered was a kinder and gentler—read: softer—version than Jordan faced because of the change in defensive rules. The infamous Jordan Rules that allowed the superstar to be knocked about—and which prodded him to bulk up in his off-seasons—are said to reflect a rougher time in the NBA, a time when Kobe might not have fared as well because he couldn't handle the hand check or the tougher measure of play. But it's a safe bet that Kobe could handle the pressure just fine, thank you. "With guys like Michael Jordan and Kobe Bryant, the rules don't matter," says Mark Jackson. "So I wouldn't dumb down their greatness and give any credit to rules."

What's not often spoken of is how, during Jordan's era, a team couldn't play zone the way it can now—keeping a player on the other side of the floor, basically playing two defenders on an opponent—thus encouraging duels and shootouts between gifted players in a one-on-one matchup. If one player was on the left side, say, everyone else had to be on the right side. With such one-on-one coverage, highly gifted shooters enjoyed a field day—in fact, they enjoyed many such days. In today's game, two or three people can flock to the ball and force a player to pass it. Or a player can go to the other side, double-team an opponent, sit in the paint for two and a half seconds and clear out on the same side of a player's isolation. In Jordan's era, if a player even looked like he was coming on the other side of the court, he was nabbed with a defensive violation. Thus one-on-one was king, playing to the strengths of a gunslinger like Jordan—and for those who were even more gifted scorers, like Kobe, that would likely have yielded quite a scorer's payday.

"If you gave any one of us guys that can score at a high level [such] one-on-one coverage, it's to our advantage every time," Durant says to me. "We don't talk about that [in comparing Kobe and Jordan]. We only talk about hand checking and physicality. So imagine if the best scorers in our game today—Kobe Bryant, LeBron James, Steph Curry, Russell Westbrook, guys like that—played all one-on-one, all the time. Imagine the points they would score. Imagine the averages we would see."

It must be said, too, that Jordan never faced the athletic competition that Kobe had to face. "Once he was in his prime they started to breed the 6–8 super-athletic shooting guard, and he was out there holding his own against everybody," Durant says. Jordan was a bit more muscular than Bryant, and MJ's direct competition at his position wasn't as tall, talented or athletic. "I look at the type of athlete that Kobe faced," Ice Cube tells me. "All of them were Jordan-like in some ways as far as athleticism [goes] in the League; [the competition for Kobe] was on a whole 'nother level. So Jordan was [one of] the most athletic of his time, and the most dominating. I don't know if Kobe was, but he still got the [same] results."

The more athletic competition forced Kobe to make far more complicated shots than Jordan, a difference that even Phil Jackson admits. Kobe has routinely made circus shots with hands in his face, bodies strewn in his path, forcing him to launch inconceivably difficult shots that swished the net many more times than it seemed possible. "So I've had to figure out how to shoot over double teams and shoot pull ups," Kobe says. "And defenses were able to disguise their traps and their schemes a lot better. So I think out of necessity I've had to figure out how to hit those tough shots over those defenses." The ballyhooed defensive rules that supposedly made Jordan the tougher player didn't force him to make the tougher shots.

And Kobe was every bit the killer as Jordan, using similar willpower to impose his desire and design on the game. "It didn't matter whether you were his teammate, whether you were his opponent, whether you were his coach," Shaw says. "If he sensed any weakness in you at all, he's going to try to rip your throat out."

Cleveland Cavaliers star guard Kyrie Irving recognized that killer instinct in Kobe when he mercilessly swatted away one of his idol's shots in the year he retired. "Even [Kobe's] block on Jordan in Jordan's final year— everybody criticized him for it, but that's what makes Kobe Kobe," Irving says to me. "Jordan would've done the same thing if he was playing against Julius Erving. It's just that competitive drive that we all try to emulate."

That willpower of course led Jordan to some highly iconic moments, none more dramatic than his famous flu game in the 1997 Finals against the Utah Jazz when Jordan proved his physical courage and valiance by playing a Championship game while his body was wracked and depleted. It was indeed a remarkable sight, seeing his comrade Scottie Pippen walk him from the court, exhausted and spent, everything left on the floor in a critical victory.

Still, less sexy but far more remarkable is how Kobe played the balance of a season with a broken finger. For Kobe, it was everyday necessity, not heroism, valor or physical courage. "I basically played with a soft cast for the rest of the ['09–'10] season. And we had to face the Celtics in the Finals, which is a physical team, and they went after that finger every chance they got. So I just had to figure it out. I always looked at it as if, 'History is not going to remember the fact that I had a broken finger as to why we didn't win a Championship.' So there's no sense in complaining and whining about it. I just need to figure out how to do it." Figure it out he did. He moved the ball more to the center of his palm and started using the middle finger and the ring finger, instead of the index finger, to follow through on his release.

"Well, he had the highest pain threshold of anybody I've been around," Shaw says. "I've seen him come down where he would roll his ankle all the way to the floor, and he'd be writhing in pain. But he'd just sit on the floor for a minute and then he would tell himself eventually that it didn't hurt and he was OK. And he might take a play off and go over to the bench and kind of work his ankle around. And then he'd get back up and come in the game." Most remarkable is how Kobe ruptured his Achilles while being fouled and then shot his two free throws before walking under his own power off the court. "I can remember coaching the game where he tore his Achilles," Mark Jackson says. "And I'm sitting there and telling my team, 'Don't go for the okey-doke. You know, he's fine, he's going to try to take over this game,' not aware of the fact that he was seriously hurt. Because I watched him time and time again in those situations tell his body: not now."

Beyond the finger and Achilles, however, Kobe was tested in a far more trying psychological fashion when he faced sexual assault charges in Colorado that damaged his reputation for a time. Bryant is reflective about that period and philosophical about how he played through the turmoil and pain.

"Basketball has always been an escape," Kobe says. "It's always been a sanctuary. It's taking all those emotions that I've had within me and using basketball as the outlet for them. It's always been there for me since I was a kid. It's always been the place where I can release these emotions, these pent-up frustrations. So to me it wasn't a matter of having a strong focus and being tough minded, and all sort of stuff. It was more therapeutic."

It is nearly inconceivable that Bryant, while facing the possibility of losing his freedom for the rest of his life, would often travel by private plane from court appearances earlier in the day to play in a game that night. Less than 11 hours after he pled not guilty to sexual assault charges in Colorado, Bryant flew to Los Angeles to appear in a playoff game against the San Antonio Spurs where he scored 42 points. "Do you know the mindset that it takes to allow that to wear on you physically and mentally and still go out and do your job?" Jackson asks. In response to Kobe's "sanctuary" argument, Jackson says, "It's fine to say that's where you express yourself. And there are guys that would feel the same way, but nobody would've done it like he did. I mean, he went out and still performed at an all-time great level in the process of going through it. And I would bet my last dollar that only two guys in the history of the game could've done it, and that's Michael and Kobe. And one had the platform to do it, so we know he did it."

What he also did was win titles with, comparatively speaking, less help than Jordan, a point that veteran guard Brandon Jennings made in 2014 on social media when he proclaimed that Kobe is "the greatest ever" and tweeted that "Kobe had Shaq. MJ had Pippen, Dennis [Rodman], Ron Harper, Horace Grant, Steve Kerr, Toni Kukoc, John Paxson, BJ Armstrong."

Players like Rick Fox, Glen Rice, Derek Fisher, Robert Horry and Brian Shaw himself might quibble with Jennings in suggesting that Kobe was exclusively dependent on Shaq, but his point about the pedigree of help Jordan had stands—and, we might add, the consistency of Jordan's "supporting cast" and his coach, while Kobe had more coaches and players to contend with as he contended for his chips. Many folk contend that, unlike Kobe, Jordan never had a dominant center like Shaq to depend on, to go inside-out, to rely on to pound and patrol the paint. That's true, but Jordan also never had to defer to another ego as strong as his, to another player as dominant as he was. Jennings also tweeted that "MJ never won without Pippen. Kobe won 2 rings without another great on his team. Kobe is the Goat."

The social medium on which Jennings expressed his views about Kobe's greatness is one that Kobe has carefully migrated to, expressing his opinions and, unlike Jordan, even speaking a bit about social issues.

"Well, I think it's about speaking your mind," Kobe says. "A big misunderstanding is that when an athlete speaks his mind the perception is, 'Oh, the athlete's right,' or 'The athlete's wrong.' I think that's not good. The important thing about having a stage, or having a platform from which to speak, is [that] you create conversation. And hopefully the conversation that's created is a healthy one that advances the particular topic forward versus the silliness of, 'Ah, I don't agree, he's an idiot.' 'No, you're an idiot; he's right.' That's really sandbox, immature dialogue. So for us as athletes, and any of us who have a voice, when we speak up about a particular issue, or a particular cause, there are people out there who disagree that an intelligent conversation can be had [despite there being] a disagreement. But we must have the idea of advancing the cause forward, versus winning an argument."

When I ask Bryant about the toxic political environment in which the country is embroiled with figures like presidential nominee Donald Trump all the rage, he is considered and thoughtful, discreet even, but not neutral in his assessment of the fallout from our political folly.

"I think you have, obviously, different opinions," he says. "This is the beauty of living in such a democratic culture. Everybody's entitled to their own opinion. Everybody has a platform to have their voice heard. Especially with social media and all of these outlets you have. And I think it sparks conversation. Now the question to ask is, does it spark a healthy conversation, or does it create friction to the point of negativity? I believe our leader should be a person that creates healthy dialogue versus creating a negative friction."

Bryant is also fond of entertainers like Kendrick Lamar and Beyoncé, finding a social register in their artistry, risking controversy to make important political interventions. As for Lamar's racially charged Grammy appearance this year, Bryant had nothing but praise. "I love what Kendrick Lamar's doing. I thought his performance was outstanding. I think he has an idea of how his music can be greater and live longer than simply being music. I think he's communicating that voice in a grand way." Bryant is equally supportive of Knowles, who caused quite a stir with her Super Bowl halftime performance of her song "Formation" that pleads for a cease in police killings of unarmed Blacks and revels in the undervalued luxuries of Black self-love. "Beyoncé's sparking intelligent conversation. And it's our job as artists to create those conversations. And now us, as a culture, it's our responsibility to take these conversations and move them forward. What she did was great. I thought it was beautiful."

Also beautiful, though little known or remarked on, is how Kobe, behind the scenes of his withering focus and killer competitive urge, is also a deeply caring man. As Shaw argues, figures like Magic and Jordan are more loved by the public, while Kobe "has been more demonized than them. But there's a side of him that's very, very generous that people don't know." I witnessed Bryant's generosity up close: a woman from another country contacted me on Twitter because she knew Bryant followed me, and because her brother had battled a serious illness and she wanted nothing more than to have his favorite player wish her brother a happy birthday. When I relayed her wishes to Bryant, he not only obliged, but he did so in spectacular fashion: instead of complying with her wish to have a simple video made on a cell phone, Bryant sent a professionally produced video to the young man wishing him continued recovery and a bright future. It was a moving, compassionate gesture.

When I asked Kobe how he'd like to be remembered, he replied, "As a person that left no stone unturned and did everything possible to try to reach his full potential. And years from now, hopefully, what I've done [will] inspire others to be able to approach their craft and their lives much the same way."

Amen. Speaking of which, the Christian church, my Christian church, still has backwards ways when it comes to gender, but we've also made significant strides in addressing justice for women and other minorities. So what was once deemed blasphemous and worthy of expulsion may now be considered prophetic. Maybe my words on Kobe as the globe's greatest basketball player ever will one day soon enjoy a similar fate.

25

Currying Favor

Steph Curry has changed the game of basketball, literally. The way he "stretches the floor" and shoots the ball from unimaginable depths and lengths on the court has altered how defenses counter such skill and transformed how players and teams think about offenses and hoisting balls up from the three-point line and beyond. Off the court, his fame has cast a spotlight on the many talents of his gifted wife and charismatic children, and shed light on the character of his faith and how it shapes his social and political views. This essay appeared online in 2016 for the ESPN website The Undefeated, *which is dedicated to probing the intersections of race, sports, culture, and society.*

If, like me, you've witnessed Stephen Curry swish the nets on an other-worldly three-pointer from near half court and said to yourself, "My God, that shot was miraculous," you might have stumbled on the key to Curry's life and game. If anything is certain about the reigning two-time NBA MVP—besides the supernatural arc of the ball as it leaves his hands and finds its corded destiny with record-breaking accuracy—it's that Curry believes in himself because he believes in God. His faith is his pillar.

"It just keeps me grounded," Curry says to me on the night he got the 2016 Maurice Podoloff MVP Trophy from NBA commissioner Adam Silver before he and the Warriors dispatched the Portland Trailblazers and clinched a spot in the Western Conference Finals. "It keeps me focused, and with the hoopla that goes on around me, my faith doesn't change, my family doesn't change. And that allows me to be myself and enjoy what I do for sure."

Curry's faith has steadied him as he enjoys the perks of a superstar, and as he faces its challenges too, especially when his wife and daughter share the spotlight. Even off the hardwood court, Curry and his family set tongues to wagging about fatherhood, marriage, feminism, family values, and the politics of color. Faith shaped Stephen Curry's consciousness from the start. "Every morning through middle school and high school we did devotions from six to six-thirty before school for thirty minutes," Sonya

Curry told me. "And it was just basically reading the Word. I didn't feel that [it] was my place to teach them about the word of God. As God says, He'll write on the tablets of our hearts. And so I think that's what you're seeing coming to fruition in [Stephen's] life right now."

Sonya Curry also thinks that her son avoids the pitfalls of too many Christians: being judgmental and preachy. Sonya alludes to a famous Biblical passage to offer a divinely prescribed division of labor. "Some people are called to preach, some people are called to teach," Sonya says. "His job is to glorify God in everything that he does, and that comes through his talents. And so from that standpoint, he's not *over*doing it. God says, 'Just let me shine through you. You just be the vessel. And be relatable.'"

Curry's most relatable trait is the pronounced lack of athletic prowess that undoubtedly binds him to the men who fantasize about the glory he's nevertheless achieved. Curry's slight, non-muscular build belies his ball-handling wizardry, his unquenchable work ethic, his three-point mastery, his adroit passing, his revolutionizing the game through his command of small ball, his lightning-quick release of the ball when shooting (one-tenth of a second at last count), and his rapid ascent as arguably the game's best player. If his body of work is housed in a frame that looks like your average American amateur, his humility seems to exist in inverse proportion to his hoops genius.

When I asked his father, Dell, one of the NBA's most clear-eyed sharp-shooters over a 16-year career, about the most important element he passed on to his son as a man and a ball player, he didn't hesitate.

"Just to stay humble," Curry told me. "Don't get too high when you're playing well; don't get too low when you're playing bad. Continue to rely on your work ethic, and get that routine and stick with it. Whether you're playing well or not. Your routine is something you can fall back on to get you through." Stephen Curry's wife, Ayesha, admires that quality most in her husband. "He's not boastful," she tells me. "After his speech the other day [accepting the MVP award], we had a dinner and he didn't say much about it. It was just like the basics of trying to win this championship. So even in our house that's not much talked about unless there's a game on. Everything's very normal around here." Ayesha sees Curry's humility as the mark of his quiet faith, less the showy evangelism of Tim Tebow and more of the understated self-possession of Jimmy Carter. Ayesha believes Stephen's humility is his most valued asset in proclaiming God to the world. "They see Stephen and they wonder why he's so nice," Ayesha says. "They wonder why he's so humble. I think that's the whole mission of this all—for him to shed light that way. It's never projecting views onto people, it's just living your life for the Lord."

* * *

As an ordained Baptist minister for 35 years, I can testify that living for the Lord isn't always smooth sailing. As the old gospel song goes, its protagonist dramatically embodying the plight of all Christians, "Nobody told me that the road would be easy." Curry has had his share of bumps, too, including, most recently, the perceived shade thrown his way by four-time MVP LeBron James, who, while acknowledging that Curry deserved the honor, nevertheless tacked ever so slightly, some might say tackily, toward a distinction without a difference: most valuable player versus best player. There appeared to be a hint of whatever is the opposite of schadenfreude, not outright jealousy, mind you, but a laudatory toast to a friendly foe with a twist of post-Beyoncé lemonade. Curry's response was far more literal and hence unsusceptible to colorful literary interpretation: "I've gotten good at ignoring people." Like Stephen off the dribble in a hotly contested game, shots were fired.

But it's off the court where Stephen and Ayesha, and their daughter Riley, too, have made a powerful impression, and where they have also endured their share of flagrant fouls. Stephen and Ayesha have brought a verve and wholesomeness to Black coupledom that is only rivaled by Barack and Michelle Obama. Curry takes as much pride in his marriage as in his transcendent basketball achievements—maybe even more. "I think everybody knows that nothing comes before his family," Curry's teammate Draymond Green told me. "It's incredible to see, especially firsthand. But it's not a façade." Stephen's brother Seth, who plays with the Sacramento Kings, agrees. "It's not like he's putting on a show for anybody," Seth tells me. "What people see on Instagram, Twitter, and on TV is who he is." Their authenticity draws people to the couple as a role model for healthy togetherness.

"The beauty of it is, we just try to be ourselves," Stephen tells me. "And the biggest compliment I think we've gotten is that people that know us, on and off the court, feel that we're the same people we were when we first got married almost six years ago. And not let this whole scene change us, even though it is a huge platform to be an influence, not only to young couples, and young parents. It's just pretty special."

Stephen's boyish handsomeness and Ayesha's radiant beauty have made them the darling of a Black America hungry for the public affirmation of

Black love—for its steely persistence amidst social forces that crush the Black family beneath stereotypes of pathology and dysfunction. In a time where hip hop's cynicism about love's edifying possibilities shadows the culture, Stephen and Ayesha's sexy embrace of cheerful monogamy stands out.

Stephen's parents provided a sturdy blueprint for him to follow. "They're a great example of a marriage sticking together, especially through their professions, and their children," Stephen says. "That was a great help for me growing up to know it's possible. It's not easy; it's definitely hard work. It's very taxing, especially on my wife, with the schedule that we have, so it's nice to have that kind of vision that they've given us."

And ever since their two-year-old daughter Riley joined her famous father on the podium for a postgame press conference after the Warriors defeated the Rockets in Game 1 of the 2015 Western Conference Finals, she has become a famous little figure in her own right. Riley instructed her father to "be quiet" and played peekaboo with the audience beneath the curtained podium, melting the nation's heart with her adorable antics. Just last week Riley renewed her status as America's Most Famous Toddler as she made a dramatic entrance and flashed a gesture with her two-fingers above her eyes, interchanged with one finger pointing to the front row press, suggesting "I'm watching you"—a gesture filled with irony since some of the press had been irritated by Riley's debut a year before and deemed it inappropriate and unprofessional.

Stephen, on the other hand, became for many the very picture of a doting father patiently indulging his daughter's cute behavior. After all, Riley had accompanied him to the podium because Ayesha was pregnant with their second daughter, Ryan, and the two-year-old was antsy and wanted to be with Daddy. Stephen answered questions and felt for Riley beneath the table, making sure to keep her within arm's reach. Beyond the surface feel-good story, the symbolism was inescapable: here was a Black parent who, with the simplest measure of affection, and without even trying to do so, was rebutting the myth that the vast majority of Black men are absent fathers.

"It's kind of ridiculous when you think about it," Ayesha Curry tells me as she reflects on the dyspeptic portrayals of Black fathers in the media. Ayesha sees the benefit of her husband being heralded, although she knows it is hardly unique. "It's nice to have that change, and to show what's really going on. 'Cause there's *plenty* of amazing young Black fathers out there and not enough light is shed on that."

Ayesha says Curry is a great dad even away from the spotlight. "He is super hands-on," Ayesha says. "He's not afraid to have a tea party with our girls and play dress-up with them when they want to play dress-up. He's like the perfect dad for little girls. He's not so into himself that he loses himself in his manhood."

If Stephen has become a national inspiration as husband and father, Ayesha has become the model of an ideal woman for millions of folk around the country. "You got a *lot* of people aspiring to be that," Draymond Green says, noting the huge popularity in social media of "a meme . . . saying, 'Oh, I'm just looking for my Ayesha Curry.'"

Ayesha is proud to be the face of happy marriage, but she insists she's no random part of grammar. "I think it's cool that people think that I'm a great wife," she says. "But I'm not an adjective, I'm a person," Ayesha laughs as she tells me. "And fortunately, I'm taken."

Ayesha is flattered by the attention because it highlights the value of mothers and stresses the importance of families in a culture too quick to forget both. She believes that in families "everybody holds each other accountable," and that the sense that it's important for families to have meals together has been tragically lost. "I feel like it's our duty now to keep that message alive, that family is important, and togetherness is important. And it's okay to want to be with somebody and to want to have a family and to want to take care of your family."

Ayesha has been taken to task on social media for what appears to be a traditional view of womanhood that undermines feminist self-expression. A recent Instagram post chastised her for exploiting her ties to a famous spouse to tout plans for a pop-up restaurant instead of encouraging women to seek higher education. "Use your fame wisely," the post read. "Women around the world should strive to be more than just 'great' mothers/cooks. Tailor your marketing and partnerships to inspire the next generation of doctors, lawyers, professors, public leaders, etc." Ayesha politely responded on Instagram that she is an entrepreneur who would continue to quietly challenge assumptions with work that speaks for itself.

"I do have a career, and I do work on a weekly basis," Ayesha tells me. "I have my own passions, I have everything. But what I'm most proud of is my family. And so that's what I project out there. And I feel like there's nothing wrong with that." Her perspective underscores the belief that feminism fights for women to be able to work independently of their husbands and to carve out their own identities—*and* the ability to become homemakers and housewives if they choose to do so. College-educated Curry's role as a "mompreneur" embraces a feminist ethic of choice.

Ayesha has also been accused of fueling the politics of respectability when she sent out a series of tweets noting that contemporary women's fashion trended toward sparse clothing. Ayesha said that she preferred to "keep the good stuff covered up for the one who matters," and that she chooses "classy over trendy." The social context in which Curry's comments are interpreted must be acknowledged: women who choose to dress provocatively are "slut shamed" and mercilessly pilloried by the same men who applaud Curry's modesty, and whose patriarchal prerogative to prescribe the right dress or sexual behavior for women is hardly challenged. Of course, these same men fail to see the looming paradox of their desire: in order to snag "an Ayesha Curry" they might want to first be "a Stephen Curry," an apparently faithful and loving husband who encourages his wife's passions and tends to the needs of his children.

As for Ayesha, she wasn't aiming to degrade or insult women who disagreed with her, just to state her preference *not* to have her dress or style dictated by a sexist culture that overly sexualized women for the material and sexual benefit of the male gaze. She is surprisingly feisty in defense of her position. "I think if you don't make people a little uncomfortable, you're not doing something right," she confidently told me. "I think my words were misconstrued greatly. So I think people were seeing different versions of what I said, and not actually going to the source and seeing what was really said." Ayesha says she stated her own preference, and that her reference to "the one that matters" could be oneself, one's mate, or whomever one might deem important. "But people's conscience took over [and] maybe they felt some type of way about what they were doing, and I think that's what started it." Ayesha does believe, however, that today's young folk are saturated with overly sexed messages that less is more.

"I think what's being mass communicated to our youth in particular is a little bit sad," Curry tells me. "Every woman has her positives; every woman has her negatives. I want everybody to succeed. I want everybody to win. I've never projected my views on anybody." Curry thinks that much of the blowback she received from Black Twitter was misplaced and rooted in misperception about her real identity. "It's crazy how a group of people can shape [the perception of] a person. Everybody has an opinion and a view on who I actually am. I feel like my message may have gotten a little misconstrued." When I ask her what exactly has been misconstrued, she points to the "holier than thou" view of her. "I've done nothing to spark that."

* * *

Stephen and his family have done even less, other than be born in their skin, to enflame a far more subtle racial wound that may be invisible to folk outside the culture: the plague of colorism, or skin tone, that has yet to be vanquished. Stephen's light skin, and its relation to—some would argue *the* crucial reason for—his broad cultural appeal, has not gone unnoticed in some Black circles. "James Harden doesn't stand a chance to win the MVP," a college professor on the West Coast proclaimed in his class when I visited his school last year, referring to Curry's closest competitor for the award. "He's too dark and 'too Black.'"

Not all the mentions of Stephen's light skin are as dramatic or negative. In fact, Curry appeared on a panel with Harden, Anthony Davis and Kevin Durant in 2014 to promote the release of the NBA2K video game, where Durant recalled first meeting Curry when they were both 10 years old while playing on the AAU circuit. "I thought he was white," Durant said. "He was this yellow kid, right? I'm just being real now, right? Where I come from, in the hood, we don't see that. We don't see the light-skinned guys around. It was all guys like me." As the darker-skinned Durant told the story, Curry was engulfed in guffaws as he rested his left hand on Harden's back, who was bowled over in laughter. There was clearly no offense meant or taken. More recently, the light-brown-skinned retired superstar Allen Iverson took to the air to laud the incredible Mr. Curry. "That light-skinned dude," Allen Iverson said in praising Curry's skills as the host laughed. "I never seen anything like this in my life. I was a certified serial killer. But this dude has it all."

Durant and Iverson were clearly displaying affection for Curry, while also reflecting widely held views of light-skinned players, especially surprise at their abilities. Earlier this year, brown-skinned Laker legend Kobe Bryant admonished his lighter-skinned teammate Jordan Clarkson not to drive to the basket like a "light-skinned dude," presumably soft and hesitantly, leading Clarkson to comment that "I've got to start doing it like a dark-skinned [dude]." But beneath the playful banter of athletic colleagues the hidden injuries of race slip into view. Many Blacks are far less sanguine about the matter of skin tone.

"I would like to think that Steph Curry's apparent marketability has nothing to do with it but if I made that false assumption that would be as silly as me thinking that Beyoncé is the top woman in music because she actually sings better than Jill Scott or Jennifer Hudson," writes Tay Jordan on the website theblackjuice.com. "I mean who cannot notice the media's clear favorability to Stephen Curry? He's of fair complexion . . . and his eyes are a pretty cool color too."

On the Sports Nut blog, a 2015 post entitled "Steph Curry's daughter and the epitome of light skinned privilege" argued that Riley Curry's adorability was enhanced by her fair skin and that her behavior was "completely unacceptable for a child not suffering from any cognitive issues." The author asks if we notice how "every jet Black athlete who would never go out of their way to compliment a Black child tweeted about how gorgeous this racially ambiguous little girl was" and how "every light skinned person automatically get[s] labeled adorable or beautiful." The author says that if the kids of dark-skinned stars Dwyane Wade, LeBron James or Curry teammate Draymond Green had been "up there acting a fool," the narrative would have been, "Somebody get this little crispy urchin off the stage."

Iverson and Durant's comments, as well as those on the internet, nod to a pecking order where lighter Blacks were perched atop the racial hierarchy of rewards. "Light, bright and damn near white" was an expression used to capture the superior social appeal of fair-skinned Blacks who were believed to be both biologically and culturally closer to white culture than their darker and more distant Black kin. Lighter-skin Blacks were deemed to be smarter and more culturally refined; darker Blacks were believed to be dumber and cruder.

Blacks have often internalized in our minds and culture the vicious stereotypes associated with skin color. We have often unconsciously circulated harmful beliefs about ourselves that are tied to skin tone: deferring to some Blacks because their skin is lighter, demonizing other Blacks because their shade is darker. I remember several years ago speaking at a higher education conference where I was praised by a Black attendee for being "much lighter in person" than I appeared on television. I said in a CNN documentary on Black America that I thought my imprisoned brother Everett, equally as bright as me, but darker skinned, wasn't nearly as encouraged in his studies as I was. And I witnessed firsthand how whites, and many Blacks, too, disparaged my blue-Black father, Everett, Sr., for no other reason than his dark skin.

To be sure, many whites may view Curry differently than they would, say, LeBron James or James Harden. A study of Google searches for Curry reveals that a great deal is made of his ethnic origins, questioning whether he is mixed race or if he is truly "just" Black. Although Curry isn't biracial like his teammate Klay Thompson, he is sometimes thought to be so, as Durant's remarks prove, though I suspect more whites than Blacks mistake him for anything but a light-skinned Black person. When a white fan attempted to ascribe Curry's marksmanship to his white genes, his sister Sydel took to Twitter to correct him, saying with a "laugh out loud" acronym that Stephen wasn't half-white, just light skinned.

The unconscious correlation of skin tone with mental or physical ability is a bugaboo that cuts both ways: Stephen is assumed to be white, or to play white, because he lacks commanding physical presence, because he doesn't often slam the ball down the hole in vicious dunks, because he's more finesse than forceful, and because he's a towering shooter, a trait some folk more readily associate with white players like Kyle Korver and Curry's coach Steve Kerr than Ray Allen, Reggie Miller or Curry's father, Dell. In such a genetic mapping of ability, Stephen's basketball pedigree seems to derive from the white side more than the Black one.

But there is also a worrisome knee-jerk reaction, certainly not equal to the unconscious preference for lightness-as-whiteness, but one that roils beneath the surface and occasionally flares, if not quite with the contempt that bludgeons Black psyches and despises dark skin, and which nevertheless chafes in resentment at a presumed superiority that is often projected without proof onto light-skinned Blacks. Beyoncé must want to be white, what with all the acclaim she wins for her talents and the rumors that her magazine covers are getting lighter and lighter over the years. (Then too, given Kerry Washington's recent complaint about being photoshopped on the cover of *AdWeek*, and the brouhaha over Serena Williams's photoshopped image in *People* magazine, darker-skinned female celebrities are particularly prey to the cultural desire to lighten their skin or reshape their bodies.)

But Beyoncé has emerged as a prominent feminist and a strong advocate for Black pride and political freedom—much like other lighter-skin celebrities of the past, including Lena Horne, and in the historic wake of light-skinned freedom fighters like Adam Clayton Powell and Malcolm X in the past, and Benjamin Jealous and Louis Farrakhan in our day. This recognition doesn't deny the legitimacy of light-skin privilege and the need to combat its dangerous premises—and the benefits and advantages it offers to those of us who are lighter. But it also suggests caution in automatically ascribing complicity with a color regime that in different ways has harmed all Blacks.

* * *

Of course, the reason any of this matters—his faith, his family, Ayesha's take on gender, and quarrels over the politics of Black skin—is because Stephen Curry is, right now, arguably our most uniquely gifted basketball phenomenon. Dell Curry argues that the weapons in his son's arsenal—the clutch shots, the way he's defended and yet is able to get shots off the dribble when his team needs them the most, his fearlessness and competitive spirit—have been with him from the start. "That skill's been in him his whole life," Dell says. "He's always been a guy who hated to lose. He wanted to be the determining factor of whether his teams won or lost. And I think it's helped get him here to this point now."

Stephen tells me that he's always had "that kind of creativity" that defines his style of play, "the juice for the game." Even in college at Davidson, Curry says he was "trying to push the envelope and do something nobody thought we could do. That experience really boosted my confidence." After he got to the NBA, Curry sought, first, to establish himself, and then to push himself to get better each year. "I was put in a position where I needed to accelerate my game pretty quickly, and that helps. And opportunity helped obviously. So I just took it and ran with it."

Curry's work ethic is already becoming legendary; his yen to get better pushed him to become, in the same year, both the league's most valued, and unofficially, its most improved player too (he placed fourth on that list this year). That the league's reigning MVP could grow by leaps and bounds to embrace further reaches of his greatness is simply astonishing. "It's incredible, some of the things that he's doing on the court," Draymond Green says to me. "So someone will say, 'Oh, my God, how does he win MVP then get better?' Well, the amount of work that he put in, that's how it happens."

It is easy to forget that Stephen Curry's draft report read like a litany of weaknesses that doubted his NBA success—he wasn't a true point guard, he made questionable shot selections, he lacked lateral quickness, he had a limited upside, he possessed average athleticism, average size and an average wingspan, and he relied too heavily on his outside shot. It is poetic justice that Curry has turned being a long shot as a superstar into being a superstar because of his long shot. His malady has become his meal ticket; his deficiency became his defining gesture. Now widely viewed as the league's greatest shooter ever, and a player with many more championships on the horizon, Wardell Stephen Curry II is as much a miracle as the awe-inspiring baskets he routinely makes.

To Live Up to Their Own Constitution

In Politics

26

The Root of Jesse

Jesse Jackson is among the greatest Black leaders ever. In a lot of historical reckoning with the 1960s, I see an unfortunate historical revisionism that tends to slight Jackson's huge accomplishments in every field of endeavor, from civil rights to politics, from opening the doors of corporate America to Black folk to democratizing capital on Wall Street, from providing the access of Black business folk to the automobile, sneaker, and technology industries to bringing racial equity to the classroom—and so much more. I first met Jackson in 1984, when I prayed on a program during his presidential campaign stop at Knoxville College, and then again, in earnest, in 1989, when I taught his namesake son at Chicago Theological Seminary and soon thereafter got signed on to write his autobiography. Jackson is one of the great preachers, storytellers, raconteurs, political minds, and public intellectuals of our age. I have traveled the country with Jackson, and despite the claims that he's self-aggrandizing and egotistical to a fault, no one has ever outworked him or committed more time to bettering the lives of vulnerable people. When Jackson calls you, there's never any small talk. "This is your brother," his familiar voice usually announces, "and I want to talk to you about . . ." as he parses the complications, complexities, subtleties, and nuances of one problem or the next, suggesting a way through moral morass or social chaos, with an incredible wealth of knowledge rolling effortlessly off his tongue. These days, with his announcement of his battle with Parkinson's, the words don't always come in the bunches of parables, paradoxes, and paradigms as in olden, golden times, but his mind is just as sharp, his determination to serve God and his people just as great as it has ever been. More than a champion or icon, even a hero, he is, too, in many ways, with the warts that all of us possess, a modern-day saint of social struggle. This is the foreword to David Masciotra's magnificent 2020 study, I Am Somebody: Why Jesse Jackson Matters.

J esse Louis Jackson was born poor and Black in the South seventy-five years after slavery ended. Even though the shackles were removed, oppression remained. American apartheid seemed to get the last laugh by extending the warranty of oppression and etching "colored" on his birth certificate. Jim Crow filled the sky of Black destiny. The wings of segregation shadowed the lives of colored children in its destructive flight. His mother, Helen Burns, was barely in her teens when she delivered him into poverty and personal peril. At sixteen, she was more than half the age of Noah Robinson, the married man next door who had a son with her that he would seldom see except through the mirror of his child's desperate nostalgia—and then not till fame had kissed him into a precocious legend. The brutal mark of his "bastard's" origin was branded on his generous forehead like an invisible "B." The circumstances of his birth sometimes blurred his eyes with grief and at other times moistened them with lament. His foremost biographer, Marshall Frady, noted his "propensity for tears" at an early age, showing just how wrong are those who say he only sobs with cameras in view.

Jackson came of age when it was literally against the law for Black folk to drink water, or ride buses, or share a meal, or stay in hotels, or vote, or go to school with white folk. It was nearly illegal to imagine that you could do something about it. If you dared to dream that you could rise above your station, there were policemen standing by to remind you of your place by clubbing you upside your head in a show of racial sadism. He came of age when Black women were routinely raped and Black men were castrated and lynched at the drop of a rope. He came of age when Black servicemen returning home from war in their uniforms were murdered by vengeful bigots at bus stops where they waited to join the families they left behind. Dodging the bombs and bullets of exotic enemies, they met death at the hands of domestic terrorists who hid behind religious cloth and crosses.

When it came time for him to get his lesson, as the old folk described formal education in their charming vernacular, he called on a rich cast of characters who bathed him in love: coaches who instilled discipline on the gridiron and around the hoop; teachers who fed his huge intellectual appetite; neighbors who saluted his eerie self-confidence even as a boy; college presidents who spotted his academic promise and egged him on; and ordinary men and women who lent him encouragement in the often proud and affirming Black world that segregation had no idea that it had helped to create. We often said to oppressors who forced us to live together back then what Joseph in the Hebrew Bible said to his brothers who sold him into slavery but only made him greater: "you meant evil against me, but God meant it for good."

While Negroes divided ourselves by shade of skin and pocketbook, racism imposed a lovely and efficient unity on Black life—a practical solidarity. Whether we were doctors or ditch diggers, lawyers or landscape architects, automobile mechanics or accountants, carpenters or chemists, nurses or nannies, farmers or pharmacists, secretaries or social workers, or judges or prisoners, we were all colored and just didn't count that much in the white world. Our grand sororities and fraternities didn't impress them. Our big churches didn't make them testify to our spiritual genius. Our thriving colleges and universities didn't make them see how much sense we had. True, the way we hit a hanging curveball or a high C eventually made the white world take notice, but the ordinary Negro rarely crossed the average white person's mind except when he served him a cold drink or passed him by on the street with his hat in his hand to show proper deference. No matter our pedigree or profession, we were often just another nigger. And when white folk took the time to worry about Negroes, it was either our sexual menace or our uppity attitudes that called for adjustment or retaliation.

This is the Black and white world that shaped Jesse Jackson. This is the world that called forth his stirring oratory, his vital leadership, his gift of prophecy. He had already cut his teeth on local protests in Greenville, South Carolina, where he was born, and later, in Greensboro, North Carolina, where he went to school, before he burst onto the national scene during the events that led to the famous protest in 1965 at Selma, Alabama. His eagerness to serve and his ambition to lead caught the eye of Ralph Abernathy, the veteran activist and best friend of the movement's greatest leader and mouthpiece, Martin Luther King, Jr. Jackson soon earned his way as an apprentice prophet of sorts, throwing in with the band of men and women who helped to change the world before there was an internet or social media. They didn't have Facebook to market their revolution; instead, they faced being booked into jails and relied largely on black-and-white television to beam their unjust imprisonment to the world. They couldn't use Twitter to tweet their message of social redemption, but they could set the nation atwitter with their bold and daring efforts to tweak social change. Before he became a commanding general in the war to remake America, Jesse Jackson was a street soldier who did grunt work to turn the nation even further toward true democracy and real freedom.

When King met his bloody end in Memphis, Tennessee, Jesse Jackson was there with him at the Lorraine Motel that evening. Some folk have held this chance occurrence, or this divinely appointed rendezvous with destiny, against him, as if he had something to do with King's demise, as if he sent that bullet hurtling across air to collapse time and space to a crushing few seconds where, as the rapper The Game brilliantly says, "the future took a head shot." But The Game amplifies the suspicion of Jackson when he asks in his rap devoted to King: "I wonder why Jesse Jackson didn't catch him before his body dropped/Would he give me the answer? Probably not." The Game's piercing questions echo the sentiments of those who believe that Jackson was overtaken by an ambition so fatal that he would as soon see King die than live and prosper. But that's a mix of bad history and terrible sociology. King was already symbolically dead before he got sent into the ground with an exploding report inside his skull. He was wildly unpopular, he didn't routinely draw big crowds, his former allies fell off, and he would have hardly earned a national holiday had he not been blasted into martyr-dom when he got caught in a bigoted assassin's crosshairs.

Yes, Jackson had a big ego to match his big Afro. You'd think rappers—and for that matter, preachers and politicians too—would be the last folk to complain about anybody's big ego. You can't be great unless you have what Quaker spiritual writer D. Elton Trueblood called "the habitual vision of greatness." And not only do you have to see it, you've got to want it bad enough to sacrifice your way there. The late great Kobe Bryant saw greatness in Michael Jordan and wanted some championships of his own. Al Sharpton saw greatness in Jesse Jackson and wanted some civil rights victories of his own. Nicki Minaj saw greatness in the Queen Bee Lil' Kim and wanted some honey of her own. Yes, Jesse Jackson wanted to be great; yes, Jesse Jackson wanted to lead. But he got what he got the old-fashioned way: he worked hard for it, as hip hop stars Method Man and Notorious B.I.G. admonished us to do. Nobody works harder than Jesse Jackson.

Before his historic gait was slowed and stiffened by the onset of Parkin-son's disease, he got up earlier than most and went to bed later too. Even now as the disease progresses, he defies its deadening lethargy with every fiber of his considerable being. For more than fifty years he's been speaking, agitating, writing, thinking, marching, protesting, strategizing, building, traveling, organizing, arguing, resisting, and fighting for us. I've been with him in London when he worked from sunup till sundown, meeting with Mandela in a leader's home, lunching with a billionaire media titan, preach-ing in churches full of common folk, kibitzing with songstresses Anita Baker, Natalie Cole, and Patti LaBelle, and then talking, talking, talking, like Sinatra sang, into the wee small hours of the morning. I've been with him in Texas when he worked with union laborers to get a fair wage and a decent standard of living. I've marched with him in Illinois as he argued against zero tolerance policies that jilted the future of young Black males.

Jesse Jackson has led us with style and substance, with flair and formidable intelligence. While King's rhetoric reflected a jazzman's pace and improvisational instincts, Jackson upped the oratorical ante by sprinkling street speech in his lyrical dance; he laced dazzling displays of urban authenticity and verbal bravura into his melodic rhetoric. He was dropping couplets and rhymes a full decade before the Sugarhill Gang and Kurtis Blow. "Down with dope/up with hope." He was spinning mantras before Tina Turner or Oprah or Deepak Chopra: "Keep Hope Alive." In 1966 he was already saying it, and I heard him say it forty-five years later, on a bright Sunday in 2011, in renowned pastor Freddy Haynes's magnificent Friendship-West Baptist Church in Dallas: "I am—Somebody. I may be poor, but I am—Somebody! I may be on welfare, but I am—Somebody! I may be uneducated, but I am—Somebody! I must be, I'm God's child. I must be respected and protected. I am Black and I am beautiful! I am—Somebody!" It makes perfect sense, indeed it seems inevitable, even necessary, that David Masciotra would choose this title for his masterly meditation on the meaning and importance of one of the greatest public moralists in the nation's triumphant and tragic history.

Jesse Jackson closed the distance between the sacred and the secular and taught us that we could embrace Moses in the Bible—and Black Moses Isaac Hayes and his Hot Buttered Soul with his bald pate shining Black sensuality to the world. Jesse Jackson looked good while doing good: he donned dashikis, sported sideburns, blew out his 'fro, draped his neck in medallions—his version of a Jesus piece—and jumped into leisure threads or Brooks Brothers suits to make his point. He was a Country Preacher— and a country's preacher. He has been a public moralist who has preached redemption to the masses and elites alike. He visited the short—and short-tempered—singer Little Willie John in prison long before another Weezy or T.I. got locked up. He shot hoops with Marvin Gaye, hung out in the studio with Stevie Wonder, preached on Aretha Franklin's second gospel album—her Daddy, the legendary preacher C. L. Franklin had, after all, helped to ordain him—performed the wedding of *Ebony* magazine's heir apparent Linda Johnson Rice, and preached the funerals of everybody from Ron Brown to Sammy Davis, Jr. "Let Mr. Bojangles rest," he pleaded over Davis's body. "He has earned it."

Jesse Jackson has been our leader and prophet at one of the most difficult times in our people's journey. After King forecast his demise the night before he was slain, Jesse Jackson had to play Joshua to his Moses. "I just want to do God's will," King thundered in Mason Temple. "And He's allowed me to go up to the mountain. And I've looked over. And I've seen the Promised Land. I may not get there with you. But I want you to know tonight that we as a people will get to the Promised Land."

Jesse Jackson has not been, like King wasn't, the only leader of our people. So many brave souls and sharp minds have helped to fashion our fate with their words and actions. But he was the most visible and vital Black leader since King's death. But unlike King, who was aided immeasurably by his martyrdom, Jackson has had to stick around and see his fortunes rise and dip even more sharply than King's. But King only lived to be thirty-nine and only had twelve years to serve. Jackson has been in public service for nearly half a century and will be seventy-nine this year, more than twice King's number. Though we wish the martyr's death on no one—and no one can detract from the ultimate price paid by King, and by Malcolm, and by Medgar, and hundreds more who gave their lives—there is a historical advantage to early death that often escapes the survivors. Jesse Jackson has endured the loss of reputation, and the battle with self-destructive forces, in public, that King only briefly engaged. Jesse Jackson has lived from the time when Black folk could barely make the news to where they become fodder for the tabloid industry. He has seen his greatest flaws magnified in a celebrity-obsessed culture hungry for details about the lives and hypocrisies of icons and flashes in the pan alike. But through it all, he has stayed the course. He has fought the good fight from the sixties till this third decade of the new millennium.

He celebrated the beauty of Blackness and shouted that it was "nation time" for Black folk in the early seventies. He led us through the wilderness of white backlash in the mid-seventies. He helped navigate us through the assaults on affirmative action in the late seventies and on through the eighties till today. He helped to combat cultural listlessness during the simultaneous rise of Black narcissism and the epidemic of crack in the late eighties and early nineties. He helped defend the Black poor at all times. He called on parents to turn off the television and teach their children to read and to take them to school. He fought the policies of racially insensitive presidents and urged racially sensitive presidents to do more for the vulnerable and dispossessed. He rescued prisoners on foreign soil, met with heads of state around the world, retrieved hostages, and encouraged political bullies to behave better. He did brilliant battle with right-wing ideologues, bested conservative intellectuals in conversation, and marshaled a dizzying array of facts in hundreds of speeches, sermons, and lectures every year he has been in, and outside, of the spotlight. And by the way, he twice ran for president of the United States, and paved the way for Barack Obama's successful pilgrimage to political power twenty years after Jackson's last run.

And now, after the Age of Obama, a lot of folk have written Jesse Jackson off. A lot of folk wonder if he's still necessary, if he still matters, as Masciotra states. A lot of folk say he should shuffle off-stage and shut up. A lot of folk just wish he would go away. Well, there's definitely always a need for new blood and fresh ideas and other leaders. But there will always be a unique place for Jesse Jackson. Without Jesse Jackson our Black prophetic ministry wouldn't be as vital as it is today. With Negro preachers addicted to the pornography of prosperity, he has constantly begged us to pay attention to the folk who are locked out of this nation's vast riches. It's not that he doesn't want Black folk to get a bigger piece of the economic pie; after all, he has hosted a Wall Street initiative to bridge the gap between major centers of capital and destitute and needy communities. His push for Black businesses has created the economic infrastructure of today's Black wealth. His targeted boycotts of certain industries opened the door for Black folk to get more franchises and licenses. But he has never caved in to the vicious play of materialism. Instead of pushing a Lexus, he cried to let us do right by the poor. He has never forgotten from whence he came.

That's why rappers and other young folk who take delight in dissing him ought to recognize that he's more like them than most other leaders. Mama was a teen mother? Check. Grandmother was thirteen when she birthed your mother? Check. Grew up poor without really knowing who your Daddy was? Check. People clowning you because you were "illegitimate"? Check. Big ego while spitting venom at folk who want to destroy your crew? Check. Enough self-confidence to start a small nation and to inspire your folk to believe in your genius? Check. Mad because folk are sleeping on the hard work you did to lay the path of success for the cats who come behind you? Check. Folk "pray and pray on your downfall"? Check. Folk love you when you're on top and try to play you to the left, to the far left, when you're down? Check. Baby-Daddy drama? Check.

But without Jesse Jackson we wouldn't have the Black leadership that we enjoy today. Without Jesse Jackson there would be no Al Sharpton, who has brilliantly morphed into a world-class advocate for Black folk and the poor. And without Jesse Jackson we wouldn't have the Black political clout that we enjoy today. There would be no fiery Maxine Waters or a soulful Barbara Lee. And there wouldn't be a Barack Obama.

Sure, Jesse has clashed with Barack; Jackson has differed greatly with Obama. The prophet has called the president to task. But that's his job. Yes, to be sure, to say that you want to sever the future president's private parts is not the way to gain the love and loyalty of young Black folk. But it was the public parts of Obama's condescending speech to Black folk that Jackson thought the president-to-be should have kept private that motivated him. In any case, Jackson apologized for his remarks, and though the president said he forgave him, Jesse Jackson lived in political exile from the man for whom he blazed a path. It is indeed curious that alleged allies like Joe Lieberman pulled for the other team and yet weren't stonewalled like Jackson. White conservatives who prayed for Obama's downfall received more play than a Black leader whose greatest fault is that he loved Black folk so much he was willing to go nuts for us!

We shouldn't cast aside our prophets because they say unpopular things. We shouldn't discard our rhetorical geniuses because their speech is still freighted with unadulterated love for Black folk. We shouldn't diss our leaders because they get long in the tooth but still manage to flash their fangs on our behalf. We shouldn't forget that we wouldn't enjoy the extravagant prosperity we enjoy today without his critical voice. We shouldn't forget that Jesse Jackson has prayed for us, preached for us, pleaded for us, prophesied for us, been proud for us, and has prodded us to do better for more of our folk for more years than most can even remember. He has been faithful to his calling even when it didn't gain him access to the White House. He has been faithful to his calling even when it didn't earn him Brownie points with the powers that be. He has been faithful to his calling even when he has been crushed by media and panned by pundits. He has been faithful to his calling even when he was caricatured and dismissed. He has been faithful to his calling even when those he has loved have been unfaithful to him.

And he has pressed toward the mark of greatness—which is defined by Jesus as willingness to serve. He has served us with his head and heart, and with his mouth and feet. He has been courageous when we have been scared; he has given ready answer to the enemies of our people when our minds have faltered. Has he been flawed? Yes, like Moses was flawed, like David was flawed, like every prophet who ever opened his or her mouth to utter what thus sayeth the Lord has been flawed. But he has been faithful despite his flaws, valiant despite his shortcomings, useful despite his imperfections.

Those of us who know him simply love Jesse. We love the way he rhymes his speech and makes us remember his ideas almost against our will. We love him for working himself every year into an appointment with the hospital for several days just to get a break from the inhuman pace he kept. We love him for the long hours and miles he logged to tell Pharaoh to let our people go. We love Jesse for being a self-assured, supremely confident Black man who thought enough of us to believe that nothing should limit us except our talent and vision. We love Jesse for teaching us to Keep Hope Alive. We love Jesse for making us believe we are somebody. We love Jesse because, despite what anyone says, he loves us so much that he is willing to live for us until he dies. David Masciotra's *I Am Somebody: Why Jesse Jackson Matters* is a brilliant glimpse into the monumental life of a modern-day prophet. It is an eloquent and timely reminder of the mettle and morality of a towering public sage who has shared with us his wisdom and inspiration for more than half a century. Read this book and get a portrait of a gifted and courageous visionary who dared to seek the truth of our political and social lives and lived to tell about it.

27

ALRIGHT

Al Sharpton, one of the most unique Black leaders in the nation's history, is an American original. Sharpton draws on his experience in the hood to swim in a sea of political sharks. He relentlessly speaks for a constituency that often lacks the ability to amplify its concerns. He effortlessly channels and pivots among a variety of moods in the collective Black psyche and its accompanying rhetorical offshoots: ironic observation, angry declamation, joyful celebration, humorous remarks, edifying encouragement, sanctified exclamation, spiritual admonition, and political uplift. Few could have predicted that Sharpton would become President Obama's most trusted and go-to Black leader. After all, Sharpton's reputation as a racial firebrand and verbal flamethrower had marked him for the margins of the culture. But his incurable knack for self-reinvention saw him become, literally, half the man he had been before he lost weight—while losing as well the nettlesome infelicities that stalk the street preacher and urban activist in awkward fury. Sharpton smoothed out the rough edges of his rhetoric, carved a new sartorial stratosphere among the suited and booted, and carried himself like a statesman who had lost none of his know-how about the also-rans and the never-made-its who compose a large part of his portable congregation. No matter how high he ascends, he is there, every Saturday, at his National Action Network headquarters in Harlem, delivering the Word to the faithful who have stuck with him through his thickest incarnation and his thinnest refashioning. This is the foreword from Sharpton's 2020 Rise Up: Confronting a Country at the Crossroads.

Martin Luther King, Jr., conquered the American imagination because he was cut from the most majestic moral and ministerial cloth. Barack Obama captured the Oval Office because he was a dream candidate plucked from central casting and featured as the nation's first Black president.

Jesse Jackson seized the nation by its lapels when he rose from modest southern roots to global acclaim as a freedom fighter. And Fannie Lou Hamer shattered convention and the racial sound barrier with her earthy and eloquent demands for emancipation.

Still and all, there has never been anyone quite like Al Sharpton on the American scene. Like King he's a preacher, but far grittier and rawer. Like Obama he's a politician, but presidents, governors, mayors and all the rest bow at his throne even though he never held elected office. Like Jackson he's the brilliantly evolved product of the Black bottom, but his bottom seems more, well, bottom. And like Fannie Lou he's got vivid vernacular, but he can make it resonate in the White House or on Harlem streets. Although it's cliché to say so, it is really true that Al Sharpton is an American original. He is a man who can, at the funeral for the martyred George Floyd, talk about how roaches flee when the light is switched on in ghetto homes, just as the light of justice makes roaches of racism scatter.

The reason Sharpton can pull it all off is because he has never stopped being himself, even as that self has matured over the years. He is an unashamed preacher, called to deliver the word at the age of four, taking as his text John 14:1—"Let not your heart be troubled: ye believe in God, believe also in me." (That verse undoubtedly gave him comfort a few years later when his heart was broken, and he plummeted from middle class to poverty when his father left his mother to start a family with Sharpton's half-sister. I told you his bottom was more bottom.) If you've ever heard him preach, you can hear how he was born first in Pentecostal tongues of fire and then reborn in swirling Baptist waters of prophecy. He preached his first sermon the year I was born. He has honed his craft in churches high and low, Black and white, and beyond, over the last 62 years. And he's been mentored by some of the best Black folk in the land.

Sharpton went out on tour with gospel great Mahalia Jackson as a youth, sat under preaching legends Bishop Frederick Douglas Washington and Dr. William Augustus Jones, was tutored by the political maverick Adam Clayton Powell, nurtured by the electrifying evangelist for justice Jesse Jackson, and, perhaps most famously, he got taken under wing by the Godfather of Soul, James Brown. It is well known by now that it was Brown who, in exchange for his support and for making Sharpton his tour manager, got the minister to style his hair after the famous impresario of funk. As Sharpton has combed through controversies and criticism, he has maintained a permanent allegiance to his follicular forebear.

People readily identify with Sharpton because, despite his fame, he is a

Black Everyman. When he first broke through as an activist, he was clothed in the tracksuit and sneakers favored by young folk in his generation. Later he was sheathed in Brooks Brothers suits and other tailored fashions. He lost significant weight when he fasted in 2001 to protest military exercises on the island of Vieques, Puerto Rico, and has since shed half a man, and with it, the unjustifiable image of a racial arsonist, to become the most well-respected leader of his generation. Sharpton is arguably the last great figure of a dying breed of charismatic Christian leaders thrust into a prominence he has maintained for decades. Along the way he was youth director for the presidential campaign of Shirley Chisholm, youth director for the New York City branch of Jesse Jackson's Operation Breadbasket, founder in 1971 of the National Youth Movement to raise funds for poor youth, and 20 years later, founder of the National Action Network to increase voter education, registration and turnout, help the poor, and to stimulate local community businesses. And he ran for president in 2004.

But it is as an on-the-ground activist who couldn't be ignored that Sharpton made his mark. When Bernhard Goetz shot four Black men on a New York City subway in 1984, for which he was eventually cleared of all but the most minor charge, Sharpton protested in the streets the weak prosecution of the self-styled vigilante. When three Black men, including Michael Griffith, were assaulted in the Howard Beach section of Queens in 1986 by a white mob, and chased onto the Belt Parkway, Griffith was struck and killed by a passing motorist. Sharpton led a protest march a week later through Howard Beach as its residents spewed race hate and epithets at the mostly Black marchers. His actions compelled New York governor Mario Cuomo to appoint a special prosecutor in the case.

In 1989, four Black teens were violently set upon by up to 30 Italian youth in the Brooklyn neighborhood of Bensonhurst. One of them shot and killed 16-year-old Yusef Hawkins with a handgun. Sharpton led protest marches in the immediate aftermath of the event, again after one of the two ringleaders was acquitted of the most serious charges against him, and later after other members of the gang were given light sentences. It was before that last demonstration that Sharpton was stabbed in the chest, and when he recovered, he pleaded for mercy for his assailant when he was sentenced in court. Sharpton was involved in the Tawana Brawley controversy, where a young Black woman claimed to have been raped by four white men in Wappinger, New York, though it turned out later to be a hoax. Amid the firestorm of criticism of the civil rights leader, few pointed out then, and few have said since, that Sharpton's greatest fault may have been that he took Brawley seriously and at her word. As the motto of the #MeToo movement suggests, Sharpton believed a young Black girl making an accusation of sexual abuse. He did it long before social media hashtags and the concerted demand in the broader culture for gender justice.

It is perhaps his involvement in several high-profile cases where Sharpton has proved especially prescient about what has become the defining civil rights issue of our day: police brutality against Black folk. Among the most notable is the case of Amadou Diallo, a Black immigrant from Guinea who was shot to death by cops from the NYPD, whose unjust death Sharpton protested. (I was arrested alongside him and Rev. Jim Forbes in a protest march in 1999.) Or the Tyisha Miller case that same year, where a Black teen was shot in her car during a health crisis as she held a revolver on her lap, lay in a comatose state, and when awakened, was startled, and clutched her gun. She was shot 23 times by cops who had been called to the scene by relatives to assist her.

There was also the case of West African immigrant Ousmane Zongo, who was shot by an undercover cop in Manhattan. Or the case of Sean Bell, a young Black man whose body was unjustly pumped full of lead with 50 bullets by plainclothes cops the day before his planned wedding. Or, more recently, the cases of Eric Garner, and just this year, of George Floyd, two Black men who were killed by cops as they pleaded for their lives in chilling similarity of expression: "I can't breathe." In these cases, and in many more, Sharpton has led protests and highlighted injustices. He has proved to be ahead of the curve in understanding just how fundamental such cases are to the safety and well-being of Black America. He understood early how they reveal our essential vulnerability in the face of law enforcement that is supposed to protect and serve us, and instead, in too many instances, has harmed and killed us. Thus, the greatest civil rights leader of our time has tackled the greatest civil rights issue of our time. He did it long before many others had an inkling or others gave him credit. He also did it at a time when so many dismissed police brutality as a problem for poor and working-class Black folk. Thus, Black elites and white officials were brought up short when it was clear that it was a plague for all Black folk.

Al Sharpton has risen to cultural heights and wields enormous political authority because he came from the lowest rungs of society but kept his compassion and love for the people. Although he has been a trumpet of conscience, he has not played just one song or sounded just one note. As a prophet, he brings Black evangelical believers further into a progressive political arc; he chastises Donald Trump, a white man who has described himself as a nationalist; he decries alternative facts; he champions women's rights; he supports LGBTQIA rights, and in fact embraced gay marriage before the Black president he advised; he speaks and protests on behalf of immigrants; he tackles global warming, climate change and environmental racism; and he provides a powerful model of principled activism, political resistance and profound proclamation of the social gospel.

Al Sharpton never claimed to be the Almighty. But Rev. Al is certainly the best *Al*ternative to the *Al*ienating effect and the *Al*arming ignorance of many political leaders. While that bit of wordplay may be hokey, or goofy, or corny, there is nothing of the sort in the leadership of Al Sharpton. This man is a gift from God to the world. This book is a gift from Al Sharpton to us. Let's appreciate them both.

CHAPTER

28

When Robin Becomes Batman

I was on an Amtrak train to New York in 2012 when suddenly a phalanx of official-looking men swooped through the first-class car demanding that everyone get off. I insisted that I could stay because I had reserved a handicap seat due to a foot injury. The conductor confirmed that they couldn't force me to move. I gathered that they were clearing the way for Vice President Biden's regular jaunt home to Delaware. "I know him," I insisted. They flashed me that "yeah right" look before resigning themselves to my nattering presence as I chatted away on my iPhone. Then, before you know it, Biden swept in, and upon spying me as the lone occupant of the cabin, he effusively greeted me. "Professor!" "Mr. Vice President, how goes it, Sir?" "Come on over and join me!" I relocated across the aisle and us two voluble gents fell quickly into a convivial conversation. Biden had recently forced Obama's hand on gay marriage. Obama had previously said his views were evolving and apparently hadn't planned to endorse same-sex marriage until after the 2012 presidential election—when Biden said during an appearance in early May on Meet the Press *that Obama was "absolutely comfortable" in letting gays and lesbians marry. Obama soon endorsed the idea. I couldn't help but kid Biden. "They tell me, my friend, that the Holy Ghost got into Obama and freed him to tell the truth about his thinking on gay marriage. I didn't know the Holy Ghost spelled his name, J-O-E B-I-D-E-N!" We shared a good chuckle. His gaffe became a spur to righteous advocacy. In many ways, as his presidency has proved, Biden is more progressive than Obama, both because he can afford to say and do things as an older white man that Obama couldn't and because times have changed. The left is far more vocal in Democratic circles. But it also has something to do with Biden's fundamental decency, his sweet-souled disposition, his basic niceness. I caught a glimpse of this when I was invited to the White House with seven other scholars to advise President Biden about different aspects of American history. I spoke to him about religion and Lincoln, LBJ, and Clinton, and how their conceptions of faith and belief translated, transferred, and transformed religion in the public realm. I ended by thanking him for his political ethic of care and his noble embrace of the politics of empathy. Portions of this essay appeared in 2020 in various places, including* The Grio.com, The Vanderbilt Project on Unity & American Democracy, *and as a foreword to Steven Levingston's terrific 2019 book,* Barack and Joe: The Making of an Extraordinary Partnership.

I

The buddy film is an American staple that mostly portrays the virtues of male bonding and rejects stereotypes of men as unemotional and uncaring creatures. The genre often pairs men of clashing styles and conflicting worldviews, and in the last few decades, it has brought together men of different races to combat the belief that we can't get along in the real world. There was surely progress in getting Black and white men together on screen, but that didn't keep stereotypes from melting the celluloid. Black men were, at best, adjuncts to the white world, or its convenient facilitators, as long as they were subordinate to the white star. At worst, Black men were fall guys in a cinematic alchemy where history was reversed, and Black accomplishment was deceitfully turned into white heroism. The buddy film occasionally careened onto "Magical Negro" territory where the Black male foil transformed the white protagonist in a quest for salvation, that is, if the white man didn't turn out to be the savior himself.

Near the end of the first decade of the new century, we watched a political version of the biracial buddy film play out in the nation's capital for eight years. It might even be argued by their followers that a dynamic duo took up revolutionary residence in Washington, D.C. Barack Obama and Joe Biden swept into town as an interracial Batman and Robin out to vanquish the harmful specter of George W. Bush and Dick Cheney and to bring light to a land languishing in darkness. This is where the buddy film adapted a superhero script and substantially upped the stakes of their partnership. Unlike most buddy films, the Black guy was the biggest star; unlike most Magical Negro films, the Black guy was not only the source and symbol of salvation, but the savior himself; and unlike most superhero films, at least before *Black Panther*, the Black guy was the swashbuckling lead.

Barack and Joe were important to the nation's politics because they embodied an edifying symbiosis—let's cheekily call it an *Obidenosis*. Obama was the country's first Black president, a tall, brilliant, charismatic slice of Americana whose blended racial pedigree lent credence to his claim that we didn't live in a Black or white America, but—and his mixed genes proved it—the *United* States of America. Biden had been a commanding force in the nation's dealings for decades, a sui generis political prodigy who won a Senate seat at 29, and a proud Irishman who quoted Seamus Heaney and backslapped his way into the hearts of large swaths of the American people. Obama's superior political ingenuity spilled from his sophisticated brain and his nose for uncanny timing, for knowing what was needed when. Biden, despite his extraordinary run in the Senate, failed twice to leave its chambers in unsuccessful presidential runs, depending on Obama's choice of him as vice president to boost his standing in the political hierarchy. In this buddy film it was clear who was the man and who was the man next to the man, reinforcing his sublimely subordinate position by occasionally massaging "the boss's" shoulders.

Obama and Biden's spectacular partnership thrived because both men agreed to swap out meaningless duties and trifling symbolism in the vice presidency for substantive engagement and hearty brotherhood. When Obama came calling—and at first, it didn't seem likely, since Biden's proclivity to gaffe included an impolitic and racially charged assessment of Obama's "clean" and "articulate" status as a Black presidential candidate when they both vied for the Oval Office in 2008 before Biden dropped out—Biden, though honored, insisted that, among other things, he get weekly private time with Obama and that he be in on every major presidential deliberation. And, perhaps most important, Biden wanted to be able to tell the truth as he saw it. Obama ate it up, and for the most part, despite Biden's predictable stumbles and unpredictable missteps, the two men flourished as a model of political fraternity in service of the nation's highest good. (Plus, one of Biden's most high profile "mistakes," getting out ahead of Obama in support of gay marriage, proved that Biden's courage and honesty forced a reticent head of state to take the sort of stand he had already privately affirmed. While Obama enjoyed a fictional "anger translator" on television's *Key and Peele*, Biden, if not quite an Obama whisperer, may have been, on occasion, the former's sturdier public conscience.)

Steven Levingston, a gifted diviner of our political ethos and an eloquent chronicler of our national tendencies, delves purposefully into the relationship between Obama and Biden in his book *Barack and Joe: The Making of an Extraordinary Partnership*, showing how it was the magical melding of two forceful personalities who were quite dissimilar in many ways, but no less capable of turning their differences into national benefit. If Obama was a bookish introvert, Biden was a literate extrovert, yet together they read the national mood, combining Barack's scholarly pensiveness and Joe's emotional intelligence to lift the country from a seemingly intractable recession.

Levingston helps us to see how much of what drew Obama and Biden to each other—both were athletes who sprinkled their speech with sports metaphors, both loved their kids (and Biden his grandkids), both fawned over their wives, both eagerly deflected acclaim for their achievements and instead heaped praise on their numerous collaborators and staff—existed off the books and beyond the stage. Yes, Obama and Biden shared an incurable love for the dreams and ideals of America, but they found in their mutually supportive ideas of empathetic manhood a portal to true intimacy and genuine camaraderie. They weren't afraid to openly root for each other, admire each other, and, rather quickly in their luminous fellowship, love each other.

Still, Levingston isn't afraid to show the uglier side of things too. Obama, like all good, or at least effective, politicians, could be calculating and strategic. When Obama stood for reelection in 2012, he let concern about his political fortunes fuel behind-the-scenes discussions about whether Hillary Clinton should replace Biden as Barack's running mate. There appeared to be real teeth to the consideration, and yet, ultimately, Biden prevailed, and so did Obama, winning reelection and preserving their friendship. When Biden was weighing a run for the presidency in 2016 as Obama left office, Barack steered him clear of the field and discouraged him from running, a development that hurt Joe. He believed that Obama was understandably looking out for his legacy, feeling that Hillary, given the political landscape, could best protect it and carry it forward. But it still stung.

And even now, as Biden has entered the 2020 presidential race, Obama has met with other hopeful candidates and touted the need for new blood in the Democratic party, all while playing it cool on endorsing Biden—or even embracing him as the heir apparent to his presidency. Similar to how he publicly loved the Black people who overwhelmingly supported him, Obama could on occasion be less enthusiastic about those who adored him, and he could fail to return in equal measure the love that was given to him.

As long as they were in the White House, Obama gave Joe royal treatment and, for the most part, remained resolutely loyal to his second in command. Once they flew the coop, Obama, while still warm and friendly, has been noticeably different, a cooler, less demonstrably supportive partner to a man whose cheek he kissed at the funeral of his son Beau, a man around whose neck he placed the Medal of Freedom eight days before they left office. As was true with Black folk, Obama could be heavy on symbolism but, when it counted, sometimes faulty in the delivery of substance, such as public love in the form of policy, or vigorous advocacy from his bully pulpit.

While the Obama presidency lasted, and as its meaning continues to unfold, the connection forged between Barack and Joe is one for the history books, even the first run at that history in the book, *Barack and Joe*, that you hold in your hands. This is as fine a reading of a unique and consequential political relationship—a partnership, a friendship, a brotherly affection sealed by genuine love—as we are likely to find. Steven Levingston has written a lovely and important book that touches on race and manhood at the heart of American politics. This buddy film come-to-life is a magnificent story told with poetic verve by a writer who sets his study up like a thriller and crafts it with the pace and surprise of a first-rate novel.

The only way the story could have gotten better is if Biden lived out one of Obama's rare gaffes—something that might be read later as a Freudian slip that revealed a hidden truth. When he was first introducing Biden to the public as his vice-presidential choice in 2008, Obama blew the line. "So let me introduce to you the next president," Obama said before quickly revising his line after catching his error and proclaiming his running mate the next vice president of the United States.

As Biden's third quest for the Oval Office heated up, all of his previous experiences came back, not only to haunt him, but, in some ways, to aid him, even the gaffes. After all, the 45th occupant of 1600 Pennsylvania Avenue precipitously lowered the presidential bar so that Biden's errors—even his huggy, kissy, "embraceable you" rituals of social intimacy that must be adapted for the #MeToo era—may lose their menacing repercussions, or, at least, may not be viewed nearly as badly now as they were then, especially since Biden, as a plainspoken politico who calls it as he sees it, is Trump without the bile, Trump without the viciousness, Trump without the hate, Trump without the unapologetic ignorance, Trump without the racist and misogynist furor that hugged his presidency to death and squeezed from it most displays of humanity and compassion.

History has proved that Obama's faux pas, instead of an error, turned out to be an unintended prophecy, and thus, Levingston's book is even more than the considerably insightful study that it manages to be. It turns out to be, too, one of the first, and finest, passes at assessing a man who holds, not simply a venerable role in history as arguably the most important vice president ever, but one who now plays Batman to Kamala Harris's Robin.

II

"I know Joe. We know Joe. But most importantly, Joe knows us."

Most everything you need to know about Joe Biden and Black folk is contained in these brief declarative sentences that border on philosophical aphorism—but not from the stoic mind of Marcus Aurelius or the paradoxical pen of Ludwig Wittgenstein. The author of these sentences is neither a Roman ruler nor an Austrian prodigy, but South Carolina congressman Jim Clyburn—an American sage of sorts. He's also a Black political force whose endorsement of Biden in February 2020 resurrected Biden's campaign from political oblivion and swept him into the Oval Office. Sure, there was lots of elbow grease and coalition building, but for once a Black mark became a stamp of approval.

What exactly did Black folk know about Joe? For starters, that you can't judge a man by a single inning in his life, and certainly not one in a metaphoric ballgame way in the past. When news surfaced that Biden had opposed busing in 1975, Black folk of a certain age—say those over 60—were nearly ho-hum. A lot of white folk they knew had opposed the practice, so it was no skin off of Black backs to realize that a white man for whom they voted, whom they had grown to admire and like a great deal, had vigorously disputed the virtue of busing. That's because Biden premised at least part of his opposition to busing on a familiar Black nationalist argument—at least familiar to him because he'd been paying attention in a way that lots of white folk hadn't—that Black folk needed to build their own schools and institutions and stop craving white acceptance. Biden argued that desegregation was "rejection of the entire Black awareness concept, where Black is beautiful, Black should be studied; and the cultural awareness of the importance of their own identity, their own individuality."

This shouldn't be confused with the notion that sixties Black nationalist leaders and their white supremacist antagonists could at least agree that they couldn't stand each other and that separation of the races—with adequate resources, at least from the Black side—was best for all involved. (Let's not forget that ten members of the American Nazi Party attended a 1961 Nation of Islam rally where Malcolm X delivered a speech, "Separation or Death," with Nazi Party leader, George Rockwell, telling the media, "I am fully in concert with their program.") Instead, Biden was acknowledging an edifying catechism of race pride that promoted Black power and collective self-determination and that preferred Black equality to white proximity. Could some white politicians endorse this view of race to escape the responsibility to direct political capital and financial resources to Black communities? Of course, and the fact that Biden initially supported busing when he ran for the Senate in 1972 before changing his mind when he encountered strong gusts of white opposition among his constituency means that his views weren't driven by pure motives. As to those motives, and whether they revealed a racist inclination, Biden says he turned to the Blacks on his staff to ask if there was something "in me that's deep-seated that I don't know." That might sound contrived, or hopelessly naïve, but there is something to be said for seeking to determine one's level of racial self-deception.

Black folk, rather than archiving Biden's missteps and cataloguing his wrong thinking, were far more interested in the dominant bent of Biden's career, the evolution of his racial consciousness, his effort to get things right on race over the years, and, especially, his effort to stand by, and behind, Barack Obama, our first Black president. Biden's familiarity with Black culture, its rhythms and designs, its desires and frustrations, endeared him to Black folk over the long haul. You could fairly taste his comfort with Black culture at his annual Black History Month shindigs at the vice-presidential manse, which were funkier and more intimate than their White House counterparts. I remember attending the Black History Month Celebration at the vice president's residence in February 2014, when Biden quoted Martin Luther King, who said that voting "is the foundation stone for political action." Biden concurred. "As a Caucasian American, that suggests that the single most significant fight for African Americans was the right to vote," the vice president said. "Without the right to vote nothing else much mattered. It all rested on the largesse of the rest of the community." It was the exercise of that fundamental right that had been unjustly denied to Black folk that helped put Biden in the White House.

Of course, the Black vote alone didn't win Joe Biden the presidency, but he knows that we were the ones who believed in him and stood by him when many others harbored doubts. Our community's faith in Joe Biden proved true, and not only did he continue to perform well with Black voters, he assembled a broad coalition that also included white, Latinx, Asian, and Indigenous voters, young and old, urban and rural, LGBTQ+. Biden even managed to snag an impressive cross section of political ideologies—not only Democrats, but some Republicans, and even larger numbers of independents and progressives, and a healthy dose of moderates and conservatives. That broad coalition of more than 80 million Americans rejected the politics of hatred and division embodied by Donald Trump for the last four years. That was the first step: Donald Trump, an unreconstructed racist and supporter of white supremacy, was convincingly defeated and had to leave the White House.

The Biden administration's hearty embrace of diversity is a vital weapon against the virulent anti-Blackness awash in the land. People and representation matter, of course, but more important than only having a Black face in a high place is that the *policies* that a diverse and representative administration can put in place are what's needed to protect and improve Black lives. The African American experience has long fallen short of the so-called American Dream, but the recent syndemic—the synergy of medical and moral pandemics in 2019—has exacerbated inequities in Black life. The lethal spread of the global virus COVID-19 collided with the racial pandemic that Black Americans have lived with since 1619. The Trump administration failed miserably at responding to both and became a megaphone for America's worst instincts and a bullhorn for the most vicious denunciation of our humanity.

The tragic deaths of George Floyd, Breonna Taylor, and many others opened the minds of millions of people in America and abroad. "Black Lives Matter" gained widespread support from large numbers of citizens, corporations, and even the NFL. White Americans now appear to recognize that in encounters with police, it's not how Black people behave or react, it's the color of our skin that too often dictates how we are treated.

If the broad coalition, including white Americans, that elected Joe Biden understands that race is too often a determinant in how justice is served, they can also see how it's too often a determinant of achieving the American Dream—of home ownership, of small business success, of school quality and graduation rates, of surviving a pregnancy, and yes, of surviving a global pandemic. The country needs leaders to end the disparities that have besieged our existence for hundreds of years. This won't be easy and will require struggle and bitter fights with conservative and right-wing opponents. Joe Biden is not flawless and will not be a perfect president. There will be disagreements, and when needed, I will be the first to use my voice to demand that we—and he—do better.

Throughout his career and his young presidency, Joe Biden has shown that he will listen to different viewpoints and try to forge connections and find common ground. As Biden concluded his speech at his vice-presidential residence during Black History Month in 2014, "this kind of malarkey can't go on. This fight has been too long, this fight has been too hard, to do anything other than win." That same spirit of empathy with Black struggle and appreciation for Black loyalty rang loudly in some of his memorable words to Black voters: "You've always had my back, and I'll have yours."

In all my years of listening to presidential rhetoric, and in all my studies of presidents interacting with Black folk, I'd never heard a president be that bold, that explicit and that transparent in acknowledging his debt to Black voters. But that's the message that President-elect Joe Biden had for the Black community in his victory speech on November 7. It was a tip of the hat to Congressman Jim Clyburn, then the nation's highest-ranking Black politician. Jim Clyburn who had essentially saved his candidacy and guaranteed him the presidency. It was a resounding gesture of gratitude in particular to the Black women who turned out in record numbers to boost his third quest for the Oval Office into the winner's circle.

III

For many Americans, it was their first time hearing Biden speak frankly and openly about his warm relationship to the Black community. But for many Black folk, especially older citizens, Biden's deeply loyal service as vice president to the nation's first Black president more than compensated for his gaffes, faux pas and flaws. For instance, Biden's visible support for Obama more than wiped clean his slate after he praised Barack, during Biden's second run for the Oval Office, for being the first "articulate . . . and clean" Black candidate for the presidency. It's not that Black folk don't keep score; it's that they generally give higher marks for intent versus a flub or flop and place more weight on noble aspiration than on poor performance. Biden was hammered by younger Black folk for his support of the infamous nineties crime bill that had pernicious consequences on Black America. And yet many older Black folk remember that quite a few brothers and sisters were in queue to support the bill because of the menace of crack cocaine and its heartless ravaging of Black communities. To indict Biden out of context was to manipulate history for convenient and shortsighted politics; it was to insert ideology to obscure unlikable facts.

Clyburn understood that the masses of Black voters, especially older voters, know that politics is chess, not checkers, that it's the long game, not the instant satisfaction or immediate payoff. Older Black voters were Aristotelian in their understanding of how character is shaped by habits and dispositions, by long practice and repetition of virtuous acts that fill in the blanks of one's political persona. They knew they could trust Biden, that he wouldn't undercut the first Black president, that he would stand up in defense of Black interests as he learned more and more over the decades of exactly how Black folk needed meaningful education, substantive health care, good jobs, better housing and relief from social misery.

Biden took these things in moderate stride and in centrist swings at the plate of social reform. As a Black progressive, I can acknowledge that there is distance between me and Biden on what to do about law enforcement and the plague of police brutality—but then, that same gap existed between me and Obama. Beyond our political differences, beyond our vigorously contrasted views of how we can stop Black blood flowing in the streets from a cop's pistol, baton or knee, I have come to trust that Biden's political instincts, and his developed intuition, are at least oriented toward making things far better rather than leaving them far worse. That's by no means perfection in public policy, but it is a great improvement over what we've seen in the last four years.

It is, perhaps, Biden's experience of grief, the way he publicly mourns his losses, the way trauma has tracked his life and hounded his happiness, that offers insight about the compassion that hugs his worldview. It also opens a natural simpatico between Black folk and the Irishman who draws strength from the poetry of Seamus Heaney, and seems at the ready, always, to meet Yeats's insistence that the center cannot hold with a political pedigree that proves that it will. There is something about the suffering Biden has endured that endears him to Black folk who, collectively, have withstood the withering assaults on our psyches by insensitive bigots, and by shrewd and cruel systems of oppression. And there's something about the visceral pain of Black folk that shapes our bodies and attunes our spirits to those who lose greatly what they love and labor over, an experience that binds Biden and Black folk in metrics of misery. But there is, too, improbable and stubborn hope that inspires Biden and lots of Black folk to break the shackles of enduring tragedy. This sense of empathy doesn't show up in predictive algorithms, or in polling, but it registers in the bodies of Black folk and in the souls of seasoned veterans of social struggle—and in the efforts of ordinary Black folk just to survive. That gives Biden far deeper resonance in Black circles than it might seem when younger Blacks dispute Biden's political agenda.

The most dramatic display of Biden's deep Black appeal may be measured in his simple, direct, yet profound humanity. After Trump, that can never again be taken for granted; it can never be presumed that a kindly gracious approach that revels in humaneness and the felicity of niceness will again be what we can expect. Biden's return to decency is more than a foundational moral virtue; it is a political asset that generates the sort of connections between citizens that should prevail, finally, even above the din of partisan fractiousness. To progressives, Biden's impulse to reach across the aisle can be seen, with some justification, as a surrender of precious ideological territory that could otherwise preserve political gain. But the bigger impulse must not be lost in the fray, and that is Biden's strong suit: no matter what differences we have as a people this nation must not be ransomed to politics that put party above country.

After four years of disconcerting assaults on the American spirit, and vicious tirades against our formidable institutions from the highest echelons of power, Biden's grace and demeanor are a huge benefit to the nation. His virtues in this arena need not be a deficit for Black progress. Even his centrist politics can help soothe a nation embroiled in battle with its identity and undergoing a reckoning with race. We need support from all quarters as we fight to restore the balance of power to "we, the people." The ruinous neo-fascism of Donald Trump has also opened the eyes of many citizens to the horrors of racial injustice; both ills gained scary intensity under the same figure.

All of this must be kept in mind when we measure Biden's moral and political rebukes of racial intolerance. Biden is keenly aware of what he owes to Black America. No president has been as direct in acknowledging this debt as the basis of both cultural recompense and political payback. Biden has convincingly begun the effort to make good on that debt. More than 20 cabinet officials have been selected; half of them are women, 12 of them are people of color, including 5 who are Black, 3 who are Latinx, 3 who are Asian American Pacific Islander, and one who is Indigenous—and one is gay. Those numbers are quite solid and suggest that Biden will keep his word as he keeps adding to his cabinet.

Biden's choice of a Black and Southeast Asian woman as vice president is a remarkable gesture of investment in Black political possibility—and a dramatic extension of the Black political future: he has put Kamala Harris in position to possibly become in a relatively few years the first Black female president. Moreover, he has pledged to put a Black woman on the Supreme Court. But beyond the numbers and calculations of diversity lies the understanding of how race works, of what is owed loyal Black voters, of how the nation can hardly begin repair without grappling with the persistent racial inequalities that mar the national character.

Joe Biden is a healing force and redeeming voice amidst the racial carnage left in the wake of the Trump presidency. He has clearly shown that he has a far more robust understanding of how national unity and racial togetherness work: they don't rest on the suppression of racial difference or the silencing of healthy conflict. Rather, Biden understands that we must wrestle with the bloody cultural wars that have sapped our will to embrace diverse identities and unorthodox bodies. The last four years have eviscerated the substance of true multiracial democracy. Trump and the right wing have crafted policies to contain the exaggerated threats of immigrants and to fight the mythical menace of people of color.

Nowhere was this more clearly seen than in the melee on the Mall when Trump partisans engulfed the nation's capital in an anti-democratic miasma—all in the belief that the nation had turned its back on them because it had rejected their Bigot in Chief. If, as Howard Thurman argues, a bigot is a person who makes an idol of his commitments, then the poisonous prejudice that polluted the land also infiltrated the reasoning of the 45th president's followers. A president's reckless rhetoric convinced them that BLM is the scourge of democracy and baited them into self-destructive behavior. In this shameful instance of disloyalty to democracy, our racial "what if" clashed with our political "couldn't be": what if this had been BLM protesters? They would have hardly been treated with such high regard. But the reason the militants on the Mall got the kid glove treatment is because much of our society—and law enforcement that was present—insisted at the outset that it couldn't be true that these white citizens were domestic terrorists carrying out a vile act of sedition. An anemic view of patriotism failed to expose traitorous action and insurrectionist impulse. But in the era of Trump the yearning to secede from the nation is often read as an enduring sign of loyalty.

As we welcome a new administration, and, hopefully, a new destiny, Joe Biden looms as a healing Lincoln ready to bring us out of the long night of racial catastrophe into a new daylight of a just and righteous national unity. Or perhaps he will be a savvy FDR offering a racial and political New Deal. Perhaps he can even bring back a commitment to the poorest and most vulnerable as in LBJ's Great Society. Or he might pick up Clinton's will to racial conversation, or Obama's artful grappling toward a more perfect union. Or, maybe, just maybe, he will be Joe Biden: a sensitive soul, equal parts poetry and politics, laying claim to rational deliberation and spiritual aspiration to make us live up to our motto: *E pluribus unum*—Out of many, one.

Cooler Than
the Other Side of the Pillow

In Black Masculine Style

29

Brother, Can You Spare a Nod?

I have always been fascinated by the semiotics of Black cultural expression and how Black folk communicate meaning with every part of our bodies, with even minimal gestures. I wrote this in 2001 for Savoy magazine.

Recently, my friend Al told me a story that highlights the special way Black men communicate with one another. Al saw a nattily dressed man walk by a homeless brother perched against a grocer's wall. "What's up?" the brother saluted the indigent man, who merely nodded his head. A world of meaning lies behind that brief encounter between two brothers from what might as well be different worlds. One brother is paid, the other penniless. One brother is well educated; the other may not be.

Despite their differences, these two men found camaraderie in a culturally loaded gesture: a nod of the head. Like these brothers, countless Black men "hear" one another without speaking a word. In fact, the cooler you are, the less verbal your greeting. It's as if the need to speak in the presence of the nod is redundant. (Of course, it's also a waste of energy, a major breach of the unwritten rule of Black male cool.) If you've nodded, you've spoken. 'Nuff said. That's not to say that nods shouldn't sometimes be accompanied by speech. A little "'Sup?" "Yo," or "What's happenin'?" can't hurt. And for those more formally inclined, "How are you?" or "Hey, good to see you" is appropriate. But be warned: The latter phrases are used only by those who lack expertise in the higher echelons of Black vernacular.

The fun of Black speech is its elasticity and its spontaneous combustions of grammar that break wildly along synapses of logic that capture the meanings formal language often misses. For instance, when I was in graduate school, my German instructor said of a particular phrase that the only available tense that could accommodate its meaning was summed up in the Black English styling "It be's like that." As the only Black member of the class, I smiled smugly and gave a high-five in my mind to all those Black folk who had been called backward for their "improper" speech. As a code, the nod draws energy from the irreverent twists of speech and flashes of style that flood Black masculine culture. So, the grittier the greeting—that is, the more racially suggestive the gesture—the better to bring brothers together. The point, after all, is to unify Black men across barriers of cash, color or culture into a signifying solidarity. The nod is visual Ebonics. It ain't taught, but you be knowin' what it is when you see it.

Black men have perfected the nod. Anonymous brothers nod with the same panache Denzel oozes with his on-screen swagger. And they do it with the flair of a grace note from Wynton's horn. Like the basketball dunk, a move Black men have stylized over the years, there is variety in the nod. There is the flip nod, composed of a quick up-and-down movement of the head. There is the double-jerk nod, a quickly repeated gesture of the head in a decidedly upward motion, found especially among the hip hop generation.

There is the smooth nod, the older Black gentleman's agreement on style. It is a longish gesture stretched out to signify a compliment, like, "Nice coat" or "Sharp shoes." Then there is the half nod, the too-cool-to-care-but-I-don't-want-to-dis-you gesture that gives props while maintaining stylistic advantage. If the smooth nod is driven by altruism, the half nod is clipped by self-aggrandizement, a hybrid of recognition and narcissism.

There is, too, the grace nod, the basic Black suit of armor put on by Black men everywhere that takes sheer exuberance in our existence as Black men. It is as simple and supple as Black style itself, a warm and affectionate up-and-down gesture that says, "I know you because I am you."

To be sure, the Black male head nod grows out of a complicated racial history. In slavery, our forebears had to devise a means of communication that slipped the notice of the majority culture, since what they had to say sometimes challenged the status quo.

Enslaved women sewed directions to freedom in coded patterns on the quilts they hung in open fields for the world to see, but not really *see*. They sang songs that had dual meanings. Spirituals were meant to soothe Black souls while entertaining white folk.

After slavery, the need for codes persisted. Since Black men continued to be barred from white male societies, they developed their own formal and informal clubs, groups and cliques. They performed an esoteric handshake of their own design. After all, Black folk could scarcely afford to reveal their true feelings or inner beliefs to a hostile white world.

So, a culture of intimate communication was built on the way our voices rose, our way of emphasizing certain words, our use of double entendres and the exchange of stylized salutations. Those traits signified that we were from the same place, fighting the same battles, no matter.

Of course, we have to be careful, even guarded, about the head nod, lest it go the way of all Black affectations that shine in the glare of public attention and is co-opted by the Backstreet Boys, or worse yet, Britney Spears. (It wouldn't be so bad if Eminem sampled our nods, sans his tired homophobic routines. But Dr. Dre must promise to cram his videos with all manner of Black nodding heads, dreaded and blunted heads, corn-rowed and bald heads, too, and give a portion of his royalties to start the BHN Foundation, to preserve the art of Black head-nodding.)

The truth is the head nod is a potentially endangered specimen of Black cultural cool. It is one of the last vestiges of sensually styled communication that Black men completely own.

Thankfully, few know how to rip it off, since its subtlety and complexity are often lost on the larger society. Still, that can't stop the inevitable nod envy that is in the offing should the Black head nod become the subject of anthropological evaluation.

At its root, the nod may be most useful for its affirming role in the politics of acknowledgment among Black men. American society remains reluctant to recognize our humanity. Or more fundamentally, that we exist at all. The nod is a way of literally and figuratively saying, "I know you exist. I see you. I acknowledge your being." That's why it's important to reach out to each other no matter where or who we are, like the homeless man and his snappy number.

And like them, Black men must nurture the gift of hearing one another without uttering a word. Such a gift, and the acknowledgment of humanity that lies beneath it, is something that Black men can give one another for free. All it costs is a nod.

30

Behind the Mask

For a few issues of Essence *magazine, I served as an advice colum-nist of sorts, channeling Black male perspectives on masculinity, why men cheat, whether it's important to men that (their) women know how to cook, why men get women's "math" and don't call back, and the like. I secretly harbored the delusion that I was following in the footsteps of Martin Luther King, Jr., who penned an advice column for* Ebony *magazine for fifteen months near the beginning of his ca-reer. I can't help but acknowledge that since we are all wearing masks during the pandemic, this chapter takes on a different meaning. This essay wasn't technically one of my columns, but it has the sensibility I hoped to convey in advising Black men to better access, and exhibit, our humanity, confess our vulnerability, and become better partners.*

Styling. Profiling. Representing. Posturing. Flossing. These keywords from Black vernacular suggest that any way you look at Black men, we are experts at putting a good face on a situation. A Black man might have lost his job, his partner and his pride in the span of a half hour, then turn around and say with a smirk, "You know, it ain't no thing but a chicken wing." We can make it look so smooth because we have been doing it so long. Our mask-wearing tradition did not start on the streets of Boston or Cleveland or Dallas. Our male ancestors in West Africa, facing a do-or-die initiation into manhood, donned masks to summon the unshakable strength of those who came before to help them make it on through.

Today, we still wear the mask.

We wear these guises because they allow us to move in and out of character, without people knowing who we really are. And we use them to throw off our opponents, while hiding the injuries we have sustained doing battle with society. That is how we survived slavery, and that is how we are navigating the slippery steps of corporate America. If we did not have our game face on, we would all still be in the bowels of the Fortune 500 companies, running errands for white folks.

Too often, however, we hold on to our mask so long that we lose our grip on who we really are. We wear the thing at home with our partner. We sport it when we run out to play ball with the boys. And many of us forget to take it off because we no longer know the difference between us and the mask. If a Black male has been showing the world the only face he wants it to see, this is where it has to end. And it is not about the white man, or keeping his male counterparts at bay, or even preventing a partner from boxing him in. This is about where he meets himself. It is about allowing himself to be known and understood. It is about his capacity to be real.

RECOGNIZING THE MASKS

Anytime a Black man focuses more on what he does not have to do rather than on what he should do, he is defining his manhood in the negative. Black men need to remember that the word *improvement* begins with *I*. We have got to learn to negotiate, compromise—even give in sometimes—be open to criticism and let go of the notion that any dissent is a betrayal. Many of our partners have been suing us for nonsupport in the court of emotions, and it is time to face up to the truth of how we are living.

And Black women need to step up as well. Hold a mirror up and show a Black man what he has been hiding behind. As I said, some men do not remember that they put the mask on in the first place. Black women have got to gently insist to their man that it is there, and that it is blocking him from his highest good. Black women often know when he is being less than honest because they can feel it. It is like opening the freezer and feeling the air blowing over the ice. You have to help him understand that he is not all there. That he is not only missing in action, but he is also truly missing out.

Say something like, "I understand that you are going into a hostile environment, but here it is safe for you to let your guard down. The way you are being now is coming between us, and I would like us to be closer."

If you share this truth, and he responds, "Cool, thank you," or "Let me think about that," you may have some grounds for growth. But if his response is defensive, something like: "You are lying, and this is not about my mask, but about your failure to see me," then you may have to move on. Just tell the truth gently.

THE MASK OF INVULNERABILITY

We learn who we are through our interaction with other human beings. But unless we have a secure enough sense of ourselves it is hard to absorb these lessons without hostility or resentment. And that sense of personal identity comes when we wrestle with our true selves.

If we have hurt ourselves with our lack of self-awareness, we have also hurt the women in our lives by failing to take the risk of telling them the truth. Without truth-telling there will be little trust, and a great deal of manipulation. The more honest we are with our partners, the less inclined any of us will be to twist, cajole, spin or strong-arm each other. To have healthy relationships, we have got to be honest about our fears of commitment, our avoidance of accountability and our tendency to hug the surface of our feelings in fear of drowning in their depths.

Intimacy demands discipline—an open, honest vulnerability that is maintained while in close proximity to the beloved. A lot of Black men are scared of the nearness. We pour the fear into our raw sexuality. Our clichéd mantra is, "Hit it, then quit it." We have so many "commitment-phobes" because we do not want to have that vulnerability uncovered.

Black men have to learn how to code-switch. In the same way that we go from Ebonics to the King's English, we have to know when to slip into survival mode and when to check out. Home should be a no-harm zone, the place where we choose to be known and understood. Our emotional health depends on it. But that means we must select partners who can handle who we really are, and then cultivate that sacred space.

Sisters, you often say you want a sensitive man, but when a brother shows his insecurities and fears, you worry that he is going to "punk out." For a man to get to intimacy, he has to feel safe. It is imperative to communicate that, no matter what he says about his fears and feelings, the relationship can bear it. In the meantime, you need to manage your own expectations. The man you were expecting to have versus the brother you got. What you have been told a real man is versus the man before you. There is no hard-and-fast definition of what it means to be a real man. We are figuring it out as we go.

THE MASK OF MATERIALISM

Black men are often afraid to admit that it is much more than sex keeping them in a relationship. There is a deeper hunger, for which sex is merely a symptom. There is a hunger for joy, a hunger for unconditional affirmation, a hunger, in the end, for love. Brothers have to stop trading away what we need for the hot rush of what we crave. We have got to pull out of the crotch-notch sweepstakes, stop measuring by the crude mathematical equation: $M = HMWB$ (manhood equals how many women bedded).

On the surface, this behavior may seem harmless. But these rituals reek of dishonesty and often block the flow of meaningful communion. The nasty little paradox, though, is that the closer we get to our women, the further we feel from ourselves. Part of this has to do with how we view self. In a capitalist society, we are taught to hold on to our possessions and defend them to the death. Too often, the self is seen as a commodity as well.

For Black folks, it is not hard to see how such beliefs might penetrate our thinking. After all, for centuries we were sold as possessions. That collective memory of being owned, and not owning, leaves deep scars and creates profound insecurities in Black men and women. Slavery and modern-day racism help provide the context for understanding how Black folks have learned to relate to this society and, more important, to one another.

So, when Black men "floss" and flaunt their gadgets and material goods, it is an understandable racial reflex ingrained in a people who have had to do without for so long. Still, it is a poor substitute for the sort of love that says regardless of what things we do not have, we have each other. Atomistic, me-focused capitalism must yield to the greater good of being a part of something bigger—and better—than our individual selves. In the process, we are also affirmed.

THE MASK OF DISHONESTY

Black men lie to make themselves look good. They lie to preserve your feelings and to give themselves room to do what they really want to do. And they lie to compensate for how bad they feel by saying how great they are. That is why hip hop is so powerful. You just add a little boast, bravado and braggadocio into the mix, and you are good to go. The problem, however, is that self-deception erodes a brother's esteem in the eyes of the person he seeks to deceive, as well as in his own. It is a particular kind of psychic torture to which Black men subject ourselves. If you are lying to yourself about your most intimate relationship, you are lying in your relationship to God.

Men rarely come to grips with this guise until they collapse from the sheer exhaustion of keeping all the lies straight, or the lies stop having their intended effect. They pay in the cost of losing the bond with their wives or girlfriends and in the disconnection from their children. For the fortunate ones, another man, whether it is a minister or an elder or a father-in-law, will pull a brother's coat and let him know he has got to stop it.

Sisters can help this process by understanding that silence in the face of their men's dishonesty equals complicity. Black women often lie to themselves not to feel the full effect of the man's lie. The late comedian Robin Harris used to joke that he only liked to deal with ugly women, because he could say, "Baby, I'm going to the moon," and she would say, "Okay, baby, you be careful!" It is not about looks; it is about insecurities that make a lot of Black women endure men's dishonesty. She wants to believe this man will be better than his failures, bigger than his weaknesses, grander than her low expectations. But this is a hell of an act of generosity, and ultimately it allows him to leave his facade intact. It is time to make him accountable, not in a brutal or vicious way, but in a straightforward one. Give the brother a mirror and say, "Here is what I see." But first you must be honest with yourself about what his dishonesty is doing to your self-esteem.

THE MASK OF CONTROL

Let's be honest, many Black men hold a suspicion that Black women are trying to rule them, believe that sisters want to put their stamp on them. Black men are insecure about our women's independence. Like brothers, Black women today can often pick and choose. They are not necessarily driven by the need to have men support them financially. That throws a kink into the Black-male psychological and emotional game plan.

Any human relationship is about power and love, and Black men need to determine how to let love prevail. Instead of telling themselves, "If I compromise, I'm less than," or "I can't let her tell me what to do," they need to ask, "In what ways am I trying to control her, because I can't control the relationship—or myself?"

Control is an illusion. Some days the woman's going to have more influence, other times, the man will. We must be willing to concede that our mates have strengths we do not have and shape the relationship around what works best. Keep it dynamic—not controlled—and then watch how it grows and evolves.

Society throws a wrinkle in here as well. There are vicious stereotypes at play. The same society that tells Black men negative, hateful things about ourselves tells us negative and hateful things about Black women. One is that Black women emasculate their men. That is just another psychological tool to make Black men feel less-than—another weapon in the divide-and-conquer arsenal keeping the Black family torn asunder. We must define ourselves for ourselves: The patriarchal vision of relationships, where men rule and women and children submit, has a high frustration and failure rate, anyway. We can do better.

THE MASK OF DISTRUST

A great deal of the dissension between the sexes draws on a deep mutual distrust of the other's ultimate agenda. The only way to lessen such distrust is through friendship. That means we must focus on the fundamentals: our lover's outlook on life, her approach to problem solving, her spiritual values, her moral vision, her social conscience. Those things do not sound very sexy. But it can make for dynamite sex and blissful erotic communion because sparks fly when both mates are rooted in such security. Too often we have got it wrong. We think that flying sparks create long-lasting love. But sparks can only ignite what has been stored and accumulated; they cannot store and accumulate. We must tenderly encourage each other to develop strengths, prune weaknesses, discipline reckless urges and harness raw, untapped energy and talent.

Permit me to offer this warning: We are living in a culture of complaint. Too many of us choose to air disagreements and diatribes about our mates in a ritual of same-sex bonding, creating and exacerbating the very conditions we try to avoid. That kind of talk makes us closer to the men we are commiserating with, but not the women we are complaining about. If you're just letting off steam and then going home less stressed, that is one thing; if you use your dissatisfaction to short-circuit closeness, that is another.

FACING THE FUTURE UNMASKED

How do we make do with what we have, even as we fight valiantly to get what should justly be ours? How do we take what is possible as the arena of struggle until what is impossible comes into view? How do we sow seeds of inspiration for a future that will benefit from what seems to be fruitless labor? And how do we love in the midst of pain?

In the end, we must remove the masks that now wear us. We must cut through the dishonesty, the emotional immaturity, the fear of intimacy, the hunger for control and the inability to take responsibility for ourselves by owning ourselves, by owning up to our shortcomings. We need not fear that if we do, it will then be open season on Black men. That will continue no matter what we do. But we must live for the integrity of a Black manhood that is willing to become stronger by shedding the crutches that cripple. We must embrace Black women as our soul mates and fellow pilgrims going forward to spiritual and moral maturity.

When we find a way with the face we have, we come to know who we are. We can wade into our own fears and anxieties, confronting them, challenging them, defeating them. We make choices in keeping with our best selves, and manage life with our own energy, power and purpose—not the borrowed strength of the mask.

We also have a better sense of who we are in a relationship with another person. We get a chance to see the outlines of our faces, our characters, our souls. We come to be known and loved for our real selves.

Besides, a relationship is going to have much greater potential to go the distance if the foundation is created by two people who have the courage to lay themselves bare. Dropping our cover encourages our partners to drop theirs.

Then our erotic joy and sexual passion will increase immensely. And the pride of our manhood will be in turning our masks into monuments, sturdy reminders of where we have come from, suitable signs of what we still must accomplish.

THE LIFE OF THE MIND

I have always thought of the academy as a site. One, it's my job, and I needed a job, but also a site, one of the few sites that did still allow for a space and thinking and access to forms of knowledge, and a site where it was possible to create something, and it was possible to create Black Studies . . . How do I make the academic space where I am more open and more available . . . to audiences that were not necessarily elite cultural institutions or academic institutions?
—Farah Jasmine Griffin, *An Insurgent Praxis: Interview with Farah Jasmine Griffin*

There is a sense in the African American community, and always has been the sense, that A's are what you are to strive for. I don't think there has ever been any deviation from this notion that you need to *get the grade*. The question is: what are you getting the grade for? . . . One final point: we shouldn't leave without looking critically at the academy and the place of the academy either in supporting and facilitating our role as positive and effective persons within our community; or, on the other hand, making that endeavor more difficult.
—Margaret Burnham, "On the Responsibility of Intellectuals"

I was in an awkward and highly unusual position: I had completed my first book, *Reflecting Black: African-American Cultural Criticism*, set to come out on June 2, 1993. But I hadn't yet written my dissertation. Let me back up: I hadn't even written my proposal, or the prospectus, for my dissertation. It was already February, and I had to get going to even become "ABD," all but the dissertation. That's if I could get my Princeton committee to agree to me writing a doctoral thesis with a convincing proposal. But there was surely no way I could get my Ph.D. before my book came out, which, for some reason, stuck in my craw. My committee agreed to convene in April to read my proposal and give me an oral examination. The prospectus usually runs to thirty or forty pages and lays out the subject one proposes to undertake and the method of doing so while citing the relevant scholarship to support one's case. The oral examination might last for three hours, attended by one's committee, other professors, and one's academic peers. (I can still see the eagerly inquisitive face of Eddie Glaude, who arrived as a graduate student in the religion department after I had physically left campus to teach in Hartford, sitting at the opposite end of the long table from me.) After the grueling and exhaustive oral examination, you are asked to step outside the room as the committee discusses the merits of your proposal and whether it meets the demanding guidelines to proceed to writing a dissertation.

My committee consisted of three intellectual heavyweights: Cornel West, whose name I had submitted to a search committee at Princeton to direct the Afro-American Studies program and who would shortly jet to fame with the publication of *Race Matters*; Jeffrey Stout, a well-respected religious ethicist and the teacher with whom I spent the most time in the rigors of writing and rewriting papers, taking courses, and critically reading challenging books; and Albert Raboteau, the prominent religious historian and author of the classic *Slave Religion*. After they grilled me for a few hours, I was asked to leave the room as they weighed my case. Upon being invited back into the room, and taking my seat at the head of the table, I was informed that I had passed the exam and that my prospectus was approved.

Of course, I was elated. But my dissertation was still years away from being written, thwarting my plan to have my Ph.D. in hand before my first book came out. Or so it seemed. As my teachers and peers congratulated me, the true reason for my happiness quickly became apparent. I reached under the table and pulled out my completed dissertation, handed copies to my committee members, and said, "Here it is." I had taken a huge risk, perhaps even a foolish one, especially since my committee might have demanded big changes to my treatment, topic, or approach. Thankfully they hadn't. There was a collective gasp in the room, and I heard my fellow graduate student Obery Hendricks, now a renowned biblical scholar and writer, mutter audibly under his breath, "Got dayuuuum." I received corrections and queries from my committee, addressed them in the finished dissertation, submitted it, had it approved, and was able to graduate on June 8, 1993, as Marian Wright Edelman joined August Wilson in receiving an honorary doctorate.

In a manner, my sidestepping educational norms wasn't all that unusual. I had repeated the eleventh grade when I gained acceptance at Cranbrook, a prestigious Michigan secondary school attended in earlier days by

Daniel Ellsberg of Pentagon Papers fame and Senator Mitt Romney. I got kicked out after a year and a half there—I couldn't quite make the adjustment from going to school in the ghetto in segregated all-Black settings to floating in the cream of the cream with mostly white students—and got sent back to Detroit to collect my GED in night school. I didn't start college until I was turning twenty-one, and I didn't finish until I was twenty-six. By the time I got my Ph.D. at thirty-four, I'd already taught at two seminaries and was an assistant professor at Brown armed only with a master's degree from Princeton. I got my doctorate in 1993, and the next year, I was tenured and promoted to full professor at the University of North Carolina.

From the time I was quite young, I have believed that smarts should serve the common good, that learning is for oneself and one's community, and that scholarship should address both abstract ideas and concrete concerns and issues. I have written books that fit all sorts of categories for all sorts of purposes: Because I earned tenure within a year of getting my Ph.D., I have been free to write as I please about what interests and drives me, in as clear and direct a fashion as possible. I rarely preach or lecture from a manuscript, so my extemporaneous explorations of ideas have permitted me to range over a number of disciplines even as I remain keenly attuned to audiences and respond to cues about their excitement, or interest, or boredom, or irritation, or anger, at my ideas. The life of the mind remains for me a satisfying and thrilling vocation, habit, and practice, as I explore ideas that have intrinsic value as sources of enormous intellectual pleasure, while lending social and moral support to the effort to make the world a better place.

Class Notes

At the Lectern

Contesting Racial Amnesia

The culture wars were at their height well into the 1990s. Higher ed-
ucation was perceived as a safe space for and a bastion of progres-
sive thinkers and scholars who tried out their "bizarre" theories of
pedagogy and social change. Feminists, critical race theorists, liber-
als, lefties, radical democrats, and an assortment of other odd aca-
demics made up what conservatives and the far right deemed to be
an army of politically correct intellectuals (who were the poisonous
predecessors to today's so-called woke mob). In 1993, professors Mi-
chael Berubé and Cary Nelson convened a conference at the Univer-
sity of Illinois Urbana-Champaign on the conflicts, contradictions,
and possibilities in higher education. My lecture situates the rise of
identity politics in historical and racial contexts often overlooked or
downplayed by critics like Todd Gitlin, who also spoke about identity
politics at the conference. This lecture appeared in the 1995 volume of
published papers from the conference edited by Berubé and Nelson,
titled "Higher Education Under Fire: Politics, Economics, and the
Crisis of the Humanities."

I'm going to tell a story about the rise of identity politics and the background assumptions against which it is articulated. After telling this
story—without knowledge of which it makes no sense to criticize identity
politics—I'll then move toward what I'm going to call post-multicultural
politics. There are three features that I want to highlight at the outset, to
which I'll return throughout in discussing universalism, memory, and traditions, which are key concepts in discussions of historicizing the rise of
identity politics as a symptom of the collapse of insightful dialogue about
race in the United States. These three things are the moral hinges of my
cautionary tale about rushing too quickly to de-essentialize without trying
to account for the rise of—and the impulses for—essentialism. We've got
to get beyond essentialism, but we've got to understand what produced es-

sentialist impulses and how they were elaborated within African American culture specifically, and how people have taken these issues as a defense mechanism against white racist hegemony and dominance, which is itself undertheorized because it's so often assumed to be universal.

The first hinge of my cautionary tale comes from Alasdair McIntyre. In his book *After Virtue*, McIntyre talks about the dissolution of a common vocabulary within which concepts like "the good" and "virtue" make sense. McIntyre is trying to argue, of course, against a kind of rule-governed conception of morality derived from rational principles, arguing against utilitarian calculuses, and so on. He's trying to get to a conception of the moral life that depends on the revival of a neo-Aristotelian sense of community, because he's seen the dissolution and unraveling of this vocabulary—a vocabulary in which "the good" and "the virtuous" make sense—insofar as there's been a shattering, a fragmentation, of our own lives as moral beings. So "the good" means one thing to one community and another thing to another community; we no longer have a unitary sense of what "the good" means, or what constitutes "the good." And as a result of that, he sees a return to what has been characterized as communitarianism—a return to sustaining virtues, habits, forms of thinking and life, within a community, such that it makes sense to claim those virtues as something relevant to be pursued. So, in his understanding, the status of the universal was buffeted by fragmentation; the solution is a kind of reconstitution of community within these neo-Aristotelian pockets that sustain habits of life and thought that instantiate coherent beliefs about the common good. It's very important to remember McIntyre's argument as we discuss the various enticements and dangers of pursuing a notion of universality.

Second hinge. Michael Kammen, in his book *The Mystic Chords of Memory*, speaks about the notion of selective memory. The selective memory is employed, in his understanding, for the aims of reconciliation, because it preserves dimensions of traditions that unify, versus traditions that are fragmented. And what he says is that selective memory is employed to reconcile this fragmentation precisely because it has the explicit and implicit need and desire to depoliticize and to cause amnesia, at which expense it maintains its tradition. So to criticize and to remember, for Kammen, is to confront uncomfortable aspects of traditions, forcing confrontation with precisely those hidden, obscured, denied features of the tradition that constitute alternate memories. To politicize is to problematize the tradition, and to remember is to recall the very elements that would undermine the possibility that the tradition could be sustained in the way in which it currently operates. Hence the need for selective memory, which reconciles the tradition, consolidates it by forgetting and depoliticizing.

Third and last hinge: Michael Rogin's notion of political amnesia, where he tries to combine certain aspects of Jameson's work in *The Political Unconscious* with Jacoby's work in *Social Amnesia*. The creation and reproduction of structured forgetting sustained by mechanisms of invisibility gives us as a paradigm Edgar Allan Poe's "Purloined Letter": it is rendered invisible precisely because it is hidden in common view. And then, at the boundary of my cautionary tale, a word from Henry Kissinger, who says that the politics of the academy are so vicious because there is so little at stake. That is worth remembering, because when we have all of this fuss about the academy, and we feel a sense of crisis, when you think about McIntyre narrating the dissolution of this vocabulary in which the crisis has arisen, the point is to remember that people whose lives are really desperate can rarely afford the luxury of pessimism; they're too busy living on the surviving fragments of hope. This is a powerful caution for us to remember, and use to interrogate our own subject positions. As academics and public intellectuals trying to rethink and reconceptualize the prevailing forms of oppression in American culture, we have got to understand that people who don't speak the kinds of languages that we speak are already giving us evidences of their survival beyond the crises that we've imagined.

With these three frontispieces (or four, with Kissinger) operating, I want to narrate the following story. The civil rights struggles were, in a broad sense, about the sacred trinity of social goods: justice, equality, and freedom. When we look at the quest for civil rights, then, there are three things that have to be kept in mind as we try to rethink higher education and its relationship to a so-called Balkanized academy.

First, the "bloodless" revolution in civil rights legislation was achieved through a coerced adherence to declared principles of democracy. The Civil Rights Movement was a long-deferred elaboration of egalitarian tendencies in American political culture, and it was not simply the reorganization of American life in a linguistic sense, such that the language changed, and people's conceptions and self-understanding were mobilized in different directions. It was actual political practice that forced the rearticulation of certain conceptions of justice, and freedom, and equality to take place. There were bodies on the front line in Birmingham and Selma, and in Georgia; there was actual, sustained, concrete, political resistance and opposition that forced the academy and the larger American society to rethink their conceptions of race.

Second, the Civil Rights Movement was about the casting of the historic quest for freedom in the modes of behavior and the language of civic piety that linked the Black freedom struggle to the ideological center of democratic culture. So when we talk about the exhaustion of the language of rights for articulating Black concerns, we have to pay attention to the way in which what happened in the Civil Rights Movement was the appropriation of the language of civic piety, which was quite resonant in American traditions of civic response and contestation; likewise, when we talk about notions of civil religion, we also have to understand that Martin Luther King, Jr., was an enormously dexterous and skillful manipulator of both the rhetoric and the means of civil religion. He articulated his specific subject position as a Black Baptist preacher, whereby he supposedly awoke from his dogmatic slumber at Boston University, and he linked his specific appropriation and understanding of freedom to a larger culture which was already in place. The language of rights is already in place, and so what he does is appropriate this language and use it. In one sense the argument can be made that what King was doing was showing the ideological flexibility of foundational political documents. In truth, he showed the interpretive flexibility of the Constitution and the Declaration of Independence to accord with notions of freedom, justice, and equality that were produced by concrete political praxis and opposition.

But we've got to get the order right here. It's not that people in the academy were having discussions at the Unit for Criticism and Interpretive Theory about what we're going to do about these Black people. They were out there being bitten by dogs, bicuspids and incisors were tearing into their flesh, and that rearticulated and reorganized conceptual practices and discursive formations. That's what went on—actual political practice. I was thinking, during Todd Gitlin's presentation, what difference does it make when we tell that story? And the difference it makes is that you not only understand the priority of certain forms of praxis to theory, but you understand the ways in which, unless we can theorize them in adequate ways, the practices don't even make sense.

Thirdly, there was the fusion of the pursuit of racial reconciliation with the concomitant rejection of narrow interpretations of racial equality, distancing both Black nationalists on the one side and white racialists/nationalists on the other side. This, then, in my understanding, put in place the realization of certain features of democratic equality—that is, the realization of access to social spheres and social goods, the more equitable distribution of social goods like education, employment, transportation, and so on. But it failed to fully satisfy the cultural and even the psychic demands embodied in the quest for freedom, equality, and justice.

So when we talk about the social structure of realities, we must see as its condition the immediate foregrounding of certain narratives of self-esteem that only make sense in relationship to these larger social structures and economic realities. When we talk about notions of self-esteem, then, they are never depersonalized realities; they are always linked to larger social realities. For instance, if you live in a culture that mediates conceptions of negative Black identity to you through television, media, theological tracts, discourses from centuries before until now, in an uncontested, unproblematized, unitary fashion, then it is fundamentally disingenuous to problematize and conceptualize essentialism, and theorize about it in the context of African Americans who have appropriated these identities, without talking about those forces to which they had to respond.

And it is disingenuous precisely because the very problem to which they were responding in the Civil Rights Movement was the problem of the bourgeois liberal opposition, which did not pay attention to the psychic demands of the movement. Of course, King picked up on this right near his death. He sounds like a nationalist when he says that the problem is to revive the Olympian manhood of Black people. That's a page right out of Molefi Asante, in one moment, and Malcolm X in a certain sixties Black nationalism. Hence the prominence of sixties Black nationalism centered on a crucial question of life's identity.

"Identity"—for several reasons. First of all, there was the devalued African past, constructed such that narratives of recovered racial identity became crucial precisely because this element was most obscured, distorted, and elided. Not only social goods were at stake; there was also an explicit appeal to the centrality of the quest for identity, because people were trying to figure out, are there Africanisms, are they being continued over in American culture, how should we understand the debate between Frazier and Herskovits, what is all this history about? It is about the quest for identity that was deliberately withheld from people of color. Linked to this, then, are narratives of self-esteem that are crucial to people whose denial was predicated on their supposed intellectual and personal inferiority, not simply as individuals, but collectively as Blacks. The uncritical notion of

Blacks being evil, and inferior, and unintelligent informs personal perceptions and how people feel about themselves.

This third feature played on the desire to be liked by people who formerly—or formally—despised African Americans. To be accepted as intelligent, as beautiful, as worthy. White validation and legitimation, all signified partially in the Civil Rights Movement's quest for inclusion, which also included elements of reconciliation that undercut its own racial memory, were being almost avoided. So we get the phenomenon of Black intellectuals who, after a quest for white legitimation and validation in the academy, continually seek the validation of white people in order to say "I'm OK—and if I'm OK and you like me, then I'm really all right." And this is part of the engine that drives the revival of a certain category of racial formation that is essentialist, and a kind of identity politics that is central to various forms of Black nationalism. It may distort the social, political, and economic structures that make it possible, but Black nationalist politics also provided an important check to the fantasies of unproblematic reconciliation and inclusion. It focused on identity, both civil and personal, as a crucial pillar of racial advance. It rejected the premise of "I'm OK because you like me" not simply because it was personal, but because it was the basis of group ambition and achievement. Thus there was a tension between the quest for inclusion and reconciliation, on one hand, and autonomy and recognition on the other.

This is one of the central tensions between the Black bourgeois liberal response and opposition to white racist dominance, and the Black nationalist upsurges in the sixties. In part, then, the politics of racial essentialism arose as a defense mechanism against the ominous gaze of white authoritarian regulation of Black being. That mechanism doesn't acknowledge the flexible, fluid boundaries of race, the socially constructed means by which race is reconstituted over space and time that is both a source not only of irreducible categories for social theorizing, but of the stakes of "personal" identity as well. Therefore, what arise are rhetorics of authenticity that are reasserted—especially in times of crisis of identity precipitated by white racist attack, whether in Alabama and Georgia, or in the narrowing of boundaries of political meanings in the Reagan-Bush era. Racial essentialism is linked to the assertions of identity politics precisely because this era has erased the memory of the context of struggle that helped, in one sense, determine this present historical moment. Depoliticization and amnesia have created, then, an artificial legacy that obscures the real problems, and encourages the circulation of stories that are only half-true. Identity politics is not, for instance, a "private" politics of special interest. What constitutes identity, personal or collective, is quite public—socialization processes, ranges of images that create and reinforce perceptions that are the basis of self-identity, and so on—and the critics of identity politics often miss that point. We can say that if racial essentialism and identity politics are linked, not naturally but by social choices and imposed constraints, then their advocates are not the sole owners of the means of reduction.

On the other side, the critics of identity politics and essentialism (myself included in certain ways) who appeal to conceptions of unity and universality mask their roots in particular and specific traditions which masquerade as universal. Thus universality and unity are often achieved by racial amnesia, because the goal of unity is the reconciliation of difference and oppositional discourses at a certain level, even though the discourse of multiculturalism ostensibly concedes space to oppositional practices within an environment. But again, we run into the operation of depoliticization and amnesia, and in regard to race, critics of identity politics rightly criticize a narrow focus on authenticity and loyalty to the race that are the governing tropes of identity politics. In one sense you can never adequately answer Billy Paul's question: "Am I Black enough for you?" And when you start down this slippery slope, you can never determine who is really Black. As a result, you come up against a perennial contestation over an increasingly narrow sphere of racial identity that is up for grabs in interpretive warfare.

So, against an uncomplex criticism of identity politics that fails to understand why Blacks are suspicious of such criticism, I want to try to pose a few plausible explanations about why some people, in this case African Americans, but also other so-called minority peoples, may be suspicious of the de-essentializing impulses that persons like myself and Cameron McCarthy and others want to press. Then we can try to figure out how we can move beyond these essentialist impulses to this radical post-multiculturalism that I want to imagine.

First of all, this notion of de-essentialized racial politics tends to mask the reasons for differentiation, and to rearticulate Blacks and others as special interest groups. Over the last twelve years, we've seen the collapse of the will to undo the legacy of past racism with immediate intervention, both in the private and public spheres. And what is often not talked about, even by Bill Clinton, is that the fierce rivalry among previously denied groups for the politics of public attention masks the anxieties of the real source of that contestation, because one rule seems to prevail: One at a time. Not Latinos and African Americans, and gays and lesbians and so on, we can't have all of them competing for the politics of public attention. One at a time. What seems to apply is an implicit rule that the distribution and regulation of social goods can only be governed by this zero-sum thinking, to which the system is hostage.

Moreover, there is a deep suspicion among many people that it is the height of hypocrisy to caution and chasten African Americans about identity politics in a land that has continually witnessed the appropriation and commodification of Black identity for its own uses. We don't have to talk about slavery under this heading, we can see this in terms of Black popular culture. We can see the commodification and appropriation of Black gay identity, so that it's not that Sylvester becomes the famous person necessarily, it's KC and the Sunshine Band. It's not the Black agrarian blues of Little Richard that gets the play, it's the rock 'n' roll of Elvis Presley. It involves the commodification of Black cultural imagination at the site of the hip, the chic, and the cool.

And even though Michael Jordan gets paid big-time, funky-fresh, dope, stupid money, most people do not realize the benefits of it, particularly those Black kids who look at Chicago Stadium and who can never buy a ticket to get into where Michael is doing his airtime, even though his will to spontaneity, his will to edifying deception, and his notions of deifications of accident, as Herskovits talks about, are all beautiful, and I love to see them. But when Black people then reappropriate notions of cultural identity, all of a sudden it becomes an off-limits game—after their very identity has been appropriated and domesticated and diluted and commodified for the interests of American capital and the larger society.

Now that I've said all of that, I want to move toward what I consider a post-multicultural politics. First of all, I'm aware of the kind of faddish title that this represents—post-everything. I think, though, that we have to find some way of problematizing the implied consensus that places unitary conceptions of multiculturalism with discourses of pluralism and diversity at the center.

First of all, my conception of post-multiculturalism would dismiss the quest for legitimacy that strangles so-called minority cultures from within and without. Part of the problem that has not been addressed in a serious way by the left—and again I refer to Todd Gitlin's provocative paper, which I'm trying to argue with him about, because I do think we have to transcend identity politics somehow—is that we've got to find a way of respecting the integrity of particularity, and to understand what forces drove the engine of quests for, and rhetorics of, authenticity, legitimacy, and loyalty. I have tried to narrate a bit of that.

But in my own post-multicultural sense, we would dismiss the quest for legitimacy that strangles not only from without but from within. I think of my students at Brown, who try to say that certain people can rap and certain people can't rap; Black people can rap and white people can't rap; white rappers can't criticize Black rappers as being inauthentic because they're not Black. And I say, what's the problem? Then they invoke Malcolm X and they say that if Malcolm X were here today he might call you the biggest sellout because you're attending an elite white institution debating forms of Black culture and consciousness and not being linked to progressive forms of realization of that within the larger society. So you can never stop it. The quest for legitimacy is perennial precisely because nobody has the markers and boundaries, and they're always slippery and sliding, which teaches us profound lessons about the nature of race to begin with.

Second, we have to move beyond modified universalisms, glimpsed in a multiculturalism that buys into consensus and a notion of wholeness, and link particularity to the possibility of reconceiving the whole so that *coherence*, and not unity, is the operative category. Now, this could be splitting hairs, but I think there is a difference between talking about notions of coherence and notions of unity. Some might see one as predicated on the other, or claim that they're synonymous, but I disagree. I think unity designates an uncontested terrain where people are brought together, whereas resonant notions of solidarity imply that these diverse coalitions can be brought together with a coherent conception of opposition to forms of practice within higher education and larger American society.

Third, I think we can have this coalition of interests that respects the integrity of particularity, while seeking, in this case, race-transcending grounds of common embrace, so that we move beyond pluralism to a concrete interpretation of what diversity really means, of what Cornel West and Henry Louis Gates talk about in terms of interrogating the moral content of our identities. And when we interrogate that moral content, what we begin to do is then automatically link them to other like-minded people, whether they be gay or lesbian, whether they be environmental activists, whether it be white men and women who are interested in resisting forms of oppression, and so on. The moral content of our identities is not merely shaped by our own historical and personal experience, but we refer to them as we make expansions across the barriers that divide us.

And finally, and most forcefully, I think that what this compels us to do in a post-multicultural moment is to move beyond the academy, which is why I opened up with Brother Kissinger. Kissinger is right on very few things, but I think he's absolutely right that, in one sense, the university is an artificial environment. And of course, we want an artificial environment to protect young seekers after truth, those who are obeying the Delphic oracle's injunction to know thyself. We want to have a protected environment, but we want to contest who those selves are, how they get constructed, who has a say in making them who they are, so that the narrow, militaristic conception of "be all you can be" gets problematized, and so that when we begin to expand the range of understandings about what persons are and who persons are, a post-multicultural moment moves that range of understandings beyond the academy.

Because the university is necessarily an artificial environment, it is an insufficient environment within which to test the greatest ideals that we can generate within the academy. So I am arguing for a public intervention that is not simply predicated upon an elitist condescending stance, but a stance that takes seriously the actual people for whom we seek to speak, and on whose behalf we speak, so that our own understandings will not only be rooted in a provocative theoretical base, but linked to understandings of people's actual, everyday lives.

CHAPTER

32

Dreams of the Drum

This lecture allowed me to offer an extended riff on Kanye West's infamous interruption of Taylor Swift as she was being awarded an MTV Video Music Award for Best Female Video. I texted JAY-Z when I saw the backlash Kanye received for his actions, saying that there was a broader historical backdrop for his admittedly rude intercession. Jay asked me to email him my thoughts, which he passed along to Kanye, after which we struck up a friendship of sorts, which has been sorely tested over the years as Kanye has grown far more conservative and I have publicly weighed in on his actions. This lecture was the keynote presentation at a 2010 Black Arts Festival held at Bucknell University. It was published in In Media Res: Race, Identity, and Pop Culture in the Twenty-First Century, *edited by James Braxton Peterson.*

Tonight, I want to talk about "Dreams of the Drum," and speak to the importance of Black arts. Since this Black arts festival is occurring here at this remarkable university, it is important to reflect upon the critical acumen that has often been associated with the most noteworthy artists in American society, who also happen to be people of color. In this case, I am especially thinking of Black artists. This topic suggests an outline to think about how the Black arts have been influential in our culture. But for me, "Dreams of the Drum" immediately conjures *Dreams from My Father*. It is not that Mr. Obama has overtaken Langston Hughes in terms of the Black dream discourse.

But in the recent collective imagination of America, dreams of Black people have become intimately webbed with the dreams of this African son, who is now the President of the United States of America. I still have to pinch myself each time I say it. Sometimes I think it is like a hoax. It might be just a dream. I wake up sometimes and say, "Boy, I just had the craziest dream that America actually elected a Black man as president." So, this is my first thought—my first association when I think about dreams *of* the drum, dreams *from* the drum, or dreams associated *with* the drum.

When we consider the impact of the Black arts in American history, we think about the drum as a central metaphor for how Black arts have had to exist, often in veiled and signified relationships to, and within, hegemonic societies. It could also be argued that the drum exists within the context of multiple and simultaneous African and African American cultures as well. By saying veiled and signified I am actually being repetitive and redundant, because signifying is the way in which veiled meanings are communicated [to] exempt the signifier from moral and social suspicion because they have covered their language and intention in such a way as to misdirect. The "Dream of the Drum" is to veil the meaning, hide the meaning, make the meaning implicit, or imply the meaning, rather than explicitly saying it. An explicit expression has often meant the destruction or the interruption of Black community, and in some cases, the distortion of Black art itself.

Signifying became a practice that was deliberately refined. Misdirecting communication is not the only source, or the only findable and traceable origin, for signifying practices, but it is one of the most remarkable ones, and one of the most useful ones, because Black folks as minorities didn't have the opportunities sometimes just to tell the truth that they were thinking. Let me give you an example of what happens when you don't signify, and you just say it straight up: Kanye West.

I was there when Kanye went up on the stage at the 2009 MTV Video Music Awards and snatched the microphone. There was no signifying going on there. Although ultimately it can be argued that the moment was rife with significance, and certain signifying elements, he was, in that moment, rather direct. Like a blunt instrument, he literally snatched the means of amplification away from a talented young artist who happened to be a young white woman, Taylor Swift, a country musician. She is as sweet and innocent as she can be. She was stunned, as were the rest of us sitting there. I was with several MTV executives. You know they were not too happy. Kanye West went up and snatched the microphone while Swift was being awarded for Best Female Video, and said, "Yo, Taylor, I'm really happy for you. I'mma let you finish. But Beyoncé had one of the best videos of all time! One of the best videos of all time!" Now, that wasn't no signifying. There wasn't any implication. There was no misdirection. There was no suggestion; no shadow of potential meaning that could go either way, that philosophers call multi-evidential. That was just straight up breaking and entering into the public space of Taylor Swift.

Now, I don't want to assign any uncontested value or pure moral interpretation to this. There is a way of [appropriately] signifying and getting communal affirmation. I think that it was rude, crude, bombastic and typically Kanye Westian. He has a big ego. But it is more than that, isn't it? Kanye West snatched a microphone, a means of amplification of what he thought of as an untruth. He had this weird idea that people should get awards that they deserve. Who is he to be the arbiter of who deserves an award? People voted after all. But historically, award shows have been problematic for Black folk because when we knew certain Black artists deserved an award, and they did not receive recognition, they didn't have a means to amplify their disgruntlement. Mr. West [committed] an act of cultural compensation—please note that he didn't intend this. I don't want you to think I am inventing his consciousness. I'm not suggesting that Kanye West consciously had this in mind. But he didn't have to.

That's my job to determine the significance and his job to speak a truth. He did something serious in this moment. He says, and I'm paraphrasing, "Look, everybody knows that the moon man"—the award that is given to those who win MTV honors—"should have gone to Beyoncé." Alhough Taylor Swift is a very talented woman, even roaches and rats were singing "Single Ladies." Everybody was singing that song, and there's a video that has been remade and remixed in some of the most pervasive, democratic ways. I thought to myself that Chuck Berry probably wished Kanye West had been around when they were giving the award he deserved to Elvis. Maybe Little Richard was so satisfied that finally after 50 years, some Black person had the position, the assertiveness, the ego, the self-centeredness, and also the courage to step up and say, "Damn it, stop giving away what belongs to Black people to somebody else. Give me my Grammy. Shut up. Whhhooo!" [in Little Richard's voice]

I am not suggesting that Kanye West was a part of a soul patrol that was policing the boundaries of appropriate awarding of artistic merits for Black artists. After all, Beyoncé isn't exactly without awards. The point is that Mr. West bluntly bludgeoned the moment—he beat the drum—and as a result, he felt the bloodcurdling response from the American audience. They punished him. They had to stop his tour. He had to go on Jay Leno's program [*The Tonight Show*] for him to break down publicly, as Mr. Leno asked him about his mama and what she would feel. That was awful. It was horrible.

Then on the other hand, Ms. Swift was awarded every award under the sun. I think she is set to receive a Nobel Prize, and maybe male artist of the year the year after that. You get my point. The overwhelming sense of protection for this laudable young white girl in light of this Black man having unfairly accosted her—[obscured] the legitimate undergirding principles,

principles that were lost in the exchange, the brutally rude exchange, be-tween Mr. West and the audience, and Ms. Swift by extension. When you don't signify and you are blunt and brutal, there are consequences that are fierce.

That is why people rely upon inferential, implicatory, suggestive, and signifying languages, so you can survive your own communication. Kanye enjoys his own privilege as a rich pop star. Of course, there have been many millions of young people of color, and some white people, for that mat-ter, who have been "Taylor Swifted" every day; who never get a chance to recover the means of amplification as did Ms. Swift. That night on that program, she was handed the microphone by a member of the tribe that had offended her—by Beyoncé—by the same person on whose behalf Mr. West ostensibly acted. That was an act of poetic and rhetorical justice that is often denied to others.

Now, you might say, why do I start here. I start here to show why it is criti-cal, crucial and central to the Black arts traditions that they have more or less dealt with the implied and inferred, the signified aspects of Black identity—usually it is humor, or veiled critique through humor—often using music to veil critiques of American society. Even Sam Cooke singing "Any Day Now," not the later song made famous by another artist, but a two-minute-and-nearly-fifty-second song that was imagining the prospects for heaven, but was really a veiled critique of the lack of heaven [for Black folk] here on earth.

Black artists, from the very beginning, and the drum speaks directly to this, have engaged in signifying practices that veiled their critique of the dominant and mainstream society so that they could exist long enough to create a livelihood out of that art. So that they could use that art to revisit the scene of the injury to Black identity for which Black art was called into existence. It was not exclusively, not necessarily or even primarily so, but it was central.

And so, the drum is a metaphor for that veiled activity in the way that the drum in the Congo Square in New Orleans was a means by which Black people communicated to each other. They could communicate explicitly, and speak widely, even though they had different languages and were from different tribes and different cultures. They also had suspicions and skep-ticisms about each other. Imagine a bunch of Americans taken from every stage and thrown together into slavery. They might speak the same lan-guage, not [as] in the case of Africans, but they might be from the South versus the North, different sensibilities, different traditions, or some could have even spoken different languages. Some are primarily Spanish speaking versus those who were primarily English speaking. They had different re- gions and geographies and cultures and expectations, all seen as American, not [for example] Arkansan.

So, imagine the eradication of all that complexity and cultural diversity in Africa, subject to the brutal weight of the Middle Passage and slavery. Individuals thrown together, deliberately taken out of their element so that they could not communicate. What happens of course is that the drum maintained itself as a signifying device to communicate where the voice had failed. The voice was interrupted. The voice was muffled. The mouths of slaves were muffled. There was a systemic [effort] to prevent Black people from communicating for fear that they would somehow undermine the dominant culture that had enslaved them.

So Black art—at least in this country, at least since 1619, in the context of slavery and Reconstruction and legalized segregation and Jim Crow, and then on into the late part of the twentieth century and then into the twenty-first century—had its origins in the determination of Black people to preserve their humanity and to communicate with each other in a hostile environment. Black artists had a moral purpose thrust upon them from the very beginning without being asked why or if they were okay with the fact that [their art] was suffused with such unintended but necessary meaning. The signifying conditions in which they engaged always had im- plications beyond themselves, or their own families or communities—but they had implications for the broader community.

We argue now about the meaning of Black art, and whether a rapper should pay attention to why his or her words might have an impact on young people, or why an artist, who is a visual artist, should pay attention to why the stereotypes [by] which she experiments may have particular meaning for those who understand the stereotypes, and a different one for those who don't. [But] the question of moral utility and social function attach rather immediately to the prospects of Black art. Black art never ex- isted in isolation from either the moral or the social consequences on Black American communities. The drum was the signifier of that. The drum [is], literally, the percussive tonality and texture of Black artistic expression, the very means by which we beat it, the means by which we express the tones and temper of Black existence. The very character of Black artistic imagi- nation beats itself out on surfaces that were stretched taut between poles of denial and opportunity. As a result of that, the drum became a signifying and symbolizing measure of Black humanity and Black artistic expression. The drum itself became eventually outlawed because people figured out that Black folk were communicating through the drums. They couldn't talk. They couldn't speak. But they could beat out the meaning.

Eventually they had to stop beating the drums, but the drum continues to signify the best of the Black arts. It becomes a metaphor handed down from one generation of Black people to another. The drum is a signifying condition. The drum contains implicit meaning. The drum is the signified meaning. The drum is the meaning that might be veiled for people to catch on—[except] for the literal Kanye West–like in-your-face meaning, although some Black art certainly does that as well. But Black art works along the edges of traditions, through implied and inferred response, working in a medium that has as its rich reward the ability of Black people to hibernate inside that drum from where the very rhythms of lived experience are emanating. Generated at the very base of that drum, these rhythms allowed them to amplify their deepest and most refined aspirations without being caught. That is why Black language has a kind of percussive, throbbing and rhythmic tonality.

That is why there is a profound difference between George Bush and Barack Obama. It is in the way they talk—the way that they walk. I don't want to make any other claims, but the most significant point of Obama being in the White House may not be his color. You can hear and feel the difference when Obama is speaking and talking: "Yes we can, yes we can." There is a rhythm that he gets from the Black church. The Black church affords its ministers a platform to speak out rhythms in their own speech. Listen to the best rhythmic intensity and poetic agitation that is mediated through the artistic expression of preaching. I know that preachers are not usually thrown into Black arts, but tell me what is more poetic and artistic than a real Black preacher who knows what he or she is doing? There are all kinds of Black preaching. Martin Luther King, Jr., is one variety. There is the Al Sharpton variety, and the Jesse Jackson variety is more well known. But even with King, you can chart the beautiful rhythmic intensities. King's voice was like a trumpet, not a drum. "I may not get there with you, but I want you to know tonight, that we as a people, will get to the Promised Land." Isn't that beautiful? Or when he delivered the "I Have a Dream" speech: "Five score years ago . . . The emancipation proclamation." [Black preaching suggests] you can say it another way, [with] the trademark of Black dialect in the rhythmic tonality and the rhythmic intensity, and the drum-like tonality of Black speech as the common character—that Black vernacular force found in the voices of the best Black preachers. Some of them nearly sing their meaning.

Catholic priests may say the same thing, but there is a rhythm to Black speech, and that rhythm is from the drum. The drum is from the same location. The beats per minute articulated, you can hear it even in the artistry of Black speech. "It's not God bless America, God damn America." Now, I know that many people miss the rhythmic intensity and the well-formed oratorical conventions in their efforts to grasp the literal interpretation of what Reverend Wright was saying, even though I have taken him out of context here. Many white brothers and sisters were appalled at Reverend Wright's comments. I am still talking about Black art, the pounding on a drum, the rhythmic intensity. I'm talking about Black preaching as one of the very elements of Black art. Reverend Wright was beating the drum. White folk thought: "My God, I thought you people went to church and talked about Jesus. How dare you speak about AIDS and white supremacy and who runs America and the like?" Well, in Black churches, that is the kind of stuff that we talk about, and we will talk about these matters in a certain way.

Some Black folk think that Jesus is about speaking in tongues, and wearing the right dress, and the right makeup and the like, just like some in the white conservative fundamentalist churches. But then there is the rhythmic intensity of Black preaching. The preaching itself becomes the articulable sound of Black survival. Black preaching becomes the way in which the interpreter of the Word speaks to the lived experiences of Black folk. The Word. The Word was seminal. It gave voice and birth. It gave birth to the voice and voice to our birth. The Word was seminal, and it had a tremendous amount of possibility wrapped up in it. The Word itself gave birth to new vision, new imagination, new ways of organizing life. The Black preacher was central to the artistic expression of Black euphony, Black sounding. The drum, the syncopation of the sound, the tonality, the rhythmic intensity, all of that stuff from Congo Square got compressed and some would say distilled in the vocal cords of the Black preacher. How they talk is just as important as what they say. A lot of people give that a twist and they think that Black people just sound stylish, but they aren't saying a damn thing.

Some people think that Black rhetorical performances have no meaning and significance, that they have no logic because they are passionate, so they have no reason. America is skeptical, especially white America, of emotional expression. You have to be tight, straightforward. There is something beautiful about that too, and it has its purposes. You don't want a person with her hand on the [nuclear] button acting the fool. There's something to be said for calm and reasoned articulation, which is of course central to many African and African American traditions. But there is skepticism about emotion and passion. It is as if when you say something like you mean it, you therefore cannot be saying much of substance. But Black people and their use of Black artistic expression are fusing style and substance. Just because LeBron James looks fierce when he is dunking doesn't mean that he ain't scoring two points. Just because Kobe Bryant led the league in scoring, the youngest to do so at 21 years of age, averaging a little bit over 30 points a game—just because he has style and he looks a different way than Larry Bird, it doesn't mean that what he is doing is not efficacious and effective, that it is not literally substantive.

Black preaching invites the discussion of our tendency to bifurcate passion and intellectual respectability. If you don't say it with a kind of calm, cool, distance, clinical dispassion, then somehow you lack the substance upon which any coherent expression of truth rests. Black art, through Black preaching, Black art from the drum of Congo Square and also through Black comedy [is meaningful]. You can hear it in a Chris Rock. You can hear it in a Bill Cosby. You can hear it in a Richard Pryor. They deploy a wide range of expressions, and sometimes, explicit expressions. Here is where my argument about veiled expression and signifying as an inferential means of Black identity is to be reasonably challenged. Of course, in terms of Black comedy, there is the more explicit expression, but even that explicit expression is a signification upon both our needs *within* the context of Black culture, as well as signifying our needs *beyond* Black culture.

Some people like Bill Cosby are bridge figures. "Jell-O pudding pops. Frozen pudding on a stick." Mr. Cosby is one of the original geniuses. Mark Twain meets Nipsey Russell. If you ever see Mr. Cosby in 1984's *Bill Cosby: Himself* you will see a man with a microphone get up and share wisdom on a stage, entertaining Americans for nearly an hour and a half with un- stinting genius. He is able to weave narratives and make that patchwork of extraordinary humor into completed meaning. And then use that to force Americans to reflect in a non-racially specific fashion upon the context of their common existence. Bill Cosby's rhetorical genius was never ex- plicit about race, though subsequently his social critique has been almost exclusively about race. Thus, his genius of signifying in nonracial terms has been compromised when it makes the transition from the stage to the podium. He didn't have that much practice at the value of interpretation within social critique. As a result, he is rather flat. I think he is ineffectual as a social critic because he lacks the insight of figures who are far more talented and sophisticated in thinking about race.

Richard Pryor, after him, was a man in full anger about the limits imposed on him because of race. Now the drum becomes articulate. Richard Pryor used his talent as an incredibly powerful drum, wielding it in defense of poor and vulnerable Black people in a way that Mr. Cosby could not. Mr. Pryor told of the angry passions that occupy the breasts of common, ordinary Black folk. He told stories about Black folk life. He told stories about people who are character types that we didn't often see on the American stage. He brought them into full view. The power of speech, that drum radiating out, beating the story, not simply of signifying, but of explicit expression. He told numerous stories that try to reveal the heart of American darkness. Joseph Conrad was a Black eye. (Many of us would have liked to have given Mister Conrad a black eye.) But when Richard Pryor gave him a Black tongue, the heart of African darkness, he turned it in on itself, so to speak. He shone the light deep in the heart of the African American struggle, striving for existence and subsistence. The interesting thing is that Mr. Pryor is taking the drum in a different direction. He is trying to articulate subversive meanings that have been submerged. That is what Richard Pryor was. He wasn't just Joseph Conrad. He was *the savage* with a microphone on stage, telling jokes.

Richard Pryor [may have] strung himself out on drugs, freebasing, but he simultaneously exposed the interior struggles of Black people trying to make sense of the world. What is more absurd than living in a country that tells you that you can't be seen as equal because of your skin color even as it exploits your genius to build the nation? What's more absurd than Americans calling Black folk lazy when they worked for 350-plus years for free? What's more absurd than putting forth the notion of white supremacy when white brothers and sisters knew it was a lie to begin with? They knew about their cousins and uncles who were attracted to even the so-called worst Black person. It was the dirty light of whiteness that we didn't want washing up in our racially bifurcated reality. Richard Pryor's voice became the archiving of the attempt to overcome white supremacy and to expose the lunacy of the mythologies of whiteness, often burning himself along his path toward clarity. In the light of his own self-destruction, he illuminated the context of Black mythology, and the pathology that made Blackness a sin. So, the drum kept beating. It beats now in Martin Lawrence and Chris Rock too, and Mo'Nique. She was vicious in *Precious*—anything but precious. A lot of Black people are mad. This is what Black art does. It often exposes the fault lines of Black identity that white folk don't know about.

Obviously, there are many arguments about the film *Precious*. "Why do we have nothing depicted in film aside from pathological characterizations?" "Black people acting crazy; white folk love that." When I went to see *Precious*, I was maybe one of four Black people in the theater that is double the size of this hall. White brothers and sisters. And I said this one is going to be a hit. I knew it was going to be a hit because white people were coming out to see a Black film. Are white folk attracted to the stories of Black pathologies? Or is it that white brothers and sisters don't see genius beyond Black pathology? Is it that white brothers and sisters would rather give Denzel an Oscar for *Training Day* and not for *Malcolm X*? Black folk were pissed about that too. But I love Denzel in *Training Day*. He was evil and I was tired of him playing the "good Negro." I loved that "luminous darkness." People are mad, but he should have also won it for *Malcolm X*. The drum beats in all kinds of explicit ways in Black cinema because in Black cinema, the drumbeat commands much more money. The percussive tones are sometimes stretched out, maybe even more percussive on some surfaces, and sometimes muffled on others. With *Precious*, the argument was why do Black people have to be pathological for white people to come see us? Why can't we just be good and positive?

The question of Black art, Black moral status, the burden of representation—this is where the drum gets even louder. Are Black arts responsible for Black people? Does Black art represent positive aspects of Black existence? Do white folk even care about that? Is Tom Cruise obsessed with representing whiteness positively? And Tom is my man, Scientology and all. But for the most part, if Tom goes down, he has Brad, Ashton Kutcher, and on, and on, and on, and on. If Denzel goes down, you have Laurence Fishburne, about a couple other brothers, maybe Terrence Howard and that's about it. So, the dearth, the paucity, the lack of depth and density of Black representations of authority places undue burdens on the backs of Black artists and freights Black art with even more meaning and menace. This is where the drum begins to beat most loudly, and you *see* it amplified through varieties of microphones.

What is a Black artist to do? Is the first obligation of Black art to Black convention? Black art can't really do that because art sometimes is used to challenge people and get in their faces. It can't just represent your positive character because sometimes what you think is positive rests upon the broken dreams of people whose voices you've muffled. It doesn't mean that we are not obsessed with the negative because we know many people are. That's the Catch-22 that we are in. In a sense, on the one hand, we don't have enough art out there from Black people to balance and counterbalance some of the negative stuff that we see. There may be Guru *and* 50 Cent, but 50 Cent is the one on the poster with the money. 50 Cent is the one people respond to. All of the so-called negative forces, which have a legitimate right to exist, are exaggerated and seen as representative. That is part of the problem. The problem is the so-called negative, the so-called dark, the so-called subversive is seen as the utterly authentic expression of Blackness. So we get trapped in that box, and so people think that pathology is the norm. Yet at the same time, people have every right to explore pathology or what you think is pathology and to raise questions about what it truly means.

Black art does that. It makes us uncomfortable. When Kara Walker does her cutouts right there in Austin, Texas, and people consider her brilliant visual play on Black and white—and the human body—she forces people to think, and rethink their own understandings of what the stereotypes are. What is a stereotype but a shortcut that is made lucid in the minds of thinking people? Stereotype is a lazy person's way of negotiating difference. How do we continue to explore the biases that require stereotypes? How do we play with that? Some subversive art does just that. Some gangsta rap art really is funny, even though it is vicious and powerful and pathological and dark and brilliant all at the same time. Some of the stuff that I listen to from Snoop is just sheer genius. Some of it makes my toes curl. Sometimes it's at the same time, on the same record. Do we get rid of Snoop? Hell no. Snoop Dogg now is making commercials with Lee Iacocca. He is a GPS system. He's mainstream. Snoop Dizzle, fa shizzle my nizzle.

So, the drum beats. It continues to grow louder. It's this drumbeat that demands responsibility of artists. And in their hands, it makes us believe that everything they do implies something—that unavoidable representationality of Black art that cannot be helped. Whether it wants to or not, it becomes representative. The significance of Blackness literally is inscribed into the Black body. My point simply is to propose that a lot of these young people say things in their hip hop music, things that are worthy of studying. If we do not acknowledge this fact, we will miss in our own culture the evidence that it is part of the Black arts tradition, part of the drum—speaking, preaching and informing the percussive tonality of Black rhetoric.

CHAPTER

33

Critical Race Theory in Action

This lecture was the keynote address in 2013 for the Tenth Annual Wiley A. Branton / Howard Law Journal Symposium in Washington, D.C. It was the morning after my fifty-fifth birthday, which I celebrated in New York City with a lovely party of friends and family. I got up in the morning and took an Amtrak to D.C. to make it in time for my 2 p.m. lecture. I meditated on my subject and let the ideas flow in my presentation. Although I had been giving lectures without notes for most of my academic life, I can remember the moment I committed to such a practice in the academy. I was in my second year of graduate school, sitting next to my mentor, Jeff Stout, as we listened to the great Brazilian political and legal theorist, and Harvard Law professor, Roberto Mangabeira Unger deliver a series of lectures as part of the Gauss Seminars in Criticism at Princeton without a single note. Unger spoke about "Reinventing Democracy." I remember it like he spoke just yesterday. I was astonished. He was eloquent, fluid, brilliant, and expansive, as if he were reading from a manuscript. Speaking in such a fashion allowed him to make observations in the moment that kept him relevant and yet he also stayed on track. This keynote appeared in 2014 in the Howard Law Journal, *vol. 57, no. 3.*

Thank you so much for that very gracious introduction and for that very kind birthday shout-out. To all the Scorpios in the house! Today is Drake's birthday—"Started from the bottom now I'm here." Alright.

What an honor it is to be here today, to come to this conference, named in honor of one of the great legal minds of our community and an extraordinary dean and a man who rendered service at the heights of both his talent and our community. I'm honored to be here in the presence of many of his family members and to be invited by Dean Dark, who is doing an extraordinary job here at Howard Law School. [Applause] The Reverend Dr. Barbara Arnwine is sitting up here in the front, an evangelist in the legal community. I want to thank her for her co-sponsorship of this extraordinary event here today with Dean Dark.

You know Black women are always leading the way, always leading the way. So, it's a real honor. My mentee Cadene Russell has been doing an extraordinary job over here, 2L—second-year law student—and I had two of my T and A's, cause they're teaching *and* assisting, from Georgetown last year, sister Amanda [Butler-Jones] and sister Sierra [Wallace], two of the finest from Howard Law School over at Georgetown dropping seditious science. [Laughter] They were hard on those students too. Tough! So it's an honor to have all three of them here; and so many others. I gotta give a shout-out—there are so many who are here, I hesitate to name any names—but I gotta shout-out Professor Kimberlé Williams Crenshaw [Applause]—one of the great legal minds in America, the founder of critical race theory. That's big. That's big time. You know, we celebrate LeBron James, for those who do, [laughter] we celebrate Michael Jordan, for those who do, or the greatest player of all time, Kobe Bryant. [Laughter] Stop hating. But we need to celebrate cerebral giants who found entire fields, who create paths, and who open up vistas of possibility. I want Professor Kim to stand up again. I know you all have seen her already; I want her to stand up again, way in the back. [Applause]

And speaking of women leading the way, the great Susan Taylor is in the house today. And as you know, Susan Taylor, the Queen of Black America, a remarkable, iconic figure, a woman of tremendous devotion to our community, is now leading the CARES Mentoring Movement, which is attempting to mentor more than a million young people in our community and to call upon responsible adults to do so. So, before she leaves out, if ya'll get a chance and you want to sign up and help out with that tremendous program—because white women are the first to respond, white men are the second to respond, then Black women, then Black men. So we can't be talking about kids if we ain't going to help them. We can't point *at* them without pointing the way. So she is here along with her partner, beloved husband Khephra Burns, one of the great writers, poets, playwrights, raconteurs, smooth dressers [laughter], smooth criminals, and a remarkable human being, one of the smartest men on earth. I want both of them to stand up so you can see them: Khephra Burns and Susan Taylor. [Applause]

I'mma go on but I'm a Baptist preacher [laughter], so I gotta do a little introduction. I saw one of the great orators, arguably, arguably the greatest orator of our generation, who fuses spiritual acumen and political commitment along with ethical and moral enlightenment, and does it with such beautiful and powerful prose, the Reverend Dr. Frederick Douglas Haynes III is in this house from Dallas, Texas. Stand up, Dr. Haynes. [Applause] What's up, Doc? We'd be like a jazz session, let him come up here and spit a little bit. Y'all wouldn't mind that would you? At the end, when I'm flunking, I want him to come on up here and say a few words. He's a tremendous and brilliant young man.

Now, today what I want to do is talk about—as Dean Dark's excellent leadership and the phrasing of Attorney Arnwine and this great school [says]—"Critical Race Theory in Action: Civil Rights Law at This Critical Juncture," [about] the crisis that we are enduring as a community, and especially among you, a community of lawyers. I haven't been among this many lawyers since I was in trouble. [Laughter] And when I think about the extraordinary responsibilities that lay before you—look at the cover of the *New York Times* today. Something about the healthcare law above the fold on the right side; the NSA stuff above the fold on the left side; and immigration law, ruled on by the highest court, with Haitian immigrants, in the Dominican Republic. All three of those are relevant to what you do. All three of those point to the extraordinary relevance of your particular commission as lawyers, as legal minds, as jurists, as activists within the law. And we know that other communities have the leisure of believing in the essential divorce between jurisprudential rationality on the one hand, where they can talk about legal principles that transcend their mark in space and time, and on the other hand, a kind of activism that is relegated to the periphery because that is seen to somehow besmirch the integrity of the law, which is neutral to the contaminating influences that surround it. But y'all know better than that.

I mentioned Professor Kimberlé Crenshaw because [of], among other things, what critical race theory invites us to understand: her notion of intersectionality, that the simultaneous convergence of conflicting forces that specify the degree to which we are both indebted to a more complicated and nuanced analysis of the problems that prevail, and how our lives are lived at those dangerous but productive intersections. And then to understand that ain't nobody sees—as the philosopher Leibniz calls it, *sub specie aeternitatis*—from the gaze of God. There's a bunch of Latin words flowing around in legal theory. A lot of that stuff has to do with our indebtedness to an Enlightenment rationality that predicates reason upon its neutrality and its inability to intervene except in specifically objective fashion. But the reality is the very shaping of the categories that are referred to owe a debt to the historical context and the radical contingency of the very notions that we produce. In other words, all of this argument [is] about philosophy being part of a conversation, about theory being part of a conversation, and the conversation is indebted to the life worlds of the very people to which it refers.

We have always understood from the very beginning—the best traditions of law in our community have always understood—that the law should be used as a weapon for those who are vulnerable, and those who are the weak, and those who underrepresented. And so y'all ain't becoming lawyers just to make mad cheddar. Cheddar can be had and should be made. Nice houses, nice cars, and sparkling reputations and living high on the hog—that's all good but that's not your ultimate purpose. Your ultimate purpose is to fulfill the great tradition of the Howard Law School. We talk about Dean Wiley Branton. We talk about Dean Okianer Christian Dark. We talk about Dean Kurt Schmoke. We can talk about Dean Charles Hamilton Houston. We speak about Thurgood Marshall and Constance Baker Motley. There are so many people who emerge from these halls where you sit, where you study, where you learn, so that the application of what you study is so incredibly important to our community.

There are many young people trying to figure out what they're going to do. "Is what I do relevant? Studying polymers or studying theoretical math or trying to figure out the application of some principle of thermodynamics, or some principle of physics; can this have particular material consequence on our people's lives?" Well, y'all working in a field where it's pretty obvious what you do is so relevant to the condition of our community, and especially now.

It's interesting; we got two Black lawyers in the White House, as president and first lady, right? Now we had Bill and Hillary—two lawyers, Yale lawyers, then they upgraded. [Laughter] I mean we ain't going to give Cambridge that much love but y'know [Laughter], since a brother and sister went there.

Now, we've got two lawyers in the White House, and so among other things, what's critical about that is that supposedly, ostensibly, they bring to bear a critical form of analysis—a way of thinking. [President] Obama, as a constitutional lawyer—people have challenged him in terms of the application of that constitutional law pedigree. Because it's one thing to be theoretical about it, another thing when you get up in the spot, and you are now the subject of a lot of analysis about how the Constitution can be rejiggered to conform to the anatomy of your present desire. So now, that constitutional law background becomes quite significant because the president himself, as a constitutional lawyer, is keenly aware of the contradictions and conflicts between the embodiment of his office and the theoretical ascription of power to that particular office.

Now, all of this is a matter of introduction to get down to my major points. [Laughter] So, I just wanted to clear a little bit of intellectual landing so we can get into some specific stuff, or as the brothers say, "'pecific" stuff, or is that Pacific stuff, as opposed to Atlantic stuff? [Laughter] And so, when we think about it more broadly, your particular vocation is critical, because as a nation of laws, as a nation that says it's governed by rules that are predicated upon the finest legal representation, and the articulation of objective principles, lawyers must adjudicate between competing claims—and estimations of truth. And so you're taught in law school like they ain't taught in other places—about how to think, and about logical processes, and about deductive and inductive reasoning, about the application of legal principles, and it ain't necessarily got nothing to do with what's right or wrong, it's gotta do with what you can prove in a court of law. That's why the few victories we end up getting, we get real excited about, especially when the tables get turned and now folk on the outside feel what we been feeling on the inside for a long time—like what happened with O.J. I don't want to go old school, and I'm not trying to make O.J. a hero. The general rule of thumb is, if you get away with murder, go somewhere and be quiet. [Laughter] I ain't naming no names, I'm just saying, that's a general principle.

But people now are mad, they want to change the law, "the law is messed up, the law is jacked up"—the law was jacked up when it was applied to us too. In the same way, it never was about whether you're right or wrong or what's moral, it's about what can be proved—evidentiary hearings, disparate treatment and effects, all these big old terms y'all be slinging around like crack dealers. [Laughter] And so now, when applied to us, when we use the law in defense of our vulnerable humanity, it is a highly charged arena because the nation's major lawyer is under assault, besides the two lawyers in the White House. They jumping on Eric Holder like he done stole something from them. Done got $14 billion from Goldman Sachs or JPMorgan, one of them big companies with a lot of money, and at the same time trying to protect the Voting Rights Act—"Oh you deny us on [Section] number four, we hook up number two." Black people play the numbers. [Laughter] But thank God he's there, because if he wasn't there, what would happen to us? What would happen when, immediately, everybody from Mississippi, Texas, North Carolina, waiting to apply that law [to us], put out voter ID laws to try to rob us and deprive us of our freedom? All I'm saying in this introductory part here is what you do is important. Now, let me get to the main part. I ain't gon' take but two hours, and we'll be out of here. [Laughter]

Let me say this: the ongoing Civil Rights Movement is at a critical juncture. Why? Because what we thought was sacred, what we thought was permanent, what we thought was inviolable—and some elements of our rights are certainly inviolable—is also vulnerable to rebuff because a Supreme Court can make a decision about the application of that law in ways that we find problematic—consternating to be exact. So now, the very success of the Civil Rights Movement, which produced the law which protected the people who were victimized formerly, is used to prove why it no longer is necessary. When, from the very beginning, if the universal principles that are, if you will, the proxy for enlightenment rationality in America were working, if you had universality and it was already working, you wouldn't need the specific and the particular. The Civil Rights Movement is a judgment against an offensive notion of universality because [if] it was already evident that it was true and powerful and necessary, the Civil Rights Movement would not be necessary. The reason there was a Civil Rights Movement is because it was already attacking this spurious, mythical notion of objectivity and universality. It ain't universal; it ain't objective. It is created for particular communities to defend themselves by appealing to principles that, when charged and challenged and scrutinized, can be put forth as the basis for messing folk up, in bigoted fashion, without looking like it. Now, that ain't exactly legal rationality I just gave you there, but that's what be happening. [Laughter]

And so, when I think about Civil Rights right now, the relationship between Civil Rights law and Civil Rights activity was at one point seen as necessarily parallel in our culture. Now, we know there was tension. There was Tupac versus Biggie tension between Thurgood Marshall and Martin Luther King, Jr. You know Thurgood Marshall thought you should be in the courts—you should be out there (and thank God he was) arguing the case, using Kenneth Clark or whoever, whatever psychologist was necessary in order to justify what was going on in *Brown versus [Board of Education]* in the mid-50s. He understood the necessity for legal reasoning. Martin Luther King, Jr., said direct action is critical as well because direct action led to a change in behavior, custom, convention and tradition, and the transformative possibility of Dr. King's movement forced the courts to take, if you will, cognizance of what was going on in the streets, and to challenge the law as the legal architecture of American bigotry.

And so, you've got to understand that philosophical argument in order to understand the parallel track that the Civil Rights Movement was on, on the one hand, and [what] Civil Rights law was doing on the other hand. They were parallel movements; without one, the other would never make sense. Martin Luther King, Jr., fought to change the law. The March on Washington was about policy and about law—Civil Rights Act, Voting Rights Bill, and after his death, the Fair Housing Act of 1968. This enshrined in American society a profound reorientation of this culture, toward a different way of thinking, legally, and in terms of public policy, about the future of Black folk.

When I think about this being a critical juncture now, I think about the fact that we need more lawyers who are willing to stand up and understand that their legal education becomes a vehicle for us to make arguments on behalf of vulnerable people. Not only in terms of making arguments against those who would try to rob us of our freedoms with these spurious ID laws. Eric Holder is already suing folk. Left and right. Why? Because he's not going to be intimidated by the Supreme Court which made a *judgment* about the necessity of the Civil Rights law being expired because the South was no longer as bigoted and racist and fanatic as it once was. Where you livin' dude? [Laughter]

Now we know that our civil rights obligations are not exhausted by the vitality of the Black voterate, which is part of the argument that was ironically being used: the fact that so many Black people were voting, that Black people were voting in disproportionate numbers to white folk, [the Supreme Court] was saying, "Obviously there ain't no problem, 'cause y'all gettin' out there and votin'." So now, the very success of our movement, despite the limitations, is used against us to try to justify snatching away what we already got. And we need y'all to be on the front line using them Latin words in defense of Negro people. [Laughter] We need you on the front line, preparing briefs like you just sent out, in defense of African American and Latino and other native, and First Nation, and Indigenous people. We need you on the front line talking about what happens with people who are immigrants. We need you on the front lines, as you're talking about in your conference here, with environmental justice. We need you making arguments that are crisp and clear, that are compelling, that articulate a [persuasive] viewpoint, that challenge the specious objectivity and transcendence of this so-called Enlightenment tradition, 'cause you understand from the get go—Black people's power and Black people's passion was a driving force for our own agency, but the oppression we endured was a measure of the failure of the dominant society to recognize us as human beings.

Wasn't it the Supreme Court that said we ain't got no rights that white folk are bound to respect? That's the law of the land. So when these crazy politicians out here talkin' 'bout "Obamacare is like slavery"—"Slow down Mase, you're killin' 'em." [Laughter] "Whatchu talkin' 'bout Willis?" Fugitive Slave Act is parallel to Obamacare? You know, isn't it interesting, isn't it ironic, isn't it crazy that the dominant American society fails to recognize our plight and predicament as vulnerable citizens in the United States of America? And so they will use the very appeal to slavery—by the way, the people they come from wasn't checkin' for us when slavery was here, wasn't checkin' for us when Jim Crow did reign, wasn't checkin' for us when the Supreme Court was mauling and mugging our humanity—[and] see it as a litmus test for the vitality and the humanity they possess, when they stood tooth and nail against [our humanity] from the very beginning.

Now these kinds of arguments don't necessarily make it out to the broader public. Here you got to do deep thinking. You gotta put your thinking caps on. You got to be willing to stay up late at night and pore over, you know, judgments that have been made and rendered. This is not an easy thing you do. This demands the most rigorous form of logic. This demands the most powerful form of thinking. This demands counterintuitive knowledge and in order to do that you got to study *hard*. And so civil rights in terms of the parallel between the Civil Rights *Movement* and Civil Rights *law* was powerful. Yes, there was tension, but there was also cooperation. Because what these men and women understood ultimately was that we will never make any serious progress unless we can protect it in court and pursue it in policy in society. What we need you to do is to continue to make those arguments.

Yes, we know affirmative action is next after the Voting Rights Act. Now folk goin' 'round making the arguments about affirmative action, feeling all superior, askin' you how you got that job and how you got up into Howard and how you got into Howard Law School and how you went to them schools you went to and got the jobs you [got, with them] *assuming* that you are somehow inferior. Now that's a hell of a jump in logic right there, 'cause half the folk askin' you questions, ain't really got no ground to be standing on to begin with. It's like those poll taxes and those literacy tests. Half the white folk administering literacy tests couldn't pass them. Ain't that something? The ignorance was so deep and lethal, the bigotry so profound and poisonous that they didn't understand the degree to which they had more in common with the Negroes they were trying to lambaste than the white supremacists of elite standing who used them as pawns in their broader game.

And so, the reality is when we think about Civil Rights law and when we think about affirmative action—affirmative action don't mean hookin' nobody up that don't deserve to get it. Affirmative action means what? When you've got two people of comparable standing appealing for a particular position, competing for a particular slot, the nod goes to the person of color, or the woman, or the other minority who has been historically underrepresented in the mainstream institutions of America. Now that don't sound like to me you getting the hook up 'cause you Black. That sound like to me: We been out here doin' the darn thing for a minute and now because of the creative edge we've been able to leverage as a result of our historically recognized minority status, we get a nod because the society itself has deprived us of the benefit of participation and the society has deprived itself of the benefit of our knowledge.

Affirmative action ain't just for us; it's for them too. If a society that doesn't want Michael Jordan playing basketball, or John Coltrane blowing his sax, or Toni Morrison writing—when Toni Morrison writes, or Coltrane blows, or Satchmo plays his trumpet, or when Jordan, or Kobe, or LeBron or whoever does their thing, that's not a way of compensating for intellectually inferior people, that's a way of expanding the boundaries of your society so you will be blessed by Black genius. So, now they say, "Well all y'all ain't geniuses." All of y'all tryin' to keep us out ain't geniuses. I know, I teach your kids! Now all my kids [I teach] are smart, but I'm just sayin'.

So what happens is: affirmative action is critical because it becomes a means toward radical justice. Diversity on its own is not a good merit; but diversity as a means toward an end is a radical measure. See you could have a Black person, an Asian person, a Native American person who are all homophobic. That's diversity, but inequality. Y'all are just diversifying your bigotry. We all agree, gay people should step off. So you go to your church, and your church is Black, your church is white, your church is red, your church is brown, your church is yellow. Y'all all agree gay people should mean nothing, have no [. . .] moral standing in our community. That's diversity toward inequality. But real equality demands diversity become a vehicle toward the realization of a broader goal, and that broader goal is about the transformation of our vision about who is a human being.

That's why the beauty of Civil Rights law teaches us we shouldn't be tryin' to hate on nobody. You know I know a bunch of Black preachers was mad when Obama came out for gay marriage. Like we really believed Obama wasn't for gay marriage from the get-go: [in Obama voice] "The Lord has spoken to me." [Laughter] Jesus's name was Joe Biden. [Laughter] That's the Blackest thing in the White House right there. [Laughter] So Joe Biden got up, [in Biden voice] "Hell yeah, I think it's good!" [Laughter] Obama's like, "Damn! This dude keeps trying to out me as a Black man." [Laughter] So Obama has to go on with Robin Roberts—signifying, subtly, and confesses [Obama voice], "I've had a change of mind. I've evolved in my thinking." And now all of a sudden, gay people are good for marriage.

And, the thing is, y'all, all these Black preachers messed up. Now, the Black preachers don't speak out over incarceration. Black preachers ain't speaking out in terms of one out of two Black boys being kicked out of school. Black preachers ain't speaking out when it comes to fundamental injustice and disparity between suburban schools and urban schools. But, the Black preachers gon' speak out on some gay marriage. Now even in terms of empirical verification of the numbers, that's just the wrongheaded methodology, 'cause you got more folk who gonna be kicked out of school, more folk who in prison, more folk who are subject to all those other forms of vicious mistreatment and bigotry than gay marriage. You ain't even marrying nobody who's gay or [lesbian] hardly in your church. You don't even know no gay people who want to get married. Now they're there, you've just suppressed them through the rigorous identification with an evangelical piety that's beat up on people. You're supposed to be worshipping a God that frees you up [but] your religion is reproducing the pathology of bigotry. [Applause]

So, you got all these gays, right? I mean all these gay and lesbian people in the church. Everybody know they gay. [Laughter] It ain't a secret. And I don't want to get into, you know, what James Baldwin terms the "burden of representation," about the symbolic articulation of *différance* and otherness. You know. Going to the choir. [Laughter] After you done preached a homophobic sermon and the choir director gotta get up. [Gestures for people to stand up.] [Laughter] Get that extra swag on. [Gestures as if conducting a choir.] [Laughter] You know. Everybody know. But what everybody don't know: some of them people preaching them sermons gay too. I ain't never been to a Black church that turned down gay tithes. So the hypocrisy of the movement is that it refuses to be thorough and committed to its own principles because it compromises constantly with its own bigotry.

My point more broadly is this: We get outraged about gay and lesbian people, but legally we shouldn't be mad at nobody trying to claim their rights. And Negroes get real proprietary when it comes [to comparing civil rights to gay rights]: "That's our movement. We own it. We don't own much but we own the Civil Rights Movement, Incorporated." [Laughter] Then you start looking back at it. King was borrowing it from a brown dude in India. I don't know, he didn't pay no royalties. Legal principles themselves that are borrowed from more ancient European, and for that matter even African, societies. So, really, all of us are sweetly promiscuous when it comes to sharing principles and knowledge. How we gon' own something? Why would we be upset that gay people get inspired by Black people? Because people can be both Black and gay at the same time. [Applause] "At the same damn time." [Laughter] And so, what's interesting is that Civil Rights law now puts us in the odd position of working against the intuitive and bigoted beliefs of conservative communities of color while we're trying to open up space for the permission of "whosoever will," that we claim to be the basis of our religion. So, my point is, your law should cut against the bigotry of your religion. The law in terms of civil rights, not only in terms of voting rights, but in terms of people's ability to marry who they want. And Black folk shouldn't be complaining about nobody when it comes to getting married. Our numbers are low; we gotta raise them up. So [. . .] count all the gay people. [Laughter] And if roaches and rats want to get married, if they're in our houses, we should count them, too.

The point is, how we gonna be talking about the health of the Black family and turn around and hate on the health of the Black family because it doesn't conform to a narrow conception? Now that's your *moral* problem, but your legal rationality, your jurisprudence, ought to be driven by a consideration of the integrity of the "other," and the basis of your identification with them should not be the faith you possess, but ultimately, your understanding that in a secular society no matter what your religion, no matter what your tradition, no matter what your sexual orientation, no matter what your faith tradition, no matter what your ethnicity, you are a human being who is a subject of the state. You should be protected by every law that can be mustered, and every logic that has been generated, and a place like Howard should be used and deployed to defend those folks. That's what you should do. [Applause]

A couple more things and I'm done. But the nitty-gritty of it, of course, is that your generation, which has been much maligned, talked about, beat up on [a timecard is held up]—my time is limited. [Laughter] But in your generation, which has been beat up on and which has been downplayed, talked about because y'all into social media, well, social media becomes an interesting arena [for sure,] not only to contest intellectual property, and to figure out legal bases in terms of ownership, but it also becomes a way of disseminating a message and getting information and coordinating a movement that can jump-start an entire people into a way of conscience that is necessary in 2013. In other words, a lot of good stuff happens on social media besides TMZ showing Kanye and Kim Kardashian. There's a lot of other good stuff going on there. Even though I don't want to diss watching "Bossip," "World Star Hip Hop," or whatever [else there] is.

All of that is good, but what's greater is to figure out ways in which your generation connects with each other, forges connections that are about liberation, about freeing people from their narrow constraints and about understanding the relationship between older and younger generations. The beauty of that, of course, is that in that social media space you begin to not only organize, you begin to share information, you begin to dig up archives that used to take us a long time to [get by] going to the library; and then step up and use that information, all the knowledge at your fingertips. I don't want to get down to a Nicki Minaj ethic, but "Google me B%#@h" and check it out. [Laughter] But be careful about everything that you Google because everything you Google ain't got good information. So you still gotta use some old shoe leather and you gotta stay up late at night and read them books and understand what's going on. But you gotta combine the social media impetus of your generation with a good old-fashioned appreciation for [the] strategic advantages of deep thought.

And then finally, let me say this. I'm so proud of all of you for choosing to devote your life to this critical moment in civil rights, when immigrants are being dissed, people deploying xenophobic narratives talking about "our land versus their land." And it's interesting to see these conservative Black people join in this jingoistic, xenophobic narrative, when you have been owned, when you have been bought, when you have been sold and distributed—now talking about "us versus them." This Manichean distinction; you've got to get rid of that. Folk getting mad: "Them immigrants taking our jobs." First of all, you ain't even have them jobs. [Laughter] You was not working—not "were," but "was"—them jobs. You weren't competing with José to get up at 4:30 in the morning, to get on a truck, that was not your "stilo." [Applause] "Negro, I'm not doing that. Been there done that." I understand that. But we shouldn't be mad at José. We should be mad at American monopoly capitalism and global crises of capitalism that exploit Indigenous people the world over, that fail to pay them a good wage.

And so, that critical juncture of Civil Rights law suggests that you expand the horizon of opportunity for those who have been historically excluded. Now that doesn't mean we're ignorant. We know that many Latino immigrants come to this country with deep and profound racial bias because Blackness is demonized the world over. Even within Latino communities, darker is worse, lighter is preferred. There's a difference between being a white Cuban from Miami than a Black Dominican from Washington Heights. There's a big difference. If Elián González had been from Santiago de Cuba as opposed to Habana de Cuba, they would have "gave" him a Snickers bar and told him to take his Black ass home. [Laughter] So we know when we go to Cuba, when we go to Brazil, and we see the gradations predicated upon light versus dark, we know we are in the face of a pathology so deep and persistent that it is resistive to even our most sophisticated analysis, because at base we have a deep down, deeply ingrained revulsion to *Blackness*. So what you and I must do is to continue to fight against that, even as we deploy our legal education against some of the greatest forces of oppression in the modern world.

And then finally in terms [. . .] of what is going on with our environment. I know Dr. Bullard is here, and others. You know when Hurricane Katrina hit, we saw what happened. Black people and people of color are still the most vulnerable. They say, "Well the storm didn't have no color involved; storms don't segregate." That may be true. It may not be segregated in intent, but it sure is in terms of its consequence. If you live higher, you're usually richer and whiter. If you live lower, you're usually darker and poorer. That means already it's pre-determined that those who are most vulnerable to natural disaster are the folk who are subjects of unnatural disasters in our political economy. Those who are in prison, those who get poor healthcare, those who are on the margins of society, those who don't get good education, those who don't do well in school, those who drop out early, all of those people happened to be victimized by the same forces of an environmental disaster that we continue to see perpetuated even now.

And so, in your day and age, as I end my little speech, I would say this to you. We have a real smart guy, who's a Black lawyer, in the White House. Our people looked forward to his coming a long time. Now we know it's been a lot more complicated than we thought. And Black folk [are] divided. On the one hand you got some people who are very critical, some to the point of hate. Criticism is not hate, but there is hate. Haters hate. [Laughter]

But there is legitimate criticism, too. The Obama contingent on the other hand don't wanna hear nuthin' wrong. "Don't be saying nuthin' about him. That's my man." [Laughter] Like he paying your child support right there in the spot. [Laughter] "That's my daddy." [Laughter] "That's my boo." [Laughter] I ain't mad, but I'm telling you that [for real], that ain't what lawyers do. Lawyers understand principles applied in as objective a fashion as possible. Ain't no objectivity; there is fairness, though. Fairness means I put my biases on the table and examine them as part of the process by which I examine any particular issue. But the point is we can't pretend that everything been rosy, peachy keen with a Black lawyer in the White House who's creating some awful powerful conflicts for lawyers who understand the Constitution. Let that be an object lesson to you, about [how] power tends to corrupt. And let this be an object lesson to you, stuff you think you can change is hard to change once you get in, but you must maintain some cutting edge of critique. [. . .]

[Obama should know that] you don't have to rebel in terms of the symbolic appropriation of Blackness, and the tropes and metaphors that have gone on consistently; but what you could do is create just a little space of dignified humanity in the midst that acknowledges us publicly and loves us unapologetically. Now if [Obama] can't do that with all his lawyer information, with his JD's and his law professorship, if at the end of the day he is not capable of acknowledging [ordinary Black folk]—even with the vicious, bigoted edge of America that [concludes that] everything Obama does they hate, because they have an unconscious and sometimes conscious resentment of anything Black, so that his very presence occasions such opprobrium and such hatred that they don't even know how to explain it to themselves—then we are in bad shape. When he steps up in the spot, [all] they see is an angry, hateful Black man.

And all I wanna say to you is that we protect him and love him, but at the same time we got to demand something of him. When I look back on the best lawyers in our tradition—these were rigorously engaged, arguing lawyers, but they also expected something of their community, and they expected something of their leadership. And if you are serious, not just simply asking for Obama to be responsible, you gotta be responsible, too! What do you do with your time? What do you do with your resource? What do you do with that knowledge? What do you do with that economic base you create? Some of the richest Black folk in America will be lawyers, but they will be poor of spirit if they are not committed *ultimately* to the redefinition of our people's freedoms! That's what you must do! [Applause]

And I'll end by saying this. And you gotta be there already. You gotta be thinking about that now! Already, even as 1L and 2L and 3L, you got to be laying strategy and plans about how you gonna deploy all this great information you get. Yes, it's gonna change, yes, the exact picture may alter, but you've already got to be involved in getting there! Migrating your spirit! Migrating your mind! Migrating your soul! Migrating your knowledge! You already gotta be where you're heading so when you get there, something will stand with you, and the power of your conviction will never waver! When you do that, then you live up to the great traditions of all these great lawyers who have done a marvelous and majestic job of bringing freedom and justice to our people. God bless you. [Applause]

Think About It

In the Study

34

More Than Academic

I was invited by historian, fellow Georgetown professor, and Dissent *co-editor Michael Kazin to reflect for the magazine on the topic "Intellectuals and Their America." The two other participants were* New York Times Book Review *editor Sam Tanenhaus and the social ethicist and political philosopher, and public intellectual, Jean Bethke Elshtain, who was a professor at the University of Chicago and before that at Vanderbilt. This essay appeared in Spring 2010 in* Dissent.

There may have been a day when American intellectuals had the luxury of thumbing their noses at pop culture. Magazines and journals devoted to serious reflection enjoyed healthy circulations. Weighty thinkers won notice for their big ideas rather than their tony digs or cushy university perches. And the lines between high and low culture weren't nearly as blurred as they are now. American intellectuals can still take refuge in obscure journals that thrive on abstract jargon. And they can write esoteric books and thump their chests in pride that they're pursuing lines of inquiry that are too important to be trusted to the newspaper or the daily blog. And they'd have a point, too, because such work (caricatures aside) is quite valuable, but it isn't the only kind of work that now matters for a respectable intellectual.

Depending on your view of these issues, the standards of intellectual work have either been thrown out the window or the snooty gatekeepers of knowledge have lost the battle to silence folk from whom we wouldn't otherwise hear. The old debate of access versus quality doesn't hold as much sway as before because some of the smartest thinkers have taken to cyberspace to air their views to an increasingly paperless nation. True, you've got to take the good with the bad in such a world, but at least as you pan for intellectual gold you can navigate gigabytes quicker than you can wade through papyrus. (For the record, I'm an unreconstructed Luddite when it comes to the disappearance of the traditional book. I inhale like an addict the dense odor of literacy that comes from leafing through books on library or bookstore shelves as I'm hijacked by serendipity and fix on volumes I wouldn't have known existed had it not been for the visceral pleasures of browsing.)

I assume, too, that we're way past the time when intellectuals have to apologize for listening to music that wasn't made by Europeans a couple of centuries ago or going to movies that aren't art house staples, although even that bit of snobbery was hard earned because the medium itself was doubted for its intellectual vitality by some of the nation's brightest lights and biggest mouths. But what has been grist for the scholar's mill can also churn in the nation's collective unconscious and appear on silver screens or in hip hop albums. (Can you even say album anymore in this largely post-vinyl era? And compact disc doesn't exactly solve the problem either in this age of digital downloads and streaming services.) A lot of deep thinking goes into JAY-Z's lyrics about hustling and fatherless Black homes, and Francis Ford Coppola's *Godfather* trilogy, well, at least the first two films, wrestles brilliantly with the role of respect and outlaw behavior in ethnic communities. Even the laziest intellectual and the most uninspired thinker can summon enough opportunism to exploit these artifacts of pop culture in the classroom or on television as a talking head.

If it's anywhere near true that most young folk turn to cable television and social media instead of network anchors to satisfy their news jones (and that's already a comedown for those who think they should get it only from the *New York Times*), then like Jesus and the woman at the well, you've got to meet folk at the symbolic level of their unspoken need—for the Jewish prophet's needy female protagonist, it was a water bucket standing in for her spiritual thirst; for the masses, it might be a hot book or a pop film speaking to their existential and romantic quagmires, like comedian and radio talk show host Steve Harvey's phenomenal bestseller *Act Like a Lady, Think Like a Man*, or Tyler Perry's gloriously gutbucket gospel stage play, later turned into a film, *I Can Do Bad All by Myself*. It's long since time for intellectuals to, well, get over ourselves and, as legendary Motown crooner Marvin Gaye implored, "come get to this—." And if that's not quite the Kantian *Ding an sich*, the thing in itself, it is at the very least the cultural thing in itself: a novel, a video, a song, anything that represents the good or ill of our society and what it's wrestling with at a given time as we seek to illumine the culture with our insight and analysis.

Let's not pretend that quarantining the life of the mind to the academy hasn't at times made the rest of the culture sick. Those who dare to write or speak in an accessible fashion are still too often looked at sideways by academic purists who pooh-pooh the value of scholars' opening our mouths in earshot of American society or forming our thoughts in eyesight of popular culture. It's bad enough to be deemed inferior for wanting to talk to more than a narrow cloister of academic colleagues; but if doing so makes us seem like we're putting the guild at risk or of relinquishing our duty to be above the fray, then that's downright comic, but tragically so.

I understand that the academy's self-image takes a hit when professors take to the small screen in shouting matches where we're paired up with hacks from either end of the political spectrum and end up looking like the buffoons we seek to expose. But that doesn't mean that there's not value to weighing in on important social and cultural matters in a medium where millions of eyeballs are glued. Even better to spar with literate television or radio hosts in a civil manner where ideas are taken seriously. Whether measured in sound bites or megabytes, the voices of smart folk who study one thing or another for a living are too much a treasure to be artificially restricted to the academic arena. If what we're saying or doing in the academy is to make a difference, we've got to be able to make it make sense in the world that needs our brains.

The need for bright minds and gifted pens, or cursors, is heightened in our current political climate. Crucial ideas are at stake, but so are the lives of millions who will never get the opportunity to speak for themselves about how those ideas affect them. American Empire is a big deal these days, especially as it's being played out in the mouth and mind of the nation's first Black president. What a looming paradox that begs for illumination among the masses.

For that matter, being the first Black president is a big deal too, even if that president thinks he can't say so except in passing, and even when the dominant culture has bet its bottom dollar that electing a Black president means that race is officially over. The race to get to the White House may be over (well, alright, the race started again as soon as it was over), but race itself can't be disposed of that easily, and that needs to be said among the majority (of) folk who may disagree with that proposition on behalf of the minority (of) folk who know in their guts it just ain't so.

Our era cries out now more than ever for bright Black minds to tell uncomfortable truths about race. And by the way, I do mean uncomfortable for everybody, even the Black folk who love their first Black president and don't want to offer him even legitimate criticism. That can be explained in part by Black folk not wanting in any way to look like the Tea Partyers who despise him, but which often means that they don't want to bother him with just demands for representation that any constituency that helped someone get into office have a right to claim.

The need for just such Black minds was never clearer than when, during the 2008 presidential campaign, Obama was pelted by conservatives and others as being a communist, a socialist, and a traitor to America for his refusal to wear a lapel flag pin, and honestly, for others, because of his color. That circumstance begged for historically sophisticated commentary by smart Black folk and white allies—though the allies often got a crack at explaining Black culture by proxy more than Black folk themselves got the chance, as any cursory look at the Sunday morning news shows will prove, which is often when people are even asked to speak on race.

There's a long history of Black folk loving America enough to tell the truth of how we were willing to lift the nation's flag high on foreign soil and die in its name even as we were denied our rights back home. That's the kind of critical patriotism that has been practiced by American heroes like Frederick Douglass and Martin Luther King and like Ella Baker and Fannie Lou Hamer. That's the kind of patriotism that most of us Black intellectuals have practiced, too: our willingness to criticize the nation is an index of our healthy love for America, a more noble gesture than the blind adoration of country that passes for loyalty. And that's the same kind of loyalty to social and political ideals that Black intellectuals must show in our willingness to criticize Obama, especially as he tries to wiggle free of a conversation on race that his election benefited from and can potentially spur.

Of course, race is the last thing Obama wants to discuss, because it upsets the thin ice on which he skates in the white mainstream in a kind of implicit racial bargain he struck (and here Shelby Steele is right in discussing the bargain, though I disagree about its implications): if whites won't remind him that he's Black, then he won't remind them that they're white. That's good news if you're a fan of historical amnesia and political cowardice, but it's bad news for those of us who must wrestle with the consequences of race among the masses of Black folk who'll never get to visit with, or walk in the shoes of, the most famous Black occupant of public housing in the nation's history.

Sure, a lot of Black folk aren't feeling the need to engage in such criticism, but it's an intellectual's job to point out why that needs to happen and why it's good for all of us, and ultimately, the president too. Thus, we prove at once that we're loyal to the nation in the same way we prove our loyalty to our tribe and vocation: by rigorously examining our practices and ideals in the light of our best thinking on pressing issues in service of humanity. That's more than academic; that's a matter, often, of life or death.

CHAPTER

35

The Life of the Black Mind in the Age of Digital Reproduction

I have written at length in my books about the role and responsibility of the intellectual, especially the public intellectual, in particular the Black public intellectual. I have always tried to make space for younger voices piercing the intellectual horizon. I suppose one reason I do that is because I faced such hostility and resentment from older Black thinkers and scholars as I was rising. When I told one of my mentors that I was promoted from assistant to full professor with tenure less than a year after I received my doctorate, his icy retort froze the air between us: "Well, if you want to sidestep the rules and do things differently from the rest of us, then go ahead." I was stunned. After all, he had been acclaimed early in his career and was the object of great jealousy as well. This essay grapples with the significantly different ways that scholarship and public intellectual work is carried on in the digital era. Although it was originally entitled "Think Out Loud: The Emerging Black Digital Intelligentsia," I renamed it for this book. The name of my essay now harkens back to Walter Benjamin's The Work of Art in the Age of Mechanical Reproduction, *playing off Benjamin's notion that mechanical reproduction, removed from the traditions and rituals that give art meaning in culture, robs artistic expressions of their uniqueness and value. This essay appeared in October 2015 in* The New Republic.

Twenty years ago, less than two years after I'd received my doctorate in religion from Princeton, I appeared with three other prominent African American intellectuals—Cornel West, Derrick Bell, and bell hooks—in a fold-over cover illustration for *The New Yorker* to highlight an essay about the rise of a new generation of Black public intellectuals. The image was a McDavid Henderson mixed-media collage of our portraits, with a ghostly image of Frederick Douglass, a Black intellectual from the nineteenth century, conjured just beneath Bell's chocolate visage. Those were heady times.

"A new African American intelligentsia has become part of this country's cultural landscape," wrote literary scholar Michael Berubé. "It's a development as noticeable as the ascendancy of the New York intellectuals after the Second World War."

The comparison was apt. Like the New York intellectuals, we had come to prominence as a group, our race a defining feature of identification and struggle in the same way that their Jewishness had supplied inspiration and subject matter. Many New York intellectuals were leftists searching for a Marxist and anti-Stalinist alternative to Soviet Communism; many Black public intellectuals were also leftists, who grappled with the enchanting, if insular, siege of Black Nationalism while combating the unheroic ubiquity of white supremacy.

Both cohorts were decidedly public. The social and literary criticism of such New York intellectuals as Lionel Trilling, Edmund Wilson, Philip Rahv, Alfred Kazin, Mary McCarthy, Daniel Bell, and Irving Howe were published in the pages of political journals like *Partisan Review, Dissent*, and, before its 1970s ideological migration to the right, *Commentary*. If Irving Kristol, Sidney Hook, and Norman Podhoretz later pioneered the rise of neoconservatism, Black public intellectuals, including Thomas Sowell, Walter Williams, and Shelby Steele, bypassed progressive politics and embraced the stony irreverence of its Black conservative counterpart.

Black public intellectuals had our own literary outlets: magazines and journals like *Reconstruction, Transition,* and *Emerge*, among others. We published trade books, snagged lucrative speaking gigs, and appeared on highbrow and popular radio and television shows. "Whether lecturing in churches or testifying on Capitol Hill," as Berubé put it, we had "the burden and the blessing of a constituency, a public—which is something most so-called public intellectuals can only invoke."

As with our New York predecessors, there was blowback to our ascension. Berubé's story, and a similar one later that year by Robert Boynton in *The Atlantic*, inspired a slew of contrary responses (Sam Fulwood III in the *Los Angeles Times* touted a Third Renaissance—after the Harlem Renaissance and the Civil Rights Movement—of Black scholars who were "the primary beneficiaries of the expansion of education and equal opportunity laws"), rebuttals (Michael Hanchard argued in *The Nation* that Jewish intellectuals weren't our true precursors, but Black thinkers who argued "over various crises within Black communities in New York during the 1930s, '40s, and '50s"), and, of course, nasty disputes. In the *Village Voice*, Adolph Reed dissed nearly every Black intellectual cited in Berubé's essay, arguing that while "Baldwin and Ellison bristled at the Black Voice designation, today's public intellectuals accept it gladly," out of a meek, if convoluted, sense of Uncle Tomism. "Maintaining credibility with their real, white audience requires that they be authentically Black, that their reports on the heart of darkness ring with verisimilitude." Besides excoriating us for interpreting Black life for white America, Reed accused us of lathering each other with praise: "[Henry Louis] Gates, West, and [Robin] Kelley lavish world-historical superlatives on Dyson, who, naturally enough, expresses comparable judgments about them." (Ironically, Reed's accusations of lost academic rigor, celebrity-mongering, and trading one's intellectual integrity for cameras, book deals, and assorted commercial seductions echoed in my public contretemps with West published in *The New Republic* earlier this year.)

Despite the similarities, there were crucial differences between the New York and Black public intellectuals. For the most part, the New Yorkers were journalists and critics who wrote and thought outside of academia. We were nearly all scholars from the start, the first generation of Black thinkers to gain broad access to the Ivy League and other elite institutions of higher education. Jewish intellectuals had been excluded from most elite colleges and universities until the late 1930s. Lionel Trilling became Columbia University's first tenured Jewish professor in 1939. Jews faced quotas because of deeply rooted prejudice—and because of the profound fear of the Jewish intellect. Jews were savaged by anti-Semitic tropes of greed and the lust for commercial control, and yet they were also viewed as bookish people who valued literacy and what Hannah Arendt famously called "the life of the mind." The stereotypes used to define us were less flattering: Black people were uninterested in ideas and addicted to ignorance. Our public performance of intelligence—in the media and in lecture halls and political forums—contradicted entrenched stereotypes of Black stupidity. Paradoxically, our success gave rise to furious criticisms of sullied academic standards—affirmative action as devolution—and compromise of the scholarly craft.

Perhaps the most difficult notion for the mainstream to reckon with was that our generation of Black intellectuals was not just racially representative but representative of the wider American intellectual enterprise. And when erudite and persuasive Black public intellectuals began to hold forth on race, politics, and culture on *Charlie Rose*, or *All Things Considered*, or the opinion pages of *The New York Times*, or before a U.S. Senate Committee on "gangsta rap," we did far more than shatter the myth of Black intellectual inferiority. We proved that, as with basketball and music, the dominant American thinkers were Black. Which brings us to the present.

* * *

We are entangled, yet again, in fratricidal feuds and internecine squabbles over who and what a Black public intellectual should be and do. In 2013 Princeton professor Eddie Glaude argued in a digital forum for The New York Times that Black intellectuals ought "to be the moral conscience of their societies: that what we write, say and do should reflect intelligent efforts to provide a critical account of who we take ourselves to be as a nation." According to him, Black intellectuals had failed in their responsibilities in this regard, to their communities and to a democracy undercut by race. We had in fact reached a "new nadir" for critical thought, one in which too many Black intellectuals—those, he claims, who "can spin a phrase and offer a soundbite"—have "either become cheerleaders for President Obama or self-serving pundits" instead of doing the "hard work of thinking carefully in public about the crisis facing Black America." Glaude argued that too many Black intellectuals had sold their souls "while the misery in Black America deepens." He liked his own prospects for not selling out and heeding the suffering of the Black masses: "Those of us committed to the work of thinking carefully in public with others must model the value of seriousness amid the white noise of our current media landscape." How? By tapping their social networks to do critical thinking and recommitting themselves to reading and writing and cultivating the "habit of public intellectual work" and offering interpretations of democratic failures and possibilities.

Glaude's dismal assessment of Black intellectual failure was striking to me for many reasons, but none more so than this: The sort of work he had called for was in fact being done, by many people, in many places, with great diligence and care. It just wasn't being done by people like him or, to an extent, like me. A new generation had come onto the scene, with pedigrees that didn't include terminal degrees, but who were driving the conversation nonetheless. Between the World and Me, which currently holds the second spot on the Times' non-fiction bestseller list, was written not by a professor but a young Black thinker who did not graduate from college: Ta-Nehisi Coates. He has seared America's conscience by eloquently insisting that the Black body be spared the myriad terrors that stalk its flesh and form its fate. Coates established his reputation as a first-rate thinker outside the academy, honing his craft not in scholarly publications but through popular blog posts and articles for The Atlantic magazine.

Along with Coates, a cohort of what I would like to call the "Black digital intelligentsia" has emerged. These post-analog Black intellectuals wrestle with ideas in a Digital Age, stake out political territory during our current crises, and *lead*, very much in the same way that my generation did, only without needing, or necessarily wanting, a home in the Ivy League—and by making their name online. They include, to name only a few, Jamelle Bouie at Slate.com, Jamil Smith at *The New Republic*'s magazine and web site, Nikole Hannah-Jones at Politico.com and the *New York Times Magazine*, and Jamilah Lemieux at *Ebony*. There is also Joy Reid, a formidable intellectual and journalist who formerly hosted a show on MSNBC, was formerly editor in chief of the online Black news magazine thegrio.com, and is author of the book *Fracture: Barack Obama, the Clintons, and the Racial Divide*. These figures are all brilliant, eloquent, deeply learned writers and thinkers grappling with important ideas in the digital public square, television or wherever they can.

Academics haven't disappeared, of course, as many of them are trained in the nation's graduate schools where they earn doctoral degrees in disciplines like American Studies and political science. Their influence, however, isn't exclusively dependent on validation at the university level. These Black digital intelligentsia reach beyond the academy as they forge a scholarly presence on podcasts, blog posts, social media, and television shows. Among this number I would also include brilliant thinkers like Marc Lamont Hill, James Braxton Peterson, Tracy Sharpley-Whiting, Brittney Cooper, Jelani Cobb, and Melissa Harris-Perry.

This mixture of scholars and thinkers outside the academy is nothing new. For every Black scholar like the sociologist E. Franklin Frazier, author of *Black Bourgeoisie*, and historian John Hope Franklin, who wrote *From Slavery to Freedom*, there were Zora Neale Hurston, Ralph Ellison and James Baldwin. For every sociologist like St. Clair Drake, there was an independent thinker like Horace Cayton, who teamed with Drake to write the classic *Black Metropolis: A Study of Negro Life in a Northern City*. For every Michele Wallace and bell hooks in the academy, there were Carol Cooper and Jill Nelson outside it (although Nelson temporarily took up residence at the City College of New York, a not unfamiliar path for other thinkers, like Margo Jefferson). And for every Gerald Early, Kimberlé Williams Crenshaw and Patricia Williams in academe, there were Stanley Crouch, Nelson George and Greg Tate in the trenches.

Yet today's Black digital intelligentsia, both academic and otherwise, has found greater communion with its own members than earlier generations did, in large part, I believe, due to the impact of technology, especially the internet. Popular publications like *Emerge* may have brought scholars and thinkers outside the academy together in the past, but the internet has provided far more outlets, and far greater likelihood of interaction. In the battle against police brutality, for example, activists and thinkers in the #BlackLivesMatter movement have been able to forge direct links with Black academics engaged in the intellectual resistance to the unjust use of authority by law enforcement. And a prominent Black thinker with 250,000 Twitter followers has a better chance of opening a dialogue with her favorite academic than someone who, in the past, had just sent along a letter.

Despite all the talk of the digital divide—the very real gulf that separates those with access to technology from the Black and brown folk who lack it—the Black digital intelligentsia has ingeniously used technology to extend and explore thought and fight injustice. Black folk, and particularly well-educated, elite Black folk, have taken more quickly and creatively to technology than their white peers, and turned its myriad functions to our social and professional use. "Black Twitter" may be infamous for scorning white women like Rachel Dolezal who think they are Black, but it has also pioneered the idea of hashtag activism such as #SayHerName, which highlighted the invisibility of Black women in discussions of police violence in Black communities, or #SoldarityIsForWhiteWomen, with its allusion to tensions between Black and white feminists, to offer but two examples.

The Black digital intelligentsia uses blogs, Twitter, Facebook, and podcasts in the same way that intellectuals of my generation used publications, television, and speaking engagements: to fight social injustice, to channel Black frustration with inequality, to combat white supremacy, to chastise the powers that be for their lack of principled public policies, to hold politicians accountable, to scold the disengagement of the elite, to tell as much of the truth as they can about the worlds they observe and occupy. This is perhaps the most pleasing contradiction of the internet era: It's nothing new, but it is.

* * *

In the late 1980s and throughout the 1990s, Black public intellectuals created enormous excitement in new generations of scholars by speaking on college campuses and in the media. Yet the bread and butter of these scholars, myself included, remained the academy, where we achieved highly. Cornel West and William Julius Wilson climbed to the highest rung of academe by being named university professors at Harvard, the same title

I hold at Georgetown. Henry Louis Gates, Jr., a widely celebrated public intellectual who has also become a gifted documentary filmmaker, wrote the most sophisticated work of literary criticism of his generation, *The Signifying Monkey*. Tricia Rose wrote *Black Noise*, a pioneering study of hip hop culture, while historian Robin D. G. Kelley penned the rigorous and elegant *Race Rebels*, a nuanced set of essays on the politics and culture of the Black working class. And Patricia Hill Collins published her seminal *Black Feminist Thought*.

Another cohort of Black public intellectuals came between the current one and my own. Our generation of Black public intellectuals had the good fortune through our success to assure younger scholars that they no longer had to hide, or make incidental, their interests in, and study of, the various dimensions of Black life and society. This cohort engaged the study of slavery and its various aftermaths in a far more sophisticated fashion; they tracked the sociology and ethnography of Black urban life; and they examined the literary and musical dimensions of Black cultural expression, from pioneering novels to burgeoning jazz studies. They devoted themselves to the oeuvre of directors like Spike Lee, John Singleton, and Euzhan Palcy, and to the hip hop of Public Enemy and 2Pac. This wave of Black public intellectuals included scholars like Duke University cultural critic Mark Anthony Neal, who published the groundbreaking *What the Music Said* in 1998, and Dwight McBride, whose essay collection, *Why I Hate Abercrombie & Fitch*, is a pioneering exploration of the public consequences of gay Black male identity.

They were different from us in terms of subject matter, style, and intellectual pursuits, but one thing remained the same: The book was their scholarly sine qua non, the achievement that made all other ambitions possible. Derrick Bell took a public stand for Black female professors at Harvard Law School only after the publication of his path-breaking and genre-blending book *Faces at the Bottom of the Well*. bell hooks "turned up" in the pages of *Esquire*—in both the traditional meaning, and in the contemporary slang sense of the phrase, which means to get loose and wild. But she appeared in an article "Feminist Women Who Like Sex," penned by Tad Friend, in which he coined the phrase "do-me feminism," after she wrote *Feminist Theory: From Margin to Center*. Yale Law School professor Stephen Carter went on the *Today* show to discuss the complexities of affirmative action because he had written *Reflections of an Affirmative Action Baby*. Today, though, the game done changed—in fact, quite a bit.

The book is no longer exclusively dominant in the realm of Black ideas.

The Black digital intelligentsia flourishes in an epistemic ecology in which the scholarly impulse has been sheared by the cutting edges of new technology and the desire for instant knowledge and commentary on current ideas and events. Today, legitimate thinkers take to blogs, Twitter, Facebook, and even Instagram to hash out ideas, try out theories, and explore intellectual options. The digital world serves as a forum for a kind of perpetual work in progress, or an extension, or remix, of existing work.

For example, scholar Courtney Baker, in advance of her recently published book *Humane Insight: Looking at Images of African American Suffering and Death*, published a blog post entitled "Sandra Bland's Face," at the *Los Angeles Review of Books* web channel. The post explored the competing and conflicted uses of Bland's image as the country attempted to interpret her death in a Texas jail cell—the same kind of work Baker explores in greater detail in her book. While Vincent Brown, a Harvard history professor, explores slavery and death in *The Reaper's Garden: Death and Power in the World of Atlantic Slavery*, he explores those same ideas, and others, in multiple media: He is the principal investigator and curator for the online animated thematic map "Slave Revolt in Jamaica, 1760–1761: A Cartographic Narrative," and was producer and director of research for the PBS documentary *Herskovits at the Heart of Blackness*.

Salamishah Tillet is a professor at the University of Pennsylvania and the co-founder of a nonprofit that uses art therapy to fight sexual violence against women and girls. But her reach has been extended by her online columns in *The Nation* and her regular appearances on MSNBC. And Peniel Joseph, a history professor at Tufts University and author of *Dark Days, Bright Nights: From Black Power to Barack Obama*, uses his online column at *The Root* to amplify his views on politics and current affairs. Even traditional outlets reflect the digital influence: newspaper columns and articles yield the geography of print and ink to the provenance of the internet as their offerings now come with a battalion of links to relevant articles, books, and even visual references to support the argument.

Savvy and immensely gifted Black scholars like Morehouse College professor and CNN contributor Marc Lamont Hill, and Lehigh University professor and MSNBC contributor James Braxton Peterson, also take full advantage of these cyber means to address social ills. Hill and Peterson have both published academic books. They also commented on the Ferguson uprisings: Hill in an online column for CNN, Peterson in a Reuters column that was widely circulated on the internet. Both discussed Ferguson, at length, on Twitter and on television. A noteworthy article in an academic journal, or even a popular publication, may still garner the offer to extend one's ideas in a book-length project, but nowadays the process is sped up by measures and leaps of bandwidth: Digital columns may lead to television appearances and thus more quickly to publishing or academic opportunities. Hill's trenchant commentary and television reporting on the ground in Ferguson on CNN, combined with his high profile in social media, helped him to land a book deal addressing the rebellion in Ferguson. Peterson's incisive commentary on a range of social and political issues on MSNBC, for web sites and in social media, significantly elevated his academic prominence.

Beyond the rewards of online success are the intellectual advantages of the immediacy that characterizes the digital vocabulary. The Black digital intelligentsia is able to quickly judge where an argument needs to be revised, redrawn, or withdrawn altogether; previously, in my generation, an essay's first draft may have circulated among trusted friends and no further. Now, publication online, as an essay or a tweet, permits strangers, some of whom may be terrifically skilled interpreters, to weigh in on one's scholarship. Airing ideas online offers a potential aid to refining one's argument. It doesn't replace the need to sweat over the work, but it does provide eyeballs and eardrums in ways never before available to thinkers.

More important, Black intellectuals who might not easily snag a hearing in traditional editorial circles—maybe they went to a second- or third-tier school, or didn't have access to scholars who might recommend them for plum gigs in the classroom or for publication—might, by the force of their ideas online, arouse the attention of administrators or faculty in search of new talent. Brittney Cooper, a Rutgers professor who has not yet published a book, is nonetheless a highly regarded commentator on race, culture, politics, and feminism, having made her start with her "Crunk Feminist" blog. Cooper's rise, and Hill's and Peterson's emergence, too, may have taken more time, and been more difficult, in an earlier era, but their conspicuous brilliance illustrates the benevolence of digital acclaim. They are simply being smart about showcasing what they can do in a number of venues, or to use the appropriate term, on a number of platforms.

Jelani Cobb, a professor at the University of Connecticut and the author of three books—on hip hop, Barack Obama, and a collection of essays on Black culture—has written brilliantly on contemporary Black life. This is befitting his graduate training under David Levering Lewis at Rutgers, a renowned historian and author of two Pulitzer Prize–winning biographies of W. E. B. Du Bois. Long before protests about how the movie *Straight*

Outta Compton neglected to broach the vicious misogyny of the group's DJ and producer, Dr. Dre, Cobb had done so in his 2007 essay collection, *The Devil and Dave Chappelle*. As smart and as eloquent as he has been in his books, however, Cobb is a public intellectual based on his prowess as an online columnist, and now, on the strength of those digital efforts, a staff writer for *The New Yorker*. If Coates, as has been suggested, is this generation's James Baldwin, then Cobb is surely our era's Ralph Ellison: an erudite and scholarly writer whose sentences are gracefully freighted with a profound knowledge of the range and depth of Blackness. While Ellison, Baldwin and Richard Wright published in magazines like *Harper's*, *Esquire* and *Look*, Coates and Cobb blog at *The Atlantic* and *The New Yorker*; same aspiration, same scope of interest, same literary and intellectual pedigree, just a different form.

Perhaps no scholar better embodies the Black digital intelligentsia than Melissa Harris-Perry. A professor at Wake Forest University and talk-show host on MSNBC, Harris-Perry has written two books; but she is best-known for turning the media into her classroom. She can—and did— school a Black president about his "Daddy issues" and educate America about why *Magic Mike XXL* is a feminist film. Harris-Perry possesses a formidable capacity to translate complicated subject matter into understandable language. Consider her withering deconstruction of Michelle Cottle's attack on Michelle Obama in *Politico*, which brought the historical sweep of Black female stereotypes in the public sphere to a mainstream format.

She has brought onto her show, and thus introduced to the nation, as wide and diverse a selection of scholars and intellectuals as has been collected on television before—including transgender writer Janet Mock, Australian feminist critic Chloe Angyal, historian and Schomburg Center director Khalil Gibran Muhammad, and social activist and hip hop artist Jessica Disu. What's more, Harris-Perry's show has bucked the trend of the Sunday news shows—which, in 2014, featured around 75 percent white guests—by bringing to her roundtable a majority of guests of color, a large percentage of whom, like Black University of Pennsylvania religious studies scholar Anthea Butler and University of Massachusetts anthropologist Jonathan Rosa, are fellow academics who might not otherwise receive the airtime that Harris-Perry offers.

At *The Atlantic* blog Ta-Nehisi Coates called Harris-Perry America's "foremost public intellectual," an assertion that former *Politico* journalist Dylan Byers criticized on Twitter, saying it undermined Coates's intellectual credibility. But Coates contended that her academic credentials—a

Ph.D. from Duke; her professorships; the two books, the first of which, *Barbershops, Bibles, and BET: Everyday Talk and Black Political Thought*, won awards in 2005 from the American Political Science Association and the National Conference of Black Political Scientists; having been the youngest scholar to deliver the Du Bois lectures at Harvard—showed that Harris-Perry more than deserved the recognition. "I believe Harris-Perry to be among the sharpest interlocutors of this historic era—the era of the first Black president," Coates wrote. "And none of those interlocutors communicate to a larger public, and in a more original way, than Harris-Perry."

Before the digital era, Hill, Peterson, Cooper, Cobb, and Harris-Perry would certainly have stood out. Their gifts would have distinguished them sufficiently to win a place in the academy, or in whatever venue they chose to aspire. But there is little doubt that their membership in the Black digital intelligentsia has procured for each the sort of broad cultural recognition that would not have been possible before.

* * *

Today's generation, as with my own, must always be wary of the pitfalls of public exposure, of too-quick fame, of chasing bright lights rather than doing the sort of work that is sometimes, perhaps even often, quiet, and which runs counter to the digital demands of nonstop, 24-hour connectedness. This is not a new worry. In the 1802 Wordsworth sonnet "The World Is Too Much with Us," we are warned against the gross materialism of the Industrial Revolution—"getting and spending." The Black digital intelligentsia must not cede to fluttering activity, to distracting if enticing preoccupations, however measured, in whatever bandwidth, the necessary time to develop as deeply and profoundly their scholarly gifts and intellectual abilities. By its nature, the scholarly enterprise, even the public intellectual practice that rests on it, runs counter to the logic and need of the hour, and counsels retreat and withdrawal, saying no.

To be sure, there is danger in the belief that everything—every idea, issue, conflict, disagreement, or difference of perception—can be solved, or even usefully summed up, in 140 characters, or in a posting on Facebook. There are contemporary problems that must be acknowledged. But each generation of Black thinkers has confronted intellectual challenges inherent to the age and usefully overcome them. Some things take time, and if the considered opinions of traditional journalism are the first rough draft of history, then digital journalism is the *dry run* of the first draft. There is value, and even political utility, in speedy responses to serious issues that demand thoughtful and critical reflection. But there is value, too, in pulling back for the long view over the long haul.

These two notions need not be in competition; snobbishness—or, to be fair, squeamishness—about weighing in too quickly, too lightly, ignores the challenge that short bursts of intellectual reflection present, the clarity demanded, the energy required to express a meaningful thought without lapsing into obscure erudition or alienating jargon. We pretend that online writing is easy at our own risk. Intellectuals of the digital age, Black or otherwise, must remember what all great thinkers know: The best work flourishes when discipline is geared to the task at hand.

The lesson of doing one's work well, and thoroughly, is a crucial lesson for young Black scholars, both those in graduate school and non-academics striving to find their place online. The virtues of the digital era for Black thinkers are many: the archiving of past scholarship that minimizes the time spent in excavating critical historical documents and resources; the communication with other like-minded thinkers, across disciplines, regions, and literally across the world; the vetting of ideas and the practice of intellectual habits with others who harbor similar desires; the interaction with populations that one hopes to study, creating a potentially stronger feedback research loop than might otherwise exist; and contact with inspiring role models who in earlier times may not have been nearly as accessible. While the Luddite in me still loves to serendipitously discover treasures in secondhand bookstores, to smell the decaying papyrus and browse over the cornucopia of cerebral achievement catalogued in texts hewn from trees, I have learned to be almost as excited about downloading the latest essay or blog post online from a first-rate thinker leading me through the cadences of critical reflection in the digital gymnasium of the mind.

TALK BACK

I don't believe American democracy, founded on gross inequalities—gendered, racial, class-clotted—will ever be fully democratic and inclusive. With that said, we should continue to move that project along, to as close to the finish line as possible. We have always had to drag our more recalcitrant white citizens along the road to progress kicking and screaming.

—Tracy Sharpley-Whiting

I mean we really are invisible people. And I just kind of went nuts. And I am saying, I am here now, and I am doing it now, and you are not going to ignore me.

—Hortense Spillers

have always been attracted to books of interviews. Things are said that don't normally get said in well-prepared paragraphs. Of course, the live performance of speech will inevitably be policed by the rules of grammar and the edicts of editing when preparing such occasions for publication. But enough of the pop and sass and pizzazz of thinking on one's feet can survive that process to offer the reading audience greater insight about a subject.

I find it joyful to speak to the younger generation. First, I want to know what they're reading, and I don't necessarily have to ask them that, I can overhear their literary protocol in the literature they cite. Then I want to learn how they think about what they read.

And yes, I'm eager at times to do verbal battle and rhetorical combat, to vigorously engage in rigorous discourse about matters important to millions of folks around the globe. The more controversial or uncomfortable the topic, the more likely one is to wring edifying truth from harrowing disagreement. Words are important; how we say what we say is terribly important; who we say them to, and on whose behalf, is more important still.

Tete-a-Tete

In Conversation with the Younger Generation

36

In Baldwin's Shadow

Ta-Nehisi Coates is one of America's most talented and renowned writers, delving deeply into many genres, from essays, magazine writing, and blogs, to fiction, comic books and screenplays. Although he is profoundly driven to be the best, he is never full of himself, and always willing to be self-critical in his efforts to master his craft. I had occasion to blurb his first book, a lovely memoir titled The Beautiful Struggle: A Father, Two Sons, and an Unlikely Road to Manhood. *I have known Paul Coates, his father, for decades. He is a gorgeous blast of Black manhood, a highly gifted, self-determined and proud guardian of Black literacy. The senior Coates invited me in 1997 to write an introduction, alongside Derrick Bell, for William Owens's* Black Mutiny: The Revolt on the Schooner Amistad, *one of the countless books he has reissued in his tireless effort to preserve Black literary efforts with his heroic Black Classic Press. A shorter version of this conversation appeared in* The Washington Post *in 2017.*

Michael Eric Dyson: There have been many deserved comparisons between you and James Baldwin, but do you think Baldwin could have written your latest book, *We Were Eight Years in Power*? Remember Baldwin was once quite nervous about debating Gunnar Myrdal and Sidney Hook, wondering "what in the hell [I'm] supposed to say to them in there about all this sociology and economics jazz?" But that's what you're doing in this book: all that sociology and economics jazz. Talk a bit about how this book differs from *Between the World and Me*, which was a memoir, and written in such an elegiac and profoundly literary style, and *We Were Eight Years in Power*, that has a command of the sources in a scholarly fashion.

Ta-Nehisi Coates: Well *Between the World and Me* is actually informed by a lot of stuff in [*Eight Years*]. I understand Baldwin, and even Ellison's, deep suspicion of sociology, especially at that point, the academic, overdone study of Black people—this sort of Negro-ology. I think some things have changed in the past twenty years. I think you've got a school of folks, maybe themselves who've read Baldwin and Ellison, who are more self-aware, whose gaze is a little different. So I think his apprehension about that has as much to do with time and place as it does with any intrinsic difference between the two of us. What amazed me is that if you go back and read *The Fire Next Time*—I know you know this—and any of his other essays, he has a kind of understanding that is now being borne out by a lot of the stuff in the academy. Baldwin would make these broad claims about America, which sound overheated and overstated, except when you study the history, they just prove to be true. So, I always wondered what he was basing his stuff on.

Dyson: That makes sense. You speak honestly of the aching sense of failure you felt about being a college dropout. Probably you and Kanye are among the most famous Black college dropouts who speak about it in a self-reflective fashion. You say in general that the classroom wasn't a place where you remembered lessons that were taught. So is it paradoxical that now you're studied in classrooms, not just in high schools, but in universities?

Coates: It's bizarre. I was at this thing the other day, and somebody said, "What do you say or tell the educators who are teaching your work? Do you have any thoughts on how it should be taught?" And I was like, "no." And I don't. And I mean that. I told her, "Listen, this was not a place where I was like a successful student." If it helps, I'm happy to help. If it touches kids, I'm really, really happy it touches kids. But it's bizarre. Because I think a lot of the stuff I've written is actually in reaction to failure in school. So I haven't studied it. I don't completely understand it. I don't know what happened.

Dyson: Think about all the rap stars who were failures in school: Tupac. Jay. Nas, who dropped out in the eighth grade. Those guys are probably your only peers in terms of fame, recognition and impact on the culture who went through that same process of being rejected by the institution of school. And yet that very classroom depends upon the insight and eloquence that they offer, even though initially it was not a safe space for them.

Coates: Yeah. And I think the other thing is that education does not have a monopoly on curiosity. That's just true. There is a long, long history— again, you know this—in this country of Black folks who took control of their own education and their own curiosity. That's what Frederick Douglass's story is [about]—especially the last book. To a large extent, that's also what Malcolm's autobiography is about, this kind of self-education [. . .] And there was a Black women's society, I believe in Philadelphia, in late antebellum [whose leader said] "self-education and reading are my liberation." [. . .] My dad was a high school dropout. And he always said that one of the great attractions for him to the Black Panther Party was that it was the first time he was surrounded by people that were reading. You could critique where they came out, but there was going to be a discussion, there would actually be a conversation. And that was liberating.

Dyson: Literacy was the Black Panthers' basic thrust. The quest for literacy has been the founding impulse of African culture in America from the get-go. But that fact has been obscured. Your experience as an autodidact contrasts with the surrounding ethos of education. Because everybody now says, "Get that schooling, get that degree." And of course I'm promoting that every day. But for an outlier like you who is self-trained, it's a critique of schooling as the repository for education. 'Cause everything in school ain't really educating us in a fundamental way.

Coates: No! When I was in elementary school there was an effort made by Black educators, some of whom I'm still in contact with today, to make sure that Black kids [like me] in the inner city had access [to the Gifted and Talented program]. It was the only place where I felt like these questions about curiosity were actually being asked of me, and being answered. I did it for second, maybe third and fourth grades, then my parents pulled me out because I was not doing well in my other classes. Now, I don't say that to critique my parents. They were working from a mode of rightful fear: "This ain't about curiosity, man, I'm trying to keep you from getting killed."

Dyson: There you go, man.

Coates: That's what this is.

[. . .]

Dyson: So what do you make of social media? We both know it has exponentially increased over the last ten years. It's done amazing and great things. It can allow you access to an archive in a very moment that took you and me going to the *Reader's Guide to Periodical Literature* in the library. I tell kids that 187.6 ain't the R&B station on your radio dial, dude, it's where the social science section is noted on the library card catalog. I'm sounding like a Luddite and a technophobe. But there's something to be said for using shoe leather to go to the library, and extracting that volume, and then browsing and discovering other books and saying, "Oh,

I didn't know that book was there too." Do you think social media has destroyed that kind of browsing and curiosity?

Coates: No, no.

Dyson: Or do you think it's made it more available?

Coates: No, I don't think it's done either. You can find thin, top-layer facts through the internet. Dates, what happened here, who did that. But you still gotta read to actually comprehend, to get the truth. There are always going to be people who only want to get a thin layer. That's always been the case. But if you are curious in your own right, you want to understand, you've got to do something else. I've got a son, he's seventeen, and he reads. He has all that stuff on his phone too. But he knows books.

Dyson: What's your writing process? Do you do your research and then begin to winnow it down, filter through the welter of data, look at the analyses and then you begin to write? Or are you writing all along? Do you get up in the morning, write three hours at a time and then go away? Is it writing as rhythm? How do you do it?

Coates: Usually, for the kind of pieces that are in [*Eight Years*], the first thing is research. I tend to read a lot at first. Then I tend to go talk to people based on what I've read. And then I write. I've found, especially recently, that if I have impressions I try to write them down as I go so I'm not just starting cold. But that's basically been the process. A lot of writers have a heavily structured process in terms of when they write; I could probably use one. But I don't have one. I was telling my wife, it's like cattle grazing. I need a big field of time. If you give me that field, I'll be done eventually.

Dyson: And you've got to say no to other stuff. You've got to say no, I can't do this.

Coates: I do. I do. But, you know, I find that, again, the curiosity is such that I don't have a hard time doing that. Eventually it just bugs me, man, that I haven't done X, Y and Z. And that'll be deeply, deeply compelling, such that, if anything, other commitments suffer.

Dyson: That's good. I mean, writers write and rewrite, right?

Coates: That's true.

Dyson: I was preaching yesterday in Chicago, and I was coming at Trump with both barrels blazing. Then I talked about the white ministers with lots of Black folk in their congregations who support him, like Joel Osteen and Paula White. And I said that two of our greatest writers in this generation, Ta-Nehisi Coates and Jelani Cobb, are atheists who do not believe in your God, and yet you turn to them for insight that feeds your spirit. I asked the congregation if they could actually say they've got more in common with these white ministers who support Trump, and who undercut everything they believe in, than they do with you and Cobb. And they clearly favored you and Jelani. It's interesting to me that despite your explicit renunciation of religious "myths," that you still have a kind of preacherly rhythm. I'll put it this way: there's a spiritual, if not a prophetic, cast to some of the stuff that you do. Is that also interesting to you?

Coates: Yeah, it is. Honestly. When *Between the World and Me* came out, my dad was like really afraid of what Black folks in church would make of it. I can only be me, you know what I mean? I'm happy to see that. I don't know how you grow up Black in this country and not have tremendous respect for the church, even though I was raised outside of it. You can't read and see everybody you love, and see that that was the institution that nurtured them. So even as I articulate my beliefs, I try to be really respectful. I'm happy that it's received. I often wonder what is the place where the two things cross? Am I drawing some sort of conclusion, or some sort of feeling, that folks get in church anyway, regardless of their belief in Jesus Christ as their Savior? Is there a route that they're traveling in their religion that leads to a similar place that I go, even with my lack of religion?

Dyson: That's right. Is it a more spiritual, or an intellectual, or even a moral kind of feeling? Because Baldwin is post-religious in any significant fashion, and yet Henry James and the King James Bible keep bubbling and eddying in his own language.

Coates: Yeah. He can't get away from it. Especially given how he was raised. But I wonder about that. I am inside the box, so I can't see, but I often wonder what I am saying. I think about Dr. Mable Jones, Prince Jones's mom, who is a seriously, seriously religious woman. And she read that; she knows what's in that book. And we've talked about it. And there is something in that book that sounds to her, and I guess to a lot of people, like what they hear in church. And I just don't mean the fact of politics being discussed in church. But there's something else. And I don't really have the capability to analyze that.

Dyson: Look, if you were in one of these churches that I often preach in, they'll say, "The Lord just using him. Don't worry, it don't matter what he saying."

Coates: Yeah, and that's probably exactly how they feel.

Dyson: Of course. They're like, "Honey, like the Bible says, it's better to say you ain't gonna go somewhere, and then you go, than to say you're gonna go, and don't end up going. So [Ta-Nehisi] said he ain't going to our truths, but he there." So, look, their hermeneutic is reinterpreting you in beautiful fashion, man. You're just extending their prophetic tradition. You know, in some instances it could look condescending, but it's not. It's really—

Coates: No, I don't take it that way. I don't take it that way at all. I appreciate that folks have the openness to consider it. And that's like a highlight of Black folks and Black experience that doesn't get enough credit. People often say, "Well, you're a Black atheist. Have you ever felt alienated?" I said, well, not 'cause of that. For other reasons, but no, that has not been my Black experience. Were I in a small town in Texas, like had I been raised that way, maybe I would feel different there. But that hasn't been my experience.

Dyson: Isn't that something that really flows through so much of your writing—the underestimated humanity of Black people, that you take as the starting point for your discussion? And the presumed universality of Black intelligence and humanity is the basis of our negotiation with the world.

Coates: Yeah. I try not to get in the pose of arguing for it. But, as you said, to take it as the premise, as the jumping-off point. I worry about it in my work. Toni Morrison talks about how you become trapped by saying, "Do you see me? I'm a man. I'm a woman." If I go to a university, talk to a history department, and I say something like: "White supremacy is at the root of this country, because this country would not exist without enslavement." And that's taken as a given. Well, then, people are asking higher order questions that really make you think. And I often wonder the price I pay for arguing about, frankly, lower order questions. African American Studies 101 questions. When I was [at Howard], for instance, the level of engagement was much higher when I was a student here. Much, much higher. Because basic stuff didn't have to be dealt with. But the level of education in this country, about African American history, and thus about American history, is extremely poor. It's low. And people who are paid, in media, to know this, like just have a basic [lack of knowledge]. I was looking at this article by Jonathan Chait. And he was saying "white supremacy" should only apply to people who out and out make explicit appeals to white power. I thought about that for a second. I was talking to a buddy of mine. I went back, because I wanted to reread [George] Wallace's "Segregation Now" speech. By [Chait's] definition, this is not white supremacy. This is not an explicit call for white power.

The White Citizens' Councils very much tried to differentiate themselves from the Klan. Even the doctrine of separate but equal—which says "equal," by the way—is presumably not white supremacy.

Dyson: Not on its face.

Coates: But people who are paid to do this, like, they've never been in a classroom with somebody who'd look at you like you were stupid if you said that, and then spell it out for you. It is the case that where one's privilege, one's whiteness, is in a certain way *not* a privilege. It is blindness; it's a kind of ignorance.

Dyson: It's a disadvantage.

Coates: It's a disadvantage. You can't apprehend the very country you live in. You don't understand it.

Dyson: And that's what King meant when he said, white supremacy hurts white people too. Because the very point you're making, intellectually, is that they are then deprived of a critical lens onto the landscape of their own experience. And the frightening thing is that Chait et al., who are supposed to know this, are writing books about Obama and interpreting race! And they sometimes miss the fundamental premise, which, metaphorically is this: either the cell phone is on silent, or the ringer is loud, but a signal is still being sent, and a call is still being made either way. So whether it's explicitly articulating the notion of white power and white privilege, or if it's implicitly suggesting it, radiating in that atmosphere, it's the same thing.

Coates: It's incredibly sad. I don't say that with any glee. Because I get my shit for being pessimistic. That's what makes me pessimistic.

Dyson: Of course.

Coates: When you look at folks who are in very elite positions who, as you said, are weighing in on the legacy of the first Black president, and just have a basic apprehension of American history—that is scary.

Dyson: It is frightening. When people ask me, I say my working definition of white supremacy is the conscious, or unconscious, belief in the inherent superiority of the white race and the intrinsic inferiority of Blacks and others. And the nearly limitless and creative ways that it manifests itself. What do you think the resistance to acknowledging white supremacy is about? Is it that white liberals don't want to be seen as part of a tradition that would include them—'cause ultimately King, at the end of his life, was saying, "I hate to tell y'all, but most Americans are unconscious racists." And white liberals participate in that too, not just the Ku Klux Klan.

Coates: You know what I think? I think you have to be sympathetic to people in the sense of understanding what the education system is. It's not particularly surprising. You know, Hillary Clinton in the 2016 primaries said something really stupid about Lincoln and Reconstruction. But the thing I had to remind myself of is, when she was in school, that was the working knowledge [of Lincoln]. And even when she was in college in the '60s, that was what people thought. That was the basic story that was told. It pervades, not just the classroom, but the culture. Like *Gone With the Wind* being what it is in American culture. With HBO feeling like it's okay to do a show like *Confederate*. What you see, across the board on multiple levels, is that this is an assumed belief. It took a terrorist attack in Charleston for people to take down the flag. That says there's a thick fog. You know, when you're Black, I actually think it's easier to climb out. You have such an incentive to get out. But with whiteness, you've been born into something. And you would have to be a special person, a particularly possessed person, to climb out. So I think there's that. But I think also, it must be really, really hard to confront the idea that you're in 2016, and this white supremacy stuff is not dead. That it actually explains a lot.

Dyson: It's uncomfortable, right?

Coates: We're born uncomfortable. We just got to be uncomfortable.

Dyson: From the get-go.

Coates: From the get-go. You just have to be. So there has to be a level of discomfort. You know, when people say things like "America," ultimately, you have to look at that kind of off a little bit. You just have to. That's your natural position.

Dyson: Of course. It's a default position.

Coates: Right. But these folks have to actually struggle to get there.

Dyson: You argue that, in the nineteenth century, there was a tight relationship between the soldier and notions of masculinity and citizenship. As I read, I thought, that's the real issue with Colin Kaepernick and white owners like Jerry Jones, who threatens his mostly Black players that they won't play if they bow their knees during the playing of the national anthem before the football game. What are folk like Jones defending? They ain't defending Black Lives Matter. They're not defending our ability to protest. They're defending capital, their bottom line. Trump says, "Hey, boycott the games if these guys don't bow to our demands." That suggestion undermines the dollars they make. But there's so much arrogance, ignorance, and white innocence tied up in the refusal to acknowledge that all

Kap is doing when he takes a knee is trying to protest, as gently as possible, the vicious consequences of white supremacy—and even that's an offense. What do you make of the white response to Kaepernick's protest?

Coates: I think the thing that keeps getting lost is that the original protest was not taking a knee, it was sitting down. And then, sympathetic to the idea that this might be seen as disrespectful to the American military, he goes and talks to a veteran. He says, "Okay, got it. How can I better do this?" And the veteran says to him, "Well, you could take a knee. That would not be upsetting." He says, "Okay, I'll do that." And even that's [a problem]. So there is no acceptable protest. I think that's what people need to understand. There will not be, there never has been, there is not any protest that will be acceptable.

Dyson: It's not what we do, it's who we are. Even the concession is rejected as un-American, when an American veteran defined it for him as an act of reverence.

Coates: Right.

Dyson: Finally, you were one of the very few people to call Obama to account for the harsh and judgmental way he talked about Black people.

Coates: You also, though. You also. I wasn't alone.

Dyson: Bless you. When you say that white folk have to pull themselves out of the fog, I think that's why it was especially painful to hear that kind of talk from Obama. Who knew better—at least we think. What do you make of how his speech functions in the broader discourse of respectability politics?

Coates: Here's the question I always had. I don't know that he knew better. And here's why. Like, people have asked me, "Is this a calculated thing?" I'm gonna be real here. That kind of sounds like some South Side Negroes to me.

Dyson: Of course.

Coates: It's not like I asked, where'd that come from?

Dyson: Right, right, right.

Coates: And listen, I'm not defending this. Obviously I got problems with it, right?

Dyson: You stated you did.

Coates: But the fact of the matter is, like—

Dyson: Your uncle, your aunt say such things all the time—

Coates: I mean, that's where they are.

Dyson: But the difference is, they ain't got a megaphone and they ain't got a bully pulpit.

Coates: Right. But they don't think he's wrong. In that [Cosby] piece [I wrote for *The Atlantic*], I watched Black people in the worst [conditions] actually cheer for [his attacks on the poor]. So I wonder—actually, and I never got to verify this, but given his background, given that he comes from a more hippy-ish family—whether he got that conservative aspect of looking at Black folk [in] Chicago.

Dyson: Interesting.

Coates: You know what I mean? It is not far from the South Side.

Dyson: Well, you're absolutely right. Because I tell people, you can go to any church, barber shop and hood stoop and hear that. And the difference is, of course, is that your uncle in the barber shop, or somebody in the church, ain't got millions of people around the world listening to them.

Coates: He ain't president, also. And my fault with it was like, you represent America now. You're not a Black dude, you're not Raheem on the corner. You're not even a pastor. You are a representative of the people. So it's just intolerable for you to do that.

Dyson: Yes, no question.

Coates: And besides, I disagree with the analysis; it's completely wrong as president of the United States to do that. You can't represent the author of the crime and then say, "Well, I'm going to speak like Raheem right now." No, no, no. You ain't gonna have Raheem's policies to deal with folks.

Dyson: Right. I remember I was at Oprah's house when she threw that first big fundraiser for Obama in 2007. And me, Obama and Chris Rock were huddled in a corner. And Chris Rock told us his famous story about the fight between heavyweight champ Larry Holmes and the great white hope boxer Gerry Cooney. Rock said Holmes was whipping his behind. And then, after Holmes knocked him out, the judges' cards revealed that two of them had Cooney ahead in the fight. Rock then told us that his daddy told him that you can't beat white folk—as in outpoint them in a fight—but you have to knock them out! As much as Obama loves to quote Rock, that particular message never gets cited. Instead, Obama quotes Chris Rock saying that Black folk always want credit for things they should be doing; but he never quotes Rock's relentless assault on white supremacy. I think that's what you're getting at.

Coates: It's true, it's true.

37

Race, Racism, Racists, Antiracists

Ibram X. Kendi is a brilliant thinker, a careful scholar, and an engaging conversationalist. And simply one of the nicest young men I know. Why is that important? Because the academy, including the Black academy, can be one of the most cutthroat places on earth. It teems with jealousy, is rife with ill-tempered denunciations of visible scholars and public intellectuals, and often seethes with contempt for those who manage to hit it big like Kendi did with his third book. This conversation, moderated by the ever witty and discerning NPR host Steve Inskeep, was conducted before Kendi's massive success with How to Be an Antiracist. *We dialogued in September 2017 at the National Book Festival. It was great fun.*

Steve Inskeep: Before we seek answers, gentlemen, I'd like to frame a question. When you think about the issues that you focus on, what is the question that America faces right now?

Ibram X. Kendi: First of all, I'd like to thank you all for coming to hear this conversation on race. And of course, I'd like to thank my co-panelist. And it's truly an honor to be here. The irony of this is that it's really been the same question throughout the history of the United States. I think the major question today is the same question that the United States faced in 1776 or in 1787 when the U.S. Constitution was written. And that is, why does racial inequality exist in this country? Why, in 1776, were so many Black people enslaved and so many white people free? Why is it today there are so many Black people in another type of slavery, in prison, and so many more white people are free? Why are Black people on the losing and dying end of American society and whites are on the sort of winning and living end of American society? And we've been debating this question for quite some time. And there's largely been two major answers. The first is that this inequality exists because there's something wrong and inferior about Black people. That Black people are reckless with the police, and that's why they're being shot in more cases than white people are. That Black people are more criminal-like, and that's why 40 percent of the incarcerated population in this country is Black. The other side of the equation is racial discrimination. Racial discrimination causes racial inequality. And then some Americans have argued both: that it is the case that Black people are inferior, but it's also the case that racial discrimination exists. And really, this three-way debate is the debate I chronicle in *Stamped from the Beginning*, seeking to answer this singular question.

Inskeep: I appreciate your raising that. Because you look back, even the period of the Civil War, when people were arguing about slavery. Many of the people even who argued against slavery nevertheless did not feel African Americans were equal and didn't want to give them equality. It's a complicated question then and you're saying it is now. What is the question on your mind, Michael Eric Dyson?

Michael Eric Dyson: Well, to pick up and echo Dr. Kendi's—

Inskeep: It'll be a better panel if you say he's wrong about something. [Laughter]

Dyson: We'll wait and see. [Laughter] He ain't said nothin' wrong yet. But it's an honor to be here with such a distinguished journalist and a great intellectual. You know, the question is to what degree is America prepared to go in order to preserve a myth that it knows is a lie. [Applause] That's building rhetorically on an intellectual genealogy, in both a Nietzschean and Foucauldian sense, that Professor Kendi has laid out in brief but powerful form. Because the bottom line is, what you gonna do in the face of obvious mischaracterizations of human beings and your situation? 'Cause you ain't just lying about Black folk; you gotta lie to yourself about who you are. In order to maintain Black inferiority, you gotta exaggerate white superiority. To be redundant. White superiority in terms of exaggeration. Right?

Now, the only thing I can say is that the present administration is the most irrefutable evidence of the mythology of white superiority. [Applause] And I gotta tell you, I probably owe an apology to George Bush. I was like, "The soft bigotry of low expectations, that's autobiographical, with dumb presidents doing stupid stuff. Excuse me, sir. By far, you were not the worst. The guy in office now is." So to me, Donald Trump is the easy translation for what Black folk have been trying to tell white folk and others for so long. Like, white supremacy is narcissistic. It's self-involved. It's self-aggrandizing. It is unconscious of its own privilege. And the extension of that privilege is the predicate of a kind of victimizing discourse.

It's interesting to me that bunches and bunches and googogs and googogs of white folk tell Black folk, "Stop playing the victim." How do you explain what's going on now? The white working class has been led to believe, and white people in general have been led to believe—and not just older white folk, but those in the millennial generation too—that we talk about race too much. That Black folk get too much ink. And they believe that some of the greatest victims of race are white. So, when you think about that, how in the hell did we get to that position? The victimization, the victim-mongering, the self-pitying that has collectively been articulated as the basis of American politics is rather astonishing. So, the question for me is to what degree are white people willing to commit themselves collectively to the delusion of white supremacy and understand that until we get rid of that we won't be able to shatter the real bonds that continue to manacle us? And we won't be ultimately free until we can free each other.

Inskeep: Go ahead. You can applaud if you'd like to. [Applause] This might be a good moment to mention that Michael Eric Dyson's book takes the form of a sermon. [Laughter]

Dyson: I'm gonna get that collection at the end. Don't worry about it. [Laughter]

Inskeep: So you raise the present administration. Let me mention a number of ways that people try to discuss the relationship of race to the politics of this moment. People will say President Trump is a racist. Or, he's not a bigot but the people around him are. Or he's taking advantage of race. Or, there may be racists among his supporters. Or, this is all a bunch of bunk, and why are you raising this issue so much? The guy is actually just saying things that need to be said. And when you talk to voters you hear all kinds of things from people, ranging from racial remarks to genuine economic concerns to a lot of confusion. Is the politics for this moment really all about race?

Kendi: I wrote a book about the history of racist ideas. In order to truly write this book, I had to show the ways in which race was constantly intersecting with other identities or other phenomena. So, in other words, I had to show that this book was really a history of anti-Black racist ideas or a collection of racial groups or a collection of racialized groups. And so you don't just have Black people, you have Black women, you have Black men. You have the Black core, you have Black elites, you have Black professors, right? You have many of these different groups, and each of these groups have been targeted by racist ideas. But depending on the group, chances are the idea itself sort of intersected with another type of idea. So, in other words, the idea that poor people are lazy and the idea that Black people are lazy comes together to say that Black poor people are lazier than white poor people. Does everybody sort of see the way that sort of works? Or the sexist idea that women are weak, and the racist idea that Black women are not really women intersects to create this idea of the strong Black woman, which is sort of the opposite of the idea of the pinnacle of womanhood, which is the weak white woman. I had to sort of show all of these other intersections. And so race is constantly sort of intersecting with class and with gender.

Inskeep: Is that the way you see politics now? It's race intersecting with these other issues.

Kendi: Oh, precisely. I mean, I don't think it's just Black people who are outraged by the 45th president. Black people aren't the same people who—I mean, women are outraged. Poor people are outraged. [Applause] Disabled people are outraged. Muslims are outraged. I mean, I'm looking for somebody who's not outraged. Right?

Inskeep: What do you think about people who say that [what's behind] the Trump phenomenon is economic anxiety, or unhappiness with elitism? You're rolling your eyes practically there. [Laughter] Go on.

Kendi: Well, I think some of these people are—the easiest way to understand them is sort of post-racial progressives. And what I mean by that is, they're progressive in the sense that they recognize that class or even poverty or even economic inequality is a problem. But they simultaneously want to reduce everything to economic anxiety, to income inequality. And so that's where the post-racialism comes in, because in their mind race is no longer a problem. All of these issues are issues of class.

Inskeep: Michael Eric Dyson.

Dyson: Well, the two are not diametrically opposed, are they? You can be anxious economically and racist. So is it really relevant to ask a kind of deconstruction of the psychological mendacity that is purveyed by 45? Racist is as racist does. I'm not a Freudian or neo-Jungian archetypal, analytical psychologist. Or a Carl Rogers indirect approach where I can put him on a couch and psychoanalyze him. The thing is, I ain't really interested in the existential anxieties that fuel and feed your demonization. I'm just saying the shit you doin' is racist. [Applause] That's what it is. So look, Donald Trump is proud of being name-checked in rap music. Look at the jarring juxtapositions that confuse us. A guy who's proud of the fact that rappers have name-checked him.

Inskeep: That's given as evidence he's not racist.

Dyson: That's what I'm saying. He's hanging out with Black people; he's got Black friends that come to him. What does that have to do with—this is our problem. The guy, Justin Volpe, who plunged the plunger up the anus of Abner Louima, was dating a Black woman. So? You can sleep with a Black woman and still be a racist. So you can be name-checked by Black folk and still be racist. Even a champagne company was being name-checked by [rappers] so much that they said, "Hey, we don't even want to be name-checked by them anymore." So they had to go from Cristal to Ace of Spades. But that's inside knowledge. Don't worry about it. [Laughter] So my point is that in this culture in which we live, racism is not simply bigotry, right? Howard Thurman said a bigot is a person who makes an idol of his or her commitments. Bigotry is real. But racism is also structural. It's also a set of ideas. Racist ideas—[Kendi] didn't say racist people. His book is a genealogical analysis—in the finest philosophical and historical form—of ideas that motivate people. Even people who ostensibly lay claim to being white and liberals may be subject to racist ideas. Martin Luther King, Jr., said it's not the bigot, it's not the KKK that turns me off. I see them. I know who they are. It's the white moderate who tells me to slow down who's a problem. [Applause]

So what I'm saying to you is that if you've got a president who stands up and tries to draw a functional equivalence, and a moral and ethical parallel, between neo-Nazis and fascists and white supremacists and anti-fascists and Black Lives Matter folk, you're dealing with a guy whose corrupted sensibilities are manifest, and whose inability to make a distinction between the two reveals the very racist logic that is so evident to us. So we don't want to admit the fact that here's a guy who seems pugnacious and willing to fight—but he also reinforces the pathological beliefs about race that have been the basis for what Professor Kendi has talked about in his book and what we know to be the case for interactions with Americans across the board.

And then, finally, [many] white folks say, "Look, it's just my anxiety. It's just that I'm nervous about the future." So you elect a billionaire as your president? I ain't really sure that you are that anxiety-stricken that you get in office a guy who has no understanding of what the everyday person is. Martin Luther King, Jr., is in jail, in Birmingham. And his white jailers come to him and say, "You know what, Dr. King? Segregation is right and integration is wrong." He said, "No, it's not." Then they start arguing, and he says, "How much money do you make?" And when they tell him he said, "Hell, you need to be out here marching with us." [Laughter] So this is what I began with. The white working class is now being celebrated as an ideal prism through which to view things.

First of all, they can be racist too. In fact, white working-class people tend to be a bit more egregious in the external manifestation of race, 'cause they're in direct competition with Black people over scarcer resources. Economic anxiety is the translation of racial resistance and Black animus at the level of the pocketbook. So white folk who say, "Oh yes, all people should live together" [actually] live in suburbs away from Negroes who don't have to deal with housing, who don't have to deal with their kids going to the same school. They leave the burden to white working-class people to work out the mathematics and algebra of racial conciliation.

So yeah, these are the people who don't want Black people in unions. They don't want them in pipefitter unions. They want to dominate the concrete industry. In other words, white working-class people have done some of the most vitriolic things against Black working-class and Latino working-class people. So to elevate them automatically as the kind of paragon of virtue is problematic. And then I'll end it by saying this: what trips me out even further, though, is even in the aftermath of the election, Bernie Sanders . . . joined with other people on the right, and on the left, who said, "Hey, identity politics is killing us." So in other words, concern about queer people. Gay, lesbian, transgendered, bisexual people. Concern about Black people, about women's issues.

Inskeep: Wait a minute. Is identity politics killing you, by the way?

Dyson: Yeah. It's called whiteness, the greatest identity [politics of all]. Let me tell you: It's the Keyser Söze approach. It really is. From the movie *Usual Suspects*. White folk going around talking about "Oh, my God, it's identity politics." What in the hell do you think whiteness is? Whiteness is the greatest identity politics perpetrated as a hoax upon American consciousness in history. So yes, I think identity politics are destroying us. And there were no identity politics—notice this—until Black people, brown people, people of color, Indigenous people, began to challenge the unspoken hegemony of whiteness as a universal norm. Look at what Professor Kendi did. So the idea is this. White people think that they are human. They are not white. "We are American, not white." When [white] people come along saying "Oh, why don't you stop being Black and be human, and be American?" That's because whiteness has been co-equivalent with what it means to be human, and white people don't see themselves as white. White folk got to come out the closet and be a race and an ethnicity as well. [Applause] Sorry.

Inskeep: That's okay. There's a lot to say. And there's a lot more to say. You made a reference there to the Charlottesville situation, the tragedy there around demonstrations trying to preserve a statue of Robert E. Lee. Which, last I saw on the news, has been placed under a sheet? Is that right?

Dyson: So to speak. [Laughter] So to speak.

Inskeep: I'm just leaving it right there. Well, that raises a question. The president himself raised this question, and other people have been raising this question and talking about other things they want to take down. Statues of the founding fathers. Other things. What monuments stay, if it's up to you gentlemen?

Kendi: I think, for me, let me just say that as an African American it's very difficult to live by, walk by, even work or go to school in a place named after somebody who, if they were still living, I would be enslaved. In the case of the Confederacy, I think it was crystal clear what they intended if their nation lived. I mean, the vice president of the Confederacy, Alexander Stephens, weeks after the Confederacy was founded in 1861, stated that our new government is founded upon the great truth that the Negro is not equal to the white man and that slavery as subordination to the superior race is his natural and normal condition.

And Jefferson Davis—who of course was the president of the Confederacy—my book, *Stamped from the Beginning*, is named after, when he said inequality between the Black and white races was stamped from the beginning. So it's clear and obvious what these Confederate leaders stood for. But we should also remember that these Confederate leaders were inspired by American leaders. Jefferson Davis was named after Thomas Jefferson. His father specifically named him after Thomas Jefferson because he admired Thomas Jefferson. And so [there are] all of these ideological relationships between the Confederacy and the slaveholding America. And a slaveholding America that dominated America before, of course, the Civil War. And so one of the things I think about is that people state that you can't really take down the monuments of presidents. That's the president. Like, how do you take down a monument for George Washington or Thomas Jefferson or one of these other people? But then when I look at Germany, and I remember that Hitler was the leader of Germany, and I don't see monuments to Hitler even though he was the leader of that nation. So for me, if it was up to me, I would allow those monuments of people who truly represented what America says itself to be. Which is freedom, which is equality, which is meritocracy. You see I say "says itself to be." It's not necessarily that, right?

Inskeep: It's not that they were perfect, but that they stood for this idea.

Kendi: Precisely. And I think slaveholders did not stand for that idea. And I think people who are clearly racist, who instituted discriminatory policies—not just sort of racist, but bigoted people who divided people, who discriminated against people, who rendered particular groups to be inferior. These are not the people who should be represented and honored—honored—by a monument. We have to remember that monuments, or when you're named after something, that's an honor. We're honoring people this way.

Inskeep: What about Thomas Jefferson? Slave owner. In some ways the classic kind of liberal progressive who's delaying progress, that you described, and yet he wrote the Declaration of Independence and the phrase that got millions of people free: "all men are created equal." What would you do for him?

Kendi: For me, again, the concept all men are created equal has long been rendered an antiracist idea. When in fact I demonstrate the way in which that's actually a foundational assimilationist idea. Which, in my work, I classify as a racist idea. And the way that works is, you can believe that the racial groups were created equal. But then Black people were raised in that pathological culture. Black people were raised in barbaric Africa. Black people were raised in Southeast D.C. And so they became inferior. And so now it's my job, either liberals today or Thomas Jefferson then, to civilize and develop people. So like that idea, the notion of "created equal" is actually not by its very nature an antiracist idea. What actually is an antiracist idea is if we say groups are equal. You see the difference. [Applause]

Inskeep: So great monuments on the mall. Washington Monument, the Jefferson Memorial, the Lincoln Memorial. I hope Lincoln stays. Does Lincoln stay? Is Lincoln okay?

Kendi: I think Lincoln, we can have a little debate.

Inskeep: All right. How about you?

Dyson: Well, I'm getting schooled. But here's the thing.

Inskeep: You would've said something different five minutes ago? Is that what you're saying?

Dyson: I'm gonna say it now. I mean, you wanted us to disagree. Now you've got your wish fulfilled. But not ultimately. Here's the deal. I think what Professor Kendi has broken down there is extremely important. Especially in the ideological and philosophical argument about creation versus existence, right? You know, what the philosophers would call both an ontological assertion about the being of people, and a category mistake—how we convince ourselves to lump them under the rubric of a particular description. So that's really sophisticated and nuanced. But when it comes to the monuments, for me to apply that thinking, here's my thought. There is a distinction between Jefferson Davis and Thomas Jefferson. For me. Right? In the sense that at least one of them was trying to articulate an ideal that could be governing and regulative of the notion of democracy. So that his words could be used, even if not with original intent, to subvert his own beliefs and to include Martin Luther King, Jr. To include Fannie Lou Hamer. Who could use those words as powerful arguments on behalf of the very people who have been excluded.

In other words, there was interpretive flexibility. There was what we might call an interpretation that was counter to the dominant one, of the original one, but came later on: "We hold these truths to be self-evident." When King says [those words] in 1963, August 28th, in front of Lincoln, he makes us think about them in a fresh way. So for that matter, to me, Lincoln, Washington and Jefferson would be different than Jefferson Davis and Stonewall Jackson. You know why? Because first of all, they were not patriots. Right? [Applause] You gonna have a statue of Huey Newton before you got one of Stonewall Jackson. 'Cause Huey Newton wasn't trying to go nowhere but here. Right? Bobby Seale, Angela Davis should have a statue long before Stonewall Jackson. [Applause]

So my point is, why? Because they were Secessionists. They didn't even love your country. They wanted to leave your country. They said it was inferior. It was the wrong argument for the protection of democracy. So how are you celebrating an anti-patriot? That would be like if you had a president who was selling the election to Russia. That stuff could never happen. [Applause/laughter]

So for me, I think that frail, flawed human beings—'cause there's another monument there, to Martin Luther King, Jr. And some have tried to argue, "He plagiarized his dissertation." He used other men's words to substantiate his claim as an intellectual, and other things that we don't need to get into up in here. Some have argued, "Well, the moral depravity of the man contradicts the ethical ideas for which he gave his life." And yet [. . .] in my books on King I've tried to say, "Anything you gonna say, I'm-a take that, deal with what it means, and still argue that he's the greatest American we've ever seen." Why? Because those flaws do not mitigate the incredible degree to which he poetically, prophetically and analytically put forth the ideals of American democracy in such a fashion that he made this nation better.

I would argue that Lincoln, at his best—especially [after] reading Kendi's book—and Washington and Jefferson and a few others, as flawed as they were, laid the groundwork for [a political] reinterpretation that subverted their very moral trajectory and gave rise to a movement that contradicted them. I would keep them. And I'm gonna tell you why I would get rid of the monuments for the Confederacy as well. People say, "Well, this is a teachable moment." Ain't nobody teaching nothing. Ain't no teaching going on. I don't see white Southerners taking their children to a Confederate flag or to a monument and going, "You know, we want to deconstruct white supremacy at its base." No. Because when you have a monument, as Professor Kendi said, you are celebrating an ideal. In a neutral environment we could teach everything. This is not a neutral environment. And when you celebrate on sacred soil the public rituals of American democracy, everything that's rooted there must have the ultimate intent of embracing the democratic energy that has made this nation what it is today. That's why I would keep them and get rid of the other cats as well. [Applause]

Inskeep: I want to ask two more questions, if I can. We've just got a few more minutes. I invited people on this social media platform known as Twitter—I just said, I'm going to be talking to these gentlemen. Anything you'd like to know? And two questions stick in my mind from people. I don't know who they are, actually. But one of them said, "Would you ask them, you gentlemen, if they feel they have done anything that has worsened racial divisions in America? As public figures, as public speakers weighing in on controversial topics, is there anything you think didn't work out the way you would hope it would?"

Dyson: Well, that's a different question. [Laughter] It ain't always worked out. Now I'm not presuming that whoever asked that question is one of the many kvetching and complaining white people who say, "You're a race baiter because you acknowledge race." I'm not going to presume that. Let's make it a legitimate question. See, here's the irony. I meet many white people who think because I talk about race, I'm creating race. I ain't created it; I'm revealing it to you. I'm just showing you the chasm, the abyss. I'm showing you the ugliness. And I'm not perfect.

Am I flawed? Of course. Have I made statements that ultimately may not serve the interests I claim to serve? Absolutely. But here's the problem, here's the difference. Many white people who are themselves racist will see me and my mistake as the unalterable manifestation of an inherent inferiority and a race-baiting that they never see in themselves or other white brothers and sisters, number one.

And number two, at the end of the day, what we are here to do—and I don't want to speak for Professor Kendi. He's going to speak for himself. But I'll say this. As a guy who's been a public intellectual for 30-some years, and has been on this front line in writing books and thinking out loud and stuff, I have never claimed to be perfect. But Grace Jones said, "I'm not perfect, but I'm perfect for you." [Laughter] So the great philosopher Grace Jones is sufficient for me. And I think ultimately we are trying to do the right thing. We're trying to make things better. We're trying to bring a spotlight to issues, including our own. I'm trying to squeeze out the sexism in myself. As a feminist, am I perfect? Absolutely not. Do I need to be reprimanded constantly? Yes. Should I reexamine my own principles daily? Yes. But what we must commit ourselves to, together, is not demonizing each other, but looking at the problems that exist so we can concretely eradicate the possibility of white supremacy. That's what I'm about every day. [Applause]

Kendi: I'm actually struggling with this question because I'm actually seeking to answer this question for my next book. I think early, in *Stamped from the Beginning*, I talked about—

Dyson: Don't give it all away, though. Let 'em read it. [Laughter] Just tease it. Just tease a little bit, don't give them the answer. You gotta pay $25 for that.

Kendi: Yes. So I'm not going to give you that much. So I think early in *Stamped from the Beginning* I state that the only thing wrong with Black people is that we think something is wrong with Black people. And the only thing extraordinary about white people is that—anybody want to take a guess? They think something is extraordinary about white people. But going back to Black people, through studying the history of racist ideas, I realized the fundamental function of racist ideas, and that function was to prevent people from resisting racial discrimination, and [prevent] people from even seeing racial discrimination. Because they are so infected by racist ideas that when they see inequality, they see what's wrong with Black people.

So that means those who are discriminating against Black people and those who are creating those inequities, those who are benefiting from those discriminatory policies, are able to continue to do so. Because we can't even see, we're not even looking for the racial discrimination, right? Because we think Black people are criminal-like. We think Black people are poor. We think Black people are hypersexual. So we're not even going to look for the discrimination in the criminal justice system.

So I asked myself very simply, are these ideas affecting Black people too? Do you have Black people blaming Black people for racial inequality? Do you have Black people who are refusing to resist racial discrimination because they think that the problem fundamentally is Black people? And clearly the answer is yes. And so in writing *Stamped from the Beginning*, before I could chronicle and study and reveal anyone else's racist ideas, I first had to chronicle and reveal my own. I first had to come to grips with the fact that I had spent the better part of my life thinking that there was something wrong with Black people.

And so, to answer your question, yes. I mean, I grew up in the 1980s and 1990s. Particularly in the 1980s and 1990s all the racist ideas that were swirling, even within Black neighborhoods, which people were patting Bill Clinton on the back for, for passing and pushing through the crime bill and antagonizing Angela Davis, who weeks before was saying he should not do that, 'cause that's going to lead to what we now see is a mass incarceration. Right? You know, you had Black people who were pushing for that. Because they were so scared of—who? Black people.

So I realized that I too had consumed racist ideas. I also realized that really racist ideas had principally, historically targeted Black minds. They didn't want you to run away. Because they wanted you to believe that you should be enslaved because you were Black. They did not want you to think that you should have more resources. That you should have more wealth. That you should not be in poverty. That you should not be in that impoverished neighborhood. They didn't want you, Black people, to think that, because then, if Black people did, they would resist. And those Black people who recognized that inequality is abnormal, who do not think that white people are superior, these are the very people throughout our history who have resisted.

And so I realized again that I had not done enough resisting in my life because of the racist ideas I had consumed. So I mentioned a new book. I'm actually writing a book that really takes the reader through my own upbringing, consuming racist ideas, and how I ultimately strove to be an antiracist. Because really, we like to talk a lot about non-racism. Everyone in America likes to stand up and say, "I'm not a racist." But really, there's no such thing as non-racism. Either we believe in racial hierarchy or we believe in racial equality. Either we look at racial disparities and see what's wrong with people, or we see what's wrong with policies. There's no in-between in that. So I'm sort of writing about how I came to realize that there's nothing wrong with people and everything wrong with this nation's policies. [Applause]

Inskeep: One final question. Also from Twitter. The question was, is there any hope?

Kendi: Oh, I think reading Dyson's *Sermon to White America*. I mean, I should say that philosophically I believe that change is possible. And what I mean by that is, I feel like an activist [. . .] somebody who desires to bring about change has to believe that change is possible. How are you going to bring about change if you don't even believe it's possible? That's the first step. So I feel like I have all of the evidence as to why we should not be hopeful. I know all the evidence. Trust me, I do. And I know it throughout history. I actually read through some of the most vicious things that have ever been said and done to Black people. But at the same time, somehow those Black people who were victims of that viciousness still had hope. And I think that's the very reason why they resisted. And I think that's the very reason why I'm sitting here right now talking to you. [Applause]

Dyson: I'm sure this is true for Professor Kendi. Every day I get threats from white people. That they gonna kill me. Call me nigger. I got so much nigger discourse my only hope is, "Could you call me Professor Nigger? [Laughter] Every now and again just say Doctor Nigger?" They're bold and emboldened. They go on my Facebook page. They send me emails. They threaten me. They say Dylann Roof had the right idea. Why does a nigger like me exist? This is from white people. And you can imagine, I'm sure, if you haven't had the experience yourself, what that's meant to do. The kind of language it is meant to discourage, the kind of rhetoric it is meant to sidetrack, the kind of ideas that it is meant to implant, and the kind of fear that it is meant to impart.

And furthermore, trying to tell other white brothers and sisters who believe it can't be that bad, it can't be that rough. "It's not us." [Yet] it's your culture that is reproducing the pathogens that lay waste to the moral ecology of this culture. So the same people who think it is a farce not to believe in global warming don't understand that racism, in the moral ecology, is such a warped and warping experience, and it is system-wide to a degree that many white brothers and sisters may be afraid to acknowledge, or fearful because their parents and their cousins and their uncles and their children agree with it.

So I think that in light of that, Howard Thurman, who I end my book with, to echo what Professor Kendi said, and I'm paraphrasing, "Our slave foreparents faced long rows of cotton in the interminable heat. The rawhide whip of the overseer. And yes what did they do? They envisioned a future beyond where they were." He said, "Never allow the horizon of your dreams to be reduced to your present experience." That that present experience could not hold you. He said, either you're going to be a prisoner of an event, or a prisoner of hope. And so I must say that I am a prisoner of hope. That's the reason I can talk about the negativity and the darkness, and then take it—because my pastor used to tell me, "Don't fight *for* victory, fight *from* victory." And in an anticipatory sense—in a theological sense we call it eschatology—the end is realized in the present.

So for me, I am a prisoner of that hope, and I think that there has to be a way that we can change. Having written this book, I meet so many white brothers and sisters, among many others, who say, "I gave this to my uncle, my cousin. I read your book. It challenged me. It was straight, no chaser. You tried to show love but you demanded that we deal with something." I think those people are real. Those people who are willing to give their lives, like Sister Heather Heyer. Those people like Viola Liuzzo. Those people like Rev. James Reeb. Those white brothers and sisters who were willing to pay the ultimate price in alliance with, and in fraternity and sorority with, us. Those of us who can come together—we are the manifestation, the evidence, of the very thing for which we fight. So yes, I am a prisoner of hope. That's why I'm able to swing against the vicious pathology of white supremacy, male supremacy, homophobia and all of the rest of the "isms" that have distorted the real true democratic spirit of this nation. And for that, I'm willing to continue to give my life. [Applause]

CHAPTER

38

We Matter, We Care

Alicia Garza is, quite simply, a star: a very smart social and cultural critic, a lovely human being, a deeply committed social activist, and one of the three co-founders of one of the most influential and triumphant social justice movements in history: Black Lives Matter. She is also a gifted talker and a lucid explainer of ideas. That made this conversation a pure pleasure, as did the expert moderation of talented Washington Post *journalist Eugene Scott. This is a slightly condensed version of the conversation that took place virtually in July of 2020 during the Aspen Ideas Festival.*

Eugene Scott: So there are so many places we can start right now. But I'm very interested, when you look back on these past three or four weeks that have led to the national uprising, and deep disgust and concern with anti-Black racism and white supremacy across the country, in places where we perhaps have never seen this type of response, what are some of the first thoughts that come to your mind, Alicia?

Alicia Garza: Well, first and foremost, it's amazing to see twice in my lifetime now such transformation happening across the country. I know when I talk to my elders, there's a sense that everything is possible right now. And that is also true when I talk to folks in my peer group. I think that, while this is an incredible moment of uprising and an incredible moment of reckoning, I really long for this to also be a moment for change. I think there are a lot of rules that have been rigged against Black communities for a very long time. That we need to see the courage and drive, the political will, to actually start to shift. I think the other thing that's really important right now that is finally becoming a robust national and global conversation is a conversation around policing and safety in our communities. And I feel really good about the reckoning and grappling that is happening right now. Whether you feel comfortable or uncomfortable with the slogan of Defund the Police, I think it's important for us to be grappling with what actually keeps communities safe in this moment. And when it comes to Black communities in particular, is safety only achieved through punishment or is safety achieved through making sure we fix and rebuild the infrastructure that has been denied Black communities for so long?

Scott: What about you, Professor Dyson? What are some of the first things that come to your mind about this moment?

Michael Eric Dyson: Well, like Miss Garza, it is striking that we have seen yet another uprising, rebellion, resurgence, and revival of a spirit of resistance that has barely been seen in this country since the civil unrest of the 1960s. And it is directly attributable to the work that Miss Garza and her colleagues have done by ingeniously fostering an environment where a hashtag becomes a statement and principle, an ideal, an aspiration and a movement. I mean, that's remarkable. That's like joining Chuck Berry, Martin Luther King, Jr., Ida B. Wells-Barnett and throwing in some Aretha Franklin. That's just a convergence of so many different aspects of our identities. The Civil Rights Movement stated the goal, the aspiration, to gain voting rights in 1965 and, before that, civil rights in '64. And then in the aftermath of Dr. King's death, the Fair Housing Act in 1968.

But Black Lives Matter is the articulation of an ideal. It's the articulation of a principle. It's the articulation of an aspiration. And it's an articulation of a reaffirmation of Black people. Yeah, Black lives matter. And they ought to matter. And [it's amazing] to see what's going on now, the pushback of Black people to insist that this is the moment. You know, people keep asking me, what's different now? What's different now is, it's different now. It's different because I've been doing interviews all over the world. They didn't do that before on Mike Brown. And Mike Brown had a national circumference within which his memory took place. But this is a global, if you will, acknowledgment. To match the global pandemic, it's a global explosion of consciousness. And that is attributable to our young brilliant Black people like Miss Garza and others who have led the way. Young people have always led the way. SNCC, John Lewis, Diane Nash, Julian Bond. Led, of course, by many leaders at multiple sites. It is not a leaderless organization, it is multiple sites of leadership that are articulating goals, ideals and aspirations.

So I am heartened when I see the world has finally caught up to where Black people have been. And I can imagine some Black people are tired. And I know that Black people are frustrated, and they say, "We ain't here to teach white folk what to do." I was doing this at George-town and my students were saying, "We didn't come here to teach young white people what to do." And I got in with them. I said, "Yeah, we didn't come here to teach . . ." I said, "Oh, but I'm a professor, so actually I *did* come here to do that, 'cause that's my job." And I tell white people, if you meet one Black person that's tired, go on to the next one. Because we run in a relay here. So somebody had the baton and they wore out. But the next person running the leg may not be worn out. So Black communi-ties are heterogenous, they are differentiated, they are complicated and nuanced.

And it is a time not only for white supremacy to be assaulted, which I'm glad—it is not only a time for the dominant white supremacist ide-ology to be attacked, it is also time for Black people to look inward and understand the resources at our disposal, and in connection with other people who have joined the movement. And hallelujah. You got Latinx people, you got Asian folk, you got First Nation folk, you got Indigenous folk. You got the Rainbow Coalition for real joining the movement.

So when I look out and see the devastating denial of Black life, Black life as the premise and predicate of American democracy— which it has been—the death of Black aspiration, which is what slav-ery was about, reinforcing an ideal that we were nothing, to see the uprising of Black people in claiming global recognition has been a re-markable thing. And despite the deaths of Miss Breonna Taylor and Mr. George Floyd and Mr. Ahmaud Arbery and so many countless others—trans people, women and Black men alike—we have at this moment the possibility of truly and fundamentally transforming the politics of the police.

And, I think, I'll end by saying yes, Miss Garza's right. You might be uncomfortable with the notion of defunding the police, but you might not be uncomfortable with the results of what that means. We done tried everything else. We done tried police-community relations, we've tried enhancing relations between law enforcement and Black communities, we've tried making them live in the same neighborhood so they would see a difference—that ain't helping. This is not a policy problem; it is a philosophical problem, and it is a culture problem.

The immediate response to see me as a threat and to demonize me; we've got to purge out of the consciousness of officers—Black people as well, and brown and red and yellow people who police us—an instinct to murder us. You know, when you're driving along, and they've done these psychological studies, when you see somebody come across your horizon, the first thing is to drive toward them before you drive away from them. And so with Black people, we have been that object.

You may not be for *defund*ing the police, but I want to take the *fun* out of killing us. I want to take the *fun* out of murdering and massacring us, and I want to *fund* those programs and policies, like the ones put forth by Miss Garza and others, that will have the chance of transforming this society in which we live. I will not talk this long again ever. But I had to get that out. I had to recognize Garza, I had to recognize Black Lives Matter, and I had to recognize the moment we're in.

Scott: Absolutely. I remember, I was a political reporter in 2012, after the Trayvon Martin killing, which was my introduction to Black Lives Matter. I was in Phoenix, Arizona. As you know, Phoenix is not a place with a bustling large Black population. So you would hear about it, but it wasn't what was happening to the degree that we saw in metropolitan areas with a large Black populace. But then I remember Mike Brown in Ferguson. By that time, I was up in grad school in Boston, and I saw so many protests and responses. And there was some traction that was happening. But this time, I saw marches in Alaska and Idaho and Wyoming. And, Miss Garza, I would like to hear your thoughts, as someone who has seen Black Lives Matter go from being painted as this fringe movement by its opponents to this idea, this value, that recent surveys say the majority of Americans are behind. What's your thought and your reaction to that?

Garza: I couldn't agree with you more. And judging by what my email in-boxes look like—threats and praise alike—I can say this is 100 percent a different moment. I think one of the things I'm grappling with, though, is not around where were Black folks at. Because I feel like Black folks are very clear about the fact that Black lives should matter. And we may have different approaches to how we do that. But I will say that seven years later it is important to see white folks now joining this movement. I think there are folks who might say things like, "Where've y'all been?" Because we have been here for almost a decade.

But I will also echo the sentiments of Prof. Dyson and say that it's important that you're here now. And the question that I think I grapple with a lot in this moment, when we look at the trajectory and the history of Black Lives Matter, and also the embracing of it now, is that it really is up to us to make this a moment that we capitalize on. And by capitalize I don't mean everybody slap Black Lives Matter on your website or on a T-shirt and profit off of it. What I mean here is to actually make Black lives matter where you are.

The fact of the matter is, if we were together right now in Aspen, we would be having this conversation with an audience that actually doesn't look like this panel. And there's nothing wrong with that. I think actually what needs to happen here is that when we talk about divesting from systems that don't benefit us, we also have to divest from practices and procedures and policies that don't benefit us either.

And so part of what divesting looks like, in this case, would actually be to figure out not just how do we diversify our environment, but how do we change how we lead in this moment. How do we change who is leading us in this moment? How do we change how we direct resources and power in this moment? And how do we also shift the way that we understand what Black Lives Matter can mean in our immediate environment as well as in our communities and in our country and across the globe?

And I make this point in particular because I think that, again, judging by what my inbox looks like, both threats and praise, what is true is that there is a major backlash that's happening to the popularity of Black Lives Matter. Black Lives Matter has not been as mainstream as it is right now. In 2013, when we started Black Lives Matter, and leading all the way until the 2016 election, saying Black Lives Matter was almost like political suicide. And that's why you couldn't get any major candidate to say it without taking a gulp of water first, right? Because they were very worried about the perceptions that were attached to and wrapped around Black Lives Matter.

Of course, we have not been concerned about that, because we've always known we've been on the right side of history. But I can say it just to make a quick parallel that the same way people tell us now to change the slogan of Defund the Police to Make the Police Better or Transform the Police or whatever, people told us this also in 2013 and said, "Well, how can you make your slogan more appealing to people like me?" And I'm really glad we didn't change our slogan to All Lives Matter or Black Lives Matter Too. We've got to be able to, as a part of the reckoning that this moment is offering us, we have to be able to sit with the discomfort of the shifts that we are being asked to make right now.

So lastly, I just want to say that, for me, when it comes to reimagining what this moment can and should look like, it also means reimagining the role of white folks in our communities and in our decision-making bodies. It means reimagining the roles that decision makers have taken up that frankly have disenfranchised Black communities from being able to make decisions about our own lives. And to be able to do that in partnership and interdependence.

I want to be very clear here and very specific that policing is just the tip of the iceberg. Rules and practices and policy and culture need to shift in our boardrooms, in our C-suites, in our schools, our economy, all throughout our society. So, don't think that to be a part of Black Lives Matter all you need to do is slap it on a T-shirt or on your website, or send out an email talking about how you're committed to diversity and inclusion. Actually think about what that looks like in your boardrooms. Think about what it looks like in your churches and in your workplaces and in your homes. You can make Black Lives Matter exactly where you are right now.

[. . .]

Scott: I think what this movement has given us is a deep awareness of the toll that being an advocate for racial equality has on someone mentally and physically and spiritually. And we're having conversations [. . .] about the importance of self-care and taking care of yourself mentally in ways that perhaps were not as common in years past. I write about identity politics for the *Washington Post*, and I write about these issues every single day. And when I'm interviewed, I'm often asked, how do you do it? How do you handle it? And I say I have a great family and an awesome group of friends, but most importantly I have a really good therapist. And I'd love to hear you all talk about, as we're wrapping things up, the importance of self-care and what you're doing to make sure you don't burn out as quickly, or maybe even at all. Because there are so many people who are very new to this moment, and this movement, and becoming overwhelmed already and don't know how to process a lot of what they're taking in. So it would be great to hear your insight and counsel.

Garza: I can start here. It's a very important question and I think it's one that deserves a broad answer. For me, of course, there's a number of different things I do. I ride the Peloton bike four times a week, 45 minutes a day. I have a therapist, and weekly get to talk about all the things I'm dealing with in relationship to the world and life. I also have a great partner and a great set of friends who keep me in deep belly laughs most of the time, when I really need it. And I have to be honest that I have realized over the last decade that I can't yoga my way to care, I can't bubble bath my way to care. But actually, care and caring and connection and interdependence is a cultural value that we have to adopt. If I'm doing things to buy myself care, then there are still people in my community that can't access that. So I like to talk about self-care as a function of community care.

And I do the work that I can to make sure the environments I'm building—the work that I do at the Black Futures Lab and the Black to the Future Act Fund and other institutions and organizations—we really build into our culture that we need people to be long-distance runners. So what that means is a different mindset and approach to how we do this work, and connecting to purpose in addition to connecting to outcomes. So every week when my team and I are talking about the work we're getting ready to move, we start with just checking in with each other. What do people need? Are you feeling anxious? How can we show up for you? And that's different than telling people to take a day off or take a week off or take a bubble bath or sending somebody a pass for yoga.

And I think this is important, because so often—at least over the last decade—there's been lots of debates over self-care. And whether or not self-care is accessible. Whose idea is that? People quote Audre Lorde, but then they quote her wrong. We have to understand that part of what it means to be in active political warfare is to change the way we orient and organize ourselves around the work that has to be done. The work of changing policies and changing laws is not separate from the work of changing culture and changing our relationships to each other, that have been shaped by systems that deem us disposable. And so if we are adopting those practices and habits, and trying to wash over them and call them something that they're not, without fundamentally changing them, then we are literally just advancing a political agenda that is not ours and it's not beneficial to us.

And so, in this moment where we are constantly pivoting, because the systems that organize our lives are actually deeply unsustainable, and so they tend towards crisis, we have to do a readjustment of ourselves in this moment. Not just to provide mutual aid, which is important. Not just to make sure that people are caring for themselves, which is important. But to actually change our practices so that care is at the center of the work that we do externally and internally. And it provides infrastructure, or a safety net as some people might say, to not just the freedom fighters who are out in the streets right now, but all of the people who are working to make social change real. So I think we have to readjust our way of understanding care from an individual's responsibility to access as they can, to environments and cultures that we nurture, that care for each other as much as we care for ourselves.

Scott: Prof. Dyson, thoughts on self-care? How individuals can care for themselves as they engage these really difficult topics?

Dyson: Well, Miss Garza has brilliantly, eloquently articulated it. I'll just add a couple things. When you think about that ethic of care she speaks about, a radical ethic of care [must be] pervasive and not just concentrated. Because if it's concentrated, it's me and mine and we take care of each other and it's good. But pervasive means we look at the structures that encourage people [and] seduce them into non-care. Into believing they're not worthy of care. That you're not worth a bubble bath, you're not worth a massage, you're not worth a meditation. You're not worth standing back and listening to Luther Vandross and Anita Baker. You are not worthy of some other elements that you think are extraneous to your being when they are central and determinative in a fundamental fashion. And we have not been allowed, we have not been permitted, to think of ourselves in that way. But Gandhi said, "Look, if I don't take care of myself first, I can't really help you."

And so even when you on the plane and they give you the announcement, they say, "When the oxygen mask comes down, put your mask on first." Because if you ain't breathing, you can't help your kids. And so that kind of ethic of self-care is not simply utilitarian, it has a function of survival. But it also, as Miss Garza suggested, has a nationwide, a global character—a community's self-care. Black people have been seduced into self-destruction. To not care. We don't care about each other, because we don't care about ourselves. And not caring about ourselves because we've been taught the other person is not worthy of consideration.

That's why I'm always careful not to say, "Treat me like you want to be treated." Well, slow down with that, 'cause you treating yourself pretty funky too. So don't do that to me. So at that level, the Golden Rule still prevails, but a Golden Rule that has political and social consequence. That is to say, how we teach people to love and embrace each other and nurture each other. And that's [why I'm so critical of] cancel culture and its nastiness and snarkiness. We ain't got to do all that. And you ain't going to cover that up being Gen Z or millennial or . . . I don't care. If you rude, you rude. If you a rude old fool, you were a rude young fool. You're just rude. And don't be trying to dress it up like it's a political ethic of assertion. No, you just rude.

And so, at the same time however, we understand that, as a people who have been disrespected, the politics of self-care bleed out into a politics of respect for the other. And I see so much disrespect of people of all ages and stages that we have to really discourage. So in that sense, I think self-care is extremely important. I'm listening to some Luther, I'm listening to some hip hop. I go old school, I chill out. I used to go to the movies, but the pandemic . . . We have a dual pandemic going on. One about race and one about the virus. But they share in common, "I Can't Breathe." The police beating us down, we can't share the oxygen of freedom, on the one hand, and we literally can't breathe on the other; and they're both interconnected. That's the vicious underside of an intersectional reality of our lives.

But at the end of the day—and when I get back out, I'mma get a therapist too. I had one. I'mma be like y'all. Y'all therapy shaming and stuff, you know what I'm saying? [Laughter] I got a therapist too, man. Come on. But it's extremely important. I'm an ordained Baptist minister for 41 years. And Black people say, "Aw, no, you just need Jesus." "No, you need a little bit more than Jesus now. You need a little bit more." That Scripture that says when the Disciples came to Jesus, and "we could not cast out the demon." And Jesus says, "Well, do you know why?" And they said, "because of prayer and fasting." And Jesus said, "And Prozac. You Negroes need Prozac. You need some chemicals; you need chemical remediation."

And so I think once Black people embrace the necessity of therapy, of talk therapy, of sometimes chemical intervention, because of the dopamine or whatever else is being released in our brains, and the chemicals, the endorphins that we need to release, when we find the way to have radical, revolutionary Black joy, in the midst of Black pain, then the therapeutic possibilities are opened up and we learn to embrace them without shame. Let's not shame each other, but let's embrace the possibility of our self-care because we care for each other. Self-care is critical, other-care is mandatory, and care for each other is the fundamental premise, I think, of Black survival in this country.

Battling Brains

On the Debate Stage

CHAPTER

39

It Ain't the Demos, It's the Demon

Eddie Glaude is one of the smartest people I know: an erudite scholar, a learned professor, an eloquent conversationalist, a superb public intellectual, and an elegant throwback to 1950s Black male charisma rooted in disarming self-possession. He is a fierce broker of complex ideas, and in conversation he is earnest and transparent. This rather heated yet cordial disagreement took place in 2016, the morning before Hillary Clinton addressed the Democratic National Convention as the party's nominee, when we appeared together on Democracy Now! *as host Amy Goodman guided us through a debate about whether progressives and Black folk should support Clinton in the effort to defeat Donald Trump. Like Noam Chomsky and Angela Davis, I said yes. Glaude was not convinced. This is a condensed version of our conversation.*

Amy Goodman: Professors Michael Eric Dyson and Eddie Glaude, thanks so much for joining us.

Eddie Glaude: Thanks for having us.

Michael Eric Dyson: Thanks for having us.

Goodman: Well, let's start with you, Professor Dyson, on this issue of why Hillary Clinton, you say, will do more for African Americans than President Obama.

Dyson: Well, I was making that argument in the context of a host of things—not the least of which is that President Obama, for a variety of reasons, has been hamstrung, has been disinclined to deal with race, has been hesitant and procrastinating about engaging race. And I think that Hillary Clinton, for many of those reasons, will be more forthcoming. She's spoken, I think, very intelligently about implicit bias. She has asked white people to hold themselves accountable vis-à-vis white privilege. She's been talking about systemic racism, as well as individual acts of bigotry and violence. So, I think, in the aggregate, when we look at the degree to which she is capable, because of that very white privilege, to speak about race, in a way that Obama, even if he chose to be more forthcoming, would be categorized and put in a Black box, in a certain way—that she has both the drive, the intelligence, the ability and the privilege to speak about it in a way that he is perhaps not only disinclined to do so, but maybe restricted, in his own mind.

Goodman: Professor Eddie Glaude?

Glaude: Well, you know, I understand the claim around the limits, or the constraints Obama faced, but I think the claims around Hillary Clinton are basically aspirational, because there's no real evidence in her immediate past of any kind of genuine and deep concern about the material conditions of Black life. And so, in other words, what I'm suggesting is that part of what—the problem is that we can't infer from anything that she's done that when she gets in office, that she's going to change and address the circumstances of Black folk in any substantive way, or the most vulnerable in any substantive way, because at the end of the day, I think, Hillary Clinton is a corporate Democrat, that she is committed to a neoliberal economic philosophy.

Goodman: What does "neoliberal philosophy" mean?

Glaude: Well, a neoliberal economic philosophy involves a kind of understanding that the notion of the public good is kind of undermined by a basic market logic that turns us all into entrepreneurs, where competition and rivalry define who we are, where the state's principal function is to secure the efficient functioning of the economy and the defense, and creating the market conditions whereby you and I can pursue our own self-interest. And part of what that does, if we only read it as an economic philosophy and not understand it as a kind of political rationale producing particular kinds of subjects, who are selfish, who are self-interested, who are always in competition with one another, then we lose sight of how neoliberalism attacks the political imagination. So the interesting question that I ask of Hillary Clinton is that, will she fundamentally change the circumstances that are at the heart of the problem facing this country? In fact, I think she's illustrative of the problem confronting the country.

Dyson: Well, I mean, that's interesting.

Goodman: Professor Dyson?

Dyson: I mean, obviously, I agree with your analysis of neoliberalism. But in terms of dissecting the constitutive elements that make up what neoliberal vision is, given what you were talking about in terms of self-interest and competition, we'd have to say Bernie Sanders exhibits, in a profound way, some of the same elements, if that becomes the litmus test.

Glaude: No, we're all in it, though.

Dyson: Right? So, if we're all in it, that means then the distinction makes no difference. Because, ultimately, if you're talking about affecting material conditions of Black people, I think that not only does she vote 93 percent of the same way that Bernie Sanders voted, say, as one, if you will, lodestar for what a progressive politics might look like. It's not simply about inference. It's about the fact that she's spent her time working with Marian Wright Edelman. It's about the way in which, as a first lady, she championed causes that Black people could not only be concerned about, but were involved with. It's not only the fact that, as a senator and then as a secretary of state, her awareness of ethnicity and race and, of course, gender, [and what] those differences might make at least provides the platform for her to articulate that vision. And more especially, in the aftermath of racial crisis in America, she has responded in a way to mobilize the public understanding of those interests.

So, for me, if material interests are the predicate for us determining the legitimacy or efficacy of a particular policy, yeah, it's aspirational, but I want that aspiration to be about taking Black life seriously. I want that aspiration to be about what we can do to transform the fundamental condition of our people.

[. . .]

Glaude: What I'm saying is, we need to understand who Hillary Clinton is, just as we need to understand who Barack Obama is.

Dyson: No doubt.

Glaude: And part of what these folks are, they're representatives of the corporate wing of the Democratic Party. These folk—

Dyson: Right.

Glaude: —it's been on their watch.

Dyson: Let me say this—

Glaude: Crime bill, the welfare bill, dismantling Glass-Steagall—it's been on their watch.

Dyson: Ain't no doubt about that. But here's the bottom line, and here's the context.

Glaude: All right.

Dyson: As they say in basketball, you've got to deal with what the defense gives you. We are talking about Donald Trump. We're talking about Hillary Clinton in [that] context. Let's bring it back to reality. We're talking about within the—

Glaude: We haven't been in reality, though, Mike?

Dyson: We've been in a serious reality that is abstract in considering the philosophical consequences of particular ideologies. What I'm saying, in light of the real-life circumstances we face now, we're talking about the choice between Donald Trump and Hillary Clinton—and, of course, Jill Stein and the Libertarian candidate, but I'm talking about those who've got a real chance to win. If we're concerned about the very people you're speaking about—you and I are going to be fine whether Donald Trump is president or whether Hillary Clinton is president, in terms of our material conditions.

But the people that we claim ostensibly to represent, those whose voices we want to amplify by our visions, by our own reflections upon the conditions they confront—ain't no doubt in my mind that Hillary Clinton represents [for them] the only possibility to at least address the undeniable lethargy of a political system—neoliberalism, in particular; more broadly, the kind of epic sweep and tide of capital and its impact on the conditions of working-class and poor Black people. But I'm saying, ain't nobody got a possibility of doing none of that in a context where Donald Trump is the president. It may mobilize and galvanize grassroots movements that will articulate their resistance against him. What it will *not* be able to do is leverage the political authority of the state in defense of those vulnerable bodies. It's not been perfect, but it certainly represents a huge advantage over a possibility of a Donald Trump presidency.

[. . .]

Glaude: It is the case that Freddie Gray's mother is still grieving, right?

Dyson: That's right.

Glaude: Rekia Boyd's mom is still grieving.

Dyson: I'm with you.

Glaude: Right? We can call the roll.

Dyson: I'm with you.

Glaude: Call the roll. So, part of what we're saying is that we have to do two things simultaneously. One is keep Donald Trump out of office. And two—right?—announce that business as usual is unacceptable.

Dyson: Yeah, but—

Glaude: So, what does that mean?

Dyson: Are they competing?

Glaude: Of course. If it's going to mean that if the—

Dyson: It's a priority.

Glaude: No, if it's going to mean—hold on, let me make the claim.

Dyson: Right.

Glaude: It's going to mean that the fear of electing Donald Trump cannot be the principal motivation of how we engage politically. So, part—

Dyson: Absolutely, right now, it must be *the* principal motive—

Glaude: No, no, no. No, no.

Dyson: No, no. Let me tell you why.

Glaude: That's a very limited conception of what democratic—

Dyson: No, no, no, because—because your—

Glaude: —democratic action—

Dyson: —your ideals will be subverted, undermined, marginalized and totally put to the periphery, if Donald Trump—

Glaude: You have an anemic conception of demos, brother.

Dyson: No, no, no. I'm saying it ain't the demos, it's the demon I'm talking about. And the demon right now, in my mind, is Donald Trump. I'm saying, if we don't make that the priority—preventing the flourishing of an ethic, of a politic and of a conception of the state, much less of the global theaters within which America operates. If we don't prevent Donald Trump from ascending, so to speak, to that throne, all the legitimate stuff that you and I agree on, any analysis you make—if you read my book on President Obama, I lay all that stuff out there. I lay out the way in which Black lives have been decentered in terms of their economic and social stability.

And, furthermore, when you talk about the degree to which Black life matters, in a Donald Trump presidency, not only can we not acknowledge that Black lives matter, we can't even see if Black lives can exist on a particular kind of plane that represents anything like democracy. So, I'm saying *that's* the priority. And if that is addressed—I don't want to reduce all of the complicated political energy in America to electoral politics, but electoral politics is a crucial wedge that can be inserted into the contemporary political scene to at least be able to make a change.

[...]

Glaude: How [can] a Democratic candidate [...] come into our community, come into this moment, where all of this suffering—where you and I have laid it out in both of our books—all this suffering is engulfing our communities, when we look at the back of Barack Obama's head, what's going to be behind it are the ruins of Black communities, the ruins of the most vulnerable in this country.

[...]

Dyson: Well, first of all, the importance of [Obama's] statement [in defense of Clinton] was to mitigate the vicious, lethal legacy of sexism that has become so normalized that we don't even pay attention to it.

But let me get back to the point we were making before the break of Obama's rhetoric. Why is it that we reduce the complicated legacy of our freedom struggle to present moments? Howard Thurman, the great prophetic mystic, said, refuse the temptation to reduce your dreams to the level of the event which is your immediate experience. And what I'm arguing for, Brother Eddie, is that we pull upon the very romantic, in the best sense of that word, conceptions of self-determination and the flourishing of Black agency—all those technical terms. In other words, for Black people to get stuff done under impossible circumstances.

The reason I can maintain the hopefulness—and Niebuhr, since you brought him up, talked about the difference between optimism and hope. Optimism is a shallow virtue; hope is a deep virtue. Even in the face of impossibility, I happen to believe in a religious and spiritual reality that has been manifest politically, that has motivated Black people from the get-go. And what that says is, I don't care what you put before me, I don't care what's going on, I'm not going to give in to what's happening. If you're talking about it's tough now, Martin Luther King, Jr., Ralph Abernathy, Ella Baker were operating under conditions where Black people didn't even have the franchise.

Glaude: Right.

Dyson: If Black people were able to leverage their political authority, and especially their morally compelling arguments, their narratives and their stories in defense of their vulnerable bodies, who are we now, with enormous access to the vote, to lament the impossibility of the situation? As if this choice between maintaining a conception of the flourishing of Black people under impossible circumstances, versus [not] putting Donald Trump in office—let's do both. Let's both acknowledge that Donald Trump is the most immediate priority to be prevented, and then, at the same time, as you say, speak about these other interests. But it doesn't mean it has to be either-or. Why can't we do both? Why can't we put Hillary Clinton in office, the way you have conversation with Cory Booker, the way you have engagements in an elite white institution? You ain't teaching at Howard, and neither am I.

Glaude: Right.

Dyson: All of our hands are dirty.

Glaude: Morehouse.

Dyson: Right, but you ain't—I'm saying—

Glaude: I know. I got you.

Dyson: I got you. My son graduated from there. Marc Hill, what's up? Professor there. But my point is that it's not an either-or situation. And I think that what you say, I agree with. But what I don't agree with is deferring the legitimacy of the priority of Donald Trump being stopped from occupying space that will bring—if it's bad now, it's going to be [worse]—it's a Bobby Womack ethic. "If you think you're lonely now, wait until the night," until Donald Trump becomes president.

Goodman: Professor Eddie Glaude, who do you want to see as president?

Glaude: With these two choices?

Goodman: In this election.

Dyson: That's no other choice for you, those three, four.

Glaude: I have no interest. Neither one.

Goodman: You don't think it matters whether—

Glaude: I don't want Donald Trump to be in office. I can only put it in the negative.

Dyson: Well, that's good enough. That's good enough.

Glaude: Right. Yeah, so I'm only going to put it in the negative.

Dyson: I'll run with that.

Goodman: And if you don't want Donald Trump to be in office, how would you prevent that from happening?

Glaude: So, part of what I've been arguing—and I wrote a piece with Fred Harris, a political scientist at Columbia—is that we should vote strategically. And that is to say, if you're an African American or if you're a person of color or you're a progressive of conscience, who's—where the word actually means something—in a swing state, it makes all the sense in the world to me, in a battleground state, that you vote for Hillary Clinton, because one of the objectives is to keep Donald Trump out of office. But if you're in a red state, like my mom and dad—my mom and daddy are in Mississippi. Right? They're Democrats, but we know Mississippi is going Trump. Right? What do you do? You can actually blank out. You can leave the presidential ballot blank. You can vote for a third-party interest. Right? Because what will happen? In that moment—

Dyson: Wow!

Glaude: —you will actually, 2020, given the turnout of how many people vote for the presidential—the Democratic candidate, will actually impact the number of delegates that come from that state to the convention in 2020. I'm in a blue state.

Dyson: Right.

Glaude: I'm talking straight, because part of what we have to do is shift the center of gravity of how African Americans engage the political process, because this is what—1924, James Weldon Johnson says it's almost as if the "Negro vote"—quote—has already been prepackaged and sealed to be delivered before they vote.

[. . .]

Dyson: I wish that Black people were political scientists who could adjudicate competing claims about rationality, on the one hand, and demagoguery, on the other. I'm telling you, at the end of the day, the Black people you're concerned about, the vulnerable people you're concerned about, can't make distinctions—if you're in a blue state or in a red state—they can't color-book like that.

What they have to understand is, the junta that is in the offing with Donald Trump coming into office has to be resisted. Go out and vote for Hillary Clinton, because a vote for Hillary Clinton preserves the possibility that the very dialogue that Professor Glaude and I are having, the very possibility of evoking a grand tradition of Du Bois and Malcolm X and James Weldon Johnson—however, none of them got you the vote. Martin Luther King, Jr., Thurgood Marshall, Ella Baker, those are the linchpins in the narrative of Black resistance to white supremacy, social injustice and economic inequality that have delivered [the vote]. I agree that we should study this in class, but on your ass, you should go out and vote for Hillary Clinton, who makes a tremendous difference.

Glaude: See, no, no, no. See, now, this is the thing. You have to have a fundamental faith in everyday, ordinary people.

Dyson: I've got [faith in them].

Glaude: What you're—what you're representing as abstract, it's actually condescending to them.

Dyson: Not at all. I preach to them every Sunday.

Glaude: What you tried to suggest is that everyday, ordinary people can't distinguish between blue and red. What we're talking about is organizing.

Dyson: No, no, no, no, I did not say that. No, no, I didn't say that.

Glaude: Yes, you did suggest that, Mike.

Dyson: I said they can't distinguish the kind of abstract political principles you're talking about, in terms—

Glaude: I wasn't talking about abstract principles.

Dyson: Wait a minute—in terms of if you're a red state and a blue state. I'm
saying the BYP [Black Youth Project 100] youth—

Glaude: I'm saying organizing, organize, organization.

Dyson: But wait a minute. But it's not either-or. It's not either-or.

Glaude: But, see, this is the thing.

Dyson: But it's not either-or.

Glaude: If it's the case—

Dyson: It's not either-or, Eddie.

Glaude: If it's the case, Mike—

Dyson: Is it either-or?

Glaude: Let me ask you this question.

Dyson: No, I'm asking you, is it either-or?

Glaude: The strategic plan that I'm suggesting suggests that it isn't either-or.

Dyson: I'm telling you what I'm doing. I'm telling you I'm in churches with
Black people, preaching every Sunday. I'm talking about the way in which
we leverage the political, moral and spiritual authority of ordinary Black
people. When you and I walk out this place, ordinary Black people are going to look at me and see me as the embodiment of their dreams. I'm sure
it happens to you, as well. They stop me and tell me, "Thank you." They
congratulate me for at least having the authority, the courage. I don't take
that [claim] seriously, but what I take more seriously is their identification
with me as a voice piece for their aspirations and hopes.

And all I'm saying to you, sir, is that I agree with you in the full sweep
of your analysis. I'm saying the everyday, ordinary Black folk I know,
that I'm in contact with, that I'm with at political organizations, and I'm
[with] on the front line [are with me]. When I spoke yesterday for the
Black caucus of the Democratic National Convention, those thousand to
two thousand people said, "What you say represents that." All I'm saying
to you, Eddie, is that at the end of the day we cannot afford the luxury of
engaging in abstract reflections on the conditions of Black people, when
what's at stake is a demagogue, that you and I both resist, that you and
I both think is problematic, getting into office. Once that happens, then
we begin to leverage BYP. We begin to also articulate a countervailing
narrative that says it ain't either-or, it's both-and. I believe in the spirit of
our people to overcome and prevail against the odds.

CHAPTER

40

Mean, Mad White Man and the Pugnacious Black Preacher?

In May 2018, New York Times columnist Michelle Goldberg and I crossed the Canadian border into Toronto to debate conservative icon Jordan Peterson and actor Stephen Fry about political correctness in the famed Munk Debates. I warned Michelle that no matter how well we did, the audience wouldn't vote us as winners because they were hardly familiar with the intricacies of our American political moment, and, therefore, we should have as much fun as possible while mounting arguments in behalf of our adopted stance to defend a version of political correctness. Of course, both of us harbored great doubts about many aspects of PC, but we also understood that there were bigger political issues—of gender, of race—at stake that would hardly be engaged unless we brought them to the fore in front of an audience not keenly attuned to the sort of racial fracas we routinely confront in America. And yet I also understood that there were serious racial and ethnic issues roiling beneath the surface of Canada, where their famous niceness, much like that of the American South, contained a host of inelegant contradictions. Although Goldberg and Fry made brilliant comments, for the sake of clarifying the tension between me and Jordan, the present excerpts focus on me and Peterson in debate (Peterson edited his comments; mine appear nearly as originally spoken)—with Rudyard Griffiths moderating—about race, whiteness, postmodernism, ethnic identity, ideology, political correctness, and national narratives of social difference.

Jordan Peterson: Hello. So, we should first decide what we're talking about. We're *not* talking about my views on political correctness, despite what you might have inferred from the last speaker's comments.

This is how it looks to me: we essentially need something approximating a low-resolution grand narrative to unite us. And we need a narrative to unite us because otherwise we don't have peace.

What's playing out in the universities and in broader society right now is a debate between two fundamental low-resolution narratives, neither of which can be completely accurate, because they can't encompass all the details. Obviously human beings have an individual element and a collective element—a group element, let's say. The question is, what story should be paramount? This is how it looks to me: in the West, we have reasonably functional, reasonably free, reasonably productive, stable hierarchies that are open to the consideration of the dispossessed that hierarchies generally create. Our societies are freer and functioning more effectively than any societies anywhere else in the world, and than any societies ever have. As far as I'm concerned—and I think there's good reason to assume this—it's because the fundamental low-resolution grand narrative that we've oriented ourselves around in the West is one of the sovereignty of the individual. And it's predicated on the idea that, all things considered, the best way for me to interact with someone else is individual to individual, and to react to that person as if they're part of the psychological process by which things we don't understand can yet be explored, and things that aren't properly organized in our society can be yet set right. The reason we're valuable as individuals, both with regard to our rights and our responsibilities, is because that's our essential purpose, and that's our nobility, and that's our function.

What's happening, as far as I'm concerned, in the universities in particular and spreading very rapidly into the broader world—including in the corporate world, much to what should be its chagrin—is a collectivist narrative. And, of course, there's some utility in a collectivist narrative, because we're all part of groups in different ways. But the collectivist narrative that I regard as politically correct is a strange pastiche of postmodernism and neo-Marxism, and its fundamental claim is that, no, you're not essentially an individual, you're essentially a member of a group. That group might be your ethnicity and it might be your sex and it might be your race, and it might be any of the endless numbers of other potential groups that you belong to, because you belong to many. And that you should be essentially categorized along with those who are like you on that dimension in that group—that's proposition number one.

Proposition number two is that the proper way to view the world is as a battleground between groups of different power. So, you define the groups first and then you assume that you view the individual from the group context, you view the battle between groups from the group context, and you view history itself as a consequence of nothing but the power of maneuvers between different groups. That eliminates any consideration of the individual at a very fundamental level, and also any idea of free speech. Because if you're a collectivist at heart in this matter, there is no such thing as free speech. It isn't that it's debated by those on the radical Left and the rest of us; it's that in that formulation, there's no such thing as free speech because for an individualist, free speech is how you make sense of the world and reorganize society in a proper manner.

But for the radical Left type of collectivist that's associated with this viewpoint of political correctness, when you speak, all you're doing is playing a power game on behalf of your group. And there's nothing else that you *can* do, because that's all there is. And not only is that all there is in terms of who you are as an individual now, and how society should be viewed, it's also the fundamental narrative of history. For example, it's widely assumed in our universities now that the best way to conceptualize Western civilization is as an oppressive, male-dominated patriarchy, and that the best way to construe relationships between men and women across the centuries is one of oppression of women by men.

No hierarchy is without its tyranny. That's an axiomatic truth; people have recognized that for thousands of years. And hierarchies do tend toward tyranny, and they tend toward usurpation by people of power. But that only happens when they become corrupt. We have mechanisms in our society to stop hierarchies from becoming intolerably corrupt, and they actually work pretty well.

I would also point this out: don't be thinking that this is a debate about whether empathy is useful or not, or that the people on the "con" side of the argument are not empathetic. I know perfectly well, as I'm sure Mr. Fry does, that hierarchies tend to produce situations where people stack up at the bottom, and that the dispossessed in hierarchies need a political voice, which is the proper, necessary voice of the Left.

But that is not the same as proclaiming that the right level of analysis for our grand unifying narrative is that all of us are fundamentally to be identified by the groups we belong to, as to construe the entire world as the battleground between different forms of tyranny as a consequence of that group affiliation.

And to the degree that we play out that narrative, that won't be progress, believe me, and we certainly haven't seen that "progress" in the universities. We've seen situations like what happened in the Wilfrid Laurier University instead. We won't see progress: what we'll return to is exactly the same kind of tribalism that characterizes the Left. Thank you.

Rudyard Griffiths: Thank you, Jordan. Michael Eric Dyson, your six minutes start now.

Michael Eric Dyson: Thank you very kindly. It's a wonderful opportunity to be here in Canada. Thank you so much. I'm going to stand here at the podium—I'm a preacher, and I *will* ask for an offering at the end of my presentation!

This is the swimsuit competition of the intellectual beauty pageant, so let me show you the curves of my thought. Oh my God, was that a politically incorrect statement I just made? How did we get to the point where the hijacking of the discourse on political correctness has become a kind of Manichean distinction between us and them? The abortive fantasy just presented is remarkable for both its clarity and yet the muddiness of the context from which it has emerged. What's interesting to me is that, when we look at the radical Left—I'm saying, "Where they at?" I want to join them. They ain't running nothing. I'm from a country where a man stands up every day to tweet the moral mendacity of his viciousness into a nation he has warped with his perilous narcissism. Y'all got Justin; we got Donald.

So what's interesting, then, is that political correctness has transmogrified into a caricature of the Left. The Left came up with the term "political correctness," shall I remind you? We were tired of our excuses and our excesses and our exaggerations; we were willing to be self-critical in a way that I fear my *confreres*—my compatriots—are not. Don't take yourself too seriously. Smile. Take yourself not seriously at all, but what you do, do with deadly seriousness. Now it has transmogrified into an attempt to characterize the radical Left. The radical Left is a metaphor, a symbol, an articulation. They don't exist; their numbers are too small. I'm on college campuses, I don't see much of them coming.

When I hear about identity politics, it amazes me. The collectivist identity politics? Uh, last time I checked race was an invention from a dominant culture that wanted groups at their behest. The invention of race was driven by the demand of a dominant culture to subordinate others—patriarchy, right?

Patriarchy was the demand of men to have their exclusive vision presented. The beauty of feminism is that it's not going to resolve differences between men and women; it just says men don't automatically get the last word. Of course, in my career, they never did.

And so, identity politics has been generated as a *bête noire* of the Right, and yet the Right doesn't understand the degree to which identity has been foisted upon Black people and brown people and people of color from the very beginning, and on women and trans people. You think that I want to be part of a group that is constantly abhorred by people at Starbucks? I'm minding my own Black business walking down the street; I have group identity thrust upon me. They don't say, "Ah, aha, there goes a Negro—highly intelligent, articulate, verbose, capable of rhetorical fury at the drop of a hat—we should not interrogate him as to the *bona fides* of his legal status." No, they treat me as part of a group, and the problem—which our friends don't want to acknowledge—is that the hegemony, the dominance of that group, has been so vicious that it has denied us the opportunity to exist as individuals.

Individualism is the characteristic moment in modernity. Mr. Peterson is right. The development of the individual, however, is predicated upon notions of intelligence—[upon the beliefs of] Immanuel Kant and David Hume, and others. Philosophically, Descartes comes along, introducing knowledge into the fray, saying that knowledge is based upon a kind of reference to the golden intelligence, the reflective glass that one possesses. And yet it got rooted in the very ground of our existence.

So, knowledge has a fleshly basis, and what I'm saying to you is that the knowledge that I bring as a person of color makes a difference in my body, because I know what people think of me, and I know how they respond to me, and that ain't no theory.

Am I mad at trigger warnings? The only trigger warning I want is from a cop: Are you about to shoot me? Not funny in America, where young people die repeatedly, unarmed, without provocation.

And so for me, identity politics is something very serious. And what's interesting about safe spaces—I hear about the university, I teach there. Look, if you have a safe space in your body, you don't need a safe space. Some of that [dialogue about safe spaces] is overblown, some of it is ridiculous, I understand. I believe that the classroom is a robust place for serious learning. I believe in the interrogation of knowledge based upon our mutual understanding of the edifying proposition of Enlightenment. At the same time, some people ain't as equal as others, so we have to understand the conditions under which they have emerged and in which they have been benighted and attacked by their own culture.

And I ain't seen nobody be a bigger snowflake than white men who complain: "Mommy, Mommy, they won't let us play and have everything we used to have under the old regime, where we were right, racist and supremacist and dominant and patriarchs and hated gays and lesbians and transsexuals!" Yeah, you've got to share. This ain't your world; this is everybody's world.

And let me end by saying this: You remember that story from David Foster Wallace: "Two fish are going along, and an older fish comes in the opposite direction. He says, 'Hello, boys, how's the water?' They swim on, they turn to each other: 'What the hell is water?'" Because when you're in it, you don't know it; when you're dominant, you don't know it. Remember that Keyser Söze said that nothing the devil did is more interesting than to make people believe he didn't exist. That's what white supremacy is.

[. . .]

Peterson: Well, I guess I would like to set out a challenge in somewhat the same format as Mr. Fry did, to people on the moderate Left. I've studied totalitarianism for a very long time, both on the left and on the right in various forms. And I think we've done a pretty decent job of determining when right-wing beliefs become dangerous. I think that they become dangerous when they, and the people who stand on the right, evoke notions of racial superiority, or ethnic superiority, something like that. It's fairly easy—and necessary, I think—to draw a box around them and place them to one side. We've done a pretty good job of that.

What I fail to see happening on the left—and this is with regard for the sensible Left, because such a thing exists—is for the same thing to happen with regard to the radical Leftists. So here's an open question: If it's not diversity, inclusivity, and equity as a triumvirate that marks out the too-excessive Left—and with equity defined, by the way, not as equality of opportunity, which is an absolutely laudable goal, but as equality of outcome, which is how it's defined—then exactly how do we demarcate the too-extreme Left? What do we do?

We say: "Well, there's no such thing as the too-extreme Left"? Well, that's certainly something that characterized much of intellectual thinking for the twentieth century, as our high-order intellectuals, especially in places like France, did everything they could to bend over backwards, to ignore absolutely everything that was happening in the catastrophic Left world in the Soviet Union and in Maoist China, not least. We've done a terrible job of determining how to demarcate what's useful from the Left from what's pathological.

And so, it's perfectly okay for someone to criticize my attempts to identify something like a boundary. We could say, diversity, inclusivity, and equity—especially equity, which is in fact equality of outcome, which is an absolutely abhorrent notion. If you know anything about history, you know that. And I'm perfectly willing to hear some reasonable alternatives. But what I hear continually from people on the left, as my opponents did, is to construe every argument that is possibly able to be construed on the axis of group identification. And to fail to help the rest of us differentiate the reasonable Left, which necessarily stands for the oppressed, from the pathological Left, which is capable of unbelievable destruction.

And what I see happening in the university campuses in particular, where the Left is absolutely predominant—and that's certainly not my imagination, that's well documented by perfectly reasonable people like Jonathan Haidt—is an absolute failure to make precisely that distinction. And I see the same thing echoed tonight.

Griffiths: Michael, give us your rebuttal.

Dyson: I don't know what mythological collective Mr. Peterson refers to. I'm part of the Left. They're cantankerous. When they have a firing squad, it's usually in a semicircle.

Part of the skepticism of rationality was predicated upon the Enlightenment project, which says we're no longer going to be subordinate to superstition; we're going to think and we're going to think well.

Thomas Jefferson was one of the great arbiters of rationality, but he was also a man who was a slave owner. How do you reconcile that? That's the complication I'm speaking about. That's not either/or; that's not a collective identity. Thomas Jefferson believed in a collective identity—that is, during the day. At night he got some Luther Vandross songs, [and metaphorically] went out to the slave quarter, and engaged in sexual relations, and had many children with Sally Hemings. His loins trumped his logic.

And when Mr. Peterson talks about postmodernism, I don't know what he's talking about. I teach postmodernism; it's kind of fun. Jacques Derrida—just to say his name is beautiful. Michel Foucault talked about the "insurrection of subjugated knowledges" as people who had been marginalized now began to speak. The "subaltern," as Gayatri Spivak talks about in postcolonial theory. The reason these people grew up and grew into existence and had a voice is because they had been denied. As Ms. [Michelle] Goldberg said, our group identity was foisted upon us;

we were not seen as individuals. Babe Ruth, when he broke the home run record, didn't bat against all the best ballplayers; he batted against the best white ballplayers. When it's been rigged in your favor from the very beginning, it's hard for you to understand how much you've been rigged. You're born on third base, then [think] you hit a triple.

And here we are, deriving our sense of identity from the very culture that we ignore. Look at the Indigenous names and the First Nation names—Toronto, Saskatchewan, Winnipeg. Tim Horton. [Laughter]

But I'll tell you, there's an envy of the kind of freedom and liberty that people of color and other minorities bring, because we bring the depth of knowledge in our body. There's a kind of jealousy of it. As the greatest living Canadian philosopher, Aubrey "Drake" Graham, says, "Jealousy is just love and hate at the same time."

I agree with Mr. Fry: we shouldn't be nasty and combative. And yet, I don't see nastiness and combativeness from people; I see them desiring to have their individual identities respected. When I get shot down for no other reason than I'm Black, when I get categorized for no other reason than my color, I am living in a culture that refuses to see me as a great individual.

[. . .]

Griffiths: Some great rebuttals there, and strong opening statements. Let's move now into the moderated cross-examination portion of this debate and get both sides engaged on some of the key issues here. I think what we've heard here is a bit of a tension—let's draw it out a bit more—between, on the one hand, the rights of groups to feel included and have the opportunity to define a group identity, and, on the other hand, a belief that there's something under threat when these groups are overly privileged through affirmative action or other outcome-oriented processes.

So, Michael, to start with you. Why isn't harm done to groups by privileging their group identity, whether it be a group identity of race or of gender, and not immediately treating them as individuals in the way that Jordan and Stephen would like you to see them first?

Dyson: Well, first of all, there was no arbitrary and random distinction that people of color and other minority groups made. When I talked about the invention of race, the invention of gender, the invention of groupthink, that was not done by those groups that have been so named, as Ms. Goldberg said. So, first of all, you've got to acknowledge the historical evolution of that reality. The concept of group identity did not begin with them. It began with a group that didn't have to announce its identity. When you are in control, you don't have to announce who you are. Many white brothers and sisters don't see themselves as one among many ethnicities or groups. They see themselves as, "I'm just American, I'm Canadian, can't you be like us? Can't you transcend these narrow group identifications?"

And yet those group identifications have been imprinted upon them by the very people whose group power has now been challenged. Let's make no mistake about it: there's a challenge. I agree with Mr. Fry, in a kind of Neverland, about how sweet it would be to have a kingly and queenly metaphor about how it got resolved; that ain't the real deal, homie. In the real world, there's stuff at stake. What's at stake are bodies. What's at stake are people's lives. What's at stake is that people are still being lynched, killed. What's at stake is that people, because of their sexuality and their racial identity, are still being harmed.

So, what I am suggesting to you is not that we are against being treated as individuals—that's what we're crying for. Please don't see me as a member of a group that you think is a thug, a "nigger," a nihilist, a pathological person. See me as an individual who embodies [concrete] realities.

I'll end by saying this: what Michelle said is extremely important. The people who have individual rights did not have to fight for them in the same manner as people of color and others have had to. When Mr. Fry talked about enslavement, he named them. Read Orlando Patterson's comparative history of race and slavery over sixteen civilizations. The Greeks did not have the same kind of slavery that Americans did. It was chattel slavery. In Greece you could buy back your freedom. You could teach the children of the people who enslaved you, and because of your display of prodigious intellect, you could secure your freedom. That was not the case in America; you were punished and killed for literacy.

My point is simply this: I am all for the celebration of broader identities, and I think that often those who are minorities, and others, are not celebrated to the degree that we [should be].

In America, we have the Confederate flag. We have white guys, mostly, in the South, but others as well, flying those Confederate flags that represent a part of the South that refused to cede its legitimate conquest at the hands of the North. They are waving that flag, not the American flag. They are not American; they are celebrating a secession, a move away from America. And a man named Colin Kaepernick, who is a football player, saying, "I want to bring beauty to that American flag," has been denied opportunity.

So we have to really set the terms of debate in order before we proceed.

Griffiths: Thanks, Michael, good point. Jordan, let's have you jump in on this idea of what you see as the pernicious danger of groupthink when it comes to ethnicity and gender. Why do you think that's one of the primal sins, in your view, of political correctness?

Peterson: Well, I think it's one of the primal sins of identity-politics players on the left *and* the right, just to be clear about that. Personally, since this has gotten personal at times, I'm no fan of the identitarian Right. I think that anybody who plays a conceptual game where group identity comes first and foremost risks an exacerbation of tribalism. It doesn't matter whether it's on the left or the right.

With regard to the idea of group rights, this is something we have fallen into terribly in Canada, not least because we've had to contend with Quebec separatism. The idea of group rights is extraordinarily problematic, because the obverse of the coin of individual rights is individual responsibilities. And you can hold an individual responsible, and an individual can *be* responsible, and so that's partly why individuals have rights.

But groups—how do you hold a group responsible? It's not a good idea to hold a group responsible. First of all, it flies in the face of the sort of justice systems that we've laid out in the West, which are essentially predicated first on the assumption of individual innocence, but also on the possibility of individual guilt—not group guilt. We saw what happened in the twentieth century, many, many times, when the idea of group guilt was able to get a foothold in the polity and in the justice system. It was absolutely catastrophic.

And so, okay, fine—group rights. How are you going to contend with the alternative to that, the opposite of that? Where's the group responsibility? How are you going to hold your groups responsible? "Well, we don't have to talk about that, because we're too concerned with rectifying historical injustices, hypothetical and otherwise." And that's certainly not to say that there wasn't any shortage of absolutely catastrophic historical injustices—that's not the point. The point is how you view the situation at the most fundamental level, and group rights are an absolute catastrophe in my opinion.

[. . .]

Dyson: Well, first of all, you said, "Be empirical." Now, as far as I know, the word "empirical" means that which can be verified or falsified through the senses. But my point is simply this: I'm suggesting to you that people use the weapons at hand. Now, it was Abraham Joshua Heschel, the rabbi, who said that everybody's not guilty, but everybody's responsible. There's a distinction there.

Clearly, everybody is not guilty, but what's interesting is to look at the flip side. If you have benefited from three hundred years of holding people in servitude, thinking that you did it all on your own—"Why can't these people work harder?" For three hundred years, you ain't had no job. So the reality is that for three hundred years, you hold people in abeyance. You hold them in subordination; you refuse to give them rights. Then all of a sudden you free them, and say, "You're now individuals"—not having the skills, not having—

Peterson: Who's this *you* that you're referring to?

Dyson: I'm talking about American society first of all; I'm talking about North America; I'm talking about every society where enslavement has existed, but I'm speaking specifically of the repudiation of individual rights among people of color in America, who were denied the opportunity to be individuals.

I obviously and ideally—and I think Michelle Goldberg does too—agree with the emphasis on individuals. What we're saying to you is that we have not been permitted to exercise our individual autonomy and authority. And the refusal to recognize me as an individual means that when you roll up on me and I'm a twelve-year-old boy in a park, and you shoot first in ways you do to Black kids that you don't do to white kids, you are not treating that person as an individual.

Griffiths: The pot is getting stirred here—I like it.

Peterson: Let's assume for a moment that I've benefited from my white privilege, okay?

Dyson: That's a good assumption.

Peterson: Yeah, well, that's what you would say. So let's get precise about this, okay?

Dyson: Mm-hmm, let's get precise.

Peterson: To what degree is my present level of attainment or achievement a consequence of my white privilege? Do you mean 5 percent? Do you mean 15 percent? Do you mean 25 percent? Do you mean 75 percent? And what do you propose I do about it?

How about a tax? How about a tax that's specialized for me so that I can account for my damn privilege, so that I can stop hearing about it?

Now, let's get precise about one other thing, okay? If we can agree—
and we haven't—that the Left can go too far, which it clearly can, then
how would my worthy opponents precisely define when the Left that
they stand for has gone too far? You didn't like equity—equality of outcome—I think that's a great marker. But if you have a better suggestion
and won't sidestep the question, let's figure out how I can dispense with
my white privilege, and you can tell me when the Left has gone too far,
since they clearly can.

And that's what this debate is about—political correctness. It's about
the Left going too far, and I think it's gone too far in many ways, and I'd
like to figure out exactly how and when, so the reasonable Left could
make its ascendance again and we could all quit this nonsense.

[. . .]

Dyson: Jordan Peterson, this is what I'm saying to you: Why the rage, bro?
You're doing well, but you're a mean, mad white man, and you're going to
get us, right? I have never seen so much whine and snowflaking. There's
enough whine in here to start a vineyard. And what I'm saying to you,
empirically and precisely, when you ask the question about white privilege, and ask it in the way that you did—dismissive, pseudo-scientific,
non-empirical, and without justification—is that, first, the truth is that
white privilege doesn't act according to quantifiable segments; it's about
the degree to which we are willing, as a society, to grapple with the ideals
of freedom, justice, and equality upon which it's based.

The second thing that was interesting to me was that you were talking
about not having a collective identity. What do you call a nation? Are
you Canadian? Are you Canadian by yourself? Are you an individual?
Are you part of a group? When America formed its union, it did so in
opposition to another group.

So the reality is that those who are part of group identities in politics
deny the legitimacy and validity of group identity for others, while denying their identities were also created that way. They have unwarranted
resentment against other groups. All I'm asking for is for us to have the
opportunity to do the same.

The quotation you talk about—the difference between equality of
outcome and equality of opportunity—that's a staid and retried argument, a hackneyed phrase, derived from the halcyon days of the debate
over affirmative action. "Are you looking for outcomes that can be determined equally, or are you looking for opportunity?"

If you free a person from slavery after a whole long time of oppression and say, "Now you are free to survive," if they have no skills, if they have no quantifiable means of existence, what you have done is liberated them into oppression. And all I'm suggesting to you—as Lyndon Baines Johnson, one of our great presidents, said—is that if you start a man in a race a hundred years behind, it is awfully difficult to catch up.

So I don't think Jordan Peterson is suffering from anything except an exaggerated sense of entitlement and resentment, and his own privilege is invisible to him, and it's manifest with lethal intensity and ferocity right here on stage.

Griffiths: Jordan, I'll let you respond to that, if you will.

Peterson: Well, what I derived from that series of rebuttals is twofold: the first is that saying that the radical Left goes too far when they engage in violence is not a sufficient response by any stretch of the imagination, because there are sets of ideas in radical Leftist thinking that led to the catastrophes of the twentieth century, and that was at the level of idea, not at the level of violent action. It's a very straightforward thing to say you're against violence; it's like being against poverty. Generically speaking, decent people are against poverty and violence. It doesn't address the issue in the least.

And with regard to my privilege or lack thereof, I'm not making the case that I haven't had advantages in my life, and disadvantages in my life, like most people. You don't know anything about my background or where I came from, but it doesn't matter to you, because fundamentally I'm a "mean white man." That's a hell of a thing to say in a debate.

Dyson: Let me just say that the "mean white man" comment was not predicated upon my historical excavation of your past; it's based upon the evident vitriol with which you speak, and the denial of a sense of equanimity among combatants in an argument. So I'm saying again, "you're a mean, mad white man," and the viciousness is evident.

[...]

Peterson: Well, I think I'm going to point out two things again. The first is that my question about when the Left goes too far *still* hasn't been answered. And the second is that it's conceivable that I am a mean man—maybe I'm meaner than some people, and not as mean as others (although I think that's probably more the case). But I would say that the fact that race got dragged into that particular comment is a better exemplar of what the hell I think is wrong with the politically correct Left than anything else that could have possibly happened.

Dyson: Imagine the hurt, the anxiety, the insult that you might genuinely feel, according to what I felt was an appropriate comment of description at the moment of its expression. But imagine now, those hurt feelings and—

Peterson: I'm not hurt.

Dyson: Okay, you feel great! You feel great about it!

Peterson: That's really different. I'm not a victim. I'm not hurt. I'm appalled.

Dyson: You're not hurt, okay. You wouldn't be a victim. So, what's interesting is that whatever non-traditional feelings of empathy you endure at this particular point, imagine, then, the horrors that so many other "others" have had to put up with for so long, when they are refused an acknowledgment of their humanity.

Now, I take your point seriously. What I'm saying to you is that, when you said that you were upset that I added the element of race when I said, "mean, mad white man," what's interesting is that you may have felt that you were being ascribed a group identity to which you do not subscribe. You may have felt that you were being unfairly judged according to your particular race. You may have felt that your individual identity was being besmirched by my rather careless characterization of you. All of that qualifies as a legitimate response to me. But it also speaks to the point we've been trying to make about the refusal to see our individual existence, as a woman, as people of color, as First Nation people and the like.

My point simply has been: the reason I talked about race in that particular characterization is because there's a particular way in which I have come to a city—I don't know if there are a lot of Black people out here . . . I'm not sure. But I constantly come to places and spaces that are not my natural habitat—other than for intellectual engagement and the love and the fury of rhetorical engagement, yes. But I often go into hostile spaces, where people will not vote in favor of my particular viewpoint, because I'm interested as an individual in breaking down barriers so that people can understand just how complicated it is.

So, what I'm saying to you is that I would invite you, in terms of the surrender of your privilege—to give you a specific response—to come with me to a Black Baptist church. Come with me to a historically Black college, come with me to an Indigenous or First Nations community, where we're able to engage in some lively conversation, but also to listen and hear.

And when I added race to that, I was talking about people's historical inability to acknowledge others' pains equally to the ones that they are presently enduring.

So, as a human being, I love you, my brother, but I stand by my comment.

Peterson: Well, I've seen the sorts of things that you're talking about. I happen to be an honorary member of an Indigenous family, so don't tell me about what I should go see with regard to oppression. You actually don't know anything about me.

Dyson: You asked me a question, I gave you a response.

Peterson: You gave me a generic response, a generic race-based response.

[...]

Dyson: I got a pretty good idea here today. All of us have studied history, but what's interesting is that I don't recall these debates about political correctness happening when people who were in power were in absolute power, unquestioned power.

Political correctness becomes an issue when people who used to have power, or who still have power but think they don't, get challenged on just a little bit of what they have and don't want to share—toys in the sandbox of life. So, all of a sudden it becomes a kind of exaggerated grievance.

Now, the things you named—the bullet points and the cisgender and the heteronormativity and heteropatriarchy and the capitalist resurgence and the insurrection of subjugated knowledges, to give Foucault some more love, or the Derridean deconstruction—all that stuff; the French phase is still going on with the french fries in America. What's interesting is that I didn't hear many complaints of political correctness at the height of the dominance of one group or another, but when Martin Luther King, Jr., who argued for group identity, as a Black person, to provide an opportunity for individual Black people to come to the fore, they began to make that claim.

Now, they didn't call it political correctness. "You're siding with those who are against free speech; you're siding with those who don't want me as a white person to be recognized in my humanity." And what I mean by political correctness is the kind of politics of *ressentiment* that are articulated by various holders of power at certain levels, at various levels.

One of the beautiful things about Foucault is that he said power breaks out everywhere. I would think a person who is critical of political correctness like you would appreciate this. As opposed to Max Weber, who said that power is over there in a hierarchical structure, where subordination is the demand, Foucault said, "No, power breaks out even among people who are disempowered." So, you can hurt somebody in your own community.

What's more politically incorrect than a Black Baptist preacher identifying with a first-century Palestinian Jew and still loving atheists? What's more politically incorrect than a Black intellectual going on Bill Maher and defending his ability to continue to have his show, despite using the N-word?

I, sir, believe in a politically incorrect version of the world. When I go as a Black Baptist preacher to chastise my fellow believers about their homophobia, that goes over like a brick cloud. When I come into arenas like this, I understand that my back is up against the wall, but—

Stephen Fry: Then come and sit over here!

Dyson: So, what's interesting is that when we look at what is seen as political correctness in our societies—in a free Canadian society, in a free American society—to me it has been a massive jumble that has been carved out of the politics of resentment that powers once held are no longer held; freedoms once exercised absolutely must now be shared.

So, I am in agreement with both of the gentlemen to my right, who believe that political correctness has been a scourge, but not necessarily the way you think. I think it's been a scourge because those who have been the deployers of power and the beneficiaries of privilege have failed to recognize their particular way. And at the end of the day, I think that those of us who are free citizens of this country, and of America, should figure out ways to respect the humanity of the other, to respect the individual existence of the other, and also respect the fact that barriers have been placed upon particular groups that have prevented them from flourishing. That's all I mean by political correctness.

[. . .]

Peterson: Look, I don't like identity-politics players at all. I don't care whether they're on the left or the right. I've been lecturing about right-wing extremism for thirty years. I'm no fan of the Right, despite the fact that the Left would like to paint me that way, because it's more convenient for them.

Dyson: How has the Right gone too far recently?

Peterson: It's threatening to go too far in identitarian Europe, that's for sure. It's gone too far in Charlottesville; it went too far in Norway. How long a list do you want? And why am I required to produce that? To show you that I don't like the identitarian Right?

Dyson: You asked me, so I just thought I'd ask you.

Peterson: I was actually asking you a question. So, your assumption is somehow that I must be on the side of the Right. Look, the Right hasn't occupied the humanities and the social sciences. It's as simple as that for me. If they had, I'd be objecting to them.

Dyson: Say that again, I didn't hear.

Peterson: The Right has not occupied the social sciences and the humanities, and the Left clearly does—the statistical evidence for that is overwhelming.

Dyson: So, what about IQ testing in terms of genetic inheritance?

Peterson: We're here to talk about political correctness, and we've done a damn poor job of it.

Dyson: Oh, I see. I gave you an example and you can't answer. Okay, all right.

[. . .]

Griffiths: Michael, I'm going to put three minutes on the clock for you.

Dyson: Thank you so much for that compliment, Brother Fry. [He accused me of "huckstering snake oil pulpit talk."] I'm used to [not exclusively] white men who see Black intelligence articulated at a certain level feeling a kind of condescension. A kind of verbal facility is automatically assumed to be a kind of hucksterism and snake-oil salesmanship. I've seen that. I get it. I get hate letters every day from white brothers and sisters who are mad I'm teaching their children. "You are just trying to co-opt our children; you are trying to corrupt them." Yes, I'm trying to corrupt them so that they will be uncorrupted by the corruptibility that they've inherited from a society that refuses to see all people as human beings.

The death threats I have received constantly for simply trying to speak my mind . . . it's not about a politically correct society that is open-minded and that has some consternation about my ability to speak. I'm getting real live—you want empirical—death threats that talk about killing me, setting up to hurt me and harm me, simply because I choose to speak my mind.

I agree with my *confreres* and my compatriots that we should argue against the vicious limitations and repercussions against speech. I believe that everybody has the right to be able to articulate themselves. And the enormous privilege we have to come to a space like this means that we have that privilege, and we should be responsible for it.

No matter where we go from here, me and Brother Peterson will go to a Black Baptist church. I'm going to hold him to that; he said it on national TV. We're going to go to a Black Baptist church and have an enlightening conversation about the need for us to engage not only in reciprocal and mutual edification but in criticism—even hard and tough criticism. But in a way that speaks to the needs and interests of those who don't usually get on TV, whose voices are not usually amplified, whose ideas are not usually taken seriously. And when they get to the upper echelons of the ability of a society to express themselves, they are equally subject to vicious recrimination and hurtful resistance.

There's an old story about the pig and the chicken going down the street and saying, "Let's have breakfast." The chicken just has to give up an egg; the pig has to give up his ass in order to make breakfast. We have often been the pigs giving up our asses to make breakfast. Let's start sharing them asses with everybody else. Thank you.

Peterson: I'm not here to claim that there's no such thing as oppression, unfairness, brutality, discrimination, unfair use of power—all of those. Anyone with any sense knows that hierarchical structures tilt toward tyranny, and that we have to be constantly wakeful to ensure that all they are isn't just power and tyranny.

It's interesting to hear Foucault referred to; it's unfortunate, but it's interesting, because Foucault, like his French intellectual *confreres*, essentially believed that the only basis upon which hierarchies were established was power. And that's part of this pernicious politically correct doctrine that I've been speaking about. When a hierarchy becomes corrupt, then the only way to ascend it is to exercise power—that's essentially the definition of a tyranny.

But that doesn't mean the imperfect hierarchies that we have constructed in our relatively free countries don't at least tilt somewhat toward competence and ability, as evidenced by the staggering achievements of civilization that we've managed to produce. It doesn't mean that the appropriate way of diagnosing them is to assume, without reservation, unidimensionally, that they're all about power, and as a consequence, that everyone who occupies any position within them is a tyrant in the making. And that is certainly the fundamental claim of someone like Foucault. And it's part and parcel of this ideological catastrophe that is political correctness.

I'm not here to argue against progress. I'm not here to argue against equality of opportunity. Anyone with any sense understands that, even if you're selfish, you're best served by allowing yourself access to the multiplicitous talents of everyone, and to discriminate against them for arbitrary reasons unrelated to their competences is abhorrent. That has nothing to do with the issue at hand. It isn't that good things haven't happened in the past and shouldn't continue to happen—that's not the point. The point is the point my compatriot Fry has made, which is: well, we can agree on the catastrophe and we can agree on the historical inequity, but there's no way I'm going to agree that political correctness is the way to address any of that. And there's plenty of evidence to the contrary, some of which I would say was displayed quite clearly tonight.

41

What's Love Got to Do with It?

Recently I was preaching at a prominent Black Baptist church in the Midwest, and after the sermon, during a book signing held for me in the church's great hall, a Black woman approached me and said, bluntly, "You know you're going to hell." "Did Jesus tell you that this morning?" I quickly retorted. "'Cause I spoke to him and he ain't tell me that was the case. Well, I guess I don't have to watch my cholesterol then." I suppose that was a non sequitur; but my slight, if nonsensical, humor was an effort to lighten things up. "You know why you're going to hell. You preached that God made gay people." "Oh," I said. "I see. But wait, you think I'm going to hell? You're clearly a polytheist. You think there's a God for gay people, and one for straight people. Plus, what do you think happened? God took off on Wednesday of the week of creation, and said, 'Lord, this making the world stuff ain't no joke. I need a day off.' And then a lesser deity came along and created gay people? Guess what, lots of white folk used to believe that that was true of Black people, and that we weren't human and that we were children of a lesser god, if of any god at all." I paused a bit as she got madder and was turning on her heels to leave. "Either God made everybody, or God ain't made nobody." This is a condensed version of a debate between me and Bishop Harry Jackson that is a far more solemn and sophisticated take on the conversation I had with that Black woman in church, but, I'm afraid, with the same frustrated results. It took place on NPR on Michel Martin's show, Tell Me More, *in May of 2009. Sadly, Bishop Jackson, who had become a spiritual adviser to President Trump, died in November 2020.*

Michel Martin: But first, our regular "Faith Matters" conversation. That's where we talk about matters of faith and spirituality. Earlier we spoke with former Washington, D.C., mayor and current city councilman Marion Barry. He was the only member of the 13-member council to oppose a measure that would've allowed D.C. to recognize same-sex marriages legally performed elsewhere.

[...]

Martin: Let me ask each of you how you arrived at the decision, at the place you are now on the issue of same-sex marriages and sanctifying, particularly sanctifying those relationships. I'm interested to know whether this is an issue you struggled with either personally or theologically or spiritually? And Bishop Jackson, why don't you start.

Jackson: Well, I'm against same-sex marriage. I struggled with the issue of the civil rights question. I think it's [a] little bit trumped up. And I'm looking at the next generation. It's not really about me or folks who want to get married. It's about what's going to happen when you redefine marriage, family, parenting? And then in the schools we've got *Heather Has Two Mommies,* we've got all those kinds of things. Do I want to go down this slippery slope where I begin to change what has been established, I believe by God, in the Scriptures? So I think the fight is about what the next generation will think.

Martin: But is the core of your view theologically driven? Would that be accurate to say this is your understanding of what Scripture requires and demands?

Jackson: Absolutely, that's where my starting point is. Absolutely.

Martin: And Reverend Dyson, can I ask you, is this a question you struggled with personally, theologically, spiritually? And what animates your point of view on this issue?

Dyson: There's no question that I struggled with it theologically. I suppose that I inherited the same vocabulary and worldview as most Black Christians do, most Christians in general, to be sure. It was heterosexist in the sense that it took the heterosexual orientation as the norm from which to start as the given. And everything that fell outside of that was not acceptable. But as I began to dig deeper into the Scriptures, where I read, [to paraphrase] "Love the Lord thy God with all thy soul, heart and mind. Love thy neighbor as thyself." That's what the law of the prophets comes down to, Jesus says. There's no asterisk, "Oh, except the gay or lesbian or transgender or bisexual people." Unlike Bishop Jackson, I think it is a matter of extending a trajectory of civil rights, along with theological reflection, into our consideration here.

He says we're redefining marriage. Well, look at what the heterosexuals are doing with it now. "Heather has two mommies," "Shaniqua got four baby daddies"—and I defend Shaniqua!

[Laughter]

My point is that not all heterosexual arrangements [. . .] have led to an endorsement of what those arrangements might look like, [especially] if the ideal is failed. So, I believe ultimately that God is a God of love, God is a God who creates human beings in splendorous difference. And I think we must embrace all of those differences, and be careful about applying a biblical stricture against homosexuality, when the same biblical stricture was applied to Black people by white supremacists who sought to use the Bible as a cudgel to beat Black people over the head and keep them enslaved and to keep women subordinate to men.

Martin: What about that, Bishop Jackson? There are those who say, well, for every person who cites Scripture in defense of their view against same-sex marriage, there are those who say you can certainly cite Scripture that was used to warrant slavery, that has been used to warrant child abuse, that has been used to warrant the abuse of women partners. What do you say about that?

Jackson: Well, I will say that they are correct, but those are not appropriate and correct interpretations of the Scripture. Anyone who looks at this Scripture doesn't see child slavery as being endorsed in the Bible. It's not there. [One] does not see, if you really read the New Testament, a male-oriented bashing of women. It's not really there. The culture, as Dr. Dyson has already discussed, brought its eyeglasses to the Scriptures, instead of seeing what the Scripture has to say. So, we profoundly disagree. Most African American clergy agree with me.

Martin: But how do you know that your interpretation is correct on this point given that throughout history, you would agree, I know, that as you just said that other interpretations of Scripture have been, in the current view, incorrect?

Jackson: Well, it's one of those things about faithfulness to what you believe to be the truth of the Scripture and the council of folks who are the faith community. As Dr. Dyson knows, people decided in the early days of the faith these particular books would be in the Scriptures, and these would not be. And essentially, the elders of the faith have gathered together and said, this is the orthodox path. This is truth as we understand it from the written word of God and how we understand Scripture to be inspired. And we as a community say, this body of truth means this. Now could that group be wrong? Certainly, but I don't think that I really have the right to play with the Scripture.

Martin: When you said that earlier that you've struggled with the civil rights aspect of that, what do you mean?

Jackson: I mean, individuals. I've got gay family members. I have folks who are in all kind of walks of life. And as a Black person thinking about 400 years of slavery, thinking about the stuff we've gone through, I would not want to keep anybody from a genuine right. I think most of us Black people feel like that.

On the other hand, Black folks, it seems to me, have a penchant for calling right, right and wrong, wrong. Meaning that I may not even be living right but I say, "That's wrong even though I'm not doing the right thing." And in that spirit, I think we are very much in danger as a whole culture of letting people do whatever they want in the name of, "It's not my business, I'm not in your bedroom," whatever. And Dr. Dyson, I've read some studies by Dr. Stanley Kurtz of Harvard that say that in places that have allowed same-sex marriage, there is an acceleration of a kind of breakdown in the family that we already see in Black families.

Martin: You are talking about overseas? You're talking about in other countries?

Jackson: Overseas, other countries, like in Europe. And so [. . .] 40 percent of the young single women probably will never be married in the Black community, and we're looking at my grandbabies coming into a world that is spiraling out of control—this is not the only aspect of the problem. But somewhere, I got to say stop the madness, I'm going to stop this negative influence and then I'm going to do marital intervention. I'm going to try to heal marriages. I've been married 33 years and that's what I want to promote.

Martin: Reverend Dyson, what about that? Bishop Jackson says right is right and the Bible may have been wrong on some things but it's right about this thing?

Dyson: Well, you know, you pressed him on the critical issue. I don't think, with all due respect to the brilliance of the Bishop, that he gave sufficient answer to you because it is arbitrary, ultimately. And it depends upon poll-driven analysis of the Scripture, which is contrary [to what] Jesus said, paraphrasing him, "wide is the way that leads to destruction." In other words, 80 percent of the people. "[But] narrow is the way that leads toward heaven." The smaller percentage. So, the minority is in the right here, according to Jesus. And "slaves obey your masters" was applied during child slavery.

When you look at the house codes in Ephesians, for instance, [we read, to paraphrase] "slaves obey your masters, women obey your husbands, children obey your fathers." Get this, if you are that dude, if you're the guy, because you could be a slave master and a husband and a father, you rollin' big. And the Bible is being written by people who look like you. So, I disagree, I think that the philosophical architecture of gender oppression got written into the Scriptures. I think that the bias and bigotry toward the vulnerable was written there, but the Bible is big enough and deep enough and profound enough to argue with itself and to allow various interpretations to prevail. I ultimately think that what we are responsible for is to interpret this Bible according to love. I don't think, finally, in ending, that [sexuality is] an experiment. I understand Bishop Jackson when he talks about this experiment and the crushing numbers in Europe.

Let's do an analysis right here on the ground in America: Given[. . .] heterosexual communities that generate marriage, or the lack of marriage, in African American communities—gay marriage ain't the problem, 'cause there ain't many gay people married. And when people say, well, it's a lifestyle choice—look, when did you decide to be heterosexual? Let me see, at seven years old, you went to your momma, and said, "look, check this out. I'm going to need that Corvette at 16 because I'm about macking the ladies, and I need that Black book so I can appeal to them?" There is no conscious choice of heterosexual identity any more than there is a homosexual one. Given the bigotry they confront, the last [people] in the world who want to be homosexual, for the most part, are homosexuals.

Martin: Bishop Jackson, what about that? What about Reverend Dyson's point, that the Bible is a living document and that a love-based perspective would sanction marriage for those that love each other, and that the core of that is the love and the commitment of the parties as opposed to their gender. What do you say to that?

Jackson: Well, I disagree. It's really not good hermeneutics, good exegesis of the Scriptures. A word, "obey," that he talked about, [should] be translated slightly different in terms of arrange yourself, adjust yourself. So, I don't think that . . .

Dyson: All of which remain problematic. I just want to throw that in—all of which remain problematic.

Jackson: Well, they do, but most theologians don't come out where you come out. And so, you make a good statement that hey, the path is narrow that leads to truth. But right now, it feels as though in our culture, especially in our communications field, that everybody is pro-gay marriage, pro-this, pro-that. It's popular, and I think there's a difference between being biblically faithful and being politically correct.

Martin: Is the core of your view, Bishop, that homosexuality is indeed a matter of moral choice as opposed to biological determination? Is that, do you think, the core of your difference between you and Reverend Dyson?

Jackson: I think so, because the complexity of choosing your gender—let's say you feel you're gay—there's so many psychological aspects that could cause you to feel like you're gay. But I believe that God has put a divine sentence in every individual, a reflection of himself, that maleness and femaleness are a part of this divine revelation of who God is put in human form.

In other words, he wired men to be men, women to be women, to reflect something of his glory. And he did that on purpose. He wasn't confused, he didn't stutter, he didn't stammer. If that's the case, then we've got somebody who's trying to mar and reverse the indelible image of God that has been put there, on purpose, by the God who put the stars in the sky. The people that say they can see God in nature and creation, that God said male and female.

Martin: Can I just ask at one point, though, a point that I had made with Councilman Barry earlier, which is—for many people the proof of justice, the proof of right and wrong, is not a matter of what is popular. And you'd said that most African American clergy, in your view, and most African American citizens, in your view, agree with you on that. Is that dispositive? Is that what makes it right?

Jackson: No, that doesn't necessarily make it right. It's really the Scriptures as I see it. Again, Reverend Dyson comes from more of a liberal interpretation of the Scriptures. I come from a more conservative, in terms of a Scriptural approach, and that means we're miles apart. And anyone listening to us would say hey, I agree with one or the other, based on how they value and approach the immutability or the surety of the word of God.

Martin: Reverend Dyson, what about you? Go ahead.

Dyson: Well, the words certainly may be immutable, but not our interpretation of them. "When I was a child, I thought as a child, I spake as a child; when I became a man, I put away childish things," to paraphrase Paul. But he said "now we see through a glass darkly. Then we shall know, even as we are also known." So, there's an epistemic gulf. There's a knowledge division between us and God.

Jackson: Yeah, but what makes you right?

Dyson: That's what I'm saying to you, but let me finish. So, I'm saying to you the fact is that as human beings who are marred, to use your word, limited, fractured and therefore provisional, we can't make absolute statements about truth because we don't know them—because we're not God. And in that sense, to say that we're giving the absolute, inerrant, infallible word of God is a contradiction in terms, because as Paul says, "we have this treasure in earthen vessels."

We don't know the whole deal. And Howard Thurman, the great African American mystic and preacher, said: look, you can go to the Atlantic Ocean, you can dip your glass in the Atlantic Ocean, it may be full of the Atlantic Ocean, but it's not all of the Atlantic Ocean.

Black people need to be the last people in the world, number one, to tell anybody who they need to get married to. Because look, I'm just amazed that gay and lesbian people want to get married after seeing what we heterosexuals have done to the institution. That restores my faith in marriage more than heterosexuals doing it. And number two, at the end of the day, it is about love. The love of God mediated to all human beings. And since we can all acknowledge we are fallible, and we are limited, and we're imperfect vessels, and we don't know the whole truth, let's in the meantime, until we find out, love each other into the next stage.

PUBLICS

My hope is that we are able to find . . . space between absolutely refusing to perform because the stakes are *too* high and absolutely rushing to perform because they *are* so high.

—D. Soyini Madison, *Performance, Personal Narratives, and the Politics of Possibility*

How important it is for scholars to take big ideas and translate them into smaller, but still substantial, bits that can be compelling to lay readers.

—Tera Hunter

It was the women freedom fighters who lit a fire in my soul. It was the Angela Davises, the Sojourner Truths, and the Assata Shakurs of the world. While fighting for both civil rights and, undoubtedly, their respect among men, the women leaders took just as much risk but received little of the recognition. There was no ego involved when women strapped on their boots and lent their lives to the movement. There was not recognition to receive. Just a belief and passion in the quest toward the liberty of Black America.

—Tamika Mallory, *State of Emergency: How We Win in the Country We Built*

When I was eleven years old, in the seventh grade at Webber Junior High, notice of an upcoming oratorical contest was broadcast over the loudspeaker during the daily morning announcements. At the end of the school day, I convinced my best friend, Greg White, to go with me to the appointed classroom so we could see what this was all about. We headed to the third floor to Mr. Otis Burdette's homeroom.

"Hey, fellas, how are you?" he greeted us.

"Fine, sir," we said.

"What's an oratorical contest?" I asked Mr. Burdette. "What does that word mean?"

"It means giving a speech," he said.

"Oh, okay. That's alright. Let's go, Greg."

"Why don't you fellas stick around?" Mr. Burdette suggested.

"No, I'm not really interested in doing that," I told Mr. Burdette.

Perhaps I had spoken too soon. After all, I had been reciting set pieces from memory ever since I was a youth in Sunday school. And Dr. King was a huge influence on me even then. When he had been killed in 1968, I used all of my allowance money to purchase through the mail a 45-rpm recording of excerpts from his most famous speeches. I quickly followed up on Mr. Burdette's gentle plea: "What do we have to do?"

"Well, you have to write a speech and then commit it to memory and deliver it."

The contest was sponsored by the local Optimist Club. I knew what *optimist* meant since I was my elementary school's spelling bee champ in both the fifth and sixth grades. Still, I wasn't feeling very upbeat about my prospects of prevailing if I entered a speech contest. But the more Mr. Burdette talked, the more Greg and I listened and thought maybe we'd give it a shot. Greg's brother, Barry, was a local phenomenon, a prodigy who had graduated from high school at fourteen and college at eighteen. We knew full well we weren't on that track of achievement, but both of us had drawn notice for our smarts, so we made a pact to give it a go.

Eventually, two years in a row, I won the school contest, then a district one, and made it to the regional contest, where I lost each time to much older boys. I can still see the headline in the *Detroit News* after winning my first district contest: "12-Year-Old Boy's Plea Against Racism Wins Award." Each year I won, I was invited to give my speech—the first year it was titled "This I Believe," the second year, "Our Challenge: Involvement," the titles having been assigned by the Optimist Club—to many organizations, including, the first time around, at a luncheon sponsored by Black businessmen. I was astonished to see that the event's cost, in 1972, was $12.50, a fee that was unimaginable to me, although my mother and I gained entree for free. From that time on I wrote and gave speeches, and eventually began to write, too, a play here, an oration for a protest gathering there, and I kept a periodic journal of sorts where I recorded my thoughts. I lost it long ago, but I remember a verse I composed, when I was perhaps fourteen: "These thoughts, these thoughts/In my head/If not written/Soon lie dead."

In many ways I am still that twelve-year-old boy relishing the opportunity to express myself and, hopefully, in the process, to bless someone's life.

The Right Address

Speeches on the Public Stage

CHAPTER

42

A Shovel or a Rope?

I was gratified that my 2005 speech about Bill Cosby—sandwiched between Henry Louis Gates, Jr.'s speech on the color line and Barack Obama's famous race speech "A More Perfect Union"—appeared in the book Say It Loud: Great Speeches on Civil Rights and African American Identity. *Cosby was one of my boyhood idols. I entertained no glee in opposing Cosby's brutal and bitter attack on poor Black folk, since his films, comedy albums, and recorded stand-up routines provided me and millions more so much joy. But, given his celebrity and wealth, I felt I had no choice but to write and speak on behalf of poor Black folk, many of whom, sadly but predictably enough, supported his views right along with millions of white folk looking for a Black voice to validate and amplify their low view of Black life. My speech has taken on even greater weight because of sexual assault allegations against Cosby, and his conviction for aggravated indecent assault in 2018 before his sentence of three to ten years was vacated by the Supreme Court of Pennsylvania in June of 2021, due to violations of his constitutional rights.*

Thank you so very kindly, Miss [Belva] Davis, for that warm introduction and for the opportunity to address such an august and distinguished audience about topics that are central, not only to African American culture but, indeed, to the American mainstream. I'm honored to be here today to engage you in discussion and dialogue, and perhaps open debate, about the issues of race and class and culture and generation.

I wrote my book on Bill Cosby—rather more directly, his remarks, now infamous as Miss Davis has indicated—precisely because those remarks did not appear out of or get driven into a vacuum. The remarks Mr. Cosby made on May 17, 2004, to an equally distinguished audience gathered together at Constitution Hall in Washington, DC, were sponsored by Howard University—along with the NAACP Legal Defense Fund and the NAACP at large—where Mr. Cosby was to receive an award on behalf of his extraordinary philanthropy and generosity and that of his wife, Dr. Camille Cosby.

Instead of giving the usual "thank you very kindly" speech, Mr. Cosby lapsed into one of the most remarkable rants of recent times—remarkable for its vigor, remarkable for its rancor, even more remarkable for the acrimony and the bitterness that it poured upon the heads of the Black poor. Mr. Cosby began a rhetorical rampage against the vulnerable by indicting them for failing to live up to the great promise of the Civil Rights Movement. He looked around that august crowd and called on the great cloud of witnesses who had gathered either symbolically or literally, calling upon Dorothy Height and others who were similarly distinguished for their extraordinary sacrifice in contributing to the Civil Rights Movement, and wondered aloud what they must think in the face of the degrading disappearance of dignity marked by the infamous and scandalous and even dangerous rise of the Black poor, and the way in which their habits so vehemently denied the incredible uplift that was delivered by the Civil Rights Movement.

He said, among other things, that poor Black people, in letting down the Civil Rights Movement, didn't speak the right way. In fact, Mr. Cosby offered that he was scarcely capable of speaking the way "these people speak." He went on to suggest that they didn't speak English. Everybody knew to speak English except "these knuckleheads." Mr. Cosby went on to suggest that Black poor people were especially licentious, having four and five children with two and three different men in the house at any particular time, and that, as a result of that licentiousness, they had communicated and transmitted a virulent virus of immorality to their children.

In fact, he suggested that perhaps one would have to have a DNA card in the ghetto pretty soon to determine if they were making love to their grandmothers. He said that a grandmother is a woman who had a baby at twelve, her child has a baby at about thirteen or fourteen, do the math—they're about twenty-six years old, he said, and they could be a grandmother and, therefore, he was trying to prevent the kind of incestuous relations that might result from people being incapable of determining genetically that one was related to a woman that one was pursuing, because she was so young.

He went on to suggest that people who give their children names like "Shaniqua, Taliqua and Muhammad and all that crap"—that's a direct quote—and "all of 'em are in jail"—another direct quote—are the very ones who are tearing away the fabric of conscience in the community. Mr. Cosby, among many other things, suggested that this poor Black community was especially anti-intellectual, uninterested in investing in education. Why? They spent $500 on gym shoes as opposed to $250 on "Hooked on Phonics."

On and on he went, in a kind of improvisational rant, where Charlie Parker meets Dennis Miller. [Laughter] And he remonstrated extravagantly against the poor. And when he made his initial comments, *The New York Times* called me. I responded to them. Mr. Cosby got me on the phone. We spoke. He told me that perhaps I hadn't heard the entire balance of his comments. I didn't understand the context within which they were delivered. And as a result, he offered to send me both the audio and the transcript of his speech.

And when I received that audio and transcript, I was mortified. Dumbfounded. Bewildered. Befuddled to a certain degree. But incensed, at another level. He incensed me to action, to reaction to be sure, and to bleed my pathos on the page, the results of which are contained in *Is Bill Cosby Right?: Or Has the Black Middle Class Lost Its Mind?* So, for me, such an incendiary title, of course, evokes an equally incendiary response. To be sure, I expect that. And yet, one remarks upon and observes with, not this mythological objectivity, with not even bemused interest, but with a kind of a shudder that people might be offended by such a subtitle who were not offended by the initial assault on the poor. A drive-by by a prominent figure within the community. A ghastly, almost conscienceless assault upon them in the name of their betterment. That kind of tough love was mostly tough, not love.

And so I began to think about these issues in the broader social and political and moral contexts within which they inevitably resonate. And when I began to think about it, I tried to put Mr. Cosby's career in context. I began in my first chapter speaking about the interesting irony of Mr. Cosby delivering such a broadside against the vulnerable and disadvantaged, himself having emerged from the Richard Allen Projects in Philadelphia. Of course, back then, the Richard Allen Projects were probably like new condominiums to folk who were poor, and the landscape was quite different forty and fifty years ago than it is now, as poverty itself has undergone radical transmutation—is a different animal. The DNA of impoverishment is quite different. It adapts to different circumstances now than even when I was poor, say twenty-five to thirty years ago.

And so out of this tremendous groundswell of anxiety that Mr. Cosby spoke from, we remember his childhood of poverty, after being middle-class. We also remember his remarkable rise, going to school, and in the sixth grade his teacher recounting that Bill would rather clown than study. How good that is, since he's a comedic genius.

And then, in the tenth grade, he flunked not once, not twice, but three times. After flunking out of school, and dropping out, he went to the Navy. And after going to the Navy, received a GED, then enrolled in Temple University. And after two years he dropped out to pursue his legendary comedic career. Later on, he was given the BA from Temple University, based upon life experience, then invited to study for the Master's and Doctor of Education degrees at University of Massachusetts at Amherst, where he wrote a dissertation on *Fat Albert and the Cosby Kids*. Then, one of his dissertation advisors lamented the degree, saying it was an empty credential. I think that lamentation is far too harsh. And yet, it does underscore the ironic pedigree of Mr. Cosby's educational attainment in light, especially, of his vigorous assault upon those who have not been equally vigorous about pursuing education.

But when we see the backdrop, we see a great inspiration like Dr. Cosby, having himself overcome impediments and obstacles that were in the way to achieve at the height of the terminal degree in America, and yet, when we began to peel back the layers, with the forceps provided by critical analysis, we began to see beneath the skin, subcutaneously, some of the contradictions. Like, folk done helped you out along the way. Given you stuff, in acknowledgment of your genius. That's fine. But in terms of the same patterns that other people have to pursue: It's a good thing that Bill Cosby wasn't around when Bill Cosby was a child, else he might not have become Bill Cosby.

The interesting irony, as well, is in one sense exacerbated, or compounded, at least, when one recalls that Mr. Cosby, for most of his career, has shirked his representative faculty as a Black icon. He's resolutely refused to represent the race, saying that his fame and celebrity meant that he was a great comedian, not a leader. Time after time, Mr. Cosby demurred, in sometimes colorful fashion, saying that, and I'm paraphrasing, "I am not a leader, I'm a comedian, that's all. Why do people insist that I make statements about the race? Why must I make all of the statements about the race? Why must I carry what James Baldwin calls the burden of representation?" "Why must I," Mr. Cosby said on one occasion, "represent the race in that fashion?" In 1985, when he appeared on *The Phil Donahue Show*, Mr. Cosby said, in answer to a question, "I am not an expert on

Blackness. Why are you asking me this question? Why don't you let me be a h-u-m-a-n b-e-i-n-g?"

Mr. Cosby said, "In my comedy I will not depend upon color." Initially, of course, he was in the mode of a Dick Gregory—acerbic, witty comments upon the acid realities of race in America. But then he chose a different path. He said, I'm paraphrasing, "I want to be a race transcender. I want to speak universally to all Americans, and therefore I don't think you can speak about the things that divide us. We must speak about the things that bring us together." Fine. And yet, in that path that he has pursued rather diligently and conscientiously, Mr. Cosby has reneged upon the necessity thrust upon others in similar positions to speak for, or on behalf of, the race.

He has given extraordinary amounts of money. His philanthropy is unquestionable. The genius of his giving has inspired remarkable response, just in recognition of what he has done. And yet, that philanthropy must never cause us to be silent in our dissent. Otherwise, elsewhere—sprinkled out in his rant—was the notion that young Black people were pimping their parents. Otherwise, the pimp/ho metaphor would be applied with vicious particularity to us and Mr. Cosby. Giving money can never be the litmus test for great Black leadership. Otherwise, Bill Gates would be the greatest Black leader we've ever had.

Mr. Cosby's background, to be sure, is relevant, but I spend most of my time not on him but on the issues, lest people think I have devolved into an ad hominem attack full of animus against a great icon. No. I want to deal with the issues he raised. And they're quite interesting. He says that he doesn't know how to talk like these people "be talkin'." Oh, I be disagreein' with that. [Laughter] I think if one examines the speech that night, it was full of Ebonicisms, witty articulations predicated upon pigmented linguistic and verbal invention. "Standin' on the co'ner."

When one thinks about the speech that night, and listens to it, it is full of the bristling integrity of street speech. It fairly glimmers with the possibility of the faint recognition—no, even more than faint—a powerful recognition of the power of speech, Black speech, Ebonics, Black articulation, Black English. And so full was that speech of these Ebonicisms and witticisms drawn from Black culture, that one must remark that Mr. Cosby is unconscious of his facility. But let's be honest. He's made a whole bunch of money off of Black English, too. I mean, Fat Albert didn't exactly speak the King's English to the Queen's taste. Didn't go around spouting Tennyson,

Though much is taken, much abides; and though
We are not now that strength which in old days
Moved earth and heaven; that which we are we are;
One equal temper of heroic hearts
Made weak by time and fate, but strong in will
To strive, to seek, to find, and not to yield.

No, he said, "I'm-ba gone-ba be-ba back-ba soon-ba." [Laughter] An interesting contrast, to be sure, even if you're not in for, say, metaphysical poetry from Donne, or even the high vernacular of Dunbar, who could switch from "I know why the caged bird sings" to "Little brown baby wif' spa'klin' eyes." Code switching is always in order.

And, of course, Mr. Cosby is right. We want our children to be able to move from one vernacular to the other. After all, don't be deceived—even Standard English has its vernacular intonations. If you contrast this to, say, what's going on in Europe right now, even in England, the English we speak here is not standard to the English being spoken there. Standards are dictated by local communities and circumstances. Standards are judged by societies that have the power to reinforce a variety of a language as uniformly, universally recognized and accepted. Never misunderstand the fact that language is always implicated in notions of power. Who has the power to tell you what's right and wrong, to speak "American," or to be in California with its nativist xenophobic passions unleashed across the board? And yet, the grand irony, perhaps God's *grande blague* and great joke—to have Schwarzenegger as the governor. Oh, the delicious irony of it all. It's too much not to comment on. "Coll-i-forn-ya." And you against Ebonics!

And so the suggestion here, of course, is to say, as James Baldwin said, "If Black English isn't a language, then tell me what is." The literal name of an essay that one of the great masters of the eloquence of the English language imbued with the sense of the King James rhetoric that his family transmitted to him, and you can hear it broiling beneath the rhetorical surface in his novels, but especially in those majestic essays—some of the best in the English language—that rival the best speakers of the tongue.

And yet he said that the purpose of Black English was for Black folk to be able to speak in such a fashion as not to be murdered in the face of white folk who were trying to murder them—in slavery and on plantations, and in Jim Crow regions and arenas, where American apartheid reigned. And so, Mr. Baldwin suggested that the virtue of Black English is the ability to facilitate a communication that will not be easily spotted in the dominant culture with the power to crush the minority. So the moral utility of the language must be examined and acknowledged as one makes dissertation upon the faults and failures of that language. Of course, Cosby is right. We don't want folks going to their jobs and saying, "Break me off dat application. You know what I'm siz-ayin' riz-ight niz-ow? Yeah, 'cause I'm tryin' to get dat job." That's probably not the best thing to do, unless you're applying, say, at the local hip hop establishment. And even there, Puffy might not dig that.

So the point is, we know we got to be able to code switch. Sociolinguistics speak about it all the time. When you're with your people—Italian, Irish, Jews, Poles, African Americans—then talk the way you do. Oy vey. Schlemiel. Schlimazel. Do your thing. Yiddish intonations, however, through brilliant comedians, have marked the linguistic landscape of American society. And so even there, the specific vernacular intonations bleed beyond their linguistic and, indeed, native boundaries, beyond their ethnicities, to seize the American scene. And they shaped them in profound ways. As has Ebonics. I mean, I saw two elderly white women, or an elderly white woman and an elderly white man.

"What choo doin'? Where you at?"

"Oh, just chillin' with my peeps, tryin' to get my groove on."

Networks—UPN, WB—[are] making millions of dollars off of Ebonics. As has Mr. Cosby, through his movies. And through that Saturday morning entertainment, of a cartoon [*The Adventures of Fat Albert and the Cosby Kids*] where we saw the moral propriety of the ghetto brought to bear upon American society. [It] reversed what Du Bois fathomed in 1903 as a cruel irony, that Black people must ever judge themselves according to the tape of another world, seeing themselves through the prism of a white world that miscomprehended them. And yet the script has been flipped, so to speak, and now America sees itself through the eyes of its minorities, through jazz and hip hop as well. Pop culture. Entertainment. We measure ourselves, the durability of the American genius, in the postmodern sense, in Black and brown and colored flesh.

And so Mr. Cosby is right to say we want our kids to be able to perform well. But he was misinformed about the complex realities of the languages we speak and hear in your neighborhood, up in Oakland, over across the Bay. The reality is that when those teachers are part of the Oakland School District, they were not trying to teach Ebonics to kids. They already be knowin' it. You ain't got to do it. They be comin' there speakin' it. The point is, can you meet them where they are to take them where they need to be? To facilitate a transition from where they are to where they need to be. If you come to school, you're French, somebody gotta speak French to you to try to teach you to speak English. *"Ce n'est pas difficile d'apprendre français. C'est facile."* Now, if you understand that, either you're advanced or you're Haitian. You're in the wrong class. Or you're a refugee from France somewhere. So get in the right class. But for the rest of us, we got to meet people where they are, [and know] what they speak. The linguistic features of these Indigenous communities must be recognized so that we can teach well.

And yet, there is some furious disregard, and remarkable indifference—sometimes evinced by people of standing who used to speak it when they mamas prayed for them. Now they done got they degrees, and they high and mighty, and they's up on the hog or, as they used to say, "[bleeping] in high cotton and wiping with the top leaf." Now we've forgotten. We have Afro-amnesia, a kind of Black forgetfulness. Now that we've succeeded, we forgot our mama and them used to pray for us in that language [that] we now look down upon. "Thank you, Lord, that the walls of my room was not the walls of my grave. My sheet wasn't my winding sheet, and my bed wasn't my cooling board. And you let the golden moments roll on a little longer. I'm like an empty pitcher before a full fountain." Lord, have mercy. If I were in church I know somebody might say "amen." Commonwealth Club got the Holy Ghost. [Laughter]

So the reality is that those people deployed those linguistic leftovers, 'cause folk always, who against the wall, be makin' it on broken pieces—and rhetorical chitlins, for all we know. Now, these chitterlings are being sold as future markets. [Laughter] And so, my brothers and sisters, the point being simply that, yes, we must facilitate transition from where people are—status quo—to where they need to be—the ideal. But we must do so recognizing the integrity of their speech. America finds it difficult to think about difference without hierarchy. Something's different and therefore it's better. No, it's different. Standard in this community is not standard in that community. When you're in the hood . . . I grew up in Detroit. They say, "Watch out for that alley apple." "Excuse me, is that fruit that grows in an alley?" No, that was a brick in my community. So if you didn't speak the Standard English of my community, you might be in the emergency ward tonight. Having been hit in the head with an alley apple.

It's contingent upon circumstance. Local color adds insight and meaning to words, and power is always at stake. Here you are in California,

[with] the power to say we're only going to speak English. Isn't it interesting that America is so arrogant and yet ignorant, that it would be proud of the fact that we are mono-linguistic? The cabdrivers you look down on speak four dialects of one language and about six other languages, and you feel superior. Of course, you can tell them to take you to the airport, 'cause your pockets are "swole"—as the young people say; you have significant capital.

Well, Mr. Cosby went on and remonstrated against the poor in so many other ways. He said, "You give your kids these names. Shaniqua, Taliqua and Muhammad, and all that crap. And they're all in jail." Now, Bill Cosby ain't got no business telling you what to name your kids, unless he's paying your child support. Now, if he's doing that, you might want to consider his linguistic choices. [Laughter]

Well, there was a study done in 2003 that said [you were in jeopardy] if your name was Shaliqua, Taliqua or Shenehneh, or Kenya or Kenyatta, something sounding Black—like the beautiful young lady at the desk here whose name is Shantell. She's a white woman, I thought she was a sister. [Laughter] Just on the name. So we be signifyin' on the name. So [it's tough] when you got them kind of Black sounding names. I said [to her], "I bet your application got rejected a whole bunch of times 'til they saw you were a white woman." Just joking with her. Sort of. [Laughter] Right?

That's what they said in 2003—economic study that said that you can't even get in the door anymore. Used to be you could get in the door to be rejected, despite your Harvard degree. "Don't call us, we'll call you." Now you can't even get in through the door, because your name is Shantell. Shaquille. So should we therefore say, "Aha, Black people should not name their kids that?" That's one approach. But dad gum, how 'bout challenging the bigger thing in society that refuses to acknowledge your virtue? Despite your name?

'Cause Oprah ain't got no regular name. ["Go ahead!" shouted from audience] But when you see "Oprah," what do you see? You see greatness, grandiloquence, magnificence—just formidable. You see something almost incomprehensibly huge. Gargantuan—let's appeal to Swift—Brobdingnagian. Thank you, *Gulliver's Travels*, for your postmodern application. You see something huge in the culture, a colossus bestriding the society with such ascendancy and power. And so the reality is, you learn to love Oprah; you have to learn the name. And you love to learn the name and you learn to love the name. In fact, you appreciate what she is and who she is. You see greatness. You see a billionaire. You see one of the most well-respected women—if not the most well-respected woman—in the country.

But if someone had told her, "Your name is Oprah, you need to change it 'cuz you just look like a ghetto queen," it would have been destructive to her. Perhaps she endured enough as it was. Think about Shaquille O'Neal. Would Mr. Cosby step up to him and tell him to change his name? Perhaps not. "I will beat you down right now, Mr. Cosby. Get you on the court and treat you like a little child. [Laughter] Thank you very much." That monotone would reinforce, with his muscles, his superiority. Mr. Cosby would not challenge him.

How about Condoleezza? I know she was here recently. Lord have mercy. [Laughter and cheers] Conda-leeza. That ain't no regular name, you all. [Laughter] Let me see—leasing a condo. You know. What happened there? Mama was a musician, inspired by the musical Italian signatures. That's like naming your kid *basso profundo*. Right? Con dolcezza. Condoleezza. That's a musical signature in Italian. That's what Africans do—make up stuff based on what they like. Condoleezza? And don't tell me about the Condoleezzas and the Shaquilles and the Oprahs. These are people of extraordinary achievement who have done well.

And so, if we learn to create a society that is against the bigotry that denies them opportunity, we're doing better. Otherwise, if we concede the legitimacy of bigotry toward these names, we're telling King he was wrong, he should have accepted the status quo. Instead, he challenged it.

People ought to be able to name their kids what they want. This ain't the first generation to name their kids after consumer products in African American culture. Africans have always been creative. If your name is Akua, your name means "Born on a Wednesday." Black people name their kids after days of the week, name their kids after the months—June, July, August. Name their kids after the circumstances of their birth—Hard Times, Pleasant Times, Good Times. Black people have always done this. I have an entire chapter on this in the book. And then, what they did in the 1930s, 1940s and 1950s, they named them after consumer products— Listerine, Cremola, Hershey Bar, Cadillac, El Dorado. Oh, you thought it started with Alizé and Versace? And Lexus? Black people always named their kids after stuff they want and can't have. Mercedes. Good Lovin.' Whatever they want and can't get access to. [Laughter]

And the point is, we don't want to sanctify the bigotry. Plus, to me, it ain't the Negroes. It ain't the Africans. It ain't the Black folk named Shaniqua that are problematic. Oh, Pookie might steal your car. But he ain't going to write no judgment against you on the Supreme Court that will affect millions of lives now and in the future. Clarence! It's those good old

American-named Negroes, Africans and Black folk who have been problematic. The high bourgeois-attaining, English-named figures who have
been so subversive of the potential of democracy to be spread.

And on and on Cosby went, and on and on I respond. A couple of more
points before I end.

Mr. Cosby said that Black people are more licentious than others. And
the Black poor—look, they're more vulnerable. They're more easily target-
able. Am I arguing that Black poor people ain't got no problems? No. I've
been Black and po'. Do you think I'm crazy? The people who are most upset by Black people who are poor who do terrible things are Black people
who are poor who do the right thing. Which is most of them. The blur of
stereotypes obscured Mr. Cosby's visions, distorted his perception of the
problem, rendered him as a comedic observer with ingenious artistic skill
but real low social analysis. Given his career of denying the legitimacy of
speaking about race and refusing to engage it [. . .] he lacks the skill to do
it now. I'm not saying he's a Johnny-come-lately and therefore he doesn't
have the authentic right to engage in race discourse. I'm saying he doesn't
have the skill to parse eloquently and complexly the nuances, in a sophisticated fashion, of public discourse about race in America.

We are not interchangeable as Black people. So that any Black person
will do who just happens to be famous and gave a [school or museum a]
bunch of money. That don't qualify you as a social critic. [Some say], "Oh,
Cosby saying nothing different than Leroy on the corner." Leroy ain't on
C-SPAN, [or] your cousin Bubba in the barber shop, funny as he is. And
Craig Mayberry has a beautiful new book about barber shop discourse—
it's great. But [Leroy or your cousin] ain't on *Nightline* in a 30-minute space
to debate the serious and insidious issues of African American culture. Because Black folk are not interchangeable despite the internalization of the
white supremacist predicate.

Folk be doin' stuff because they got skills at it. It takes time to develop it.
And what other culture turns only to a comedian and claims that he is the
greatest leader we've ever produced? Better than King and Garvey and Ella
Baker and Fannie Lou Hamer and James Baldwin or Angela Davis? Better
than Ida B. Wells-Barnett and Du Bois? And Frederick Douglass? This is
the *greatest leader*? Wow. Where ya' been, bruh?

In America now, especially the right wing, the acid conservatism in this
country, heaps huge praise upon Mr. Cosby's head by saying, "Finally a Black
leader has spoken about responsibility." Where have you been? Any Black
leader worth his or her salt speaks about this weekly, daily. Any intellectual

worth his or her salt talks about it as a necessity for forward progress. The problem is, Mr. Cosby spoke about personal responsibility outside of the context of social responsibility. They are reciprocal and dynamic [. . .] We don't wait for social responsibility to behave right.

But behaving right will not solve the problem Mr. Cosby pointed to. Good behavior will never stop job flight. Can never stop capital bleeding. Can't stanch the bleeding of downsizing and outsourcing. Can't stop the exploitation of indigenous marketplaces in Indonesia. When you call a takeout taxi tonight because you don't want to cook, the person answering you might be in Burma. And when you make a local call, "You know that place right around the corner from 595, on Market Street? You know that place?" "Sir, I am in India." International processes have been absorbed by multinational corporations which control 70 percent of the business transfers in America. When you think about [it], 300-and-some-odd companies control the expansion of global wealth, and you're speaking about local responsibility. It's critical, it's necessary, but it's not sufficient in philosophical terms. Good behavior is its own reward, and most Black people I know urge it upon their children with vigor and intensity.

And yet, as I come to my close here, the reality is that that taking of personal responsibility which is critical in terms of moral character in the Black community will never solve the fundamental economic and social problems where concentration of poverty is the problem. You see, good behavior won't keep billboards out of your neighborhoods—that are Black and poor, or Latino—that celebrate drugs, in terms of liquor and in terms of smoking. Why is it the fact that rich white kids and rich Black kids have to come into the ghetto to get their relief? [Get] their chemical transgression on? To engage in that? Why must they come there? Because zoning laws keep that stuff out of the suburbs. So the concentration of poverty is a result of political and public policy decisions. And if you are already fragile, with your back against the wall, you don't have any political power, then you don't have the power to keep this stuff out of your community.

And please don't correlate morality with class status. That would mean the richest people were the best. Oh, Lord, have mercy. I ain't mad at her, but what about your girl, Miss Hilton? Miss Paris. I'm going to be quiet here, because I know I got to shut up, but I got to say this before I shut up. Or, as my uncle used to say, from Alabama, "Er, uh, Miss Hilton?" She had great parenting, I suppose, but maybe the parenting can't be coordinated with the cash you've got. Maybe people who are rich [. . .] I mean, she's got not one but two sex tapes. I have to watch these things. I'm a cultural critic. [Laughter] It's very difficult for me to endure *One Night in Paris* and its follow-up. But, alas, for you, the people, I engage in that sacrifice. Then she's got a show on TV whose ratings are through the roof. And building a multimillion-dollar empire on being [irresponsible], what Cosby accused the Black poor of being . . .

The problem is, my friends—as we interrogate and scrutinize this peculiar conundrum—that we can never correlate class status and social status and moral attainment. Because, in the end, we know that some of the best people in the world have no money, and some of the worst people have money. So we can never associate exclusively the province of impropriety with those who are poor.

As I end for real—a Baptist preacher got to end about three times—as I end for real here, we want all people to be responsible. But how can Mr. Cosby overlook himself in this alleged and ostensible self-critique? The last time I checked, you've got to critique yourself in order to be self-critical. If you're rich, self-critical means criticizing the rich folk. Not the poor folk. Otherwise that's criticizing other folk. Just want to hip you to that term. "He was being self-critical." Against who? I didn't hear him mention many rich Black people. See, Black people defended Mr. Cosby. "Well, we've got to get our dirty laundry out there and get it aired and cleaned." Let me see: Do you want everybody's dirty laundry or just the poor people's dirty laundry?

I wrote a book on Dr. King, called him the greatest American who ever lived. Talked about promiscuity and plagiarism. Black people went crazy on me. [Whispering] "Why you got to let that out?" First of all, because it happened. Secondly, because I'm trying to anticipate those tapes that will be released in about twenty, thirty years. And if I've already called him great, having anticipated their release, and knowing what they said, and [I] still said he was great, then I'm ahead of the game. It's a strategic and intellectual choice. It's a methodological and procedural one. It's also intellectually honest. We claimed about dominant white culture: "They just choose the stuff they like and the stuff they don't like—they don't talk about it. Thomas Jefferson. They romanticize him. Don't speak about the slaves." Well, you can't talk about Dr. King without talking about the foibles and faults. But you don't want that dirty laundry out there, because we're not interested in putting [out] Black dirty laundry, we're interested in putting *poor* Black dirty laundry out there . . .

Do we want to put [out the laundry of] Black ministers who rail in their pulpits with theological certitude against being gay or lesbian, themselves closeted gay? Do we want to tell that truth? Do we want to "out" that story?

No. When [the film] *Barbershop* came out, nobody said what Cedric the Entertainer's character said about Dr. King was wrong. We just didn't want it out there. So the point is, if it's good for the goose it's good for the gander. Let's love all of our people. And let's be honest and self-critical and desirous of virtue.

In the post-Emancipation culture, Black former slaves were looked down upon by the Black elite, because the Black elite felt embarrassed. Bill Cosby said in his speech, "The white man must be laughing at us." He still feels the gaze of a dominant white culture that he has sought to please, but rarely chosen to challenge. And now, because he has spilled the venom and directed anger and hostility against his own, he is being uplifted as a hero. And yet, we fail to challenge him, with his perch high in dominant culture . . .

So my point is—as I take my seat—that Mr. Cosby has delved deeply into pools of profound, critical issues [. . .] He's brought a sledgehammer to the surgeon's table, where a scalpel is necessary. And as my dear friend and his dear friend, Rev. Jesse Jackson, says, "When you're in a pit, do you want a shovel to dig you deeper or do you want a rope to pull you out?" I think Mr. Cosby threw down a shovel. I'm trying to let down a rope. Thank you so very kindly.

[Applause]

43

Like Hemingway Being Mugged
by Morrison

In October 2019, I got a lovely email from the Newswomen's Club of New York, a professional association founded in 1922 to support women in journalism. They wrote: "We would be honored if you would consider attending the Front Page Awards and present The New York Times' *Nikole Hannah-Jones with her Journalist of the Year Award." I'd first met Hannah-Jones five years earlier when we both appeared on CBS's Sunday morning news show* Face the Nation, *although I'd been reading her for years, especially as she weighed in on the re-segregation of American public schools. That's the topic host Bob Schieffer asked her about, particularly as it related to "No Child Left Behind," the Bush-era 2001 act of Congress that reauthorized the Elementary and Secondary Education Act, including Title 1 provisions applying to disadvantaged youth. Hannah-Jones was sharp and eloquent. "To me, one of the fundamental flaws with No Child Left Behind that we don't talk about is it still is attempting to make separate schools equal. It's still saying that yes, these schools are all Black, all Latino, and poor, but if we just put enough resources in, we can turn those schools around. There's almost no money devoted to programs that would help schools integrate, that would help schools break up the poverty that leads to the achievement gap. And so until there's a real conversation about that, because I think there's a fundamental misunderstanding of* Brown. Brown v. Board of Education *was not about resources. By the time* Brown *came before the Supreme Court, Southern states who believed that a ruling was going to come against their interests had begun to equalize funding, all of those types of tangibles.* Brown *was about the separation in itself, in that in a nation with a history of a racial caste to separate Black students from the mainstream was inherently unequal. And we still don't want to talk about that separation." Boom! I loved her style im-*

mediately, and that same honest, transparent, rigorous, and fearless approach to telling the truth is what shines so brilliantly in the 1619 Project. It was that same brilliance that in 2021 led the University of North Carolina to offer Hannah-Jones a presigitious tenured position as the Knight Chair in Race and Investigative Journalism at the Hussman School of Journalism and Media. When the UNC Board of Trustees scuttled the tenured part of Hannah-Jones's appointment, she was instead offered a fixed-term contract with the option of being reviewed for tenure within five years. The decision sparked enormous outrage, a contemplated lawsuit by Hannah-Jones, and an outpouring of national support from intellectuals and scholars, even some who opposed Hannah-Jones's 1619 Project. The public pressure on UNC to reconsider its decision was to strike a blow for academics to work free of political intolerance or interference. After UNC reversed course and offered her tenure, Hannah-Jones instead chose to teach at the HBCU Howard University. It was easy to take to the podium and speak from the heart about Hannah-Jones's importance to the culture.

Americans are curious creatures. On the one hand, they love history. They cannot get enough of books on Lincoln. How many? More than 15,000 books have been written about him. Books on George Washington. Even Aaron Burr. The Founding Fathers, the Founding Mothers, the Founding Brothers, the Founding Sisters. Or [many folk can't get enough of] the reenactment of the Civil War.

And yet when it comes to Africans in America, when it comes to Black people, when it comes to a contingent of other minorities, [we hear], "Can't you get over it? Do we need yet another film on enslavement? Do we need yet another Black feminist remonstration against the moral indifference of a dominant culture?"

And yet, the paradox is that we are obsessed with history, on the one hand, and determined to avoid it at the same time. And so the terrain upon which she walks elegantly, with radical, visceral sophistication, is letting the impossible intervene between amnesia and historical fatigue.

And what she has brilliantly done is given totemic power to a number—the ostensible innumeracy of Black people notwithstanding. She has given totemic power to a number that joins 1776. 1812. 1919—the red summer where Black blood flooded this earth. 1968, where a King stood a few years before in the sunlit summit of expectation and articulated his vision. And the death of a man, the scion of a political family, who died in a hotel ballroom trying to bring justice to America.

She has added to 2008, when the first Black president rose like a phoenix from the political ashes to which he'd been consigned because he had a different name. And 2016, where a man has seized social media to excrete the feces of his moral depravity into a nation he has turned into his psychic commode. [Applause]

She has rescued 1619. [Applause]

The record says, "20 And Odd. Negroes." I see 20 odd Negroes in this room. [Laughter] Extracted from their resting in African soil and brought here to America. Consigned against their will; forced immigrants. And what Nikole Hannah-Jones has done, she has stood with Orlando Patterson, whose magisterial tome on freedom argues that we could not even conceive of American freedom without the corollary of American enslavement. She stands in the gap between Orlando Patterson and Langston Hughes, who said, "America never was America to me."

But Nikole Hannah-Jones has argued in her brilliant and insightful essay that begins that 1619 Project that America was never America to America itself, without the contributions of these sun-kissed children, these citizens of a despised minority. These people who have been rendered persona non grata. That they are the woof and warp, they are the predicate of American democracy. That they are the basis for us understanding who we are. How dare she have the unabashed temerity to insert the centrality of people who have been forced to the margin? She has translated, in eloquent terms, deep and profound historical commentary and made it accessible to everyday people.

They have those 1619 books on the corner like they selling crack. [Laughter] I walked into *The New York Times* building today—true story—and one of the officers who knew who I was and congratulated me for being there indicated that Miss Nikole Hannah-Jones herself had promised him an issue so he could send it to some folk down in Southland. And he was so proud. This is the level of everyday access she has given people the power to have.

We talk, blindly, sometimes abstractly, about public intellectuals, those who take ostensibly difficult concepts and render them transparent to those who don't have the particular energy or the commitment to study hard and long. But a public intellectual makes plain the basis of a particular argument or a sphere of thought so that people can understand why it is important.

Look at what she has wrought. And we can tell the magnitude of it by the opposition that it has engendered. Even in her own ranks among journalists: "Is this political correctness run amok?" "What have Arthur and Dean done at *The New York Times*? Have they capitulated to that?" Did we say this when the eighteenth anniversary of 9/11 came? Was this political correctness? Or is this the attempt of a nation to wrestle with the infernal intensity of terror unleashed upon its vulnerable citizens?

What she has done is shown that 9/11 was *not* the date of origin of terror in this nation. Not even 1921, with the Tulsa Massacre. But in 1619, when human beings of inestimable worth, and of Godly value, were brought to this nation to work against their will to build it from the bottom up. Brick by brick, sentence by sentence, brain by brain, sinew by sinew.

And the epic sweep of her brilliantly beautiful prose, like Hemingway being mugged by Morrison. [Applause]

Short declarative sentences in the service of an expansive truth.

She has willed it, yes, it is true, through her genius. We didn't need the MacArthur Foundation to announce to her and to ourselves what she is. Women's genius is never as routinely recognized as that of men. Black women, even more rarely. Look at her. Her physiology is itself representative and emblematic of a powerful expression of unapologetic Black female identity. Look at that fiery follicular formation. [Applause]

That ink inscribed upon her body. Dimples deep enough to swim in. [Laughter] And a brain, an ocean, that contains the beautiful flora and fauna and the algae and the life of Black existence. What she and *The New York Times* have done is to give back to this nation a heritage of engaging the "other" by looking deeply in the self, to see our own ethical complicity and our moral courting of forces we claim not to represent.

Martin Luther King, Jr., quoting Arnold Toynbee, said, and I'm paraphrasing, it may be the Negro who will inject new meaning into the veins of the civilization of the West. What Nikole Hannah-Jones has done! And long even before 1619, when she's writing about re-segregation of schools, she could've won that award then. Or talking about redlining in housing, and the degree to which we were incapable of living equally in society. The vast movement of Robert Moses with urban renewal, which James Baldwin has said [is really] "Negro removal," she documented this as an ethnographer, a faithful and powerful conscience. And so, it is with great glee and deep joy that I'd like you to look at this film of this beautiful Black genius who has given us back to ourselves. And given this nation its raison d'être rooted in the element of race that it has refused to recognize. [Applause]

The Right of the People Peaceably to Assemble

Protest Orations

CHAPTER

44

When That Flag Goes Down
America Comes Up

My dear friend the incredible performer, writer, thinker, and actress Aunjanue Ellis—who confirmed her genius in her role as Clark Sisters matriarch and gospel music maven Mattie Moss Clark in The Clark Sisters: First Ladies of Gospel, *a film directed by my brilliant Detroit homegirl Christine Swanson—invited me to join her at "Take It Down America Rally: X the X," at the United States Capitol on Flag Day in 2016, to demand the removal of the "Stars and Bars" of the Confederate flag from the left corner of the state flag of Mississippi, from whence Ellis hails. Ellis eloquently explained the rationale for the protest at the Capitol. "We are holding the rally in Washington, D.C., to make the case to the country that if it happens in Mississippi, it can happen anywhere. We are insisting on a national discussion, not just about the flag, but what it does. We live in a time where . . . what's happening in Mississippi is happening everywhere. Mississippi is contagious." Tragically, it was not until the protests in the aftermath of George Floyd's murder, along with persistent protests over the years from folk like Ellis and state business leaders, religious groups, and national sports organizations, that the Mississippi House of Representatives sent legislation to Governor Tate Reeves to sign a bill removing the Confederate battle emblem and designing a new version of the state flag.*

I am happy to join with you today with Sister Aunjanue Ellis, a remarkable, radiant, powerful artistic presence, and Attorney Carlos Moore, a brilliant legal mind that articulates the values of true democracy and Black humanity in the midst of a culture that has refused to cede our legitimacy as citizens in this country by flying under the banner of bigotry. We must join together today our voices, our visions, the virtue of our democracy on this Flag Day, to say what this Mississippi flag represents is antithetical to the true spirit of American democracy. It is against every understanding we have of the beauty, the power and the promise of what it means to be an American.

Isn't it strange that this particular flag represents the repudiation of the value of American unity—*E pluribus unum*—out of many, one? And yet this flag reminds us that we are essentially divided, because it flows in an air that has been poisoned by racial hate and the retaliation against Black humanity.

And so how can we truly be seen as fully American when we embrace a flag that does not celebrate America's wholeness? Isn't it interesting that those who oppose this flag are seen as un-American, and those who participated in an effort of secession, of separating themselves from the United States of America, are now being protected on American soil that has been purchased by blood, that has been deepened by the visions of Black soldiers for justice to respond to the inequality that prevails in this culture? [Applause]

Nearly a year ago, a young mad, crazed racist draped himself in the Confederate flag and then went into a church where people were at prayer to mow them down—nine souls, praying to their God. He was so full of hate that that flag spoke for him in a symbol of renunciation of the beauty and spirit that that prayer meeting represented. So, these great Black martyrs went to their reward, sent there by the bullets of an evil man who wrapped himself in this banner of bigotry.

But in Mississippi that is not just a Confederate flag; that is the alternative to the state flag. It is literally woven into the fabric of Mississippi's culture and consciousness. It is literally the flag that represents the state. It is literally the flag that articulates its value. The pledge of allegiance to the state of Mississippi is a pledge to the sovereignty of the state that continues to be in open rebellion against the democratic values of our American state. [Applause]

And it is interesting that from 1906 to 2001, they ain't even had no official flag in Mississippi. They readopted that flag in 2001 because of an inadvertent oversight that precluded the flag from being officially integrated into the rituals of governance. In other words, they didn't even have no flag. And so they're defending something that is essentially the byproduct of hate and not heritage. Or, if we want to be real about it, their heritage is hate. [Applause]

Ain't no essential contradiction. Some people feed on hate. We saw what happened the other day in Orlando. We saw the vicious expression of hate against gay or lesbian or transgender or bisexual or queer people. And I'm here to tell you today, if you use your religion to make God cosign your bigotry, you are a part of a confederacy of hate. [Applause]

If you are a Christian who believes that God will send gay or lesbian or transgender or bisexual or queer people to hell, you are part of a confederacy of hate that rejects the essential premise of not only American democracy, but the spirit of God. And I say to you that this flag must come down, because it represents everything that America is supposed to *not* be. We are a country of promise and potential and greatness, expanding upon the backs of, yes, coerced immigrants called slaves, and immigrants who came here of their own will. Mississippi is the product of Black genius and imagination. [Applause]

Mississippi is the product of a blues delta so rich in the power of song to tell the truth about the suffering masses in the world. So, they will take our blues music from Mississippi, but impose greater blues upon the folk who are there even today. [Applause]

And as I end, this is a problem, as Miss Ellis said, for America. This ain't no Mississippi problem. This is a problem for the United States of America. How dare America continue to extract from us taxes to support our own demise? We are in effect supplementing our own oppression. And we say no. We will no longer participate in the drama and pageantry of American bigotry with a flag that is unfurled at the behest of white supremacy. White supremacy hurts everybody. Not just people of color. It hurts the white folk who have been seduced into the delusion that they are somehow superior. [Applause]

And so I say, take that flag down. When that flag comes down, love goes up. When that flag goes down, beauty comes up. When that flag goes down, America comes up. When that flag goes down, God comes up. When that flag goes down, the spirit comes up. When that flag goes down, American democracy is raised to its highest height. [Applause]

CHAPTER

45

Golgotha in Memphis

Every time I visit the National Civil Rights Museum in Memphis, Tennessee, constructed around the very motel where Martin Luther King, Jr., met his fateful end, I cry like a baby, especially when I make it to Room 306, where he lodged, the room preserved just as it was the evening King was assassinated at 6:01 pm CST. I have written two books about him, penned countless articles and essays about him, have read nearly every major book about him, and yet my curiosity about his life, and my need to know even more, as much as possible, remains. Even in light of the upcoming revelations contained in the FBI documents to be unsealed in 2027, I believe that King is the greatest figure ever to grace the American scene. Standing in what was once the parking lot of the Lorraine Motel where Dr. King gave up the ghost was both eerie—because it put me squarely at the scene of my great hero's death—and comforting, because, just for another moment, I could tread the ground he traversed for the last time on earth. This speech was delivered in 2018 at the fiftieth anniversary of King's death—at the site that his murder transformed into a monument to the memory of a great man and an even greater movement for freedom, justice, and equality.

Thank you, Brother [Roland] Martin. What an honor and privilege it is to be here today on the very real estate where the greatest witness for freedom, justice and democracy met his end, on this lonely and desolate balcony where the future, in the words of one rapper, "took a head shot." Martin Luther King, Jr., gave his life so that we could be free. And yet so many of us have failed to take advantage of that freedom. We live in a nation where we continue to see a roll call of vitriol and hatred expressed against those King loved the most.

He came to Memphis because his brothers who were sanitation workers were on strike. He came here and stayed in room 306 because he wanted to identify with the least, the lost and the lowliest. He came here because radical injustice was rising up and economic inequality was a reality. He came here because white supremacy had reared its ugly head yet again.

And at the end of his life there were few who were willing to follow him. And now we stand today in the midst of a culture where a man gets up every morning at 5:30 a.m. to tweet. He talks about shithole countries, but we know where the shithole is: Beneath his nose and above his chin. [CHEERS]

We know what justice looks like. This is not it. We must speak out against a president who refuses to acknowledge the humanity of the most vulnerable people in this nation. We must rise together to declare that justice "must roll down like waters and righteousness like a mighty stream," but only if we are willing to facilitate and foster that conversation.

We must realize now that there are other "others" who are here who were not as prominent when Dr. King was alive. Our queer brothers and sisters, our Indigenous brothers and sisters, those who continue to fight against radical invisibility because of their economic inequality. Dr. King loved all of them. And we should embrace all of them, because we can't afford to have our pet peeves and our bigotries and biases against nobody. We all in the same boat. [Applause]

And so, I come here today to remind you what you already know: that Dr. King has been appropriated by people who are trying to pretend that he was an advocate for a narrow version of color blindness. Thirty-four words he uttered when he was thirty-four years old: "I have a dream one day my four little children will live in a nation where they will not be judged by the color of their skin but by the content of their character." But that was not yet a reality. That was a dream, that was hypothesis, that was a vision that was not real.

And so we know that racism is still real today. Black lives matter because people refuse to acknowledge the humanity of Black people still in 2018. And here we are, fifty years after this man gave up the ghost. Fifty years after he made the ultimate sacrifice, we are still fighting for recognition of those who are most vulnerable.

And if we are to make America realize the dream that this man had, we've got to confront the nightmare he continually confronted. He came to Memphis because not a lot of people were loving those who were garbage workers and sanitation workers. Now we are obsessed, even in the Black church, with the gospel of prosperity. We trying to get paid and get cars and homes. And ain't nothing wrong with that, but you cannot pursue wealth at the expense of your soul. And Martin Luther King, Jr., understood that. [Applause]

And if you are obsessed with those trinkets and those material gifts, and you do not care about those who are poor, you know not Jesus. Don't claim to rise with God on Easter while you are crucifying those who are poor on Monday right after it. Don't claim to be a servant of God, but you hate people who ain't like you. Don't claim to know Jesus, but you are an Evangelical who sides with a president who doesn't know anything about the poor and the vulnerable in this nation. [Applause]

We got a man who's mad at the Mexicans. It ain't the Mexicans. It ain't the Puerto Ricans. It ain't the Dominicans. It's the right-wing Republicans who are out here trying to destroy the legacy of Martin Luther King. And so, King, at the end of his life, was joining with other freedom fighters— Cesar Chavez, the Rev. Jesse Jackson, the Rev. Andrew Young, Dorothy Cotton—making sure that we could forge a connection between those who should join together because we had much more in common than we had fighting each other.

And so now we must have a big tent philosophy and a large vision about what constitutes America. And my brothers and sisters, if you gonna drink from King's fountain, you got to taste the bitterness of sacrifice for those who are lower on the totem pole. There are people who are working forty and fifty and sixty hours who still can't make ends meet. There are young Black and brown and Indigenous children who are getting kicked out of school at earlier and earlier ages while we criminalize our children, police people in the schools criminalizing our kids. And then, in the streets, we are being shot down like dogs. If you are afraid of a Black person because they are Black, get out of the policing business. [Applause]

The police are our servants, not our dictators. We do not hate the police; we hate bad policing. We hate the inequality that clouds, consciously and unconsciously, the minds of police people who tase us and baton us and whip us and shoot us and handcuff us and then hunt us down like dogs to murder us in the streets. And so, we gotta speak out against that.

And in speaking out against that we must talk about this prison industrial complex. You can be a Black person with a college degree, and sometimes you can't get the same job that a white person who went to prison got. We must address this inequality and the sexism, the homophobia and the patriarchy that prevail too.

They'll use your religion as a justification for your bigotry. Don't make God cosign your hate. The God I love says, whosoever will, gay or straight or Black or white or red or brown or yellow or poor, it doesn't make a difference. We are all children in the eyes of God. And so I say to you today, as we remember Dr. King, we remember what he stood for. We remember what he preached about.

The last sermon he was going to preach before he was murdered, the next Sunday in his church, is "Why America May Go to Hell." Now, I know some of y'all good Christians and good religious people don't know how to pronounce hell, even though you living in it. You mad at young people 'cause they cussing on a rap album. You better listen to these young people. You better hear the young prophets who are raising their voices to talk about the pain that they confront.

And so, what I want you to do is to be a Trojan horse. You know what a Trojan horse is. You get in some places 'cause you light-skinned and got curly hair. You get in some places 'cause you got a degree, and you speak the King's English to the Queen's taste. You get in some places because people celebrate you because of your achievement. But when you get in, let all of those Negroes out of you. Let all of those poor people out of you. And let them know that they are your people, and that you love them too. God bless you. [Applause]

Read the Papers!

Opinion Pages

46

King's Dream, Rihanna's Demand

In March 2021, Newsweek *magazine invited me to weigh in on reparations, especially since it has gained currency in the culture, even filtering up to Congress with its decision to finally agree to study the measure as one way to fulfill justice to Black folk. I say one way because the fear among some Black folk is that if, and when, we get reparations, our white brothers and sisters will say, "Enough already. Don't say a damn thing more about racial injustice in America." It should be apparent that on that view, reparations would be too costly a price to pay for a greater goal of righting what is wrong in this nation tied to its past, and the ongoing mistreatment of Black folk. Americans needn't worry; money isn't the only way—even if it is a crucial one— to compensate Black folk for the trauma, trouble, and terror. How about America being just as ingenious at helping Black America as it was in harming us? How about no taxes for Black folk for the next fifty years or double that time? Sure, that won't help Marvin Gaye—"Natural fact is, Oh honey that I can't pay my taxes"—Joe Louis, or even Wesley Snipes, Ron Isley, Dionne Warwick, and legions more, but it can help millions more in the future. And how about free tuition for all Black folk attending college for the next century? The point is for the nation to put on its thinking cap to figure out ways to make reparation to its most tenaciously loyal citizens in the land.*

"Bitch better have my money," the songstress snarls in hypnotic cadence. "Pay me what you owe me." For many people, Rihanna's 2015 anthem serves as the soundtrack to the movement for Black reparations.

Her tune profanely echoes Martin Luther King, Jr.'s urgent cry to the nation in 1963 in "I Have a Dream," his most famous oration. King argued the case for Black compensation in that address to the March on Washington when he declared that "in a sense we've come to our nation's capital to cash a check." King claimed that the Founding Fathers, in the Constitution and the Declaration of Independence, "were signing a promissory note to which every American was to fall heir."

King insisted that it "is obvious today that America has defaulted on this promissory note in so far as her citizens of color are concerned." The nation had instead "given the Negro people a bad check, a check which has come back marked 'insufficient funds.'" But King said that Black folk refused to believe that "the bank of justice is bankrupt," that there was inadequate currency in "the great vaults of opportunity." Hence, Black folk had "come to cash this check." To paraphrase Rihanna, *Nation better have my money*.

When it comes to Black reparations, money is hardly the only issue at stake. Our women and culture were raped. Our flesh and time were stolen. Our men were castrated and lynched. What America owes us is far more than material. The nation's debt to us gets at the very moral composition of the nation.

It is a matter of conscience, too, and the nation's will to do right by the folk whose blood and brawn, and yes, whose brains and spirit, lifted America from a brazen upstart to the world's most fabled empire. We were bought or kidnapped from Africa and transported to the New World. We tilled soil we couldn't build on. We erected edifices we couldn't own. We constructed schools we couldn't attend. We defended a democracy that didn't return the favor. And we generated untold wealth from which we have been systemically barred.

The ethical perversion of the Atlantic slave trade bred myriad and interlocking brutalities. These atrocities were rooted in the collective psyche of a nation hell-bent on turning Sigmund Freud into both analyst and prophet. There was a determined repression of the incalculable loss of Black life and limb that led to a pathological denial of responsibility. That fateful denial joins the esteemed founder of psychoanalysis to the Jamaican reggae star Shaggy in America's claim, despite abundant proof to the contrary, that "it wasn't me."

But in addition to the rape and pillage of Black Americans, the nation continues to deny slavery's willful erasure of our humanity. It denies its primary role as the tragic source of our suffering in the past and present. But that denial compels us to recover our moral memory and to make reparation for the harm the nation has done to Black America. That damage continues to this day. Persistent racial inequality proves the grave error of those who dismiss the call for Black reparation. Some contend that our downfall happened so long ago that nobody is alive who suffered and therefore we don't owe anyone Black anything. That is a nifty if nasty rhetorical ploy. It is also a grievous gesture of moral cowardice.

It is this denial, in addition to the material theft, that reparations are needed to ameliorate. It overlooks how the nation would not admit in real time the colossal injury that slavery imposed on Black people. The denial of the injury was initially rooted in the belief that bad stuff couldn't happen to soulless animals who didn't technically, or constitutionally, count as full citizens or human beings. (For an update of this belief, see *The Godfather*, as Don Zaluchi issues a warning against peddling drugs in schools or to children, as he exclaims, after pounding the table, "In my city, we would keep the traffic in the dark people, the coloreds. They're animals anyway, so let them lose their souls.") When folk who endured the crime of slavery passed off the scene, their offspring suffered its traumatic aftermath. But their plight was chalked up to their inherent inferiority. Or they supposedly lacked the gumption to overcome the obstacles that any poor and struggling people face.

That was a triple whammy of denial. First, the denial that slavery happened the way its opponents claim it did. Second, even when some of slavery's ills were conceded, there was the denial that it was all that bad. Thirdly, there was the denial that it was qualitatively different than the challenges poor whites routinely confronted.

Of course, in the eyes of many whites the moral statute of limitations had run out a decade or two after slavery's end. It was only much later that many whites could in hindsight admit that slavery and its immediate aftereffects were damaging. But they believed that we were way past all of the brutality and that Black folk had decades to recover and move on. The blame once again fell on Black folk for their own oppression.

The notion of reparation has been awfully difficult for white folk in America to accept. That's in part because such acceptance rests on acknowledging that many of their ancestors were often grimy and inglorious. This contradicts the whitewashed textbook portraits of the Founding Figures who created this nation. For a moment, let's take race out of the equation, well, not altogether, but let's remove it from the divide between Black and white in America.

Other nations have been far less arrogant and willing to admit error. For the last 35 years, New Zealand has been making reparation to the Indigenous population it colonized and abused. It has given them checks totaling hundreds of millions of dollars, land, and an apology. American selfishness has prevented the nation from offering Black folk any money.

Its cultivated amnesia has precluded the return to Black folk of stolen property. American arrogance has even kept us from offering a meaningful apology. If pride goes before the fall, then humility precedes the rise. Even South Africa learned that lesson. They established a Truth and Reconciliation Commission to come clean about the white minority's horrid institutional racism before genuine reconciliation with post-apartheid Black society could take place.

Here in the United States, a number of cities and states made gestures toward racial compensation. Tulsa, Oklahoma, and Elaine, Arkansas, grappled with making payments to Black survivors of racist violence. Nashville, Atlanta, Dallas, Cleveland, Chicago and Detroit passed legislation offering symbolic support for racial reparation to Black folk. And the state legislatures of New York and California passed bills that addressed various aspects of reparations.

Of course, the most successful reparations legislation is the Civil Liberties Act of 1988. That bill authorized the payment of reparations to Japanese Americans for their incarceration in concentration camps during World War II. Reparations for Black people have not yet made it past the psychology of whiteness and the dogma of white omnicompetence that frames it. In the psychology of whiteness, group invincibility goes hand in hand with imperious self-making. This psychology keeps many whites from seeing that privilege and power more than merit and hard work give them several legs up over Black folk. Society is shaped at every level to support white life, white identity, white enterprise, white beliefs, white striving, and white justification of inherent superiority.

Ira Katznelson's illuminating sociological study, *When Affirmative Action Was White*, shows how advantages, opportunities and benefits were rigged for white society. The G.I. Bill, for instance, secured the white middle class and opened an even bigger income and wealth chasm between Blacks and whites. The bill offered mostly white veterans low-cost mortgages, low-interest loans to jump-start businesses, unemployment compensation, and tuition payments and living expenses to attend high school, vocational school or college. Of the mortgages insured by the G.I. Bill in New York and northern New Jersey suburbs, 67,000 went to whites while fewer than 100 went to Blacks and other non-whites.

The myth of white omnicompetence discards Black folk and others as unworthy impostors and undeserving inheritors of the American Dream. It was the vision of the American Dream as uniquely for white folk that King brilliantly hijacked in his most noted speech. King used it as a central metaphor of American possibility and linked Black struggle to its realization. King insisted that without Black life and labor that dream is hardly complete or legitimate. And justly treating Black folk is a significant sign of the dream's fulfillment.

Black reparation should take various forms: scholarships for Black children and youth, transfer payments to the neediest Black families for a period, lower interest rates for homes, and a genuinely fair crack at training for decent jobs. Reparation should take whatever form the American imagination can conjure; it should be developed with the imperative to be just as creative in making progress as it was in creating mayhem. America should apply to reparation the same ingenuity it used to fashion restrictions and limitations on Black life in chattel slavery and Jim Crow, ingenuity it used a million ways to make Black life miserable, and to hold us back, to undereducate us, and to make us poor, a system so cruelly sophisticated that it is still in place hundreds of years later. Only then will that nation show how serious it is about making true reparation to the Black folk who made this country what it is today.

As Martin Luther King, Jr., argued: "Whenever the issue of compensatory treatment for the Negro is raised, some of our friends recoil in horror. The Negro should be granted equality, they agree; but he should ask nothing more. On the surface, this appears reasonable, but it is not realistic." King concluded, "A society that has done something special against the Negro for hundreds of years must now do something special for the Negro." Well, if not special, then at least America must do what it did, and continues to do, for white folk. Let the reckoning and counting begin.

47

Model Minorities?

In April 2021, I was invited by legendary performer and television host Jada Pinkett Smith to participate in her venerable Facebook talk show, Red Table Talk, with her talented mother, Adrienne Banfield-Jones, and her gifted daughter, Willow. We were joined by the noted Asian American journalist Lisa Ling to speak about the unconscionable assaults on Asian American and Pacific Island folk, some by Black folk, and the tensions brewing between Black and AAPI communities. Of course, the utterly detestable role played by the forty-fifth president in fomenting hate and generating violent attacks on Asian folk in light of the global pandemic cannot be overlooked. I was invited to participate in large measure because of a version of this March 2021 opinion piece that ran in The Washington Post. *There can be no tolerance for bigotry of any sort against Asian brothers and sisters, and the more quickly we come to realize, to paraphrase Dr. King, that injustice against any group is an injustice against all groups, the better off we will be as a nation.*

The struggles of the Black American narrative—the arc from slavery to Barack Obama—are celebrated, contested and even sometimes disparaged. But there is no denying that this narrative is well known. We all grasp the importance of Black history to the American story, even if we argue over the proper emphasis. The relationship between Asian American and Pacific Islanders and their place in American history is not, to many, nearly as obvious. The American racial conversation, in which African Americans are the default minority group, has impoverished our understanding of—and provided a poor platform for—the stories of others.

Of course, there is no such thing as a monolithic Black experience. Yet it is not uncommon for the multihued complexities of Blackness to be neatly folded into a sweeping generalization about Black life. While such an approach obscures the vast reaches of Blackness, it offers a convenient paradigm to comparatively interpret the lives and experiences of other groups. Even though the Latino community overtook Black folk as the nation's largest minoritized group—those defined in contrast to the white majority—Black folk remain the standard when speaking of non-white, non-majority experiences. The relation between Blacks and Asian Americans in particular can offer us great insight about the nation and the future of freedom struggles.

To be sure, the Black American template as racial arbiter among minoritized folk exists for a reason. African Americans may have worked out our identities and cultural traditions on the margins of the nation, but our inventions and imagination long ago claimed center stage in the unfolding American drama. Our spirituals and blues, our jazz and hip hop, our preaching and prophesying, our styles and performances, articulated the American soul.

Without Black folk—from Frederick Douglass to John Lewis, from Mahalia Jackson to JAY-Z—America couldn't possibly be what it is today. Even those who would deny the weight of racial oppression in America—and the toll taken by the uphill climb against it—won't deny the centrality of Black America's role in the nation's story. As even our race-baiting former president, Donald Trump, said in 2020 at Mt. Rushmore, "the Tuskegee airmen, Harriet Tubman . . . Jesse Owens . . . the great Louis Armstrong . . . and Muhammad Ali . . . only America could have produced them all."

But neither would America be as viable without the Pulitzer Prize–winning writing of Jhumpa Lahiri, the poetry and hip hop artistry of Mona Haydar, the trailblazing ceramic art of Toshiko Takaezu, Feng Zhang's innovations on the CRISPR technique for altering DNA, or the pioneering work in semantics and politics of scholar-turned-senator S. I. Hayakawa, a polymath who earned a shout-out on "Black Man," Stevie Wonder's epic tribute to the multicultural roots of the nation. Despite their rich contributions to this country, stereotypes persist: Asian American men have been tagged as predatory misogynists. Asian American women have been crudely exotified as "China dolls" and "Geisha girls" who eagerly submit to men's sexual desires.

If marginalized and minoritized groups have made America a singular force in the global community of nations, the suffering and oppression of Indigenous, Latino, and Asian American peoples is, like that of Black folk, undeniable. The genocide of native peoples explains how their stories and truths have been buried beneath an avalanche of dismemory. They weren't engaged; they were eviscerated. Latinos have been too numerous to sink beneath the weight of amnesia. Instead, they were thought of in proximity to Black identity, as with Dominicans, or viewed as white when they hailed from Cuba. They may have been joined by language, but they were separated by culture, color and custom. Asian Americans split the difference: they weren't subject to ethnic cleansing so much as they were constrained into peaceful oblivion or passive indifference.

Each of these groups has also been relentlessly compared to Black folk, usually in more positive fashion. Latinos, especially immigrants, were said to work harder and for far less money than Black folk. Native folk were said to be far more clever than Black people because they figured out a way to extract a measure of reparation through casinos. And Asian Americans were said to be plain smarter and to hardly cause any trouble in society.

The perceived gulf between Asian Americans and Blacks is perhaps the largest of all ethnic and racial groups. True, just as Black folk could also be Latino, and perhaps less recognizably Indigenous, they could also be Asian American. That pairing seemed to stretch the cultural imagination further, and arguably offered the most exoticized racial mixture. "Blasian" seemed to be an intriguing fusion. But there were huge differences between, say, the fashion model Tyson Beckford, a product of an Afro-Jamaican mother and a Panamanian father with Chinese blood, and Kamala Harris, whose parentage intertwined Jamaican and Indian roots. Still, it seemed to be the oddest of couplings because Black and Asian American cultures, especially Japanese, Chinese and Korean, seemed so disparate, so distinct, so dissimilar, so unagreeably opposed.

Despite negative comparisons to other groups, the Black narrative remains dominant while the Asian American story is largely obscured, often invisible. That is why, in a year with thousands of anti-Asian assaults, civil rights violations and instances of verbal harassment reported even before the Atlanta-area shootings in March 2021—in which six of the eight slain were women of Asian descent—most Americans are just beginning to engage with the Asian American struggle. That is why we sense that race is near the core of the Atlanta killings but have a harder time putting the tragedy in context or agreeing on whether these were, in a legal sense, hate crimes. That is why former president Donald Trump wasn't immediately drummed out of public life after calling COVID-19 a "Chinese virus" or "Kung flu" and appearing to give sanction to those who would exclude or attack people of Asian ancestry, rather than affirming Asian Americans' place in the American family.

In our popular imagination, the snarling legacy of Black disenfranchisement does not as easily attach to Asian America, writ large. Asian

Americans were not wiped out, like Native Americans, under the marauding imperatives of empire. A Civil War was not waged over their previous
condition of servitude. There is not an Asian American figure as universally lauded for his contributions as Rev. Martin Luther King, Jr., or, for
that matter, Mexican American civil rights leader Cesar Chavez, whose
likeness now sits behind President Biden in the Oval Office.

And yet there has been plenty of systemic racism, traumatic oppression
and disenfranchisement of Asian American populations. Chinese immigration was severely curtailed from the 1870s well into the 1920s because
they were viewed as a "yellow peril" to white society. It led, on the night of
October 24, 1871, to the "Chinese Massacre" in Los Angeles, fueled by propaganda that Chinese Americans were "barbarians taking jobs away from
whites." On that night a bloodthirsty mob of 500 white folk swept through
Chinatown in downtown Los Angeles, killing at least 18 people. The brutal
lynchings were set in motion when a white man claimed he got caught in
a melee between rival Chinese gangs. Even though seven white men were
held to account, their convictions were overturned on a legal technicality.

This led to the passage of the horrendous Chinese Exclusion Act in
1882, the first law to explicitly ban immigration based on race. Filipinos
were demonized in the early twentieth century for their alleged uncivilized
and unclean bodies. Franklin Roosevelt issued the infamous Executive
Order 9066 to force into internment camps Asian American citizens who
were labeled enemies of the state. Vietnamese commercial fishermen in
Texas faced racist confrontations with the Ku Klux Klan in the late 1970s,
and six people were gunned down at a Wisconsin Sikh temple in 2012.

Blacks and Asian Americans have also confronted the profound skepticism about their loyalty to the nation. From the start of the country, suspicion has lingered about how committed Black folk were to the nation's
principles and goals. That had to do in large part with the willingness of
enslaved Black folk to listen to offers to fight on behalf of the British, who
promised them freedom. The doubt about Black loyalty has been deeply
entrenched in the culture. It flares when Black citizens express outrage
at the American denial of rights to people of color around the world. It
flashes, too, when, closer to home, they criticize domestic politics aimed at
undermining the Black franchise.

Asian American citizens faced that litmus test in bitter fashion during
World War II when their loyalty to the nation was challenged for no other
reason than their ethnicity. There was no widespread or visible denunciation of American politics or practices by Asian American communities. In

fact, Chinese American physicist Chien-Shiung Wu worked on the Manhattan Project and Japanese American future senator Daniel K. Inouye was earning the Medal of Honor for his service in combat during the same war that Japanese Americans were rounded up and put into internment camps. During the Vietnam War era, members of the Hmong community fought a clandestine war in Laos on the side of American forces but experienced some of the same antagonism faced by other Southeast Asian refugees.

One reason is that vastly different communities are gathered under the AAPI umbrella, among them Korean Americans, Taiwanese Americans, Indian Americans, Native Hawaiians, and Chamorro and Carolinian Americans in the U.S. territory of Guam and the U.S. commonwealth of the Northern Mariana Islands. Each group was either already here or established itself here in different eras, for different reasons. Each has faced different hurdles. The "model minority" myth—a notion developed in the 1960s to suggest that Asian Americans thrived despite marginalization—helps obscure wealth inequality within Asian America, which recently supplanted African Americans as the group with the widest disparity between the wealthy and poor within its circles. The concept also makes Asian American achievement a metric—or cudgel—by which to assess, or criticize, Black and Latino progress. Think of how former New York magazine columnist Andrew Sullivan once evoked a shopworn trope about Asian Americans' "solid two-parent family structures" to taunt Black communities and their allegedly inferior moral habits and domestic arrangements.

What's more, many of our debates about American authenticity and meaning revolve around the Black-white binary. The equal protection guarantee of the 14th Amendment was first intended as a prohibition of legal discrimination against African Americans. The resistance from so many quarters to the New York Times' 1619 Project, which argues that Black America and the racism it has confronted since the nation's earliest days are integral to our understanding of the American founding, speaks to the generations-old clash of interpretations that put Black history at the center of the American story.

By contrast, Asian American history is often footnoted or compartmentalized, recounted and analyzed as a subplot in the bigger national narrative. For one, Asian Americans have been unjustly perceived as less assertive than African Americans in the fight for equality. For the same reasons that the AAPI community is a collective, the comparison makes no sense. The struggles and needs and timing of its constituent groups have always been different, but no less needed. And the persistence of stereotypes of Asian Americans—pernicious, clashing notions of passivity, on one hand, and subversion of American norms of decency and purity on the other—mock their contributions to national life.

Still, Asian American and Black history share something crucial: the burden of stereotype and scapegoating for the nation's ills. Think of the hatred Colin Kaepernick absorbed for kneeling during the national anthem. Think of the ordeal Fred Korematsu endured to challenge the legality of Japanese American internment all the way to the Supreme Court. And think of martyrs, from George Floyd to Vincent Chin—a Chinese American brutally beaten to death in Detroit, my hometown, in 1982 by two white autoworkers who associated Chin with the success of the Japanese auto industry. At their core, attacks on people of color, whether Black, AAPI, Latino or Native American, are about blaming the other. It's something most minoritized groups have in common.

Disparate groups, having overcome oppression, have made this country whole. Until we understand the ways in which the Asian American story is in many ways like the African American story, we won't be able to reckon with tragedies like Atlanta. Vincent Chin ought to be as well known, and as righteously mourned, as George Floyd. The best way to set us on our path is for the lived experiences of Asian Americans, like those of African Americans, to be viewed as essential to an understanding of the nation's identity.

Graduated Tax

On the Commencement Stage

48

The Weltanschauung of Lil Wayne, or What Can You Do with a Harvard Degree?

I have spoken many times to various Harvard audiences over the years. In June 2008, I was more than happy to address 300 undergraduates, faculty, alumni, and family members at their Sixth Annual Black Commencement Celebration. The fact that Harvard Law School graduate Barack Obama had just made history by clinching victory in the contest to become the nation's first Black presidential nominee of a major party the night before my speech on June 4, 2008, added even more excitement to the proceedings. I would speak again in the W. E. B. DuBois lectures, which began in November, the day after Obama was first elected president. When I returned to address Black Harvard graduates in May 2011, things were quite different: Obama was three years into his first term, expectations and perceptions of his performance in office had shifted, and the vulgar racist assault on his presidency had galvanized a great deal of Black America.

I want to speak to you about the subject: "What Can You Do with a Harvard Degree?" [Laughter] We is in a church, so "amens" are certainly appropriate, and other rhetorical ejaculations in the midst are quite welcome.

But when you think about what you can do with a Harvard degree the first thing that pops into mind is that you can get a good job. We're living in an extremely difficult period in American history and even, most especially, the history of African Americans, who are dealing with enormously difficult times when it comes to employment. The employment rate has risen for some, the unemployment rate has doubled for others. The unemployment rate for Black people right now is about 15.5%. That's an extraordinarily high rate, when the rate of unemployment for the majority community in America is beneath 10 percent. And so getting a good job is not something that is guaranteed to people, even if you get a college degree. A Harvard degree, of course, is quite valued, but it's even tough out here for

Harvard graduates. And the thing is that, as a Harvard graduate, you have the opportunity to do something that others can't take for granted in seeking and securing employment: The prestige of the university from which you emerge, the pedigree vouchsafed in hundreds of years of incredible intellectual achievement, suggests that you can get a good job.

And why is a good job important? Well, first of all, you do want to earn some money. Cheddar is important in cheeseburgers and on your dinner table. "Cash rules everything around me/Got to get the money/Dollar dollar bill y'all." Sure. That old Wu-Tang Clan saying is still true. But money is critical, not simply as a symbol of the aspired wealth to which you might aim, but also to transact commerce, and to sustain family, and to expand community, and to deepen your reach in an economy that has been made unsure by a variety of forces. So getting a good job is good to have money, because you need money to eat and survive. You can talk about, "Well, I can live without so much money," but try it out first before you assert that.

And then it's good not simply for making money, but for also allowing you to warehouse and showcase the extraordinary talent that you have that led you to Harvard, that got you into these walls of ivy, these halls of excellence, but allows you then to show off what you've learned while you're here. And getting a good job permits you to correlate between your appreciation for knowledge and your acquisition of certain skills—your erudition on the one hand and your ability to be able to apply that knowledge in a very functional and empirical fashion as you work your work. Whether that's as an engineer, a lawyer, a doctor. Maybe not an astronaut anymore, since NASA's closing down. I don't have any conspiracy theories, [but] when the brother gets to be the head of NASA, then it closes down. There are enough conspiracy theories about brothers from Harvard doing big things in public housing, but we'll say a bit about that later.

And so what's interesting is that the good jobs you're able to secure often give you a sense of real achievement. Because one of the most nefarious consequences of joblessness and unemployment is the lack of personal involvement in community and in family and, as a result of that, a lack of feeling of strength and security about one's place in the world. And so having a good job should not be assumed to be something that is automatic, because when difficult times have come, people need to get as much purchase as they can upon the economy. And a job certainly is the key.

Of course, being a Harvard graduate with a Harvard degree suggests that you've got a leg up and a step ahead of those who don't have that degree. And in getting a good job, it means not only getting the kind of money that you need, and not only being able to warehouse and showcase your talents, but it also suggests a meaningful existence. Because a lot of folk without jobs report that they don't feel so important, that they don't feel meaningful, that they don't feel significant, that they don't feel they're making a vital contribution.

Now it is true, we tell people all the time, don't become so closely identified with your job. You are not what you do. And yet that may be the luxury of those who possess enough of an abundance—abundance of opportunity, abundance of ability to work—to say that. We certainly don't want to reduce the tension between who we are as human beings and the things that we're able to do in the world. You are, after all, not clearly, not finally reduceable to the things you do in life. A job cannot exhaustively define you. And yet at the same time, if your vocation comes in your job—not just something you do just to be doing it, but a sense of mission and purpose driving what you do—then gainful employment is more than having a good paycheck or having compensation for the enormous skills you have. It's a sense of bountiful and abundant participation in the lives of your fellow citizens. But also in the lives of your family. And to enhance what you feel about yourself. The pernicious consequence of unemployment and joblessness is that people feel that they are not worthy. Or some people look at them and cast aspersions against them, castigate them for not having a job.

We got politicians out here who are throwing darts at people, suggesting that they don't want to work. We look at New York and we see that one out of two of every Black men is unemployed in New York City. Ain't that many lazy people in America. People ain't working, not because they are lazy. Well, not all of them. Not most of them. We know some people are just downright lazy, and it ain't color coordinated. We know that people across the board—Lithuanian, Italian, Jewish, Polish, and, yes, African American too—we don't want to exempt ourselves from that. In the vernacular, we got cousins "and them" [who are lazy]. We understand what the deal is. But the reality is that most people are not lazy. Most people want to work. Most people want to derive a sense of meaning from the work that they do and to make a contribution to the world in which they live.

And so having a good job is not a given. You don't want to take that for granted. But it is critical and vital in this particular era. Why? Because here we are, living through all of this massive shift in the economy. The shift from manufacturing to service industries has depleted the resources for so many people. People who used to work by the sweat of their brow and their physical brawn and the magnificence of their muscle are now shifting into other areas and arenas of competitive labor. And now we're not simply competing with what's going on in America. We see a global workplace, we see a global economy, where China owns a bunch of American "paper." Which means then that now we expand, and we get global. When you call the information system on your telephone, what do you get? You're not getting somebody around the corner up in Cambridge or over in Dedham. You're getting somebody in Delhi. You be trying to say, "You know that place next to Tony Roma's down the street?" "Sir, I am not in America." Right? So now the information system is global. The dynamic system of exchange of commerce is global. Dollars are not the only media through which we can talk about the accumulation of wealth. The dollar's not as dominant as it used to be. We look at the European market. We look at what's going on in the Middle East. We look at the challenge to America and the American-based economy rooted in certain things. Oil, for one. And then we begin to rethink who we are. So having a good job is not simply a matter of having a local vision. It's about a global understanding of our contribution to our families and to ourselves, and having a sense of meaningfulness in what we do.

But not only can you get a good job. I've been hinting at this: You can also have a meaningful life. And, you know, having a meaningful life means that as much as it is important to have a good job and to make good money and to support yourself and your family, and to be able to showcase the talent you gained here, or at least the talent that got you here, and showcase the skills that you've acquired here to be able to refine what you do. You also want to be able to lead a meaningful life. A Harvard degree, or a degree from any school, for that matter, should help out. A lot of people pooh-pooh education. They make fun of what it means to read and to write and to think critically and systematically.

I was sitting at the press conference the other night for the Miami Heat after they had defeated the Chicago Bulls. And I'm sitting in the press conference, because I talk to a few of these guys and engage with them. And Dwyane Wade and LeBron are at the podium, and they're speaking about Chris Bosh. And you know Chris Bosh has been getting a lot of heat, no pun intended. He's been catching a lot of dreck and a lot of "wreck" because they say he's soft, and it's [only] two-and-a-half men on the Miami team. When Dwyane Wade and LeBron James and Chris Bosh signed there, they said that [Bosh] is too cerebral. And so one of the questioners from the media asked, "Isn't it interesting that Chris Bosh is having such success, but he prepares in a way different from you all?" And Dwyane and LeBron get that knowing smile on their face. And Dwyane said, "Yeah, most people, when they prepare for the game, they're listening to music. But Chris has his head in a book." He says, "And given how he's been playing the last few days, we gonna buy him as many books as we can find." And isn't it interesting? And I'm sitting there thinking, why is that so funny and odd that a brother would be reading? Thinking critically. Engaging in reflection upon ideas as a preparation for the game. I mean, I'm not mad if you're listening to your iPod, and you got your favorite music on. Maybe Murray Perahia's Beethoven concertos. Maybe Waylon Jennings's bluegrass album. Maybe some JAY-Z or Nas and Lil Wayne. Maybe even Nicki Minaj.

But why is it that if he's actually reading and thinking and engaging his mind, that that's all of a sudden a cause of suspicion or derision or even lighthearted humor? Why is that? Because we live in an anti-intellectual culture. And I ain't talking about Black folk. I'm talking about America. Now, a lot of people try to put this at the feet of African American culture. We know that ain't real. Now, we got our share of people who look down at the pointy-head professors, intellectuals. I remember when I was a kid, they called me "Professor." They kept saying it. I just thought I'd become one. But we know that for the most part we're not speaking about African American culture and the derisive perspective on learning. This is an American phenomenon. America is deeply and profoundly anti-intellectual. Don't want to think critically. Don't want to engage in the life of the mind. And those who do are seen as somehow antithetical to the very vibrancy of American democracy. And yet the truth is, without the fund of ideas from which to draw, to underwrite the incredible and exponential increase in democracy, America would not be what it is today. And so the life of the mind is critical, not only to the culture, not only to the country, it's critical to our individual existence.

Now, one of the things you should've learned while you were here is that education ain't gonna stop with you graduating. If you're done with learning—I can understand being done for a minute. Ain't got to get up, ain't got to go to class, ain't got to go to lab, ain't got to hear no professor talk. And after Dyson finishes, "ain't got to hear nobody else spitting venom at me about my lack of getting up." Professor Frederick talked about senioritis. Some of y'all caught it as freshmen. [Laughter] And so nobody has to dictate to you any further what to do.

But I ain't talking about schooling. I'm talking about what my daddy from Albany, Georgia, used to call "learning." He said, "Boy, what they learning you?" Now some people would say, "Oh what a solecism. What a grammatical construction that is outside the bounds of normal discourse and acceptable rhetoric: 'What are they learning you?'" Like it was a disease. Like it was a virus. Well, it is. I know it ain't grammatically correct to talk about what they learning you, 'cause you have to learn yourself. That's an existential assertion of the possibility of opening your mind to grand ideas. But "learning you" suggests that there's something to epistemology, just a big old word to talk about knowledge. There's something to expanding the horizon of your consciousness and deepening your love affair with ideas.

And that's different than schooling. Schooling is the institutional matrix that receives the impulse to learn. Learning is the lifelong process of gaining new information, grasping new knowledge and learning how to use it to your benefit and the benefit of the people around you. So when you learn something, you get excited. And I want you to have a meaningful existence, because I want you to be excited about learning new things.

I mean, one of the reasons I listen to hip hop is, I learn new stuff. I know people say, "You crazy? Whatcha' learning, new cuss words?" Yes. [Laughter] Quite frankly, yes. But—but—but you can learn new ways to say stuff that puts you in a different framework. Witty, some of it is. Some of it just for the sheer rhetorical mastery that is displayed. I was listening last night to a new Lil Wayne song. I was late to the Lil Wayne celebration and coronation. I was old school. I was still listening to Rakim. I was on Nas, I was on Jay, I was on Lauryn Hill. I wasn't trying to hear nothing about Lil Wayne. I said, "What is he saying?" [Laughter] And my man said to me, "Man, you getting old. I thought you was a hip hop intellectual. You're getting old, Dyson." I said, "Yeah, I'm just trying to make distinctions. I ain't trying to hate, I'm trying to relate."

But I'm trying to also understand. Deconstruct, demythologize, insinuate myself into the Weltanschauung of Lil Wayne. What is he saying? "We are not the same, I am a Martian." [Laughter] I said, "I hear that. But what he sayin'?" So then I got it. I said, "Oh, it's the way he says it. The way he flips verses. I get it." The kind of intricate, ironic use, the parodic use of language." "I'd rather be underground pushing flowers than in the pen sharing showers." [Laughter] Oh, okay. Of course, you did go to the pen. I don't know how many showers you shared. But learning something. Listening to young people saying something differently. Like JAY-Z said, "Now all my teachers couldn't reach me/And my mama couldn't beat me/Hard enough to match the pain of my pop not seeing me/So with that disdain in my membrane/Got on my pimp game/ [. . .] My defense came." Oh. Now I see. A different way of understanding fatherlessness in one's own life, and the effect it may have. The deleterious consequence of a father absent in an African American community, in a project.

And so I began to listen. Because I began to see that a lot of these young people are in love with learning. They may not be in love with schooling. Nas dropped out in the eighth grade. But ain't nobody gonna call him dumb. Who was wrong, Nas or the school? Tupac dropped out before he graduated. Who's wrong, him or the school? Because the reality is this: not all schools are created equal. Schools are subject to, and vulnerable to, the particular perspectives and political ideologies that drive the construction of curricula and the agendas for their particular school in local communities. That stuff is up for grabs, debate and argument. And as a result of that, some of the institutional matrixes that construct knowledge are not friendly to young people of color.

But learning is different. A lot of people assume these young people don't have a desire to learn. I know that ain't true. I know you know that ain't true. Here you are: you are the living repudiation of the notion that young Black people or young people of color are not in love with learning. You don't come to Harvard to play basketball. Well, maybe, but not primarily. [Laughter] Y'all here for some serious business, for some learning. And, in that learning, it's not simply something you get that you can apply to your job, it's something that you can also apply to your life. The intrinsic value of thinking well. The beauty of reading and understanding what you read. Do you know how many people are illiterate in America?

And so the wild and delightful beauty of being able to understand what you read, and having the freedom to do so. The ability to learn. There's something that's intrinsically valuable about that, and I don't want you to lose that, I don't want you to miss that, even after you leave the halls of ivy. I want you to understand you cannot simply read a book and learn something new, you can then engage in the process of using that knowledge to create a world that can fundamentally transform the prospects for human community for millions beyond your own shop, beyond your own bailiwick.

And so one of the things you can also do with a Harvard degree is learn to tell the truth accurately but compassionately. And, you see, that's a hard thing to do in the culture in which we live. Because truth telling ain't something people necessarily be in love with. And a lot of us—most of us, all of us—are subjective, so what we think is true in our perspective might be informed by what politics we have, what religion we have, what culture we grew up in, what race and the like.

But the reality is, my brothers and sisters, that we are hungry in this culture for truth. Because lies have been spoon-fed to us, lies have been piped to us, lies have been told to us. And I'm talking about lies about culture, about race, about gender, about human beings, about vulnerable human beings, and people don't necessarily want to hear the truth. We don't always want to hear the truth. We often, like that Jack Nicholson character in *A Few Good Men*, believe that "you can't handle the truth." And so we live in a culture that tells lies about young Black people. Dumb. Stupid. Disinclined to literacy. Don't want to be concerned about the broader community. Getting drunk, smoking weed, getting high. Though those may not be mutually exclusive categories. One can make a contribution, be concerned about community and get high. I'm not suggesting that, neither am I advocating that. I'm simply noting it observationally. [Laughter] But this is the school of Timothy Leary as well.

What's interesting is that lies about young people of color are especially destructive because people make a lot of hay out [of] them. One suggests why they don't want young [white] people in schools with young Black people or brown people, because they will somehow communicate the virus of their illiteracy or their cultural immorality or their lack of ethical orientation. Then there are lies about gender, whether women can be scientifically inclined. Whether they can appropriate the requisite knowledge to substantiate their claim to being scientists. That they can hang with Dr. [Allen] Counter. That they can be informed about the world in which we live through physical phenomena. So lies about who women are and what they can study and what they can learn and what they can appreciate. Lies about gay and lesbian or transgender or bisexual brothers or sisters. Lies about what they want. How, if you're gay or lesbian, transgender or bisexual, you're going to undermine community. My God, you might catch it!

Especially in Black communities and in communities of color, we got to be very careful about this. We been living with gay and lesbian and transgendered and bisexual people for so long, whether we knew it or not. What are we going to do, be retroactively homophobic? "Oh my God, had I known you were gay I wouldn't have taken that tuition payment from you." [Laughter] "I wouldn't have listened to that great sermon you preached." And to tell the truth about gender or sexual orientation in this country, and even in our culture, challenges some of the shibboleths and platitudes, challenges some of the narrow notions that we have incubated, but not in the heart of learning.

And what I say to you, what I beg of you, what I plead with you, is to use your Harvard degree to challenge the lies. Lies people tell constantly. Lies people tell repetitively. Lies about race, lies about religion, lies about who is in and who is out in terms of acceptable American patriotism.

Now, we've been living through this with our president. People been— you know, the Birther movement, going around challenging his birth certificate like he wasn't real. His bona fides. Like he got to show his slave pass. [Laughter] Like this is under Black Codes. Like this is apartheid. "Show us your papers." [Applause] I just wish once for a joke he'd have pulled out some weed papers. [Laughter] Marijuana wrap, is what I'm saying. Just say, "Here my papers right here. They not mine, they were left in my car last night." [Laughter] I just wish once he'd go out on the White House lawn with some tube socks and maybe a skull cap, getting his morning paper. I wish he would barbecue and have some chitlins in the White House, just to live down to the derisive stereotype of what they thought a Black man was gon' be. What did they think he was gon' do?

And so these stereotypes about his Otherness: he's not one of us. Lies about who this man was. Lies about this Harvard graduate. Lies about a man who did everything they said they wanted. Go to a good school. Marry a brilliant woman who's fine as well. Simultaneity is not a sin. [Laughter and applause] Harvard graduate herself, Princeton undergraduate. Children looking good. They're just a Black Norman Rockwell postcard. ["Amen!"] We just love to see them walk down Air Force One. [Applause] "I'm not a player, I just crush a lot." [Laughter] We love to see him thrust and parry. We love to see him look at Benjamin Netanyahu like, "Are you out of your damn mind?" [Applause] Ain't got to say a word, it's all in his face. Cultural significance, racial signification of Blackness, all in his face.

I'm almost done. So we love to see what this brilliant, beautiful Black man has wrought. And the questions about his character, about whether or not he is American, are so unfounded. And here Donald Trump was leading the parade. And the Birther movement. And Glenn Beck. And Rush Limbaugh. I don't have to narrate their personal maladies, their existential foibles for you. The reality is, is that Barack Obama—Barack Hussein Obama, President Barack Hussein Obama—deserved the legitimacy and authenticity, the assumption that he was an American, that any other president has earned and deserved. [Applause]

And if they gon' do it to him, they gon' do it to you. So just 'cause you got a Harvard pedigree, just 'cause you got a Harvard degree, don't mean they ain't gonna challenge you. And ask you, "Did you write that paper? Did you do that experiment?" I know y'all don't experience that here, but at other schools I've heard they ask questions. "Are you really that intelligent? Are you really that articulate? Are you that cold with your rhetoric that you're able to understand a gerund and a participle, and that a dangling participle is not a piece of lettuce? Are you that cold that you can understand stochastic motion? Do you know thermodynamics? Do you know Maxwellian principles or Brownian motion? Do you understand quantum mechanics? Do you really understand what Busta Rhymes is saying?" [Laughter]

Now, as I end and take my seat, but the thing is we want the president to understand, if they doin' it to him, and we love and protect him, he's got to love and protect us. [Applause] It's not easy to do. Folk don't want to even acknowledge he's a Black man. He talked about a policeman up here in Cambridge and people went crazy. First of all, he didn't call the man stupid, he said "acting stupidly." That's different. He's presupposing a fundamental ground of intelligence that was radically departed from, at least for that instance. So the presumption was itself proved that Mr. Obama did not believe—President Obama did not believe—the very thing with which he was charged. Yet, at the same time, we got to be open and honest here, to tell the truth. And the truth is that in America people are afraid for Obama to tell the truth about race, and therefore, if he can't do it, and we know he's in a tight box, those of us who have the ability and the leisure and the freedom and the intelligence and the learning must do so ourselves.

And when we do so, we must do so with respect. We must not be mean-spirited or vicious or personal. We must be prophetic and principled. We must tell the truth in love. We must speak truth to power with accuracy and compassion. And when we do that, then we preserve the dignity of our opponent and we make sure that we don't believe that we know all of the truth ourselves. Be that humble to recognize that truth.

I end by saying this: what else can you do with a Harvard degree? You can help somebody. Now, my friends, we live in an era where people are self-enclosed, narcissistic, self-interested, want to do stuff for themselves and don't want to help nobody else. I know it sounds like a cliché, maybe even a tag to a sermon, a coda to a homily. But the reality is, is that in America a lot of folk are concerned about self. What *I* can do. What *I* can get for me. How *I* can hustle. How *I* can make dough. How I can expand *my* particular bailiwick, *my* particular home, *my* particular kingdom, the cars I have.

And I ain't mad if you get a new car, and a nice one. The rapper Flo Rida wanted to talk to me a couple nights ago, so he sent a car. He said, "I'll send a car for you." I thought cool. He'll send a nice sedan. He sent an all-white Maybach. [Laughter] I was like, "My Lord, what have I done wrong? Did I offend God?" But what was interesting to me is that—as I'm taking a ride in this $500,000 car—that he could afford to send that to me because he was getting [in] a $1.8 million Bugatti. My wife said to him, "You're driving our house." [Laughter] That's beautiful. I'm glad for him. He's a humble young man. He's brilliant. Get as much as you can.

But what I tried to suggest to him, as I leave with you, is that even the accumulation of all of these magnificent toys, and this magnificent wealth, that you come from a people who fundamentally have loved humanity and served their brothers and sisters and helped somebody else. Why is that important? Because even creeping up into bourgeois Black culture is the notion "I did it myself. You do it yourself." You know, if you read all the treatises on the Black middle class, you'll discover that Black middle class people understand, and upper middle class people understand, when you make it, that's "we" made it. That's you and your mama "and them," your baby mamas, your related people. That is everybody included.

And that means, my brothers and sisters, that when you make it, there's a sense of vicarious participation in "we" making it. Why? Because you didn't make it by yourself. Somebody prayed for you. Somebody sacrificed for you. Somebody gave you fifty dollars, that was their last fifty dollars, and it meant the world to them. Somebody got out there and got into a car wash or sold chicken for you. Somebody labored for you. And you must remember to do the same. [Applause] That means you got to help. And you know this: when you help them, you help yourself. And when you help yourself, and you help them, you help our community get better. We have got to do away with this narcissistic individualism, with this me-ism, this myopic concentration on self. We got to love community.

Millions of Black people will go to bed tonight and will not be able to eat. Millions of Black people do not have a job. Millions of Black people are being demonized by people with education and who have political connections. Millions of Black people and poor white people and poor brown people have nobody to advocate for them.

And so what I say to you to do with your degree is to help somebody. You can help individuals, tutor a child, mentor a young person in your community, reach out and help somebody who needs to learn how to read. Who may be 55 or 60. You can engage in the fundamentally radical act of being a self-giving and sacrificial servant of powers that are higher than you.

And when you do that you have earned the beautiful power of a Harvard degree. But more than that, you have become a full-fledged member of the beautiful heritage of your community that continues to live on in your lives, to walk in your lanes, and to think brilliantly in your mind. And when you do that, you will have made the most significant and profound contribution to our community.

God bless you. I congratulate the class of 2011.

CHAPTER

49

How We Become Who We Are

Historically Black colleges and universities remain vital sources of Black education, cultural formation, and group pride, and an important crucible for shaping rituals of racial cohesion, identity, and purpose. All three of my children graduated from HBCUs, and I began my trek in higher education at Knoxville College. I have had the privilege of speaking at several HBCU commencements. One of my fondest memories is when I had the magical opportunity to be a co-commencement speaker with the late, great Cicely Tyson at Dillard University in May 2009. She recited Langston Hughes's immortal poem "Mother to Son," in which the mother tells her son, "Life for me ain't been no crystal stair," encouraging the students to soldier on. I was inspired to remind them that as the "Katrina class"—they entered school the same year as the devastating hurricane of 2005—they could be proud and refuse to be cowed by critics like Cosby who berated the citizens of New Orleans for their irresponsibility. As I said that morning, "A lot of people go around the country lecturing folk about how to be responsible, even as they are irresponsible. America tells you to be responsible for what the past has wrought, and yet America refuses to live up to its responsibility to do the right thing."

I delivered this commencement address at Hampton in May 2016. Hampton is one of the most storied HBCUs in the nation, and its president, William Harvey, is one of the most captivating and legendary figures to lead one of our finest institutions.

What an honor it is to be here today with one of the legendary figures in all of American education. When the names of the great presidents of our greatest institutions are called, when that list is enumerated, Dr. Harvey will be near the top. The Benjamin Elijah Mayses and the William Harveys signify such deep and profound commitment to American education, but especially to African American education as well. [Applause] I told Dr. Harvey on the ride over here, he's like the pastor of millions. And we thank God for his incredible intelligence, for his unstinting passion. He is unrelentingly obsessed with the magnificent purpose of making this institution greater. And Dr. Harvey told me I would be speaking today—not invited me, but he told me, at the funeral of my beloved mentor Dr. William Douglas Booth, whose brilliant and lovely wife (both of them long-standing friends of mine), Mrs. Ruth Booth, serves as one of his assistants and receptionists, that I would be speaking. Because when Dr. Harvey speaks, it gets done. So I canceled everything else I had on the books, and I am here this morning because of this legendary figure. Let's give it up for Dr. Harvey. [Applause]

I see so many of my friends and associates over the years, but I got to shout out Dr. Linda Malone-Colon, who is the Dean of the Liberal Arts here. Looking like a schoolgirl herself, even this morning. And I want to say to all of the mothers here, "Happy Mother's Day." As Dr. Harvey indicated, my son Mwata graduated from here. And indeed, all of my children—my two sons and my daughter—graduated from HBCUs. My daughter, Maisha, from Spelman, my son Michael from Morehouse, after four other HBCUs—my name might as well been Lou Rawls, I was a one-man United Negro College Fund. And I started at Knoxville College myself. And my son Mwata Omotiyo Dyson, the president of his class, 1993, spoke during his graduation. He is now a distinguished anesthesiologist and entrepreneur. And it's because of Hampton University. Some tell me the real "HU." [Applause and cheers]

And so what a great honor it is to be here today. I'm not going to take long, because y'all ain't here to hear me. You are here to hear that you are officially graduated from this great institution. I want to reflect with you today about "How We Become Who We Are." It's a paradox in one sense. Because we think that our identities are already shaped. We think that who we are has been settled. But we know until we draw our last breath we continue to evolve.

The first thing that you ought to know about becoming who you are is that you got to have perspective. And the perspective that you ought to have is that you come from a great people. You have emerged from people who beat back the vicious demons of white supremacy and social injustice and economic inequality and oppression. You come from a stock of people who have made America what it is today. You come from people who came over in hulls of ships that were filled with bodies that were intended to do the work of American culture that we are not often given credit for. And that perspective is important, because some of us think that old school happened ten years ago. That ain't old. I remember hearing the great intellectual P. Diddy say once, "Back in my day, back when I was young, back in 1989." Now that might be old to some of y'all, but that ain't real old to nobody else.

And so some of us, because we are addicted to Twitter, with 140 characters, and Facebook—back in my day we had to face the book and read it ourselves. [Laughter] We ain't had no Google to look stuff up. We had to go to the "li-berry." That's where the lies are buried. You better go there and dig 'em up. [Laughter] We had card catalogues. Y'all don't know nothing about that. One eighty-six, where the Sociology was, where we were digging deep into the li-berry. Now y'all, just with a click, can archive—which is beautiful—massive amounts of gigabytes and information. But in one sense the old school leather on the pavement yielded some insight as well. There were some folk like Du Bois, who didn't have social media. But he dug deep into the souls of Black folk and saw that we were made of something powerful and something persistently great and glorious. And you ought to have perspective about that.

I know you want to "mess up some commas and mess up some commas. Forty thousand to a hundred thousand, hundred thousand, another hundred thousand. Three hundred thousand, five hundred thousand, a million. Let's make the money shower." I know you want to do that. [Applause] But you better understand that some folk came before that. [Sings Negro spiritual "Hold On."] "Keep-uh your hand on-a that plow. Hold on!" You had some folk who ain't had no money. But they had a sense of God in their hearts and a hint of the Spirit in their own noble aspirations. They understood that they were blessed by God. They had no dough, but they had determination. They didn't have education like you got today, but they knew how to call upon the name of a God who could get them over. "How I got over."' [Applause]

I know y'all got some scribes going on now. I listen to the great philosopher Tupac, who said, "Somebody wake me, I'm dreamin'/I started as a seed in semen/Swimming upstream, planted in the womb while screaming/On the top was my pops, my mama hollering stop, from a single drop, this is what they got/Not to disrespect my people but my papa was a loser/Only plan he had for mama was to blank her and abuse her/And even as a seed I could see his plan for me/Stranded on welfare, another broken family." Even the great philosopher Christopher Wallace: "Used to fuss when the landlord dissed us/No heat, wondered why [crowd completes line] Christmas missed us. Birthdays was the worst days/Now we [crowd completes line] sip champagne when we thirsty. Damn right I like the life I live, 'cause I went from [crowd completes line] negative to positive. And it's all good/ And if you don't know [crowd completes line] now you know."

All I'm saying to you is that you got perspective rooted in some serious existential and political realities. But don't forget where you came from. Don't forget the people who birthed you. Don't forget whose womb you emerged from. Stop demonizing women as Bs and Hs and skeezers and sluts and hood rats and chicken heads, and recognize that is a fine form for a fantastic female that produced what you are today. ["Come On Now" shouted from the crowd] You got muscles on your body and you looking at some gray-haired old man. But don't forget that gray-haired old man took what you couldn't take to get what you were able to take today. When people called them "boy" and "girl," and when they got 60 [years of age] called them "Uncle" and "Aunt." Don't forget that that person you think is a sellout allowed you to buy in, and raise up, and deepened your analysis of what you are and where you are. Don't forget that perspective.

But not only that. Not only in becoming who you are do you have to have perspective. But you've got to understand as well the reality of the power you possess. Now, some of us don't understand what that power is. Here we are in America right now, enduring some difficult times. The difficult times that we are enduring have to do with class, have to do with gender, have to do with sexual orientation, have to do with race. Here we are under the administration of the first Black president of the United States of America. We ain't never been prouder to have a Black family living in public housing. [Laughter] Don't you apply for that when you get your Section 8. You ain't getting 1600 Pennsylvania Avenue. He ain't perfect, but as Grace Jones said, perfect for the situation in which he finds himself. We know that from the very beginning folk didn't even want him to succeed. He says yes, they say no. He says wet, they say dry. He says up, they say down. But the reality is he kept on fighting through. And now, nearly at the end of his presidency we see what has come about when he has exercised that power.

And you also have to exercise your power to hold him accountable for what he's doing in the White House and what you are responsible for doing with your life. The reality is, my brothers and sisters, we live in a nation where we have been denied legitimate access to what we ought to possess because of what our parents struggled for. In the Civil Rights Movement, they struggled for the right to vote. And yet some of us have been denied that right, not because we don't seek to vote, but because of the political machinations of a culture that continues to undermine us. And so I say to you, exercise your power. Exercise your power to get to the polls. Don't act like it's raining, too un-sunshine-y, for you to pull that lever and dimple that chad. You better get up like you going to a Beyoncé concert and you drinking some lemonade. "You know I gave you life." [Laughter] Get up because somebody got up before you to allow you to exercise that power.

And no matter what you are becoming, whether you are a dentist or a psychologist or a ditch digger, whether you are an engineer or a college professor, exercise the power that God gave to you and that your people fought for you to be able to exercise. But also, the power to love other people. The power to affirm other people. The power in your life not to be arrogant, but to be humble. Not to assume you got where you are 'cause of all that. You ain't the only cute person in the world. You ain't the only fine person in the world. You ain't the only educated person in the world. There are a lot of folk in your own neighborhood who are finer, better looking and more intelligent, but they didn't get the opportunity that you have today. So you better take advantage of that opportunity to exercise that power to do the right thing in your personal relationships.

Not only that, you ought to be able to speak on behalf of—join with the chorus of voices that have arisen during —Black Lives Matter. Your generation has reminded us you ain't got to be old to be useful. You ain't got to be old and aged to be wise. Your Black Lives Matter movement has been important. It has reminded us that Black lives do matter. We ain't saying nobody else's lives don't matter. But we know white lives matter, because we live in a culture that affirms that day in and day out. The reason we say Black Lives Matter, because Black lives matter *too*. Our intelligence is important. Our work ethic is important. Our sweat is important. Our industry is important. Our spirit is important as well. [Applause]

And you gotta remember to speak up for those who ain't like you. Black people ain't got no sense beating up on no gay people. Some of the people who have blessed you the most have been gay or lesbian or transgendered or bisexual or queer. You just didn't know it. Some of y'all trying to use God to cosign your bigotry. Don't bring God into that. [Applause] God is no respecter of human beings, which means God shows no partiality. God ain't worried about your sexual orientation, God is worried about your moral orientation. What are you doing to help somebody else? What are you doing to spread the Gospel of love? What are you doing to make sure justice is real in America? What are you doing to become a vehicle for God's divine destiny?

And then I'm going to leave you with this: To become who you are, you've got to understand that you've got to challenge the patriarchy of an oppressive culture. Why do I single that out? It's Mother's Day. A lot of our mothers had to deal with a lot of trauma. Black mothers still don't get their just due. They get demonized as welfare queens, they get dismissed and marginalized as women who are standing in the way. But without Black mothers and white mothers and yellow and red and brown mothers, we wouldn't even be here today. We ought to remember that patriarchy can have vicious consequences. If you're a real man you shouldn't be scared of a real woman. [Applause] Real men ain't mad at real women. 'Cause your manhood ain't about your muscles, your manhood ain't about your bass voice, your manhood ain't about how tall you are, your manhood is in your ability to love and affirm your family and to embrace the vulnerable and stand tall upon the principles of self and other love. [Applause]

And so men are viciously treated by patriarchy too. Trying to outdo each other. Trying to show who's the biggest and baddest, and then we end up murdering each other and hurting each other and dogging each other's reputation. We can't even affirm each other as men, because we are so involved in a corrosive competition, we can't affirm the beauty of the next brother. You ought to learn to do that. If God gave somebody else a gift it ain't taking nothing away from you. You do you. Do what God gave you. Express the genius of your own soul and spirit and God will lift you up. If you are faithful to what God gave you, you ain't got to be a Xerox of nobody else, be an original. [Applause] You ain't got to retweet nobody else. Tweet yourself.

Then I say to us, we got to love our women. We got to love our women because they are the wombs from which we have emerged. They are the beautiful standards by which we understand God has blessed us. We are the basis in our community of appreciating those women because those women have sacrificed to make it possible to do what we do. We love our fathers, because we know they are there, standing strong, standing tall and affirming. But on this Mother's Day we must acknowledge that the women in our lives deserve to be respected and deserve to be celebrated and deserve to be embraced. [Applause]

I take my seat, but that's why we ought to celebrate strong women, 'cause strong women make strong children, make stronger men, make stronger communities, make stronger universities, make stronger worlds for us to operate in. That's why Harriet Tubman gonna be on the money, dog. [Applause] And do you think Harriet Tubman wasn't a strong woman? What do you think she said? "Excuse me. There's a thing called the Underground

Railroad. I want you guys to come along. It's really cool." That ain't what she said. She said, "Be here tonight at 8:30. And don't be late." And then some of them changed their minds. "Ms. Tubman, we was gonna go, but we done changed our minds. But we ain't gwon to tell nobody." She said, "Oh, I know you won't." She had a Bible in one hand and a shotgun in the other. "Don't call it a comeback. I been here for years. Mama said knock you out." And she had to knock some of those Negroes out. And when they woke up, they asked, "Where I is?" "Negro, you free. We done drug your butt to freedom." And women are still doing it today. Some of y'all wouldn't be here without a mama who told you, "Take your butt to Hampton University and graduate." That's how you become who you're meant to be. Peace. [Applause]

50

Is America Still a Dream?

I was a professor in the Department of Communication Studies at the University of North Carolina, Chapel Hill, when the students requested that I speak at the winter 1996 commencement before an audience of 6,000 in the iconic Dean Smith Arena. In my speech, I argued that, contrary to commonly held beliefs, particularly in the South, young folk were not killing the American Dream with their destructive pop culture and their abortive narcissism. I defended youth culture and wrestled with some of its figures, like Kurt Cobain, Alanis Morrissette, Snoop Dogg, and Jenny McCarthy. I quoted the rapper The Notorious B.I.G., defended affirmative action, and gently criticized my friend Michael Jordan for his approach to philanthropy. Although there was no social media back then, the local newspapers pilloried me and derided my speech as "a political screed dressed up in trendy gobbledygook." My chancellor took me to task in the press. An editorial cartoon featured a caricature of me sitting on a commode using toilet paper to write my next speech. There were calls for the university to fire me, and a flurry of angry columns and letters to the editor denouncing me and my commencement address. And of course, the vitriol was accompanied by death threats. This is one of the rare commencement addresses that I wrote down ahead of time for the occasion. (Given its reception, I was convinced to go back to extemporaneous addresses.) You can read for yourself whether the criticism was warranted.

Thirty-five years ago, in a commencement address he delivered at Lincoln University in Pennsylvania, Martin Luther King, Jr., said that "America is essentially a dream, a dream as yet unfulfilled." Two years later, in the symbolic and rhetorical shadow of Abraham Lincoln in Washington, D.C., King riveted our nation with his monumental reinterpretation of what fellow Nobel laureate Toni Morrison calls "that well-fondled phrase, 'the American Dream.'" Four years after dreaming out loud about the wondrous possibilities of American democracy, King confessed, in a BBC broadcast of his "A Christmas Sermon on Peace," that "not long after talking about that dream I started seeing it turn into a nightmare." Church bombings, ghetto poverty, riots and war had tempered King's extravagant optimism and sparked his broad reassessment of our country's commitment to social justice.

Is America still a dream?

In the minds of millions of our citizens today, the prospect of America expanding its geography of hope and strengthening its democratic impulses is hampered by the downward drift of youth culture. Like the American Dream itself, the story of American youth's moral bankruptcy— its nihilistic bent and its narcissistic base—has been greatly exaggerated. While America has not yet turned to eating its young, its rhetoric of "discipline and punishment," to pinch a well-worn phrase from philosopher Michel Foucault, is staggering. America is prosecuting a war against its youth, and the casualties are piling up.

Every other week or so, a new report from the front is issued. Kurt Cobain's self-indulgent death is said to be a barometer of the ethical eclipse of Generation X, the first age group to collect the term of a mathematical equation as a badge of identity. Perhaps that's because older folk—shall we call ourselves Generation Y, as in "Why do young folk act that way?"— refuse to pose possible solutions to what we in our algebra of despair conclude are intractable problems. Tupac Shakur's violent end is read as a cosmic order of justice shoring itself up, a karmic down payment on a self-determined bad existence in this world and the world to come.

All the while C. Delores Tucker and Bill Bennett, ideological soulmates in the alleged battle to save our youth, congratulate themselves—Ms. Tucker raising high the banner of racial purity, Mr. Bennett waving the flag of American pop culture's moral poverty. But what Ms. Tucker and Mr. Bennett fail to mask, especially in their attack on gangsta rap and the corporate interests that support it, is that their biracial coalition of conscience is really a self-righteous campaign of moral policing that departs radically from the ethical integrity of prophets like Martin Luther King. Indeed, the King estate would be embarrassingly rich if it could collect royalties on every use of his rhetoric to defend present moral posturing among the truly morally impoverished—from the crusaders against rap to the Republican Party of California in its defense of the ill-named California Civil Rights Initiative.

King would certainly have been disturbed by the way gangsta rap glamorizes violence and verbally assails women—that is, after he would have freed his own house from the plagues of patriarchy. But King understood that even literal acts of violence committed by Blacks during riots, though morally detestable, paled in comparison to the forces that provoked their violence. He said, "Let us say boldly that if the total slum violations of law by the white man over the years were calculated and compared with the lawbreaking of a few days of riot, the hardened criminal would be the white man."

The misuse of King's memory and spirit of protest in the war against gangsta rap, which in truth is a war against youth, is mirrored in the equally faulty adaptation of King's image and words in the war to trample affirmative action. For those who argue that King stood against preferences for Blacks, emphasizing content of character over color of skin, his words are a stern rebuke. "It is impossible to create a formula for the future which does not take into account that our society has been doing something special *against* the Negro for hundreds of years," King wrote. "How then can he be absorbed into the mainstream of American life if we do not do something special *for* him now?"

These are not the words of the King who has inspired us to make him the Archetypal African American or the Model Moral Man when it comes to race. But his words, and more important, his example, suggest a strategy for recovering the dangerous dimensions of the American Dream, for making it an instrument of collective redemption only after it has been engaged to measure our failure to achieve our highest destiny as a nation. For the real, hopeful danger of the American Dream is that it will burst the seams of the expected; that it will suggest promise where there was none and that it will sow urgency on the very ground where initiative had been murdered.

By making the American Dream so promiscuous, in other words, by making it tangible and within the grasp of ordinary folk, especially those not imagined in its early versions, the guardians of high optimism and shallow vision are incurably vexed. They believe that there must be some secret to preserving our national identity, a secret passed along to the masters of American history, as opposed to those who, like Fanon's wretched of the earth, "live inside history." Such thoroughgoing elitism, of course, trumps the original complexity of the American Dream, a dream of immigrants who fled tyranny and terror in the people-making embrace of the New World. The only hope for extending the American Dream is an acknowledgment that for many it has not been achieved, and that perhaps its greatest support will come after we wrestle with the dystopias of those Malcolm X aptly termed "victims of democracy."

The value of youth culture is partly in its blistering detail about how the American Dream has not only been fondled, but molested. Obviously, I'm not referring to Jenny McCarthy's frenetic blond-bombshell meets dizzy broad redux—the late Marilyn Monroe and early Goldie Hawn joined at the breast, sheathed in pop culture's conflicted desire for a postmodern babe who looks nothing like mom but who, like her, despite appearances, is beyond approach. Modernism in a miniskirt. Neither am I referring to some youth's mindless imitation of their parents' "obtuse pedantry," in philosopher Walter Kaufmann's wonderful phrase, the stodgy, stolid and stale beliefs of the past sent along on the wings of feckless tradition. Brahmins in Bugle Boys.

I'm referring to those youth who inspired terms like "slackers," "Generation X," and "lost generation." Berated for lacking initiative and a work ethic, these youth confront, sometimes heroically, sometimes self-destructively, the limited life options that both wealth and poverty offer. The thin solidarity provided by age is made thicker by anger: against brutalizing authority, against narrow beliefs about what is worthy in life, against simplistic, reductive thinking about a complex youth culture. But it is simply easier to dismiss our youth than to hear them. Sure, part of youth culture is built on keeping old folk out—Kurt Cobain's screaming voice was calculated to send shivers up our spines; Snoop Doggy Dogg's vigorous vulgarity is not for the rhetorically fainthearted; Alanis Morissette's ode to fellatio in the theater melts our stiff resolve, so to speak, to listen with an open mind; and the Notorious B.I.G.'s boasting of his phallic prowess is jarring.

But the bravura and braggadocio, and the self-deprecation and cynicism, too, sometimes conceal, at other times reveal, personal and social pain, the stark underside of the American Dream. It is true that the film *Kids* is brutally graphic in depicting the self-destructive sexual behavior of teens. But it shouldn't be lambasted; it should be lauded for delivering a wake-up call to youth about the lethal consequences of unsafe sex. It is true that the film *Set It Off* stylishly portrays the possible consequences of a life of crime for four Black women; but the real crime is the lack of economic and social resources available to keep Black women safe and sane in a culture that often renders them a triple minority. It's true that gangsta rappers often denigrate women in their lyrics, mirroring the more sophisticated misogyny of the corporate world and higher education.

But there is also a celebration of the freedom of lyrical creativity, rhetorical dexterity and racial signification. It's glimpsed when Snoop Doggy Dogg flows:

> *Fallin' back on that ass, with a hellified gangsta lean*
> *Gettin' funky on the mic, like an old batch of collard greens*
> *It's the capital S,*
> *Oh yes I'm fresh*
> *D O double G Y*
> *D O double G ya see*
> *Showin' much flex when it's time to wreck a mic*
> *Pimpin' hoes and clockin' a grip like my name is Dolemite*

But Snoop's extraordinary craft is also peeped when he attempts to place his speech in the context of theological and sociological debates about the nature of evil and undeserved suffering. Snoop says:

> *Wake up, jump out my bed*
> *I'm in a two man cell wit' my homie lil' half-dead*
> *Murder was the case that they gave me*
> *Dear God I wonder can you save me?*

In both theology and sociology, the problem of evil is addressed in the issue of theodicy. For theologians, theodicy occurs when there is a rupture in the relationship between God and human beings, when evil challenges claims about God's goodness and complete power. In sociology, Max Weber, according to social ethicist Jon Gunnemann, contended that theodicy occurs when there is an "incongruity between destiny and merit." In other words, when there is a disjuncture between what you get in life and what you think you deserve. In both interpretations, theodicy is operating in the lyrics of some rappers, a strong and sharp protest against the limits of Judeo-Christian morality and the American Dream.

There is, too, at work in some hip hop lyrics, an awareness of the shift in social and economic conditions that account for lost opportunities among young people, especially poor Blacks. The Notorious B.I.G. states it when he says:

> *Back in the day, our parents used to take care of us*
> *Look at 'em now, they're even fuckin' scared of us*

Callin' the state for help, because they can't maintain
Damn things done changed
If I wasn't in the rap game
I'd probably have a key knee deep in the crack game
Because the streets is a short stop
Either you slingin' crack rock
Or you got a wicked jump shot
Damn it's hard being young from the slums
Eatin' five cents gums
Not knowin' where your meal's comin' from
What happened to the summer time cook out
Every time I turn around a nigga's bein' took out

While that may not appear to be cutting-edge, theoretically dense, historically sophisticated analysis, it's a powerful interpretation of the cultural consequences of shifts in our economy that have gutted public spaces for recreation for poor youth. These changes have also shifted power away from older to younger youth—especially with the rise of what Mike Davis calls the "political economy of crack," where illicit drug dealing, possibly with the complicity of the CIA, has placed millions of dollars in the hands of young Black and Latino teens and young adults.

My point here is not to uncritically celebrate rap or the cultures that produce it. My point is not to romanticize American youth culture. My point is that often the American Dream is talked about without consciousness of its darker side. The American nightmare about which King spoke is often considered un-American. Not in its utter existence, mind you; it would be a fine thing to make poverty, illiteracy, repression of youth, racism, sexism, homophobia and the like un-American.

But it is considered un-American to mention that these things exist because of anything other than people being lazy, or stupid, or trifling, or unwilling to grasp hold of the American Dream through good old-fashioned elbow grease. If we say that some of the guardians of the American Dream keep others living in the basement of that dream—keep the nightmarish conditions alive for some—we're considered un-American, or at the least, which is almost a morally equivalent term, PC, or politically correct. The only PC I'm worried about for Americans is post conscience: when America strays beyond the boundaries of justice, truth and democracy because it has forgotten its history, the good and the bad.

As you graduate today, I encourage you not to be PC. The only way you can do that is to get rid of the amnesia that clogs the arteries of American national memory. The only way you can do that is to remember that the American Dream has been long in the making, and that your piece of it today as a college graduate has come at great expense. Some white folk who are graduating today are the products of so-called poor white trash, from Appalachia or other parts of the South. Don't forget that you're not better than your parents who might not have learned their ABCs but who can spell love and support real well. Some women are graduating today in families and communities where gender oppression continues to rule. Don't take your degrees for yourself, but take them for all those women who wished they had formal training so they could dismantle informal structures of sexism that remain rooted in our culture.

Some Black folk are graduating today out of families where you might be the first generation to go to school. Don't forget to reach back to help those who look like you. I was glad when Michael Jordan, that enormously important genius, a great UNC alumnus, gave a million dollars to the School of Social Work. But I was disappointed to learn that he believed that had he given money to the Black Cultural Center he would have been giving money to just one group instead of the entire university. But the School of Social Work is not the whole university. So white seems to register as cheerfully universal while Black seems to come across as hopelessly limited. One of the greatest lessons you can learn is what Jordan failed to learn: it's all right to give back to Black folk who loved you before you became a star, who were human before the law declared it, who were universal the moment they were conceived in their mother's womb. Mr. Jordan, giving money to Black folk might have helped them achieve the dream you've attained, and might have sent a message to others that it's all right to support your own, even as you participate in the larger drama of American citizenship.

As you graduate today, keep striving for the American Dream, but a deeper, more complex version of that dream. Keep making it possible for everybody to enjoy the beautiful domain of American democracy. And never forget to be yourself. As the old Black woman said a long time ago, "Be who you is and not who you ain't; 'cause if you is what you ain't, you am what you not." Peace.

Notes

Chapter 2

1. Michael Eric Dyson, *Why I Love Black Women* (New York: Basic Civitas Books, 2003), p. 202.
2. *One in 100: Behind Bars in America 2008*, Pew Center on the States, pp. 5–7.
3. Sohail Daulatzai, "Protect Ya Neck: Muslims and the Carceral Imagination in the Age of Guantanamo," *Souls* 9, no. 2 (Spring 2007), pp. 132–147.
4. Sonia Murray, "Hip Hop Stars Behind Bars," *Arizona Daily Star,* October 10, 2005.
5. Soledad O'Brien interview with Everett Dyson and Michael Eric Dyson, April 2008. All future quotes from Everett are from this interview.
6. Jon Schecter, "The Second Coming," *The Source* 55, April 1994, pp. 45–46, 84.

Chapter 13

1. I have in mind here how the literacy of exemplary Black figures is implicated in debates about Black intelligence, Black humanity, and Black culture. For instance, Phillis Wheatley's eighteenth-century verse was the putative proof of Black intelligence to white critics (including Thomas Jefferson) who disbelieved Blacks' ability to achieve abstract reasoning and sophisticated literary expression. For a brilliant reading of Wheatley's case, see Henry Louis Gates, Jr., *Figures in Black: Words, Signs, and the Racial Self* (New York: Oxford University Press, 1987), pp. 61–79. However, there is another historical debate about representative figures that draws from Ralph Waldo Emerson's *Representative Men: Seven Lectures* (1850), in *Ralph Waldo Emerson: Essays and Lectures,* edited by Joel Porte (New York: Library of America, 1983), where Emerson articulates his conception of the personal qualities and cultural functions of leaders and great men, or representative men. For a provocative and insightful examination of the intellectual pitfalls, ideological distortions, historical inaccuracies and gendered misrepresentations that attend the application (by nineteenth-century Black figures like Delaney and Douglass themselves, as well as by contemporary intellectuals) of the category representative man to nineteenth-century Black leadership, see Robert S. Levine's *Martin Delany,*

Frederick Douglass, and the Politics of Representative Identity (Chapel Hill: University of North Carolina Press, 1997).

2. Of course, there have been countless scholars in religious studies who have critically appropriated cultural studies, critical social theory and poststructuralism into their work. A random list might include excellent works like *Changing Conversations: Religious Reflection and Cultural Analysis,* edited by Dwight N. Hopkins and Sheila Greeve Davaney (New York: Routledge, 1996) [cultural studies]; Evelyn Brooks Higginbotham, *Righteous Discontent: The Black Women's Movement in the Black Baptist Church* (Cambridge, Mass.: Harvard University Press, 1993) [critical social theory]; and Mark C. Taylor, *Erring: A Postmodern A/theology* (Chicago: University of Chicago Press, 1984) [deconstruction/poststructuralism].

3. See Friedrich Nietzsche, *The Genealogy of Morals* (1887), in *Basic Writings of Nietzsche,* edited and translated by Walter Kaufmann (New York: Modern Library, 1968) and Michel Foucault, "'The Discourse on Language," in *The Archaeology of Knowledge,* translated from the French by A. M. Sheridan Smith (New York: Pantheon Books, 1972), pp. 215–37; and "Nietzsche, Genealogy, History" in *Aesthetics, Method, and Epistemology: Essential Works of Foucault, 1954–1984,* edited by James D. Faubion, translated by Robert Hurley and others (New York: The New Press, 1998), pp. 369–91.

I am not suggesting that either Nietzschean or Foucauldian genealogy is about tracking and tracing origins. As Foucault wrote, genealogy is rather about a "patience and a knowledge of details;" and that it required a "relentless erudition" since genealogy "does not oppose itself to history" but rather, "opposes itself to the search for origins" ("Nietzsche, Genealogy, History," p. 570). Rather, it is the rich sense of history that the genealogist needs to discern the "basis of all beginnings, atavisms, and heredities" (p. 373). I simply mean to stress the historicity of rhetorical practices and oral traditions, and that a genealogical approach helps to situate the history of how such traditions and practices have been read, and how they have functioned within the context of (African) American culture. As such, their beginnings far exceed the dry details of when they started; rather, their histories of emergence register the political conflict and racial experience that led to their use to begin with. The emphasis in such a genealogical approach is on the historical and cultural circumstances under which such traditions and practices emerged, how they survived, what uses they serve, and what needs they fulfill.

4. I mean the "invention of tradition" in a positive fashion, with the intent of establishing a specific, productive relationship with the past, as Eric Hobsbawm states in *The Invention of Tradition* by Eric Hobsbawm and Terence Ranger (Cambridge: Cambridge University Press, 1984). Thus, when I argue for invented traditions of racial memory, I am pointing to deliberate acts of racial self-preservation through mobilizing memories of achievement, resistance, opposition, sacrifice and survival. Of course, it is perhaps just such gestures

that rile figures like Arthur Schlesinger, Jr., who rail against multiculturalism, especially Afrocentrism, as an "invention of tradition." For a balanced critical reading of Afrocentrism against Schlesinger's assault, see Leith Mullings, *On Our Own Terms: Race, Class, and Gender in the Lives of African American Women* (New York: Routledge, 1997), pp. 189–193, esp. 191, where she calls Schlesinger's claim "at best disingenuous and at worst blatantly dishonest." Mullings, of course, is responding to Schlesinger's negative commandeering of the phrase "invention of tradition" to distinguish multiculturalism from ostensibly more established, ancient, authentic traditions. But it would behoove Schlesinger to regard Hobsbawm's point that traditions "which appear or claim to be old are often quite recent in origin and sometimes invented" (p. 1). (Although Hobsbawm has apparently forgotten this as he has recently joined the attack on multiculturalism as well.) For Schlesinger's attack on multiculturalism, and his claim against Afrocentrism, see his The *Disuniting of America: Reflections on a Multicultural Society* (New York: Whittle Communications, 1991).

5. Walter J. Ong, *Orality and Literacy:* The *Technologizing of the Word* (New York: Routledge, reprint, 1988).

6. I briefly map the complex expressions of race and racism, and the various ways in which they are manifest—including the subtextual predicates of racial discourse and practice, which I term "racial mystification"—in my *Race Rules: Navigating the Color Line* (New York: Vintage, reprint, 1997), pp. 33–46.

7. I deal with the issue of how Black cultural practices are related to a hegemonic white culture in my chapter on critical white studies, titled "Giving Whiteness a Black Eye," from my book, *Open Mike: Reflections on Philosophy, Race, Sex, Culture and Religion* (New York: Civitas Books, 2002).

8. Robert Farris Thompson, *Flash of the Spirit: African and Afro-American Art and Philosophy* (New York: Random House, 1983); Peter Linebaugh, "All the Atlantic Mountains Shook," in *Labour/Le Travailleur 10,* 1982; Peter Linebaugh and Marcus Rediker, "The Many-Headed Hydra: Sailors, Slaves and the Atlantic Working Class in the Eighteenth Century," *Journal of Historical Sociology,* 3(3), 1990, pp. 225–252; and Paul Gilroy, *The Black Atlantic: Modernity and Double Consciousness* (Cambridge, Mass.: Harvard University Press, 1993) and *Small Acts: Thoughts on* the *Politics of Black Cultures* (London: Serpent's Tail Press, 1993).

9. See, for example, the following anthologies: *Black British Cultural Studies,* edited by Houston Baker et al. (Chicago: University of Chicago Press, 1997); *Cultural Studies,* edited by Lawrence Grossberg et al. (New York: Routledge, 1992); *Black Literature and Literary Theory,* edited by Henry Louis Gates, Jr. (New York: Methuen, 1984); *Home Girls: A Black Feminist Anthology,* edited by Barbara Smith et al. (New York: Kitchen Table/Women of Color Press, 1983); *Reading Black, Reading Feminist: A Critical Anthology,* edited by Henry Louis Gates, Jr. (New York: Meridian Books, 1990); *Changing Our Own Words,*

edited by Cheryl A. Wall (New Brunswick, NJ: Rutgers University Press, 1991); *The Essential Frankfurt School Reader*, edited by Andrew Arato and Ike Gebhardt (New York: Continuum, 1982); and *Critical Race Theory* (New York: The New Press, 1995), edited by Kimberlé Crenshaw et al.

10. I have in mind here the fierce exchange between critic Joyce A. Joyce (now the head of African-American Studies at Temple University) and Henry Louis Gates, Jr., and Houston Baker, whom Joyce accused of hoisting extraneous, European theories onto indigenous Black literary and cultural practices. I also have in mind the skepticism expressed by Barbara Christian about the value and utility of theory in African American discourse, and her insistence that theory does not function (and is not viewed) in the same way in the West and the non-West, in her well-known essay, "The Race for Theory," in *The Nature and Context of Minority Discourse*, edited by Abdul R. JanMohamed and David Lloyd (New York: Oxford University Press, 1990).

11. I have in mind here the work of Julia Kristeva, the late Jean-Francois Lyotard, Roland Barthes, Jacques Lacan, Jacques Derrida, Michel Foucault, and so on. I will cite the relevant texts by selected authors below.

12. For example, see the essays by figures like David Hume, Immanuel Kant, Thomas Jefferson, and G. W. E. Hegel, in *Race and the Enlightenment: A Reader*, edited by Emmanuel Chukwudi Eze (Oxford: Blackwell Publishers, 1997).

13. See the postcolonial theory of figures like Edward Said, *Orientalism* (New York: Random House, 1978), and *Culture and Imperialism* (New York: Alfred A. Knopf, 1993); Gayatri C. Spivak, *In Other Worlds: Essays in Cultural Politics* (New York: Methuen, 1987), and *The Post-Colonial Critic: Interviews, Strategies, Dialogues*, edited by S. Harasym (New York: Routledge, 1990); and Homi K. Bhabha, *The Location of Culture* (New York: Routledge, 1994).

14. Jacques Derrida, *Speech and Phenomenon*, translated by David Allison (Evanston: Northwestern University Press, 1973); *Of Grammatology*, translated by Gayatri Spivak (Baltimore: Johns Hopkins University Press, 1976); and *Dissemination*, translated by Barbara Johnson (Chicago: University of Chicago Press, 1982).

15. The phrase is James Baldwin's.

16. Richard Rorty, *Philosophy and the Mirror of Nature* (Princeton: Princeton University Press, 1979). Hans-Georg Gadamer, *Philosophical Hermeneutics*, translated and edited by David Linge (Berkeley: University of California Press, 1976); and Paul Ricoeur, *Hermeneutics and the Human Sciences* (Cambridge: Cambridge University Press, 1981).

18. The phrase *verstehen* (understanding) is adapted from Wilhelm Dilthey. For an insightful reading of Dilthey's distinction between "understanding," which is suited for the human sciences (*Geisteswissenschaften*), and "explanation," which is suited for the sciences (naturwissenschaften), see Richard E. Palmer, *Hermeneutics: Interpretation Theory in Schleiermacher, Dilthey, Heidegger, and Gadamer* (Evanston, Ill.: Northwestern University Press, 1969), pp. 98–123, esp. 105-b. Of course, the Diltheyan distinction between understanding and

explanation—as well as Kantian idealism's distinction between cognitive and aesthetic judgments—is one to which I am opposed on pragmatist grounds, for reasons best expressed by Richard Rorty in his "Texts and Lumps," from *Objectivity, Relativism, and Truth: Philosophical Papers,* Volume 1 (Cambridge: England: Cambridge University Press, 1991), pp. 78–92. For an excellent examination of the complex intellectual issues involved in the assertion of meaning(s) in the interpretation of texts, see Jeffrey L. Stout, "What Is the Meaning of a Text?," *New Literary History* 14 (1982), pp. 1–12.

19. Barbara Johnson has brilliantly illumined this deconstructive approach over a series of engaging books: *The Critical Difference: Essays in the Contemporary Rhetoric of Reading* (Baltimore: Johns Hopkins University Press, 1980); *A World of Difference* (Baltimore: Johns Hopkins University Press, 1987); *The Wake of Deconstruction* (Cambridge, Mass.: Blackwell, 1994); and *The Feminist Difference: Literature, Psychoanalysis, Race and Gender* (Cambridge, Mass.: Harvard University Press, 1998). In fact, it was from her that I first heard this formulation (or something very much near it), in a lecture at Brown University, circa 1992.

20. Henry Louis Gates, Jr., *The Signifying Monkey: A Theory of African-American Literary Criticism* (New York: Oxford University Press, 1988).

21. Michel Foucault, *Power/Knowledge: Selected Interviews and Other Writings: 1972–1977,* edited by Colin Gordon (New York: Pantheon Books, 1980), p. 81.

22. Louis Althusser, *For Marx,* translated by Ben Brewster (London: Verso, 1979 [reprint]).

23. I first used the term performative epistemology in 1994, in a lecture at the University of North Carolina, before reading Derrida's notion of performative interpretation later the same year in *Specters of Marx: The State of Debt, the* Work *of Mourning, and the New International,* translated by Peggy Kamuf (New York: Routledge, 1994). Derrida says "performative interpretation" is "an interpretation that transforms the very thing it interprets" (p. 51), which jibes with my notion of performative epistemology in Black sacred rhetoric. Also see Henry Giroux's notion of "performative pedagogy" in "Where Have All the Public Intellectuals Gone?: Racial Politics, Pedagogy, and Disposable Youth," *JAC: A Journal of Composition Theory (Special Issue: Race, Class, Writing)* 17(2) (1997), pp. 191–205, where he writes that performative pedagogy "opens a space for disputing conventional academic borders" and which "reclaims the pedagogical as a power relationship that participates in authorizing or constraining what is understood as legitimate knowledge, and links the critical interrogation of the production of the symbolic and social practices to alternative forms of democratic education that foreground considerations of racial politics, power, and social agency" (p. 199). Also see Giroux's powerful *Channel Surfing: Race Talk and the Destruction of Today's Youth* (New York: St. Martin's Press, 1997).

24. It is also interesting to note that in hip hop culture, a phrase that is currently popular is "doing the knowledge," accenting, as in its religious rhetorical counterpart, the active, agential process of engaging, encountering and enacting—indeed, performing—knowledge. On the religious score, with an account that accentuates the performative moral dimension of religious knowledge, see Enda McDonagh's *Doing the Truth: The Quest for Moral Theology* (Notre Dame: University of Notre Dame Press, 1979).

25. Of course, there have been some excellent studies, but the richness and complexity of Black sacred rhetoric cries out for more serious study. For a few interesting examples, see Alice Jones's 1942 Fisk University master's thesis, "The Negro Folk Sermon: A Study in the Sociology of Folk Culture"; William Pipes, *Say Amen Brother! Old-Time Negro Preaching: A Study in American Frustration* (Detroit: Wayne State University Press, 1992 [1951]); Henry H. Mitchell, *Black Preaching* (Philadelphia: J. B. Lippincott, 1970); Bruce Rosenberg, *Art of the American Folk Preacher* (New York: Oxford University Press, 1970); Gerald L. Davis, *I Got the Word in Me and I Can Sing It, You Know: A Study of the Performed African-American Sermon* (Philadelphia: University of Pennsylvania Press, 1985); Carolyn Galloway-Thomas and John Louis Lucaites, editors, *Martin Luther King, Jr., and the Sermonic Power of Public Discourse* (Tuscaloosa: University of Alabama Press, 1993); and Walter Pitts, *Old Ship of Zion: The Afro-Baptist Ritual in the African Diaspora* (New York: Oxford University Press, 1996 [1993]), esp. pp. 59–90 and 132–75.

26. C. L. Franklin's rich sermonic history, fortunately, has been preserved on over seventy recordings, initially produced by Chess and Jewel record labels, and now available on audio cassette recordings sold both in gospel music stores and also in large retail chain music stores. Franklin's magisterial art has also been transcribed, edited, and analyzed in Jeff Todd Titon, ed., *Give Me This Mountain: Reverend C. L. Franklin, Life History and Selected Sermons* (Urbana: University of Illinois Press, 1989). The sermons of Charles Adams are also on audiocassette, both from his church, Hartford Avenue Memorial Church in Detroit, as well as from sermons preached around the country in various ecclesiastical and social venues, including the Progressive National Baptist Convention. In both cases, of course, as with all great Black preaching, Franklin and Adams must be heard to get the full impact of their verbal and religious artistry.

27. Sometimes spelled "hoop": see Robert Franklin, *Another Day's Journey: Black Churches Confronting the American Crisis* (Minneapolis: Fortress Press, 1997), pp. 68–69, 75. For more on the "hooped," or folk, sermon, see Albert Raboteau's splendid essay, "The Chanted Sermon," in *A Fire in the Bones: Reflections on African-American Religious History* (Boston: Beacon Press, 1995), p. 151.

28. Jürgen Habermas, *The Structural Transformation of the Public Sphere: An Inquiry into a Category of Bourgeois Society*, translated by Thomas Burger with the assistance of Frederick Lawrence (Cambridge, Mass.: MIT Press, 1993). For insightful treatments and criticisms of Habermas's concept of the public

sphere, see the essays in Craig Calhoun, ed., *Habermas and the Public Sphere* (Cambridge, Mass: MIT Press, 1992); and the essays in Bruce Robbins, ed., *The Phantom Public Sphere* (Minneapolis: University of Minnesota Press, 1993).

29. Nancy Fraser, *Justice Interruptus: Critical Reflections on the "Postsocialist" Condition* (New York: Routledge, 1997), p. 77.

30. Ibid., p. 101; also pp. 99–120, and esp. 80–98.

31. Nancy Fraser, *Unruly Practices: Power, Discourse and Gender in Contemporary Theory* (Minneapolis: University of Minnesota Press, 1989), pp. 113–43. For another examination of the social and theoretical effects of the differential exclusion of women from the public sphere in the bourgeois era, see Joan Landes, *Women and the Public Sphere in the Age of the French Revolution* (Ithaca, N.Y.: Cornell University Press, 1988).

32. See the essays in Black Public Sphere Collective, ed., *The Black Public Sphere* (Chicago: University of Chicago Press, 1995), esp. those by Houston Baker, Steven Gregory, Michael Hanchard, and Michael Dawson, which criticize various aspects of Habermas's concept of the public sphere in regard to race. See also the essays in Toni Morrison, ed., *Race-ing Justice, En-gendering Power: Essays on Anita Hill, Clarence Thomas and the Construction of Social Reality* (New York: Pantheon Books, 1992); Evelyn Brooks Higginbotham, *Righteous Discontent*; and Fraser, *Justice Interruptus* (on Anita Hill, Clarence Thomas, and the Black public sphere), pp. 99–120.

33. Craig Calhoun, *Critical Social Theory: Culture, History and the Challenge of Difference* (Oxford: Basil Blackwell, 1995), p. 244.

34. Ibid., pp. 240–48, esp. 245; Fraser, *Justice Interruptus*, pp. 69–98, esp. 80–81 and 89–93; *Unruly Practices*, p. 167.

35. For alternate publics, see Calhoun, p. 242; for nineteenth-century women's groups, see Fraser, *Justice Interruptus*, p. 74. See also Mary P. Ryan, *Women in Public: Between Banners and Ballots, 1825–1880* (Baltimore: Johns Hopkins University Press, 1990), and her "Gender and Public Access: Women's Politics in Nineteenth-Century America," in *Habermas and the Public Sphere;* Brooks Higginbotham, *Righteous Discontent*; and Geoff Eley, "Nations, Publics, and Political Cultures: Placing Habermas in the Nineteenth Century," in *Habermas and the Public Sphere.*

36. Habermas's Enlightenment project fails to account for the complexities of identity formation that he relegates to the private sphere (Calhoun, *Critical Social Theory,* pp. 244–45). A postmodern, or even a sociological conception of identity, versus an Enlightenment concept where identities are stable and uniformly evolve to structure the development of the person over space and time, would help underscore the interpenetration of public/private spheres in constructing the conditions of identity formation. See Stuart Hall on these three types of identity (Enlightenment, sociological, and postmodern), in *Modernity and Its Futures,* edited by Stuart Hall, David Held, and Tony McGrew (Oxford: Polity Press), pp. 275–80.

37. I am not arguing against what Martin J. Beck Matustik calls Kierkegaard's "performative holism" in his *Specters of Liberation: Great Refusals in the New World Order* (Albany: State University of New York Press, 1998), p. 30. By referring to a leap of discursive imagination by Foucault to overcome the Kierkegaardian either/or, I mark the ironical, even paradoxical, reinscription of Kierkegaard in the text (leap of faith); one must go through Kierkegaard to overcome elements of his thought.

38. However, for Rorty's argument that Foucault exhibited the traits of *Geistgeschichte*, "the sort of intellectual history that has a moral," in Foucault's *The Order of Things*, see the third volume of Rorty's philosophical papers, *Truth and Progress: Philosophical Papers*, Volume 3 (Cambridge: Cambridge University Press, 1998), pp. 271–72.

39. Hall et al., *Modernity and Its Futures*, pp. 292–93.

40. Michele Barrett, *The Politics of Truth: From Marx to Foucault* (Stanford: Stanford University Press, 1991), p. 126.

41. Not a substitute, however. For more on this distinction, see Barrett, *The Politics of Truth*, pp. 123–24.

42. It is important, however, to acknowledge that Marx never used the term "false consciousness" (Engels did in a letter to Franz Mehring in 1893, long after Marx's death). See Barrett, *The Politics of Truth*, pp. 5–17.

43. Michel Foucault, "Truth and Power," in *The Foucault Reader* (New York: Pantheon, 1984), p. 60. See Barrett's exploration of Foucault's take on the distinctions between ideology and discourse in *The Politics of Truth*, pp. 123–56.

44. Stuart Hall in *Critical Dialogues in Cultural Studies*, edited by David Morley and Kuan-Hsing Chen (New York: Routledge, 1996), pp. 135–36. Also, in the same volume, John Fiske sees Hall's suspicion of Foucault as "uncharacteristic" (p. 217). Hall concedes, in the interview (with Larry Grossberg) cited above, that Foucault's objection to ideology, and his advocacy of discourse, may be more "polemical" than "analytical" (p. 135).

45. For an interesting application of Foucauldian theory—especially notions of "authorfunction" and "empirico-transcendental doublet"—to King's rhetoric and the Civil Rights Movement, see Richard King, *Civil Rights and the Idea of Freedom* (New York: Oxford University Press, 1992), pp. 111 and 121. However, Richard King also suggests the limited use of domination theories (advanced by Frankfurt School theorists [Theodor Adorno, Max Horkheimer, and Herbert Marcuse] and Foucault), and the concept of hegemony articulated by Antonio Gramsci, in helping to explain the complex functions and achievements of the Civil Rights Movement (p. 203).

46. Michael Eric Dyson, *Making Malcolm: The Myth and Meaning of Malcolm X* (New York: Oxford University Press, 1995), p. 85.

47. Ibid., pp. 89–90.

48. Ibid., p. 90.

49. Ibid., pp. 89–90.

50. For a rigorous, broadly stimulating and provocative psychoanalytic-Marxist reading of Malcolm X that draws on the insights of Marx and Freud, see Victor Wolfenstein's *Victims of Democracy: Malcolm X and the Black Revolution* (London: Free Association Books, 1989).

51. Despite the lack of Marx's "authorship," the notion of false consciousness may work in the effort to explain Malcolm (or at least his self-conception) because, unlike Foucault, he believed that there was a truth from which one could depart, thus marking error as the distance between false practice and truth. However, Foucauldian discussions of discursive regimes of truth remain salient in discussing Malcolm and the Nation of Islam, since the dispersion of powers over the field of discursive practices constituted within the Nation's social and moral order can be explained by understanding how white supremacist forces and political powers prohibited the articulation of Black self-determination within the logic of the state apparatus. In short, certain ideas were made reasonable (white domination) by being rendered normative. Moreover, the power of white supremacist thought to veil itself—to make its operations discrete, and hence, unquestioned—in the logic of the political status quo and underwritten by the rhetoric of democracy, was formidable indeed. In such a light, the very idea of Black self-determination—or for that matter, Black intelligence, rationality, and humanity—were ruled out of play, or in Foucauldian terms, were suppressed from emergence within the discursive parameters of American nationalism. Still, as Stuart Hall argues, the discursive, at crucial points, bears remarkable analytical resemblance to the ideological. As I stated above, Hall acknowledges that Foucault's strike against ideology might have been more polemical than analytical. In any case, dimensions of both Foucauldian and Marxist theories offer insight into Malcolm's rhetorical and social practices. For the Marxist take on Malcolm's ideological battles with white supremacy as a false consciousness, see Wolfenstein, *Victims of Democracy*.

52. Initially, King was much less ambitious about the sort of radical social transformation he envisioned near the end of his life, when he began to argue for a revolution of values and a more aggressive approach to social change. For a fascinating study of how major news magazines (*Time, Newsweek,* and *U.S. News & World Report*) changed their coverage of King as he grew more radical, and their coverage grew more critical, see Richard Lentz's *Symbols, the News Magazines, and Martin Luther King* (Baton Rouge: Louisiana State University Press, 1990).

53. I discuss this in greater detail in *Reflecting Black: African-American Cultural Criticism* (Minneapolis: University of Minnesota Press, 1993), pp. 221–46, 304–8.

54. I am not suggesting that rhetoric alone, without concrete social practice, achieved the ends King and his cohorts sought. I am merely suggesting the materiality of discourse, that is, that it carries weight, and that it can lead to profound social transformation.

55. See Mae Henderson's remarkable essay, "Speaking in Tongues: Dialogics, Dialectics, and the Black Woman Writer's Literary Tradition," in *Feminists Theorize the Political*, edited by Judith Butler and Joan W. Scott (New York: Routledge, 1992), pp. 144–66, which argues the difference between glossolalia—the capacity to "utter the mysteries of the spirit," and is, thereby, speech that is "private, non-mediated, nondifferentiated univocality"—and heteroglossia, which signifies "public, differentiated, social, mediated, dialogic discourse." Heteroglossia is the "ability to speak in diverse known tongues" (p. 149). Such a notion, I believe, marks the polyvocal, multiarticulative character of Black rhetorical practices, and suggests the seminal, constructed publicity within which Black sacred speech can signify.

Index